최신경향 완벽반영

지텔프 공식 기출 문제+인강
200% 환급반

출석 NO 성적 NO 시작만 해도 50%, 최대 200% 환급!

0원으로 최단기 목표점수 달성

KB198546

빠른 합격을 위한 역대급 구성!
지텔프 200% 환급반 끝장 혜택 한 눈에 보기

01

출석/성적 무관
50% 즉시 환급

02

수강료 부담 NO
최대 200% 환급

03

목표 미달성 시
+120일 무료연장

+120일

04

생애 첫 지텔프 응시료
50% 할인쿠폰 제공

66,000원 → 33,000원
50% 할인쿠폰

COUPON

* 시원스쿨LAB 홈페이지(lab.siwonschool.com)에서 지텔프 환급반 패키지를 할인가로 구매하실 수 있습니다.
* 환급조건 : 출석 60일 + 목표성적 달성 성적표 + 2년 이내 목표점수 미달성 내역 + 수강후기 작성 + 네이버 블로그 포스팅
* 제공하는 혜택 및 환급조건은 기간에 따라 변경될 수 있습니다.

2025 최신 지텔프 공식기출 UADATE!

시원스쿨 지텔프 공식 기출 시리즈

시원스쿨LAB 연구진 총 출동! 퀄리티가 다른 G-TELP 교재
G-TELP 공식기출 라인업으로 목표점수 완벽대비!

시원스쿨 지텔프 교재가 특별한 이유

01

G-TELP KOREA 공식 기출문제로 구성된
최신&최다 기출문제집

02

최신기출문제 유형 및 출제패턴 분석으로
실제 시험 출제패턴 예측

03

파트별 출제 포인트 및
목표점수 달성 공략 가이드 제공

04

초보자 맞춤 꼼꼼한 해설과 함께
매력적인 오답에 대한 해설 추가제공

2025 최신 G-TELP KOREA 공식 기출 문제

지텔프 LEVEL 2
공식
기출문제집

부록

시원스쿨 LAB

지텔프 영역별 공략 가이드

특강 바로가기 QR ▶

지텔프 Level 2 시험을 처음 준비하는 학습자를 위한 지텔프 전문강사 서민지 강사님의 특별 수업이 마련되어 있습니다. 문법, 청취, 독해 3개의 영역에 대한 기출문제를 기반의 유형별 패턴 분석과 고득점을 위한 문제 풀이 전략 가이드를 확인해보세요! 문법의 출제 경향과 문제 풀이 방법에서부터 청취 노트테이킹 비법과 키워드 찾기, 독해 지문 분석과 패러프레이징에 관한 내용으로 학습자 여러분의 성적을 확실하게 수직 상승시켜드립니다. 이 특강은 부록으로 제공해드리는 자료와 함께 위의 QR코드 접속하여 서민지 강사님의 강의 영상으로 학습할 수 있습니다.

문법 유형별 파트별 공략 가이드

• 문법 유형별[Grammar] 영역 구성

지텔프 문법은 총 26문항으로 구성되어 있으며 문법 풀이 시간은 총 20분 주어집니다. 지텔프 문법은 매 회차의 시험마다 정해진 유형의 문제가 정해진 문항 수만큼 출제되며, 그 중 22문항은 정답의 단서가 명확하게 주어지기 때문에, 정답의 단서와 연결되는 공식과 단어를 단순 암기함으로써 정답을 쉽게 고를 수 있습니다. 이 22문항에 해당하는 유형은 (1) 진행시제 (6문항), (2) 가정법 (6문항), (3) 준동사(6문항), (4) 당위성의 나타내는 동사원형 (2문항), (5) 관계사 (2문항)입니다. 나머지 4문항은 문제에서 주어지는 문맥을 파악하여 가장 자연스러운 단어를 정답으로 골라야 하므로 해석 능력이 필요한 문제입니다. 여기에 해당하는 유형은 (1) 조동사 (2문항), (2) 연결어 (2문항)입니다.

구분		문항 수
진행시제	현재진행, 과거진행, 미래진행 현재완료진행, 과거완료진행, 미래완료진행	6
가정법	가정법 과거 (3문항) 가정법 과거완료 (3문항)	6
준동사	동명사 (3문항) to부정사 (3문항)	6
당위성을 나타내는 동사원형	당위성을 나타내는 동사/형용사 뒤 that절의 동사원형	2
조동사	will / can / must / should / might 등 (해석이 꼭 필요한 유형)	2
연결어	접속사 / 접속부사 / 전치사 (해석이 꼭 필요한 유형)	2

지텔프 문법 주요 특징

• 공식 및 정답 단서를 완벽히 암기하면 영포자도 22문제를 확보할 수 있습니다.

• 정답 단서는 주로 빈칸이 포함된 문장이나 빈칸 주변에서 확인할 수 있습니다.

• 문항 수 기준 가장 개수가 많은 **진행시제, 가정법, 준동사** 유형은 문법 공식이 비교적 어렵지 않고 미리 학습한 내용이 그대로 시험 문제로 출제되므로 초보자도 쉽게 풀 수 있습니다. 따라

서 32점 이상이 목표일 경우 문법만 고득점을 확보해서 단기간에 목표 달성이 가능합니다.

- 문법 시험시간은 20분이지만 10~15분 사이에 26문항을 모두 풀 수 있어서 남는 시간 동안 청취나 독해 영역을 미리 풀 수 있습니다.

• 진행시제

문법 영역에서 시제 유형 문제는 진행시제만이 정답으로 출제됩니다. 진행시제는 「be동사 + 동사의 ing」의 형태로 특정 시점에 진행 중인 동작을 의미하는 시제입니다. 총 6개의 진행시제 유형이 1문제씩 출제되며 특정 시제에 대한 단서들을 꼭 암기해서 문제에 적용하면 쉽고 빠르게 문제를 풀 수 있습니다.

구분	형태 (be + -ing)	단서
현재진행	am/are/is + -ing	Now, right now, currently, at the moment, as of this moment, at present, presently
과거진행	was/were + -ing	• When/Before + 주어 + 과거동사, 주어 +_____ • While + 주어 +_____, 주어 + 과거동사 • ago, yesterday, last + 시간 표현
미래진행	will be + -ing	• When/Until/If + 주어 + 현재동사, 주어 + _____ • tomorrow, next + 미래 표현 • in / until / by + 미래 시점
현재완료진행	has/have been + -ing	• Since + 과거시점(과거동사) + 주변시제 현재 • Ever since + 과거시점(과거동사) + 주변시제 현재 • for + 숫자기간 (+ now)
과거완료진행	had been + -ing	• Before + 주어 + 과거동사, 주어 + _____ + for 기간 • When / until / by the time + 주어 + 과거동사, 주어 + _____
미래완료진행	will have been + -ing	• By the time + 주어 + 현재동사, 주어 + _____+ for 기간 • By / In + 미래시점, 주어 + _____ + for 기간

• 가정법

가정법은 총 6문항이 출제되며 현재 혹은 과거의 사실을 반대의 상황으로 가정하여 말하는 문장입니다. 일반적으로 현재 사실을 반대로 말하는 가정법 과거(3문항), 과거 사실을 반대로 말하는 가정법 과거완료(3문항)이 출제됩니다. 가정법 과거완료 유형은 도치의 유형이 출제됩니다. 또한 1년에 1~2문제 정도의 빈도로 과거의 사실을 반대로 말하면서 현재의 결과를 가정하는 혼합가정법이 출제되기도 합니다.

구분	문장 구조 공식
가정법 과거	If + 주어 + **과거동사(were)**, 주어 + **would/could/might 동사원형**
가정법 과거완료	If + 주어 + **had p.p.**, 주어 + **would/could/might have p.p.** *도치 유형: Had + 주어 + p.p., 주어 + **would/could/might + have p.p.**
혼합가정법	If + 주어 + had p.p., 주어 + **would/could/might + 동사원형**

문장 구조 공식에서 밑줄로 된 부분 중에 하나만 실제 문제에서 빈칸으로 출제됩니다. 가정법 과거에서 일반동사는 해당 동사의 과거형이 나오고 be동사의 과거형은 원래 was와 were가 있지만 가정법 과거에서는 항상 were만 사용합니다.

•준동사

준동사란 동사가 형태를 바꾸어 다른 품사(명사, 형용사, 부사 등)로 활용되는 형태를 말하며, 대표적으로 to부정사와 동명사가 있습니다. 지텔프 문법 영역에서는 to부정사와 동명사가 준동사 문제로 출제됩니다.

2022년 이전에는 동명사 3문항, to부정사 2문항이 출제되었지만 최근 2022년 초부터 동명사 3문항, to부정사 3문항으로 출제되고 있습니다. 그래서 준동사 문제 중에 1문제가 to부정사인지 동명사인지 헷갈린다면 해당 시험지에서 to부정사가 정답인 문제가 몇 문제인지, 동명사가 정답인 문제가 몇 문제인지 확인하여 1문제가 덜 출제된 유형을 바로 그 문제의 정답으로 고를 수 있습니다. 이를 '숫자 맞추기'라고 하며, 정해진 유형의 문제가 정해진 수만큼 출제되는 문법 영역에서 유용하게 쓸 수 있는 방법입니다.

to부정사와 동명사 유형의 문제는 항상 to have p.p.나 having p.p.와 같은 완료부정사, 완료동명사가 선택지에 제시되는데, 이는 문장의 동사보다 부정사나 동명사의 동사의 시제가 더 앞선 경우에만 쓰이는 형태이며, 지텔프 Level 2 문법에서는 다루어지지 않는 내용이므로 오답으로 소거하실 수 있습니다.

구분	출제 포인트
동명사	• 타동사 뒤에 목적어로 쓰이는 동명사 • 동명사가 포함된 관용표현
to부정사	• 타동사 뒤에 목적어로 쓰이는 to부정사 • 타동사의 목적어 뒤에 위치하는 목적격보어로 쓰이는 to부정사 • 수동태(be p.p.) 뒤에 위치하는 to부정사 • 명사를 수식하는 to부정사 • '~하기 위해서'라는 의미로 부사로 쓰이는 to부정사 • 형용사를 수식하는 to부정사

• 당위성을 나타내는 동사원형

이 유형은 2문제로 출제되고 있으며, 제안/추천/요구/주장/명령의 의미를 나타내는 동사 또는 형용사 뒤에 위치한 that절에서 동사의 자리가 빈칸으로 출제되는 문제에 해당하는 유형입니다. 제안/추천/요구/주장/명령의 의미를 나타내는 동사 또는 형용사의 의미로 인해 that절의 동사가 '~해야 한다'라는 조동사 should의 의미까지 내포하면서 that절의 동사는 시제나 인칭에 상관없이 항상 동사원형으로 쓰입니다. 그래서 이 유형의 문제는 항상 동사원형이 정답입니다. 따라서 이 유형의 문제를 풀기 위해서 정답의 단서로 활용되는 제안/추천/요구/주장/명령의 의미를 나타내는 동사/형용사를 암기하는 것이 필수적입니다.

문장 구조
주어 + 동사(제안, 추천, 요구, 주장, 명령) + that + 주어 + _____ (동사원형이 정답)
주어 + be동사 + 형용사(제안, 추천, 요구, 필수) + that + 주어 + _____ (동사원형이 정답)

• 관계사

관계사 유형은 총 2문항이 출제되며, 크게 관계대명사와 관계부사로 나뉘어 출제됩니다. 그 중에서 관계대명사가 더 자주 출제됩니다.

관계대명사란 명사를 수식 또는 설명하기 위해 주어, 동사 등이 포함된 절이 쓰일 때, 그 절 안에서 수식 받는 명사(선행사) 대신 쓰이는 단어를 말합니다. 그래서 관계대명사는 그 절에서 주어 또는 목적어로 쓰이기 때문에, 관계대명사가 포함된 절(관계대명사절)은 관계대명사 뒤에 주어나 목적어가 없는 불완전한 절이 이어집니다. 관계대명사절에서 주어 역할을 하면 주격 관계대명사, 목적어 역할을 하면 목적격 관계대명사라고 합니다. 소유격 관계대명사는 명사와 함께 쓰여서 관계대명사절 안에서 「소유격 관계대명사 + 명사」가 하나의 주어나 목적어로 쓰입니다.

관계대명사는 명사를 수식하는 절에서 주어나 목적어 역할을 하지만 관계부사는 명사를 수식하는 절에서 부사 역할을 한다는 점이 다릅니다. 주로 장소 부사, 시간 부사로 쓰여 장소 관계부사인 where, 시간 관계부사인 when이 자주 출제됩니다. 부사는 문장성분이 아니기 때문에 관계부사 뒤에는 주어, 동사, 목적어 또는 보어 등 필요한 문장 성분이 모두 갖춰진 완전한 절이 이어집니다.

관계사	관계사절 구조	출제빈도
주격 관계대명사 who / which / that	선행사(사람) + who / that + 동사 + … 선행사(사물) + which / that + 동사 + … * 빈칸 앞에 콤마(,)가 있으면 that으로 시작하는 선택지는 오답으로 소거 * 관계사 바로 다음에 주어 없이 동사가 나와서 불완전한 문장	상
목적격 관계대명사 who(m) / which / that	선행사(사람) + who(m) / that + 주어 + 동사 (+ 수식어구) 선행사(사물) + which / that + 주어 + 동사 (+ 수식어구) * 빈칸 앞에 콤마(,)가 있으면 that으로 시작하는 선택지는 오답으로 소거 * 관계사 바로 다음 문장에서 목적어가 없는 불완전한 문장	상
소유격 관계대명사 whose	선행사(사람 / 사물) + whose + 명사 (+주어) + 동사 + … * 빈칸 앞에 콤마(,)가 있으면 that으로 시작하는 선택지는 오답으로 소거 * whose + 명사 뒤에 주어나 목적어가 없는 불완전한 문장	하
관계부사 when	선행사(시간) + when + 완전한 문장 * 빈칸 앞에 콤마(,)가 있으면 that으로 시작하는 선택지는 오답으로 소거	하
관계부사 where	선행사(장소) + where + 완전한 문장 * 빈칸 앞에 콤마(,)가 있으면 that으로 시작하는 선택지는 오답으로 소거	중

· 조동사

조동사는 총 2문항이 출제되며, 문맥상 빈칸에 들어갈 알맞은 조동사를 골라야 하는 문제이므로, 우선 출제되는 조동사의 종류와 의미를 파악해두고, 주어진 문제의 문맥과 어울리는 조동사를 고르는 연습을 해야 합니다.

조동사	의미
should	(1) 의무, 당위성 : ~해야 한다 (2) 충고, 조언 : ~하는 것이 좋겠다

must	(1) 강한 의무, 금지 : ~해야 한다, 하면 안된다(must not)
	(2) 확신 ~임에 틀림없다 **출제빈도 낮음
can	(1) 능력 : ~할 수 있다
	(2) 가능성 : ~할 수 있다
	(3) 허가 : ~해도 좋다 **출제빈도 낮음
could	(1) can의 과거 : ~할 수 있었다
	(2) 가정법 : ~할 수도 있다 **출제빈도 낮음
will	(1) 미래 : ~할 것이다
	(2) 주어의 의지 : ~할 것이다
	(3) 확실히 정해진 상황 : ~할 것이다
would	(1) will의 과거 : ~할 것이었다
	(2) 과거의 불규칙한 습관 : ~하곤 했다 **출제빈도 낮음
	(3) 가정법 **출제빈도 낮음

• 연결어

연결어는 접속사, 접속부사, 전치사가 포함되며, 총 2문항이 출제됩니다. 주로 접속사와 접속부사가 출제되는데, 전치사는 출제 빈도가 매우 낮습니다. 조동사 유형과 마찬가지로 문맥상 빈칸에 들어갈 알맞은 연결어를 고르는 유형으로 출제되므로, 출제되는 연결어의 종류와 의미를 모두 파악해두고 주어진 문제의 문맥과 어울리는 연결어를 고르는 연습을 해야 합니다.

접속사와 접속부사는 둘 다 뒤에 주어와 동사 등이 포함된 절이 이어지는데, 둘 사이의 차이점은 접속부사 뒤에는 반드시 콤마(,)가 있고 그 뒤에 절이 이어진다는 것입니다.

전치사는 뒤에 주어와 동사가 포함된 절이 아니라 명사가 이어지는데, 형용사나 수식어구가 많이 붙은 명사구일 수도 있으며, 동명사일 수도 있습니다.

•빈출 부사절 접속사

논리	
이유	because, as 때문에 since, now that ~이므로
시간	when, as ~할 때 as soon as ~하자마자 until ~할 때까지 after ~후에 before ~전에 since ~이후로 while ~하는 동안
양보	although, though, even though 비록~ 하지만 even if ~라 할지라도

조건 경우	If 만약 ~라면 unless ~하지 않는다면 as long as ~하는 한 once 일단 ~하면 in case(that) ~할 시에는, ~하면 given (that) ~라 가정하면 provided (that) ~라면, ~라는 조건으로
대조	while, whereas 반면에
목적	so that, in order that ~하기 위해서
결과	so+형용사/부사+that 너무 ~해서 ~하다 so 따라서

• 빈출 접속부사

논리	
역접	However 하지만 Instead ~대신에 Conversely 정반대로 On the contrary = In contrast 대조적으로 On the other hand 반면에
양보	Nevertheless = Nonetheless 그럼에도 불구하고, 그렇지만 Otherwise 그렇지 않으면 Even so 그럼에도 불구하고
결과	Therefore =Thus = Hence 그러므로 As a result 결국 Accordingly 따라서 Consequently 결과적으로
예시	For example = For instance 예를 들어
첨가	Besides = In addition = Moreover 게다가 Furthermore 더 나아가서 Also 또한 (*However 하지만 – 추가설명이 뒤에 이어짐)
부연	After all 어쨌든 In fact 사실 In particular = particularly 특히 Specifically 특히 In other words 다시 말해서
강조	Of course 물론 Absolutely 틀림없이 Certainly 분명히 Undoubtedly 의심의 여지가 없게 Indeed 정말로 Naturally 당연히
시간	Meanwhile 한편, 그와 동시에 Presently 현재 Eventually 결국
기타	Fortunately 다행히도 Unfortunately 안타깝게도

• 꼭 구별해야 하는 전치사/접속사/접속부사

	전치사	접속사	접속부사
~때문에	because of	because	
	due to	since	
	owing to	as	

~에도 불구하고	despite in spite of	although though even though	nevertheless nonetheless
~대신에	instead of		instead
~의 경우에	in case of	in case (that)	

문법 문제 풀이 가이드

• 진행시제 문제 풀이

1. **빈칸 위치 확인**: 문제에서 빈칸의 위치가 동사 자리라면 시제, 가정법, 당위성을 나타내는 동사원형 유형 중 하나이다.

2. **선택지 확인**: 「be동사 + -ing」 형태의 선택지가 3개 이상일 경우 진행시제 문제이다. (단순시제 소거)

3. 빈칸이 포함된 문장에서 시제에 관련 단서를 찾아 동그라미로 표시한다.
   (right now, currently, ago, yesterday, 「when+과거동사」 등)

4. 단서가 불명확한 경우, (1) 주변 시제를 확인해보고, (2) 헷갈리는 2개의 선택지를 표시하고 다른 문제에서 정답으로 나온 시제를 소거한다.

5. 각 시제는 1문제씩 출제되기 때문에 출제된 시제 문제 개수를 검토한다.

• 예제 풀이

Keith usually works at company headquarters, but this week he needs to inspect other branches. ② Right now, he ①_____ to Texas to examine the operations of the Houston branch. ③ (a) is traveling 　　(b) had traveled 　　(c) travels 　　(d) will have been traveling	STEP ① 빈칸의 위치가 동사 자리인 것을 확인한다. STEP ② 빈칸 뒤에 현재진행시제의 단서 Right now인 것을 확인한다. STEP ③ 보기 중에서 단순시제인 (c), 완료시제인 (b), (d)는 오답이며 현재진행시제인 (a) is traveling을 정답으로 선택한다.

• 가정법 문제 풀이

1. **빈칸 위치 확인**: 문제에서 빈칸의 위치가 동사 자리라면 시제, 가정법, 당위성을 나타내는 동사원형 유형 중 하나이다.

2. **선택지 확인**: 선택지 중에 「would / could / might have p.p.」, 「 would / could / might + 동사원형」, 또는 「had p.p.」 형태의 선택지가 있을 경우 가정법 문제이다.

3. 빈칸의 위치가 주절에 있고 빈칸 앞 또는 뒤에 있는 if절에 과거시제 동사가 있다면, 선택지에서 「would / could / might + 동사원형」을 정답으로 고른다.

4. 빈칸의 위치가 주절에 있다면 빈칸 앞 또는 뒤에 있는 if절에서 과거완료(had p.p.) 동사가 있다면 선택지에서 「would / could / might + have p.p.」를 정답으로 고른다.

5. 빈칸의 위치가 if절에 있고, 빈칸 앞 또는 뒤에 있는 주절에서 「would / could / might + 동사원형」이 있다면 선택지에서 과거시제 동사를 정답으로 고른다.

6. 빈칸의 위치가 if절에 있고, 빈칸 앞 또는 뒤에 있는 주절에서 「would / could / might + have p.p.」가 있다면 선택지에서 과거완료시제(had p.p.) 동사를 정답으로 고른다.

· 예제 풀이

Laura's apartment lease is almost up, and she is concerned about rising rent prices in her neighborhood. ② If her landlord were to keep her rent at the same amount, she ①_____ the agreement for another year. 　(a) would have happily renewed ③ (b) will happily renew 　(c) would happily renew 　(d) will have happily renewed	STEP ① 빈칸의 위치가 동사 자리인 것을 확인한다. STEP ② 빈칸 문장 앞에 If로 시작하는 절이 있고 그 절의 동사가 be동사의 과거형 were인 것을 확인한다. STEP ③ 보기 중에서 「would / could / might + 동사원형」 형태인 (b)를 정답으로 선택한다.

· 준동사

1. **빈칸 위치 확인:** 빈칸 앞에 동사가 위치하거나 명사가 위치해 있다면 준동사 유형이다.

2. **선택지 확인:** 선택지가 to부정사와 동명사로 구성되어 있다면 준동사 유형이다.

3. 선택지에서 완료부정사(to have p.p.), 완료동명사(having p.p.)를 오답으로 소거한다.

4. to부정사는 「to + 동사원형」, 동명사는 「동사 + ing」 형태가 정답이다.

5. 동명사 3문항, to부정사 3문항이 출제되므로 to부정사와 동명사 중에 정답이 헷갈리는 경우, 해당 회차의 문제 중 to부정사가 정답인 문제와 동명사가 정답인 문제의 개수를 확인해서 정답을 고른다.

· to부정사 예제 풀이

Jolene's neighborhood is experiencing a wave of car thefts. As a result, the local police have ② agreed ①_____ patrols in the area, and a closed-circuit security system will soon be installed.
 	
    (a) having increased
③ (b) to increase
    (c) increasing
    (d) to have increased
	STEP ① 빈칸의 위치가 목적어 자리인 것과 선택지가 to부정사와 동명사로 이루어져 있음을 확인한다.
	
	STEP ② 동사 agree가 to부정사를 목적어로 취하는 동사임을 표시한다.
	
	STEP ③ 보기 중에서 「to + 동사원형」형태인 (b)를 정답으로 선택한다.

· 동명사 예제 풀이

Most people do not realize how many objects they touch throughout the day or how easily germs transfer between surfaces. It is important that people ② avoid ①_____ with their hands until they have thoroughly washed them.
 	
    (a) to eat
    (b) having eaten
    (c) to have eaten
③ (d) eating
	STEP ① 빈칸의 위치가 목적어 자리인 것과 선택지가 to부정사와 동명사로 이루어져 있음을 확인한다.
	
	STEP ② 동사 avoid가 동명사를 목적어로 취하는 동사임을 표시한다.
	
	STEP ③ 보기 중에서 「동사 + -ing」형태인 (d)를 정답으로 선택한다.

· 당위성을 나타내는 동사원형

1. **빈칸 위치 확인:** 빈칸 앞에 접속사 that과 그 앞에 제안, 추천, 요구, 주장, 명령을 나타내는 동사나 당위성을 나타내는 형용사가 있다면 당위성을 나타내는 동사원형 유형이다.

2. **선택지 확인:** 선택지 중에 동사원형이 포함되어 있다면 당위성을 나타내는 동사원형 유형이며, 그 문제의 정답이 동사원형이다.

The National Weather Service just issued a tornado warning for the town of Holmville. Local government officials ② advise that residents ①_____ indoors and away from windows to avoid being injured.
 	
  (a) will stay
  (b) are staying
  ③ (c) stay
  (d) stayed
	STEP ① 선택지 (a)~(d)에 동사원형이 포함된 것을 보고 당위성을 나타내는 동사원형 유형일 것이라고 추측한다.
	
	STEP ② 빈칸 앞에 접속사 that이 있고, 그 앞에 제안, 추천, 요구, 주장, 명령 동사 중 하나인 advise가 현재시제로 언급되어 있는 것을 확인한다.
	
	STEP ③ 선택지 중에서 동사원형 형태인 (c)를 정답으로 선택한다.

· 관계사

1. **빈칸 위치 확인:** 빈칸 앞에 명사가 있거나 명사와 콤마(,)가 함께 있는 경우 관계사 유형이다.

2. **선택지 확인:** 선택지가 모두 관계사절로 구성되어 있으므로 다른 유형과 혼동되지 않는다.

3. 선택지에서 what, why, how로 시작하는 선택지는 오답으로 소거한다.

4. 선행사가 사람이면서 빈칸 뒤 문장이 불완전한 문장이라면 who 또는 that이 정답이다.

5. 선행사가 사물이면서 빈칸 뒤 문장이 불완전한 문장이라면 which 또는 that이 정답이다.

6. 빈칸 앞에 콤마(,)가 있는 경우 that으로 시작하는 선택지는 오답으로 소거한다.

7. 장소 명사 뒤에 「which/that + 불완전한 문장」이 이어지면 정답이며, 장소 명사 뒤에 「where + 완전한 문장」가 이어져도 정답이다.

8. 시간 명사 뒤에 「which/that + 불완전한 문장」이 이어지면 정답이며, 시간 명사 뒤에 「when + 완전한 문장」이 이어져도 정답이다.

· 관계사 예제 풀이

2001: A Space Odyssey is known for its innovative special effects. ① The film, ②_____, used practical features such as spaceship models, rotating sets, and high-contrast photography to craft a realistic portrayal of space.
 	
    (a) who won the award for best visual effects
③ (b) which won the award for best visual effects
    (c) what won the award for best visual effects
    (d) that won the award for best visual effects
	STEP ① 빈칸 앞의 선행사 The film이 사람명사가 아닌 것을 확인한 다.
	STEP ② 관계대명사 which나 that으로 시작하는 (c), (d) 중에서, 빈칸 앞에 콤마(,)가 있어서 쓸 수 없는 that으로 시작하는 (c)를 오답으로 소거한다.
	STEP ③ which로 시작하는 (b)를 정답으로 선택한다.

· 조동사

1. **빈칸 위치 확인**: 빈칸 앞에 주어, 빈칸 뒤에 동사원형이 있다면 조동사 유형이다.

2. **선택지 확인**: 선택지가 모두 조동사로만 구성되어 있으므로 조동사 유형임을 알 수 있다.

3. 규칙, 법률, 의무, 행동의 목적, 기한이 언급에 관련된 내용일 경우 must가 정답일 가능성이 높다.

4. 행동의 목적, 기한, 충고, 당위성에 관한 내용일 경우 should가 정답일 가능성이 높다.

5. 가능성, 능력, 확률에 관한 내용일 경우 can이 정답일 가능성이 높다.

6. 미래시점이 언급되거나 접속사 when, if절에 현재시제 동사가 쓰인 경우 will이 정답일 가능성이 높다.

7. 자연 현상, 질병, 의학 관련하여 추측하기 어려운 사항에 대한 내용일 경우 may 또는 might가 정답일 가능성이 높다.

Tesla is one of the world's top manufacturers of energy-efficient electric cars. What makes the company popular is that its vehicles ① _____ be driven farther on a single charge than most others on the market.
 	
    (a) will
    (b) must
    (c) might
  ③ (d) can
	STEP ① 빈칸의 위치와 선택지를 확인하여 조동사 유형임을 파악하고 빈칸 앞 뒤 문맥을 파악한다.
	
	STEP ② 전기 자동차가 한번의 충전으로 다른 전기 자동차보다 더 멀리 운행된다는 의미를 나타내는데, 이것은 테슬라의 전기 자동차가 가진 능력을 나타내는 것이므로 능력, 가능성에 대한 내용임을 확인한다.
	
	STEP ③ '~할 수 있다'라는 의미로 가능성을 나타내는 조동사 (d) can를 정답으로 선택한다.

· 연결어

1. **빈칸 위치 확인:** 빈칸 뒤에 완전한 문장이 위치하거나, 콤마(,) 뒤에 완전한 문장이 있거나 명사구가 위치한다면 연결어 유형 문제이다.

2. **선택지 확인:** 선택지가 접속사, 접속부사, 전치사로 구성되어 있는 것을 보고 연결어 유형임을 확인한다.

3. 빈칸 뒤에 주어와 동사가 포함된 완전한 절이 위치하면 접속사가 정답이다.

4. 빈칸 뒤에 콤마(,)가 있고 그 뒤에 완전한 절이 위치하면 접속부사가 정답이다.

5. 빈칸 뒤에 명사구 또는 동명사가 위치하면 전치사가 정답이다.

· 연결어 예제 풀이

Wolfgang Amadeus Mozart was a classical musician and composer who is still widely known today. ② As a child prodigy, he started composing music ① _____ he was five and could play multiple instruments by age six.
 	
    (a) in case
    (b) until
    (c) now that
  ③ (d) when
	STEP ① 빈칸이 문장과 문장 사이에 콤마(,) 없이 연결되어 있는 것을 확인하고 접속사 문제임을 확인하고 빈칸 앞뒤 문장의 문맥을 파악한다.
	
	STEP ② 빈칸 앞 문장에서 동사가 started이므로 과거 시제임을 알 수 있고, 빈칸 뒤의 문장의 동사도 was로 과거시제임을 확인한다.
	
	STEP ③ 문맥상 '그가 5세 때 음악을 작곡하기 시작했다'라는 의미가 가장 자연스러우므로 '~할 때'를 나타내는 부사절 접속사 (d) when이 정답이다.

청취 파트별 공략 가이드

• 청취 (Listening) 구성

- 구성: 4개의 PART로 구성 (PART 1~4)
- 음원 진행 순서: [1차 질문 – 대화/담화 – 2차 질문]의 순서로 진행
- 음원 길이 및 총 문항 수: 총 27-28분, 총 26문항 [6문항(파트2, 3)-7문항(파트1, 4)]
- 성우: 남, 여 전원 미국인
- 특징: 시험지에 질문은 나와 있지 않고 각 문항별로 (a)~(d)의 선택지만 표시
- PART별 지문 종류 및 문항 수

구분	지문 종류	문항 수
PART 1	2인 대화 (남자와 여자의 일상 대화)	7
PART 2	1인 담화 (행사나 제품에 대한 광고, 설명)	6
PART 3	2인 대화 (남자와 여자의 일상 대화 – A, B의 장/단점)	6
PART 4	1인 담화 (특정 주제에 대한 팁 또는 과정 및 방법 설명)	7

• 청취 풀이 과정

음원 순서	General Direction	PART 1 Direction	PART 1 1차 질문	PART 1 지문	PART 1 2차 질문	PART 2 Direction
소요 시간	1분 30초	20초	1분 5-10초	3분 30초 내외	1분 45초	20초
할 일	PART 1 선택지 분석		질문 노트테이킹	들으면서 문제 풀기	PART 2 선택지 분석	

음원 순서	PART 2 1차 질문	PART 2 지문	PART 2 2차 질문	PART 3 Direction	PART 3 1차 질문	PART 3 지문
소요 시간	1분 5-10초	3분 30초 내외	1분 45초	20초	1분 5-10초	3분 30초 내외
할 일	질문 노트테이킹	들으면서 문제 풀기	PART 3 선택지 분석		질문 노트테이킹	들으면서 문제 풀기

음원 순서	PART 3 2차 질문	PART 4 Direction	PART 4 1차 질문	PART 4 지문	PART 4 2차 질문
소요 시간	1분 45초	20초	1분 5-10초	3분 30초 내외	1분 45초
할 일	PART 4 선택지 분석		질문 노트테이킹	들으면서 문제풀기	

· **PART 1**: 2인 대화

PART 1은 남자와 여자의 일상적인 대화가 제시됩니다. 주로 개인의 일상과 경험에 관련된 이야기로 구성되며, 아래와 같은 내용으로 전개됩니다.

구분	질문 내용	빈출 문제 유형
대화 초반	대화의 중심 소재 최근 경험에 대한 질문	What did ~ do last weekend? Why did ~ go yesterday?
대화 중반	세부 내용	세부 정보
대화 후반	대화 후 여자/남자가 할 일	What will ~ do after the conversation? What will ~ do ~ weekends?

■ PART 1 예시

[질문]

> 27: Why has Tessa not visited the Roadhouse Restaurant recently?
> 28: According to Tessa, what will customers appreciate about the renovations?
> 29: What did the restaurant do to improve the quality of their steaks?
> 30: How can a customer get a gift card for the restaurant?
> 31: Why does Tessa think that keeping the live country band is a good thing?
> 32: Why will more people be eating at the restaurant?
> 33: What will Tessa most likely do next Saturday?

1. 첫 번째 문제는 대부분 화자들의 대화 주제나 한 화자의 계획 및 일정에 대한 목적을 묻는 질문으로 출제되므로 대화 첫 부분에서 언급되는 주요 키워드를 잘 듣고 정답을 고릅니다.

2. 마지막 문제는 대부분 둘 중 한 화자가 대화가 끝난 후 할 일에 대해 묻는 질문으로 출제되므로 대화가 마무리 될 때 질문에서 언급된 화자가 무엇을 할 것인지 듣고 정답을 고릅니다.

3. 28~32번중 2문제 이상 지문을 듣고 풀 수 있어야 합니다.

4. 2인 대화이므로 남, 여 화자의 이름과 각 화자가 주장하는 내용을 구분하여 문제에서 둘 중 누가 언급되었는지 확인합니다.

5. 대화 내용의 진행과 문제의 순서가 동일하므로 문제의 키워드를 미리 노트테이킹하여 대화 중에 순서대로 키워드가 언급되는 것을 듣고 문제를 풉니다.

Part 1

27. (a) because it has been closed for renovations
    (b) because she dislikes the food there
    (c) because it has gotten a bad reputation
    (d) because she has been working a lot

→ 최근 경험에 대한 질문 (필수 풀이 문제)

28. (a) the more spacious layout
    (b) the beautiful views outside
    (c) the more comfortable seating
    (d) the fresh paint on the walls

→ 세부정보

29. (a) They altered the cooking process.
    (b) They changed their meat supplier.
    (c) They used different seasonings.
    (d) They replaced their head chef.

→ 세부정보

30. (a) by entering an eating contest
    (b) by giving the best karaoke performance
    (c) by winning a physical challenge
    (d) by answering the most trivia questions

→ 세부정보

31. (a) because the music is popular with the customers
    (b) because the band plays for free
    (c) because the music is her favorite genre
    (d) because the band takes requests

→ 세부정보

32. (a) The staff are friendlier.
    (b) The menu has been expanded.
    (c) The portions are larger.
    (d) The prices have been lowered.

→ 세부정보

33. (a) eat out with her officemates
    (b) bring a meal to Drake's house
    (c) visit a restaurant with her husband
    (d) have a meal with Drake's family

→ 마지막으로 여자, 남자가 대화 후 할 일을 언급 (필수 풀이 문제)

· PART 2: 1인 담화

PART 2는 특정 주제에 대한 전문가의 강연이 담화 형태로 제시됩니다. 주로 행사나 제품의 홍보 및 소개의 내용으로 구성되며, 아래와 같은 내용으로 전개됩니다.

구분	질문 내용	빈출 문제 유형
담화 초반	전문가가 전달하는 중심 소재 프레젠테이션의 목적	What is this talk mainly about? What is the talk all about?
담화 중반	세부 내용	세부 정보 (What / How / Why / When)
담화 후반	제품: 할인 방법, 제품 받는 방법 등 행사: 행사 티켓 구매/예약/할인 방법	How can one get / receive ~?

■ PART 2 예시

[질문]

34: What is the subject of the presentation?
35: What does the Air Calendar help its users with?
36: How can the Travel Atlas help users plan their itinerary?
37: What can users do with the Basics feature?
38: How can the product help users communicate while traveling?
39: How, most likely, can one get the product with all its features?

⊙ PART 2 문제 공략

1. 첫 번째 문제는 주제 또는 목적에 관한 문제이므로 지문 첫 부분에서 무엇에 대해 이야기하는 지 잘 듣고 선택지의 패러프레이징에 유의하여 정답을 선택합니다.

2. 35~39번중 2문제 이상 지문을 듣고 풀 수 있어야 합니다.

3. 1인 담화이므로 화자(the speaker)가 전달하는 내용에 집중하여 질문의 키워드가 언급되는 부분이 들리면 미리 분석해 둔 선택지 중에서 해당되는 선택지를 정답으로 고릅니다.

Part 2

34. (a) a social media site for travelers
    (b) a travel-themed convention
    (c) a useful gadget for travelers
    (d) a travel-related resource
→ 중심소재, 목적 (필수 풀이 문제)

35. (a) researching flights
    (b) choosing destinations
    (c) reviewing airlines
    (d) booking hotels
→ 세부 정보

36. (a) by rating nearby accommodations
    (b) by displaying points of interest
    (c) by listing local guides
    (d) by showing transportation options
→ 세부 정보

37. (a) They can contact other travelers.
    (b) They can buy necessities online.
    (c) They can find useful facilities.
    (d) They can make hotel reservations.
→ 세부 정보

38. (a) by translating speech
    (b) by suggesting useful phrases
    (c) by listing vocabulary
    (d) by correcting pronunciation
→ 세부 정보

39. (a) by giving it a positive review
    (b) by buying the premium version
    (c) by downloading it immediately
    (d) by joining the mailing list
→ 추론

• **PART 3**: 2인 담화

PART 3은 두 개의 항목(이하 A, B) 중에서 한 화자가 선택을 고민하는 내용이며, 다른 화자가 A와 B의 장점과 단점에 대해 함께 이야기를 나누고 대화 마지막에 A와 B 중에 무엇을 선택할 것인지 말하고 대화가 마무리됩니다.

구분	질문 내용	빈출 문제 유형
대화 초반	40번: 최근에 고민하게 된 일에 대한 질문 최근에 경험한 일에 대한 세부 질문	What did ~ do last weekend? Why is ~ thinking of ~?
대화 중반	41, 42번: A의 장점, 단점에 관한 질문 43, 44번: B의 장점, 단점에 관한 질문	세부 정보 (What / How / Why)
대화 후반	45번: A와 B 중에서 선택한 것에 관한 질문	What will ~ probably do after the conversation? What will ~ decide to do?

■ PART 3 예시

[질문]

40: Why was Jenna shopping for an air conditioner?

41: How could a central air conditioner help Jenna sleep?

42: Why is Jenna hesitant to install a condenser in her backyard?

43: What did Jenna notice about the window air conditioners at the appliance store?

44: How might a window air conditioner prevent Jenna from enjoying her bedroom?

45: What will Jenna probably do after the conversation?

PART 3 문제 공략

1. 첫 번째 문제는 대부분 화자들의 대화 주제나 한 화자의 계획 및 일정에 대한 목적을 묻는 질문으로 출제되므로 대화 첫 부분에서 언급되는 주요 키워드를 잘 듣고 정답을 고릅니다.

2. 41~44번중 2문제 이상 지문을 듣고 풀 수 있어야 합니다.

3. 대화에서 다루어지는 두 항목(A, B)의 장점과 단점을 구분해서 노트테이킹합니다.

4. 마지막 문제는 항상 두 항목(A, B) 중 무엇을 선택할 것인지에 대한 질문인데, 대화 중 언급된 A, B의 장점과 단점 중 하나를 다시 언급하는 것이 정답의 단서로 제시됩니다.

[문제 선택지]

Part 3

40. (a) because she is in a new home
    (b) because hers is broken
    (c) because she needs it for work
    (d) because hers is old
    → 화자의 상황 (필수 풀이 문제)

41. (a) by reducing the humidity
    (b) by adjusting the air flow
    (c) by keeping the house quiet
    (d) by making a soothing sound
    → 세부 정보

42. (a) It would damage her flowers.
    (b) It would cost too much money.
    (c) It would take a long time.
    (d) It would take up too much room.
    → 세부 정보

43. (a) that they use minimal electricity
    (b) that they are affordable
    (c) that they need little maintenance
    (d) that they are powerful
    → 세부 정보

44. (a) by restricting the sunlight
    (b) by leaking water
    (c) by reducing the temperature
    (d) by blocking the view
    → 세부 정보

45. (a) install air conditioning throughout her house
    (b) request an estimate for installation
    (c) install air-conditioning in her bedroom
    (d) ask for a discount on installation
    → 대화 후 할 일 / 결정할 것은? (필수 풀이 문제)

· PART 4: 1인 담화

PART 4는 1인 화자가 특정 주제에 대한 팁 또는 과정 및 방법 설명하는 담화 형식의 지문이며,
First, Secondly, … Lastly 또는 Number one, Number two, … Number five와 같이
과정이나 여러 항목을 순서대로 열거하는 형식을 취합니다.

PART 4	질문 내용	빈출 문제 유형
담화 초반	담화의 주제	What is this talk mainly about?
담화 중반	항목 1~5번에 관한 세부 정보	세부 정보(What / How / Why)
담화 후반	마지막 항목에 대한 세부 질문	세부 정보(What / How / Why)

■ PART 4 예시

[질문]

46: What is the speaker mainly talking about?
47: According to the speaker, what is the whole idea of mindfulness meditation?
48: According to the speaker, why is it necessary to set an alarm for the session?
49: Why, most likely, should one stretch before meditating?
50: What advice does the speaker give about the proper posture when meditating?
51: According to the speaker, what should one do during meditation?
52: How should one end a meditation session?

PART 4 문제 공략

1. 첫 번째 문제는 대부분 주제에 관한 문제이므로 지문 첫 부분에서 무엇에 대해 이야기하는지 잘 듣고 선택지의 패러프레이징에 유의하여 정답을 선택합니다.

2. 47~52번 중 2문제 이상 지문을 듣고 풀 수 있어야 합니다.

3. PART 4에서 다루어지는 주제가 상식적으로 널리 알려진 내용일 경우, 지문에서 정답의 단서를 놓치더라도 질문 노트테이킹만으로 지문의 주제를 토대로 정답을 추론할 수 있습니다.

Part 4

46. (a) advice on teaching meditation
    (b) tips on group meditation
    (c) advice on starting meditation
    (d) tips on advanced meditation
→ 담화의 주제 (필수 풀이 문제)

47. (a) to imagine oneself in different places
    (b) to focus on what will happen in the distant future
    (c) to learn how to ignore daily annoyances
    (d) to pay attention to a specific moment in time
→ 첫 번째 항목에 관한 세부 정보

48. (a) to signal the start of the session
    (b) to avoid being distracted
    (c) to keep the same session length
    (d) to prevent sleepiness
→ 두 번째 항목에 세부 정보

49. (a) to avoid feeling uncomfortable
    (b) to assist breathing techniques
    (c) to allow more frequent practice
    (d) to focus the mind for the session
→ 세 번째 항목에 세부 정보

50. (a) Sit with legs crossed.
    (b) Keep the arms folded.
    (c) Sit on the floor.
    (d) Keep the back upright.
→ 네 번째 항목에 관한 세부 정보

51. (a) focus on staying still
    (b) visualize a pleasant location
    (c) concentrate on breath control
    (d) recall a happy memory
→ 다섯 번째 항목에 관한 세부 정보

52. (a) by noticing the benefits
    (b) by doing some gentle movement
    (c) by resting with eyes closed
    (d) by thinking about the day ahead
→ 여섯 번째 항목에 관한 세부 정보

청취 문제 풀이 가이드

• 청취 문제풀이 핵심 전략 4가지

1. 선택지 분석은 꼭 미리 한다.

질문은 시험지에 기재되어 있지 않고 선택지만 인쇄되어 있기 때문에 대화나 담화를 듣기 전에 선택지를 먼저 확인해두는 것이 중요합니다. 특히 2인 대화 혹은 1인 담화에서 다룰 중심소재나 핵심 키워드들을 미리 파악하고 지문을 들을 수 있기 때문에 들으면서 선택지에서 빠르게 정답을 고를 수 있습니다.

선택지 분석 세부 전략

(1) 핵심 키워드에 표시하기

모든 단어가 아니라 핵심 키워드에만 표시(동그라미, 밑줄 등)를 하면 문제를 풀 때 한 눈에 키워드를 파악하여 정답을 선택할 수 있습니다.

(2) 단어별 표시 방법

핵심 명사나 형용사, 부사는 동그라미를, 동사는 밑줄을 그어줍니다. 때에 따라 증감을 나타내는 동사의 경우, 증가는 윗방향 화살표, 감소는 아래방향 화살표로 표시하며, 장점, 이점, 혜택 등과 같은 긍정적이거나 이득을 나타내는 단어는 +로, 단점, 불이익 등 부정적인 단어는 -로 표시합니다.

ex) That the speaker lacks the confidence. ↓

(3) 선택지 단서로 질문의 의문사 추측하기

아래와 같은 선택지를 보고 질문의 의문사를 추측할 수 있습니다.

ex) by celebrating her son's achievement
→ by -ing는 방법을 나타내므로 의문사 h(how) 미리 적기

Because he didn't like the food
→ because는 이유를 나타내므로 y(why) 미리 적기

to explain how to learn English
→ to부정사가 '~하기 위해'라는 목적을 나타내므로 y(why) 미리 적기

when he will return
→ 선택지에 when, after, before 등의 시간부사 접속사가 있다면 when 미리 적기

(4) 모든 선택지를 한글로 번역할 필요는 없다.

모든 선택지를 모두 번역하는 것은 너무 많은 시간이 소요될 뿐만 아니라 지문을 들을 때 정답의 단서나 정답과 관련된 구문을 나타내는 키워드를 놓칠 가능성이 높습니다. 선택지에서 키워드가 될 수 있는 동사나 명사에 표시를 하는 정도로 시간을 절약하되, 정답률이 높은 각 PART의 첫 번째 문제의 선택지는 한두 단어 정도로 요약해서 한글로 적는 것은 좋습니다.

(5) 선택지 분석의 타이밍

문법 시험 시작 후 20분, 청취 시험이 시작되면서 음원이 방송으로 재생됩니다. 이 때 나오는 청취 시험 안내인 General direction과 각 PART가 시작되기 전 PART별 direction이 재생될 때가 바로 선택지를 분석할 최적의 타이밍입니다. 기출 문제집의 청취 문제를 풀면서 이 direction 시간에 선택지 분석하는 것이 어렵다면 문법을 빨리 풀고 나서 빠르게 PART별 선택지 중에서 아래와 같이 일부를 먼저 분석해두는 것도 좋습니다.

PART 구분	분석 문항
PART 1	첫 두 문제, 마지막 문제 미리 분석
PART 2 & 3	첫 문제와 마지막 문제 미리 분석
PART 4	첫 문제 꼼꼼히 분석 후 이어지는 2문제 키워드 분석

2. 질문 노트테이킹

질문이 시험지에 나오지 않는 청취 문제를 풀기 위해서 질문 노트테이킹은 필수적입니다. 노트테이킹은 질문의 핵심 키워드를 위주로 적어야 하며, 이를 통해 대화나 담화에서 핵심 문장을 포착하고 오답 선택지 키워드를 소거하여 정답 확률을 높일 수 있습니다. 이를 위해 매일 최소 1~2지문씩 질문 노트테이킹 연습을 하면서 어려운 질문도 키워드를 빠르게 적을 수 있도록 사전에 철저히 훈련해야 합니다.

질문 노트테이킹 세부 전략

(1) 기본 문장 구조: [의문사 – 동사 – 마지막 핵심 키워드]

청취에 출제되는 질문의 문장 구조는 다양한데, 구조뿐만 아니라 질문의 핵심이 형용사와 부사, 고유명사와 시간 표현까지 매우 다양합니다. 따라서 질문의 기본 문장 구조를 바탕으로 노트테이킹할 부분의 뼈대를 파악하고, 질문을 들으면서 추가로 적어야 하는 부분을 파악하는 훈련이 필요합니다.

(2) 자주 나오는 단어들은 축약해서 쓰는 연습하기

내용	축약 노트테이킹
의문사	why = y
	how = h
	what, which = w
증가 / 감소	↑ / ↓
부정어구 (not, never 등)	X
benefit advantage useful beneficial advantage 등 이익, 혜택에 관한 어휘	+
disadvantage downside drawback 등 부정적 어휘	–

(3) 사람 이름은 첫 글자를 대문자로 적기

남자와 여자 성우의 대화로 구성된 PART 1/3의 경우, 질문에 남자와 여자의 이름이 언급되는 경우가 많습니다. Jane 이 언급되었다면 J를, Matthew가 언급되었다면 M을 적는 식으로 사람 이름의 노트테이킹은 이름의 첫 글자를 대문자로 적습니다. 질문이 "According to Jane"이라고 시작하는 경우, 같은 주제에 대해 Matthew도 언급을 했더라도 Jane이 말하는 부분에서 정답의 단서가 언급되므로 질문에서 누구를 지칭하는지를 확인해야 합니다. 특히 동일한 주제에 대해 남자와 여자가 모두 언급하기 때문에 이를 이용한 오답 선택지도 반드시 있으므로 사람 이름을 노트테이킹하지 않으면 오답을 고를 확률도 높아집니다.

(4) 까다롭고 긴 단어는 한글로 적기

영어로 빠르게 적기 까다롭거나 길이가 긴 단어의 경우는 한눈에 알기 쉬운 짧은 한글 단어로 적거나 발음 나는 대로 적을 수 있습니다. 단, 그 단어를 봤을 때 바로 영어가 연상될 수 있어야 하며, 한글로 적으려다 오히려 막혀서 시간을 낭비하는 상황이 발생하지 않도록 미리 연습을 많이 해 두어야 합니다.

(5) 질문 노트테이킹 연습 문항 수 늘리기

　　질문 노트테이킹 연습 시 초반에는 문항 순서별로 한 문항씩 연습하다가 점차 3개에서 7개
문항까지 한 번에 노트테이킹을 쭉 이어가는 연습을 합니다. 실제 시험에서는 6~7개의 질문
이 출제되며, 각 질문 사이에 5초의 간격이 있으므로 이 시간에 맞춰 질문 노트테이킹을 빠짐
없이 할 수 있도록 준비해야 합니다.

3. 패러프레이징(paraphrasing)에 유의한다.

지텔프 청취 영역은 듣고 이해하는 능력을 평가하는 영역이므로, 문제와 지문, 그리고 선택지에
각각 동일하거나 유사한 의미의 다른 말로 표현하는 패러프레이징(paraphrasing)이 많이 적용
되어 있습니다. 따라서 평소에 패러프레이징을 분석하고 정리하는 연습을 통해 동의어와 유사
표현에 익숙해져야 합니다. 독해에 비해서 패러프레이징이 어려운 편은 아니지만, 평소에 연습을
많이 한다면 정답 선택이 수월해질 수 있으며 독해 문제를 푸는 데도 도움이 되기 때문에 청취 영
역의 패러프레이징 분석도 필요합니다.

4. 청취 전략을 수립한다.

지텔프 청취는 지텔프 전체 3개의 영역 중 난이도가 가장 높은 영역이라고 볼 수 있습니다. 따라
서 시험을 위한 전략 설정이 매우 중요합니다. 실제 시험에서 청취 4개의 PART를 모두 풀 때 시
간이 부족하다고 느낀다면 2~3개의 파트만 푸는 전략을 설정합니다.

(1) PART별 시간 분배

　　시간이 부족하지는 않지만 특정 PART에서 점수가 항상 좋지 않을 때, 차라리 그 PART를
포기하고 자신 있는 PART의 선택지 분석 및 마킹 시간으로 활용하는 것도 효율적입니다. 예
를 들어, PART 2에서 항상 1~2개의 정답률을 보이는 경우, PART 2를 하나의 선택지로 답
안지를 채우고, PART 2가 진행되는 시간에 PART 3이나 PART 4의 선택지를 미리 분석
하여 해당 PART의 정답률을 높이는 것이 더 효율적입니다. 이를 위해서 기출문제집 TEST
별 청취 점수를 비교해보면서 PART 1~4 중에 정답률이 높은 PART와 정답률이 저조한
PART를 파악하는 것이 좋습니다.

(2) 추천 전략

독해 풀이 시간 및 청취 PART 선호 성향	집중 공략 PART 추천
• 독해 시간이 부족한 편이다. • 대화 유형이 더 편하다.	PART 1, 3 집중 공략하기!
• 독해 시간이 부족한 편이다. • 전체적인 구조가 딱딱 떨어지는 PART 3, 4만 푼다.	PART 3, 4 집중 공략하기!
• 독해시간이 부족하지는 않으나 거의 딱 맞춰서 끝내는 편이다.	PART 1, 3, 4 집중 공략하기!

(3) 문제 풀이 전략 – 키워드 문장에서만 정답 찾기

청취도 독해처럼 질문의 키워드가 포함된 문장에서만 정답을 찾아야 합니다. 질문의 핵심 키워드를 벗어나면 유사하게 들리거나 관련이 있을 것으로 예상되는 단어는 반드시 오답으로 제시되므로 단순하게 핵심 키워드가 언급된 부분에서 들은 단어를 정답으로 선택합니다.

• 청취 문제풀이 전략 적용

청취 문제풀이 전략은 단순히 이론으로 정리하기보다는 실제 문제에 적용하는 연습을 통해 자신만의 문제풀이 방법을 활용하는 것이 효율적입니다. 따라서 아래의 예시와 같이 문제풀이 핵심 전략을 적용해보고, 실전에 적용할 수 있도록 매일 연습을 해봅시다.

1. 선택지 분석하기 및 노트테이킹

(a) their first experiences in an internship 첫 인턴 경험
(b) their impressions of an educational tour 교육 견학
(c) their plans to visit a broadcasting studio 방송국 방문 계획
(d) their dreams of becoming television actors 배우 꿈

(a) a collection of plant care videos 식물 관리 동영상
(b) starter kits for new gardeners 초보자 세트
(c) a list of local plant growers 식물 재배업자
(d) plans for unique garden designs 독특한 정원 디자인

2. 질문 노트테이킹

27: What are Rose and Marvin mainly talking about?
노트테이킹: *W R/M (R&M) T?*

28: What surprised Rose the most about a live set?
노트테이킹: *W surprised R 라이브 세트?*

29: What made Marvin feel dizzy in the monitoring room?
노트테이킹: *W M dizzy 모니터링?*

30: How did Rose assume that studios displayed weather maps?
노트테이킹: *H R weather map(웨더 맵)?*

31: Why will Rose's sister be interested in hearing about the studio tour?
노트테이킹: *Y R's interested 투어?*

32: According to Rose, what was unexpected about Veronica Miller?
노트테이킹: *R, W unexpected V.M.(밀러)?*

33: What advice did Veronica Miller probably give the students?
노트테이킹: *W 조언 V.M.(밀러) → (give) 학생?*

3. 패러프레이징 적용 및 정리

(1) 질문 – 스크립트 – 정답 순서로 정리한다.

(2) 질문의 포인트 키워드가 적용된 부분을 질문과 본문에 각각 형광펜으로 칠하고 패러프레이징 된 부분은 밑줄을 긋는다.

(3) 본문과 정답의 패러프레이징 표현을 빨간 펜으로 표시하고 연결해 본다.

(4) 패러프레이징된 단어/구를 아래에 정리하면서 리뷰한다.

Q. What does SunGrown Online offer gardening enthusiasts?

[SCRIPT]
Now, for the gardening enthusiasts, check out SunGrown Online's plant section. There, you can shop for a variety of colorful greenery and flowering plants supplied by the best growers in town. For beginners, we also offer seedling sets complete with basic planting tools and care instructions. If you are not sure what type of plants to look for, check out the plant section's catalogue on the app for an overview of all our garden products.

정답: (b) starter kits for new gardeners

패러프레이징
For beginners → for new gardeners / seedling sets ~ → starter kits

• 청취 관련 자주 묻는 질문 5

Q1. 32~50점 목표인데 청취를 풀어야 하나요?

No! 청취는 지텔프에서 가장 어려운 영역이며 토익 LC 350점 이상 점수를 받았던 학생도 지텔프 청취에서 한 번에 46점 이상 받은 경우가 거의 없습니다. 청취 실력이 어느 정도 갖춰진 상황이더라도 청취 없이 충분히 목표 달성이 가능합니다. 선택지 하나로 쭉 밀고 나가면 됩니다.

Q2. 32~50점 목표인데 청취에서 어떤 선택지로 찍을까요?

일반적으로 청취는 정답 선택지가 골고루 분포되어 있기 때문에 (a)~(d) 선택지 중 하나를 정해서 동일한 답으로 마킹할 경우 23~27점 사이의 점수를 받을 수 있습니다. 해당 회차의 시험의 정답 분포에 따라 운좋게 31점까지도 나올 수도 있습니다.

Q3. 청취 점수가 잘 안 나오는데 청취를 꼭 공부해야 하나요?

각자 지닌 청취 실력이 다 다르기 때문에 현재 자신의 수준을 제대로 파악하고 접근해야 합니다.

(1) 지문의 내용이 잘 안 들리며 어휘력이 좋지 않고 문장 해석 또한 초보의 수준인 경우

지금은 청취 문제를 풀 단계가 아닙니다. 기출 문제는 너무 버거운 수준입니다. 지텔프 문법 영역을 우선 학습하면서 동시에 어휘 암기, 구문 독해 연습을 통한 기초 학습을 꾸준히 3주 이상 진행하시기 바랍니다. 기본적인 어휘력이 바탕이 된 상태에서 해석 실력도 향상된다면 그 때 청취 학습을 시작할 수 있습니다. 문장 해석 및 어휘력이 부족한 상태에서 청취 학습은 전혀 효과가 없습니다.

(2) 지문의 내용을 절반 정도 이해할 수 있으며, 어휘력과 독해 실력이 중급 수준인 경우

다음의 순서대로 매일 꾸준히 청취 학습을 진행해보세요.
① 청취 PART 1~4 풀이 → ② 질문노트테이킹 연습 → ③ 패러프레이징 정리 → ④ 청취 스크립트 분석 (독해 풀이 방식과 동일) → ⑤ 잘 안 들리는 구간은 형광펜으로 칠하고 여러 번 듣기 → ⑥ 여러 번 듣고 노트에 적기

Q4. 제가 소위 "만학도"입니다. 독해는 기본기가 있는 것 같은데 청취는 도무지 들리지가 않습니다. 청취 학습을 꼭 해야 할까요?

만학도 분들께서 특히 청취 영역 때문에 고생하시는 것을 지금까지 많이 지켜봐 왔습니다. 그런데 그 중에 99%는 처음에 청취를 포기했다가 수차례의 정기시험에서 목표 점수 65점 달성에 실패하시고 결국 청취에서 점수를 올려야 한다는 결론을 깨닫게 됩니다. 그리고 나서 청취 PART 2개 정도만 듣고 문제를 푸는 것을 목표로 정말 열심히 연습하셔서 마침내 목표 달성을 이루시는 것도 많이 봐왔습니다. 청취 기본기가 전혀 없으신 분은 지문의 모든 문장을 받아쓰기로 연습하기도 하셨습니다. 총점 평균 65점이 목표라면 청취는 포기하시면 안됩니다. 앞서 설명해드린 파트별 공략 가이드와 문제 풀이 가이드를 숙지하시고 기출 문제를 풀고 분석하셔서 청취에서 최대 50점을 확보하시는 것이 좋습니다.

Q5. 총점 평균 65점이 나오려면 청취에서 몇 점이 필요한가요?

문법은 최소 92점 이상, 독해는 65점 이상이 나온다는 가정하에 최소 42점 이상이 되어야 안정적으로 점수 달성이 가능합니다. 문법과 독해에서 그 이상의 점수가 나오면 그만큼 청취에서 덜 나와도 안정적으로 목표 점수를 달성할 수 있습니다. 문법은 100점도 불가능한 점수가 아니니 도전해보세요!

독해 파트별 공략 가이드

- 독해 [Reading and Vocabulary] 구성
  - 구성: 4개의 PART로 구성 (PART 1~4)
  - 총 문항 수: 총 28문항 (각 PART별 7문항씩)
  - 특징: 각 PART의 마지막 6번째, 7번째 문제는 동의어 문제로 출제
  - PART별 지문 종류 및 문항 수

구분	지문 종류	문항 수
PART 1	Biographical Article (위인/유명 인사의 전기문)	7
PART 2	Magazine Article (잡지 기사문)	7
PART 3	Encyclopedia Article (백과사전식 지문)	7
PART 4	Business/formal letter (비즈니스 서신)	7

• PART 1: Biographical Article (위인/유명 인사의 전기문)

PART 1은 역사적 위인이나 유명 인사를 주제로 하는 지문이 출제되며, 아래와 같은 구성으로
전개됩니다.

문단	주요 내용	빈출 문제 유형
1번째 문단	인물의 주요 업적 요약 설명	What is 인물 best known for? What is 인물 (most) famous for?
2번째 문단	인물의 출생 및 어린 시절 경력을 시작하게 된 계기 진로를 선택한 시기	What motivated/inspired 인물 to do ~? When 인물 first ~? When 인물 started ~? How did 인물 ~?
3번째 문단	초기 업적	세부 정보 (What / How / Why)
4번째 문단	주요 업적	세부 정보 (What / How / Why)
5번째 문단	인물의 근황 / 인물에 대한 평가	세부 정보 (What / How / Why)

BILLIE HOLIDAY

Billie Holiday was an American jazz and swing singer. Best known for her compelling and emotional vocal delivery as well as improvisational singing skills that brought her songs to life, she is widely seen as one of the most influential jazz singers of all time.

1번째 문단: 인물의 주요 업적 요약 설명
⇒ 53. What is Billie Holiday most remembered for?

Eleanora Fagan, who later took the stage name Billie Holiday, was born on April 7, 1915, in Philadelphia, Pennsylvania. While her paternal parentage is disputed, American jazz musician Clarence Holiday is reported to be her father. He left not long after she was born, and she grew up with her mother in Baltimore, Maryland. Holiday's early life was marred by instability, leading to her drop out of school at the age of eleven and often get in trouble with the law. She found peace in music and, as a young teenager, started singing in nightclubs in the Harlem neighborhood of New York.

2번째 문단: 인물의 출생 및 어린 시절 / 경력을 시작하게 된 계기 / 진로를 선택한 시기
→ 54. Why did Holiday probably start singing in nightclubs?

Holiday's reputation grew with each performance. She made her recording debut at the age of eighteen, and it was then that she also reconnected with her father. In 1935, she was signed and began recording in earnest, showcasing her flair for adapting her voice to fit a song's mood. In 1938, Holiday made the potentially risky decision to work with Artie Shaw and his orchestra. In doing so, she became one of the first Black vocalists to work with a white orchestra. The increased exposure led her popularity to grow significantly.

3번째 문단: 초기 업적
→ 55. According to the text, how did Holiday make a breakthrough in her career?

In 1939, Holiday recorded her most controversial song, titled "Strange Fruit," about violence against African Americans in the American South. The lyrics, combined with a slow tempo and emphasis on certain words, created a hauntingly painful impression of the effects of racism, but the song met resistance in a still racially divided America. Nonetheless, the powerful feelings it evoked as well as its notoriety helped propel the song to fame.

4번째 문단: 주요 업적
→ 56. Based on the text, why, most likely, did some people dislike "Strange Fruit"?

Throughout the 1940s and 1950s, Holiday continued to perform concerts, including multiple sold-out shows at New York's famous Carnegie Hall. On July 17, 1959, she died in New York City from health complications caused by chronic alcohol and drug addiction. More than 3,000 people attended her funeral, including many famous jazz performers. In 2000, she was inducted into the Rock and Roll Hall of Fame, which cemented her influential status.

5번째 문단: 인물의 근황
→ 57. What achievement proved Holiday's lasting legacy?

PART 2는 과학, 생물, 사회, 환경 분야의 연구나 고대 유물의 발견 등을 주제로 하는 지문으로
출제되며, 아래와 같은 구성으로 전개됩니다.

문단	주요 내용	빈출 문제 유형
1번째 문단	연구 주제 설명 연구 목적/결과	What is the main topic? What is the article all about? What is the article mainly about?
2~4번째 문단	연구의 계기, 초기 실험 연구의 주요 결과 특징 / 연구 방법	세부 정보 (What / How / Why) 일치/불일치 (true / NOT true)
마지막 문단	연구에 대한 시사점 / 한계점	How can 연구 주제 have a(n) (significant) impact on ~? 세부 정보 (What / How / Why)

PART 2 예시

THE CHALLENGE OF NEW YEAR'S RESOLUTIONS

At the beginning of every year, many Americans make resolutions that they fail to follow
through on. Despite these continual failures, people still resolve to quit their old vices or start
healthy new practices whenever the new year rolls around. There are several reasons why
people struggle to change their habits, and those reasons are connected to how the human
brain works.

1번째 문단: 연구 주제 설명
→ 60. What is the article all about?

First, it is hard to keep New Year's resolutions because they go against the habits we
have already made a part of our daily routine. The connections between neurons in our brain
are responsible for our habits and, while these connections are not necessarily permanent,
they do become stronger the more often we repeat a habit. Until we incorporate resolutions
into our daily routines, they may be difficult to stick to. For example, if going to the gym
is not already a habit for someone, it will be much easier for them to give up soon after
starting.

2번째 문단: 연구의 주요 결과 특징 ①
→ 61. Based on the text why, most likely, is it hard to work new habits into a daily schedule?

Second, the act of creating resolutions on its own can be beneficial, even if they are not acted upon. Simply thinking about making a positive change in one's life, such as losing weight or exercising more, gives one a sense of accomplishment. Thus, the actual act of doing these things is not necessary for people to feel better about themselves.

3번째 문단: 연구의 주요 결과 특징 ②

→ 62. According to the article, how do people boost their mood when making resolutions?

This phenomenon can be explained by what scientists call "affective forecasting," through which people predict that what they feel in the present will also be what they feel in the future. People feel good when they create New Year's resolutions, so they assume that they will also feel good when they finally put their plans into action. However, when the time comes to fulfill the resolution—and the act does not give the positive feeling they envisioned—many people will either procrastinate or get discouraged and quit.

4번째 문단: 연구의 주요 결과 특징 ③

→ 63. According to the fourth paragraph, why do most people abandon their New Year's resolutions?

By knowing how the brain works, people can achieve resolutions more easily. One of the best ways to form new habits and to feel good about doing them is to focus on only one goal at a time and, if the goal is a large one, to break it down into smaller, easier-to-achieve tasks.

5번째 문단: 연구에 대한 시사점

→ 64. What can people do to ensure that their resolutions are successful?

• PART 3: Encyclopedia Aricle(백과사전식 지문)

PART 3은 인문, 사회, 과학, 동식물 등의 다양한 주제를 다루는 지문으로 출제되며, 아래와 같은 구성으로 전개됩니다.

문단	주요 내용	빈출 문제 유형
1번째 문단	중심 소재에 대한 소개 정의/특징	What is 중심 소재?
2번째 문단	중심 소재의 기원	세부 정보 (When 중심 소재 found? / What 중심 소재 origin? / Why ~ started?)
3-4번째 문단	세부 특징	세부 정보 (When / What / How / Why) 일치/불일지 (true / NOT true)
5번째 문단	현황/의의/시사점/과제	세부 정보 (When / What / How / Why)

ONLINE DISINHIBITION

Online disinhibition is a psychological phenomenon in which people who communicate online feel less restrained and express themselves more freely than they would in real-life interactions. Thus, people may act completely different when interacting with others online. The term was first used in 2004 by psychology professor John Suler when he published the article, "The Online Disinhibition Effect."

1번째 문단: 중심 소재에 대한 소개
→ 67. What is the article mainly about?

This phenomenon can manifest in one of two ways: benign disinhibition or toxic disinhibition. In benign disinhibition, online interactions can have positive effects on the people involved. For example, some people are able to freely express themselves on the Internet without feeling embarrassed or anxious. People who are shy or who belong to marginalized groups can easily find others with similar interests, develop friendships, and feel safe.

2번째 문단: 중심 소재의 기원
→ 68. Based on the second paragraph, why do some people find it easier to communicate online?

On the other hand, when the disinhibition is of the toxic kind, online interactions tend to have negative effects on the people involved. Toxic disinhibition occurs when people act cruelly online, using foul language or harsh insults that can be hurtful to those who are on the receiving end.

There are several factors that influence online disinhibition. One of these is the feeling of anonymity. When people believe that they can separate their actions on the Internet from their real-life identity, they are more confident about opening up. People feel like they can say anything online because they think that those actions will have no effect on their real lives.

4번째 문단: 세부 특징 ①
→ 69. According to the fourth paragraph, why are some people able to separate their online behavior from their real-life identity?

Online interactions that do not happen in real time also affect online disinhibition. Unlike in real-time communication, if someone knows that what they are posting will not be seen by the recipient right away, they might worry less about being unkind and decide to send inconsiderate messages. However, in some cases, delayed communication might also give the sender an opportunity to compose messages with more care.

5번째 문단: 세부 특징 ②
→ 70. What is most likely true about people who use real-time online communication methods?

Finally, it is impossible to see other people's facial expressions or hear their tone of voice online. This lack of nonverbal cues that would otherwise be present in face-to-face interactions can cause a person to forget that they are still talking to a real human with real emotions.

6번째 문단: 세부 특징 ③
→ 71. How does the lack of nonverbal cues online affect people?

• PART 4: Business letter / Formal letter (비즈니스 서신)

PART 4는 구매, 환불, 채용 공고, 추천서, 이직 요청 등 사업 및 거래를 주제로 하는 서신으로 출제되며, 아래와 같은 구성으로 전개됩니다.

문단	주요 내용	빈출 문제 유형
1번째 문단	편지를 쓴 이유	Why did A write a letter? What is the purpose of the letter?
2번째 문단	요청사항 답변, 주최하는 행사의 목적 등	세부 정보(When / What / How / Why)
3번째 문단	세부 정보	세부 정보(When / What / How / Why)
4번째 문단	세부 정보	세부 정보(When / What / How / Why)
5번째 문단	끝 인사 (첨부파일, 연락처, 수신인이 할 일 등을 언급)	What will A do when ~? What should A do if ~? Why probably A call/contact ~?

PART 4 예시

Audrey Hilton

Owner

Four Walls Printing Shop

Dear Ms. Hilton,

Good day! I am the manager of Mercer Office Supplies, and I am writing to address the letter you sent us complaining about your recent order.

1번째 문단: 편지를 쓴 이유
→ 74. Why is Robert Kingsley writing to Audrey Hilton?

In the letter, you mentioned that the parcel delivered to your shop on July 24 was missing two reams of XT 8.5-by-11-inch photo paper. Upon consulting our records and making inquiries with our packaging staff, we have confirmed that the package sent to you was indeed incomplete.

2번째 문단: 세부 정보
→ 75. What did Audrey mention in her letter?

On that particular date, we experienced a glitch on our website due to the surge of orders we have been experiencing this graduation season. We have never had so many orders in the history of the company. This momentary malfunction affected the processing of orders and resulted in the incorrect quantity of paper being delivered to you.

3번째 문단: 세부 정보
→ 76. Why did Mercer Office Supplies suffer a computer glitch?

I would like to apologize for our service issue. Moreover, I am requesting your patience in awaiting the delivery of the rest of your order. This is because our supplier has temporarily confined bulk orders of this particular product to one case per week, due to the current high demand. So, we will not be able to refill our stock until later this week. Rest assured that we will forward the remainder of your order to you as soon as possible.

4번째 문단: 추론
→ 77. Why, most likely, will the company's delivery of the remaining items be delayed?

To compensate for the inconvenience we have caused you, we will deliver four reams of the photo paper, two more than you initially ordered, to your address as soon as it is available. We will email you when the products have arrived in our warehouse and are ready to ship. Please contact me by email if you have further questions.

Thank you very much for your understanding.

Regards,.

5번째 문단: 끝 인사 (첨부파일, 연락처, 수신인이 할 일 등의 내용 언급)
→ 78. How does Robert plan to make up for Audrey's inconvenience?

• 독해 문제풀이 핵심 전략 4가지

1. [질문 – 지문 – 정답]의 순서로 푼다.

독해 문제는 질문의 핵심 키워드를 파악한 후 지문에 언급되거나 의미는 유사하지만 다른 말로 표현된 패러프레이징 문장을 찾으면 정답을 쉽게 찾을 수 있습니다. 첫 문제에 대한 정답의 단서는 지문의 첫 문단에 위치하고, 두 번째 문제에 대한 정답의 단서는 그 다음 문단에 위치하는 식으로 문제의 순서가 지문의 문단의 순서와 대체로 동일하기 때문에 하나의 질문을 읽고 지문에서 정답의 단서를 찾고 선택지에서 정답을 고른 후, 그 다음 질문을 읽는 방식으로 각 문제를 하나씩 푸는 것이 효율적입니다.

2. 동의어 문제는 해당 어휘가 위치한 문단에서 바로 푼다.

동의어 문제는 PART별로 2문제씩 출제되며, 한 PART 당 7문제 중에 여섯 번째, 일곱 번째에 위치합니다. 동의어 문제는 지문에서 두 단어에 밑줄로 표시되어 해당 단어의 의미가 가장 가까운 것을 찾는 유형으로 출제되므로, 첫 번째에서 다섯 번째 문제를 순서대로 풀다가 밑줄로 표시된 단어가 보이면 바로 해당 동의어 문제를 푸는 것이 좋습니다. 동의어는 사전적 동의어 또는 문맥적 동의어를 고르는 유형으로 출제되며, 최근 출제경향으로는 문맥적 동의어를 찾는 문제가 더 자주 출제되고 있습니다. 그래서 내용 흐름의 이해가 필수적이며, 같은 맥락에서 의미를 알지 못하는 어휘가 제시되더라도 문단을 읽으면서 의미를 파악할 수 있도록 문맥 이해를 위한 해석 연습을 해야 합니다.

3. 패러프레이징(paraphrasing)에 유의한다.

지텔프 독해 문제는 단순히 읽을 수 있는지를 평가하는 것이 아니라 독해 능력을 평가하기 위해 출제된 것으로, 문제와 지문, 그리고 선택지에 각각 동일하거나 유사한 의미의 다른 말로 표현하는 패러프레이징(paraphrasing)이 많이 적용되어 있습니다. 따라서 평소에 패러프레이징을 분석하고 정리하는 연습을 통해 동의어, 유사 표현에 익숙해져야 합니다.

4. 오답 소거를 필수적으로 활용한다.

의미를 알지 못하는 어휘를 만났을 때 문맥 파악을 통해 의미를 추론할 수 있지만, 일반적인 독해 문제를 풀이할 때는 함정 선택지와 복잡한 패러프레이징 때문에 한 번에 정답을 찾아내기 어렵습니다. 정답의 단서가 위치한 문단은 찾았지만 선택지에서 정답을 찾아내기 어려운 경우, 단순히 해당 문단을 반복해서 읽는 것은 오히려 시간을 낭비하는 비효율적인 방법이 될 수 있습니다. 따라서 오답을 소거하여 정답을 찾는 방법을 활용하는 것이 좋습니다.

· 독해 문제풀이 전략 적용

독해 문제풀이 전략은 단순히 이론으로 정리하기보다 실제 문제에 적용하는 연습을 통해 자신만의 독해 문제풀이 방법을 체득하는 것이 효율적입니다. 따라서 아래의 예시와 같이 문제풀이 핵심 전략을 적용해보고, 자신에게 맞는 문제풀이 방법을 만들어 보세요.

[핵심 전략 적용 예시 1]

Serena Williams is an American professional athlete recognized as one of the best tennis players of all time. She is **best known for** winning the most major tournaments, known as Grand Slams, of any female tennis player of her generation.

Q. What is Serena Williams **most famous for**?
 	
(a) being the ~~youngest professional tennis player~~ of all time
(b) securing more tournament victories than any of her peers
(c) having the ~~longest professional tennis career~~ of any player
(d) ~~winning more tournaments in a single year~~ than any of her peers
	① 질문을 먼저 확인하여 정답의 힌트를 주는 포인트 키워드 찾기: most famous for
	
	② 지문에서 most famous for가 패러프레이징 되어 있는 부분을 찾고, 그 주변에서 정답 단서 확인하기
	정답 단서: winning the most major tournaments, known as Grand Slams, of any female tennis player of her generation (그녀의 세대의 그 어떤 여성 테니스 선수들 중 그랜드 슬램이라고 알려진 가장 큰 메이저 대회를 우승한 것)
	
	③ 파악한 내용을 토대로 (a)~(d)의 내용을 확인하며 오답 소거
	  (a) youngest(가장 어린/젊은)와 관련된 내용이 언급되지 않았으므로 소거한다.
	  (b) winning을 securing으로, most major tournaments ~ of any female tennis player of her generation을 more tournament victories than any of her peers로 패러프레이징하여 정답의 단서와 동일한 의미를 나타내므로 정답이다.
	  (c) longest ~ tennis career(가장 긴 테니스 경력)과 관련된 내용이 언급되지 않았으므로 소거한다.
	  (d) winning more tournaments ~ than any of her peers는 (b)와 동일한 내용이지만 '단 1년만에'(in a single year) 최다 우승했다는 내용은 없으므로 오답으로 소거한다.

winning → securing

most major tournaments ~ of any female tennis player of her generation → more tournament victories than any of her peers

질문 What is Serena Williams most famous for?

키워드 및 정답 단서 She is best known for winning the most major tournaments, known as Grand Slams, of any female tennis player of her generation.

정답 (b) securing more tournament victories than any of her peers

매력적인 오답 (d) winning more tournaments ~~in a single year~~ than any of her peers

[핵심 전략 적용 예시 2-1]

Although Williams's forceful personality, unconventional hairstyles, and colorful on-court attire have sometimes sparked controversy, she has established herself as a leading figure in the tennis world. She has challenged the traditional image of the sport and inspired women around the world who might now have a different notion of how the game is supposed to be played and what its greatest players are supposed to look like.

Q. Based on the passage, **why, most likely**, was Williams **influential** in the **world of women's tennis**? (a) She ~~introduced~~ the game to a new generation. (b) She ~~opened the door for other Black women~~ to play. (c) She challenged the traditions of the sport. (d) She advocated for ~~gender equality~~ among players.	① 질문을 먼저 확인하여 정답의 힌트를 주는 포인트 키워드 찾기: influential, world of women's tennis ② 지문에서 질문의 핵심 키워드가 패러프레이징 된 부분을 찾고, 그 주변에서 정답 단서 확인하기 정답 단서: She has challenged the traditional image of the sport and inspired women around the world. (그녀는 그 스포츠의 전통적인 이미지에 도전하였고 전세계에 있는 여성들에게 영감을 주었다) ③ 파악한 내용을 토대로 (a)~(d)의 내용을 확인하며 오답 소거 (a) 새로운 세대에게 테니스를 소개했다(introduced)는 내용과 관련된 언급이 없었으므로 오답으로 소거한다. (b) opened the door for는 '~를 위하여 기회를 마련해주다'라는 의미로 쓰이는 표현인데, 문맥상 전세계에 있는 여성들에게 영감을 주었다고 하여 흑인 여성에만 국한하지 않았으므로 오답으로 소거한다. (c) 정답의 단서에 쓰인 She has challenged the traditional image of the sport와 동일한 내용이므로 정답이다. (d) gender equality(성평등)에 대한 내용은 언급되지 않았으므로 오답으로 소거한다.

[핵심 전략 적용 예시 2-2]

Although Williams's forceful personality, unconventional hairstyles, and colorful on-court attire have sometimes sparked controversy, she has established herself as a leading figure in the tennis world. She has challenged the traditional image of the sport and inspired women around the world who might now have a different notion of how the game is supposed to be played and what its greatest players are supposed to look like.

Q. In the context of the passage, sparked means _____?

(a) brought on
(b) flashed
(c) thought about
(d) traced

① 동의어 문제가 마지막 부분에 위치하였다고 마지막에 푸는 것이 아니라 다른 문제를 순서대로 풀다가 밑줄로 표시된 단어가 보이면 곧장 해당 단어의 동의어 문제를 풀이한다.

② 밑줄로 표시된 단어가 포함된 문장을 읽고 해당 문장에서 어떤 의미로 쓰였는지 먼저 파악한다. 해당 문장에서 sparked는 윌리엄스의 단호한 성격, 특이한 머리 스타일, 색이 다채로운 경기복장을 주어로 하는 문장의 동사로 쓰였다. sparked의 목적어는 '논란'이라는 의미의 명사 controversy이므로 이러한 문맥에 미루어 볼 때 윌리엄스의 단호한 성격, 특이한 머리 스타일, 색이 다채로운 경기복장이 논란을 일으켰다는 의미를 나타내고 있음을 알 수 있습니다

③ 선택지 중에서 '초래하다', '야기하다'라는 의미에 가장 가까운 의미를 가진 단어를 찾는다. 이때, 사전적 동의어로 의미 자체가 전혀 다른 단어를 먼저 소거한다.

(a) brought out(초래했다): 사전적 동의어이므로 정답이다.

(b) flashed(번쩍였다): spark의 다른 뜻 '불꽃을 일으키다'라는 의미일 때 유의어인 '번쩍이다'라는 의미를 나타내는 동사의 과거형이므로 소거한다.

(c) thought about(~에 대해 생각했다): 사전적인 의미로 다르기 때문에 소거한다.

(d) traced(추적했다): 문맥상 추적하는 일과 관련이 없으므로 오답으로 소거한다.

(1) 출제된 단어와 선택지에 나온 단어를 사전에서 찾아보고, 자주 사용되는 의미 중 최대 3개를 정리한다.

spark
① <명사> 불꽃, 불똥
② <명사> 번뜩임, 기폭제
③ <동사> 촉발시키다, 유발하다

bring on
① <동사> ~을 야기하다, 초래하다

Flash
① <명사> 섬광, 번쩍임
② <동사> 번쩍이다, 비추다
③ <동사> 휙 내보이다, 빠르게 움직이다

trace
① <동사> 추적하다
② <동사> (선을 따라) 그리다, 따라가다
③ <명사> 자취, 흔적

(2) 출제된 단어가 어떤 의미로 쓰였는지 문맥으로 파악한다.

Spark

Williams's forceful personality, unconventional hairstyles, and colorful on-court attire have sometimes sparked controversy.
<동사> 촉발시키다, 유발하다
윌리엄스의 단호한 성격, 독특한 머리 스타일, 그리고 색이 다채로운 경기복장이 때때로 논란을 일으켰다.

(3) 각각 단어의 유의어를 사전에서 찾아 정리한다.

spark : cause, bring on, trigger, give rise to, prompt
flash : flicker, shoot by
trace : detect, discover, find

시원스쿨 **LAB**

2025 최신 G-TELP KOREA 공식 기출 문제

지텔프

LEVEL 2

공식
기출문제집

TEST 1~7

◀ 청취 음원
MP3 다운로드 바로가기

GENERAL TESTS OF ENGLISH LANGUAGE PROFICIENCY
G-TELP ™

LEVEL 2

TEST 1

문제집 뒤에 있는 OMR 답안지를 사용하여 실전처럼 연습할 수 있습니다.

GRAMMAR SECTION

Example:

The boys _____ in the car.

(a) be
(b) is
(c) am
(d) are

The correct answer is (d), so the circle with the letter (d) has been blackened.

ⓐ ⓑ ⓒ ●

NOW TURN THE PAGE AND BEGIN

1. Laura's apartment lease is almost up, and she is concerned about rising rent prices in her neighborhood. If her landlord were to keep her rent at the same amount, she _____ the agreement for another year.

   (a) would have happily renewed
   (b) will happily renew
   (c) would happily renew
   (d) will have happily renewed

2. Blue whales were once abundant. However, excessive hunting of the creatures for their blubber to make lamp oil has reduced the population. Fortunately, blue whale hunting was banned in 1967 _____ the species from extinction.

   (a) to save
   (b) to have saved
   (c) having saved
   (d) saving

3. Jassi has spent the past few weeks rehearsing her dance for the final project of her choreography class. Later today, she _____ her dance routine in the auditorium.

   (a) performs
   (b) will be performing
   (c) has performed
   (d) was performing

4. Tyler wants to ride the new roller coaster, Steel Goliath, but the line has a one-hour wait time. _____ he is willing to wait, he will have to come back when the line is shorter.

   (a) Unless
   (b) Whenever
   (c) Because
   (d) Once

5. Most people do not realize how many objects they touch throughout the day or how easily germs transfer between surfaces. It is important that people avoid _____ with their hands until they have thoroughly washed them.

   (a) to eat
   (b) having eaten
   (c) to have eaten
   (d) eating

6. The National Weather Service just issued a tornado warning for the town of Holmville. Local government officials advise that residents _____ indoors and away from windows to avoid being injured.

   (a) will stay
   (b) are staying
   (c) stay
   (d) stayed

7. Tunde decided to drive to work yesterday. Unfortunately, he got stuck in traffic and arrived late. If he had known that the roads were going to be so congested, he _____ the train instead.

(a) would take
(b) will take
(c) will have taken
(d) would have taken

8. Brushing one's teeth regularly is among the most effective ways to prevent cavities. That is why people _____ brush their teeth after every meal and each night before bed.

(a) should
(b) can
(c) would
(d) might

9. Keith usually works at company headquarters, but this week he needs to inspect other branches. Right now, he _____ to Texas to examine the operations of the Houston branch.

(a) is traveling
(b) had traveled
(c) travels
(d) will have been traveling

10. *2001: A Space Odyssey* is known for its innovative special effects. The film, _____, used practical features such as spaceship models, rotating sets, and high-contrast photography to craft a realistic portrayal of space.

(a) who won the award for best visual effects
(b) which won the award for best visual effects
(c) what won the award for best visual effects
(d) that won the award for best visual effects

11. It seems like only yesterday that Mica was starting her new job as a staff writer for the *Penn Times*. By next month, she _____ for the newspaper for a year.

(a) will write
(b) has been writing
(c) will have been writing
(d) writes

12. The CEO is choosing between Grace and Martha to lead the sales department. If she were to ask for my input, I _____ Grace as the team leader because of her vast experience.

(a) would have suggested
(b) will have suggested
(c) would suggest
(d) will suggest

13. Layla arrived early at the music festival. One of the performers was her favorite band, Chinked Armor. She was determined _____ the band play live, even if it meant waiting for hours.

(a) to have seen
(b) having seen
(c) to see
(d) seeing

14. It can be hard to find a trustworthy babysitter, so families in my neighborhood are lucky to have Elise. She is kind and reliable, and she _____ kids since she was sixteen years old.

(a) had been taking care of
(b) is taking care of
(c) will have taken care of
(d) has been taking care of

15. Cecilia was recently diagnosed as iron deficient. That is why her new doctor recommends that she _____ foods rich in iron, such as liver, poultry, and seafood.

(a) eat
(b) ate
(c) will eat
(d) is eating

16. Peter could not afford Glenbank University's tuition fees, and the deadline to accept the admission offer has passed. If the fees had been lower, he _____ to Glenbank to earn his degree.

(a) would move
(b) would have moved
(c) will move
(d) will have moved

17. Yuki's friends invited him over for their special "Taco Tuesday" dinner the other night. However, he declined their invitation because he _____ since 6 a.m. and felt ready to collapse from exhaustion.

(a) will have worked
(b) had been working
(c) is working
(d) has been working

18. Animals such as sheep, cows, and deer are ruminants, meaning that they re-chew partially digested food. Ruminating is a feeding technique _____ to extract more nutrition from grass, which is hard to digest.

(a) when animals use
(b) who animals use
(c) what animals use
(d) that animals use

19. Tesla is one of the world's top manufacturers of energy-efficient electric cars. What makes the company popular is that its vehicles _____ be driven farther on a single charge than most others on the market.

(a) will
(b) must
(c) might
(d) can

20. The documentary that my parents streamed yesterday was at least three hours long. They started watching the film before I left for the mall, and they _____ it when I came back.

(a) were still watching
(b) have still watched
(c) are still watching
(d) still watched

21. Jolene's neighborhood is experiencing a wave of car thefts. As a result, the local police have agreed _____ patrols in the area, and a closed-circuit security system will soon be installed.

(a) having increased
(b) to increase
(c) increasing
(d) to have increased

22. Marvin transferred from the night class to a morning session. When asked why he changed classes, he said that he dislikes _____ lectures at night because he is often sleepy by then.

(a) to attend
(b) having attended
(c) attending
(d) to be attending

23. Butler University's basketball team was down two points with less than a second remaining in the game. Their captain took a long shot, but missed. If he had scored, Butler _____ the game.

(a) would have won
(b) will win
(c) would win
(d) will have won

24. Wolfgang Amadeus Mozart was a classical musician and composer who is still widely known today. As a child prodigy, he started composing music _____ he was five and could play multiple instruments by age six.

(a) in case
(b) until
(c) now that
(d) when

25. Hazel wants to become more well-read, but she is busy with her job. If she were to get more free time, she _____ more often than she does now.

(a) would have read
(b) would read
(c) will have read
(d) will read

26. Russell, who recently graduated with a degree in data analysis, has already found a job in the fraud department of a local bank. The job involves _____ accounts for suspicious activity that may indicate criminal behavior.

(a) to have monitored
(b) having monitored
(c) to monitor
(d) monitoring

LISTENING SECTION

▶ Test 1 전체 음원 재생

DIRECTIONS:

The Listening Section has four parts. In each part you will hear a spoken passage and a number of questions about the passage. First you will hear the questions. Then you will hear the passage. From the four choices for each question, choose the best answer. Then blacken in the correct circle on your answer sheet.

Example:

(a) one
(b) two
(c) three
(d) four

Bill Johnson has four brothers, so the best answer is (d). The circle with the letter (d) has been blackened.

NOW TURN THE PAGE AND BEGIN

PART 1. *You will hear a conversation between two people. First you will hear questions 27 through 33. Then you will hear the conversation. Choose the best answer to each question in the time provided.*

27. (a) because it has been closed for renovations
    (b) because she dislikes the food there
    (c) because it has gotten a bad reputation
    (d) because she has been working a lot

28. (a) the more spacious layout
    (b) the beautiful views outside
    (c) the more comfortable seating
    (d) the fresh paint on the walls

29. (a) They altered the cooking process.
    (b) They changed their meat supplier.
    (c) They used different seasonings.
    (d) They replaced their head chef.

30. (a) by entering an eating contest
    (b) by giving the best karaoke performance
    (c) by winning a physical challenge
    (d) by answering the most trivia questions

31. (a) because the music is popular with the customers
    (b) because the band plays for free
    (c) because the music is her favorite genre
    (d) because the band takes requests

32. (a) The staff are friendlier.
    (b) The menu has been expanded.
    (c) The portions are larger.
    (d) The prices have been lowered.

33. (a) eat out with her officemates
    (b) bring a meal to Drake's house
    (c) visit a restaurant with her husband
    (d) have a meal with Drake's family

PART 2. *You will hear a presentation by one person to a group of people. First you will hear questions 34 through 39. Then you will hear the talk. Choose the best answer to each question in the time provided.*

34. (a) a social media site for travelers
    (b) a travel-themed convention
    (c) a useful gadget for travelers
    (d) a travel-related resource

37. (a) They can contact other travelers.
    (b) They can buy necessities online.
    (c) They can find useful facilities.
    (d) They can make hotel reservations.

35. (a) researching flights
    (b) choosing destinations
    (c) reviewing airlines
    (d) booking hotels

38. (a) by translating speech
    (b) by suggesting useful phrases
    (c) by listing vocabulary
    (d) by correcting pronunciation

36. (a) by rating nearby accommodations
    (b) by displaying points of interest
    (c) by listing local guides
    (d) by showing transportation options

39. (a) by giving it a positive review
    (b) by buying the premium version
    (c) by downloading it immediately
    (d) by joining the mailing list

40. (a) because she is in a new home
    (b) because hers is broken
    (c) because she needs it for work
    (d) because hers is old

43. (a) that they use minimal electricity
    (b) that they are affordable
    (c) that they need little maintenance
    (d) that they are powerful

41. (a) by reducing the humidity
    (b) by adjusting the air flow
    (c) by keeping the house quiet
    (d) by making a soothing sound

44. (a) by restricting the sunlight
    (b) by leaking water
    (c) by reducing the temperature
    (d) by blocking the view

42. (a) It would damage her flowers.
    (b) It would cost too much money.
    (c) It would take a long time.
    (d) It would take up too much room.

45. (a) install air conditioning throughout her house
    (b) request an estimate for installation
    (c) install air-conditioning in her bedroom
    (d) ask for a discount on installation

46. (a) advice on teaching meditation
    (b) tips on group meditation
    (c) advice on starting meditation
    (d) tips on advanced meditation

50. (a) Sit with legs crossed.
    (b) Keep the arms folded.
    (c) Sit on the floor.
    (d) Keep the back upright.

47. (a) to imagine oneself in different places
    (b) to focus on what will happen in the distant future
    (c) to learn how to ignore daily annoyances
    (d) to pay attention to a specific moment in time

51. (a) focus on staying still
    (b) visualize a pleasant location
    (c) concentrate on breath control
    (d) recall a happy memory

48. (a) to signal the start of the session
    (b) to avoid being distracted
    (c) to keep the same session length
    (d) to prevent sleepiness

52. (a) by noticing the benefits
    (b) by doing some gentle movement
    (c) by resting with eyes closed
    (d) by thinking about the day ahead

49. (a) to avoid feeling uncomfortable
    (b) to assist breathing techniques
    (c) to allow more frequent practice
    (d) to focus the mind for the session

THIS IS THE END OF THE LISTENING SECTION

READING AND VOCABULARY SECTION

DIRECTIONS:

You will now read four different passages. Each passage is followed by comprehension and vocabulary questions. From the four choices for each item, choose the best answer. Then blacken in the correct circle on your answer sheet.

Read the following example passage and example question.

Example:

Bill Johnson lives in New York. He is 25 years old. He has four brothers and two sisters.

How many brothers does Bill Johnson have?

(a) one
(b) two
(c) three
(d) four

The correct answer is (d), so the circle with the letter (d) has been blackened.

   ●

NOW TURN THE PAGE AND BEGIN

SERENA WILLIAMS

Serena Williams is an American professional athlete recognized as one of the best tennis players of all time. She is best known for winning the most major tournaments, known as Grand Slams, of any female tennis player of her generation.

Serena Jameka Williams was born on September 26, 1981, in Saginaw, Michigan. At a young age, Williams was inspired by her older sister Venus, who had already started learning tennis. Williams showed incredible capability and started training with her father when she was only three.

Williams entered her first tournament at the age of four. Over the next five years, she won forty-six of her forty-nine matches and was ranked first in the ten-and-under division. Her parents, wanting the sisters to improve their skills further, moved the family to West Palm Beach, Florida, where they attended a tennis academy.

Following in her sister's footsteps, Williams became a professional tennis player at age fourteen. Within a year, she was the ninety-ninth best player in the world rankings, a great feat for her age. Although many expected that Venus would be the first of the sisters to win a Grand Slam, it was Serena who won the first major tournament title, the 1999 US Open, putting her on the road to her eventual number one ranking. Williams would go on to face her sister in a number of Grand Slams as she became a regular participant in the major tournament finals. Over the course of her astounding career, Williams won more than twenty Grand Slams.

Williams's playing style stood out in the world of women's tennis. Where many female tennis players projected grace and agility on the court, Williams was powerful and aggressive, and opponents found her to be a daunting physical presence. The Williams sisters were also among the few African American professional tennis players and, at times, experienced discrimination for standing out in a mostly white sport.

Although Williams's forceful personality, unconventional hairstyles, and colorful on-court attire have sometimes sparked controversy, she has established herself as a leading figure in the tennis world. She has challenged the traditional image of the sport and inspired women around the world who might now have a different notion of how the game is supposed to be played and what its greatest players are supposed to look like.

53. What is Serena Williams most famous for?

(a) being the youngest professional tennis player of all time

(b) securing more tournament victories than any of her peers

(c) having the longest professional tennis career of any player

(d) winning more tournaments in a single year than any of her peers

54. Why did Williams's family move to Florida?

(a) to give her access to advanced tennis training

(b) to enroll her in an award-winning public school

(c) to allow her to compete against mature tennis partners

(d) to encourage her to compete in high-profile matches

55. How did Williams surprise people in 1999?

(a) by tying the number one player in the world

(b) by losing to her sister in the final round of a tournament

(c) by becoming ranked number one among female players

(d) by accomplishing something before her older sister

56. What was most notable about Williams when she was playing matches?

(a) her graceful movement on the court

(b) her remarkable physical strength

(c) her bravery when faced with discrimination

(d) her unusual serving technique

57. Based on the final paragraph, why, most likely, was Williams influential in the world of women's tennis?

(a) She introduced the game to a new generation.

(b) She opened the door for other Black women to play.

(c) She challenged the traditions of the sport.

(d) She advocated for gender equality among players.

58. In the context of the passage, capability means _____ .

(a) trust

(b) agreement

(c) support

(d) potential

59. In the context of the passage, sparked means _____ .

(a) brought on

(b) flashed

(c) thought about

(d) traced

PART 2. *Read the following magazine article and answer the questions. The underlined words in the article are for vocabulary questions.*

THE CHALLENGE OF NEW YEAR'S RESOLUTIONS

At the beginning of every year, many Americans make resolutions that they fail to follow through on. Despite these <u>continual</u> failures, people still resolve to quit their old vices or start healthy new practices whenever the new year rolls around. There are several reasons why people struggle to change their habits, and those reasons are connected to how the human brain works.

First, it is hard to keep New Year's resolutions because they go against the habits we have already made a part of our daily routine. The connections between neurons in our brain are responsible for our habits and, while these connections are not necessarily permanent, they do become stronger the more often we repeat a habit. Until we incorporate resolutions into our daily routines, they may be difficult to stick to. For example, if going to the gym is not already a habit for someone, it will be much easier for them to give up soon after starting.

Second, the act of creating resolutions on its own can be beneficial, even if they are not acted upon. Simply thinking about making a positive change in one's life, such as losing weight or exercising more, gives one a sense of accomplishment. Thus, the actual act of doing these things is not necessary for people to feel better about themselves.

This phenomenon can be explained by what scientists call "affective forecasting," through which people predict that what they feel in the present will also be what they feel in the future. People feel good when they create New Year's resolutions, so they assume that they will also feel good when they finally put their plans into action. However, when the time comes to <u>fulfill</u> the resolution—and the act does not give the positive feeling they envisioned—many people will either procrastinate or get discouraged and quit.

By knowing how the brain works, people can achieve resolutions more easily. One of the best ways to form new habits and to feel good about doing them is to focus on only one goal at a time and, if the goal is a large one, to break it down into smaller, easier-to-achieve tasks.

60. What is the article all about?

(a) how to make a fresh start each year
(b) why people fail to make resolutions
(c) when it is time to quit unhealthy habits
(d) what makes resolutions difficult to keep

61. Based on the text why, most likely, is it hard to work new habits into a daily schedule?

(a) The brain needs time to adjust to changes.
(b) People do not have time for additions to their routine.
(c) The existing connections between neurons cannot be broken.
(d) People are naturally inclined to give up when challenged.

62. According to the article, how do people boost their mood when making resolutions?

(a) by reminding themselves to think positively
(b) by thinking about their past accomplishments
(c) by imagining the benefits of transformation
(d) by planning many enjoyable activities

63. According to the fourth paragraph, why do most people abandon their New Year's resolutions?

(a) because they are unsure of how to take action
(b) because they do not feel as good as expected
(c) because they never felt positive about the plan
(d) because they did not expect to encounter obstacles

64. What can people do to ensure that their resolutions are successful?

(a) try not to make too many changes at once
(b) complete the most complicated tasks first
(c) avoid rushing through the smaller steps
(d) share plans with as many people as possible

65. In the context of the passage, continual means _____.

(a) quiet
(b) frequent
(c) tempting
(d) lengthy

66. In the context of the passage, fulfill means _____.

(a) release
(b) line up
(c) prevent
(d) carry out

ONLINE DISINHIBITION

Online disinhibition is a psychological phenomenon in which people who communicate online feel less restrained and express themselves more freely than they would in real-life interactions. Thus, people may act completely different when interacting with others online. The term was first used in 2004 by psychology professor John Suler when he published the article, "The Online Disinhibition Effect."

This phenomenon can manifest in one of two ways: benign disinhibition or toxic disinhibition. In benign disinhibition, online interactions can have positive effects on the people involved. For example, some people are able to freely express themselves on the Internet without feeling embarrassed or anxious. People who are shy or who belong to marginalized groups can easily find others with similar interests, develop friendships, and feel safe.

On the other hand, when the disinhibition is of the toxic kind, online interactions tend to have negative effects on the people involved. Toxic disinhibition occurs when people act cruelly online, using <u>foul</u> language or harsh insults that can be hurtful to those who are on the receiving end.

There are several factors that influence online disinhibition. One of these is the feeling of anonymity. When people believe that they can separate their actions on the Internet from their real-life identity, they are more confident about opening up. People feel like they can say anything online because they think that those actions will have no effect on their real lives.

Online interactions that do not happen in real time also affect online disinhibition. Unlike in real-time communication, if someone knows that what they are posting will not be seen by the recipient right away, they might worry less about being unkind and decide to send <u>inconsiderate</u> messages. However, in some cases, delayed communication might also give the sender an opportunity to compose messages with more care.

Finally, it is impossible to see other people's facial expressions or hear their tone of voice online. This lack of nonverbal cues that would otherwise be present in face-to-face interactions can cause a person to forget that they are still talking to a real human with real emotions.

67. What is the article mainly about?

    (a) the change of personality a person undergoes when online

    (b) the benefits of limiting internet screen time

    (c) the important considerations of online dating

    (d) the origin of a psychological internet phenomenon

68. Based on the second paragraph, why do some people find it easier to communicate online?

    (a) They can express themselves without feeling guilty.

    (b) They can befriend others with shared concerns.

    (c) They can be more supportive of strangers.

    (d) They can avoid interacting with certain groups.

69. According to the fourth paragraph, why are some people able to separate their online behavior from their real-life identity?

    (a) because their complete freedom is guaranteed

    (b) because their actions have no lasting effects on anyone

    (c) because their personal data can be concealed

    (d) because their posts will not be seen by their family

70. What is most likely true about people who use real-time online communication methods?

    (a) They are more creative with their messages.

    (b) They spend more time composing responses.

    (c) They tend to be more mindful of what they say.

    (d) They feel closer emotionally to the recipients.

71. How does the lack of nonverbal cues online affect people?

    (a) by making them forget that they are living a real life

    (b) by making it harder to interpret tone of voice

    (c) by making them rely on their emotions when interacting

    (d) by making it easier to disregard others' feelings

72. In the context of the passage, <u>foul</u> means _____.

    (a) direct

    (b) offensive

    (c) strict

    (d) complex

73. In the context of the passage, <u>inconsiderate</u> means _____.

    (a) rude

    (b) forgetful

    (c) instant

    (d) disapproving

Celine Mitchell
9162 Belleview Street
Golden Valley Homes
Canyon Country, CA

Dear Ms. Mitchell:

As you are aware, we held our annual homeowners association meeting last Saturday. We are writing this letter to tell you about our revised rules based on residents' suggestions and recommendations. The new guidelines are as follows:

1. The gate at the main entrance to our community will now remain closed at all times. Property owners must <u>notify</u> security before a visitor is scheduled to arrive so that the visitor can be placed on a permanent or temporary guest list. Any visitor not listed will be denied access to the community. This is to ensure the safety of all residents and to prevent any suspicious people from entering our community.

2. The association fee will be increased from $300 per month to $350 per month. This is to accommodate extra personnel for the 24/7 security measures implemented for our growing community and to change our garbage collection service from once to twice a week.

3. Excessive noise coming from any residence that causes a disturbance to neighboring houses is strictly prohibited. First-time offenders will receive a written warning, while a $100 fine will be given to repeat offenders.

4. Residents are now required to park in their private garage or carport, unless their home is not equipped with one. In addition, on-street parking is allowed on only one side of the road. This is to prevent traffic congestion and to allow easy passage of emergency vehicles. Owners of improperly parked vehicles will be subjected to fines and towing fees at their own <u>expense</u>.

We expect your full cooperation on these matters. Thank you.

Sincerely,
Mark Andrews
President
Golden Valley Homeowners Association

74. Why did Mark Andrews write a letter to Celine Mitchell?

(a) to tell her about an upcoming community meeting
(b) to ask for her suggestions for new community guidelines
(c) to advise her of a problem within their community
(d) to inform her about the new rules in their community

75. What was most likely true about visitors to the community before the first new regulation was created?

(a) Some of them received a background check.
(b) They had their own code to the front gate.
(c) Some of them intended to do harm.
(d) They could only be put on a temporary list.

76. How has the association decided to make the community's handling of its trash better?

(a) by hiring a different company
(b) by placing security cameras near waste bins
(c) by increasing service frequency
(d) by introducing a daily pickup system

77. What will happen to residents who cause excessive noise more than once?

(a) Monthly fees will be increased.
(b) Legal steps will be taken immediately.
(c) A written warning will be issued.
(d) An appropriate fine will be imposed.

78. When, most likely, would residents be allowed to park on the street?

(a) when their house does not include a carport
(b) whenever spaces are available
(c) when their family has multiple vehicles
(d) whenever traffic is minimal

79. In the context of the letter, notify means _____.

(a) limit
(b) contact
(c) fight
(d) expect

80. In the context of the letter, expense means _____.

(a) budget
(b) value
(c) cost
(d) insurance

GENERAL TESTS OF ENGLISH LANGUAGE PROFICIENCY
G-TELP ™

LEVEL 2

TEST 2

문제집 뒤에 있는 OMR 답안지를 사용하여 실전처럼 연습할 수 있습니다.

GRAMMAR SECTION

DIRECTIONS:

The following items need a word or words to complete the sentence. From the four choices for each item, choose the best answer. Then blacken in the correct circle on your answer sheet.

Example:

The boys _____ in the car.

(a) be
(b) is
(c) am
(d) are

The correct answer is (d), so the circle with the letter (d) has been blackened.

   ●

NOW TURN THE PAGE AND BEGIN

1. Unlike most other birds, turkey vultures have a very good sense of smell. Using this ability, they _____ detect meat from over a mile away and often arrive at a food source before other vulture species.

(a) must
(b) would
(c) can
(d) should

2. Keith went to the optometrist for a checkup last week, and he is now wearing his new prescription eyeglasses. His eyesight _____ for three months before Keith decided to have his eyes checked.

(a) has been worsening
(b) worsens
(c) had been worsening
(d) will worsen

3. Times Square in New York City used to be called Longacre Square. The famous commercial intersection used this original name _____ The New York Times newspaper moved its headquarters to the area in 1904.

(a) since
(b) because
(c) when
(d) until

4. Hailey was picked up from school by her dad. She asked if they could grab some tacos, and her dad agreed _____ some on the way home.

(a) to buy
(b) buying
(c) to have bought
(d) having bought

5. A hummingbird's heart beats at an average rate of 1,200 beats per minute. The human heart, _____ sixty to one hundred times per minute, is significantly slower by comparison.

(a) who only beats
(b) which only beats
(c) that only beats
(d) what only beats

6. Masood was thinking about going to the beach next weekend, but he is having second thoughts because rain is expected. If the forecast were to improve, Masood _____ to the coast as planned.

(a) would go
(b) would have gone
(c) will go
(d) will have gone

7. Frank's sister told him that there are no chemical elements starting with the letter J. Unconvinced, he _____ at the periodic table for the last five minutes, trying to prove her wrong.

(a) will stare
(b) has been staring
(c) stares
(d) had been staring

8. Keeley recently repainted her living room with blue paint, but she does not like the new look. If she had known that the color would make the room look so dark, she _____ a different shade.

(a) will use
(b) would use
(c) will have used
(d) would have used

9. The Leaning Tower of Pisa is tilted because of the soft soil that it was built on. _____, it was also this flexible soil that protected the tower from at least four strong earthquakes.

(a) In other words
(b) Therefore
(c) At the same time
(d) Otherwise

10. Timothy has a photo album in which he gathers pictures of his friends. He bought it as a freshman and, by the time he eventually graduates, he _____ memories to the book for four years.

(a) is adding
(b) will have been adding
(c) will add
(d) has been adding

11. Some people assume that Mars is a hot planet because of its red color, but the planet is actually colder than Earth. This is because the extremely thin atmosphere _____ does not retain any heat.

(a) that the planet possesses
(b) what the planet possesses
(c) when the planet possesses
(d) where the planet possesses

12. Donna has been earning a good salary translating documents from French to English. However, if she were to learn German, she _____ the opportunity to attract even more customers.

(a) will have
(b) would have
(c) will have had
(d) would have had

13. Monowi is a town in Nebraska that has a population of one. As the town's only resident, Elsie Eiler's duties involve _____ as Monowi's mayor and librarian.

(a) to act
(b) having acted
(c) to have acted
(d) acting

14. Norah's computer monitor appeared to be broken but, when the technician checked it, he found a very simple issue. Had Norah known that the monitor was simply not plugged in, she _____ the problem herself.

(a) would fix
(b) will have fixed
(c) would have fixed
(d) will fix

15. Contrary to popular belief, sweat does not have any odor. However, when bacteria that live on the skin mix with the sweat, waste matter is produced, and this causes sweat _____ bad.

(a) smelling
(b) to smell
(c) having smelled
(d) to have smelled

16. James cannot find his house keys. He _____ have checked that they were in his pocket before he left the office, but he forgot to do so.

(a) should
(b) can
(c) must
(d) will

17. Hawaiian pizza actually originated in Canada, not Hawaii. In the 1960s, Canadian Sam Panopoulos _____ with a pizza recipe when he decided to put canned pineapple on pizza and call it "Hawaiian pizza."

(a) experiments
(b) would experiment
(c) has been experimenting
(d) was experimenting

18. Trevor is bored with his economics class and is thinking of quitting. If the teacher were to deliver more interesting lectures, Trevor _____ to attend the class.

(a) would likely continue
(b) will likely continue
(c) would likely have continued
(d) will likely have continued

19. Lydia intends to lose weight but does not want to drop red meat from her diet. Her dietitian recommends _____ to white meat and fish instead because they contain less fat.

(a) switching
(b) to switch
(c) having switched
(d) to have switched

20. About 300 million years ago, Earth's seven continents were connected as one massive supercontinent called Pangaea. Had the continent not broken apart, ecosystems _____ very differently up to the present day.

(a) will likely have developed
(b) would likely have developed
(c) will likely develop
(d) would likely develop

21. Willow trees contain salicin, a substance that transforms into salicylic acid, which is an ingredient of aspirin. This is why ancient beliefs prescribed that one _____ on willow bark to lessen fever and pain.

(a) is chewing
(b) chewed
(c) chew
(d) will chew

22. Rishi has been unable to attend school for three days because of the flu. When his classmate drops by in a few hours to lend him some of her notes, Rishi _____ in bed.

(a) was resting
(b) will be resting
(c) rests
(d) has been resting

23. When flying on an airplane, our senses of smell and taste can decrease in sensitivity by more than 50 percent. This is why passengers tend _____ that in-flight meals taste bland.

(a) thinking
(b) to have thought
(c) having thought
(d) to think

24. There are plans to move our office to a bigger building because of our growing sales force. In fact, the president and department heads _____ the proposed locations at this very moment.

(a) are discussing
(b) discussed
(c) would discuss
(d) were discussing

25. Our flight to the Maldives went through so much turbulence that a lot of passengers started to worry. However, the captain advised that everybody _____ calm, as the situation was under control.

(a) remains
(b) was remaining
(c) remain
(d) will remain

26. According to legend, goats were the first to experience the energizing effects of coffee. An ancient Ethiopian goat herder noticed that his goats became overly active every time they finished _____ on wild coffee beans.

(a) to feed
(b) having fed
(c) to have fed
(d) feeding

LISTENING SECTION

▶ Test 2 전체 음원 재생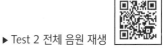

DIRECTIONS:

The Listening Section has four parts. In each part you will hear a spoken passage and a number of questions about the passage. First you will hear the questions. Then you will hear the passage. From the four choices for each question, choose the best answer. Then blacken in the correct circle on your answer sheet.

Example:

(a) one

(b) two

(c) three

(d) four

Bill Johnson has four brothers, so the best answer is (d). The circle with the letter (d) has been blackened.

NOW TURN THE PAGE AND BEGIN

27. (a) their first experiences in an internship
    (b) their impressions of an educational tour
    (c) their plans to visit a broadcasting studio
    (d) their dreams of becoming television actors

28. (a) how different it looks on TV
    (b) how rude the crew are
    (c) how cold it feels in person
    (d) how calm the anchors are

29. (a) watching from a certain angle
    (b) viewing brightly colored images
    (c) looking through the cameras
    (d) seeing multiple video screens

30. (a) by using a green screen backdrop
    (b) by showing a paper map on screen
    (c) by using a large television screen
    (d) by projecting a computer screen

31. (a) She hopes to be a weather reporter.
    (b) She wants to be a news anchor.
    (c) She hopes to become a set designer.
    (d) She wants to be a director.

32. (a) that she looked the same without makeup
    (b) that she behaved professionally
    (c) that she sounded different in person
    (d) that she dressed informally

33. (a) to make professional contacts
    (b) to develop a varied skillset
    (c) to gain academic qualifications
    (d) to specialize in one role

PART 2. *You will hear a presentation by one person to a group of people. First you will hear questions 34 through 39. Then you will hear the talk. Choose the best answer to each question in the time provided.*

34. (a) an online cooking course
    (b) a local community garden
    (c) an online shopping opportunity
    (d) a local farm tour

35. (a) by having a simple setup process
    (b) by providing a speedy payment method
    (c) by highlighting popular products
    (d) by remembering frequently bought items

36. (a) a collection of plant care videos
    (b) starter kits for new gardeners
    (c) a list of local plant growers
    (d) plans for unique garden designs

37. (a) to choose a delivery time
    (b) to benefit from a wide selection
    (c) to qualify for a discount
    (d) to make special dietary requests

38. (a) They can buy from a preferred source.
    (b) They can read customers' reviews.
    (c) They can compare competitors' prices.
    (d) They can register for a trial period.

39. (a) to get items while they are fresh
    (b) to qualify for a refund
    (c) to request same-day delivery
    (d) to access free shipping

PART 3. *You will hear a conversation between two people. First you will hear questions 40 through 45. Then you will hear the conversation. Choose the best answer to each question in the time provided.*

40. (a) Her desktop is disorganized.
    (b) She would like better security.
    (c) Her laptop has been slow lately.
    (d) She needs space for work files.

43. (a) by enabling her to share files
    (b) by allowing for faster software updates
    (c) by keeping all her files in order
    (d) by extending the laptop's battery life

41. (a) because it provides easy access
    (b) because it fits in her luggage
    (c) because it is password-protected
    (d) because it charges quickly

44. (a) because of limited access
    (b) because of security concerns
    (c) because of constant updates
    (d) because of price increases

42. (a) that it could get lost
    (b) that files could be deleted
    (c) that it could become damaged
    (d) that files could be stolen

45. (a) buy a different laptop computer
    (b) get a portable storage device
    (c) subscribe to an online service
    (d) bring paper files during her trips

46. (a) avoiding unexpected illness
    (b) planning for dangerous situations
    (c) training to be a first responder
    (d) teaching emergency medicine

50. (a) They might be unable to find help.
    (b) They may lack transportation.
    (c) They might lose contact.
    (d) They may be in unfamiliar areas.

47. (a) by live streaming news reports
    (b) by allowing time to order supplies
    (c) by connecting to rescue services
    (d) by providing key status updates

51. (a) by keeping people informed
    (b) by providing entertainment
    (c) by allowing people to signal
    (d) by charging other devices

48. (a) to find out how to avoid disasters
    (b) to become a trained professional
    (c) to learn how to care for injuries
    (d) to borrow emergency equipment

52. (a) that it has an extra set of keys
    (b) that it is full of gas
    (c) that it has emergency snacks
    (d) that it is in good shape

49. (a) contact neighbors for assistance
    (b) put out a small fire
    (c) find emergency supplies quickly
    (d) exit the house safely

THIS IS THE END OF THE LISTENING SECTION

READING AND VOCABULARY SECTION

DIRECTIONS:

You will now read four different passages. Each passage is followed by comprehension and vocabulary questions. From the four choices for each item, choose the best answer. Then blacken in the correct circle on your answer sheet.

Read the following example passage and example question.

Example:

Bill Johnson lives in New York. He is 25 years old. He has four brothers and two sisters.

How many brothers does Bill Johnson have?

(a) one
(b) two
(c) three
(d) four

The correct answer is (d), so the circle with the letter (d) has been blackened.

NOW TURN THE PAGE AND BEGIN

WANGARI MAATHAI

Wangari Maathai was a Kenyan educator, activist, and environmentalist best known for being the first African woman to receive a Nobel Peace Prize. She founded the Green Belt Movement, an environmental organization that promotes the conservation of African forests.

Wangari Muta Maathai was born on April 1, 1940, in the town of Nyeri, Kenya. Maathai's awareness of the natural environment started when she was a child. Growing up, she spent time playing in streams and fetching water and firewood for her family. Because her family obtained most of their necessities from the natural world, they associated nature with God and believed that the trees prevented disasters from happening to their land.

Although going to school was rare for girls at that time, Maathai was able to complete early education in various Catholic schools, finishing first in her classes. She qualified for a scholarship at Benedictine College in the United States, earning a degree in biology in 1964. She also undertook doctoral courses in Germany and completed them in 1971 at the University of Nairobi, becoming the first woman in either East or Central Africa to earn a doctorate.

Maathai became an active member of the National Council of Women of Kenya, advocating for the rights of poor women whose lives were affected by the destruction of the country's natural resources. Maathai sought to end the massive problem of deforestation by encouraging the village women to plant trees. This became the Green Belt Movement, which was soon adopted by neighboring African countries. The organization has since planted over fifty-one million trees and provided thousands of women with a way to earn a living.

Maathai also led anti-government protests that led to her being arrested numerous times. In 1989, for example, she staged a successful protest against the felling of trees in a recreational park that were being cleared to make room for a skyscraper. She was elected to Kenya's parliament in 2002 and appointed as Assistant Minister in the Ministry for Environment and Natural Resources the following year. In 2004, Maathai received the Nobel Peace Prize for "her contributions to sustainable development, democracy, and peace."

Wen Maathai died in 2011, an award called the Wangari Maathai Forest Champion Award was launched with the purpose of recognizing others who contribute to the preservation and management of forests.

53. What is Wangari Maathai best known for?

(a) becoming a famous politician
(b) founding religious organizations
(c) winning a prestigious award
(d) pioneering education reforms

54. Why did Maathai's family have spiritual beliefs about nature?

(a) because they attended church regularly
(b) because they depended on it for their everyday needs
(c) because they experienced disasters frequently
(d) because they lacked access to it in their daily lives

55. Why, most likely, were Maathai's academic achievements unexpected?

(a) Females were rarely given access to education.
(b) She frequently argued with her teachers.
(c) Schools seldom accepted poor students.
(d) She initially performed poorly in her classes.

56. According to the fourth paragraph, how did the Green Belt Movement come to be?

(a) through a women's rights organization
(b) through the physical labor of women
(c) through a women's advocate in parliament
(d) through peaceful protests by women

57. Why, most likely, did Maathai lead protests against the government?

(a) She was an advocate for social reform.
(b) She hoped to achieve public recognition.
(c) She was angry about its control over her career.
(d) She disapproved of environmental destruction.

58. In the context of the passage, undertook means _____.

(a) pursued
(b) abandoned
(c) opposed
(d) recovered

59. In the context of the passage, appointed means _____.

(a) planned
(b) contacted
(c) promised
(d) chosen

PART 2. Read the following magazine article and answer the questions. The underlined words in the article are for vocabulary questions.

STUDYING STUDENT ROUTINES

Getting up early for school is something most people are familiar with, but research shows that delaying school start times by as little as an hour can lead to improvements in students' academic performance.

Surveys show that more than half of high school students in the US do not get enough sleep. This can be <u>detrimental</u> to their overall development, especially in the case of adolescents, who need more sleep due to growth spurts. Health organizations therefore suggest that classes start no earlier than 8:30 a.m., to give students adequate sleep for their physical and mental health.

A study by the University of Washington set out to confirm the effects of adjusting school starting hours. For a period of two weeks, researchers worked with two sets of approximately ninety students each from two different high schools. One group followed the usual class schedule of starting at 7:50 a.m., and the other started almost an hour later, at 8:45 a.m.

Instead of asking students about their sleep routines, the researchers had them wear wrist monitors to collect data on movement and light exposure. The students also filled out a survey to report data such as daytime sleepiness and mood. The behavior of the students in class was observed with the help of two participating teachers.

The researchers found that the students who started school later got an average of thirty-four extra minutes of sleep. Although some people might have expected the late-start group to change their bedtimes accordingly—as teens are normally inclined to be night owls—both groups actually went to sleep around the same time. The students with the later school start were less sleepy and more focused in class. Their final grades in biology class were 4.5 percent higher than those of students with an earlier school start.

The study has <u>established</u> the potential benefits of scheduling classes to start at a later time. However, schools and parents are concerned about the challenges such a change could involve, such as insufficient time for afterschool activities and household chores. Nevertheless, experts say that gaining improvements in the students' mental and physical development would be worth the effort.

60. What is the article mainly about?

   (a) how exercise can improve academic performance
   (b) how daily schedules can affect student achievement
   (c) how diet can influence examination results
   (d) how school day length can impact student happiness

61. What was the purpose of the research conducted by the University of Washington?

   (a) to assess the effects of reduced homework
   (b) to confirm the connection between phone use and sleep
   (c) to verify the benefits of delayed school starts
   (d) to disprove a link between class size and performance

62. Why, most likely, were the study's participants asked to wear wrist monitors?

   (a) so their overnight activities could be recorded
   (b) so their mood changes could be observed
   (c) so their daytime naps could be tracked
   (d) so their hormone levels could be detected

63. Which of the following is NOT true about the late-start group?

   (a) They did better in an assessment than their peers.
   (b) They tended to get more sleep than they had before.
   (c) They had better concentration in their lessons.
   (d) They began going to bed later than they had before.

64. What do experts say about adopting later start times in school?

   (a) that the benefits for students outweigh the inconveniences
   (b) that it will result in very little change
   (c) that the consequences for parents make it impractical
   (d) that it will positively impact teachers

65. In the context of the passage, detrimental means _____.

   (a) unnatural
   (b) harmful
   (c) applicable
   (d) general

66. In the context of the passage, established means _____.

   (a) reconsidered
   (b) installed
   (c) demonstrated
   (d) organized

PARROTFISH

Parrotfish are a group of fish species that thrive in shallow, tropical waters. They are characterized by their beak-like mouths, which resemble that of a parrot and give the group its name. Parrotfish are known for their ability to convert dead coral into fine white sand, which constitutes the world's famous white beaches. Moreover, parrotfish are one of the key factors in maintaining the health of reefs. The fish come in a wide range of vivid colors, including intricate combinations of green, blue, orange, and yellow that can change throughout their lives.

Parrotfish are also known to shift their sex as they mature, with most fish being born female and changing to male within a few years. Younger females breed more successfully, while larger, fully developed males can effectively defend their offspring. Male fish can even change back to female when necessary.

Parrotfish are hunted by moray eels and reef sharks. In the daytime, they use their speed to evade predators but, at night, some species cover their body in a clear "cocoon" of mucus before sleeping to conceal their smell and make them more difficult for predators to detect.

The fish spend most of the day feeding on algae that grows on the coral and can negatively affect its health. This practice helps provide space for new coral to grow, keeping the coral reefs thriving. Parrotfish also eat dead coral by grinding it with their tough, beak-like teeth. The undigested waste is deposited onto the ocean floor and eventually finds its way onto beaches as fine white sand. Each parrotfish can produce up to 700 pounds of sand a year.

Although most parrotfish species are not classified as "endangered," their populations are nonetheless threatened. Some species, such as the bumphead parrotfish, are already rare in the Pacific Islands as they are continuously hunted and sold for aquarium displays and as delicacies. Destruction of their habitats is also one of the major threats to their populations. Various organizations are currently implementing measures to protect parrotfish, including regulating the extent of fishing and informing the public of the fish's importance.

67. According to the first paragraph, what is true about parrotfish?

    (a) They survive best at extreme depths.

    (b) They eat the white sand around coral reefs.

    (c) Their colors let them match their surroundings.

    (d) Their appearance can transform over time.

68. Why, most likely, is it helpful that parrotfish can change sex?

    (a) Larger females are needed for reproduction.

    (b) They can reach sexual maturity faster.

    (c) Older males are needed to protect their young.

    (d) They can achieve a more balanced population.

69. According to the third paragraph, how do some parrotfish protect themselves from predators while sleeping?

    (a) by hiding beneath the reef

    (b) by masking their own scent

    (c) by gathering in large numbers

    (d) by giving off a foul odor

70. How do parrotfish help keep coral thriving?

    (a) by attacking potential predators

    (b) by removing damaging organisms

    (c) by protecting beneficial algae

    (d) by adding vital nutrients

71. What are some organizations doing to preserve parrotfish?

    (a) breeding the creatures in captivity

    (b) trying to relocate large populations

    (c) working to raise public awareness

    (d) advocating to ban fishing practices

72. In the context of the passage, constitutes means _____.

    (a) forms

    (b) expresses

    (c) serves

    (d) inserts

73. In the context of the passage, deposited means _____.

    (a) credited

    (b) stored

    (c) arranged

    (d) released

Audrey Hilton
Owner
Four Walls Printing Shop

Dear Ms. Hilton,

Good day! I am the manager of Mercer Office Supplies, and I am writing to address the letter you sent us complaining about your recent order.

In the letter, you mentioned that the parcel delivered to your shop on July 24 was missing two reams of XT 8.5-by-11-inch photo paper. Upon <u>consulting</u> our records and making inquiries with our packaging staff, we have confirmed that the package sent to you was indeed incomplete.

On that particular date, we experienced a glitch on our website due to the surge of orders we have been experiencing this graduation season. We have never had so many orders in the history of the company. This momentary malfunction affected the processing of orders and resulted in the incorrect quantity of paper being delivered to you.

I would like to apologize for our service issue. Moreover, I am requesting your patience in awaiting the delivery of the rest of your order. This is because our supplier has temporarily <u>confined</u> bulk orders of this particular product to one case per week, due to the current high demand. So, we will not be able to refill our stock until later this week. Rest assured that we will forward the remainder of your order to you as soon as possible.

To compensate for the inconvenience we have caused you, we will deliver four reams of the photo paper, two more than you initially ordered, to your address as soon as it is available. We will email you when the products have arrived in our warehouse and are ready to ship. Please contact me by email if you have further questions.

Thank you very much for your understanding.

Regards,

Robert Kingsley
Robert Kingsley
Mercer Office Supplies

74. Why is Robert Kingsley writing to Audrey Hilton?

(a) to inform her about an issue with product quality
(b) to answer her inquiry about an estimate
(c) to respond to her recent complaint about a delivery
(d) to verify the details of her last purchase

75. What did Audrey mention in her letter?

(a) The product she ordered arrived damaged.
(b) The package in question was missing multiple items.
(c) The product she received was of poor quality.
(d) The package in question was delivered to the wrong address.

76. Why did Mercer Office Supplies suffer a computer glitch?

(a) due to an increase in the number of sales
(b) due to an oversight of the maintenance staff
(c) due to an electrical outage from a storm
(d) due to an error made by the software programmers

77. Why, most likely, will the company's delivery of the remaining items be delayed?

(a) The employees are on strike.
(b) The supplier is being replaced.
(c) The office is temporarily closed.
(d) The current stock is limited.

78. How does Robert plan to make up for Audrey's inconvenience?

(a) by providing her with promotional gifts
(b) by offering her some money back
(c) by giving her more items than she paid for
(d) by sending her a better product

79. In the context of the passage, consulting means _____.

(a) checking
(b) packing
(c) clearing
(d) forgetting

80. In the context of the passage, confined means _____.

(a) gathered
(b) weakened
(c) returned
(d) restricted

GENERAL TESTS OF ENGLISH LANGUAGE PROFICIENCY

G-TELP ™

LEVEL 2

TEST 3

문제집 뒤에 있는 OMR 답안지를 사용하여 실전처럼 연습할 수 있습니다.

GRAMMAR SECTION

Example:

The boys _____ in the car.

(a) be
(b) is
(c) am
(d) are

The correct answer is (d), so the circle with the letter (d) has been blackened.

ⓐ   ⓑ   ⓒ   ●

NOW TURN THE PAGE AND BEGIN

1. The identity of the poet who wrote
   Sir Gawain and the Green Knight is
   still unknown. _____, scholars have
   been able to determine that he lived in
   the West Midlands of England during
   the fourteenth century.

   (a) However
   (b) In conclusion
   (c) Moreover
   (d) For instance

2. Mrs. Anderson nearly missed her
   package delivery last week. She
   _____ a sweater when the doorbell
   rang, and she was so absorbed in
   her task that she barely noticed the
   sound.

   (a) will be knitting
   (b) was knitting
   (c) is knitting
   (d) has been knitting

3. Scientists are using genome
   sequencing to explore de-extinction
   of species that have disappeared.
   Further advancements are still
   needed, but if researchers were
   to succeed, they _____ extinct
   animals, such as the woolly mammoth
   or the dodo.

   (a) could have brought back
   (b) will have brought back
   (c) will bring back
   (d) could bring back

4. Jason's phone battery was very low
   on power when he left work yesterday.
   Because of this, he resisted _____
   his phone until he could get home and
   charge it.

   (a) to use
   (b) using
   (c) to have used
   (d) having used

5. Maya often bakes as a way to relieve
   stress. She has a batch of chocolate
   cookies in the oven at the moment,
   and she _____ them out in about
   twenty minutes.

   (a) will have been taking
   (b) was taking
   (c) will be taking
   (d) has been taking

6. In parts of the Southern US, some
   homeowners paint their porch ceilings
   a distinct shade of light blue. The
   color, _____, is believed by some to
   confuse evil spirits and prevent them
   from entering a home.

   (a) that is called "haint blue"
   (b) what is called "haint blue"
   (c) which is called "haint blue"
   (d) who is called "haint blue"

7. The school's fire alarm started malfunctioning during the second period of the day and has continued to do so for the last hour. Steven cannot focus on his math problems while the alarm _____.

(a) rang
(b) has been ringing
(c) would ring
(d) is ringing

8. Although never built, the Palace of the Soviets was intended to be a skyscraper topped with a statue of Vladimir Lenin. Had the building been completed, it _____ the world's tallest structure at that time.

(a) would be
(b) will have been
(c) would have been
(d) will be

9. Driving while tired can be very dangerous. Road safety officers advise that drivers _____ to rest for a while if they find themselves feeling drowsy behind the wheel.

(a) are pulling over
(b) pull over
(c) will pull over
(d) pulled over

10. This year's creative writing competition is now underway. Participants _____ submit their entries by 12 p.m. next Friday, or their stories will not be reviewed by the judging panel.

(a) must
(b) can
(c) might
(d) would

11. The interrobang is a punctuation mark that combines a question mark and an exclamation point. It was designed _____ a question asked in surprise or disbelief but has not been commonly adopted by writers.

(a) indicating
(b) to have indicated
(c) having indicated
(d) to indicate

12. Suresh's friends invited him to a party but later revealed that everyone was wearing silly outfits. Suresh decided he would not go if it involved _____ a silly costume.

(a) having worn
(b) to wear
(c) wearing
(d) to have worn

13. Amber is hoping to receive an acceptance letter from the prestigious Wexman University. She also applied to a few smaller colleges in her home state _____ she gets rejected from her dream university.

(a) in case
(b) unless
(c) even though
(d) because

14. The Winchester Mystery House is notable for its bizarre, sprawling architecture. It is said that construction crews _____ on the house nonstop for thirty-eight years until the owner died in 1922.

(a) have been working
(b) are working
(c) will have been working
(d) had been working

15. Hurricanes and tropical storms can cause serious property damage. Experts advise that, when such weather systems are approaching, homeowners _____ preparations to minimize damage, such as taping or boarding up windows.

(a) will make
(b) make
(c) are making
(d) made

16. Jin is not happy with the quality of his assignment and has decided to rewrite it. If he were to submit the essay in its current condition, he _____ a very low score.

(a) would probably have received
(b) will probably have received
(c) would probably receive
(d) will probably receive

17. Ben and Nancy's first Christmas together is coming up, and Nancy is struggling to think of a good gift. Her friend suggested _____ Ben something handmade instead of a store-bought item.

(a) giving
(b) to give
(c) having given
(d) to have given

18. When Kamila got home from work yesterday, she saw that the kitchen light bulb had burned out. Had her housemate let her know in advance, she _____ a replacement on the way home.

(a) will have bought
(b) would buy
(c) would have bought
(d) will buy

19. The Japanese island of Aoshima, also known as "Cat Island," gets its name from its huge cat population. The island's human population, however, continues to fall and _____ since the decline of the local fishing industry.

(a) had been doing so
(b) is doing so
(c) will be doing so
(d) has been doing so

20. Beth spent three hours working on her motorcycle's engine. Unfortunately, when she attempted to fire it up, the engine completely failed _____, even after all her efforts.

(a) starting
(b) to start
(c) to have started
(d) having started

21. A popular style of cooking called *sous vide* entails immersing vacuum-sealed bags of food in temperature-controlled water. One advantage of the method is that the food _____ be left underwater for long periods without overcooking.

(a) can
(b) must
(c) should
(d) will

22. Caroline prepared diligently for her conference presentation on childhood education but, while she was giving the speech yesterday, she left out important details. Had she not been so tired, she _____ a better presentation.

(a) will have delivered
(b) would deliver
(c) would have delivered
(d) will deliver

23. Frank's rubber plant has grown so quickly that it is now too big for its pot. He plans _____ it to a larger container with some fresh soil as soon as he can.

(a) transferring
(b) to have transferred
(c) to transfer
(d) having transferred

24. Lando has a lot in common with his friend Greta. However, unlike Greta, _____, Lando enjoys all kinds of meat and can regularly be found dining in the steak restaurant downtown.

(a) what is vegetarian
(b) which is vegetarian
(c) where is vegetarian
(d) who is vegetarian

25. Amelia is struggling with a heavy course load this semester. If she were to drop one of her classes, she _____ more free time, but she likes her professors too much to do that.

(a) would have had
(b) would have
(c) will have
(d) will have had

26. Josh is at the immigration office to extend his visa, but there is a long line. Josh estimates that, by the time he is able to see an official, he _____ for over two hours.

(a) is waiting
(b) was waiting
(c) will have been waiting
(d) will be waiting

LISTENING SECTION

▶ Test 3 전체 음원 재생

DIRECTIONS:

The Listening Section has four parts. In each part you will hear a spoken passage and a number of questions about the passage. First you will hear the questions. Then you will hear the passage. From the four choices for each question, choose the best answer. Then blacken in the correct circle on your answer sheet.

Example:

(a) one
(b) two
(c) three
(d) four

Bill Johnson has four brothers, so the best answer is (d). The circle with the letter (d) has been blackened.

NOW TURN THE PAGE AND BEGIN

27. (a) because the weather was poor
    (b) because it was difficult to get into the venue
    (c) because the band was terrible
    (d) because it was dangerous to be in the audience

28. (a) Traffic was heavy.
    (b) Fees were high.
    (c) Signage was poor.
    (d) Spaces were limited.

29. (a) because there was a big line
    (b) because he misplaced his original ticket
    (c) because there was high security
    (d) because he wanted to change his seat

30. (a) getting to go backstage
    (b) being close to the band
    (c) hearing all new music
    (d) socializing with other fans

31. (a) Many of them yelled at the organizers.
    (b) Some of them refused to leave.
    (c) Many of them demanded a full refund.
    (d) Some of them walked out.

32. (a) because he arrived home late
    (b) because he drove a long way
    (c) because he stayed up all night
    (d) because he danced for a long time

33. (a) go to the band's concert
    (b) have dinner with a friend
    (c) listen to the band's music
    (d) watch a movie at home

34. (a) to introduce a pet food service
    (b) to promote a new pet store
    (c) to announce a new pet care app
    (d) to educate about pet nutrition

37. (a) It ships all meals frozen.
    (b) It uses special packaging.
    (c) It adds natural preservatives.
    (d) It notifies buyers immediately.

35. (a) because the prices are low
    (b) because of the way they taste
    (c) because the portions are large
    (d) because of the way they look

38. (a) the frequency of orders
    (b) the method of payment
    (c) the variety of ingredients
    (d) the species of pet

36. (a) sign up for a trial account
    (b) call customer support
    (c) select from set meals
    (d) meet with an expert

39. (a) by reaching out to customer service
    (b) by visiting a store branch
    (c) by closing their account on the website
    (d) by submitting an online form

40. (a) whether to invite friends over
    (b) whether to take an overseas vacation
    (c) whether to join him on a trip
    (d) whether to go away for the weekend

41. (a) enjoy local cuisine
    (b) lie in the sun
    (c) read a good book
    (d) wade in the water

42. (a) the amount of traffic
    (b) the length of the trip
    (c) the cost of hotels
    (d) the time of the year

43. (a) by cleaning up her bedroom
    (b) by working on a novel
    (c) by hanging out with neighbors
    (d) by catching up on sleep

44. (a) Her television is broken.
    (b) Her favorite café is closed.
    (c) Her local area is dull.
    (d) Her housemate is away.

45. (a) spend some time at the beach
    (b) go to the office and work
    (c) get some rest at her house
    (d) try out a new hiking trail

46. (a) switching to new career
    (b) adjusting to a new work arrangement
    (c) making friends with colleagues
    (d) learning to manage a heavy workload

47. (a) by ensuring a sufficient amount of sleep
    (b) by making a detailed agenda
    (c) by keeping a steady morning routine
    (d) by setting up a recurring meeting

48. (a) to have privacy from family
    (b) to ensure sufficient space
    (c) to look professional in meetings
    (d) to maintain concentration

49. (a) by choosing a productive time of day
    (b) by working on it with colleagues
    (c) by requesting feedback from a supervisor
    (d) by dividing it into small pieces

50. (a) the end of the working day
    (b) the time to take a break
    (c) the moment to switch tasks
    (d) the point when family return

51. (a) to ensure family interaction
    (b) to transition back to personal time
    (c) to maintain an active social life
    (d) to focus on physical fitness

52. (a) Their productivity will drop.
    (b) They will miss their colleagues.
    (c) Their stress will increase.
    (d) They will need time to adjust.

THIS IS THE END OF THE LISTENING SECTION

READING AND VOCABULARY SECTION

DIRECTIONS:

You will now read four different passages. Each passage is followed by comprehension and vocabulary questions. From the four choices for each item, choose the best answer. Then blacken in the correct circle on your answer sheet.

Read the following example passage and example question.

Example:

> Bill Johnson lives in New York. He is 25 years old. He has four brothers and two sisters.
>
> How many brothers does Bill Johnson have?
>
> (a) one
> (b) two
> (c) three
> (d) four

The correct answer is (d), so the circle with the letter (d) has been blackened.

NOW TURN THE PAGE AND BEGIN

PART 1. Read the following biography article and answer the questions. The underlined words in the article are for vocabulary questions.

BILLIE HOLIDAY

Billie Holiday was an American jazz and swing singer. Best known for her compelling and emotional vocal delivery as well as improvisational singing skills that brought her songs to life, she is widely seen as one of the most influential jazz singers of all time.

Eleanora Fagan, who later took the stage name Billie Holiday, was born on April 7, 1915, in Philadelphia, Pennsylvania. While her paternal parentage is disputed, American jazz musician Clarence Holiday is reported to be her father. He left not long after she was born, and she grew up with her mother in Baltimore, Maryland. Holiday's early life was marred by instability, leading her to drop out of school at the age of eleven and often get in trouble with the law. She found peace in music and, as a young teenager, started singing in nightclubs in the Harlem neighborhood of New York.

Holiday's reputation grew with each performance. She made her recording debut at the age of eighteen, and it was then that she also reconnected with her father. In 1935, she was signed and began recording in earnest, showcasing her flair for adapting her voice to fit a song's mood. In 1938, Holiday made the potentially risky decision to work with Artie Shaw and his orchestra. In doing so, she became one of the first Black vocalists to work with a white orchestra. The increased exposure led her popularity to grow significantly.

In 1939, Holiday recorded her most controversial song, titled "Strange Fruit," about violence against African Americans in the American South. The lyrics, combined with a slow tempo and emphasis on certain words, created a hauntingly painful impression of the effects of racism, but the song met resistance in a still racially divided America. Nonetheless, the powerful feelings it evoked as well as its notoriety helped propel the song to fame.

Throughout the 1940s and 1950s, Holiday continued to perform concerts, including multiple sold-out shows at New York's famous Carnegie Hall. On July 17, 1959, she died in New York City from health complications caused by chronic alcohol and drug addiction. More than 3,000 people attended her funeral, including many famous jazz performers. In 2000, she was inducted into the Rock and Roll Hall of Fame, which cemented her influential status.

53. What is Billie Holiday most remembered for?

    (a) writing a famous American jazz song
    (b) developing a distinctive vocal technique
    (c) being the first female jazz singer in America
    (d) having a controversial musical career

54. Why did Holiday probably start singing in nightclubs?

    (a) It brought her comfort when her life was difficult.
    (b) It helped her cover her school tuition.
    (c) It brought her public recognition when she was unknown.
    (d) It helped her form valuable friendships.

55. According to the text, how did Holiday make a breakthrough in her career?

    (a) by introducing a new genre of music to audiences
    (b) by recording a pioneering collaboration with her father
    (c) by taking chances in her professional relationships
    (d) by influencing the work of established artists

56. Based on the text, why, most likely, did some people dislike "Strange Fruit"?

    (a) because it criticized a popular politician
    (b) because they disapproved of its original composer
    (c) because it promoted an illegal activity
    (d) because they disagreed with its social message

57. What achievement proved Holiday's lasting legacy?

    (a) having a famous concert hall named after her
    (b) being honored by an artistic organization
    (c) having her music featured in a popular film
    (d) being commemorated by a renowned sculptor

58. In the context of this passage, flair means _____.

    (a) approval
    (b) patience
    (c) talent
    (d) humor

59. In the context of this passage, chronic means _____.

    (a) regular
    (b) unlikely
    (c) flexible
    (d) uncertain

REMOTE WORKING BENEFITS

The COVID-19 pandemic compelled many businesses around the world to shift to a remote working model in order to avoid spreading infection. However, despite the unfortunate way in which remote working came to the forefront, studies are showing that working from home has major benefits not just for workers, but for employers as well.

One major benefit of remote working is the decrease in commuting time. While obviously a benefit for employees, less time spent commuting also benefits businesses. The mental well-being of employees has been shown to be connected to a <u>surge</u> in work productivity and a decrease in absenteeism. Some employees commute an hour or more one way, arriving to work already stressed out. Commute length can also be a major factor in how often employees take sick days from work. When working from home, employees "arrive" to work fresh and ready to go in a relaxed environment.

Remote working options have also enabled companies to have more flexibility with regard to location. This is especially helpful when businesses are looking to recruit the best people to join their team. Previously, businesses would have to choose from a pool of either local candidates or those willing to uproot and move their lives to a new city, restricting the potential employee pool considerably. With the ability to bring in exceptional individuals from across the nation, businesses benefit from a wealth of experienced candidates.

Another major benefit to businesses is the potential to reduce operating costs. With employees working from home, there is no need to budget for renting office space. This is especially handy for smaller businesses that may be operating in high-rent areas. One study estimated that businesses could save an average of $10,000 per employee per year with full-time remote working options.

While the <u>transition</u> requires serious planning to enforce set work hours, ensure effective communication with employees, and provide office equipment for home use, in the long run, remote working can improve efficiency and employee satisfaction, while allowing companies to build diverse and adaptable teams. With flexibility a key driver of success in the global market, this helps to make businesses more competitive.

60. What is the article mainly about?

   (a) how employees have adapted to remote working
   (b) how remote working can positively impact businesses
   (c) how remote working helps the national economy
   (d) how different industries can shift to remote working

61. Based on the second paragraph, how, most likely, would working from home help reduce employee absence?

   (a) by allowing workers to take more breaks
   (b) by creating a peaceful work environment
   (c) by providing more flexible working hours
   (d) by eliminating stress from traveling to work

62. According to the article, how does remote work benefit recruitment?

   (a) It widens the range of potential candidates.
   (b) It increases the chance of a candidate accepting the job.
   (c) It simplifies the task of scheduling candidates for interview.
   (d) It improves the prospect of a candidate staying in the position.

63. Based on the fourth paragraph, why might a small business choose a remote working model?

   (a) to spend less time searching for a suitable office space
   (b) to encourage employees to use their own computers
   (c) to avoid facing unnecessarily high operating costs
   (d) to allow managers to focus on expanding their departments

64. What is the purpose of the final paragraph?

   (a) to give a specific example of a company with remote workers
   (b) to remind readers of the disadvantages of remote working
   (c) to show that employing remote workers is easy
   (d) to argue that remote working is advantageous overall

65. In the context of this passage, surge means _____.

   (a) division
   (b) rise
   (c) breakdown
   (d) gap

66. In the context of this passage, transition means _____.

   (a) change
   (b) reduction
   (c) profile
   (d) conclusion

THE AMERICAN FLAG

The American flag is the national flag of the United States of America. Although the flag has always featured stars and stripes and the colors red, white, and blue, the specific design has been altered more than twenty times since 1777.

Before 1776, America consisted of thirteen colonies under the rule of Great Britain. The emerging government in the colonies decided that a flag was needed to unite them as they fought for independence. The Flag Resolution of 1777 laid out the design for the new nation's first flag, with thirteen alternating red and white horizontal stripes and thirteen six-pointed white stars on a blue background to represent the original colonies.

As new states were added to the United States, more stars were added to the flag. The fiftieth and final star was added in 1960 when the state of Hawaii joined the union. The current design retains thirteen red stripes, representing valor and bravery, and thirteen white stripes, representing purity and innocence. The blue background represents vigilance, perseverance, and justice. If a new state were admitted, the flag would need to be redesigned once more to accommodate the addition.

The United States has a Flag Code, or set of rules, that outlines how the flag should be handled. For example, when a flag is worn out, it should be destroyed in a dignified manner, such as by burning. Additionally, the flag should never be used as clothing or bedding, nor should it be used for advertising purposes. It should never be displayed upside down unless to signal great danger, and it should never touch anything below it, such as the ground.

There are various rituals associated with the US flag. It is usually taken down during bad weather unless it is weather-resistant. If flown at night, it should be illuminated. The flag can be displayed every day but, during national holidays and days of remembrance in particular, it is flown to showcase patriotism. During times of national mourning, the flag is lowered to half-mast. This may be done following the death of a government official or a military member.

67. Which statement best describes the US flag?

    (a) Its colors have been adjusted frequently.

    (b) It has remained unaltered since it was first conceived.

    (c) Its basic elements have never been rearranged.

    (d) It has taken on different looks over time.

68. Why did the emerging government probably decide to create an official flag?

    (a) to distance themselves from a ruling power

    (b) to attract new immigrants to America

    (c) to unite the colonies following a conflict

    (d) to show their loyalty to Great Britain

69. What, most likely, would happen if a new state were added?

    (a) The flag would feature more stripes.

    (b) The stars would be made bigger.

    (c) The flag would feature an additional star.

    (d) The stripes would be made thicker.

70. According to the fourth paragraph, what does the Flag Code describe?

    (a) how the flag can be properly used for advertising

    (b) how individuals should show respect for the flag

    (c) how the flag can be repaired if it becomes damaged

    (d) how individuals should be punished for mistreating the flag

71. Which of the following is NOT an example of accepted flag use?

    (a) taking the flag inside when a storm is coming

    (b) having the flag on display for a holiday

    (c) putting a spotlight on the flag when it is dark

    (d) flying the flag upside down for national mourning

72. In the context of this passage, retains means _____.

    (a) keeps

    (b) identifies

    (c) hangs

    (d) manages

73. In the context of this passage, rituals means _____.

    (a) stories

    (b) areas

    (c) customs

    (d) sayings

Derek Martin
121 W. Clark St.
Newburg, TN

Dear Mr. Martin:

Thank you for contacting us via our website. Boom Pow Fitness is a gym with a friendly and welcoming atmosphere. We are <u>committed</u> to the goal of making everyone feel comfortable about working to reach their fitness objectives and, as such, we regard all of our members as part of our fitness family. With that in mind, let me address your queries.

Your inquiry mentioned that you work long hours, and we understand how the week can fly by and your health can be neglected. That is why we offer convenient 24/7 membership access so you can fit exercise into your schedule. There are lockers available as well as showers if you desire a quick workout before heading to the office.

Our <u>spacious</u> facility has ample room for our members to work out without feeling cramped. Everything is clean and well maintained, and we have an assortment of equipment for cardio and weight training. You expressed some nervousness about beginning your fitness journey, but please do not worry. All weight machines come with guides showing how to perform each exercise.

Your request also mentioned an interest in more tailored help. We have personal trainers who are happy to work with you to build a personalized fitness and nutrition plan. Additionally, we have a wide variety of fitness classes, such as yoga, Pilates, and cycling, that run from 5 a.m. to 7 p.m. every day of the week and are included in the price of your membership.

If this sounds like the fitness experience you were looking for, please give me a call at 555-0167. I will tell you all about our membership plans and class options, and we can set a time for you to tour our facilities or even try out one of our fitness classes.

Sincerely,

Cynthia Thompson
Cynthia Thompson
Assistant Manager, Boom Pow Fitness

74. Why is Cynthia Thompson writing to Derek Martin?

(a) to ask about his current workout goals

(b) to thank him for joining the fitness center

(c) to answer his questions about the gym

(d) to offer him a discount on a new membership

75. Based on the second paragraph, why might people fail to get enough exercise?

(a) because they think gym fees are too expensive

(b) because they lack time to focus on working out

(c) because they find it hard to get motivated

(d) because they lack interest in maintaining good health

76. What, most likely, is Derek's concern about working out at the fitness center?

(a) the accessibility of convenient parking

(b) his lack of experience with gym equipment

(c) the quality of the exercise machines

(d) his prior challenges with past injuries

77. How can Derek enjoy a more customized gym experience?

(a) by consulting with experts about his workouts

(b) by having a daily session with a nutritionist

(c) by joining a program to monitor his weight loss

(d) by specifying his objectives in an online survey

78. What will Cynthia do if Derek calls her?

(a) She will put him in touch with a personal trainer.

(b) She will email him membership documents to sign.

(c) She will send him a sample exercise plan.

(d) She will arrange a time to show him around the facility.

79. In the context of the passage, committed means _____.

(a) related
(b) attracted
(c) dedicated
(d) identical

80. In the context of the passage, spacious means _____.

(a) distinct
(b) bright
(c) elegant
(d) large

GENERAL TESTS OF ENGLISH LANGUAGE PROFICIENCY
G-TELP ™

LEVEL 2

TEST 4

문제집 뒤에 있는 OMR 답안지를 사용하여 실전처럼 연습할 수 있습니다.

GRAMMAR SECTION

Example:

The boys _____ in the car.

(a) be
(b) is
(c) am
(d) are

The correct answer is (d), so the circle with the letter (d) has been blackened.

ⓐ ⓑ ⓒ ●

NOW TURN THE PAGE AND BEGIN

1. Rosie broke her new phone on the way home last night. She _____ it when she fell asleep on the subway, and it slipped out of her hand.

   (a) would hold
   (b) was holding
   (c) has been holding
   (d) will hold

2. Chicken à la King is a dish of diced chicken cooked in a cream sauce with mushrooms and vegetables. The dish, _____, is often served over rice or noodles.

   (a) what is easy to prepare
   (b) who is easy to prepare
   (c) that is easy to prepare
   (d) which is easy to prepare

3. Jupiter's gravity is so strong that it effectively protects Earth by deflecting comets that might otherwise hit our planet. If Jupiter had never existed, Earth _____ by many more comcts by now.

   (a) will likely have been struck
   (b) would likely have been struck
   (c) would likely be struck
   (d) will likely be struck

4. Joe visited his friend in Calgary and intended to go home by 10 p.m. However, they were having so much fun that when they finally finished _____, it was already late, so Joe stayed the night.

   (a) to have caught up
   (b) having caught up
   (c) catching up
   (d) to catch up

5. Magpies are some of the most intelligent birds and are known to be able to recognize themselves in a mirror. This is remarkable, as only a few animal species _____ identify themselves in such a way.

   (a) would
   (b) must
   (c) should
   (d) can

6. A partial solar eclipse will be happening today and will be visible from the town square. However, Derek and his astronomy club are planning _____ the event from the observatory because it offers a better view.

   (a) to watch
   (b) having watched
   (c) watching
   (d) to have watched

7. The okapi lives in the jungles of the Congo and looks like a cross between a deer and a zebra. _____, it is actually the only living relative of the giraffe.

(a) Therefore
(b) However
(c) Otherwise
(d) Similarly

8. Margaret hates leaving her new cat on his own, but she had to run some errands today. By the time she gets home later, poor Tippy _____ alone for about five hours.

(a) will have been waiting
(b) has been waiting
(c) will wait
(d) is waiting

9. Brianna has been baking for years, so she is always happy to give advice to those with less experience. She usually recommends _____ the baking journey with something simple, such as cupcakes.

(a) having started
(b) to start
(c) starting
(d) to have started

10. Craig had a terrible time on his recent vacation to Scotland. His friend Arthur, _____, booked awful hotels, arranged unreliable transportation, and chose overpriced restaurants that were not very good.

(a) what organized everything
(b) who organized everything
(c) which organized everything
(d) that organized everything

11. Andy's musical instrument store almost closed last year, but he managed to keep it afloat by giving lessons to customers. Offering _____ people how to play music proved to be a profitable new line of business.

(a) to have taught
(b) having taught
(c) to teach
(d) teaching

12. Jim won last year's local marathon and became an instant celebrity. If he had more time to devote to training, he _____ the event every year, just to keep his fans happy.

(a) would probably have entered
(b) will probably enter
(c) will probably have entered
(d) would probably enter

13. When Reina arrives at Harvey's house for their date tonight, Harvey will not be there. Instead, he _____ late at the office, as he needs to finish a case report. Unfortunately, he forgot to tell Reina.

(a) has worked
(b) will be working
(c) works
(d) was working

14. Most cranberries are gathered in a process known as wet harvesting. In this process, the field is flooded and, after the vines are shaken, air pockets within the berries cause them _____ to the surface.

(a) to float
(b) floating
(c) having floated
(d) to have floated

15. Tardigrades may be tiny, but they are probably the toughest animals on Earth. For example, if one were to put a tardigrade in outer space, it _____ for decades.

(a) will likely survive
(b) will likely have survived
(c) would likely survive
(d) would likely have survived

16. *Fahrenheit 451* is a 1953 dystopian novel by Ray Bradbury in which books are censored and burned. Ironically, the book itself was also subjected to censorship in some places _____ it was judged to be offensive.

(a) even if
(b) although
(c) so that
(d) because

17. Nigel forgot most of his lines in the final performance of the play last night and was embarrassed. If he had bothered to practice yesterday afternoon instead of playing video games, his performance _____ more smoothly.

(a) would have gone
(b) will go
(c) would go
(d) will have gone

18. Helena saw a group of kids playing very close to a dangerous river. Fearing for their safety, she warned them of the risk and suggested they _____ somewhere else.

(a) are playing
(b) played
(c) will play
(d) play

19. Iguazu Falls, located on the border of Argentina and Brazil, is the largest waterfall system in the world. For those who enjoy _____ incredible natural wonders, it is a great bucket list addition.

   (a) having visited
   (b) to visit
   (c) visiting
   (d) to have visited

20. Mr. Davis's Friday afternoon statistics class is unpopular with students. Many of his past students maintain that if they had known beforehand how boring Mr. Davis was, they _____ a different class.

   (a) would have chosen
   (b) would choose
   (c) will choose
   (d) will have chosen

21. Yesterday, there was an escape from Grantville Prison. Four convicts are currently on the run, and police _____ them down with tracker dogs in the local woodland, where they are believed to be hiding out.

   (a) will have been hunting
   (b) hunted
   (c) have hunted
   (d) are hunting

22. Due to the risk posed by box jellyfish and other marine stinging organisms, it is recommended that people _____ swimming off some Australian beaches at certain times of year.

   (a) avoid
   (b) are avoiding
   (c) avoided
   (d) will avoid

23. Theresa may have to give up on her dream of becoming a juggler. She _____ for six months, but she still cannot keep three balls in the air for more than about five seconds.

   (a) would practice
   (b) has been practicing
   (c) practices
   (d) had been practicing

24. In 2005, the municipal government of Rome passed new rules on animal welfare. One provision states that dog owners _____ walk their pets daily or face a fine equivalent to $625.

   (a) would
   (b) can
   (c) must
   (d) may

25. Lina finally got back to working on her thesis last week. For days, her air-conditioning unit _____ loud noises that prevented her from concentrating. Thankfully, someone eventually came to fix it.

(a) had been making
(b) is making
(c) will have made
(d) has been making

26. Assuming an average speed of about 25 mph, NASA estimates that if a person were to cycle to the moon, it _____ about 416 days to complete the journey.

(a) will take
(b) would have taken
(c) will have taken
(d) would take

LISTENING SECTION

▶ Test 4 전체 음원 재생

DIRECTIONS:

The Listening Section has four parts. In each part you will hear a spoken passage and a number of questions about the passage. First you will hear the questions. Then you will hear the passage. From the four choices for each question, choose the best answer. Then blacken in the correct circle on your answer sheet.

Example:

(a) one

(b) two

(c) three

(d) four

Bill Johnson has four brothers, so the best answer is (d). The circle with the letter (d) has been blackened.

NOW TURN THE PAGE AND BEGIN

27. (a) study abroad programs
    (b) work-related travel
    (c) company branch locations
    (d) mini-vacation spots

28. (a) He stayed at a luxury hotel.
    (b) He ate a lot of delicious food.
    (c) He met the love of his life.
    (d) He had plenty of time to relax.

29. (a) because of the people she saw
    (b) because of the work she accomplished
    (c) because of the places she went
    (d) because of the things she learned

30. (a) by wearing lighter clothes
    (b) by purchasing an air conditioner
    (c) by opening a window
    (d) by finding a spot in the shade

31. (a) because there were record low temperatures
    (b) because she lost her winter clothes
    (c) because the heater needed repair
    (d) because she is used to warm places

32. (a) to explore natural attractions
    (b) to try a new activity
    (c) to research native animals
    (d) to interview for a job

33. (a) have a meal with his colleagues
    (b) head back home to rest
    (c) celebrate his recent promotion
    (d) prepare for a meeting

34. (a) a tour for future students
    (b) a guide for new employees
    (c) a tour for visiting parents
    (d) a guide for university faculty

37. (a) because of his business success
    (b) because of his military service record
    (c) because of his generous donations
    (d) because of his educational contributions

35. (a) to earn extra credit
    (b) to learn from professionals
    (c) to meet other students
    (d) to practice public speaking

38. (a) to grab a quick breakfast
    (b) to attend study groups
    (c) to meet friends for lunch
    (d) to sign up for tutoring

36. (a) It is open to local residents.
    (b) It features rare publications.
    (c) It is accessible at all times.
    (d) It features a research lab.

39. (a) by visiting the housing office
    (b) by entering a writing contest
    (c) by taking the campus tour
    (d) by completing a survey

40. (a) a college graduation
    (b) a business convention
    (c) a company retreat
    (d) a wedding reception

43. (a) by allowing him to work anywhere
    (b) by giving him time with his kids
    (c) by allowing him to enroll in classes
    (d) by giving him more freedom

41. (a) She has a beautiful office.
    (b) She is paid generously.
    (c) She likes her coworkers.
    (d) She can retire early.

44. (a) to return to a regular routine
    (b) to stop having to look for work
    (c) to network with more people
    (d) to gain access to benefits

42. (a) so she can explore a different field
    (b) so she can improve her finances
    (c) so she can return to a previous employer
    (d) so she can complete her training

45. (a) take some vacation time
    (b) interview at another company
    (c) become a freelance worker
    (d) keep her current position

PART 4. *You will hear an explanation of a process. First you will hear questions 46 through 52. Then you will hear the explanation. Choose the best answer to each question in the time provided.*

46. (a) funding a student drama club
    (b) acting in an afterschool play
    (c) putting on a stage production
    (d) persuading kids to do theater

47. (a) one with a lot of roles
    (b) one that is manageable
    (c) one with a lot of humor
    (d) one that is challenging

48. (a) He assigned him a small role.
    (b) He invited him to audition.
    (c) He gave him time to practice.
    (d) He let him work backstage.

49. (a) going over them with friends
    (b) attending all the rehearsals
    (c) practicing them backstage
    (d) tying them to staging

50. (a) by hiring a professional team
    (b) by keeping the design simple
    (c) by asking parents to help
    (d) by using items from past shows

51. (a) because of a competing event
    (b) because he failed to advertise
    (c) because of a sudden storm
    (d) because he had limited seating

52. (a) let them solve problems on their own
    (b) invite them to suggest favorite plays
    (c) encourage them to stop the show if needed
    (d) allow them to introduce the performance

THIS IS THE END OF THE LISTENING SECTION

READING AND VOCABULARY SECTION

Example:

Bill Johnson lives in New York. He is 25 years old. He has four brothers and two sisters.

How many brothers does Bill Johnson have?

(a) one
(b) two
(c) three
(d) four

The correct answer is (d), so the circle with the letter (d) has been blackened.

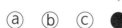

NOW TURN THE PAGE AND BEGIN

ROALD DAHL

Roald Dahl was a British writer best known for authoring children's fantasy books that mix clever storytelling with dark humor. His stories have been adapted into multiple films, plays, and television shows.

Dahl was born in 1916 in Cardiff, Wales, after his parents had emigrated from Norway. Unfortunately, when Dahl was three years old, both his sister and his father died unexpectedly. School was also a tough environment for Dahl, and he received poor grades. He was once punished by his headmaster for putting a mouse inside a jar of candy as a prank. Incidents like this were later used in his writing.

After graduating high school, Dahl avoided staying home and attending college, saying he preferred to take a job that would send him to "wonderful <u>faraway</u> places." He went to work for an oil company that sent him to Tanzania, Africa. Later, when World War II broke out, Dahl joined the Royal Air Force. While flying his first mission, he was forced to make a crash landing in Libya but was eventually rescued. The experience gave him material for his first short story collection, *Over to You: Ten Stories of Flyers and Flying*.

Initially, Dahl wrote for adults, but he later turned to children's literature. *James and the Giant Peach*, his first young adult novel, exemplifies Dahl's surreal, creative style. In the book, an impoverished young boy discovers an enormous magical peach. He befriends seven magically transformed insects and, together, they escape James's cruel aunts. James is an orphan, and many of Dahl's stories involve missing parents, possibly inspired by the loss of his own father.

Dahl told his daughters stories every night, and he tried to incorporate details he knew children enjoyed: magic and adventure, along with grotesque elements. His nightly storytelling incorporated memories of his childhood trips to Norway, where he had discovered fantastic tales of trolls and sorcerers. Although his stories often lack a clear moral, many of the characters must use their imaginations to survive in a cruel world.

Dahl died in 1990 in Oxford, England. In 2023, many of his books were censored after being <u>deemed</u> inappropriate for young readers. However, after public outcry, the books were reissued in their full versions. Despite ongoing debates over his work, Dahl remains one of the greatest children's storytellers of the twentieth century.

53. What is Roald Dahl best known for?

    (a) his tales for young audiences
    (b) his timeless mystery movies
    (c) his books for adult readers
    (d) his acclaimed children's poetry

54. Which of the following is NOT mentioned in the article about Dahl's youth?

    (a) He lost one of his parents at an early age.
    (b) He got in trouble with a school administrator.
    (c) He was taken away from his family as an infant.
    (d) He performed poorly as a young student.

55. Why, most likely, did Dahl move to another country?

    (a) to attend a prestigious university
    (b) to take a new position with his employer
    (c) to serve as a member of the military
    (d) to research material for his stories

56. What is mentioned in the article as being a common theme in most of Dahl's stories?

    (a) the search for a missing treasure
    (b) the tragedy of growing up without a parent
    (c) the quest for additional knowledge
    (d) the struggle to overcome childhood poverty

57. Based on the fifth paragraph, how, most likely, did Dahl develop his stories?

    (a) by adapting lessons from well-known fairytales
    (b) by recounting memories shared by his mother
    (c) by observing everyday events in the world
    (d) by entertaining his children at bedtime

58. In the context of the passage, faraway means _____.

    (a) relaxing
    (b) lost
    (c) distant
    (d) hidden

59. In the context of the passage, deemed means _____.

    (a) judged
    (b) made
    (c) proven
    (d) turned

PART 2. *Read the following magazine article and answer the questions. The underlined words in the article are for vocabulary questions.*

WHY BIRTHDAY CAKES ARE SERVED

At modern birthday parties, we eat cake and blow out birthday candles. Cake styles worldwide range from simple to <u>elaborate</u>. This delicious treat is also available in countless flavors, from traditional vanilla to more exotic sweet and savory concoctions. But how did the tradition of having cake on birthdays originate?

For much of human history, birthdays were not celebrated at all. The first reference to such a celebration is the Bible's description of an Egyptian pharaoh's birthday that took place around 3000 BCE. However, it is likely that this celebration did not mark the pharaoh's birth date, but rather the date when he became ruler of Egypt and was thus born again as a god.

The ancient Greeks were the first to observe a public event with cake and candles. To celebrate Artemis, goddess of the moon, they made round cakes that represented the lunar sphere and topped these cakes with candles to imitate rays of moonlight. The ancient Romans used a similar unsweetened cake (made of flour, olive oil, nuts, and cheese) for birthdays, but only to <u>commemorate</u> the fiftieth year—and only if the citizen was a famous man. Women's birthdays were not celebrated until much later.

Kinderfest, a German holiday that began in the eighteenth century, is credited for popularizing birthday cakes as we know them today. Each birthday, children would receive a cake with lit candles signifying their age, with an extra candle to bestow good luck in the following year. That evening, after dinner, when the candles had nearly burned down, the birthday child could blow them out, make a wish, and enjoy their treat.

For decades, birthdays cake ingredients were costly and the baking process labor-intensive, limiting their popularity. However, with the Industrial Revolution came not only mass production of ingredients that made them more affordable, but also a new ingredient, baking powder, which simplified the baking process. Ready-made cakes also became widely available for purchase. This made throwing a birthday party much easier, and has led to the birthday cake's worldwide popularity today.

60. What is the article mainly about?

    (a) the origin of a religious celebration

    (b) the creator of a popular dessert item

    (c) the symbolism behind a holiday event

    (d) the evolution of a common tradition

61. What was the first historical mention of a birthday celebration?

    (a) a tale inscribed on an ancient tablet

    (b) a story told in a religious text

    (c) a letter written by a famous ruler

    (d) a poem dedicated to the gods

62. How, most likely, did the ancient Romans decide whether someone would be celebrated with a cake?

    (a) They based it on the time of day in which the party was held.

    (b) They considered their reputation among other citizens.

    (c) They based it on the time of year when the person was born.

    (d) They considered their favorability among the gods.

63. When were eighteenth-century German children allowed to eat a special cake?

    (a) once they had said all of their prayers

    (b) on the morning of their birthday celebration

    (c) after blowing out all of their candles

    (d) before their midday meal was finished

64. According to the article, what has made birthday cakes more popular over time?

    (a) Prices of ingredients have fallen.

    (b) Advertising efforts have increased.

    (c) Home baking is making a comeback.

    (d) People have acquired more spending money.

65. In the context of the passage, elaborate means _____.

    (a) tidy

    (b) famous

    (c) strong

    (d) complex

66. In the context of the passage, commemorate means _____.

    (a) decorate

    (b) find

    (c) honor

    (d) make

THE TICHBORNE CLAIMANT

"The Tichborne Claimant" was a man who insisted he was the long-lost heir of a wealthy English family. The legal trials involving the man's claim were two of the longest and most controversial cases in Victorian-era England.

Roger Tichborne, son of Lady Tichborne, stood to inherit a vast fortune. In 1854, while sailing near South America, he was lost at sea. However, in 1863, encouraged by countless rumors and a fortune teller claiming Roger was still alive, Lady Tichborne placed advertisements in newspapers worldwide offering a reward for information about her son.

A man then known as Thomas Castro responded and wrote to Lady Tichborne, claiming to be Roger. He said that he had survived a shipwreck and was living in Australia. Despite many gaps in his tale, Lady Tichborne was eager to believe his story and invited him to visit. However, many speculated that grief for her lost son had made her irrational, and they questioned her mental state.

When Castro arrived in England, he was much shorter than Roger had been and had a much heavier frame. He was unable to communicate in French, a language that Roger had been raised speaking. Nonetheless, he resembled Roger in certain ways and knew specific details of Roger's private life. So, Lady Tichborne accepted him and granted him a yearly allowance. When she died, the man sued for the entire family fortune.

The Tichborne family opposed Castro in court, calling him an imposter and using his appearance, lack of bilingualism, and absence of a tattoo on his left arm as evidence. But the British public generally disliked the aristocracy and instead took the side of the man seeking the Tichborne fortune.

Castro lost his second trial lawsuit. His true identity was revealed to be neither Roger Tichborne nor Thomas Castro. Instead, he was identified as Arthur Orton, a man wanted for horse theft and murder. He was sentenced to prison time for lying under oath. After his release, he died in poverty. Still, he remained a popular folk hero for everyday people and was viewed by many as an innocent victim of elite society.

67. What is the main topic of the article?

(a) a woman who searched for a long-lost husband
(b) a man who tried to deceive a family
(c) a ship that was lost in a terrible storm
(d) a family fortune that was successfully stolen

68. What had Lady Tichborne's relative done that motivated her search?

(a) disappear while on a lengthy sailing voyage
(b) run away after an argument with friends
(c) insist on contacting a trusted fortune teller
(d) publish a mysterious letter in the newspaper

69. Why, most likely, did Lady Tichborne believe Castro?

(a) because she recognized him instantly
(b) because he knew friends of the family
(c) because she was becoming mentally ill
(d) because he visited her in the hospital

70. Which of the following is mentioned in the text about Castro?

(a) He weighed much less than Roger had.
(b) He spoke the same languages that Roger had spoken.
(c) He stood significantly taller than Roger had.
(d) He shared information only known to Roger and his family.

71. Why did the British public side with Castro?

(a) They were won over by his cleverness.
(b) They distrusted the evidence against him.
(c) They felt his imprisonment was cruel.
(d) They preferred him over the family.

72. In the context of the passage, speculated means _____.

(a) forgot
(b) disagreed
(c) thought
(d) requested

73. In the context of the passage, elite means _____.

(a) upper-class
(b) open
(c) modern-day
(d) old

Mr. Jack Reynolds
Department of Transportation
200 State Street
Watford, NY

Dear Mr. Reynolds,

I am contacting you in your capacity as Director of the Department of Transportation. For the past month, increased traffic going past my apartment in the middle of the day has made it impossible for me to get work done from home. I hope you can find a solution for this issue.

A week ago, I called your department seeking assistance. I was told that I would receive a call back from your office within two business days, but that call never came. Yesterday, I called again and was informed that the only way to <u>resolve</u> this matter was to send a letter to the department. In the future, the department should tell citizens immediately when they must send a letter, rather than wasting their time with phone calls.

Although the area is quiet at night, with construction beginning on the new Watford Sports Stadium, the noise from construction trucks during the day is unacceptably loud. This noise does not bother some residents because they are away at work during this time. However, I work from home as an illustrator, and the constant racket has made it impossible for me to concentrate in my apartment, even when I wear headphones.

I am especially annoyed because the stadium was a project that I and other residents personally opposed. We spoke at the local townhall meeting about how building a new stadium was expensive and unnecessary. Our concerns were ignored at the time, and now they have been realized.

I am aware that the next citywide election is in November. If I do not hear back from you within the week about the current situation, I will feel compelled to run for office myself in an aggressive <u>bid</u> to replace you.

Sincerely,

Rebecca Donaldson

74. Why is Rebecca Donaldson writing to Jack Reynolds?

(a) to inquire about an upcoming construction project
(b) to complain about a change in traffic noise
(c) to report safety issues in her apartment building
(d) to ask for clarification about a local parking law

75. What was Rebecca told when she first contacted the Department of Transportation?

(a) that she might want to continue calling daily
(b) that she would likely receive a response letter
(c) that she might be better off writing a letter
(d) that she would be getting a call soon

76. Why is the situation worse for Rebecca than for other residents?

(a) She has a longer commute to work.
(b) She spends a lot of time at home.
(c) She is often working late at night.
(d) She lives in a single-family home.

77. Why did Rebecca speak at the town hall meeting?

(a) to share that residents were against the project
(b) to request a change in the construction schedule
(c) to ask that the stadium be built in a different location
(d) to support a plan to repair residential buildings

78. How, most likely, will Rebecca react if she does not hear back from Jack Reynolds?

(a) She will vote for a new Director of Transportation.
(b) She will decide to move away from Watford.
(c) She will try to become the next Director of Transportation.
(d) She will run for office as Mayor of Watford.

79. In the context of the passage, resolve means _____.

(a) settle
(b) prefer
(c) choose
(d) propose

80. In the context of the passage, bid means _____.

(a) cost
(b) image
(c) stop
(d) attempt

GENERAL TESTS OF ENGLISH LANGUAGE PROFICIENCY
G-TELP ™

LEVEL 2

TEST 5

문제집 뒤에 있는 OMR 답안지를 사용하여 실전처럼 연습할 수 있습니다.

GRAMMAR SECTION

Example:

The boys _____ in the car.

(a) be
(b) is
(c) am
(d) are

The correct answer is (d), so the circle with the letter (d) has been blackened.

ⓐ　ⓑ　ⓒ　●

NOW TURN THE PAGE AND BEGIN

1. Carter has secured a volunteer position in Ecuador this summer, but it starts on the day of his upcoming graduation. Therefore, he _____ for the airport right after the morning ceremony.

   (a) will be leaving
   (b) will have left
   (c) has been leaving
   (d) would have left

2. Tin was one of the first metals processed by humans. It was first used during the Bronze Age, when it was combined with copper _____ a mixture known as alloy bronze.

   (a) to have created
   (b) having created
   (c) to create
   (d) creating

3. In the 1960s, a rumor surfaced that the Japanese had renamed a town "Usa." The idea was that this had been done _____ they could export products labeled "Made in USA." The rumor was proven false.

   (a) if
   (b) even though
   (c) unless
   (d) so that

4. My cousin Astrid wants to go somewhere warm for her winter vacation to escape Minnesota's freezing weather. Since my friends and I had already decided to go to Hawaii, I suggested that she _____ us.

   (a) will join
   (b) join
   (c) is joining
   (d) joined

5. Emery left last night's party early, just before the host entertained the guests with a few piano tunes. Had Emery stayed until the party ended, she _____ his performance.

   (a) would have seen
   (b) will see
   (c) will have seen
   (d) would see

6. Octopush is an aquatic sport that originated in England. Like hockey, it involves _____ a puck into a net. However, in this case, the sport takes place in a pool.

   (a) to have pushed
   (b) to push
   (c) pushing
   (d) having pushed

7. Ahmed will probably not be able to join the Greenburgh Fun Run on Saturday because he has a leg injury. However, if his leg were to heal faster than expected, he _____ in the event.

   (a) would surely have participated
   (b) would surely participate
   (c) will surely participate
   (d) will surely have participated

8. During its early months of operation, Silver Plate Restaurant struggled to attract customers. Luckily, the owners managed _____ this problem by advertising their business regularly on social media.

   (a) having overcome
   (b) to overcome
   (c) overcoming
   (d) to have overcome

9. Research has shown that attempts to hunt coyotes can cause them to breed in greater numbers. American ranchers, _____ to dislike coyotes, are typically cautioned to leave the creatures alone.

   (a) who are known
   (b) which are known
   (c) that are known
   (d) what are known

10. Winona was invited to interview for the position of office assistant at a financial consulting firm. Right now, she _____ for the interview by reviewing the company's background and the specific job description.

   (a) prepares
   (b) has been preparing
   (c) prepared
   (d) is preparing

11. Last night, Xavier arrived at the railway station just minutes before the train was scheduled to depart for Portland. Had he missed it, he _____ to wait for hours at the station for the next ride.

   (a) would have
   (b) will have
   (c) will have had
   (d) would have had

12. Superstitions vary widely from culture to culture. According to some Italian and Portuguese beliefs, a person _____ invite bad luck by walking backwards, as this can alert the devil to their location.

   (a) would
   (b) should
   (c) may
   (d) must

13. Although raccoons seem harmless, they sometimes carry viruses, despite the absence of obvious symptoms. Because of this, health experts advise that people _____ their hands if they come into contact with one.

(a) will wash
(b) wash
(c) washed
(d) are washing

14. Tamyra's homemade pizzas are delicious. Whenever she cooks for us, it feels like we are at a genuine Italian pizzeria. She often says that if she were able to, she _____ her own pizza restaurant.

(a) would have opened
(b) will open
(c) will have opened
(d) would open

15. Leaving a dog's nails untended can lead to leg injuries, affecting the animal's long-term mobility. Therefore, pet owners _____ trim their dogs' nails regularly if they want to keep their pets healthy.

(a) could
(b) must
(c) might
(d) would

16. The alternative rock band Dark Tide will hold its final performance this weekend. The band _____ at sold-out venues for two decades, and its final concert will be no exception.

(a) is performing
(b) had been performing
(c) has been performing
(d) performs

17. Due to the stressful workload, Homer wants to resign as his company's chief engineer. However, he intends to find a new job before quitting so that he does not risk _____ his sole source of income.

(a) to lose
(b) having lost
(c) to have lost
(d) losing

18. The renovation of Watertown Public Library is underway. Some concerned patrons _____ about its deteriorating condition for years before a renovation project was finally approved last month.

(a) are worrying
(b) will be worrying
(c) had been worrying
(d) have been worrying

19. While in college, Denzel will stay with his aunt in the city. He considered _____ his own apartment near campus, but he realized he could save money by staying with a relative.

(a) renting
(b) to have rented
(c) having rented
(d) to rent

20. The element Moscovium was discovered in 2003 by Russian and American scientists at the Joint Institute for Nuclear Research. This facility is in Moscow, _____ that the element is named after.

(a) what is the city
(b) which is the city
(c) that is the city
(d) where is the city

21. In 2011, the country of South Sudan was established upon separating from Sudan. If a referendum had not approved the split, Sudan _____ its title as the largest country in Africa.

(a) would have kept
(b) would keep
(c) will keep
(d) will have kept

22. The Taino people of the Caribbean region were thought to have been wiped out by European colonizers in the 1500s. _____, a recent study revealed that fifteen percent of Puerto Ricans have Taino ancestry.

(a) Besides
(b) As a result
(c) In addition
(d) However

23. A production crew was stationed at the mall this morning to film a commercial starring a famous actress. When I walked by, the crew _____ equipment while the actress signed autographs for fans.

(a) was setting up
(b) will be setting up
(c) is setting up
(d) has been setting up

24. Now that his final exams are over, Ezra is excited to get back into the *Silver Striker* television series. He plans _____ all nine seasons over the summer break.

(a) to have watched
(b) watching
(c) to watch
(d) having watched

25. Saturn's rings occasionally disappear
    due to a tilt in the planet's axis. If
    someone were to view Saturn through
    a telescope during one of these
    periods, the planet _____ to have
    no rings at all.

    (a) would seem
    (b) will seem
    (c) will have seemed
    (d) would have seemed

26. Bailey is the most senior employee
    in her company, and she has no
    plans to resign anytime soon. By next
    year, she _____ there for ten years
    already.

    (a) will be working
    (b) will have been working
    (c) is working
    (d) has been working

LISTENING SECTION

▶ Test 5 전체 음원 재생

DIRECTIONS:

The Listening Section has four parts. In each part you will hear a spoken passage and a number of questions about the passage. First you will hear the questions. Then you will hear the passage. From the four choices for each question, choose the best answer. Then blacken in the correct circle on your answer sheet.

Example:

> (a) one
> (b) two
> (c) three
> (d) four

Bill Johnson has four brothers, so the best answer is (d). The circle with the letter (d) has been blackened.

   ●

NOW TURN THE PAGE AND BEGIN

27. (a) hanging out at a party
    (b) getting some groceries
    (c) going to a concert
    (d) shopping for clothes

28. (a) by accidentally bumping into her
    (b) by sending her flowers
    (c) by sharing some gardening tools
    (d) by suddenly dropping by

29. (a) one that discusses horror films
    (b) one that helps improve sleep
    (c) one that features scary stories
    (d) one that hosts famous actors

30. (a) television comedy stars
    (b) teachers of comedy writing
    (c) retired stand-up comedians
    (d) people who are new to comedy

31. (a) It changes hosts weekly.
    (b) It features fun competitions.
    (c) It has plenty of episodes.
    (d) It invites audience feedback.

32. (a) because the episodes last too long
    (b) because the conversations go off topic
    (c) because the hosts interview too many guests
    (d) because the speakers have annoying voices

33. (a) have a meal together
    (b) go to a family reunion
    (c) hold a game night
    (d) attend a cooking class

34. (a) a magic shop opening
    (b) a magician's charity event
    (c) a brand-new magic show
    (d) a convention for magicians

35. (a) They promise rapid processing.
    (b) They offer a two-year repair warranty.
    (c) They promise free returns.
    (d) They offer discounts on large orders.

36. (a) a panel of experts
    (b) fellow contestants
    (c) several celebrity judges
    (d) all event attendees

37. (a) to meet a celebrity
    (b) to purchase an outfit
    (c) to enter a raffle
    (d) to receive a free gift

38. (a) to raise money for charity
    (b) to promote a local academy
    (c) to inspire kids to join in
    (d) to advertise certain products

39. (a) by registering in advance
    (b) by purchasing two at a time
    (c) by posting on social media
    (d) by joining the magicians' club

40. (a) a student advisor
    (b) a close coworker
    (c) a former roommate
    (d) a family member

41. (a) She could prepare for a degree program.
    (b) She could practice her writing.
    (c) She could study her favorite authors.
    (d) She could meet fellow readers.

42. (a) because of the strict professor
    (b) because of the final exam
    (c) because of the required texts
    (d) because of the quick pace

43. (a) the small-group projects
    (b) the funny lectures
    (c) the hands-on activities
    (d) the light workload

44. (a) because of the early start time
    (b) because of the long commute
    (c) because of the large class size
    (d) because of the online format

45. (a) enroll in both courses
    (b) sign up for the literature course
    (c) search for a new course
    (d) take the marine biology course

46. (a) packing for a music festival
    (b) creating a camping trip playlist
    (c) choosing music for a road trip
    (d) making playlists for friends

47. (a) because he failed to prepare enough music
    (b) because he forgot to make a playlist
    (c) because he remained on the same road
    (d) because he decided to travel alone

48. (a) It brought up bad memories.
    (b) It set the wrong mood.
    (c) It had poor sound quality.
    (d) It made her sleepy.

49. (a) because she refused to stop singing along
    (b) because she kept switching radio stations
    (c) because she refused to play certain songs
    (d) because she kept turning up the volume

50. (a) because his car broke down
    (b) because he ran out of data
    (c) because his phone died
    (d) because he had bad reception

51. (a) too many unfamiliar songs
    (b) songs with repetitive lyrics
    (c) advertisements between songs
    (d) songs with too much bass

52. (a) by changing styles often
    (b) by trying out new bands
    (c) by taking a friend's suggestions
    (d) by mixing up the song order

THIS IS THE END OF THE LISTENING SECTION

READING AND VOCABULARY SECTION

DIRECTIONS:

You will now read four different passages. Each passage is followed by comprehension and vocabulary questions. From the four choices for each item, choose the best answer. Then blacken in the correct circle on your answer sheet.

Read the following example passage and example question.

Example:

Bill Johnson lives in New York. He is 25 years old. He has four brothers and two sisters.

How many brothers does Bill Johnson have?

(a) one
(b) two
(c) three
(d) four

The correct answer is (d), so the circle with the letter (d) has been blackened.

NOW TURN THE PAGE AND BEGIN

HANK AARON

Hank Aaron was an American baseball player and civil rights champion. He is best known for breaking baseball icon Babe Ruth's home run record and for holding his own record for thirty-three years.

Aaron was born in Mobile, Alabama, on February 5, 1934, during the Great Depression. Aaron and his siblings grew up in poverty. He enjoyed playing sports, but his parents could not afford to buy sports equipment, so Aaron would practice baseball swings using everyday items, such as broomsticks and bottlecaps.

In 1954, after years of success in segregated high school and professional leagues, Aaron joined a Major League Baseball (MLB) team, the Milwaukee Braves. In 1957, he was awarded the National League Most Valuable Player for leading his team to their only World Series Championship. Over a long career, he set a number of hitting records and, in the spring of 1974, he was on the verge of breaking one of MLB's most important milestones: the record for career home runs, which at the time was 714 and held by the legendary Babe Ruth.

On opening day, Aaron tied the record. Then, four days later, in front of a sold-out stadium, Aaron hit another home run and made history. Although it was a <u>momentous</u> achievement, many Americans were upset to see a Black man break Ruth's record. Aaron received letters from all over the country, many of which were racially threatening. That year, he set the Guinness World Record for the most mail sent to a private citizen. While he remained fearless under pressure, the highly publicized racist letters he received drew attention to a deep-rooted societal problem.

In response, Aaron became determined to help <u>address</u> race issues in America. After retiring from baseball with 755 home runs, he donated extensively to charities, dedicated his time to creating scholarships for Black students, and encouraged the MLB to develop more diverse teams. These philanthropic efforts, partially motivated by Aaron's personal struggles, also honored the legacy of his friend, the late Martin Luther King Jr., who had been killed for leading the fight against racial inequality.

After spending many years as a business owner and philanthropist, Hank Aaron died in January 2021. Although his home run record was broken in 2007, Aaron remains one of the greatest major league players of all time and a role model for many.

53. What is Hank Aaron most famous for?

    (a) breaking the record for the fastest pitch in baseball
    (b) winning more awards than any baseball player before him
    (c) having the longest career in baseball history
    (d) hitting more home runs than any baseball player before him

54. How did Aaron practice baseball during his childhood?

    (a) by using common household objects
    (b) by getting equipment from his older siblings
    (c) by borrowing his neighbor's athletic gear
    (d) by taking items from his school's sports department

55. According to the text, which of the following is true of Aaron's major league career?

    (a) He had previously played only on high school teams.
    (b) He was named the best player for several seasons.
    (c) He played an important role in his team's championship win.
    (d) He struggled to stand out when he first began playing.

56. Why, most likely, did Aaron receive a lot of hate mail?

    (a) because he performed poorly in an important game
    (b) because he compared himself to another baseball player
    (c) because he broke a record that was held by a white man
    (d) because he was known for poor sportsmanship

57. Which of the following is NOT mentioned as a factor in Aaron's decision to donate his time to charitable work?

    (a) the lack of diversity on baseball teams
    (b) the activist efforts of his friend
    (c) the threats he received over his success
    (d) the death of a former teammate

58. In the context of the passage, momentous means _____.

    (a) significant
    (b) delayed
    (c) necessary
    (d) simple

59. In the context of the passage, address means _____.

    (a) wait for
    (b) tackle
    (c) complain about
    (d) study

THE INVENTION OF BARCODES

Today, the barcode is found everywhere: store products, library books, and even hospital wristbands. However, it has not always been this way. Before the barcode's invention, store items were priced manually, causing errors at checkout. Furthermore, without a dependable way to keep track of stock, retailers often failed to detect theft. The retail industry needed a more efficient product-tracking system.

In the late 1940s, Joe Woodland and Bernard Silver devised the concept of the barcode, a mark that would allow machines to read product information. Sitting on a Miami beach, Woodland was inspired by a design he had sketched in the sand that was reminiscent of the dots found in Morse code. By 1952, the two men had patented bullseye-shaped barcodes. However, the technology to read and process the information was not yet available.

The invention of the laser in the 1960s accelerated the development of barcode technology. In 1966, as more companies began to pursue automation in checkout lines, the Kroger supermarket chain agreed to test a new system. This spurred a competition to create the best barcode design. The Radio Corporation of America bought the patent for Woodland and Silver's bullseye design and began using it with laser scanners. On July 3, 1972, the first bullseye barcode was tested at Kroger's Kenwood Plaza store in Cincinnati, to initial success.

However, problems soon followed. The bullseye barcode smudged easily, making it unreadable. In consideration of this issue, IBM employee George Laurer created a new version: a striped barcode with a universal numbering system. On June 26, 1974, the first item to be scanned using the new barcode was a packet of Wrigley's chewing gum, which had been chosen to show that the barcode could even be printed on very small packages.

Today, Laurer's barcode is still in use and has become essential in other areas, such as healthcare. Hospitals use barcodes on patient wristbands for accurate identification and on prescription bottles for dosage and safety details. This application, which has elevated patient care and streamlined medical procedures, showcases the barcode's versatility and its global relevance in today's society.

60. What is the article mainly about?

   (a) the impact of barcodes on retail sales
   (b) the people who design barcodes today
   (c) the history of the barcode system
   (d) the person who created the barcode scanner

61. What prevented barcodes from being used in the 1950s?

   (a) There was little demand for them.
   (b) There was no way to scan them.
   (c) There was a known flaw in their design.
   (d) There was no consistent way to print them.

62. When did Kroger's in Cincinnati first test barcode technology?

   (a) before the bullseye shape was created
   (b) after a universal numbering system was developed
   (c) before lasers had become available
   (d) after companies competed to make the best design

63. Why was chewing gum used to demonstrate Laurer's design?

   (a) because it was produced by a partner company
   (b) because it was particularly small
   (c) because it was the store's bestselling item
   (d) because it was visually appealing

64. Which of the following is NOT implied about barcodes in the healthcare sector?

   (a) They are used to track admitted patients.
   (b) They help to reduce prescription errors.
   (c) They are used to regulate medication dosages.
   (d) They help to identify medical equipment.

65. In the context of the passage, detect means _____.

   (a) notice
   (b) punish
   (c) admit
   (d) explain

66. In the context of the passage, pursue means _____.

   (a) ruin
   (b) suspend
   (c) seek
   (d) repeat

BANYAN TREE

The banyan tree is a species of fig tree and a member of the mulberry family. Found in India and Pakistan, it is notable for its aerial root system that grows above ground, for the sweet fruit it produces, and for its unique relationship with fig wasps.

The name "banyan" may refer to many species of fig trees known as "strangler figs." When a banyan seed lands on another tree, it grows into a vine that <u>extends</u> toward the ground, wrapping around the tree and its roots. Eventually, the strangler fig will grow to encircle the original tree, killing it in the process.

As the banyan tree develops, it grows what are called aerial prop roots, which hang from its branches. These roots grow into the ground, eventually hardening into thick wooden structures that look like tree trunks. However, all the trunks are connected to the original banyan. A single banyan can expand outward into a broad area, creating what is often referred to as a banyan grove. The largest banyan tree currently alive is over 250 years old and can be found in Kolkata, India. With over 3,600 aerial roots, the tree covers roughly 3.5 acres, thus resembling an entire forest.

The banyan tree is pollinated by the fig wasp, a species that has evolved to have a close relationship with the tree. Figs initially develop as a structure called a syconium, or a pod with flowers on the inside. Fig wasps lay their eggs inside these pods when the tree is producing pollen. The insects then transport pollen wherever they go. Later, pods are <u>dispersed</u> by birds and other animals, which eat the mature figs.

The banyan is India's national tree and has great significance in the Hindu religion. According to Hindu mythology, the divine deity Krishna delivered a sermon while standing under a banyan tree. This speech—including its location—is described in the Bhagavad Gita scripture, one of the core Hindu texts. The banyan is often referred to as a "world tree" that grows upside down and provides blessings to those on Earth through its roots.

67. What is the article mainly about?

    (a) a tree that has edible leaves
    (b) a poisonous tree species
    (c) a tree that is becoming extinct
    (d) a type of fruit-bearing tree

68. How, most likely, do strangler figs get their name?

    (a) from the method they use to get food
    (b) from the twisted pattern of their roots
    (c) from the way they eliminate other trees
    (d) from the arm-like appearance of their vines

69. According to the third paragraph, what makes up a banyan grove?

    (a) the hardened roots of a single banyan tree
    (b) the fallen leaves of many banyan trees
    (c) the dried-out remains of several banyan trees
    (d) the flowering branches of one banyan tree

70. Based on the text, what can probably be said about fig wasps?

    (a) They eat the pods produced by banyan trees.
    (b) They carry pollen to and from their nests.
    (c) They build their homes inside thick roots.
    (d) They bring mature fruit to their hives.

71. Which is NOT stated in the final paragraph about a particular banyan tree's significance in Hindu mythology?

    (a) It was the site of an important sermon.
    (b) It is thought to be a source of divine blessings.
    (c) It was referenced in a religious text.
    (d) It is believed to house an important deity.

72. In the context of the passage, extends means _____.

    (a) stretches
    (b) slows
    (c) settles
    (d) slides

73. In the context of the passage, dispersed means _____.

    (a) thrown
    (b) spread
    (c) known
    (d) used

To: Diane Foster <diane.foster@marigoldhotel.com>
From: Horace Bramley <horace.bramley@wellnessretreats.com>
Subject: Wellness Spa Partnership

Dear Ms. Foster,

My name is Horace Bramley, and I am the owner of Bramley's Wellness Retreats. I produce retreat experiences for overstressed workers in today's fast-paced world. I am contacting you because I feel that the Marigold would be the perfect location for a wellness retreat, and I would love to partner with you.

First, let me tell you about our retreats. We combine physical activity and mindfulness practices to relieve stress for corporate employees. For example, at a recent retreat for business executives, we started the day with aerobic exercise to work up a sweat and then transitioned to gentle yoga poses. After lunch, the clients meditated, focusing on releasing negative emotions. We cater to clients who are in high-intensity occupations and require an outlet for their stress.

When I was at your hotel, I felt an amazing energy, in part due to the marvelous fragrances. Each room had a gentle smell of exotic wood and therapeutic oil, reminding me of an aromatherapy session. I asked the desk clerk about the oils and was told that you select them personally. Such beautiful aromas would complement the relaxing spa services I offer during my retreats.

A few months ago, I held a spa retreat at a small hotel, and this led to a substantial increase in their profits for that period. At a larger hotel like the Marigold, you would easily see greater financial rewards if you were to start hosting retreats.

I would love to establish an arrangement with terms that you find agreeable. I will be unavailable this weekend due to an out-of-town business trip, but feel free to email me, and we can schedule a video conference to discuss the details next week.

Best,

Horace Bramley

74. Why is Horace Bramley writing to Diane Foster?

(a) to request a discount on a group reservation
(b) to invite her to one of his wellness retreats
(c) to propose a collaboration with her hotel
(d) to ask her to invest in his business

75. Why, most likely, do Horace's clients attend his retreats?

(a) because of their poor physical health
(b) because of their stressful family responsibilities
(c) because of their need for emotional support
(d) because of their busy professional lives

76. According to the third paragraph, why was Horace impressed with the Marigold Hotel?

(a) because of the soothing scents in the building
(b) because of the skilled musicians that performed there
(c) because of the beautiful paintings in the rooms
(d) because of the abundance of plants in the lobby

77. Based on the fourth paragraph, what advantage does the Marigold probably have over other hotels?

(a) It features more available rooms.
(b) It has a more impressive architectural design.
(c) It features more experienced staff.
(d) It has a more flexible reservation policy.

78. How does Horace suggest discussing the terms of their agreement?

(a) by meeting during his weekend trip to the hotel
(b) by arranging a call for the following week
(c) by connecting during a weekend conference
(d) by having lunch the following week

79. In the context of the passage, cater to means _____.

(a) promote
(b) serve
(c) separate
(d) provide

80. In the context of the passage, establish means _____.

(a) fight for
(b) allow
(c) set up
(d) review

TEST BOOKLET NUMBER: _____

GENERAL TESTS OF ENGLISH LANGUAGE PROFICIENCY
G-TELP ™

LEVEL 2

TEST 6

문제집 뒤에 있는 OMR 답안지를 사용하여 실전처럼 연습할 수 있습니다.

GRAMMAR SECTION

Example:

The boys _____ in the car.

(a) be
(b) is
(c) am
(d) are

The correct answer is (d), so the circle with the letter (d) has been blackened.

ⓐ   ⓑ   ⓒ   ●

NOW TURN THE PAGE AND BEGIN

1. While hummingbirds are known as the smallest migrating bird, they have other special qualities. They are also the only birds that _____ fly backwards, using wings that beat up to 4,000 times per minute.

   (a) would
   (b) must
   (c) can
   (d) could

2. Jonathan and his friends want to see a movie on Friday night. Unfortunately, they all like completely different types of films, which makes _____ a movie difficult.

   (a) to choose
   (b) to have chosen
   (c) choosing
   (d) having chosen

3. The novel *Lightforce* was highly anticipated, but the author, Brad Bickley, could not finish it due to writer's block. Had the book been completed, it _____ launched at a celebrity event last month.

   (a) would be
   (b) will be
   (c) will have been
   (d) would have been

4. The city of Istanbul is one of the largest and oldest in the world. Until 1453, it was known as "Constantinople" and _____ as the capital of the Byzantine Empire.

   (a) has been serving
   (b) had been serving
   (c) would serve
   (d) will have served

5. Rebecca is replying to a friend's email invitation to a party at his house next Friday night. Rebecca is eager _____, but only if she can take a guest along with her.

   (a) to go
   (b) to have gone
   (c) going
   (d) having gone

6. Dogs understand us reasonably well when we communicate with them. This is because their advanced language processing, _____, allows them to comprehend words, tone, context, and gestures.

   (a) who resembles ours
   (b) which resembles ours
   (c) that resembles ours
   (d) what resembles ours

7. Iceland is very active geologically and has many hot springs that are popular with swimmers. If the country's volcanic activity were ever to cease, Icelanders _____ one of their favorite methods of relaxation.

(a) will lose
(b) will have lost
(c) would lose
(d) would have lost

8. Mark and Jen wanted to do some outdoor exercise this afternoon, but it is pouring rain outside. They are going to wait it out and play tennis in the park's indoor stadium _____ the rain stops.

(a) after
(b) whereas
(c) because
(d) until

9. The International Cheese-Making Competition begins tomorrow in Paris. Right now, competitors from more than twenty different countries _____ in the city, ready to demonstrate their dazzling expertise.

(a) are arriving
(b) arrive
(c) had been arriving
(d) would arrive

10. Alice has been calling her doctor for several days. She has decided that if she is not able _____ him by tomorrow, she will make an appointment with another doctor.

(a) reaching
(b) to reach
(c) having reached
(d) to have reached

11. Tamil, which is spoken in parts of India, Sri Lanka, and Singapore, is one of the oldest continuously spoken languages in the world. It is estimated that people _____ Tamil since 2500 BCE.

(a) are speaking
(b) have been speaking
(c) will be speaking
(d) had been speaking

12. Before going to bed last Thursday, Justin noticed that the batteries in his alarm clock were dead. If he had not replaced them, he _____ his appointment the following morning.

(a) might have missed
(b) will miss
(c) might miss
(d) will have missed

13. Natalie has arrived at the arena to see her favorite band, but their tour bus has broken down, causing a delay. She does not mind _____, though, as they are amazing in concert.

(a) to have waited
(b) having waited
(c) to wait
(d) waiting

14. Colin canceled his old gym membership because the drive to that gym took too long. He is looking around at other gyms and _____ to a new one next week.

(a) switched
(b) has been switching
(c) will be switching
(d) would switch

15. Peacocks are among the world's largest flying birds, weighing up to thirteen pounds. At night, they perch in trees. However, they choose _____ their nests on the ground.

(a) building
(b) to build
(c) having built
(d) to have built

16. Peter is about to complete his tenth marathon. He began long-distance running to improve his physical health, but he discovered he also loved racing. This coming September, he _____ in marathons for over two years.

(a) is competing
(b) will have been competing
(c) will be competing
(d) has been competing

17. Maria wants to get a puppy. Her best friend, Jemima, advised that she _____ one from a local shelter rather than buying one from a pet store.

(a) adopt
(b) adopted
(c) is adopting
(d) will adopt

18. The Declaration of Independence was drafted by American statesman and attorney Thomas Jefferson, _____ the third US president and the founder of the University of Virginia.

(a) that was also
(b) which was also
(c) who was also
(d) what was also

19. Chelsea was leaving her apartment in a hurry to meet her friends when she realized that she _____ her keys. Shaking her head at her forgetfulness, she rushed back to retrieve them.

    (a) is missing
    (b) has been missing
    (c) will have been missing
    (d) was missing

20. William Shakespeare is considered one of the greatest writers in history. Some people have argued that his works _____ have been written by another author, but experts have thoroughly dismissed that claim.

    (a) should
    (b) will
    (c) may
    (d) can

21. Although Bill is looking for a new house, his financial advisor has reservations about such a purchase. He suggests that Bill _____ for a while until house prices decrease significantly.

    (a) will wait
    (b) waited
    (c) wait
    (d) is waiting

22. James loves cats, but he already has too many strays staying at his home. Still, if he were to move to a larger place, he _____ every abandoned cat in his neighborhood.

    (a) will rescue
    (b) would rescue
    (c) will have rescued
    (d) would have rescued

23. Leroy usually drives the same two-hour route every year to see his family for Christmas. _____, this year, heavy flooding in the area forced him to take a much longer, more roundabout drive.

    (a) Likewise
    (b) Therefore
    (c) Otherwise
    (d) However

24. German forces came close to winning World War I in its early stages. Had it not been for the efforts of the Belgian Army, the Germans _____ the Allies, a group of powerful countries.

    (a) would probably have defeated
    (b) will probably defeat
    (c) will probably have defeated
    (d) would probably defeat

25. Ever since Janice got her license, her mom has been really nervous about letting her drive. Nonetheless, last Friday night, her mom risked _____ Janice the keys to the family car.

(a) giving
(b) to give
(c) to have given
(d) having given

26. Marcus has been frightened of the woods ever since he saw a horror movie set in the forest. If he were to overcome his fear, he _____ his friends on a camping trip next weekend.

(a) will join
(b) will have joined
(c) would have joined
(d) would join

LISTENING SECTION

▶ Test 6 전체 음원 재생

DIRECTIONS:

The Listening Section has four parts. In each part you will hear a spoken passage and a number of questions about the passage. First you will hear the questions. Then you will hear the passage. From the four choices for each question, choose the best answer. Then blacken in the correct circle on your answer sheet.

Example:

(a) one

(b) two

(c) three

(d) four

Bill Johnson has four brothers, so the best answer is (d). The circle with the letter (d) has been blackened.

NOW TURN THE PAGE AND BEGIN

27. (a) working at a department store
    (b) shopping in their neighborhood
    (c) going to a holiday party
    (d) exchanging their presents

31. (a) that he was always watching
    (b) that he was a magical figure
    (c) that he was kind to all children
    (d) that he was entirely fictional

28. (a) to take advantage of big sales
    (b) to buy items before they sell out
    (c) to avoid large crowds of people
    (d) to pay for things a little at a time

32. (a) He worried about ruining a
        celebration.
    (b) He was afraid her parents would
        be angry.
    (c) He worried it would affect their
        relationship.
    (d) He was afraid she would tell other
        children.

29. (a) She requested presents for others.
    (b) She listed all the toys that she
        wanted.
    (c) She asked for a trip to see the
        elves.
    (d) She pointed out her good behavior.

33. (a) continue gift shopping
    (b) have coffee nearby
    (c) wrap some presents
    (d) drive to a local café

30. (a) by overhearing a friend talking
    (b) by finding out from her parents
    (c) by discovering a hidden present
    (d) by seeing her dad wrap her gift

34. (a) a celebration of a war hero
    (b) the making of a historical film
    (c) a tour of a war museum
    (d) the reopening of a historical site

35. (a) when the park opens
    (b) after their performance
    (c) before the intermission
    (d) as they are rehearsing

36. (a) change into other clothes
    (b) sign a legal form
    (c) watch a training video
    (d) get a doctor's note

37. (a) to experience less engine noise
    (b) to volunteer for the robbery
    (c) to avoid breathing in the smoke
    (d) to get the most scenic view

38. (a) a meal hosted by an actor
    (b) a tour of the general's mansion
    (c) a colonial-style cooking class
    (d) a speech from the film's director

39. (a) They can download an app.
    (b) They can arrive at a certain time.
    (c) They can join a mailing list.
    (d) They can mention a specific phrase.

40. (a) to start an internship
    (b) to return to her job
    (c) to study for classes
    (d) to visit her friend

41. (a) an online class
    (b) a required class
    (c) an advanced class
    (d) a popular class

42. (a) He had trouble understanding the instructor.
    (b) He was unable to develop good listening skills.
    (c) He had trouble learning correct pronunciation.
    (d) He was unable to remember the content.

43. (a) his stories about travel
    (b) his interest in local culture
    (c) his knowledge of food
    (d) his efforts to communicate

44. (a) her extended family
    (b) her new coworkers
    (c) her future roommate
    (d) her local hosts

45. (a) brainstorm ideas for a project
    (b) start working on her new course
    (c) download a language app
    (d) concentrate on her senior thesis

46. (a) how to create books for kids
    (b) how to publish kids' books
    (c) how to get kids to read books
    (d) how to review kids' books

47. (a) on a building's fire escape
    (b) in a haunted house
    (c) on a skyscraper's roof
    (d) in a famous museum

48. (a) an imaginary person
    (b) a true story
    (c) an unlikely friendship
    (d) a strange creature

49. (a) He pretends he is a delivery man.
    (b) He sees an animal driving a car.
    (c) He pretends he is in another country.
    (d) He sees a cartoon coming to life.

50. (a) by introducing a puzzle
    (b) by using complex characters
    (c) by introducing new vocabulary
    (d) by using sudden plot twists

51. (a) the history of his apartment building
    (b) the identity of a strange woman
    (c) the contents of a hidden container
    (d) the secret lives of his parents

52. (a) being able to answer questions
    (b) finding something familiar in the characters
    (c) knowing how the tale will end
    (d) believing that the stories are real

THIS IS THE END OF THE LISTENING SECTION

READING AND VOCABULARY SECTION

DIRECTIONS:

You will now read four different passages. Each passage is followed by comprehension and vocabulary questions. From the four choices for each item, choose the best answer. Then blacken in the correct circle on your answer sheet.

Read the following example passage and example question.

Example:

> Bill Johnson lives in New York. He is 25 years old. He has four brothers and two sisters.
>
> How many brothers does Bill Johnson have?
>
> (a) one
> (b) two
> (c) three
> (d) four

The correct answer is (d), so the circle with the letter (d) has been blackened.

NOW TURN THE PAGE AND BEGIN

CHARLIE CHAPLIN

Charlie Chaplin was an English actor and director who rose to fame during the silent film era. He is known for his iconic comedy character "the Little Tramp," an innocent but mischievous individual dressed in a tattered suit and derby hat who appeared in numerous movies.

Charles Spencer Chaplin was born on April 16, 1889, in London, England. His childhood was difficult. His father left when he was very young, and his mother, a music hall entertainer, was often unable to provide for Charlie and his brother. However, her passion for performing inspired her son, and young Charlie soon harbored ambitions to be an actor.

Chaplin's talent secured him a spot in a British comedy troupe but, after traveling with the group to the US, his focus <u>shifted</u> to comic movies. In 1914, he signed a contract with Keystone Studios in Los Angeles. For one production, he chose enormous pants, an undersized coat and hat, and a fake mustache from the studio's vast costume selection. Chaplin claimed that once he put on those accessories, he knew who his new character was, and "the Little Tramp" was born.

As this new character, Chaplin rose to stardom. The Little Tramp was low in social status but possessed perfect manners, and audiences saw themselves in the character's daily struggles against authority figures. By 1918, Chaplin was earning a movie star's salary. He wrote, directed, and starred in *The Gold Rush*, a comedy that is now considered one of history's greatest silent films.

After 1927, movies began featuring sound, but Chaplin swore that audiences would never hear the Tramp talk. So, he retired the character. In 1940, he appeared in his first speaking role as the lead in the political parody *The Great Dictator*. Chaplin plays a dual role as both dictator Adolf Hitler and the barber who is mistaken for him. The barber eventually embraces the confusion, using the attention and notoriety to argue for compassion and peace over discriminatory behavior.

In later life, Chaplin was accused of having <u>ties</u> to Communist figures during a time when the US government viewed that political ideology as dangerous. In response, Chaplin relocated to Switzerland in political protest, where he died in 1975. Today, he is remembered as one of the greatest stars of the silent film era and as an actor who revolutionized on-screen comedy.

53. According to the article, what is Charlie Chaplin best known for?

   (a) portraying a famous historical figure onscreen
   (b) appearing in the first silent movie
   (c) producing award-winning romantic comedies
   (d) developing a humorous film character

54. Based on the second paragraph, why, most likely, did Chaplin decide to become a performer?

   (a) because he admired his mother's profession
   (b) because he was persuaded to by an acting agent
   (c) because he wanted to follow in his brother's footsteps
   (d) because he had dreams of becoming wealthy

55. Why did audiences relate to Chaplin's "Little Tramp" character?

   (a) They understood his ongoing romantic struggles.
   (b) They identified with his everyday challenges.
   (c) They aspired to reach his high social status.
   (d) They supported his respect for government authority.

56. In *The Great Dictator*, what did the barber's acceptance of his new identity allow him to do?

   (a) escape his many previous mistakes
   (b) launch a campaign for public office
   (c) encourage greater kindness in society
   (d) draw more attention to his business

57. How did Chaplin respond to the US government's accusations?

   (a) by quitting a political party
   (b) by relocating to another country
   (c) by making a protest movie
   (d) by resorting to legal action

58. In the context of the passage, shifted means _____.

   (a) worked
   (b) changed
   (c) listened
   (d) planned

59. In the context of the passage, ties means _____.

   (a) disruptions
   (b) additions
   (c) connections
   (d) intentions

WHY HOT DOGS ARE RARELY SOLD IN FAST-FOOD RESTAURANTS

Hot dogs—sausages served on a split roll—are one of America's most popular foods. Hot dogs, like hamburgers, originated in Germany, but they are now commonly associated with American cuisine. Many fast-food restaurants, such as McDonald's and Burger King, built their businesses by selling hamburgers. However, it is rare for an American fast-food chain to sell hot dogs.

So, why are fast-food hot dogs so unpopular? Although some restaurants have attempted to market hot dogs, most have been surprisingly unsuccessful. The "McHotDog" vanished from the McDonald's menu shortly after its release, and endeavors by other chains also flopped, with a newspaper review calling Burger King's hot dog "a disgusting disgrace." But, like hamburgers, hot dogs are simple to prepare, so they seem like a perfect fit for fast-food restaurants.

Interestingly, the food's preparation might be what has led to its failure. Fast-food hamburgers with buns can remain warm and edible under heat lamps for about fifteen minutes, allowing them to be ready before a customer even places an order. But hot dogs sweat moisture, turning their bread soggy very quickly. This means they must be either served to a restaurant-goer immediately or kept separate from their buns, which <u>hinders</u> service, making for long lines and unhappy patrons.

Hot dogs are also prepared differently based on regional preferences. For instance, many restaurants in Chicago, where hot dogs are loaded with toppings, discourage putting ketchup on their "dogs." But elsewhere in America, ketchup is <u>acceptable</u> as a topping. In New York, hot dogs often come with sauerkraut and, in the Southwestern United States, they are typically served with mayonnaise and bacon. These differences in local tastes make it difficult for chain restaurants to offer a single product that can be prepared quickly.

Hot dogs first became popular in the US during the early 1900s. They were often sold at seaside resorts or state fairs, so Americans came to associate them with leisure and summer weather. People enjoy grilling them at family picnics and ordering them at baseball games. A mental link between hot dogs, relaxation, and the outdoors may help explain why customers are less interested in buying them from fast-food restaurants.

60. What is the article mainly about?

(a) the limited market for hot dogs
(b) the increasing popularity of hot dogs
(c) the overall history of hot dogs
(d) the ingredients included in hot dogs

61. Based on the second paragraph, why might the failure of fast-food hot dogs be surprising?

(a) because they are inexpensive to produce
(b) because they are well-received by customers
(c) because they are relatively easy to make
(d) because they are highly rated in restaurant reviews

62. According to the article, what makes selling fast-food hamburgers convenient?

(a) They remain edible after preparation.
(b) They can be cooked with a heat lamp.
(c) They require only a few ingredients.
(d) They are prepared using basic equipment.

63. What is suggested in the fourth paragraph about hot dog toppings in the United States?

(a) that they are only popular in certain regions
(b) that they should be added in a specific order
(c) that they vary widely in different parts of the country
(d) that they have become increasingly expensive

64. How did hot dogs come to be associated with leisure?

(a) They were initially served at baseball games.
(b) They were originally eaten on national holidays.
(c) They were initially eaten only in the summer.
(d) They were originally sold at outdoor locations.

65. In the context of the passage, hinders means _____.

(a) expands
(b) invites
(c) creates
(d) delays

66. In the context of the passage, acceptable means _____.

(a) valuable
(b) suitable
(c) visible
(d) believable

THE CATHEDRAL OF JUSTO GALLEGO

The Cathedral of Justo Gallego, also called "the Cathedral of Junk," is a religious building in Madrid, Spain. Covering 8,000 square feet, with a dome rising 130 feet in the air, it was created nearly single-handedly as an act of spiritual devotion by a former monk.

Justo Gallego joined a monastery as a young man. In 1961, after falling ill with tuberculosis, he requested permission to leave his religious order and seek treatment. Gallego vowed that if he survived his condition, he would realize his dream of building a religious shrine. He recovered and, without any formal training, began building the cathedral on land that he had inherited from his family.

Gallego designed the building in an unusual style. He avoided straight lines in his plans, instead favoring curves and circles. As an explanation for this design, Gallego stated that God made all things round, including the planets and the earth. He also used unusual construction techniques. To make the cathedral's columns, he filled empty paint cans with concrete. To make stained glass windows, he smashed discarded colored glass into tiny pieces, then painstakingly glued the fragments into complex patterns.

Most of the materials used for the cathedral were recycled everyday objects or surplus materials donated by local companies. Though Gallego mainly funded his work through donations, he also received $45,000 from the Coca-Cola Company, which used his partially built cathedral in an advertisement. Following the commercial, approximately 1,000 tourists began visiting the cathedral each day.

For decades, Gallego worked on the cathedral daily, with little outside assistance. When local authorities deemed the building to be structurally unsound, there were fears that, when Gallego died, the still-unfinished building would be demolished. To avoid this, Gallego arranged to donate the building to a nonprofit agency. After Gallego's death in 2021, the organization began making repairs, saving the cathedral from destruction. Its members committed to completing the cathedral, and construction is ongoing to this day, according to Gallego's plans. However, the building is not registered as a church. Instead, it serves as a meditative space for followers of all religions.

67. Based on the first paragraph, why did Justo Gallego probably build the cathedral?

(a) to raise awareness of recycling
(b) to show his religious faith
(c) to stay active in retirement
(d) to attract tourists to his home

68. What caused Gallego to leave the monastery?

(a) He experienced a disturbing dream.
(b) He was ordered to by his supervisor.
(c) He needed to address a serious illness.
(d) He was advised to by a family member.

69. Based on the third paragraph, what probably influenced Gallego's choice for the style of the cathedral?

(a) his desire to simplify its construction
(b) his attempt to model it after a famous building
(c) his goal for it to be attractive to visitors
(d) his effort to imitate natural shapes in its design

70. Why did the Coca-Cola Company contribute to Gallego's building costs?

(a) because it used the site in promotional materials
(b) because it had to pay for damage it caused
(c) because it wanted to make a charitable donation
(d) because it put advertisements up at the location

71. How did a nonprofit agency save the cathedral?

(a) by registering it as a church
(b) by purchasing it from the owner
(c) by opening it to the public
(d) by making it structurally safe

72. In the context of the passage, surplus means _____.

(a) costly
(b) written
(c) extra
(d) learning

73. In the context of the passage, deemed means _____.

(a) judged
(b) hoped
(c) promised
(d) forced

TO: Baggage Services <baggageservices@defiantair.com>
FROM: Emma Lewis <emma.lewis@sparklemail.com>
SUBJECT: Baggage Issue

Dear Sir or Madam:

Last Sunday, I flew from Tokyo to Los Angeles aboard Defiant Airlines. When I arrived in Los Angeles, my luggage was declared lost. It has been three days now, and I have still not received it. I am contacting the Baggage Services Department to resolve the issue.

When my suitcase failed to appear on the carousel, I went to the nearest Defiant desk to seek assistance. However, upon hearing my situation, staff suggested only that I wait in case someone had taken it by accident. Apparently, such errors are often noticed within minutes, and bags are quickly returned. I waited as instructed, but without success.

After returning to the desk, I was given a claim number. The agent then told me that if my suitcase could not be located and returned within twenty-four hours, I would be given a voucher to purchase clothing. This was helpful but insufficient, as I needed replacement items immediately. I was traveling for business, and I hadn't worn my usual professional clothing because it was such a long flight.

Furthermore, I am an architect, and I had packed miniature architectural models for my imminent project, a multi-million-dollar skyscraper in Los Angeles. When my luggage failed to reach its destination, I was forced to put off meetings with my biggest client, placing my project in jeopardy. If the models are not returned, I will have to reproduce them, and this will involve considerable expense, for which I will hold Defiant responsible.

I have called Defiant daily without receiving any updates. Should my luggage be permanently misplaced, I will be forced to sue your airline for all damages inflicted on me by the loss. Therefore, if my suitcase is not returned to me, you will hear from my attorney.

Sincerely,

Emma Lewis

74. Why is Emma Lewis writing to Defiant Airlines?

    (a) to inquire about luggage restrictions
    (b) to complain about damaged property
    (c) to get excess baggage fees refunded
    (d) to locate belongings lost on a trip

75. What did the staff suggest may have occurred?

    (a) Emma put the wrong label on her case.
    (b) Another passenger mistook Emma's luggage for their own.
    (c) Emma waited in the wrong location.
    (d) A staff member dropped Emma's bag in error.

76. Why, most likely, did Emma require additional clothing?

    (a) because she had professional engagements to attend
    (b) because she had been unprepared for the cold weather
    (c) because she had left her jacket on the plane
    (d) because she had traveled in her business suit

77. What put Emma's architectural project at risk?

    (a) the loss of several valuable documents
    (b) the need to postpone meetings with a client
    (c) the accidental breakage of her models by the airline
    (d) the fact that she was unable to reach her coworkers

78. According to the letter, what will Emma do if the situation is not resolved?

    (a) refuse to fly with the airline again
    (b) call the airline every day for updates
    (c) bring a legal case against the airline
    (d) visit the airline's offices in person

79. In the context of the passage, insufficient means _____.

    (a) unsatisfactory
    (b) inaccurate
    (c) unavoidable
    (d) included

80. In the context of the passage, imminent means _____.

    (a) finished
    (b) affordable
    (c) common
    (d) upcoming

GENERAL TESTS OF ENGLISH LANGUAGE PROFICIENCY

G-TELP ™

LEVEL 2

TEST 7

문제집 뒤에 있는 OMR 답안지를 사용하여 실전처럼 연습할 수 있습니다.

GRAMMAR SECTION

Example:

The boys _____ in the car.

(a) be
(b) is
(c) am
(d) are

The correct answer is (d), so the circle with the letter (d) has been blackened.

ⓐ   ⓑ   ⓒ   ●

NOW TURN THE PAGE AND BEGIN

1. Megan had planned to have dinner at her favorite Italian restaurant but chose to cook instead. She _____ ingredients for her creamy pasta sauce when she realized she did not have any cream or milk.

   (a) has been gathering
   (b) was gathering
   (c) would gather
   (d) is gathering

2. Finished in 1931, *The Persistence of Memory* is one of Salvador Dali's most famous oil paintings. Art critics interpret the three melting clocks in the painting, _____, as signifying the fluidity of time.

   (a) which were inspired by melting cheese
   (b) that were inspired by melting cheese
   (c) who were inspired by melting cheese
   (d) what were inspired by melting cheese

3. Dave is having trouble at work after accidentally breaking the company laptop. His employer is demanding that he _____ for the repair, or else the laptop's cost will be deducted from his next paycheck.

   (a) paid
   (b) is paying
   (c) will pay
   (d) pay

4. The red supergiant star Betelgeuse will inevitably explode one day. Although the star is nearly 650 light-years away, if it were to explode, it _____ from Earth, even in the daytime.

   (a) will be visible
   (b) would have been visible
   (c) would be visible
   (d) will have been visible

5. Gostra is a traditional Maltese game dating back to the Middle Ages. The game involves _____ along a greasy wooden pole to grab one of three flags attached to the end.

   (a) to have run
   (b) running
   (c) having run
   (d) to run

6. Lara fell down in the street and sprained her wrist. Unfortunately, this means she cannot work her usual job as a massage therapist, so she _____ at home for a few weeks until her wrist heals.

   (a) will have been staying
   (b) stays
   (c) has stayed
   (d) will be staying

7. The peregrine falcon is considered the fastest animal in the world. While diving to hunt, it _____ reach speeds of up to 240 miles per hour, which is comparable to a Formula 1 racecar.

(a) shall
(b) can
(c) should
(d) must

8. After trying many new software programs, the manager found SurveyScape to be the only program _____ all of the company's needs. Therefore, it was installed on every workplace computer last week.

(a) what fulfilled
(b) that fulfilled
(c) who fulfilled
(d) when fulfilled

9. Wally's sales pitch was cut short after everyone was asked to leave the building for a scheduled pest control treatment. Had he been informed ahead of time, he _____ his meeting with the client.

(a) would have rescheduled
(b) will reschedule
(c) would reschedule
(d) will have rescheduled

10. Determined to quit her job, Charlotte began writing her resignation letter. She _____ it for almost an hour before she realized she wanted to stay at the company after all.

(a) had been working on
(b) works on
(c) has been working on
(d) would work on

11. *Moai* are giant stone statues of human figures carved by the Rapa Nui people of Easter Island. In some cases, the head is the only visible part _____ the torsos are wholly or partially buried.

(a) so that
(b) until
(c) even if
(d) because

12. This year, Neil's company is celebrating its fiftieth anniversary, and a committee has been put in charge of the upcoming party. They _____ activities for the past two weeks but have plenty more to do.

(a) had been planning
(b) are planning
(c) have been planning
(d) will have planned

13. Waumat is an initiation rite of the *Saleré-Mawé* indigenous group in Brazil. The ritual requires boys _____ the stings of bullet ants, which cause a burning, throbbing sensation that typically lasts for about twenty-four hours.

(a) enduring
(b) to have endured
(c) to endure
(d) having endured

14. At the age of eight, Steve became frightened when he jumped into the ocean and the waves were stronger than expected. Since then, he has disliked _____ in open water. He prefers pools instead.

(a) having swum
(b) swimming
(c) to swim
(d) to have swum

15. Using simulators, astronomers can predict the effect of an asteroid hitting Earth. For example, if an asteroid the size of Mount Everest were to collide with Earth, it _____ widespread devastation and even mass extinctions.

(a) will likely have caused
(b) would likely have caused
(c) will likely cause
(d) would likely cause

16. Bowling is a sport that is probably rooted in religious practice. Around the fourth century, Germans _____ roll a stone to knock down clubs that represented nonbelievers. This ritual signified the cleansing of sins.

(a) should
(b) might
(c) would
(d) must

17. Chan is in the middle of a speech that has lasted far too long. By the time he finishes, his very restless audience _____ to him for an hour and a half.

(a) will have been listening
(b) will be listening
(c) has been listening
(d) is listening

18. Linda will need more time to complete her thesis. She needs to do heavy revisions after one of the panelists advised that Linda _____ the focus of the discussion section.

(a) change
(b) changed
(c) is changing
(d) will change

19. Tech-Newton, a startup technology company, canceled its expansion after failing to reach sales targets. Had the company sold more products, it _____ enough money to fund the new factory.

(a) will make
(b) would make
(c) will have made
(d) would have made

20. A famous adage says that laughter is the best medicine. Psychologists have long agreed with this, as they regard _____ as an effective way to relieve anxiety and reduce feelings of depression.

(a) to laugh
(b) laughing
(c) to have laughed
(d) having laughed

21. Tom's cat, Chito, escaped last week and has still not returned. After putting up posters around the neighborhood and receiving no news, Tom has decided _____ a reward in the hope of bringing Chito home.

(a) having offered
(b) to have offered
(c) to offer
(d) offering

22. Symbiosis refers to a biological interaction between two species that is usually of benefit to both. _____, clownfish deter predators from sea anemones and, in return, benefit from the shelter provided by the anemones.

(a) Otherwise
(b) By contrast
(c) Meanwhile
(d) For instance

23. Although Vanessa wants to practice law, she is worried that she might have flunked the bar exam. If she were to receive a failing grade, she _____ making alternative career plans.

(a) would have begun
(b) will have begun
(c) would begin
(d) will begin

24. Andrea is an avid horticulturalist. Today, she will host a party for her gardening club. She _____ her azaleas and boxwoods right now so she can show them off to her guests.

(a) is pruning
(b) has been pruning
(c) would prune
(d) will have pruned

25. When Thea was young, her father often taught her simple household repairs. For example, she once learned _____ a clogged sink, which is very useful now that she lives alone.

(a) to have fixed
(b) to fix
(c) fixing
(d) having fixed

26. The film critic gave a big-budget movie a terrible review for its mediocre story. He wrote that if the acting had been as bad as the writing, he probably _____ the theater before the movie ended.

(a) would have left
(b) will have left
(c) would leave
(d) will leave

LISTENING SECTION

▶ Test 7 전체 음원 재생

DIRECTIONS:

The Listening Section has four parts. In each part you will hear a spoken passage and a number of questions about the passage. First you will hear the questions. Then you will hear the passage. From the four choices for each question, choose the best answer. Then blacken in the correct circle on your answer sheet.

Example:

> (a) one
> (b) two
> (c) three
> (d) four

Bill Johnson has four brothers, so the best answer is (d). The circle with the letter (d) has been blackened.

NOW TURN THE PAGE AND BEGIN

27. (a) their dream honeymoon
    (b) their most recent trip
    (c) their upcoming vacation
    (d) their favorite travel spot

28. (a) by making their own itinerary
    (b) by participating in a group tour
    (c) by traveling with their friends
    (d) by hiring a private tour guide

29. (a) It has life-like dinosaur models.
    (b) It has the oldest dinosaur display.
    (c) It has whole dinosaur skeletons.
    (d) It has the biggest dinosaur display.

30. (a) staying within their budget
    (b) getting a reservation
    (c) finding decent restaurants
    (d) deciding where to eat

31. (a) by taking public transportation
    (b) by walking around
    (c) by using ride-share services
    (d) by renting a car

32. (a) to try to borrow a camera
    (b) to get his camera back
    (c) to ask for advice on cameras
    (d) to have his camera fixed

33. (a) go out for dinner
    (b) cook for the next day
    (c) get some dessert
    (d) have a meal at home

34. (a) an astronomy club gathering
    (b) an astronomy course
    (c) a summer astronomy camp
    (d) an astronomy festival

35. (a) by viewing an interactive exhibit
    (b) by reading a booklet
    (c) by receiving expert instruction
    (d) by watching a video

36. (a) lecture on space technology
    (b) share his past experiences
    (c) debate with other scientists
    (d) speak about his future plans

37. (a) by ordering on the website
    (b) by visiting the souvenir shop
    (c) by participating in a workshop
    (d) by signing up for a contest

38. (a) They include original music.
    (b) They feature innovative visual effects.
    (c) They include live narration.
    (d) They feature a new sound system.

39. (a) join a mailing list
    (b) buy a raffle ticket at the event
    (c) fill out an online form
    (d) donate money to a charity

40. (a) clear snow from the street
    (b) buy cleaning supplies
    (c) remove snow from the car
    (d) get the car repaired

43. (a) She dislikes putting on the gear.
    (b) She is afraid of slipping on the ice.
    (c) She dislikes the freezing weather.
    (d) She is afraid of falling into the water.

41. (a) decorating the tree together
    (b) watching them open gifts
    (c) making cookies together
    (d) seeing them play with new toys

44. (a) because of the bad storm
    (b) because of the packed hotels
    (c) because of the travel time
    (d) because of the holiday closures

42. (a) the uncomfortable sofa
    (b) the crowded space
    (c) the unfamiliar foods
    (d) the noisy children

45. (a) visit a town by themselves
    (b) go to her parents' place
    (c) stay at home by themselves
    (d) drop by her friends' place

46. (a) how to train for a marathon
    (b) how to organize a marathon
    (c) how to win a marathon
    (d) how to recover from a marathon

47. (a) look online for races to enter
    (b) consult a running coach
    (c) find a partner to train with
    (d) make a practice schedule

48. (a) He does weight training.
    (b) He uses an exercise bike.
    (c) He takes yoga classes.
    (d) He walks on the treadmill.

49. (a) trying different running styles
    (b) getting a good pair of shoes
    (c) shopping for exercise machines
    (d) buying the right workout clothes

50. (a) reading online posts
    (b) waking up too early
    (c) eating a large breakfast
    (d) drinking too much coffee

51. (a) He was exhausted.
    (b) He felt mild knee pain.
    (c) He broke a rule.
    (d) He had a serious injury.

52. (a) by soaking in a hot bath
    (b) by doing meditation
    (c) by getting a massage
    (d) by visiting his friends

THIS IS THE END OF THE LISTENING SECTION

READING AND VOCABULARY SECTION

DIRECTIONS:

You will now read four different passages. Each passage is followed by comprehension and vocabulary questions. From the four choices for each item, choose the best answer. Then blacken in the correct circle on your answer sheet.

Read the following example passage and example question.

Example:

> Bill Johnson lives in New York. He is 25 years old. He has four brothers and two sisters.
>
> How many brothers does Bill Johnson have?
>
> (a) one
> (b) two
> (c) three
> (d) four

The correct answer is (d), so the circle with the letter (d) has been blackened.

NOW TURN THE PAGE AND BEGIN

GEORGIA O'KEEFFE

Georgia O'Keeffe was an American painter. She has been called the "mother of American modernism" and is best known for her paintings of natural scenes, such as flowers and landscapes, often inspired by places she knew.

Born in Sun Prairie, Wisconsin, in 1887, O'Keeffe was the daughter of dairy farmers. As a young girl, she knew she wanted to be an artist and took lessons with a local watercolor painter. She later studied in New York, where she won a scholarship to a summer school program for her painting, *Untitled (Dead Rabbit with Copper Pot)*. O'Keeffe's time in New York City enabled her to visit galleries that displayed work by experimental artists and photographers.

During these years in the city, O'Keeffe practiced a style known as imitative realism. Artists using this style tried to paint exactly what they saw, as if capturing a photograph. However, O'Keeffe grew bored with this. Later, when she met artist Arthur Wesley Dow, who believed that art should be a form of self-expression, his influence led her to create abstract paintings that focused on moods and emotions rather than realism.

She pursued this new style, later known as modernism, while working as an art teacher in South Carolina. She was among the few painters in the world skilled at creating this type of art. In 1915, she mailed some of her drawings to a friend in New York, who shared them with famous art critic, Alfred Stieglitz. Stieglitz realized that O'Keeffe's art was special and arranged high-profile showings of her work. Soon, O'Keeffe became one of the most famous artists in the nation.

O'Keeffe and Stieglitz married in 1924. Stieglitz loved his wife's art but misunderstood its meaning. He interpreted the abstract forms in her paintings as an expression of her femininity, which other critics agreed with. O'Keeffe, however, rejected this thinking as sexist and distanced herself from these ideas by painting more recognizable images.

Until her death in 1986, O'Keeffe continued to be a bold and experimental artist. She spent much of her life in New Mexico, where the harsh natural landscape inspired her. In 2014, a painting of a flower, *Jimson Weed/White Flower No. 1*, sold for $44.4 million. The continued value of her art is a reminder that she was not just an eminent female modernist but also one of the greatest artists of the twentieth century.

53. What is Georgia O'Keeffe most famous for?

(a) creating paintings of the natural world
(b) experimenting with different art mediums
(c) inventing techniques for landscape painting
(d) making sculptures using natural objects

54. When was O'Keeffe exposed to unconventional works of art?

(a) when she was working for a photographer
(b) when she was a volunteer at an art gallery
(c) when she was taking lessons from a local painter
(d) when she was a student in a major city

55. Which is NOT mentioned in the text about O'Keeffe's work after meeting Dow?

(a) It became boring to her after a while.
(b) It was influenced by the other artist's ideas.
(c) It departed from her realistic art style.
(d) It was an expression of her feelings.

56. How did O'Keeffe initially rise to fame?

(a) by winning a notable art competition
(b) by sharing her work with a fellow teacher
(c) by getting the attention of an industry expert
(d) by sending her work to a high-profile gallery

57. Based on the fifth paragraph, why, most likely, did O'Keeffe change her painting style again?

(a) because she wanted her art to better reflect her femininity
(b) because she was inspired by advice from her husband
(c) because she was bothered by misconceptions about her art
(d) because she wanted to attract the attention of critics

58. In the context of the passage, distanced means _____.

(a) confused
(b) separated
(c) challenged
(d) identified

59. In the context of the passage, eminent means _____.

(a) casual
(b) threatening
(c) familiar
(d) leading

WHY DID EGYPTIANS MAKE MUMMIES?

One of the most common images associated with ancient Egypt is that of the mummy. Mummies, or preserved human remains, were created by Egyptians beginning about 5,000 years ago, and perhaps even earlier. Though we do not have direct records of the reasons for this practice, Egyptologists agree that these figures served a religious purpose related to beliefs about the afterlife.

The earliest Egyptian mummies may have been created unintentionally. Egypt's climate is very hot and dry, without much rain. Because of this, some bodies that were buried in the desert did not decompose. Instead, they were preserved. This discovery may have provided inspiration to the ancient Egyptians, who then began studying how to replicate this effect.

Scholars say that by as early as 2600 BCE, Egyptians were intentionally preserving the bodies of the dead. They developed techniques for drying out corpses so they would not decompose. These methods involved removing the internal organs and coating the body in natron, a type of salt, for over a month. This dried the body and kept it free of bacteria. The body was then wrapped in sheets of linen and sometimes adorned with decorations. Rich, powerful individuals were commonly mummified, then buried in elaborate tombs with numerous passageways and chambers, such as the famous pyramids.

Historians generally agree that mummification served a religious purpose. It was thought that preservation of the body would help the individual enter the afterlife. The dead person's soul, detached from the body, would be reunited with its physical form at a later time. Because the person would need their body even after death, it was important to keep it in good condition. These ideas about immortality may also be linked to the Egyptian god Osiris, who was said to have died and been reborn every year.

Ancient mummies continue to be a useful source of knowledge for modern-day researchers. Due to the success of the Egyptians at preserving human remains, scientists have been able to use x-rays and biopsies to learn about the health of ancient people, including things like diet and disease. These findings give us a richer understanding of life in the ancient world.

60. What is the article mainly about?

  (a) a method of preserving the dead
  (b) a significant archeological site
  (c) a popular myth about the afterlife
  (d) an annual religious ritual

61. Based on the article, how were the first Egyptian mummies likely created?

  (a) by being placed in freezing tombs
  (b) by being exposed to thin mountain air
  (c) by being buried deep in the sand
  (d) by being sealed in airtight coffins

62. Which is NOT mentioned about the mummification process used by ancient Egyptians?

  (a) It involved extracting parts from inside the body.
  (b) It was done over a year-long period.
  (c) It involved encasing the body in cloth.
  (d) It was customary among the upper class.

63. According to the fourth paragraph, why did ancient Egyptians believe that bodies should be preserved?

  (a) because they would be inhabited by the soul of a god
  (b) because they would be used by the deceased in the afterlife
  (c) because they would otherwise spread deadly diseases
  (d) because they would be used later in religious ceremonies

64. According to the final paragraph, what has helped scientists learn more about ancient people?

  (a) using modern equipment to mummify animals
  (b) trying to recreate the mummification process
  (c) investigating the places where mummies have been stored
  (d) carrying out medical procedures on mummies

65. In the context of the passage, coating means _____.

  (a) carrying
  (b) calming
  (c) covering
  (d) cleaning

66. In the context of the passage, elaborate means _____.

  (a) busy
  (b) temporary
  (c) secret
  (d) complex

PEACHES

The peach tree, or *Prunus persica*, is a deciduous tree that grows a sweet, fleshy fruit. The tree has been domesticated for thousands of years and provides an important fruit crop for many across the world.

The peach belongs to the genus *Prunus*, which also includes fruit trees such as cherry and apricot. It requires both moderately cold winters and warm summers in order to mature into a fruit-bearing tree, since blossoming is triggered by a period of cold. This means that peach trees cannot usually grow in tropical areas unless they are at high altitudes. Typically, peach trees begin fruiting after three years and can live for up to twenty.

Historians believe that the peach originated in China and was first cultivated as a crop in Zhejiang Province as early as 6000 BCE. The fruit later spread throughout Asia and into the Middle East, Europe, and North America. Because the peach grew so well in Persia, or modern-day Iran, the Romans thought that the fruit had originated there. They referred to the fruit as the "Persian apple," and this is the source of the *persica* part of its scientific name.

In addition to being a delicious food, peaches have occupied an important place in the cultures of Asia and Europe. In Chinese mythology, for example, the fruit has been associated with immortality. Legend tells of a celebration called the Feast of Peaches, which occurred every 6,000 years. The gods would gather to consume peaches that helped maintain their eternal life. Later, when peaches arrived in Europe, painters such as Vincent van Gogh and Claude Monet featured the fruit in many of their works. The beautiful peaches in these artworks came to be associated with ideas about health and well-being.

Today, peaches continue to be an important food item in many countries. However, peach crops are threatened by the changing global climate. Because peaches require such specific climatic conditions, seasonal temperature fluctuations have harmed the crop in recent years, endangering this economically and culturally significant fruit.

67. What is the article mainly about?

   (a) the different characteristics of a type of fruit
   (b) the economic impact of an important fruit crop
   (c) the different varieties of a type of fruit
   (d) the sudden decline of a common fruit crop

68. According to the article, what enables peach trees to grow fruit?

   (a) being situated in a specific type of soil
   (b) receiving regular amounts of rainfall
   (c) being planted during a particular season
   (d) experiencing a well-timed change in temperature

69. Where did the peach get part of its scientific name?

   (a) from an ancient myth about its creator
   (b) from the region where it was first found
   (c) from a mistaken belief about its origins
   (d) from the person who first discovered it

70. Based on the article, how did peaches come to be associated with eternal life?

   (a) through their documented use in ancient medicines
   (b) through their portrayal in legends as a divine food
   (c) through their recurring presence in ancient poetry
   (d) through their depiction in many famous paintings

71. Why, most likely, have supplies of peaches been reduced in recent years?

   (a) The fruit is being damaged by invasive pests.
   (b) The trees have been affected by environmental shifts.
   (c) The fruit is spoiling faster due to new diseases.
   (d) The trees have been threatened by the logging industry.

72. In the context of the passage, cultivated means _____.

   (a) farmed
   (b) impacted
   (c) finished
   (d) removed

73. In the context of the passage, occupied means _____.

   (a) stolen
   (b) regained
   (c) held
   (d) symbolized

To: Burt Greenie <b.greenie@greenunicorn.net>
From: Dr. Tess Burrell <t.burrell@smilodonvet.com>
Subject: Taking Care of Spot

Dear Mr. Greenie,

This is Dr. Burrell, your veterinarian, following up about your visit today. As I mentioned earlier, your dog Spot has a bit of an upset stomach, but this is nothing serious. Following the instructions below should get Spot feeling better in no time.

First, remember to keep Spot relaxed and rested. This probably won't be difficult because he seems very tired from his illness. Limit his exercise to three short walks per day, plus additional outside time whenever he needs to go to the bathroom. We don't want him outside chasing after squirrels all day, as he needs to save his energy for recovery.

Remember to give him the pills that I prescribed today. These will help settle his upset stomach. It can be difficult to get dogs to swallow pills, so be patient. The best thing to do is put the pill in some soft dog food or a favorite treat and trick him into swallowing it. Try to use a healthy treat.

Finally, feed Spot a bland diet for a few weeks to boost his recovery. Rather than giving him his regular dog food, try plain white rice and boiled, skinless chicken, which will still provide a nutritious meal. You can also mix in pureed pumpkin from a can, like you would use for making pumpkin pie. Make sure it's plain pumpkin, though, without any added spices that could irritate his stomach. After recovery, you may resume feeding Spot his regular diet.

Following these tips should put Spot on the path to a quick recovery. If you have any other concerns or his condition doesn't improve over the next three days, please call me at the clinic. I will have my assistant check in after a few days. I hope Spot feels better soon.

Best,

Dr. Tess Burrell

74. Why is Dr. Burrell writing to Burt Greenie?

    (a) to identify the symptoms of his dog's current illness
    (b) to ask for details of his dog's current routine
    (c) to suggest ways to prevent his dog's frequent stomach bugs
    (d) to give him advice for his dog's recovery

75. According to the letter, why would it be easy to keep Spot relaxed?

    (a) He dislikes going outside most of the time.
    (b) He lacks energy due to his health issues.
    (c) He naturally has a quiet temperament.
    (d) He is taking medicine that makes him sleepy.

76. How does Dr. Burrell suggest getting the dog to take medication?

    (a) by hiding it in appetizing food
    (b) by following it with a treat
    (c) by cutting it into smaller pieces
    (d) by mixing it into his water bowl

77. Why, most likely, does Dr. Burrell recommend pausing Spot's regular diet?

    (a) to adjust his meals for more nutritional value
    (b) to remove the cause of his stomach irritation
    (c) to increase his chances of healing quickly
    (d) to avoid a reaction with his medications

78. According to the letter, what should Burt do if his pet does not get better after three days?

    (a) take the dog to an emergency care clinic
    (b) get in touch with the veterinarian directly
    (c) bring the dog for a follow-up appointment
    (d) call the doctor's assistant immediately

79. In the context of the passage, <u>settle</u> means _____.

    (a) calm
    (b) push
    (c) fill
    (d) touch

80. In the context of the passage, <u>bland</u> means _____.

    (a) constant
    (b) liquid
    (c) popular
    (d) mild

ANSWER
SHEET

G-TELP

시원스쿨 **LAB**

문항	답란	문항	답란	문항	답란	문항	답란	문항	답란
1	ⓐⓑⓒⓓ	21	ⓐⓑⓒⓓ	41	ⓐⓑⓒⓓ	61	ⓐⓑⓒⓓ	81	ⓐⓑⓒⓓ
2	ⓐⓑⓒⓓ	22	ⓐⓑⓒⓓ	42	ⓐⓑⓒⓓ	62	ⓐⓑⓒⓓ	82	ⓐⓑⓒⓓ
3	ⓐⓑⓒⓓ	23	ⓐⓑⓒⓓ	43	ⓐⓑⓒⓓ	63	ⓐⓑⓒⓓ	83	ⓐⓑⓒⓓ
4	ⓐⓑⓒⓓ	24	ⓐⓑⓒⓓ	44	ⓐⓑⓒⓓ	64	ⓐⓑⓒⓓ	84	ⓐⓑⓒⓓ
5	ⓐⓑⓒⓓ	25	ⓐⓑⓒⓓ	45	ⓐⓑⓒⓓ	65	ⓐⓑⓒⓓ	85	ⓐⓑⓒⓓ
6	ⓐⓑⓒⓓ	26	ⓐⓑⓒⓓ	46	ⓐⓑⓒⓓ	66	ⓐⓑⓒⓓ	86	ⓐⓑⓒⓓ
7	ⓐⓑⓒⓓ	27	ⓐⓑⓒⓓ	47	ⓐⓑⓒⓓ	67	ⓐⓑⓒⓓ	87	ⓐⓑⓒⓓ
8	ⓐⓑⓒⓓ	28	ⓐⓑⓒⓓ	48	ⓐⓑⓒⓓ	68	ⓐⓑⓒⓓ	88	ⓐⓑⓒⓓ
9	ⓐⓑⓒⓓ	29	ⓐⓑⓒⓓ	49	ⓐⓑⓒⓓ	69	ⓐⓑⓒⓓ	89	ⓐⓑⓒⓓ
10	ⓐⓑⓒⓓ	30	ⓐⓑⓒⓓ	50	ⓐⓑⓒⓓ	70	ⓐⓑⓒⓓ	90	ⓐⓑⓒⓓ
11	ⓐⓑⓒⓓ	31	ⓐⓑⓒⓓ	51	ⓐⓑⓒⓓ	71	ⓐⓑⓒⓓ		
12	ⓐⓑⓒⓓ	32	ⓐⓑⓒⓓ	52	ⓐⓑⓒⓓ	72	ⓐⓑⓒⓓ	password	
13	ⓐⓑⓒⓓ	33	ⓐⓑⓒⓓ	53	ⓐⓑⓒⓓ	73	ⓐⓑⓒⓓ		
14	ⓐⓑⓒⓓ	34	ⓐⓑⓒⓓ	54	ⓐⓑⓒⓓ	74	ⓐⓑⓒⓓ	0 0 0 0	
15	ⓐⓑⓒⓓ	35	ⓐⓑⓒⓓ	55	ⓐⓑⓒⓓ	75	ⓐⓑⓒⓓ	1 1 1 1 / 2 2 2 2 / 3 3 3 3	
16	ⓐⓑⓒⓓ	36	ⓐⓑⓒⓓ	56	ⓐⓑⓒⓓ	76	ⓐⓑⓒⓓ	4 4 4 4 / 5 5 5 5	
17	ⓐⓑⓒⓓ	37	ⓐⓑⓒⓓ	57	ⓐⓑⓒⓓ	77	ⓐⓑⓒⓓ	6 6 6 6 / 7 7 7 7	
18	ⓐⓑⓒⓓ	38	ⓐⓑⓒⓓ	58	ⓐⓑⓒⓓ	78	ⓐⓑⓒⓓ	8 8 8 8	
19	ⓐⓑⓒⓓ	39	ⓐⓑⓒⓓ	59	ⓐⓑⓒⓓ	79	ⓐⓑⓒⓓ	9 9 9 9	
20	ⓐⓑⓒⓓ	40	ⓐⓑⓒⓓ	60	ⓐⓑⓒⓓ	80	ⓐⓑⓒⓓ		

시원스쿨 **LAB**

G-TELP

시원스쿨 **LAB**

※ TEST DATE

MO.	DAY	YEAR

감독관인	확인

성 명		등급	① ② ③ ④ ⑤

성 명 란

초성 / 중성 / 종성 (자음·모음 표기란)

수 험 번 호

| 0 | 1 | 2 | 3 | 4 | 5 | 6 | 7 | 8 | 9 |

1) Code 1.
| 0 1 2 3 4 5 6 7 8 9 |
| 0 1 2 3 4 5 6 7 8 9 |
| 0 1 2 3 4 5 6 7 8 9 |

2) Code 2.
| 0 1 2 3 4 5 6 7 8 9 |
| 0 1 2 3 4 5 6 7 8 9 |
| 0 1 2 3 4 5 6 7 8 9 |

3) Code 3.
| 0 1 2 3 4 5 6 7 8 9 |
| 0 1 2 3 4 5 6 7 8 9 |
| 0 1 2 3 4 5 6 7 8 9 |

주민등록번호 앞자리 — 고유번호
| 0 1 2 3 4 5 6 7 8 9 |

문항	답란	문항	답란	문항	답란	문항	답란	문항	답란
1	ⓐⓑⓒⓓ	21	ⓐⓑⓒⓓ	41	ⓐⓑⓒⓓ	61	ⓐⓑⓒⓓ	81	ⓐⓑⓒⓓ
2	ⓐⓑⓒⓓ	22	ⓐⓑⓒⓓ	42	ⓐⓑⓒⓓ	62	ⓐⓑⓒⓓ	82	ⓐⓑⓒⓓ
3	ⓐⓑⓒⓓ	23	ⓐⓑⓒⓓ	43	ⓐⓑⓒⓓ	63	ⓐⓑⓒⓓ	83	ⓐⓑⓒⓓ
4	ⓐⓑⓒⓓ	24	ⓐⓑⓒⓓ	44	ⓐⓑⓒⓓ	64	ⓐⓑⓒⓓ	84	ⓐⓑⓒⓓ
5	ⓐⓑⓒⓓ	25	ⓐⓑⓒⓓ	45	ⓐⓑⓒⓓ	65	ⓐⓑⓒⓓ	85	ⓐⓑⓒⓓ
6	ⓐⓑⓒⓓ	26	ⓐⓑⓒⓓ	46	ⓐⓑⓒⓓ	66	ⓐⓑⓒⓓ	86	ⓐⓑⓒⓓ
7	ⓐⓑⓒⓓ	27	ⓐⓑⓒⓓ	47	ⓐⓑⓒⓓ	67	ⓐⓑⓒⓓ	87	ⓐⓑⓒⓓ
8	ⓐⓑⓒⓓ	28	ⓐⓑⓒⓓ	48	ⓐⓑⓒⓓ	68	ⓐⓑⓒⓓ	88	ⓐⓑⓒⓓ
9	ⓐⓑⓒⓓ	29	ⓐⓑⓒⓓ	49	ⓐⓑⓒⓓ	69	ⓐⓑⓒⓓ	89	ⓐⓑⓒⓓ
10	ⓐⓑⓒⓓ	30	ⓐⓑⓒⓓ	50	ⓐⓑⓒⓓ	70	ⓐⓑⓒⓓ	90	ⓐⓑⓒⓓ
11	ⓐⓑⓒⓓ	31	ⓐⓑⓒⓓ	51	ⓐⓑⓒⓓ	71	ⓐⓑⓒⓓ		
12	ⓐⓑⓒⓓ	32	ⓐⓑⓒⓓ	52	ⓐⓑⓒⓓ	72	ⓐⓑⓒⓓ	password	
13	ⓐⓑⓒⓓ	33	ⓐⓑⓒⓓ	53	ⓐⓑⓒⓓ	73	ⓐⓑⓒⓓ		
14	ⓐⓑⓒⓓ	34	ⓐⓑⓒⓓ	54	ⓐⓑⓒⓓ	74	ⓐⓑⓒⓓ	0 0 0 0	
15	ⓐⓑⓒⓓ	35	ⓐⓑⓒⓓ	55	ⓐⓑⓒⓓ	75	ⓐⓑⓒⓓ	1 1 1 1 / 2 2 2 2 / 3 3 3 3	
16	ⓐⓑⓒⓓ	36	ⓐⓑⓒⓓ	56	ⓐⓑⓒⓓ	76	ⓐⓑⓒⓓ	4 4 4 4 / 5 5 5 5	
17	ⓐⓑⓒⓓ	37	ⓐⓑⓒⓓ	57	ⓐⓑⓒⓓ	77	ⓐⓑⓒⓓ	6 6 6 6 / 7 7 7 7	
18	ⓐⓑⓒⓓ	38	ⓐⓑⓒⓓ	58	ⓐⓑⓒⓓ	78	ⓐⓑⓒⓓ	8 8 8 8 / 9 9 9 9	
19	ⓐⓑⓒⓓ	39	ⓐⓑⓒⓓ	59	ⓐⓑⓒⓓ	79	ⓐⓑⓒⓓ		
20	ⓐⓑⓒⓓ	40	ⓐⓑⓒⓓ	60	ⓐⓑⓒⓓ	80	ⓐⓑⓒⓓ		

시원스쿨 LAB

G-TELP

시원스쿨 LAB

※ TEST DATE

MO.	DAY	YEAR

성 명

등급 ① ② ③ ④ ⑤

감독관인 / 확인

성명란

초성 / 중성 / 종성

수 험 번 호

1) Code 1.

2) Code 2.

3) Code 3.

주민등록번호 앞자리 — 고유번호

문항	답 란	문항	답 란	문항	답 란	문항	답 란	문항	답 란
1	ⓐⓑⓒⓓ	21	ⓐⓑⓒⓓ	41	ⓐⓑⓒⓓ	61	ⓐⓑⓒⓓ	81	ⓐⓑⓒⓓ
2	ⓐⓑⓒⓓ	22	ⓐⓑⓒⓓ	42	ⓐⓑⓒⓓ	62	ⓐⓑⓒⓓ	82	ⓐⓑⓒⓓ
3	ⓐⓑⓒⓓ	23	ⓐⓑⓒⓓ	43	ⓐⓑⓒⓓ	63	ⓐⓑⓒⓓ	83	ⓐⓑⓒⓓ
4	ⓐⓑⓒⓓ	24	ⓐⓑⓒⓓ	44	ⓐⓑⓒⓓ	64	ⓐⓑⓒⓓ	84	ⓐⓑⓒⓓ
5	ⓐⓑⓒⓓ	25	ⓐⓑⓒⓓ	45	ⓐⓑⓒⓓ	65	ⓐⓑⓒⓓ	85	ⓐⓑⓒⓓ
6	ⓐⓑⓒⓓ	26	ⓐⓑⓒⓓ	46	ⓐⓑⓒⓓ	66	ⓐⓑⓒⓓ	86	ⓐⓑⓒⓓ
7	ⓐⓑⓒⓓ	27	ⓐⓑⓒⓓ	47	ⓐⓑⓒⓓ	67	ⓐⓑⓒⓓ	87	ⓐⓑⓒⓓ
8	ⓐⓑⓒⓓ	28	ⓐⓑⓒⓓ	48	ⓐⓑⓒⓓ	68	ⓐⓑⓒⓓ	88	ⓐⓑⓒⓓ
9	ⓐⓑⓒⓓ	29	ⓐⓑⓒⓓ	49	ⓐⓑⓒⓓ	69	ⓐⓑⓒⓓ	89	ⓐⓑⓒⓓ
10	ⓐⓑⓒⓓ	30	ⓐⓑⓒⓓ	50	ⓐⓑⓒⓓ	70	ⓐⓑⓒⓓ	90	ⓐⓑⓒⓓ
11	ⓐⓑⓒⓓ	31	ⓐⓑⓒⓓ	51	ⓐⓑⓒⓓ	71	ⓐⓑⓒⓓ		
12	ⓐⓑⓒⓓ	32	ⓐⓑⓒⓓ	52	ⓐⓑⓒⓓ	72	ⓐⓑⓒⓓ		password
13	ⓐⓑⓒⓓ	33	ⓐⓑⓒⓓ	53	ⓐⓑⓒⓓ	73	ⓐⓑⓒⓓ		
14	ⓐⓑⓒⓓ	34	ⓐⓑⓒⓓ	54	ⓐⓑⓒⓓ	74	ⓐⓑⓒⓓ		
15	ⓐⓑⓒⓓ	35	ⓐⓑⓒⓓ	55	ⓐⓑⓒⓓ	75	ⓐⓑⓒⓓ		
16	ⓐⓑⓒⓓ	36	ⓐⓑⓒⓓ	56	ⓐⓑⓒⓓ	76	ⓐⓑⓒⓓ		
17	ⓐⓑⓒⓓ	37	ⓐⓑⓒⓓ	57	ⓐⓑⓒⓓ	77	ⓐⓑⓒⓓ		
18	ⓐⓑⓒⓓ	38	ⓐⓑⓒⓓ	58	ⓐⓑⓒⓓ	78	ⓐⓑⓒⓓ		
19	ⓐⓑⓒⓓ	39	ⓐⓑⓒⓓ	59	ⓐⓑⓒⓓ	79	ⓐⓑⓒⓓ		
20	ⓐⓑⓒⓓ	40	ⓐⓑⓒⓓ	60	ⓐⓑⓒⓓ	80	ⓐⓑⓒⓓ		

시원스쿨 LAB

G-TELP

시원스쿨 **LAB**

성 명		등급	① ② ③ ④ ⑤

성 명 란

초성 / 중성 / 종성

수 험 번 호

1) Code 1.

2) Code 2.

3) Code 3.

주민등록번호 앞자리 − 고유번호

문항	답 란	문항	답 란	문항	답 란	문항	답 란	문항	답 란
1	ⓐⓑⓒⓓ	21	ⓐⓑⓒⓓ	41	ⓐⓑⓒⓓ	61	ⓐⓑⓒⓓ	81	ⓐⓑⓒⓓ
2	ⓐⓑⓒⓓ	22	ⓐⓑⓒⓓ	42	ⓐⓑⓒⓓ	62	ⓐⓑⓒⓓ	82	ⓐⓑⓒⓓ
3	ⓐⓑⓒⓓ	23	ⓐⓑⓒⓓ	43	ⓐⓑⓒⓓ	63	ⓐⓑⓒⓓ	83	ⓐⓑⓒⓓ
4	ⓐⓑⓒⓓ	24	ⓐⓑⓒⓓ	44	ⓐⓑⓒⓓ	64	ⓐⓑⓒⓓ	84	ⓐⓑⓒⓓ
5	ⓐⓑⓒⓓ	25	ⓐⓑⓒⓓ	45	ⓐⓑⓒⓓ	65	ⓐⓑⓒⓓ	85	ⓐⓑⓒⓓ
6	ⓐⓑⓒⓓ	26	ⓐⓑⓒⓓ	46	ⓐⓑⓒⓓ	66	ⓐⓑⓒⓓ	86	ⓐⓑⓒⓓ
7	ⓐⓑⓒⓓ	27	ⓐⓑⓒⓓ	47	ⓐⓑⓒⓓ	67	ⓐⓑⓒⓓ	87	ⓐⓑⓒⓓ
8	ⓐⓑⓒⓓ	28	ⓐⓑⓒⓓ	48	ⓐⓑⓒⓓ	68	ⓐⓑⓒⓓ	88	ⓐⓑⓒⓓ
9	ⓐⓑⓒⓓ	29	ⓐⓑⓒⓓ	49	ⓐⓑⓒⓓ	69	ⓐⓑⓒⓓ	89	ⓐⓑⓒⓓ
10	ⓐⓑⓒⓓ	30	ⓐⓑⓒⓓ	50	ⓐⓑⓒⓓ	70	ⓐⓑⓒⓓ	90	ⓐⓑⓒⓓ
11	ⓐⓑⓒⓓ	31	ⓐⓑⓒⓓ	51	ⓐⓑⓒⓓ	71	ⓐⓑⓒⓓ		
12	ⓐⓑⓒⓓ	32	ⓐⓑⓒⓓ	52	ⓐⓑⓒⓓ	72	ⓐⓑⓒⓓ	password	
13	ⓐⓑⓒⓓ	33	ⓐⓑⓒⓓ	53	ⓐⓑⓒⓓ	73	ⓐⓑⓒⓓ		
14	ⓐⓑⓒⓓ	34	ⓐⓑⓒⓓ	54	ⓐⓑⓒⓓ	74	ⓐⓑⓒⓓ		
15	ⓐⓑⓒⓓ	35	ⓐⓑⓒⓓ	55	ⓐⓑⓒⓓ	75	ⓐⓑⓒⓓ		
16	ⓐⓑⓒⓓ	36	ⓐⓑⓒⓓ	56	ⓐⓑⓒⓓ	76	ⓐⓑⓒⓓ		
17	ⓐⓑⓒⓓ	37	ⓐⓑⓒⓓ	57	ⓐⓑⓒⓓ	77	ⓐⓑⓒⓓ		
18	ⓐⓑⓒⓓ	38	ⓐⓑⓒⓓ	58	ⓐⓑⓒⓓ	78	ⓐⓑⓒⓓ		
19	ⓐⓑⓒⓓ	39	ⓐⓑⓒⓓ	59	ⓐⓑⓒⓓ	79	ⓐⓑⓒⓓ		
20	ⓐⓑⓒⓓ	40	ⓐⓑⓒⓓ	60	ⓐⓑⓒⓓ	80	ⓐⓑⓒⓓ		

시원스쿨LAB

시원스쿨 LAB

2025 최신 G-TELP KOREA 공식 기출 문제

지텔프

LEVEL 2

공식
기출문제집

G-TELP KOREA 문제 제공 | 시원스쿨어학연구소 지음

시원스쿨 LAB

최신 지텔프
공식 기출문제집

초판 1쇄 발행 2024년 12월 19일

지은이 시원스쿨어학연구소
펴낸곳 (주)에스제이더블유인터내셔널
펴낸이 양홍걸 이시원

홈페이지 www.siwonschool.com
주소 서울시 영등포구 영신로 166 시원스쿨
교재 구입 문의 02)2014-8151
고객센터 02)6409-0878

ISBN 979-11-6150-922-8 13740
Number 1-110404-18189900-06

머리말

G-TELP 최신 출제 경향 집중 공략
2025년 지텔프 시험 대비 최신 기출 문제집

G-TELP 목표 점수 달성은
시원스쿨랩 『최신 지텔프 공식 기출문제집』으로!

지텔프 Level 2 시험은 군무원 및 소방·경찰 공무원, 7급 공무원 및 세무사, 노무사, 회계사, 감정평가사 등 전문직 자격증 시험에도 영어능력검정시험으로 인정받고 있습니다. 경찰공무원 채용 과정 중 영어 검정제로서 지텔프 Level 2의 43점이 필요한 것을 비롯하여, 소방 공무원은 50점, 7급 공무원 및 세무사, 노무사, 회계사, 감정평가사 지원 자격 요건은 지텔프 Level 2 시험에서 65점이 필요합니다. 이렇게 많은 곳에서 활용되는 지텔프는 여타 공인영어 시험보다 적은 문항수, 빠른 성적확인 등의 장점이 부각되어 많은 수험생들의 선택을 받고 있습니다.

공인 영어 시험에서 목표 점수를 달성하기 위해 시험 출제 유형과 출제 형식, 그리고 출제 경향을 파악하는 것은 학습 방향과 학습 내용을 결정짓는 중요한 과정입니다. 특히 근시일내에 시험을 칠 예정이라면 최신 기출 유형이 반영된 실전 문제집으로 실전 대비 훈련을 하는 것이 가장 효과적인 학습 방법일 것입니다.

이에 시원스쿨랩은 2025년 기준 최신 지텔프 기출문제 7회분을 수록한 『최신 지텔프 공식 기출문제집』을 출간하였습니다. 정기시험의 난이도를 직접 체험하고 문제를 풀어봄으로써 지텔프 수험생 여러분이 목표한 기간 내에 완벽하게 목표 점수를 달성할 수 있도록 하였습니다.

또한 실제 시험에서 효과를 발휘하기 위해서는 실전 문제 풀이 시 부족한 시간에 가장 빠르게 정답을 찾아내는 연습도 필요합니다. 또한 자신이 어떤 유형에 취약한지, 어떤 유형을 집중 공략해야 하는지에 대해 알지 못하면 실전에 완벽하게 대비할 수 없습니다. 그래서 시험영어 연구 전문가 조직인 시원스쿨어학연구소에서는 출제 유형과 정답의 단서 및 오답의 소거 이유까지 밝히면서 매력적인 오답도 피할 수 있도록 자세하고 정확한 해설지도 함께 제작하였으며, 이를 통해 학습자로 하여금 제한된 시간 안에 최대한 많은 문제를 풀어 정답률을 높일 수 있도록 하였습니다.

뿐만 아니라, 학습자가 자신의 실력을 자가 진단을 할 수 있도록 학습플랜과 각 회차별 점수 기입표도 함께 제공합니다. 그리고 학습자 여러분의 편의를 고려하여 문제지를 분권으로 제작하여 실제 지텔프 시험지를 푸는 듯한 느낌을 받을 수 있도록 하였습니다. 본서인 해설지에는 지텔프에 대한 소개와 활용법, 목표 점수별 공략법을 실어 학습 방향과 전략에 도움이 될 수 있도록 하였으며, 부록으로 영역별 지텔프 공략 가이드는 문법, 청취, 독해 3개 영역별 소개와 특징, 그리고 문제 풀이 가이드를 제공해드립니다. 이 지텔프 공략 가이드는 특강 영상으로도 제공되오니 표지나 목차에 있는 QR코드로 확인하실 수 있습니다. 이러한 다양한 학습 편의 컨텐츠로 『최신 지텔프 공식 기출문제집』은 시중의 그 어떤 G-TELP 기출문제집보다 실전 대비 효과가 강력할 것이라고 자신합니다.

이 책으로 지텔프 목표 점수의 빠른 달성과, 나아가 여러분의 꿈이 실현되기를 기원합니다.

시원스쿨어학연구소 드림

목차

부록

| 별책 | **특강: 지텔프 영역별 공략 가이드**

◀ 특강
지텔프 영역별 공략 가이드
바로 가기 QR

| 온라인 | 공식 기출 문제 청취 음원(MP3)

◀
MP3 및 각종 자료
다운로드 바로가기 QR

시원스쿨LAB 홈페이지 (lab.siwonschool.com)
[교재/MP3] 메뉴 내 『최신 지텔프 공식 기출문제집』 교재 검색

이 책의 구성과 특징

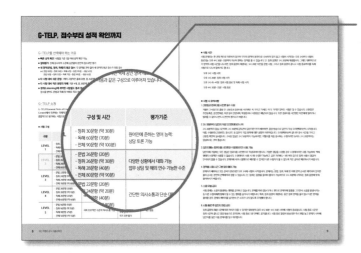

TELP Level 2 시험 관련 정보 제공

G-TELP Level 2 시험에 익숙하지 않은 학습자를 위해 시험 소개 및 정기시험 일정, 접수 방법, 그리고 성적 확인 방법 및 성적 활용표에 관한 정보를 제공해드립니다. 또한 32점부터 65점까지 다양한 목표 점수별로 문법, 청취, 독해에 대한 학습 방향과 공략법을 알려드립니다. 지텔프를 처음 학습하시는 분들에게 학습량과 학습기간, 그리고 학습 전략에 대한 막막함을 해소시킬 수 있는 구체적인 꿀팁과 공략법을 제공해드립니다.

목표 점수별 공략법

지텔프 Level 2 시험에서 출제되는 모든 문제의 유형을 분류하여 해당 유형의 출제 빈도수, 출제 경향을 파악하실 수 있습니다.

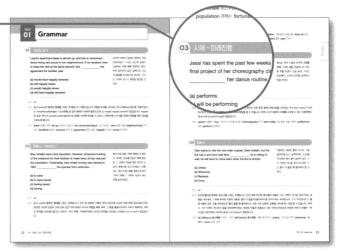

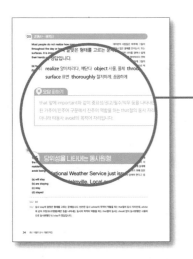

정답 및 해설
명쾌한 해설과 오답을 피하는 팁 제공

지텔프 기출 문제의 출제 포인트를 분석하여 해당 유형에 맞는 정답 단서 찾기와 정답 선택지를 찾는 방법을 명쾌하게 설명해드립니다. 또한 매력적인 오답을 피할 수 있도록 오답 소거 요령과 오답의 이유를 추가로 설명해드립니다.

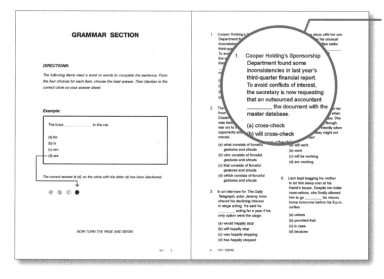

책 속의 책 – 문제지
지텔프 최신기출 문제 수록

지텔프 최신 기출 문제를 실제 지텔프 시험 형식 그대로 만나실 수 있습니다. 시험시간을 맞춰 두고 실제 시험을 치는 것과 같이 문제를 풀어보세요!

실제와 동일한 Answer Sheet 제공

문제 풀이 시 실제 답안 마킹까지 연습할 수 있도록 고사장에서 볼 수 있는 지텔프 Answer Sheet를 동일하게 구현하여 제공해드립니다. 총 4장을 제공해드리며, 더 필요하시다면 시원스쿨랩 사이트에서 다운로드하실 수 있습니다. 목차에 있는 MP3 및 각종 자료 다운로드 바로가기 QR를 이용하세요.

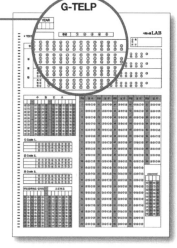

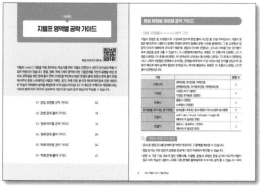

◀ 특강 바로 가기 QR

[특강] 지텔프 영역별 공략 가이드

지텔프 Level 2 시험을 처음 준비하는 학습자를 위해 지텔프 전문강사 서민지 강사님의 특별 수업이 마련되어 있습니다. 문법, 청취, 독해 3개의 영역에 대한 기출문제를 기반의 유형별 패턴 분석과 고득점을 위한 문제 풀이 전략 가이드를 확인해보세요! 문법의 출제 경향과 문제 풀이 방법에서부터 청취 노트테이킹 비법과 키워드 찾기, 독해 지문 분석과 패러프레이징에 관한 내용으로 학습자 여러분의 성적을 확실하게 수직 상승시켜드립니다. 이 특강은 부록으로 제공해드리는 자료와 함께 위의 QR코드로 서민지 강사님의 강의 영상을 확인할 수 있습니다.

G-TELP, 접수부터 성적 확인까지

G-TELP를 선택해야 하는 이유

- **빠른 성적 확인:** 시험일 기준 5일 이내 성적 확인 가능
- **절대평가:** 전체 응시자의 수준에 상관없이 본인의 점수로만 평가
- **세 영역(문법, 청취, 독해)의 평균 점수:** 각 영역별 과락 없이 세 영역의 평균 점수가 최종 점수
  ex) 문법 100점 + 청취 28점 + 독해 67점 = 총점 195점 → 평균 65점
  　　문법 92점 + 청취 32점 + 독해 71점 = 총점 195점 → 평균 65점
- **타 시험 대비 쉬운 문법:** 7개의 고정적인 출제 유형, 총 26문제 출제, 문제 속 단서로 정답 찾기
- **타 시험 대비 적은 분량의 독해:** 지문 4개, 총 28문제 출제
- **청취(Listening)에 취약한 사람들도 통과 점수 획득 가능:** 세 개의 영역의 평균 점수가 최종 점수이므로 청취에서 상대적으로 낮은 점수를 받아도 문법과 독해 및 어휘로 목표 점수 달성 가능

G-TELP 소개

G-TELP(General Tests of English Language Proficiency)는 국제 테스트 연구원(ITSC, International Testing Services Center)에서 주관하는 국제적으로 시행하는 국제 공인 영어 테스트입니다. 또한 단순히 배운 내용을 평가하는 시험이 아닌, 영어 능력을 종합적으로 평가하는 시험으로, 다음과 같은 구성으로 이루어져 있습니다.

- 시험 구성

구분	구성 및 시간	평가기준	합격자의 영어구사능력	응시자격
LEVEL 1	· 청취 30문항 (약 30분) · 독해 60문항 (70분) · 전체 90문항 (약 100분)	원어민에 준하는 영어 능력: 상담 토론 가능	일상생활 상담, 토론 국제회의 통역	2등급 Mastery를 취득한 자
LEVEL 2	· 문법 26문항 (20분) · 청취 26문항 (약 30분) · 독해 28문항 (40분) · 전체 80문항 (약 90분)	다양한 상황에서 대화 가능 업무 상담 및 해외 연수 가능한 수준	일상생활 업무 상담 회의 세미나, 해외 연수	제한 없음
LEVEL 3	· 문법 22문항 (20분) · 청취 24문항 (약 20분) · 독해 24문항 (40분) · 전체 70문항 (약 80분)	간단한 의사소통과 단순 대화 가능	간단한 의사소통 단순 대화 해외 여행, 단순 출장	제한 없음
LEVEL 4	· 문법 20문항 (20분) · 청취 20문항 (약 15분) · 독해 20문항 (25분) · 전체 60문항 (약 60분)	기본적인 문장을 통해 최소한의 의사소통 가능	기본적인 어휘 구사 짧은 문장 의사소통 반복 부연 설명 필요	제한 없음
LEVEL 5	· 문법 16문항 (15분) · 청취 16문항 (약 15분) · 독해 18문항 (25분) · 전체 50문항 (약 55분)	극히 초보적인 수준의 의사소통 가능	영어 초보자 일상 인사, 소개 듣기 자기 표현 불가	제한 없음

● 시험 시간

시험 문제지는 한 권의 책으로 이루어져 있으며 각각의 영역이 분권으로 나뉘어져 있지 않고 시험이 시작되는 오후 3시부터 시험이
종료되는 오후 4시 30분~35분까지 자신이 원하는 영역을 풀 수 있습니다. 단, 청취 음원은 3시 20분에 재생됩니다. 그래도 대략적으로
각 영역의 시험 시간을 나누자면, 청취 음원이 재생되는 3시 20분 이전을 문법 시험, 그리고 청취 음원이 끝나고 시험 종료까지를 독해
시험으로 나누어 말하기도 합니다.

　　　오후 3시: 시험 시작

　　　오후 3시 20분: 청취 시험 시작

　　　오후 3시 45~47분: 청취 시험 종료 및 독해 시험 시작

　　　오후 4시 30분~35분: 시험 종료

● 시험 시 유의사항

1. 신분증과 컴퓨터용 사인펜 필수 지참

　　지텔프 고사장으로 출발 전, 신분증과 컴퓨터용 사인펜은 꼭 가지고 가세요. 이 두 가지만 있어도 시험은 칠 수 있습니다. 신분증은
　　주민등록증, 운전면허증, 여권 등이 인정되며, 학생증이나 사원증은 해당되지 않습니다. 또한 컴퓨터용 사인펜은 타인에게 빌리거나
　　빌려줄 수 없으니 반드시 본인이 챙기시기 바랍니다.

2. 2시 30분부터 답안지 작성 오리엔테이션 시작

　　2시 20분까지 입실 시간이며, 2시 30분에 감독관이 답안지만 먼저 배부하면, 중앙 방송으로 답안지 작성 오리엔테이션이 시작됩니다.
　　이름, 수험번호(고유번호), 응시코드 등 답안지 기입 항목에 대한 설명이 이루어집니다. 오리엔테이션이 끝나면 휴식 시간을 가지고
　　신분증 확인이 실시됩니다. 고사장 입실은 2시 50분까지 가능하지만, 지텔프를 처음 응시하는 수험자라면 늦어도 2시 20분까지는
　　입실하시는 것이 좋습니다.

3. 답안지에는 컴퓨터용 사인펜과 수정테이프만 사용 가능

　　답안지에 기입하는 모든 정답은 컴퓨터용 사인펜으로 작성되어야 합니다. 기입한 정답을 수정할 경우 수정테이프만 사용 가능하며, 액체
　　형태의 수정액은 사용할 수 없습니다. 수정테이프 사용 시 1회 수정만 가능하고, 같은 자리에 2~3회 여러 겹으로 중복 사용시 정답이
　　인식되지 않을 수 있습니다. 문제지에 샤프나 볼펜으로 메모할 수 있지만 다른 수험자가 볼 수 없도록 작은 글자로 메모하시기 바랍니다.

4. 영역별 시험 시간 구분 없이 풀이 가능

　　문제지가 배부되고 모든 준비가 완료되면 오후 3시에 시험이 시작됩니다. 문제지는 문법, 청취, 독해 및 어휘 영역 순서로 제작되어 있지만
　　풀이 순서는 본인의 선택에 따라 정할 수 있습니다. 단, 청취는 음원을 들어야 풀이가 가능하므로 3시 20분에 시작되는 청취 음원에 맞춰
　　풀이하시기 바랍니다.

5. 소음 유발 금지

　　시험 중에는 소음이 발생하는 행위를 금지하고 있습니다. 문제를 따라 읽는다거나, 펜으로 문제지에 밑줄을 그으면서 소음을 발생시키는
　　등 다른 수험자에게 방해가 될 수 있는 행위를 삼가시기 바랍니다. 특히, 청취 음원이 재생되는 동안 청취 영역을 풀지 않고 다른 영역을
　　풀이할 경우, 문제지 페이지를 넘기면서 큰 소리가 나지 않도록 주의해야 합니다.

6. 시험 종료 후 답안지 마킹 금지

　　청취 음원의 재생 시간에 따라 차이가 있을 수 있지만 대부분의 경우 4시 30분~4시 35분 사이에 시험이 종료됩니다. 시험 종료 시간은
　　청취 시간이 끝나고 중앙 방송으로 공지되며, 시험 종료 5분 전에도 공지됩니다. 시험 종료 알림이 방송되면 즉시 펜을 놓고 문제지 사이에
　　답안지를 넣은 다음 문제지를 덮고 대기합니다.

2025년 G-TELP 정기시험 일정

회차	시험일자	접수기간	추가 접수기간 (~자정까지)	성적공지일 (오후 3:00)
제546회	2025-01-05(일) 15:00	2024-12-06 ~ 2024-12-20	~2024-12-25	2025-01-10(금) 15:00
제547회	2025-01-19(일) 15:00	2024-12-27 ~ 2025-01-03	~2025-01-08	2025-01-24(금) 15:00
제548회	2025-02-02(일) 15:00	2025-01-10 ~ 2025-01-17	~2025-01-22	2025-02-07(금) 15:00
제549회	2025-02-16(일) 15:00	2025-01-24 ~ 2025-01-31	~2025-02-05	2025-02-21(금) 15:00
제550회	2025-03-02(일) 15:00	2025-02-07 ~ 2025-02-14	~2025-02-19	2025-03-07(금) 15:00
제551회	2025-03-16(일) 15:00	2025-02-21 ~ 2025-02-28	~2025-03-05	2025-03-21(금) 15:00
제552회	2025-03-30(일) 15:00	2025-03-07 ~ 2025-03-14	~2025-03-19	2025-04-04(금) 15:00
제553회	2025-04-13(일) 15:00	2025-03-21 ~ 2025-03-28	~2025-04-02	2025-04-18(금) 15:00
제554회	2025-04-27(일) 15:00	2025-04-04 ~ 2025-04-11	~2025-04-16	2025-05-02(금) 15:00
제555회	2025-05-11(일) 15:00	2025-04-18 ~ 2025-04-25	~2025-04-30	2025-05-16(금) 15:00
제556회	2025-05-25(일) 15:00	2025-05-02 ~ 2025-05-09	~2025-05-14	2025-05-30(금) 15:00
제557회	2025-06-08(일) 15:00	2025-05-16 ~ 2025-05-23	~2025-05-28	2025-06-13(금) 15:00
제558회	2025-06-22(일) 15:00	2025-05-30 ~ 2025-06-06	~2025-06-11	2025-06-27(금) 15:00
제559회	2025-07-06(일) 15:00	2025-06-13 ~ 2025-06-20	~2025-06-25	2025-07-11(금) 15:00
제560회	2025-07-20(일) 15:00	2025-06-27 ~ 2025-07-04	~2025-07-09	2025-07-25(금) 15:00
제561회	2025-08-03(일) 15:00	2025-07-11 ~ 2025-07-18	~2025-07-23	2025-08-08(금) 15:00

제562회	2025-08-17(일) 15:00	2025-07-25 ~ 2025-08-01	~2025-08-06	2025-08-22(금) 15:00
제563회	2025-08-31(일) 15:00	2025-08-08 ~ 2025-08-15	~2025-08-20	2025-09-05(금) 15:00
제564회	2025-09-14(일) 15:00	2025-08-22 ~ 2025-08-29	~2025-09-03	2025-09-19(금) 15:00
제565회	2025-09-28(일) 15:00	2025-09-05 ~ 2025-09-12	~2025-09-17	2025-10-03(금) 15:00
제566회	2025-10-19(일) 15:00	2025-09-19 ~ 2025-10-03	~2025-10-08	2025-10-24(금) 15:00
제567회	2025-10-26(일) 15:00	2025-10-03 ~ 2025-10-10	~2025-10-15	2025-10-31(금) 15:00
제568회	2025-11-09(일) 15:00	2025-10-17 ~ 2025-10-24	~2025-10-29	2025-11-14(금) 15:00
제569회	2025-11-23(일) 15:00	2025-10-31 ~ 2025-11-07	~2025-11-12	2025-11-28(금) 15:00
제570회	2025-12-07(일) 15:00	2025-11-14 ~ 2025-11-21	~2025-11-26	2025-12-12(금) 15:00
제571회	2025-12-21(일) 15:00	2025-11-28 ~ 2025-12-05	~2025-12-10	2025-12-26(금) 15:00

● 시험 접수 방법

정기 시험 접수 기간에 G-TELP KOREA 공식 홈페이지 www.g-telp.co.kr 접속 후 로그인, [시험접수] – [정기 시험 접수] 클릭

● 시험 응시료

정기시험 66,300원 (졸업 인증 45,700원, 군인 33,200원) / 추가 접수 71,100원 (졸업 인증 50,600원, 군인 38,000원)

● 시험 준비물

① 신분증: 주민등록증(임시 발급 포함), 운전면허증, 여권, 공무원증 중 택1
② 컴퓨터용 사인펜: 연필, 샤프, 볼펜은 문제 풀이 시 필요에 따라 사용 가능, OMR 답안지에는 연필, 샤프, 볼펜으로 기재 불가
③ 수정 테이프: 컴퓨터용 사인펜으로 기재한 답을 수정할 경우 수정액이 아닌 수정 테이프만 사용 가능

● 시험장 입실

시험 시작 40분 전인 오후 2시 20분부터 입실, 2시 50분부터 입실 불가

● OMR 카드 작성

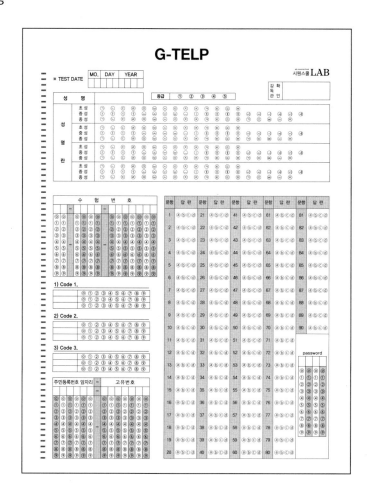

<설명>
◦ 날짜, 성명을 쓰고 등급은 ②에 마킹합니다.
◦ 이름을 초성, 중성, 종성으로 나누어 마킹합니다.
◦ 수험 번호는 자신의 책상에 비치된 수험표에 기재되어 있습니다.
◦ Code 1, Code 2는 OMR 카드 뒷면에서 해당되는 코드를 찾아 세 자리 번호를 마킹합니다. (대학생이 아닌 일반인의 경우 Code 1은 098, Code 2는 090)
◦ Code 3은 수험 번호의 마지막 7자리 숫자 중 앞 3자리 숫자를 마킹합니다.
◦ 주민등록번호는 앞자리만 마킹하고 뒷자리는 개인 정보 보호를 위해 지텔프에서 임시로 부여한 고유 번호로 마킹해야합니다. (수험표에서 확인)
◦ 답안지에는 90번까지 있지만 Level 2 시험의 문제는 80번까지이므로 80번까지만 마킹합니다.
◦ OMR 카드 오른쪽 아래에 있는 비밀번호(password) 4자리는 성적표 출력 시 필요한 비밀번호로, 응시자가 직접 비밀번호를 설정하여 숫자 4개를 마킹합니다.
◦ 시험 시간에는 답안지 작성(OMR 카드 마킹) 시간이 별도로 주어지지 않습니다.

● 성적 발표

시험일 5일 이내 G-TELP KOREA 공식 홈페이지 www.g-telp.co.kr 접속 후 로그인, [성적 확인] – [성적 확인] 클릭 / 우편 발송은
성적 발표 후 차주 화요일에 실시

● 성적 유효 기간

시험일로부터 2년

● 성적표 양식

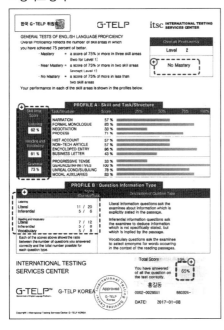 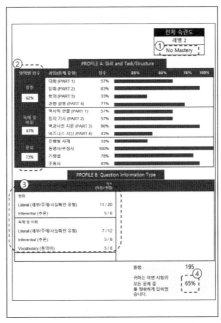

* 편의를 위해 우리말로 번역하였습니다.

① No Mastery: 응시자가 75% 이상의 점수를 획득할 경우 Mastery, 그렇지 못할 경우 No Mastery로 표기되며, 32점이나 65점,
   77점 등 점수대별 목표 점수를 가진 응시자에게 아무런 영향이 없습니다.

② 영역별 점수: 각 영역별 점수를 가리키는 수치입니다. 이를 모두 취합하면 총점(Total Score)이 되며, 이를 3으로 나눈 평균값이
   ④에 나오는 최종 점수입니다.

③ 청취와 독해 및 어휘 영역의 출제 유형별 득점: 청취와 독해 및 어휘 영역의 Literal은 세부사항, 주제 및 목적, 사실 확인 유형의
   문제를 말하며, 이 유형들은 지문의 내용에 문제의 정답이 직접적으로 언급되어 있는 유형입니다. Inferential은 추론 문제를
   말하며, 이 유형은 지문에 문제의 정답이 직접적으로 언급되어 있지 않지만 지문에 나온 정보를 토대로 추론을 통해 알 수 있는
   사실을 보기 중에서 고르는 문제입니다. 이 유형의 경우, 정답 보기가 패러프레이징(paraphrasing: 같은 의미를 다른 단어로
   바꾸어 말하기)이 되어 있어 다소 난이도가 높은 편입니다. 청취와 독해 및 어휘 영역에서는 문제가 각각 5~8문제씩 출제됩니다.
   마지막으로 Vocabulary는 각 PART의 지문에 밑줄이 그어진 2개의 단어에 맞는 동의어를 찾는 문제입니다. 총 네 개의
   PART에서 각각 2문제씩 나오므로 항상 8문제가 출제됩니다.

목표 점수별 공략법

지텔프 Level 2. 32점

1. 총점 96점이 목표

지텔프 시험은 문법 26문제, 청취 26문제, 독해 28문제로 구성되어 있으며 각 영역이 100점 만점, 총 80문제입니다. 여기서 평균 32점을 얻기 위해서는 세 영역 합산 총점이 96점이 되어야 합니다.

2. 문법 84점만 받으면 된다

각 영역별로 난이도는 "청취 > 독해 > 문법" 순으로, 청취가 가장 어렵고 문법이 가장 쉽습니다. 문법 영역은 총 26문제 중 시제 6문제, 가정법 6문제, 당위성 표현 2문제, 부정사/동명사 6문제, 조동사 2문제, 접속사/전치사 2문제, 관계대명사절 2문제로 출제됩니다. 같은 유형의 문제가 반복되어 나오고, 그 유형은 총 7개 유형이므로 이 7개 유형만 학습하면 문법 영역에서 최대 84점의 고득점이 가능합니다.

따라서 1주일에서 2주일 동안 7개 유형의 각각의 특징과 단서를 파악하는데 주력하여 학습한다면, 문제 해석이 필요한 조동사와 접속사 문제를 제외하고, 나머지 22문제를 맞추어 약 84점이 확보됩니다. (한 문제당 약 4점으로 계산) 여기서 청취와 독해에서 3문제 이상 더 맞추면 총점 96점이 훌쩍 넘어 목표 점수 32점을 쉽게 달성할 수 있습니다.

지텔프 Level 2. 65점

1. 총점 195점이 목표

평균 65점은 세 영역에서 총점 195점이 되어야 하는 점수이므로, 문법에서 92점, 청취에서 30~40점, 독해에서 63~73점을 목표 점수로 권장합니다. 지텔프 시험의 가장 큰 장점은 문법의 난이도가 낮다는 것과 독해의 문제수가 적다는 것입니다. 앞서 32점 목표 공략법에서 설명하였듯이 문법은 총 7개 유형이 반복적으로 출제되어 총 26문제가 구성되어 있으므로 해당 유형의 이론을 공부하고 실전 문제만 충분히 풀이한다면 기본적으로 84점 이상은 얻을 수 있습니다. 여기서 조동사와 접속사 유형을 풀이하기 위해 출제되는 여러 조동사와 접속사를 공부하고 문장 해석을 통한 문맥 파악에 노력을 기울인다면 최대 96점(26문제 중 25문제 정답)은 충분히 달성할 수 있습니다.

2. 65점 목표의 난관: 독해와 어휘

독해는 토익에 비하여 분량이 적을 뿐 난이도가 토익보다 쉬운 것은 아닙니다. 한 지문은 약 500개 단어로 구성되어 있으며, 이는 토익 PART 7의 이중 지문과 비슷한 분량입니다. 이러한 지문이 총 4개, 각 지문당 7개의 문제가 출제되어 있으며, 그 7문제에는 세부정보, 추론, 사실확인, 동의어 찾기 유형이 섞여서 출제됩니다. 특히 동의어 찾기 문제는 한 지문당 2문제가 고정적으로 출제되어 독해 영역 전체에서 동의어 문제는 총 8문제가 출제됩니다. 그 외의 세부정보, 사실확인, 추론 유형의 문제는 반드시 해당 지문을 꼼꼼하게 읽으면서 정답을 찾아야 합니다.

동의어 문제를 제외한 한 지문에 나오는 독해 문제 5문제는 독해 지문의 단락 순서대로 출제됩니다. 예를 들어, 첫번째 단락에서 첫번째 문제의 정답 단서가 있으며, 두번째 단락에 두번째 문제의 정답 단서가 있는 식입니다. 하지만 이것이 항상 규칙적이지는 않은데, 가령 첫번째 단락에 첫번째 문제의 정답 단서가 없으면 두번째 단락에 첫번째 문제의 정답 단서가 있기도 합니다. 그래서 문제를 풀 때는 첫번째 문제를 먼저 읽고, 문제의 키워드를 파악한 다음, 첫번째 단락을 읽으면서 해당 키워드를 찾는 식으로 문제를 풀이합니다. 여기서 가장 중요한 것은 문장의 내용을 제대로 이해할 수 있는 해석 능력입니다. 영어 문장 해석 능력은 기초적인 영문법과 어휘 실력으로 완성됩니다.

따라서 지텔프 독해에서 요구되는 수준의 어휘 실력을 갖추기 위해 기초 영단어 포함 최소 2,000단어 이상 암기해야 하며, 영어 문장을 올바르게 해석하기 위해 기초 영문법을 학습해야 합니다. 여기서 기초 영문법이란 중/고등학교 영어 수준의 영문법을 말하며, 품사의 구분부터 문장성분 분석, 각 문장의 형식에 따른 문장 해석 방법, 부정사, 동명사, 분사(구문), 관용 구문까지 아울러 포괄적으로 일컫는 말입니다. 어휘와 해석 능력만 갖춰진다면 60점까지 무리없이 도달할 수 있으며, 거기서 추가적으로 패러프레징(paraphrasing) 된 오답을 피하는 요령, 세부 정보 및 추론 문제에서 정답 보기를 찾는 요령 등 독해 스킬에 해당하는 것을 추가적으로 학습하면 70점에 도달할 수 있습니다.

3. 청취 영역을 포기하지 말 것

청취는 총 4개 지문, 각 지문당 6~7문제가 출제되는데, 난이도가 그 어떤 다른 영어 시험보다 어려운 수준이기에 많은 수험생들이 청취 영역을 포기하는 경우가 많습니다. 청취 영역이 어려운 이유는 첫째, 문제가 시험지에 인쇄되어 있지 않습니다. 즉 듣기 음원에서 문제를 2회 들려주는데, 이 때 빠르게 시험지에 메모하여 문제를 파악해야 합니다. 둘째, 한 지문이 6분 이상 재생되기 때문에, 들으면서 즉각적으로 6~7문제를 풀어야 하는 수험생에게 아주 긴 집중력을 필요로 합니다. 셋째, 문제의 난이도가 독해 영역의 문제만큼이나 어렵습니다. 듣기 문제에서 세부정보, 사실 확인, 추론 유형의 문제를 풀이해야 하는데, 이 때 성우가 말하는 단서 중 한 단어만 놓쳐도 해당 문제에서 오답을 고를 확률이 매우 높아집니다. 그렇기 때문에 약 25분 정도 소요되는 청취 영역 시간 동안 문법이나 독해 문제를 푸는 수험생이 많고, 청취는 하나의 보기로 통일하여 답안지에 기재하는 등 포기하는 경우가 많습니다.

문법과 독해에서 고득점을 받는다면 청취에서 하나의 보기로 답안지를 작성하여도 20점~25점의 점수를 얻어 총점 195점을 받을 수 있지만, 항상 변수에 대비해야 합니다. 여기서 변수는 독해 영역에서 지나치게 어려운 주제의 지문이 출제되는 경우입니다. 특히 독해 PART 2 잡지 기사문과 PART 3 백과사전 지문에서 의학, 과학, 윤리/철학 등 이해하기 어려운 개념에 대한 지문이 등장하면 어휘부터 어렵기 때문에 많은 수험생들이 제실력을 발휘하지 못하고 목표한 점수를 얻지 못하는 경우가 발생합니다. 이러한 경우를 대비하여, 청취 영역시간에는 청취 영역을 적극적으로 풀이할 것을 권장합니다. 물론 지문이 길고 문제도 적혀 있지 않기 때문에 어렵겠지만, 한 지문에서 첫 3문제는 지문의 앞부분에서 키워드만 듣게 되면 바로 정답을 찾을 수 있을 정도로 비교적 난이도가 낮습니다. 따라서 문제를 읽어줄 때 문제를 메모하는 연습을 하여 각 지문당 3문제씩이라도 집중해서 제대로 푼다면 적어도 30점 이상은 얻을 수 있습니다. 청취 영역에서 30점 보다 더 높은 점수를 받을 경우, 그만큼 독해에서 고난도의 문제를 틀리더라도 총점 195점을 달성하는데 많은 도움이 될 것입니다.

지텔프 Level 2. 65점 이상 (청취, 독해 고득점 공략법)

목표 점수가 65점 이상이라면 65점 목표 공략법과 거의 동일합니다. 여기서 문법은 96점 이상, 청취 50점 이상, 독해 70점 이상이면 충분히 달성 가능합니다. 따라서 청취와 독해 고득점 공략법을 소개해드리겠습니다.

1. 청취 문제 풀이 과정

청취는 지문과 문제가 듣기 음원으로 제공된다는 점만 다를 뿐 한 지문당 여러 문제가 출제된다는 점, 총 네 개의 파트로 이루어진 점 등 분량이나 출제 유형의 측면에서 독해 및 어휘 영역과 거의 흡사합니다. 즉 청취 영역에도 세부사항, 사실 확인, 주제 및 목적, 추론 유형이 출제됩니다. 하지만 문제를 듣기 전까지 문제 유형을 알 수 없으므로 시험지에 있는 보기를 먼저 읽고 해석하여 핵심 포인트에 밑줄을 긋거나 각 보기의 옆에 우리말로 적어 둡니다. 이 예비 동작은 PART 1은 청취 음원이 시작되기 전, 안내문과 샘플문제를 설명할 때, PART 2, 3, 4는 이전 PART의 지문이 끝나고 문제를 다시 읽어줄 때 실시합니다.

질문의 키워드를 찾는 것이 독해 문제를 풀 때 반드시 체크해야 하는 사항인 것처럼, 청취 영역을 풀 때의 첫 단계도 질문의 키워드를 찾는 것입니다. 청취 문제는 문제지에 적혀 있지 않으므로 수험생이 직접 듣고 적어야 하는데, 이때 문제 전체를 적는 것이 아니라 키워드만 빠르게 적는 것이 핵심 포인트입니다. 문제는 항상 의문사(what, how, which, where, when 등)로 시작되므로 의문사를 적는데, 이때 what 대신 '무엇/뭐'라고 쓰거나, 주어가 사람일 경우 첫 글자만 씁니다. 그리고 가장 중요한 키워드인 <동사 + 목적어/보어>는 가장 자세히 적어야 합니다. 예를 들어, "What will Jason do in the conference?"라는 질문을 듣는다면 "무엇 / J / 하는지 / 컨퍼런스"라고 메모하는 하는 식입니다. "컨퍼런스"와 같이 3글자 이상의 단어는 영어로 "conf."라고 줄임말을 쓰거나 "컨퍼"라고 쓰는 등으로 빠르게 메모 할 수 있는 방법도 있습니다. 참고로 청취에도 추론 유형이 출제되는데, "most likely", "probably"라는 단어가 문제에서 들린다면 "most likely / probably"라고 모두 적지 말고 "추론"이라고만 메모하는 것이 좋습니다.

문제를 다 듣고 지문을 들을 때는 키워드가 언급되는 부분을 반드시 짚어 내야 합니다. 지문의 내용이 전개되는 순서는 문제의 순서와 동일하므로 1번의 키워드를 듣고 정답을 체크하고나면, 2번의 키워드가 언급되는 부분을 듣기 위해 귀를 열어 놓고 있어야 합니다. 만약 2번의 키워드를 듣지 못했는데 3번의 키워드를 듣게 되었다면, 2번의 정답을 찾을 수 있는 방법이 거의 없다고 보셔야 합니다. 현재 청취 목표 점수는 50점 이상이므로 모든 문제를 맞출 필요는 없습니다. 듣지 못한 문제는 과감히 포기하고 다음 문제의 키워드가 나오는 것을 대비해야 합니다. 또한 키워드가 들린다고 곧장 정답을 찾으려 하지 말고, 해당 문장을 끝까지 읽고 반전의 내용이 이어지지 않는지 확인 후 보기에서 정답을 골라야 합니다. 예를 들어, 저렴하지만 품질보증이 되지 않는 물건을 살 것인지, 비싸지만 오랜 기간 품질보증이 되는 물건을 살 것인지 설명하는 지문(PART 3)에서 "남자는 대화 후 무엇을 할 것인가?"와 같은 질문에 대한 키워드로 여자가 "So, what are you going to do?"라고 말한 뒤 남자가 "I don't want to spend much money(나는 많은 돈을 쓰고 싶지 않아)."라고 말한다고 해서 '저렴한 물건을 살 것이다'라는 보기를 정답으로 고르면 안됩니다. 남자가 바로 뒤이어 "But I'd prefer the product with a full two-year warranty(하지만 나는 만 2년의 품질 보증이 있는 상품을 좋아해)."라고 말한다면 정답은 바뀔 수 있기 때문입니다.

2. 독해 고득점 공략법

독해의 고득점 공략법은 바로 독해 스킬입니다. 어휘 수준과 해석 실력이 뒷받침된 상태에서, 문제에서 원하는 정보가 무엇인지를 찾아야 합니다. 문제에서 원하는 정보는 바로 문제의 "키워드"입니다. 예를 들어, 문제가 '지문에서 설명하는 법안에 의한 영향이 아닌 것은?'이라면 여기서 키워드는 '지문에서 설명하는 법안'과 '영향'입니다. 그럼 '그 법안'이 언급된 부분에서 법안에 의한 인과관계가 명확한 사건들을 지문에서 찾아서 보기의 내용과 대조해야 합니다. 하지만 해당 단락에서 '그 법안'에 대한 설명에 뒤이어 다른 사건이 서술되어 있다면, 그 다른 사건이 '지문에서 설명하는 법안에 의한 영향이 아닌 것'일 가능성이 매우 큽니다. 그런데 문제에서는 '영향을 받지 않는 사건'을 정답으로 고르라고 했는데, 대부분 응시자들은 단순히 지문에서 영향을 받은 사건 뒤에 위치하였다고 해서 이 사건도 '그 법안'의 영향을 받았다고 착각을 일으킵니다. 이를 '상상 독해'라고 하며, 지문에 언급되지 않은 내용으로 지문의 내용을 오독(misreading)하는 것입니다. 특히, 문제에 most likely, probably, can be said가 포함되어 있는 추론 유형의 문제에서 이러한 상상 독해로 오답을 고르는 경우가 많으니 주의하여야 합니다.

독해 고득점을 위해서 어휘의 중요성은 너무나 당연한 것입니다. 특히 여러가지 의미를 가지고 있는 다의어는 독해 문제의 단서가 되거나 동의어 찾기 문제가 되는 경우가 많습니다. 예를 들어 address라는 단어는 명사로 '주소', '연설'이라는 의미를 나타내고 있으며, 동사로 쓰이면 '연설하다'라는 의미로만 알고 있을 것입니다. 하지만 지텔프에서 address는 '(문제를) 해결하다, 다루다'라는 의미로 출제된 적이 있습니다. 기존에 알고 있던 의미와 전혀 다른 의미이기 때문에 모르면 해석이 불가하거나 문제를 풀지 못하는 경우가 발생합니다. 따라서 독해 고득점을 위해서 어휘를 학습할 경우에는 한 단어가 여러 가지 의미를 가지고 있다면 모든 의미를 파악해 놓는 것이 좋습니다. 특히 그 중의 하나의 의미가 특정 명사, 전치사구, 부사와 함께 쓰인다면 함께 쓰이는 단어까지 함께 연어(collocation)로 외우는 것이 좋습니다.

지텔프 LEVEL 2 성적 활용표

● 주요 정부 부처 및 국가 자격증

활용처(시험)	지텔프 Level 2 점수	토익 점수
군무원 9급	32점	470점
군무원 7급	47점	570점
경찰공무원(순경)	48점 (가산점 2점) 75점 (가산점 4점) 89점 (가산점 5점)	600점 (가산점 2점) 800점 (가산점 4점) 900점 (가산점 5점)
소방간부 후보생	50점	625점
경찰간부 후보생	50점	625점
경찰공무원 (경사, 경장, 순경)	43점	550점
호텔서비스사	39점	490점
박물관 및 미술관 준학예사	50점	625점
군무원 5급	65점	700점
국가공무원 5급	65점	700점
국가공무원 7급	65점	700점
입법고시(국회)	65점	700점
법원 행정고시(법원)	65점	700점
세무사	65점	700점
공인노무사	65점	700점
공인회계사	65점	700점
감정평가사	65점	700점
호텔관리사	66점	700점
카투사	73점	780점
국가공무원 7급 (외무영사직렬)	77점	790점

* 출처: G-TELP 공식 사이트(www.g-telp.co.kr)

5일 단기 공략 학습플랜

1일	2일	3일	4일	5일
[부록] 지텔프 영역별 공략 가이드 1~6 (QR무료 특강)	TEST 1 풀이 및 채점 + 오답 리뷰	TEST 2 풀이 및 채점 + 오답 리뷰	TEST 3 풀이 및 채점 + 오답 리뷰	TEST 1~3 어휘 정리 및 암기

65점 이상 목표 공략

문법과 독해 리뷰에 중점을 두고 어휘 암기를 꾸준히 해야 합니다. 특히 문법은 만점을 목표로 리뷰하는 것을 권장하며, 독해에서는 정답의 단서와 정답 선택지의 패러프레이징의 형태를 잘 확인하며 리뷰합니다. 청취는 50점을 목표로 난이도가 높은 문제는 리뷰하지 않고 지문에서 정답 단서가 잘 들리고 정답 선택지가 쉬운 문제 위주로 리뷰합니다.

43~50점 목표 공략

문법과 독해 리뷰에 중점을 두고 어휘 암기를 꾸준히 해야 합니다. 특히 문법은 92점을 목표로 리뷰하는 것을 권장하며, 독해에서는 난이도가 높은 문제는 리뷰하지 않고 지문에서 정답 단서와 정답 선택지의 패러프레이징 정도가 어렵지 않은 문제 위주로 리뷰합니다. 청취는 비교적 난이도가 낮은 PART 1, 3에서 세부 정보 유형의 문제 위주로 리뷰합니다.

32점 목표 공략

문법은 해석이 필요한 조동사, 접속사/접속부사 문제를 제외하고 문법 84점 이상을 목표로 중점적으로 리뷰하며, 독해와 청취의 경우 각 PART에서 지문의 첫 부분에 집중하여 첫번째와 두번째 문제를 위주로 리뷰합니다. 특히 독해는 세부 정보 문제와 동의어 문제에서 득점할 수 있도록 키워드 확인과 어휘 암기를 연습합니다.

■ 회차별 채점 후 리뷰는 청취와 독해의 경우 틀린 문제 위주로 진행하며, 문법은 모든 문제를 리뷰합니다.

■ 어휘 정리는 해당 회차의 기출 문제에서 나온 단어 중 자신이 모르는 단어를 모두 정리하는 것을 말하며, 별도의 지텔프 보카 교재를 학습하더라도 기출 문제에서 정리한 단어도 병행하여 암기합니다.

Grammar

1. (c)	2. (a)	3. (b)	4. (a)	5. (d)	6. (c)	7. (d)	8. (a)	9. (a)	10. (b)
11. (c)	12. (c)	13. (c)	14. (d)	15. (a)	16. (b)	17. (b)	18. (d)	19. (d)	20. (a)
21. (b)	22. (c)	23. (a)	24. (d)	25. (b)	26. (d)				

Listening

27. (d)	28. (a)	29. (b)	30. (c)	31. (a)	32. (b)	33. (d)	34. (d)	35. (a)	36. (b)
37. (c)	38. (a)	39. (b)	40. (a)	41. (c)	42. (d)	43. (b)	44. (d)	45. (c)	46. (c)
47. (d)	48. (b)	49. (a)	50. (d)	51. (c)	52. (a)				

Reading & Vocabulary

53. (b)	54. (a)	55. (d)	56. (b)	57. (c)	58. (d)	59. (a)	60. (d)	61. (a)	62. (c)
63. (b)	64. (a)	65. (b)	66. (d)	67. (a)	68. (b)	69. (c)	70. (c)	71. (d)	72. (b)
73. (a)	74. (d)	75. (c)	76. (c)	77. (d)	78. (a)	79. (b)	80. (c)		

채점 계산표 (정답 개수 기재)		채점 계산 방법
Grammar	_____ / 26문항	Grammar 정답 개수 ÷ 26 × 100
Listening	_____ / 26문항	Listening 정답 개수 ÷ 26 × 100
Reading & Vocabulary	_____ / 28문항	Reading & Vocabulary 정답 개수 ÷ 28 × 100
총점	_____ / 80문항 ▸ _____ / 100점	총점: 각 영역 합산 정답 개수 ÷ 80 × 100 ▸ 소수점 이하는 올림 처리

TEST 01

GRAMMAR
LISTENING
READING & VOCABULARY

01 가정법 과거

Laura's apartment lease is almost up, and she is concerned about rising rent prices in her neighborhood. If her landlord were to keep her rent at the same amount, she _____ the agreement for another year.

(a) would have happily renewed
(b) will happily renew
(c) would happily renew
(d) will have happily renewed

로라의 아파트 임대차 계약이 거의 만료되었고, 그녀는 인근의 집세가 상승하는 것에 대해 걱정하고 있다. 만약 집주인이 같은 금액으로 그녀의 월세를 유지하기로 한다면, 그녀는 기꺼이 1년 더 계약을 갱신할 것이다.

정답 (c)

해설 동사 renew의 알맞은 형태를 고르는 문제입니다. If절의 동사가 가정법 과거를 나타내는 과거시제(were)일 때, 주절의 동사는 「would/could/might + 동사원형」과 같은 형태가 되어야 알맞으므로 (c) would happily renew가 정답입니다. happily와 같은 부사가 would/could/might와 동사원형 사이에 위치할 수 있으니 선택지에서 부사를 제외한 형태를 찾아 정답을 고르도록 합니다.

어휘 lease 임대차 계약 be up 만료되다, 끝나다 be concerned about ~을 걱정하다 rent 집세, 방세 neighborhood 근처, 인근 landlord 집주인 amount 금액, 양 agreement 계약, 합의 happily 기꺼이 renew 갱신하다

02 준동사 – to부정사

Blue whales were once abundant. However, excessive hunting of the creatures for their blubber to make lamp oil has reduced the population. Fortunately, blue whale hunting was banned in 1967 _____ the species from extinction.

(a) to save
(b) to have saved
(c) having saved
(d) saving

흰긴수염고래는 한때 개체수가 많았다. 하지만, 등유를 만들기 위해 필요한 그 고래의 지방을 위한 과도한 사냥이 개체수를 축소시켜왔다. 다행히도, 흰긴수염고래를 멸종으로부터 구하기 위해 그 고래의 사냥이 1967년에 금지되었다.

정답 (a)

해설 동사 save의 알맞은 형태를 고르는 문제입니다. 빈칸 앞 부분에 '다행히, 흰긴수염고래 사냥이 1967년에 금지되었다'라는 완전한 구조의 문장이 쓰여 있어 빈칸 이하 부분이 부사의 역할을 해야 하며 '그 종을 멸종으로부터 구하기 위해'라는 의미로 목적을 나타내야 합니다. 따라서 '~하기 위해, ~하려면'이라는 뜻으로 목적을 나타내는 to부정사 (a) to save가 정답입니다.

어휘 blue whale 흰긴수염고래 abundant 풍부한, 많은 excessive 과도한 blubber (고래 등의) 동물 지방 lamp oil 등유 population 개체수 fortunately 다행히 ban 금지하다 species 종 extinction 멸종 save 구하다

---

03 시제 – 미래진행

Jassi has spent the past few weeks rehearsing her dance for the final project of her choreography class. Later today, she _____ her dance routine in the auditorium.

(a) performs
(b) will be performing
(c) has performed
(d) was performing

재시는 안무 수업의 마지막 과제를 위해 그녀의 춤을 연습하느라 지난 몇 주를 보냈다. 오늘 늦게, 그녀는 강당에서 그녀의 안무를 공연하고 있을 것이다.

정답 (b)

해설 동사 perform의 알맞은 형태를 고르는 문제입니다. 빈칸이 속한 문장 앞에 미래시점을 나타내는 부사 later today가 쓰여 있으므로 빈칸이 속한 문장의 시제는 미래시제임을 알 수 있습니다. 따라서 보기 중에서 미래를 나타낼 수 있는 미래진행시제 (b) will be performing이 정답입니다.

어휘 spend + 시간 + -ing: ~하느라 (시간)을 보내다 choreography 안무 later today 오늘 늦게, 오늘 나중에 auditorium 강당 perform 공연하다

---

04 접속사

Tyler wants to ride the new roller coaster, Steel Goliath, but the line has a one-hour wait time. _____ he is willing to wait, he will have to come back when the line is shorter.

(a) Unless
(b) Whenever
(c) Because
(d) Once

타일러는 새로운 롤러 코스터 '스틸 골리앗'을 타고 싶어하지만, 1시간을 기다려야 하는 줄이 늘어져 있다. 그가 기꺼이 기다릴 것이 아니라면, 그는 줄이 더 짧을 때 돌아와야 할 것이다.

정답 (a)

해설 빈칸에 들어갈 알맞은 접속사를 고르는 문제입니다. 빈칸 뒤에 위치한 종속절의 내용은 '그는 기꺼이 기다릴 것이다'라는 내용을 나타내며, 그 뒤에 위치한 주절의 내용은 '줄이 더 짧을 때 돌아와야 할 것이다'라는 의미입니다. 그가 기다린다면 그 줄에 머물러 있는 것을 의미하므로 줄이 짧을 때 돌아온다는 것은 서로 상반된 상황을 나타낸다는 것을 알 수 있습니다. 따라서 '그가 기꺼이 기다리지 않을 것이라면'이라는 의미로 주절과 연결되는 것이 자연스러우므로 부정의 의미가 포함된 '~하지 않는다면'이라는 의미의 접속사 (a) Unless가 정답입니다.

어휘 be willing to 동사원형: 기꺼이 ~하다 will have to 동사원형: ~해야 할 것이다 unless ~하지 않는다면 whenever ~할 때마다 once 일단 ~하면

Most people do not realize how many objects they touch throughout the day or how easily germs transfer between surfaces. It is important that people avoid _____ with their hands until they have thoroughly washed them.

(a) to eat
(b) having eaten
(c) to have eaten
(d) eating

대부분의 사람들은 하루에 그들이 얼마나 많은 물체를 만지는지, 또는 세균들이 표면 사이를 얼마나 쉽게 이동하는지에 대해 알아차리지 못하고 있다. 사람들은 철저하게 그들의 손을 씻을 때까지 그들의 손으로 먹는 것을 피하는 것이 중요하다.

정답 (d)

해설 동사 eat의 알맞은 형태를 고르는 문제입니다. 빈칸 앞에 쓰여 있는 동사 avoid는 동명사를 목적어로 취하므로 (d) eating 이 정답입니다.

어휘 realize 알아차리다, 깨닫다 object 사물, 물체 throughout 내내, 전체에 걸쳐 easily 쉽게 germ 세균 transfer 이동하다 surface 표면 thoroughly 철저하게, 꼼꼼하게

⊗ 오답 피하기

that 앞에 important와 같이 중요성/권고/필수/의무 등을 나타내는 형용사가 위치해 있으므로 빈칸이 「it is ~ that절」 구조로 된 가주어/진주어 구문에서 진주어 역할을 하는 that절의 동사 자리로 혼동하지 않도록 주의해야 합니다. 빈칸은 동사 자리가 아니라 타동사 avoid의 목적어 자리입니다.

The National Weather Service just issued a tornado warning for the town of Holmville. Local government officials advise that residents _____ indoors and away from windows to avoid being injured.

(a) will stay
(b) are staying
(c) stay
(d) stayed

국립 기상국은 방금 홈빌 마을에 대한 토네이도 경보를 발령하였다. 지자체 공무원들은 주민들에게 실내에 머물 것과 부상을 피하기 위해 창문으로부터 떨어져 있어야 한다고 충고한다.

정답 (c)

해설 동사 stay의 알맞은 형태를 고르는 문제입니다. 빈칸은 동사 advise의 목적어 역할을 하는 that절의 동사 자리인데, advise 와 같이 주장/요구/명령/제안 등을 나타내는 동사의 목적어 역할을 하는 that절의 동사는 should 없이 동사원형만 사용하므로 동사원형인 (c) stay가 정답입니다.

어휘 **issue** 발급하다, 발령하다 **warning** 경고, 경보 **official** 공무원 **advise** 충고하다, 조언하다 **indoors** 실내에서 **injure** 부상을 입히다

07 가정법 과거완료

Tunde decided to drive to work yesterday. Unfortunately, he got stuck in traffic and arrived late. If he had known that the roads were going to be so congested, he _____ the train instead.

(a) would take
(b) will take
(c) will have taken
(d) would have taken

툰데는 어제 운전을 하여 출근하기로 결정하였다. 불행히도, 그는 교통 체증에 갇혔고 늦게 도착하였다. 도로가 매우 혼잡해질 것이라는 것을 그가 알았었다면, 그는 대신에 기차를 탔을 것이다.

정답 (d)

해설 동사 see의 알맞은 형태를 고르는 문제입니다. If절의 동사가 가정법 과거완료를 나타내는 과거완료시제(had p.p.)일 때, 주절의 동사는 「would/could/might + have + p.p.」와 같은 형태가 되어야 알맞으므로 (d) would have taken이 정답입니다.

어휘 **drive to work** 운전해서 출근하다 **unfortunately** 불행히도 **get stuck in traffic** 교통 체증에 갇히다 **congested** 혼잡한, 붐비는 **instead** 대신에

08 조동사

Brushing one's teeth regularly is among the most effective ways to prevent cavities. That is why people _____ brush their teeth after every meal and each night before bed.

(a) should
(b) can
(c) would
(d) might

치아를 정기적으로 닦는 것은 충치를 예방하는 가장 효과적인 방법 중에 하나이다. 그것이 사람들이 매 식사 후에, 그리고 매일 저녁 잠자리에 들기 전에 치아를 닦아야 하는 이유이다.

정답 (a)

해설 빈칸에 들어갈 알맞은 조동사를 고르는 문제입니다. 빈칸 앞 문장은 '충치를 예방하는 가장 효과적인 방법이 치아를 정기적으로 닦는 것'이라고 언급하였고, 빈칸이 포함된 문장은 사람들이 식사 후에, 자기 전에 매일 치아를 닦는 이유를 설명하고 있으므로 '치아를 닦다'라는 의미의 brush their teeth 표현과 어울리는 조동사를 골라야 합니다. 따라서 보기 중에서 '~해야 하다'라는 의미로 충고를 나타내는 조동사 (a) should가 정답입니다.

어휘 **brush one's teeth** 치아를 닦다, 양치하다 **regularly** 규칙적으로, 정기적으로 **effective** 효과적인 **prevent** 예방하다 **cavity** 충치 **meal** 식사

Keith usually works at company headquarters, but this week he needs to inspect other branches. Right now, he _____ to Texas to examine the operations of the Houston branch.

(a) is traveling
(b) had traveled
(c) travels
(d) will have been traveling

키스는 보통 본사에서 업무를 하지만, 이번주에 그는 다른 지사들을 점검해야 한다. 바로 지금, 그는 휴스턴에 있는 지사의 운영을 조사하기 위해 텍사스로 이동 중이다.

정답 (a)

해설 동사 travel의 알맞은 형태를 고르는 문제입니다. 빈칸 앞에 위치한 Right now가 '바로 지금'이라는 의미를 나타내어 현재 일시적으로 진행되는 일을 뜻하는 현재진행시제 동사와 어울려 쓰이므로 (a) is traveling 이 정답입니다

어휘 headquarters 본부, 본사 inspect 점검하다 branch 지사, 지점 examine 조사하다, 검사하다

2001: A Space Odyssey is known for its innovative special effects. The film, _____, used practical features such as spaceship models, rotating sets, and high-contrast photography to craft a realistic portrayal of space.

(a) who won the award for best visual effects
(b) which won the award for best visual effects
(c) what won the award for best visual effects
(d) that won the award for best visual effects

<2001: 스페이스 오딧세이>는 혁신적인 특수효과로 알려져 있다. 최우수 시각 효과상을 받은 그 영화는 우주의 사실적인 묘사를 만들기 위해 우주선 모델과 회전하는 세트, 고대비 사진과 같은 실용적인 특징들을 사용하였다.

정답 (b)

해설 사물 명사 The film을 뒤에서 수식할 관계사절을 고르는 문제입니다. 선택지 (a)~(d)를 보고 빈칸에 들어갈 관계사절이 관계대명사 뒤에 타동사 won과 목적어 the award, 전치사구 for best visual effects가 이어지는 구조임을 알 수 있습니다. 사물 명사를 수식하는 관계대명사는 which 또는 that인데, 빈칸 앞에 콤마가 있으므로 관계대명사 which로 시작하는 (b) 가 정답입니다.

어휘 be known for ~로 알려져 있다 innovative 혁신적인 special effect 특수 효과 practical 실용적인 feature 특징 rotating 회전하는 high-contrast 고대비의 craft (공들여) 만들다 realistic 사실적인, 현실적인 portrayal 묘사

✕ 오답 피하기

관계대명사 that은 콤마(,) 뒤에 사용할 수 없는 관계대명사입니다. 빈칸 앞에 콤마(,)가 있는 경우 that으로 시작하는 관계사절은 오답으로 소거됩니다.

11 시제 – 미래완료진행

It seems like only yesterday that Mica was starting her new job as a staff writer for the *Penn Times*. By next month, she _____ for the newspaper for a year.

(a) will write
(b) has been writing
(c) will have been writing
(d) writes

미카가 <펜 타임즈>의 전속 기자로서 새로운 일을 시작한 것이 바로 어제였던 것 같다. 다음 달 쯤이면, 그녀는 그 신문사에서 1년 동안 글을 써오는 중일 것이다.

정답 (c)

해설 동사 write의 알맞은 형태를 고르는 문제입니다. 빈칸 앞에 위치한 By next month가 미래시점을 나타내고 있고, 빈칸이 포함된 문장에 for a year와 같이 「for + 기간」 표현으로 기간을 나타내는 구문이 있어서 1년 동안 계속 진행 중일 미래의 상태를 나타낼 미래완료진행형 동사가 필요하므로 (c) will have been writing이 정답입니다.

어휘 staff writer 전속 작가, 전속 기자

12 가정법 과거

The CEO is choosing between Grace and Martha to lead the sales department. If she were to ask for my input, I _____ Grace as the team leader because of her vast experience.

(a) would have suggested
(b) will have suggested
(c) would suggest
(d) will suggest

CEO는 영업부를 이끌 사람으로 그레이스와 마사 중에서 고르는 중이다. 만약 그녀가 나에게 의견 제공을 요청한다면, 나는 그레이스의 폭넓은 경험 때문에 그녀를 팀장으로 제안할 것이다.

정답 (c)

해설 동사 suggest의 알맞은 형태를 고르는 문제입니다. If절의 동사가 가정법 과거를 나타내는 과거시제(were)일 때, 주절의 동사는 「would/could/might + 동사원형」과 같은 형태가 되어야 알맞으므로 (c) would suggest가 정답입니다.

어휘 lead 이끌다 sales department 영업부 ask for ~을 요청하다 input 정보의 제공 team leader 팀장 vast 폭넓은 suggest 제안하다

Layla arrived early at the music festival. One of the performers was her favorite band, Chinked Armor. She was determined _____ the band play live, even if it meant waiting for hours.

(a) to have seen
(b) having seen
(c) to see
(d) seeing

레일라는 음악 축제에 일찍 도착했다. 공연자들 중 하나는 그녀가 가장 좋아하는 밴드 Chinked Armor였다. 그녀는 심지어 몇 시간을 기다리더라도 그 밴드가 연주하는 것을 실황으로 보겠다고 결심하였다.

정답 (c)

해설 동사 see의 알맞은 형태를 고르는 문제입니다. 빈칸 앞에 위치한 was determined는 to부정사와 함께 '~하기로 결심하다'를 뜻하는 「be determined to 동사원형」의 구조로 쓰이므로 (c) to see가 정답입니다.

어휘 **be determined to 동사원형**: ~하기로 결심하다 **live** 실황으로, 생중계로

✕ 오답 피하기

Be caught를 제외한 수동태 형태 「be + p.p.(-ed)」 뒤에는 동명사가 아닌 to부정사가 위치합니다.

It can be hard to find a trustworthy babysitter, so families in my neighborhood are lucky to have Elise. She is kind and reliable, and she _____ kids since she was sixteen years old.

(a) had been taking care of
(b) is taking care of
(c) will have taken care of
(d) has been taking care of

신뢰할 수 있는 베이비시터를 찾는 것은 어려울 수 있다. 그래서 우리 동네의 가정들은 엘리스가 있어 운이 좋다. 그녀는 친절하고, 믿을 수 있다. 그리고 그녀는 16살때부터 아이들을 돌보고 있는 중이다.

정답 (d)

해설 동사구 take care of의 알맞은 형태를 고르는 문제입니다. 빈칸 뒤에 위치한 「since + 주어 + 과거시제동사」는 '~했을 때부터', '~이었던 이후로'라는 의미로 과거 시점에 시작하여 현재에도 진행 중인 동작이나 행동을 나타내는 현재완료진행형 동사와 어울리므로 (d) has been taking care of가 정답입니다.

어휘 **trustworthy** 신뢰할 수 있는 **neighborhood** 동네, 인근 **be lucky to 동사원형**: ~해서 운이 좋다 **reliable** 믿을 수 있는 **take care of** ~을 돌보다

15 당위성을 나타내는 동사원형

Cecilia was recently diagnosed as iron deficient. That is why her new doctor recommends that she _____ foods rich in iron, such as liver, poultry, and seafood.

(a) eat
(b) ate
(c) will eat
(d) is eating

세실리아는 최근에 철분 결핍으로 진단을 받았다. 그게 그녀의 새로운 의사가 간 요리, 가금류 고기, 그리고 해산물과 같은 철분이 풍부한 음식을 먹어야 한다고 권장하는 이유이다.

정답 (a)

해설 동사 eat의 알맞은 형태를 고르는 문제입니다. 빈칸은 동사 recommends의 목적어 역할을 하는 that절의 동사 자리인데, recommend와 같이 주장/요구/명령/제안 등을 나타내는 동사의 목적어 역할을 하는 that절의 동사는 should없이 동사원형만 사용하므로 동사원형인 (a) eat가 정답입니다.

어휘 diagnose 진단하다 iron 철, 철분 deficient 결핍된, 부족한 rich 풍부한 liver 간 요리 poultry 가금류(닭, 거위 등) 고기 seafood 해산물

16 가정법 과거완료

Peter could not afford Glenbank University's tuition fees, and the deadline to accept the admission offer has passed. If the fees had been lower, he _____ to Glenbank to earn his degree.

(a) would move
(b) would have moved
(c) will move
(d) will have moved

피터는 글랜뱅크 대학교의 등록금을 감당할 수 없었고, 입학 제안을 수용하는 기한이 지났다. 만약 그 등록금이 더 낮았더라면, 그는 글렌뱅크로 가서 학위를 얻었을 것이다.

정답 (b)

해설 동사 move의 알맞은 형태를 고르는 문제입니다. If절의 동사가 had been과 같이 가정법 과거완료를 나타내는 「had p.p.」일 때, 주절의 동사는 「would/could/might + have p.p.」와 같은 형태가 되어야 알맞으므로 (b) would have moved가 정답입니다.

어휘 afford ~을 감당하다, (~을 지불할) 여유가 있다 tuition fee 등록금 deadline 마감일, 기일 admission 입학 earn 얻다 degree 학위

Yuki's friends invited him over for their special "Taco Tuesday" dinner the other night. However, he declined their invitation because he _____ since 6 a.m. and felt ready to collapse from exhaustion.

(a) will have worked
(b) had been working
(c) is working
(d) has been working

유키의 친구들은 며칠 전 밤에 유키를 그들의 특별 "타코 화요일" 저녁 식사에 초대하였다. 하지만, 그는 그들의 초대를 거절하였는데, 그 이유는 그가 오전 6시부터 계속 일을 하고 있었던 중이었고, 탈진으로 쓰러질 준비가 되었다고 느꼈기 때문이었다.

정답 (b)

해설 동사 work의 알맞은 형태를 고르는 문제입니다. 첫 문장에 과거시제 동사 invited를 통해 과거 시점에 초대했다는 것을 알 수 있으므로 빈칸이 속한 문장에서 since 6 a.m.을 보고 유키가 오전 6시부터 일을 해오고 있었던 시점이 주절의 과거시제 동사 declined가 가리키는 과거시점인 것을 알 수 있습니다. 따라서 빈칸에 들어갈 시제는 declined보다 더 먼저 일어난 일을 나타내는 과거완료진행시제가 되어야 하므로 (b) had been working이 정답입니다.

어휘 the other night 며칠 전 밤에 decline 거절하다 feel ready to 동사원형: ~할 준비가 되었다고 느끼다 collapse 쓰러지다, 무너지다 exhaustion 탈진

❌ 오답 피하기

「since + 과거시점」은 현재완료진행시제의 단서가 되기도 하지만 과거완료진행시제의 단서가 될 수 있습니다. 주변의 시제가 과거시제이고, since 뒤에 쓰인 과거시점이 특정과거시점보다 더 앞선 시점일 경우, 빈칸에 들어갈 시제는 과거완료진행시제입니다.

Animals such as sheep, cows, and deer are ruminants, meaning that they re-chew partially digested food. Ruminating is a feeding technique _____ to extract more nutrition from grass, which is hard to digest.

(a) when animals use
(b) who animals use
(c) what animals use
(d) that animals use

양, 소, 사슴과 같은 동물들은 반추동물인데, 이는 그들이 부분적으로 소화된 음식을 다시 씹는다는 것을 의미한다. 반추는 소화시키기 어려운 풀에서 더 많은 영양분을 추출하기 위해 동물들이 사용하는 음식을 먹는 기술이다.

정답 (d)

해설 사물 명사 a feeding technique을 뒤에서 수식할 관계사절을 고르는 문제입니다. 선택지 (a)~(d)를 보고 빈칸에 들어갈 관계사절이 관계대명사 뒤에 주어 animals와 동사 use로 구성되는 구조임을 알 수 있습니다. 사물 명사를 수식하는 관계대명사는 which 또는 that인데, (a)~(d) 중에는 which로 시작하는 관계사절이 없으므로 정답은 (d) that animals use입니다.

어휘 ruminant 반추동물 chew 씹다 partially 부분적으로, 일부 digested 소화된 ruminate 반추하다, 되새김질하다 feeding 음식을 섭취하는 technique 기술 extract 추출하다, 뽑아내다 nutrition 영양분 grass 풀 digest 소화시키다

❌ 오답 피하기

관계대명사 what은 선행사(관계사절의 수식을 받는 명사)를 가지지 않는 관계대명사입니다.

---

19 조동사

Tesla is one of the world's top manufacturers of energy-efficient electric cars. What makes the company popular is that its vehicles _____ be driven farther on a single charge than most others on the market.

(a) will
(b) must
(c) might
(d) can

테슬라는 에너지 효율이 좋은 전기 자동차를 제조하는 세계 최고의 제조업체 중 하나이다. 그 회사를 인기 있게 만드는 것은 그 회사의 차량들이 1회 충전으로 시중에 판매되는 다른 대부분의 전기 자동차들보다 더 멀리 운행될 수 있다는 것이다.

정답 (d)

해설 빈칸에 들어갈 알맞은 조동사를 고르는 문제입니다. 빈칸이 속한 문장은 테슬라의 전기 자동차가 한번의 충전으로 다른 전기 자동차보다 더 멀리 운행된다는 의미를 나타내는데, 이것은 테슬라의 전기 자동차가 가진 능력을 나타내는 것이므로 '~ 더 멀리 운행될 수 있다'라는 의미를 나타내는 것이 적절합니다. 따라서 '~할 수 있다'라는 의미를 나타내는 조동사 (d) can이 정답입니다.

어휘 manufacturer 제조업체 efficient 효율적인 popular 인기 있는 vehicle 차량 farther 더 멀리 single 한번의 charge 충전 on the market 시중에 판매되는

The documentary that my parents streamed yesterday was at least three hours long. They started watching the film before I left for the mall, and they _____ it when I came back.

(a) were still watching
(b) have still watched
(c) are still watching
(d) still watched

나의 부모님이 어제 스트리밍으로 보셨던 다큐멘터리는 최소 3시간 길이였다. 그들은 내가 쇼핑몰로 떠나기 전에 그 영화를 시청하기 시작하셨고, 내가 돌아왔을 때 여전히 그것을 시청하고 계셨다.

정답 (a)

해설 동사 watch의 알맞은 형태를 고르는 문제입니다. 빈칸 뒤에 과거시제 동사(came)를 포함한 when절이 쓰여 있어 이 when절이 가리키는 과거 시점에 준비하는 일이 일시적으로 진행되던 상황을 나타내야 자연스러우므로 이러한 의미로 쓰이는 과거진행시제 (a) were still watching이 정답입니다.

어휘 documentary 다큐멘터리 영화 stream 스트리밍으로 재생하다, 데이터 전송을 연속으로 이어하다 at least 최소한 leave for ~을 향해 떠나다 still 여전히

Jolene's neighborhood is experiencing a wave of car thefts. As a result, the local police have agreed _____ patrols in the area, and a closed-circuit security system will soon be installed.

(a) having increased
(b) to increase
(c) increasing
(d) to have increased

조렌의 동네는 차량 절도의 급증을 겪고 있다. 그 결과로, 현지 경찰은 그 지역의 순찰을 증가시키기로 동의하였고, 폐쇄회로 보안시스템이 곧 설치될 것이다.

정답 (b)

해설 동사 increase의 알맞은 형태를 고르는 문제입니다. 빈칸은 타동사 have agreed의 목적어 자리이며, agree는 to부정사를 목적어로 취하여 '~하기로 동의하다'라는 의미를 나타냅니다. 따라서 to부정사인 (b) to increase가 정답입니다.

어휘 neighborhood 동네, 인근 wave (특정한 일의) 급증 theft 절도 as a result 그 결과로 agree to 동사원형: ~하기로 동의하다 patrol 순찰하다 closed-circuit 폐쇄회로 security 보안 install 설치하다

22 준동사 – 동명사

Marvin transferred from the night class to a morning session. When asked why he changed classes, he said that he dislikes _____ lectures at night because he is often sleepy by then.

(a) to attend
(b) having attended
(c) attending
(d) to be attending

마빈은 저녁반에서 아침반으로 옮겼다. 왜 반을 바꾸는지 물었을 때, 그는 종종 그때쯤 졸리기 때문에 저녁에 강의를 듣는 것을 싫어한다고 말했다.

정답 (c)

해설 동사 attend의 알맞은 형태를 고르는 문제입니다. 빈칸은 타동사 dislikes의 목적어 자리이며, dislike는 동명사를 목적어로 취하여 '~하는 것을 싫어하다'라는 의미를 나타냅니다. 따라서 동명사인 (c) attending이 정답입니다.

어휘 transfer 옮기다, 이동하다 session (특정한 활동의) 시간, 기간 dislike 싫어하다 attend a lecture 강의를 듣다 by then 그때쯤

23 가정법 과거완료

Butler University's basketball team was down two points with less than a second remaining in the game. Their captain took a long shot, but missed. If he had scored, Butler _____ the game.

(a) would have won
(b) will win
(c) would win
(d) will have won

버틀러 대학의 농구팀은 그 시합에서 1초도 남지 않은 상황에서 2점 차로 지고 있었다. 그들의 주장은 긴 슛을 시도하였지만, 득점하지 못했다. 만약 그가 득점을 했다면, 버틀러는 그 시합을 이겼을 것이다.

정답 (a)

해설 동사 win의 알맞은 형태를 고르는 문제입니다. If절의 동사가 「had p.p.」일 때, 주절의 동사는 「would/could/might + have p.p.」와 같은 형태가 되어야 알맞으므로 (a) would have won이 정답입니다.

어휘 with + 목적어 + -ing: ~하는 채로, ~하는 상황에서 less than ~보다 적은 take a shot 슛을 하다 score 득점하다

Wolfgang Amadeus Mozart was a classical musician and composer who is still widely known today. As a child prodigy, he started composing music _____ he was five and could play multiple instruments by age six.

(a) in case
(b) until
(c) now that
(d) when

볼프강 아마데우스 모차르트는 오늘날에도 여전히 널리 알려진 고전 음악가이자 작곡가이다. 신동으로서, 그는 그가 5세 때 음악을 작곡하기 시작하였으며, 6세 때는 여러 악기를 연주할 수 있었다.

정답 (d)

해설 빈칸에 들어갈 알맞은 접속사를 고르는 문제입니다. 빈칸 앞에 위치한 주절의 동사가 started이므로 과거시제임을 알 수 있으며, 빈칸 뒤에 위치한 종속절의 동사도 was로 과거시제임을 알 수 있습니다. 문맥상 '그가 5세 때 음악을 작곡하기 시작했다'라는 의미가 가장 자연스러우므로 '~할 때'를 나타내는 부사절 접속사 (d) when이 정답입니다.

어휘 classical 고전의 musician 음악가 composer 작곡가 widely 널리 prodigy 천재, 영재 compose 작곡하다 multiple 다수의, 여러 개의 instrument 악기 in case ~한 경우에 (대비하여) until ~까지 now that ~이므로, ~때문에 when ~할 때

Hazel wants to become more well-read, but she is busy with her job. If she were to get more free time, she _____ more often than she does now.

(a) would have read
(b) would read
(c) will have read
(d) will read

헤이즐은 좀 더 박식해지고 싶어 한다. 하지만 그녀는 그녀의 일로 바쁘다. 만약 그녀가 더 많은 자유 시간을 갖게 된다면, 그녀는 지금보다 더 자주 책을 읽을 것이다.

정답 (b)

해설 동사 read의 알맞은 형태를 고르는 문제입니다. If절의 동사가 가정법 과거를 나타내는 과거시제(were)일 때, 주절의 동사는 「would/could/might + 동사원형」과 같은 형태가 되어야 알맞으므로 (b) would read가 정답입니다.

어휘 well-read 책을 많이 읽은, 박식한 be busy with ~로 바쁘다

26 준동사 – 동명사

Russell, who recently graduated with a degree in data analysis, has already found a job in the fraud department of a local bank. The job involves _____ accounts for suspicious activity that may indicate criminal behavior.

(a) to have monitored
(b) having monitored
(c) to monitor
(d) monitoring

러셀은, 최근에 데이터 분석 학위를 가지고 졸업을 하였는데, 이미 한 지역 은행의 사기 전담 부서에 취직하였다. 그 일은 범죄 행위를 나타낼 수도 있는 의심스러운 행위에 대한 계좌를 감시하는 것을 수반한다.

정답 (d)

해설 동사 monitor의 알맞은 형태를 고르는 문제입니다. 빈칸 앞에 쓰여 있는 동사 involve는 동명사를 목적어로 취하므로 (d) monitoring이 정답입니다.

어휘 graduate 졸업하다 degree 학위 analysis 분석 fraud 사기, 기망 involve 수반하다, 포함하다 account 계좌 suspicious 의심스러운 indicate 나타내다 criminal 범죄의 behavior 행위 monitor 감시하다, 지켜보다

PART 1

F: Hello, Drake! How was your weekend?

M: Hi, Tessa. My weekend was great. My officemates and I had dinner at the Roadhouse Restaurant last Saturday.

F: 27 Oh, I haven't eaten there in a while. I've been too busy with work to eat out much. I heard that it was recently renovated.

M: Yes, it was. The restaurant's interior was updated. It looks more modern now.

F: Sounds great! The interior sure looked outdated the last time I ate there. The walls were faded and the overall mood was stiff and formal.

M: It looks cozier and more welcoming now with brick walls, wood floors, and overhead spotlights. You know what's really great? They added a second floor!

F: Finally, a second floor! The restaurant tends to get crowded on weekends so it takes too long to be seated. 28 I'm sure the customers will appreciate the bigger space.

M: It definitely makes a difference. The second floor also has an open balcony, so customers can dine outside in the fresh air.

F: Fresh air and high-quality meat—you can't ask for more! I really enjoy their steaks. The ingredients are so simple, but the steaks are so good.

여: 안녕, 드레이크! 주말은 어땠어?

남: 안녕, 테사. 내 주말은 굉장했어. 나의 사무실 동료들과 나는 지난 토요일에 로드하우스 레스토랑에서 저녁식사를 했어.

여: 오, 나는 한동안 거기서 식사해본 적이 없네. 나는 너무 바빠서 외식을 많이 하지 못했어. 그 곳은 최근에 개조가 되었다고 들었어.

남: 응, 맞아. 그 레스토랑의 인테리어는 최신화되었어. 지금은 좀 더 현대적으로 보여.

여: 좋은 소식이네! 인테리어는 지난 번 내가 거기서 식사를 했을 때 정말 구식으로 보였어. 벽은 색이 바래져 있었고 전체적인 분위기가 딱딱하고 격식을 차린 것 같았어.

남: 지금은 벽돌로 만든 벽, 나무 바닥, 머리 위의 집중 조명으로 더 편안하고 환영하는 분위기로 보여. 그리고 뭐가 정말 굉장한지 알아? 그들이 2층을 추가했다는 것이야!

여: 마침내, 2층이 생겼구나! 그 식당은 주말에는 붐비는 경향이 있어서 자리에 앉으려면 시간이 너무 오래 걸렸어. 고객들이 더 커진 공간을 환영할 거라고 생각해.

남: 그게 정말 차이가 있어. 또한 2층은 개방 발코니가 있어서 고객들이 신선한 공기와 함께 바깥에서 식사를 할 수 있어.

여: 신선한 공기와 품질이 좋은 고기라, 더 원할 게 없겠어! 난 그곳의 스테이크를 정말로 좋아해. 재료가 정말 간단하지만, 스테이크는 정말 좋아.

M: **29** The waiter said they're now getting their steaks direct from a ranch in Texas, which is why they're even tastier than before. Oh—and they also added a mechanical bull for customers to ride on.

F: Wow, really? I've always wanted to try riding a mechanical bull. Do they offer a prize for those who can finish the ride?

M: Of course. **30** You must ride the mechanical bull for eight seconds without falling off. If you successfully complete the challenge, you'll get a restaurant gift card worth $50.

F: That sounds fun! And a gift card is not bad for a prize. I definitely want to try that.

M: Also, they now hold karaoke night every Tuesday and a trivia night every Thursday. Anyone can join and win cash prizes.

F: Wow! They've added a lot of activities. Do they still have live country music on Saturdays by— what was the band's name?

M: The Lonely Cowboys! Yes, I actually saw them perform when I was there last weekend. I enjoyed seeing them again.

F: Nice. **31** The customers really seem to like country music, so it's good that the restaurant keeps bringing in the Lonely Cowboys. What else is new at the Roadhouse Restaurant?

M: Well, **32** they also added vegetarian options to their menu. Besides the large servings and reasonable prices, the vegetarian options are great because even people with dietary restrictions can eat there.

남: 웨이터가 말하길, 그들은 이제 스테이크를 텍사스에 있는 목장에서 직접 전달받는다고 했어. 그래서 그게 예전보다 훨씬 더 맛있는 이유야. 오, 그리고 고객들이 탈 수 있는 기계 황소도 추가했어.

여: 와, 정말? 나는 항상 기계 황소에 타는 걸 시도해보고 싶었어. 끝까지 황소를 탈 수 있는 사람들을 위해서 상을 제공하니?

남: 물론이지. 너는 떨어지지 않고 8초 동안 기계 황소를 타야 해. 그 도전을 성공적으로 완료한다면, 너는 50달러 상당의 식당 상품권 카드를 받을거야.

여: 재밌을 것 같아! 그리고 상품권 카드는 상품으로 나쁘지 않아. 난 무조건 시도해보고 싶어.

남: 그리고, 그들은 이제 매주 화요일에 노래방의 밤과 매주 목요일에 상식 퀴즈의 밤을 개최해. 누구나 참가할 수 있고 상금을 탈 수 있어.

여: 와! 많은 활동들을 추가했구나. 토요일마다 하는 그 라이브 컨트리 음악을 여전히 하는 거야? 그 밴드 이름이 뭐였지?

남: '론리 카우보이즈'! 맞아. 나는 지난 주말에 거기 있었을 때 그들이 공연하는 것을 실제로 봤어. 그들을 다시 봐서 즐거웠어.

여: 좋아. 고객들은 정말 컨트리 음악을 좋아하는 것 같아. 그래서 그 식당이 '론리 카우보이즈'를 계속 데려 와서 좋아. 로드하우스 레스토랑에서 그 밖에 새로운 건 뭐가 있어?

남: 음, 그들은 또한 그들의 메뉴에 채식 옵션을 추가했어. 분량을 늘인 것과 합리적인 가격 외에도, 채식 옵션은 식단 제한을 가진 사람들조차 거기서 식사를 할 수 있기 때문에 굉장한 거야.

F: That's a smart move. **32** I bet more people will eat there now because there are more food options.

여: 그건 영리한 조치야. 더 많은 음식 선택권이 있으니까 틀림없이 더 많은 사람들이 거기서 식사를 할거야

M: Exactly. I really recommend that you go and see the restaurant, Tessa. My officemates and I had a good time.

남: 맞아. 난 네가 그 식당에 가서 보는 것을 추천해, 테사. 나의 사무실 동료들과 나는 좋은 시간을 보냈어.

F: I really want to, especially after hearing about all of these improvements.

여: 나도 정말 그러고 싶어. 특히 이런 모든 개선점들을 다 듣고 나니까 말이야.

M: Well, **33** I'm going there again next Saturday with my family. Why don't you come with us?

남: 음, 난 내 가족들과 함께 다음주 토요일에 거기에 다시 갈 거야. 너도 같이 갈래?

F: **33** That will be great, Drake!

여: 그거 좋을 것 같아, 드레이크!

어휘 officemate 사무실 동료, 직장 동료 in a while 한동안 too 형용사 to 동사원형: 너무 ~해서 ~하지 못하다 eat out 외식하다 renovate 개조하다 update 최신화하다 modern 현대적인 sure 정말, 확실히 outdated 구식의 fade 색이 바래다 stiff 딱딱한, 뻣뻣한 formal 격식의 cozy 편안하 welcoming 환영하는 brick 벽돌 overhead 머리 위의 tend to 동사원형: ~하는 경향이 있다 get crowded (사람들로) 붐벼지다, 혼잡해지다 be seated 자리에 앉다 appreciate 환영하다, 고마워하다 definitely 확실히, 틀림없이 dine 식사하다 high-quality 고품질의, 품질이 좋은 ask for 요청하다 ingredient 재료 direct 직접, 바로 ranch 목장 tasty 맛있는 mechanical 기계의, 기계로 작동하는 ride on ~에 타다 fall off 떨어지다 complete 완료하다 challenge 도전 worth ~상당의, ~의 가치를 지닌 hold (행사를) 열다, 개최하다 karaoke 가라오케, 노래방 trivia 일반 상식 cash prize 상금 activity 활동 perform 공연하다 bring in 데려오다 vegetarian 채식의, 채식주의의 large serving 많은 분량 reasonable 합리적인 dietary 식단의 restriction 제한 move 조치, 행동 I bet 내 생각에 틀림없이 improvement 개선 why don't you + 동사원형?: ~하지 않을래?, ~할래? (제안, 권유)

---

27 세부 정보

Why has Tessa not visited the Roadhouse Restaurant recently?

(a) because it has been closed for renovations
(b) because she dislikes the food there
(c) because it has gotten a bad reputation
(d) because she has been working a lot

테사가 최근에 로드하우스 레스토랑에 방문하지 않았던 이유는 무엇인가?

(a) 개조 공사로 문을 닫았기 때문에
(b) 그녀가 그곳의 음식을 싫어하기 때문에
(c) 그곳이 나쁜 평판을 받았기 때문에
(d) 그녀는 많은 일을 해오고 있었기 때문에

정답 (d)

해설 대화 초반부에 테사가 로드하우스 레스토랑에 한동안 가보지 못했다고 말하고, 일이 너무 바빠서 외식을 많이 하지 못했다 (I've been too busy with work to eat out much)고 언급하였으므로 (d)가 정답입니다.

어휘 renovation 개조 공사 dislike 싫어하다 reputation 평판

have been too busy with work → has been working a lot

---

28 세부 정보

According to Tessa, what will customers appreciate about the renovations?

(a) the more spacious layout
(b) the beautiful views outside
(c) the more comfortable seating
(d) the fresh paint on the walls

테사에 따르면, 고객들은 개조 공사에 대해 무엇을 환영할 것인가?

(a) 더 넓은 배치
(b) 아름다운 야외 경관
(c) 더 편안한 좌석
(d) 벽에 갓 칠한 페인트

정답 (a)

해설 로드하우스 레스토랑에 2층이 생겼다는 내용의 대화 중에서 테사가 주말에는 너무 붐벼서 자리에 앉으려면 너무 오래 걸렸다고 언급하였습니다. 그래서 2층이 생겨서 더 넓은 공간으로 인해 고객들이 환영할 것이라고 확신한다(I'm sure the customers will appreciate the bigger space)고 언급하였으므로 선택지 중에서 더 넓은 공간에 대해 언급한 (a)가 정답입니다.

어휘 spacious 넓은 layout 배치 view 시야, 경관 comfortable 편안한 seating 좌석

the bigger space → the more spacious layout

What did the restaurant do to improve the quality of their steaks?

(a) They altered the cooking process.
(b) They changed their meat supplier.
(c) They used different seasonings.
(d) They replaced their head chef.

그 식당은 스테이크의 품질을 향상시키기 위해 무엇을 하였는가?

(a) 조리 과정을 변경하였다.
(b) 고기 공급업체를 바꿨다.
(c) 다른 양념을 사용하였다.
(d) 주방장을 교체하였다.

정답 (b)

해설 대화 중반에 스테이크에 대해 언급하는 부분에서 웨이터가 이제 스테이크를 텍사스에 있는 목장으로부터 직접 받고 있다고 말했고, 그게 스테이크가 이전보다 훨씬 더 맛있어진 이유라고(The waiter said they're now getting their steaks direct from a ranch in Texas, which is why they're even tastier than before) 언급하였습니다. 이는 텍사스의 한 목장으로 스테이크의 공급업체를 바꾸었다는 의미이므로 (b)가 정답입니다.

어휘 improve 향상시키다 quality 품질 alter 변경하다 cooking process 조리 과정 supplier 공급업체, 공급업자 seasoning 양념 replace 교체하다 head chef 주방장

패러프레이징

even tastier than before → improve the quality

How can a customer get a gift card for the restaurant?

(a) by entering an eating contest
(b) by giving the best karaoke performance
(c) by winning a physical challenge
(d) by answering the most trivia questions

고객은 그 식당의 상품권 카드를 어떻게 얻을 수 있는가?

(a) 먹기 대회에 참가함으로써
(b) 최고의 노래방 공연을 함으로써
(c) 신체적 도전에서 우승함으로써
(d) 가장 많은 일반 상식 문제에 답함으로써

정답 (c)

해설 질문의 키워드인 a gift card가 언급된 부분에서 드레이크가 기계 황소를 타고 8초 동안 떨어지지 않고 타야 한다고 말하였고, 그 도전을 성공적으로 완료하면 50달러 상당의 상품권 카드를 얻을 것(You must ride the mechanical bull for eight seconds without falling off. If you successfully complete the challenge, you'll get a restaurant gift card worth $50)이라고 언급하였습니다. 떨어지지 않고 기계 황소에 타는 것은 신체적 활동으로 볼 수 있으므로 (c)가 정답입니다.

어휘 enter 참가하다, 들어가다 eating contest 먹기 대회 performance 공연 physical 신체적인

31 세부 정보

Why does Tessa think that keeping the live country band is a good thing?

(a) because the music is popular with the customers
(b) because the band plays for free
(c) because the music is her favorite genre
(d) because the band takes requests

테사가 라이브 컨트리 밴드를 유지하는 것이 좋은 일이라고 생각하는 이유는 무엇인가?

(a) 그 음악은 고객들에게 인기가 있기 때문에
(b) 그 밴드는 무료로 연주하기 때문에
(c) 그 음악은 그녀가 가장 좋아하는 장르이기 때문에
(d) 그 밴드는 요청사항을 들어주기 때문에

정답 (a)

해설 질문의 키워드인 live country band에 대해 언급된 부분에서 테사가 고객들이 컨트리 음악을 좋아하는 것처럼 보인다고 말하고, 그래서 그 식당이 컨트리 음악 밴드인 '론리 카우보이즈'를 계속해서 데려 오는 것은 좋다고(The customers really seem to like country music, so it's good that the restaurant keeps bringing in the Lonely Cowboys) 언급하였습니다. 따라서 이와 같은 내용으로 컨트리 음악이 고객들에게 인기가 있다고 언급한 (a)가 정답입니다.

어휘 popular with ~에게 인기가 있는 for free 무료로 take a request 요청을 들어주다, 요청을 받아들이다

> 패러프레이징
>
> The customers really seem to like country music → the music is popular with the customers

32 세부 정보

Why will more people be eating at the restaurant?

(a) The staff are friendlier.
(b) The menu has been expanded.
(c) The portions are larger.
(d) The prices have been lowered.

더 많은 사람들이 그 식당에서 식사를 하게 될 이유는 무엇인가?

(a) 직원들이 더 친절하다.
(b) 메뉴가 확장되었다.
(c) 분량이 커졌다.
(d) 가격이 낮아졌다.

정답 (b)

해설 질문의 키워드인 '더 많은 사람들이 식사를 할 것'이라는 내용은 대화 후반부에서 채식 옵션이 추가되었다는 부분에서 언급되었습니다. 채식주의 옵션이 추가된 것에 대해 테사는 그건 영리한 조치라고 하였고, 더 많은 음식 선택권이 있기 때문에 틀림없이 더 많은 사람들이 그 식당에서 식사를 할 것(I bet more people will eat there now because there are more food options)이라고 언급하였습니다. 따라서 더 많은 음식 선택권은 메뉴가 확장되었음을 나타내므로 (b)가 정답입니다.

어휘 staff 직원 friendly 친절한, 우호적인 expand 확장시키다 portion 분량 lower 낮추다

패러프레이징

more food options → the menu has been expanded

❌ 오답 피하기

드레이크가 말한 부분에서 the large servings와 reasonable prices를 근거로 (c)와 (d)를 정답으로 고를 수 있는데, 이 둘은 '더 많은 사람들이 그 식당에서 식사를 할 이유'로 언급된 것이 아니므로 오답입니다.

---

(33) 추론

What will Tessa most likely do next Saturday?

(a) eat out with her officemates
(b) bring a meal to Drake's house
(c) visit a restaurant with her husband
(d) have a meal with Drake's family

테사는 다음주 토요일에 무엇을 할 것 같은가?

(a) 그녀의 사무실 동료들과 외식한 다
(b) 드레이크의 집으로 식사를 가져 간다
(c) 그녀의 남편과 식당을 방문한다
(d) 드레이크의 가족과 함께 식사한 다

정답 (d)

해설 질문의 키워드인 next Saturday가 언급된 대화의 마지막 부분에서 드레이크가 다음주 토요일에 자신의 가족들과 그 식당을 다시 갈 것이라고 말한 뒤, 테사에게 같이 가자는 제안(I'm going there again next Saturday with my family. Why don't you come with us?)을 하였습니다. 이에 테사가 제안에 응함으로써 그녀가 드레이크의 가족과 함께 식사를 할 것이라는 것을 알 수 있습니다. 따라서 정답은 (d)입니다.

Good morning, everyone. Welcome to our talk. We at Nomadic Crowd Company believe that traveling should be hassle-free. That's why we have developed the all-in-one companion for your travel. **34** Let me introduce our newest application for tourists and adventurers like you: the Excursions app. The Excursions app is a multifunctional smartphone application designed for travelers. Packed with useful features, it's the perfect app for adventurers who love to explore places on their own rather than rely on tour guides. Here are some of its features.

First of all, **35** the Air Calendar helps you find and book the best flights for your trips. Simply enter your desired destination in the Calendar's search engine, and it will show you the different flights available. Color-coded for easy viewing, the Calendar displays the cheapest flights in green, while the most expensive routes are in red. Just choose the flight you want and book it straight from the app!

Next, **36** the Travel Atlas feature lets you plan and organize your own itinerary. For example, if you're traveling to Paris and you're worried about not knowing what to do there, the Travel Atlas can help you out. **36** With the built-in map, you can easily find all available tourist attractions in that area. From visiting sites like the Eiffel Tower and museums to discovering street art and sampling fine wine, you'll surely find something fun to do with Travel Atlas.

Our Travel Atlas is also equipped with a Basics feature. **37** This helps you find the most convenient establishments for eating, resting, or buying necessities wherever you are. This Basics feature will show information about the shops and services

좋은 아침입니다. 여러분. 저희 강연에 오신 것을 환영합니다. 저희 노매딕 크라우드 컴퍼니는 여행은 성가신 것이 없어야 한다고 믿고 있습니다. 그게 저희가 여러분의 여행을 위해 일체형의 동반자를 개발한 이유입니다. 여러분과 같은 관광객, 모험가들을 위한 저희의 최신 어플리케이션을 소개해드립니다. '익스커젼 앱'입니다. '익스커젼 앱'은 여행객들을 위해 만들어진 다기능 스마트폰 어플리케이션입니다. 유용한 특징들로 가득하여, 관광 가이드에 의지하는 것보다 스스로 여러 장소들을 탐험하는 것을 좋아하는 모험가들을 위한 완벽한 앱입니다.

무엇보다, '에어 캘린더'는 여러분의 여행에 가장 좋은 비행편을 찾고 예약하는 것을 도와줍니다. 간단하게 '에어 캘린더'에 있는 검색 엔진에 희망 목적지를 입력하시면, 구입 가능한 각각의 다른 비행편을 보여줄 것입니다. 쉽게 보실 수 있도록 색으로 구분되어 있는데, '에어 캘린더'는 가장 저렴한 비행편을 초록색으로, 반면에 가장 비싼 경로는 빨간색으로 되어 있습니다. 여러분이 원하는 비행편을 골라서 앱을 통해 곧바로 예약하세요!

다음으로, '트래블 아틀라스'는 여러분이 여러분만의 여행일정을 계획하고 준비하도록 해줍니다. 예를 들어, 여러분이 파리로 여행을 갈 것이고, 그곳에서 무엇을 해야 하는지 몰라서 걱정하고 있다면, '트래블 아틀라스'가 여러분에게 도움을 줄 수 있습니다. 내장되어 있는 지도로, 여러분은 쉽게 그 지역에서 이용할 수 있는 관광명소를 쉽게 찾을 수 있습니다. 에펠 타워와 박물관들과 같은 방문 장소부터 길거리 예술을 찾아보고 고급 와인을 시음하는 것까지, 여러분은 '트래블 아틀라스'로 확실히 재미있는 것을 찾을 것입니다.

저희 '트래블 아틀라스'는 또한 '베이직' 특징을 갖추고 있습니다. 이것은 여러분이 어디에 있든지 식사, 휴식 또는 필수품들을 구입하는 것을 위한 가장 편리한 시설을 찾는 것을 도와줍니다. 이 '베이직' 특징은 그 지역에서 이용 가능한 매장과 서비스에

available in the area. You can even filter the results by inputting your preferences, such as your desired hotel ratings or your expected budget.

Another amazing feature of Excursions is the Language Pal. Turn your smartphone into a handy language translator! To use this feature, select your language and the language you need to translate, like English to Spanish or Spanish to English. Then simply hold your phone up so it can "listen" to what you are saying while you are having a conversation. **38** The app will automatically translate what you say into the local language. The locals can respond by talking to the app, and it will speak for them in your language. The Language Pal can also translate written text on billboards, signs, and menus. Simply tap on the camera icon and point your smartphone's camera to the sign, and you'll see the translation on your screen. You can translate over 100 languages with a Wi-Fi or data connection and 50 languages when offline.

The Excursions app will be available for download in all smartphone app stores starting next month. **39** There will be two versions—a free lite version and a premium version which costs only $12.99. The lite version will only contain the first two features.

관한 정보를 보여줄 것입니다. 여러분은 심지어 희망하는 호텔 등급이나 예상 예산과 같은 여러분이 선호하는 것을 입력하여 결과를 걸러서 보실 수 있습니다.

'익스커전'의 또다른 놀라운 특징은 '랭귀지 팔'입니다. 여러분의 스마트폰을 현리한 언어 번역기로 바꿔보세요! 이 특징을 사용하기 위해서, 영어를 스페인어로, 또는 스페인어를 영어로, 이렇게 여러분이 사용하는 언어와 번역해야 하는 언어를 고르세요. 그러고 나서 단순히 여러분의 폰을 들고 있으면, 폰은 여러분이 대화를 하고 있는 중에 여러분이 말하는 것을 "들을 수" 있습니다. 이 앱은 자동으로 여러분이 말하는 것을 현지 언어로 번역할 것입니다. 현지인들은 그 앱에 말을 함으로써 대답을 할 수 있으며, 그것은 여러분이 사용하는 언어로 말을 할 것입니다. '랭귀지 팔'은 또한 광고판, 표지, 그리고 메뉴에 있는 쓰여진 문자도 번역할 수 있습니다. 단순하게 카메라 아이콘을 눌러서 여러분의 스마트폰 카메라를 그 표지로 향하게 하세요. 그러면 여러분은 화면에서 번역된 것을 볼 것입니다. 여러분은 와이파이나 데이터 연결을 가지고 100개 이상의 언어를 번역할 수 있고, 연결이 되어 있지 않을 때는 50개의 언어를 번역할 수 있습니다.

'익스커전' 앱은 다음달부터 모든 스마트폰 앱스토어에서 다운로드가 가능할 것입니다. 무료의 라이트 버전과 불과 12.99밖에 하지 않는 프리미엄 버전, 이렇게 두 가지의 버전이 있을 것입니다. 라이트 버전은 처음에 말씀드린 두 개의 특징만을 포함할 것입니다.

어휘 talk 연설, 강연 traveling 여행 hassle-free 성가신 일이 없는, 귀찮지 않은 all-in-one 일체형의 companion 동반자, 동행 newest 최신의 tourist 관광객 adventurer 모험가 excursion 여행, 나들이 multifunctional 다기능의 designed 만들어진, 고안된 packed with ~로 가득한 useful 유용한 explore 탐험하다 on one's own 스스로 rather than ~보다는 rely on ~에 의존하다 feature 특징 first of all 무엇보다 먼저 book 예약하다 flight 비행편 enter 입력하다 desired 희망하는 destination 목적지 available 구매가능한, 이용 가능한 color-coded 색으로 구분된 straight 곧바로 itinerary 여행 일정 built-in 내장된 tourist attraction 관광 명소 discover 발견하다 sample 시음하다 be equipped with ~를 갖추고 있다 convenient 편리한 establishment 시설 necessity 필수품 filter 거르다 input 입력하다 preference 선호 budget 예산 turn A into B: A를 B로 바꾸다 translator 번역기 translate 번역하다 automatically 자동으로 local 현지의, 현지인 billboard 광고판 sign 표지 point 향하다, 가리키다 offline 연결이 되어 있지 않은, 오프라인의 starting ~부터 cost 비용이 들다 contain 포함하다

34 주제/목적

What is the subject of the presentation?

(a) a social media site for travelers
(b) a travel-themed convention
(c) a useful gadget for travelers
(d) a travel-related resource

발표의 주제는 무엇인가?

(a) 여행가들을 위한 소셜 미디어 사이트
(b) 여행을 주제로 하는 대화
(c) 여행가들을 위한 유용한 장치
(d) 여행 관련 수단

정답 (d)

해설 담화의 초반부에 관광객과 모험가들을 위한 최신 어플리케이션을 소개한다는 말과 함께 '익스커전' 앱을 언급하였고, 이 앱은 여행객들을 위해 만들어진 다기능의 어플리케이션이라고(Let me introduce our newest application for tourists and adventurers like you: the Excursions app. The Excursions app is a multifunctional smartphone application designed for travelers) 언급하였습니다. 따라서 이 담화의 주제는 여행과 관련된 어플리케이션이며, 이를 수단, 방편으로 언급한 (d)가 정답입니다.

어휘 **subject** 주제 **themed** ~을 주제로 하는 **gadget** 장치, 도구 **related** ~와 관련된 **resource** 수단, 방편

❌ 오답 피하기

Application은 스마트폰에 설치되는 응용 프로그램(소프트웨어)에 해당하기 때문에, 도구 또는 장치를 나타내는 gadget이라고 볼 수 없으므로 (c)는 오답입니다.

35 세부 정보

What does the Air Calendar help its users with?

(a) researching flights
(b) choosing destinations
(c) reviewing airlines
(d) booking hotels

'에어 캘린더'는 사용자들에게 무엇을 도와주는가?

(a) 비행편을 조사하는 것
(b) 목적지를 선택하는 것
(c) 항공사의 후기를 작성하는 것
(d) 호텔을 예약하는 것

정답 (a)

해설 질문의 키워드인 '에어 캘린더'가 언급된 부분에서 '에어 캘린더'가 여행에 가장 좋은 비행편을 찾고 예약하는 것을 도와준다(the Air Calendar helps you find and book the best flights for your trips)고 언급하였습니다. 이를 통해 비행편을 검색하는 것을 도와준다는 것을 알 수 있으므로 (a)가 정답입니다.

어휘 **research** 조사하다 **review** 사용 후기를 작성하다, 검토하다 **airline** 항공사

패러프레이징

find and book the best flights → researching flights

How can the Travel Atlas help users plan their itinerary?

(a) by rating nearby accommodations
(b) by displaying points of interest
(c) by listing local guides
(d) by showing transportation options

'트래블 아틀라스'는 사용자의 여행 일정을 어떻게 계획할 수 있는가?

(a) 근처에 있는 숙박시설의 점수를 매김으로써
(b) 흥미로운 지점을 보여줌으로써
(c) 현지 가이드를 나열함으로써
(d) 교통 수단 선택권을 보여줌으로써

정답 (b)

해설 질문의 키워드인 '트래블 아틀라스'가 언급된 부분에서, 여행 일정을 계획할 수 있다고 언급한 뒤에 그 방법에 대해 내장된 지도로 그 지역에서 이용 가능한 관광명소를 쉽게 찾을 수 있다고(With the built-in map, you can easily find all available tourist attractions in that area) 언급하였습니다. 따라서 이용 가능한 관광명소를 흥미로운 지점(points of interest)으로 언급한 (b)가 정답입니다.

어휘 rate 점수를 매기다, 등급을 매기다 nearby 근처에 있는 accommodation 숙박시설 display 보여주다 point 지점 of interest 흥미로운 list 나열하다 transportation 교통 수단, 이송

패러프레이징

tourist attractions → points of interest

What can users do with the Basics feature?

(a) They can contact other travelers.
(b) They can buy necessities online.
(c) They can find useful facilities.
(d) They can make hotel reservations.

'베이직' 특징으로 사용자들은 무엇을 할 수 있는가?

(a) 다른 여행객들과 연락을 할 수 있다.
(b) 필수품들을 온라인으로 구매할 수 있다.
(c) 유용한 시설을 찾을 수 있다.
(d) 호텔 예약을 할 수 있다.

정답 (c)

해설 질문의 키워드인 '베이직' 특징이 언급된 부분에서 이 특징이 식사, 휴식, 필수품 구매를 위한 가장 편리한 시설을 찾는 것을 도와준다고(This helps you find the most convenient establishments for eating, resting, or buying necessities wherever you are) 언급하였습니다. 따라서 유용한 시설을 찾는 것을 언급한 (c)가 정답입니다.

어휘 contact 연락하다 facility 시설 make a reservation 예약하다

convenient establishments → useful facilities

❌ 오답 피하기

단서가 되는 문장에서 필수품 구매(buying necessities)가 언급되었지만 온라인으로 구매한다는 언급은 없었고, 필수품 구매를 위한 시설을 찾는 것을 도와준다는 언급이었으므로 (b)는 오답입니다.

---

38 세부 정보

How can the product help users communicate while traveling?

(a) by translating speech
(b) by suggesting useful phrases
(c) by listing vocabulary
(d) by correcting pronunciation

그 제품은 사용자가 여행 중에 의사소통하는 것을 어떻게 도와줄 수 있는가?

(a) 말을 번역함으로써
(b) 유용한 구문을 제안함으로써
(c) 어휘를 나열함으로써
(d) 발음을 교정함으로써

정답 (a)

해설 질문의 키워드인 communicate와 관련된 부분으로 '랭귀지 팔'(Language Pal)이 언급되었습니다. 여기서 이 어플리케이션이 사용자의 말을 듣고 현지 언어로 자동으로 번역하고, 현지인은 그 앱에 말함으로써 대답도 할 수 있고, 그 말을 사용자의 언어로 말해줄 것(The app will automatically translate what you say into the local language. The locals can respond by talking to the app, and it will speak for them in your language)이라고 언급하였습니다. 이는 말을 번역하는 것을 의미하므로 (a)가 정답입니다.

어휘 product 제품 communicate 의사 소통하다 speech 말, 발화 suggest 제안하다 phrase 구문, 표현 list 나열하다 vocabulary 어휘, 단어 correct 교정하다 pronunciation 발음

How, most likely, can one get the product with all its features?

(a) by giving it a positive review
(b) by buying the premium version
(c) by downloading it immediately
(d) by joining the mailing list

모든 특징들을 가지고 있는 제품을 어떻게 얻을 수 있을 것인가?

(a) 긍정적인 후기를 제공함으로써
(b) 프리미엄 버전을 구매함으로써
(c) 즉시 그것을 다운로드 함으로써
(d) 메일링 리스트에 가입함으로써

정답 (b)

해설 질문에서 언급된 '모든 특징을 가지고 있는 제품'(the product with all its features)은 화자가 언급하지 않았지만, 담화의 마지막 부분에서 해당 어플리케이션을 다운로드 받을 때 2가지 버전이 있을 것이며, 하나는 무료의 라이트 버전, 다른 하나는 12.99달러로 구매할 수 있는 프리미엄 버전이 있다고 언급하였습니다. 그리고 라이트 버전은 첫 두 개의 특징만 포함할 것이라고(There will be two versions—a free lite version and a premium version which costs only $12.99. The lite version will only contain the first two features) 언급한 것으로 미루어 보아 프리미엄 버전은 유료인 대신 모든 특징을 갖추고 있음을 유추할 수 있습니다. 따라서 정답은 (b)입니다.

어휘 **positive** 긍정적인 **immediately** 즉시 **join** 가입하다 **mailing list** (정기적 광고물을 받아보는) 수신자 명단

PART 3

M: Jenna! What brings you here to the mall?

F: Oh, hi, Tyler! I just came from ABC Appliances. I was shopping for an air conditioner. **40** I recently moved into my new house, but it doesn't have a cooling system yet.

M: Congratulations on your new house! Hmm, air conditioning really is important nowadays because of the summer heat.

F: Yeah, but I can't choose between a window air conditioner and a central air conditioner.

M: I've experienced using both of them. Maybe we can discuss the pros and cons of each option.

F: Great idea! Let's start with central air conditioning. What's your take on it?

M: Okay. Central air conditioning cools your entire house from a single location where the condenser is installed. It sends cool air through vents in different areas of your home. So obviously, one advantage is that it will cool the different rooms in your house at once.

F: Right. **41** Another advantage is that it won't bother my sleep because it only produces a slight hum. I'm a light sleeper, so I'd really like the room to be silent while I sleep.

M: But there are downsides as well. For one, installing a central air conditioner is very complicated. You need to hire a professional to install it.

F: So I've heard. **42** Another thing is that its condenser will take up too much space in my

남: 제나! 여기 쇼핑몰에 어떤 일이야?

여: 아, 안녕 타일러! 나는 막 ABC 가전에서 나왔어. 나는 에어컨을 구매하려던 중이었어. 나는 최근에 새로운 집으로 이사를 했는데, 냉각 시스템이 아직 없더라.

남: 새 집으로 이사한 것 축하해! 흠, 에어컨은 여름 열기 때문에 요즘 정말 중요해.

여: 응, 하지만 난 창문형 에어컨과 중앙 에어컨 사이에서 고를 수가 없어.

남: 나는 둘 다 사용해본 경험이 있어. 어쩌면 우리가 각각의 선택에 장점과 단점을 논의할 수 있을지 몰라.

여: 좋은 생각이야! 중앙 에어컨부터 시작하자. 너는 어떻게 생각해?

남: 좋아. 중앙 에어컨은 너의 집 전체를 냉각기가 설치되어 있는 한 군데의 위치에서 냉각시켜. 그것은 너의 집안의 다른 곳에 있는 통풍구를 통해 시원한 공기를 보내줘. 그래서 확실히, 한 가지 장점은 한번에 너의 집에 있는 각기 다른 방들을 시원하게 해줄 것이라는 거야.

여: 맞아. 또다른 장점은 그게 약간의 웅웅거리는 소리만 발생해서 나의 수면을 방해하지 않을 것이라는 거야. 나는 잠이 잘 깨는 사람이라서, 나는 잠을 자는 동안 방이 정말 조용하기를 원해.

남: 하지만 단점도 있어. 첫째, 중앙 에어컨을 설치하는 것은 아주 복잡해. 너는 그걸 설치할 전문가를 고용해야 해.

여: 나도 그렇게 들었어. 또 다른 점은 그 냉각기가 내 뒷마당에서 너무 많은 공간을 차지할 것이라

backyard. My backyard isn't that big, and the unit will take up space that I could otherwise use for gardening. **42** That's why I'm hesitant about central air conditioning.

M: Is that so? Then that's something you really need to consider, Jenna.

F: Yeah. What about window air conditioners?

M: Well, a window air conditioner is installed in a window or other opening in the wall. It only cools the room where it's installed, so in a way, that's an advantage. You can target specific rooms instead of cooling the whole house.

F: Exactly. If I only need to cool my bedroom, then I can just install the air conditioner there.

M: That's right. **43** Another advantage is that it's very affordable. You can buy a high-quality window air conditioner for as little as $150.

F: Yeah, **43** I noticed the prices at the appliance store. Window air conditioners are pretty cheap, but the prices vary based on the power of the unit.

M: Don't forget that a window air conditioner will block the window it's installed in. Because the unit is mounted in the window, **44** you won't be able to enjoy the view or open that window anymore for, say, fresh air. That's a drawback worth considering.

F: Oh, I happen to love the view of the lake from my bedroom!

M: Another downside of a window air conditioner is the security risk. It can be removed from outside your house, and that can be an entry point for burglars if you don't properly secure the unit.

는 거야. 내 뒷마당은 그렇게 크지 않고, 그 한 기기가 정원 가꾸기로 사용할 수도 있는 공간을 차지할 거야. 그게 내가 중앙 에어컨을 주저하는 이유야.

남: 그래? 그러면 그게 정말 네가 생각해봐야 하는 거네, 제나.

여: 응. 창문형 에어컨은 어때?

남: 음, 창문형 에어컨은 창문이나 벽에 있는 다른 열린 공간에 설치되는 거야. 그건 그게 설치된 방만 시원하게 해주지. 그래서 어떤 면에서는 그게 한 가지 장점이야. 너는 집 전체를 냉각하는 대신에 특정 방만 대상으로 정할 수 있어.

여: 맞아. 내가 만약 침실만 시원하게 해야 한다면, 난 거기에 에어컨을 설치하기만 할 수 있어.

남: 맞아. 또 다른 장점은 그게 정말 가격이 적당하다는 거야. 넌 고급 창문형 에어컨을 150달러 정도의 적은 금액으로 살 수 있어.

여: 응, 나는 가전제품 매장에서 그 가격을 확인했어. 창문형 에어컨은 꽤 저렴하지만, 그 가격이 기기의 동력에 따라 다양하더라.

남: 창문형 에어컨이 설치되는 창문은 막힐 것이라는 것을 잊지 마. 그 기기가 창문에 놓이기 때문에, 너는 풍경을 즐기거나 예를 들어, 신선한 공기를 위해 창문을 더 이상 열 수 없을 거야. 그게 고려할만한 단점이지.

여: 아, 난 내 침실에서 보이는 호수 경관을 정말 좋아하게 되었는데.

남: 창문형 에어컨의 또다른 단점은 보안 위험성이야. 그건 너의 집 바깥에서 제거될 수 있고, 네가 제대로 그 기기를 고정시키지 않으면 절도범들에게는 침입 지점이 될 수 있어.

F: That sounds a bit scary. Well, thanks for helping me identify the pros and cons of both air conditioning units, Tyler.

M: No problem, Jenna. So, which one are you going to choose for your house?

F: Well, 45 I realized that I don't really need air conditioning in my entire house. I only really need it in my bedroom. Besides, I still have another window in my bedroom with a view of the lake.

여: 그거 조금 무섭네. 음, 두 가지 에어컨의 장점과 단점을 확인하는 것을 도와줘서 고마워, 타일러.

남: 별일아냐, 제나. 그래서, 너는 너의 집을 위해 무엇을 고를 거니?

여: 음, 난 집 전체를 냉각시키는 것을 필요하지 않다고 깨달았어. 난 단지 내 침실에서만 그게 필요해. 게다가, 난 그래도 호수 경관이 보이는 다른 창문이 침실에 있어.

어휘 appliance 가전 제품 air conditioner 에어컨, 냉방 기기 cooling system 냉각 시스템, 냉방 장치 central 중앙의 discuss 논의하다 pros and cons 장점과 단점 what's your take on it? 너는 어떻게 생각해? cool 냉각시키다, 시원하게 하다 entire 전체의 condenser 냉각기 install 설치하다 through ~을 통해서 vent 통풍구 obviously 명백히, 확실히 advantage 장점 at once 한번에 bother 귀찮게 하다, 방해하다 produce 발생시키다 slight 약간의 hum 웅웅거리는 소리 light sleeper 잠을 잘 깨는 사람 silent 조용한 downside 단점 complicated 복잡한 hire 고용하다 professional 전문가 take up 차지하다 space 공간 backyard 뒷마당 unit 구성 단위의 하나, 한 개의 기기 otherwise 그렇지 않으면, 그 외에 gardening 정원 가꾸기 be hesitant about ~에 대해 머뭇거리다, 주저하다 in a way 어떤 면에서는 target 대상으로 하다 specific 특정한 instead of ~하는 것 대신에 affordable 가격이 적당한, 알맞은 high-quality 고급의 as little as ~만큼 적은 pretty 꽤 vary 다양하다 based on ~에 따라 power 동력 block 막다, 차단하다 mount 놓다, 고정시키다 view 경관, 전망 drawback 단점 worth + -ing: ~할만한 가치가 있는 happen to 동사원형: ~하게 되었다, 우연히 ~하다 lake 호수 security 보안 risk 위험성 remove 제거하다 entry point 침입 지점, 입구 burglar 절도범 properly 적절히, 제대로 secure 고정시키다 a bit 약간 scary 무서운 identify 확인하다

---

40 세부 정보

Why was Jenna shopping for an air conditioner?

(a) because she is in a new home
(b) because hers is broken
(c) because she needs it for work
(d) because hers is old

제나가 에어컨을 사려는 이유는 무엇인가?

(a) 그녀가 새 집에 있기 때문에
(b) 그녀의 것이 고장 났기 때문에
(c) 그녀는 직장에 그것이 필요하기 때문에
(d) 그녀의 것이 오래되었기 때문에

정답 (a)

해설 대화 초반부에 제나가 최근에 새로운 집으로 이사를 했고 냉각 시스템이 아직 없다고(I recently moved into my new house, but it doesn't have a cooling system yet) 언급하였으므로, 새로운 집에 이사해서 에어컨을 사려는 것을 알 수 있습니다. 따라서 (a)가 정답입니다.

어휘 broken 고장 난

How could a central air conditioner help Jenna sleep?

(a) by reducing the humidity
(b) by adjusting the air flow
(c) by keeping the house quiet
(d) by making a soothing sound

중앙 에어컨은 제나가 자는 것에 어떻게 도움이 될 수 있는가?

(a) 습도를 줄임으로써
(b) 기류를 조정함으로써
(c) 집을 조용하게 유지함으로써
(d) 진정시키는 소리를 냄으로써

정답 (c)

해설 중앙 에어컨의 장점에 대해 언급하면서 제나가 잠을 자는 것과 관련하여 중앙 에어컨은 약간의 소리만 발생시키는데 제나는 잠을 잘 깨는 사람이라 잠을 자는 동안 조용하길 원한다고(Another advantage is that it won't bother my sleep because it only produces a slight hum. I'm a light sleeper, so I'd really like the room to be silent while I sleep) 언급하였습니다. 이는 제나는 조용해야 잠을 잘 수 있다는 것을 알 수 있으므로 (c)가 정답입니다.

어휘 reduce 줄이다, 감소시키다 humidity 습도 adjust 조정하다 air flow 기류, 공기 흐름 quiet 조용한 soothing 진정시키는, 달래는

⊗ 오답 피하기

제나는 에어컨이 약간의 웅웅거리는 소리가 나는 것이 잠드는데 도움이 된다고 하지 않았고, 집이 조용한 것을 원한다고 언급했습니다. 또한 hum(웅웅거리는 소리)을 a soothing sound로 보기 어려우므로 (d)는 오답입니다.

Why is Jenna hesitant to install a condenser in her backyard?

(a) It would damage her flowers.
(b) It would cost too much money.
(c) It would take a long time.
(d) It would take up too much room.

제나가 뒷마당에 냉각기를 설치하는 것을 주저하는 이유는 무엇인가?

(a) 그것이 그녀의 꽃을 상하게 할 것이다.
(b) 그것이 너무 많은 비용이 들 것이다.
(c) 그것이 너무 오랜 시간이 걸릴 것이다.
(d) 그것이 너무 많은 공간을 차지할 것이다.

정답 (d)

해설 질문의 키워드인 냉각기(condenser)가 언급된 부분에서 제나는 뒷마당에 냉각기가 너무 많은 공간을 차지할 것(Another thing is that its condenser will take up too much space in my backyard)이라고 언급하였고, 그것이 자신이 중앙 에어컨에 대해 주저하는 이유라고 언급하였습니다. 따라서 정답은 (d)입니다.

어휘 be hesitant to 동사원형: ~하는 것을 주저하다 damage 상하게 하다, 손상시키다 cost 비용이 들다 room 공간

43 세부 정보

What did Jenna notice about the window air conditioners at the appliance store?

(a) that they use minimal electricity
(b) that they are affordable
(c) that they need little maintenance
(d) that they are powerful

제나가 가전제품 매장에서 창문형 에어컨에 대해 알아차린 것은 무엇인가?

(a) 그것들이 최소한의 전기를 사용한다는 것
(b) 그것들이 가격이 적당하다는 것
(c) 그것들이 관리가 거의 필요하지 않다는 것
(d) 그것들이 강력하다는 것

정답 (b)

해설 창문형 에어컨에 대해 논의하면서 제나가 가전제품 매장을 언급하기 전에 타일러가 창문형 에어컨의 장점으로 가격이 매우 적당하다고(Another advantage is that it's very affordable) 언급하였습니다. 그 후에 제나가 가전 제품 매장에서 가격을 알아차렸다고 하면서 창문형 에어컨이 꽤 저렴하다고(I noticed the prices at the appliance store. Window air conditioners are pretty cheap) 말하였으므로 정답은 (b)입니다.

어휘 minimal 최소한의 electricity 전기 little 거의 없는, 거의 아닌 maintenance 관리 powerful 강력한

44 세부 정보

How might a window air conditioner prevent Jenna from enjoying her bedroom?

(a) by restricting the sunlight
(b) by leaking water
(c) by reducing the temperature
(d) by blocking the view

창문형 에어컨은 제나가 그녀의 침실에서 즐기는 것을 어떻게 막을 것인가?

(a) 햇빛을 제한함으로써
(b) 누수시킴으로써
(c) 온도를 낮춤으로써
(d) 경관을 막음으로써

정답 (d)

해설 창문형 에어컨의 단점을 언급하는 부분에서 타일러는 제나에게 창문형 에어컨이 경관을 즐기거나 창문을 여는 것을 못하게 될 수 있다고(you won't be able to enjoy the view or open that window anymore for, say, fresh air) 말하였고, 그에 대해 제나는 침실에서 호수 경관을 보는 것을 좋아한다고 말하였습니다. 이를 통해 창문형 에어컨이 제나가 침실에서 경관을 보는 것을 막을 것이라는 것을 알 수 있으므로 (d)가 정답입니다.

어휘 restrict 제한하다 leak 새게 하다 temperature 온도

What will Jenna probably do after the conversation?

(a) install air conditioning throughout her house
(b) request an estimate for installation
(c) install air-conditioning in her bedroom
(d) ask for a discount on installation

제나는 대화 후에 무엇을 할 것 같은 가?

(a) 그녀의 집 전체에 에어컨을 설치한다
(b) 설치 견적을 요청한다
(c) 그녀의 침실에 에어컨을 설치한다
(d) 설치에 대한 할인을 요청한다

정답 (c)

해설 대화 마지막 부분에서 타일러가 무엇을 고를 것인지 묻는 말에 제나는 집 전체에 에어컨이 필요하지 않고 침실에만 필요하다(I realized that I don't really need air conditioning in my entire house. I only really need it in my bedroom.)고 언급하였습니다. 이를 통해 제나가 중앙 에어컨이 아닌 침실에 창문형 에어컨을 설치할 것임을 알 수 있으므로 (c)가 정답입니다.

어휘 throughout 전체에 request 요청하다 estimate 견적 installation 설치 ask for ~을 요청하다 discount 할인

Welcome back to another episode of *Full Wellness*. Today, we're going to talk about meditation. Meditation is a mental exercise in which you focus on a specific object, thought, or activity to calm your mind. We've all heard about the benefits of meditation for reducing stress and improving productivity. **46** Still, some of our listeners don't meditate because they're not sure how to get started. So today, I'll teach you how to meditate.

There are many different types of meditation techniques, but I personally recommend something that's called "mindfulness meditation." **47** The whole idea is to focus on what you're feeling and observing in the present moment. I'll tell you how to do it.

The first step is to find a place to meditate. You can meditate anywhere, but it has to be very quiet and free of interruptions. Some good places for meditation are your room, the local library, or a garden—anywhere that's peaceful and where you can sit comfortably.

The second step is to set a time limit for your session. While experienced meditators usually meditate for 20 minutes, you should start with short sessions of 5 to 10 minutes. Set a gentle-sounding alarm to alert you when your time is up. **48** If you don't set an alarm, your attention will be diverted to thoughts like, "Has it been five minutes yet?" or "Should I stop now?" and you won't be able to meditate effectively.

The third step is **49** to do some stretches. When meditating, you'll need to sit in one spot for a certain length of time, and that can strain some parts of your body. Thus, it's important to loosen up your body

<풀 웰니스>의 또다른 에피소드로 돌아오신 것을 환영합니다. 오늘 저희는 명상에 대해 이야기를 해 볼 것입니다. 명상은 특정 사물, 생각, 또는 활동에 집중하여 여러분의 마음을 진정시키는 정신 운동 입니다. 우리는 모두 스트레스 감소와 생산성 향상 에 대한 명상의 이로운 점에 대해 모두 들어보았습 니다. 아직도 저희 청취자들 중 몇몇 분들은 어떻게 시작해야 하는지 몰라서 명상을 하지 않고 계십니 다. 그래서 오늘, 제가 명상을 하는 방법을 가르쳐 드릴 것입니다.

명상 기술에는 서로 다른 많은 종류가 있지만, 저는 개인적으로 "마음챙김 명상"이라고 불리는 것을 추 천합니다. 전체적인 목적은 현재 시점에 당신이 느 끼고 관찰하는 것에 집중하는 것입니다. 제가 그것 을 하는 방법을 말씀드리겠습니다.

첫 번째 단계는 명상을 할 장소를 찾는 것입니다. 여러분은 어느 곳에서나 명상을 할 수 있습니다. 하 지만 매우 조용하고 방해가 없는 곳이어야 합니다. 명상을 위한 좋은 장소는 여러분의 방, 지역 도서 관, 또는 정원과 같은 평화로운 곳이며, 여러분이 편안하게 앉을 수 있는 곳입니다.

두 번째 단계는 여러분의 명상 시간에 대한 시간 제 한을 설정하는 것입니다. 경험이 많은 명상가들은 보통 20분 동안 명상을 하는 반면, 여러분은 5분에 서 10분 정도의 짧은 시간으로 시작하셔야 합니다. 명상 시간이 끝났을 때 당신에게 알려주기 위한 조 용한 소리의 알람을 설정하세요. 알람을 설정하지 않는다면, 여러분의 주의는 "5분이 아직 되지 않았 나?" 또는 "지금 멈춰야 하나?"와 같은 생각들로 관 심이 돌려지게 될 것이며, 여러분은 효과적으로 명 상을 할 수 없을 것입니다.

세 번째 단계는 약간의 스트레칭을 하는 것입니다. 명상을 할 때, 여러분은 한 자리에 일정 길이의 시 간동안 앉아 있어야 할 것입니다. 그리고 그것은 여 러분의 신체의 일부분에 무리를 줄 수 있습니다.

before you begin. Just a few minutes of lightly stretching your neck, legs, and lower back can help prepare your body.

The fourth step is to check that you have proper posture. Experienced meditators sit on the floor with their legs crossed in front of them. However, this can be uncomfortable for beginners. Sitting in a chair works fine too, but your feet should be flat on the floor. **50** Keep your head facing forward, your upper body straight but relaxed, and your hands resting on your legs. You don't have to close your eyes, but do so if you want to.

51 The fifth step is to focus all your attention on your breathing. Notice how the air feels as it enters your nose, how the air fills up your lungs, and the rising and falling of your chest. Do the "4-7-8 breathing technique." Breathe in for four seconds, hold it for seven seconds, and exhale for eight seconds. If you can't hold your breath that long, just focus on making each exhale twice as long as each inhale. This focused attention is the thing that will relax and clear your mind.

The final step is to finish your session gently. It's not a good idea to abruptly end your meditation and resume your regular activities because it removes the calm energy that you've created in your mind. **52** Once your time is up, gently open your eyes or lift your gaze. Pause for a moment to sit and notice how you feel before you move on to your next activity.

Those are our steps for meditating. Remember, it will be hard to maintain your focus at first, but it gets easier if you meditate every day.

그러므로, 시작하기 전에 여러분의 몸을 풀어주는 것이 중요합니다. 목, 다리, 그리고 허리를 단 몇 분 동안 가볍게 스트레칭하는 것은 여러분의 신체를 준비시키는 것에 도움이 될 수 있습니다.

네 번째 단계는 제대로 된 자세를 하고 있는지 확인하는 것입니다. 경험이 많은 명상가들은 다리를 그들 앞에 교차시킨 채로 바닥에 앉습니다. 하지만, 이것은 초보자들에게는 불편할 수 있습니다. 의자에 앉는 것도 효과가 좋습니다. 하지만 여러분의 발은 바닥에 평평하게 놓여야 합니다. 여러분의 머리는 정면을 바라보게 하고, 상체를 곧게 세우되 편안하게 유지시키며, 손은 다리 위에 올려두세요. 눈을 감을 필요는 없습니다만, 원하신다면 감으시기 바랍니다.

다섯 번째 단계는 여러분의 모든 주의를 호흡에 집중하는 것입니다. 여러분의 코에 공기가 어떻게 들어오는지, 그 공기가 폐를 어떻게 채우는지, 그리고 가슴이 올랐다가 내려가는 것을 느끼시기 바랍니다. "4-7-8 호흡법"을 하세요. 4초간 숨을 들이마시고, 7초 동안 멈춘 다음, 8초 동안 내뱉습니다. 그렇게 오래 호흡을 멈출 수 없으시다면, 각각의 내뱉는 호흡을 들이쉬는 호흡의 두 배의 길이로 만드는 것에 집중하세요. 이렇게 주의를 집중하는 것은 여러분의 정신을 휴식을 취하게 하고 깨끗하게 하는 것입니다.

마지막 단계는 부드럽게 명상 시간을 마치는 것입니다. 갑자기 명상을 끝내고 일상 활동을 이어가는 것은 좋은 생각이 아닙니다. 왜냐하면 그것은 여러분의 정신에 만들어 놓은 차분한 에너지를 없애기 때문입니다. 일단 여러분의 시간이 다 되면, 부드럽게 눈을 뜨거나 시선을 들어올리세요. 잠시 앉아서 멈추고 다음 활동으로 옮기기 전에 기분이 어떠한지 주목하시기 바랍니다.

그것들이 명상을 위한 단계입니다. 기억하세요. 처음에는 집중력을 유지하는 것이 어려울 것이지만, 매일 명상하신다면 점점 더 쉬워질 것입니다.

어휘 meditation 명사 mental 정신의 focus on ~에 집중하다 specific 특정한 object 사물, 물체 thought 생각 activity 활동 calm 진정시키다, 차분하게 하다 benefit 이로운 점, 혜택 reduce 줄이다, 감소시키다 improve 향상시키다 productivity 생산성 get started 시작하다 technique 기술, 방법 personally 개인적으로 mindfulness 마음챙김 idea (~을 하는) 목적 observe 관찰하다 present moment 현재 시점 interruption 방해 peaceful 평화로운 comfortably 편안하게 session 특정 활동의 기간, 시간 experienced 경험이 많은, 숙련된 meditator 명상가 gentle 부드러운 alert 알리다, 주의를 환기시키다 set an alarm 알람을 설정하다 attention 주의, 관심 divert 주의를 딴 데로 돌리다, 관심을 돌리다 effectively 효과적으로 spot 자리, 장소 length 길이 strain 무리를 주다, 부담을 주다 loosen up 풀어주다 proper 제대로 된, 적당한 posture 자세 uncomfortable 불편한 work fine 잘 되다, 효과가 좋다 flat 평평한 forward 앞으로, 전방으로 upper body 상체 straight 곧게 relaxed 편안한 rest on ~에 놓다 don't have to 동사원형: ~할 필요는 없다 breathing 호흡 notice 주목하다, 알아차리다 fill up 채우다 lung 폐 chest 가슴, 흉곽 exhale 호흡을 내뱉다 twice as long as 2배만큼 길게 inhale 들이마시다, 들숨 relax 휴식을 취하게 하다 clear 깨끗하게 하다 gently 부드럽게 abruptly 갑자기, 느닷없이, 불쑥 resume (중단되었던 것을) 계속하다, 재개하다 remove 없애다 lift 들어올리다 gaze 시선, 눈길 pause 잠시 멈추다 maintain 유지하다 at first 처음에

---

46 주제/목적

What is the speaker mainly talking about?

(a) advice on teaching meditation
(b) tips on group meditation
(c) advice on starting meditation
(d) tips on advanced meditation

화자는 무엇에 관해 주로 이야기 하고 있는가?

(a) 명상을 가르치는 것에 대한 조언
(b) 단체 명상에 대한 팁
(c) 명상을 시작하는 것에 대한 조언
(d) 고급 명상에 대한 팁

정답 (c)

해설 담화의 첫 부분에서 화자는 일부 청취자들이 어떻게 시작하는지 몰라서 명상을 하지 않는다고 언급하며, 그래서 명상을 하는 방법을 가르쳐 주겠다고(Still, some of our listeners don't meditate because they're not sure how to get started. So today, I'll teach you how to meditate.) 언급하였으므로 명상을 시작하는 것에 대한 조언에 대해 이야기 하고 있음을 알 수 있습니다. 따라서 정답은 (c)입니다.

어휘 advice on ~에 대한 조언 tip on ~에 대한 팁 advanced 고급의, 상급의

According to the speaker, what is the whole idea of mindfulness meditation?

(a) to imagine oneself in different places
(b) to focus on what will happen in the distant future
(c) to learn how to ignore daily annoyances
(d) to pay attention to a specific moment in time

화자에 따르면, 마음챙김 명상의 전체적인 목적은 무엇인가?

(a) 다른 장소에 있는 자신을 상상하는 것
(b) 먼 미래에 무슨 일이 일어날지에 대해 집중하는 것
(c) 일상의 짜증을 무시하는 법을 배우는 것
(d) 특정 시점에 집중하는 것

정답 (d)

해설 질문의 키워드인 the whole idea of mindfulness meditation은 "마음챙김 명상"에 대해 언급하는 부분에서 현재 시점에 느끼고 관찰하는 것에 집중하는 것이라고(The whole idea is to focus on what you're feeling and observing in the present moment) 언급되었습니다. 이를 통해 현재 시점에 집중하는 것이 전체적인 목적임을 알 수 있으므로 (d)가 정답입니다.

어휘 imagine 상상하다 distant 먼 ignore 무시하다 annoyance 짜증, 골칫거리 pay attention to ~에 집중하다 specific 특정한

패러프레이징

focus on ~ in the present moment → pay attention to a specific moment in time

According to the speaker, why is it necessary to set an alarm for the session?

(a) to signal the start of the session
(b) to avoid being distracted
(c) to keep the same session length
(d) to prevent sleepiness

화자에 따르면, 명상 시간에 알람을 설정하는 것이 필요한 이유는 무엇인가?

(a) 명상 시간의 시작을 신호로 알리기 위해
(b) 주의가 분산되는 것을 피하기 위해
(c) 동일한 길이의 명상 시간을 유지하기 위해
(d) 졸음을 예방하기 위해

정답 (b)

해설 질문의 키워드인 set an alarm에 대해 언급된 부분에서, 화자는 알람을 설정하지 않으면 "아직 5분이 되지 않았나?" 또는 "지금 멈춰야 하나" 와 같은 생각으로 주의가 돌려질 것이며, 효과적인 명상을 할 수 없을 것이라고(If you don't set an alarm, your attention will be diverted to thoughts like, "Has it been five minutes yet?" or "Should I stop now?" and you won't be able to meditate effectively) 말하였습니다. 이를 통해 알람을 설정하는 것은 주의가 분산되는 것을 막기 위해서임을 알 수 있으므로 (b)가 정답입니다.

어휘 necessary 필요한 signal 신호로 알리다, 표시하다 distracted 주의가 분산된 length 길이 prevent 예방하다, 막다 sleepiness 졸음, 졸림

패러프레이징

be diverted → being distracted

---

49 추론

Why, most likely, should one stretch before meditating?	명상을 하기 전에 스트레칭을 해야 하는 이유는 무엇일 것 같은가?
(a) to avoid feeling uncomfortable (b) to assist breathing techniques (c) to allow more frequent practice (d) to focus the mind for the session	(a) 불편함을 느끼는 것을 피하기 위해서 (b) 호흡법에 도움을 주기 위해서 (c) 명상을 더 자주 하도록 하기 위해서 (d) 명상 시간 동안 정신을 집중하기 위해서

정답 (a)

해설 질문의 키워드인 스트레칭에 대해 화자는 명상을 할 때 한 자리에 일정 시간 동안 앉아 있어야 하는데, 그러면 신체의 일부분에 무리를 줄 수 있으므로 명상을 시작하기 전에 몸을 풀어주는 것이 중요하다고(When meditating, you'll need to sit in one spot for a certain length of time, and that can strain some parts of your body. Thus, it's important to loosen up your body before you begin) 언급하였습니다. 이를 통해 명상 전에 스트레칭을 하는 것은 신체의 일부분에 무리를 주지 않기 위해서임을 알 수 있으므로 이를 패러프레이징한 (a)가 정답입니다.

어휘 assist 도움을 주다, 지원하다 frequent 빈번한 practice 실천

패러프레이징

strain some parts of your body → feeling uncomfortable

What advice does the speaker give about the proper posture when meditating?

(a) Sit with legs crossed.
(b) Keep the arms folded.
(c) Sit on the floor.
(d) Keep the back upright

명상할 때 제대로 된 자세에 대해 화자가 제공하는 조언은 무엇인가?

(a) 다리를 교차한 채로 앉는다.
(b) 팔을 접을 채로 유지시킨다.
(c) 바닥에 앉는다.
(d) 등을 곧게 세워서 유지한다.

정답 (d)

해설 질문의 키워드인 제대로 된 자세(proper posture)에 대해 화자는 머리를 전방을 향하게 유지하고 상체를 곧게 하되 편안하게 유지시키고, 팔은 다리 위에 놓아 두라고(Keep your head facing forward, your upper body straight but relaxed, and your hands resting on your legs) 언급하였습니다. 이를 통해 등을 곧게 편 자세를 유지하라는 것이 화자의 조언임을 알 수 있으므로 정답은 (d)입니다.

어휘 arm 팔 folded 접혀진, 접은 back 등 upright 곧은, 꼿꼿한

> 패러프레이징
>
> keep ~ your upper body straight → keep the back upright

According to the speaker, what should one do during meditation?

(a) focus on staying still
(b) visualize a pleasant location
(c) concentrate on breath control
(d) recall a happy memory

화자에 따르면, 명상 중에 무엇을 해야 하는가?

(a) 가만히 있는 것에 집중한다
(b) 즐거운 장소를 마음 속에 그린다
(c) 호흡 제어에 집중한다
(d) 행복한 기억을 회상한다

정답 (c)

해설 화자가 말한 명상의 다섯 번째 단계는 호흡에 집중하는 것(The fifth step is to focus all your attention on your breathing)이었습니다. 따라서 이를 호흡 제어로 표현한 (c)가 정답입니다.

어휘 stay still 가만히 있다 visualize 마음 속에 그리다 pleasant 즐거운, 유쾌한 concentrate on ~에 집중하다 control 제어, 통제 recall 회상하다

> 패러프레이징
>
> focus all your attention on your breathing → concentrate on breath control

52 세부 정보

How should one end a meditation session?

(a) by noticing the benefits
(b) by doing some gentle movement
(c) by resting with eyes closed
(d) by thinking about the day ahead

명상 시간은 어떻게 끝내야 하는가?

(a) 얻은 것에 주목함으로써
(b) 부드러운 움직임을 함으로써
(c) 눈을 감은 채로 휴식함으로써
(d) 다음 날에 대해 생각함으로써

정답 (a)

해설 질문의 키워드인 명상을 끝내는 것에 대해 화자는 시간이 다 되면 부드럽게 눈을 뜨거나 시선을 들어올리고 잠시 앉아서 멈추고, 다음 활동으로 옮기기 전에 기분이 어떠한지에 주목하라고(Once your time is up, gently open your eyes or lift your gaze. Pause for a moment to sit and notice how you feel before you move on to your next activity) 언급하였습니다. 이를 통해 명상을 한 후의 자신의 지금 기분이 어떠한지 확인하는 것으로 명상을 끝내라는 것을 알 수 있으므로 (a)가 정답입니다. (a)에서 언급한 benefits는 명상을 통해 자신이 얻은 것을 의미합니다.

어휘 notice 주목하다 benefit 얻은 것, 혜택, 이득 gentle 부드러운 movement 움직임, 운동 rest 휴식을 취하다 the day ahead 다음 날

❌ 오답 피하기

화자가 눈을 부드럽게 뜨라고 하였으나 이것은 명상을 끝내기 위한 행위로서 스트레칭과 같은 부드러운 움직임을 말하는 것 아니라 갑자기 눈을 뜨지 말고 천천히 뜨라는 것을 의미한 것입니다. 이는 부드러운 움직임을 통한 명상 종료를 나타내는 것이 아니므로 (b)는 오답입니다.

PART 1

SERENA WILLIAMS

Serena Williams is an American professional athlete recognized as one of the best tennis players of all time. **53** She is best known for winning the most major tournaments, known as Grand Slams, of any female tennis player of her generation.

Serena Jameka Williams was born on September 26, 1981, in Saginaw, Michigan. At a young age, Williams was inspired by her older sister Venus, who had already started learning tennis. Williams showed incredible **58** capability and started training with her father when she was only three.

Williams entered her first tournament at the age of four. Over the next five years, she won forty-six of her forty-nine matches and was ranked first in the ten-and-under division. **54** Her parents, wanting the sisters to improve their skills further, moved the family to West Palm Beach, Florida, where they attended a tennis academy.

Following in her sister's footsteps, Williams became a professional tennis player at age fourteen. Within a year, she was the ninety-ninth best player in the world rankings, a great feat for her age. **55** Although many expected that Venus would be the first of the sisters to win a Grand Slam, it was Serena who won the first major tournament title, the 1999 US Open, putting her on the road to her eventual number one ranking. Williams would go on to face her sister in a number of Grand Slams as she became a regular participant in the major tournament finals. Over the course of her astounding career, Williams won more than twenty Grand Slams.

세레나 윌리엄스

세레나 윌리엄스는 역대 최고의 테니스 선수 중 한 명으로 인정받는 미국의 프로 운동선수이다. 그녀는 그녀의 세대의 여성 테니스 선수 중에서 그랜드 슬램으로 알려진 대부분의 메이저 대회를 우승한 것으로 가장 잘 알려져 있다.

세레나 자메카 윌리엄스는 1981년 9월 26일, 미시간주의 새기노에서 태어났다. 어린 시절에, 윌리엄스는 그녀의 언니인 비너스에게 영향을 받았는데, 그녀는 이미 테니스를 배우고 있었다. 윌리엄스는 엄청난 능력을 보여주었고 그녀가 3살 밖에 되지 않았을 때 그녀의 아버지와 훈련을 시작하였다.

윌리엄스는 4세의 나이로 첫 토너먼트에 참가하였다. 그 후 5년이 넘도록 그녀는 49 게임 중 46승을 하였고 10세 이하 유소년부에서 1위를 차지하였다. 자신의 자녀들이 그 이상의 실력으로 향상하기를 원했던 그녀의 부모님은 플로리다주의 웨스트팜비치로 이사하였으며, 그곳에서 그들은 테니스 아카데미에 다녔다.

그녀의 언니의 발자국을 따라 윌리엄스는 14세 때 프로 테니스 선수가 되었다. 그 해에 그녀는 세계 랭킹 99위가 되었으며, 그녀의 나이에는 엄청난 위업이었다. 비록 많은 사람들이 그 자매에서 언니인 비너스가 그랜드 슬램을 달성하기를 기대하였으나, 첫 메이저 대회 타이틀인 1999년 US 오픈에서 우승한 것은 바로 세레나였고, 그것이 그녀를 최종 1위의 길로 들어서게 하였다. 윌리엄스는 메이저 대회의 결승전에 자주 참가하게 되면서 수많은 그랜드 슬램에서 그녀의 언니와 계속해서 마주치곤 하였다. 믿기 어려운 그녀의 경력 동안, 윌리엄스는 20회 이상 그랜드 슬램을 달성하였다.

56 Williams's playing style stood out in the world of women's tennis. Where many female tennis players projected grace and agility on the court, Williams was powerful and aggressive, and opponents found her to be a daunting physical presence. The Williams sisters were also among the few African American professional tennis players and, at times, experienced discrimination for standing out in a mostly white sport.

Although Williams's forceful personality, unconventional hairstyles, and colorful on-court attire have sometimes **59** sparked controversy, she has established herself as a leading figure in the tennis world. **57** She has challenged the traditional image of the sport and inspired women around the world who might now have a different notion of how the game is supposed to be played and what its greatest players are supposed to look like.

윌리엄스이 경기 스타일은 여성 테니스 분야에서 두각을 나타내었다. 많은 여성 테니스 선수들이 경기장에서 우아함과 민첩함을 보여주는 곳에서, 윌리엄스는 강력하고 공격적이었다. 그리고 상대 선수들은 그녀를 신체적으로 위압적인 존재라고 생각했다. 윌리엄스 자매는 또한 많지 않은 아프리카계 미국인 프로 테니스 선수 중에 있던 선수였으며, 때때로 주로 백인으로 구성된 스포츠에서 두각을 나타내는 것에 대해 차별을 겪었다.

비록 윌리엄스의 단호한 성격, 독특한 머리 스타일, 그리고 색이 다채로운 경기복장이 때때로 논란을 일으켰지만, 그녀는 테니스 세계에서 주요 인물로서 자신을 확고히 하였다. 그녀는 그 스포츠의 전통적인 이미지에 도전하였고 시합이 어떻게 진행되어야 하는지 그리고 위대한 선수들이 어떤 모습으로 보여야 하는지에 대해 현재 다른 개념을 가지고 있을지도 모르는 전세계에 있는 여성들에게 영감을 주었다.

어휘 **professional** 전문적인, 프로의 **athlete** 운동 선수 **recognized** 인정 받는 **of all time** 역대 **major** (스포츠의) 메이저의, 주요한 **tournament** 토너먼트, 시합, 대회 **Grand Slam** 테니스 대회 중 4개의 메이저 대회 전체 우승 **female** 여성의 **generation** 세대 **be inspired by** ~에게 영감을 받다, ~에게 영향을 받다 **incredible** 믿을 수 없는, 엄청난 **capability** 능력 **enter** 참가하다 **match** 시합, 경기 **rank** 순위에 오르다 **division** 부, 분과 **improve** 향상시키다 **further** 그 이상으로, 더 나아가서 **footstep** 발자국, 발자취 **feat** 위업 **title** (스포츠) 타이틀, 선수권 **put one on road to** ~로 가는 길로 들어서게 하다 **eventual** 최종적인 **go on to** 동사원형: 계속해서 ~하다 **a number of** 수많은 **regular** 잦은, 주기적인 **participant** 참가자 **finals** 결승전 **astounding** 믿기 어려운, 경악스러운 **stand out** 눈의 띠다, 두각을 나타내다 **project** 보여주다, 선보이다 **grace** 우아함 **agility** 민첩성 **aggressive** 공격적인 **opponent** 상대방 **daunting** 위압적인, 벅찬 **physical** 신체적인 **presence** 존재(감) **at times** 때때로, 가끔 **discrimination** 차별 **mostly** 주로, 일반적으로 **forceful** 강력한, 단호한 **personality** 성격 **unconventional** 독특한, 관습을 따르지 않는 **attire** 복장, 의상 **spark** 촉발시키다, 유발하다 **controversy** 논란, 논쟁 **establish** 확고히 하다 **leading figure** 주요 인물 **challenge** 도전하다 **traditional** 전통적인 **notion** 개념 **be supposed to** 동사원형: ~하기로 되어 있다, ~할 예정이다 **look like** ~처럼 보이다

What is Serena Williams most famous for?

(a) being the youngest professional tennis player of all time
(b) securing more tournament victories than any of her peers
(c) having the longest professional tennis career of any player
(d) winning more tournaments in a single year than any of her peers

세레나 윌리엄스는 무엇으로 가장 유명한가?

(a) 역대 최연소 프로 테니스 선수인 것
(b) 다른 동료 선수들 보다 더 많은 대회 우승을 확보한 것
(c) 선수들 중 가장 오래 프로 테니스 경력을 가지고 있는 것
(d) 다른 동료 선수들 보다 1년 내에 더 많은 대회에서 우승한 것

정답 (b)

해설 질문의 키워드인 most famous for는 지문의 첫 문단 best known for로 표현되어 있습니다. 해당 문장에 따르면 그녀는 그녀의 세대의 여성 테니스 선수 중에서 그랜드 슬램으로 알려진 대부분의 메이저 대회를 우승한 것으로 가장 잘 알려져 있다고(She is best known for winning the most major tournaments, known as Grand Slams, of any female tennis player of her generation) 언급되어 있으므로 선택지 중에서 가장 많은 대회의 우승을 언급한 (b)가 정답입니다.

어휘 secure 확보하다, 얻다 victory 우승, 승리 peer 동료 single 하나의

패러프레이징

winning the most major tournaments → securing more tournament victories than any of her peers

---

Why did Williams's family move to Florida?

(a) to give her access to advanced tennis training
(b) to enroll her in an award-winning public school
(c) to allow her to compete against mature tennis partners
(d) to encourage her to compete in high-profile matches

윌리엄스의 가족이 플로리다로 이사한 이유는 무엇인가?

(a) 그녀가 상급 테니스 훈련에 대한 접근할 수 있도록 하기 위해
(b) 수상 경력이 있는 공립학교에 그녀를 등록시키기 위해
(c) 그녀를 성인 테니스 파트너와 겨루도록 하기 위해
(d) 세간의 이목을 끄는 시합에 참가하도록 그녀를 장려하기 위해

정답 (a)

해설 질문의 키워드인 move to Florida는 세 번째 문단에서 언급되었습니다. 해당 문장에 따르면 윌리엄스의 부모님은 그들의 딸이 그 이상의 실력으로 향상하기를 원했으며 플로리다주의 웨스트팜비치로 이사하였고, 그곳에서 그들은 테니스 아카데미에 다녔다고(Her parents, wanting the sisters to improve their skills further, moved the family to West Palm Beach, Florida, where they attended a tennis academy) 언급되어 있습니다. 따라서 더 나은 실력향상을 위해 플로리다로 이사했다는 것을 알 수 있으므로 (a)가 정답입니다.

어휘 give access to ~에 접근을 허가하다, ~에 접근하게 하다 advanced 상급의, 발전된 enroll in ~에 등록하다 award-winning 상을 수상한, 수상 경력이 있는 allow + 목적어 + to부정사: (목적어)를 ~하도록 하다 compete against ~와 겨루다 mature 성인의 encourage + 목적어 + to부정사: (목적어)를 ~하도록 장려하다 high-profile 세간의 이목을 끄는

패러프레이징

improve their skills further → give her access to advanced tennis training

---

55 세부 정보

How did Williams surprise people in 1999?

(a) by tying the number one player in the world
(b) by losing to her sister in the final round of a tournament
(c) by becoming ranked number one among female players
(d) by accomplishing something before her older sister

윌리엄스는 1999년에 사람들을 어떻게 놀라게 하였는가?

(a) 세계 1위 선수와 동점을 이룸으로써
(b) 한 대회의 결승전에서 그녀의 언니에게 패배함으로써
(c) 여성 선수들 중 1위가 됨으로써
(d) 그녀의 언니보다 무엇인가를 먼저 달성함으로써

정답 (d)

해설 질문의 키워드인 1999년은 네 번째 문단에서 언급되었습니다. 해당 문장에 따르면 비록 많은 사람들이 언니인 비너스가 그랜드 슬램을 달성하기를 기대하였으나, 첫 메이저 대회 타이틀인 1999년 US 오픈에서 우승한 것은 세레나였다고(Although many expected that Venus would be the first of the sisters to win a Grand Slam, it was Serena who won the first major tournament title, the 1999 US Open) 언급하였으므로 이를 통해 언니가 우승할 것이라는 사람들의 기대와 달리 세레나가 우승하여 놀라게 했음을 알 수 있습니다. 따라서 언니보다 첫 메이저 대회에서 우승을 먼저 달성한 것이므로 (d)가 정답입니다.

어휘 tie ~와 동점을 이루다 final round 결승전 accomplish 달성하다 before ~전에, 보다 먼저

❌ 오답 피하기

1999년 US 오픈에서 우승한 것은 세레나의 첫 메이저 대회 우승이었다고 언급되어 있을 뿐 여성 선수 랭킹 1위가 되었다는 내용은 없으므로 (c)는 오답입니다.

What was most notable about Williams when she was playing matches?

(a) her graceful movement on the court
(b) her remarkable physical strength
(c) her bravery when faced with discrimination
(d) her unusual serving technique

윌리엄스가 경기를 하고 있을 때 그녀에 대해 가장 주목할만한 점은 무엇이었는가?

(a) 경기장에서 보여주는 그녀의 우아한 움직임
(b) 놀라운 그녀의 체력
(c) 차별을 마주했을 때의 용기
(d) 특이한 서브 기술

정답 (b)

해설 질문의 키워드 notable은 직접적으로 지문에 언급되어 있지 않지만, 윌리엄스가 테니스 경기 중 보여주는 특징을 언급한 다섯 번째 문단에서 관련된 내용을 찾을 수 있습니다. 해당 문장에 따르면 윌리엄스의 경기 스타일은 여성 테니스 분야에서 두각을 나타내었는데, 많은 여성 테니스 선수들이 경기장에서 우아함과 민첩함을 보여주는 반면, 윌리엄스는 강력하고 공격적이었다고(Williams's playing style stood out in the world of women's tennis. Where many female tennis players projected grace and agility on the court, Williams was powerful and aggressive) 언급되어 있습니다. 이를 통해 윌리엄스는 경기장에서 강력함 힘을 보여주는 경기를 펼쳤다는 것을 알 수 있으므로 (b)가 정답입니다.

어휘 notable 주목할 만한 graceful 우아한 movement 움직임 court 테니스 코트, 테니스 경기장 remarkable 놀라운, 놀랄 만한 physical strength 체력, 신체적인 힘 bravery 용기 faced with ~을 마주한 unusual 특이한 technique 기술, 방법

패러프레이징

powerful and aggressive → physical strength

Based on the final paragraph, why, most likely, was Williams influential in the world of women's tennis?

(a) She introduced the game to a new generation.
(b) She opened the door for other Black women to play.
(c) She challenged the traditions of the sport.
(d) She advocated for gender equality among players.

마지막 문단에 따르면, 윌리엄스가 여자 테니스 세계에서 영향력을 가졌던 이유는 무엇이었을 것 같은가?

(a) 그녀는 신세대에 테니스를 소개하였다.
(b) 그녀는 다른 흑인 여성들이 테니스를 할 수 있도록 문을 열어주었다.
(c) 그녀는 테니스의 전통에 도전하였다.
(d) 그녀는 선수들 사이에서 성평등을 지지하였다.

정답 (c)

해설 질문의 키워드인 influential은 마지막 문단에서 inspired로 표현되었습니다. 해당 문장에서 윌리엄스는 테니스의 전통적인 이미지에 도전하였고 시합이 어떻게 진행되어야 하는지 그리고 위대한 선수들이 어떤 모습으로 보여야 하는지에 대해 현재 다른 개념을 가지고 있을지도 모르는 전세계에 있는 여성들에게 영감을 주었다고(She has challenged the traditional image of the sport and inspired women around the world who might now have a different notion of how the game is supposed to be played and what its greatest players are supposed to look like) 언급되어 있습니다. 이를 통해 윌리엄스가 테니스의 전통에 도전했다는 것을 알 수 있으므로 정답은 (c)입니다.

어휘 influential 영향을 주는, 영향력을 가지는 introduce 소개하다, 도입하다 advocate 지지하다, 옹호하다 gender equality 성평등

⊗ 오답 피하기

윌리엄스는 테니스 시합이 어떻게 진행되어야 하는지 그리고 위대한 선수들이 어떤 모습으로 보여야 하는지에 대해 전세계에 있는 여성들에게 영감을 주었다고 하여 흑인 여성에만 국한하지 않았으므로 (b)는 오답입니다.

In the context of the passage, capability means _____.

(a) trust
(b) agreement
(c) support
(d) potential

해당 단락의 문맥에서 capability가 의미하는 것은?

(a) 신뢰
(b) 동의
(c) 지원
(d) 잠재력

정답 (d)

해설 해당 문장에서 capability는 윌리엄스가 보여준 '능력'을 나타냅니다. 문맥상 그녀의 언니가 먼저 테니스를 배우기 시작하였고, 그 뒤에 세레나 윌리엄스가 훈련을 시작했다는 문장이 있으므로, 그녀가 보여준 능력은 '잠재력'으로 볼 수 있습니다. 따라서 선택지 중에서 '잠재력'이라는 의미를 나타내는 (d) potential이 정답입니다.

In the context of the passage, sparked means _____.

(a) brought on
(b) flashed
(c) thought about
(d) traced

해당 단락의 문맥에서 sparked가 의미하는 것은?

(a) 초래했다
(b) 번쩍였다
(c) ~에 대해 생각했다
(d) 추적했다

정답 (a)

해설 해당 문장에서 sparked는 윌리엄스의 단호한 성격, 특이한 머리 스타일, 색이 다채로운 경기복장을 주어로 하는 문장의 동사로 쓰였습니다. sparked의 목적어는 '논란'이라는 의미의 명사 controversy이므로 이러한 문맥에 미루어 볼 때 윌리엄스의 단호한 성격, 특이한 머리 스타일, 색이 다채로운 경기복장이 논란을 일으켰다는 의미를 나타내고 있음을 알 수 있습니다. 따라서 선택지 중에서 '초래하다', '야기하다'라는 의미를 나타내는 bring on의 과거형 (a) brought on이 정답입니다.

PART 2

THE CHALLENGE OF NEW YEAR'S RESOLUTIONS

60 At the beginning of every year, many Americans make resolutions that they fail to follow through on. Despite these **65** continual failures, people still resolve to quit their old vices or start healthy new practices whenever the new year rolls around. **60** There are several reasons why people struggle to change their habits, and those reasons are connected to how the human brain works.

First, it is hard to keep New Year's resolutions because they go against the habits we have already made a part of our daily routine. The connections between neurons in our brain are responsible for our habits and, **61** while these connections are not necessarily permanent, they do become stronger the more often we repeat a habit. Until we incorporate resolutions into our daily routines, they may be difficult to stick to. For example, if going to the gym is not already a habit for someone, it will be much easier for them to give up soon after starting.

Second, the act of creating resolutions on its own can be beneficial, even if they are not acted upon. **62** Simply thinking about making a positive change in one's life, such as losing weight or exercising more, gives one a sense of accomplishment. Thus, the actual act of doing these things is not necessary for people to feel better about themselves.

This phenomenon can be explained by what scientists call "affective forecasting," through which people predict that what they feel in the present will also be what they feel in the future. People feel good when they create New Year's resolutions, so they assume that they will also feel good when

새해 결심의 도전

매년 초에, 많은 미국인들은 완수하지 못하는 결심을 한다. 이러한 지속적인 실패에도 불구하고, 사람들은 새해가 돌아올 때마다 여전히 그들의 오래된 악덕 행위를 그만두려고 결심하거나 건전한 새로운 실천을 시작하려고 결심한다. 사람들이 그들의 습관을 바꾸려고 애쓰는 것에는 몇 가지 이유가 있는데, 그 이유들은 인간의 두뇌가 어떻게 작동하는지에 연관되어 있다.

첫째, 새해 결심은 지키기가 어렵다. 왜냐하면 그 결심은 우리가 이미 일상 생활에 일부분으로 만들어 놓은 습관에 반대되는 것이기 때문이다. 우리의 뇌에 있는 신경 세포들 사이의 연결은 우리의 습관을 담당하고 있으며, 이러한 연결이 필수적으로 영구적이지 않은 반면에 우리가 한 습관을 더욱 더 자주 반복할 수록 그 연결은 점점 더 강해진다. 우리가 결심한 것을 일상 생활에 통합할 때까지, 그 결심은 지키기 어려울지도 모른다. 예를 들어, 누군가에게 체육관에 가는 것이 아직 습관이 아니라면, 시작한 후 얼마 지나지 않아 포기하는 것이 그들에게는 훨씬 더 쉬울 것이다.

둘째, 결심을 하는 행위는 그 결심이 실행에 옮겨지지 않는다 해도 그 자체로 이익이 될 수 있다. 누군가의 인생에서 긍정적인 변화를 만들 수 있는 것, 예를 들어 체중을 줄이는 것이나 운동을 더 많이 하는 것과 같은 것에 대해 단순히 생각하는 것이 성취감을 준다. 그러므로, 이러한 것들의 실제 실천은 사람들이 자신에 대해 더 나은 기분을 느끼기 위해서 반드시 필요한 것은 아니다.

이러한 현상은 과학자들이 "정서적 예측"이라고 부르는 것으로 설명될 수 있는데, 그것을 통해 사람들이 현재의 기분 상태가 미래의 그들의 기분 상태가 될 것이라는 것을 예측하는 것이다. 사람들은 새해 결심을 할 때 기분이 좋아서, 그들이 마침내 그들의 계획을 실행에 옮길 때에도 기분이 좋을 것이라고

they finally put their plans into action. However, 63 when the time comes to 66 fulfill the resolution—and the act does not give the positive feeling they envisioned—many people will either procrastinate or get discouraged and quit.

By knowing how the brain works, people can achieve resolutions more easily. 64 One of the best ways to form new habits and to feel good about doing them is to focus on only one goal at a time and, if the goal is a large one, to break it down into smaller, easier-to-achieve tasks.

생각한다. 하지만, 그들의 결심을 이행하는 시간이 되었을 때-그리고 그 행위가 그들이 마음 속에 그렸던 긍정적인 기분을 주지 않을 때, 많은 사람들은 미루거나 좌절을 하고 그만둘 것이다.

두뇌가 어떻게 작동하는지 아는 것으로, 사람들은 더 쉽게 결심한 것을 달성할 수 있다. 새로운 습관을 형성하고 그 습관을 하는 것에 대해 기분이 좋아지기 위한 가장 좋은 방법 중 하나는 한번에 하나의 목표에만 집중하는 것이다. 그리고 그 목표가 규모가 크다면, 그것을 더 작고, 달성하기 더 쉬운 일로 쪼개는 것이다.

어휘 challenge 도전 resolution 결심, 다짐 fail to 동사원형: ~하지 못하다 follow through on ~을 완수하다, 끝까지 따라가다 despite ~에도 불구하고 continual 계속되는, 반복되는 failure 실패 resolve 결심하다 vice 악덕 행위, 비행 healthy 건전한, 정상적인 practice 행위, 실천 roll around 돌아오다 struggle to 동사원형: ~하려고 애쓰다 be connected to ~에 연관되어 있다 go against ~에 반대하다 daily routine 일상 생활, 매일 반복하는 일 neuron 신경세포 be responsible for ~을 담당하다, ~을 책임지다 not necessarily 반드시 ~ 은 아닌 permanent 영구적인 the 비교급 ~, the 비교급 ~: ~할수록 더 ~하다 repeat 반복하다 incorporate A into B: A를 B로 통합시키다, 합치다 stick to ~을 지키다, 고수하다 give up 포기하다 act 행위, 실천 on one's own 혼자서, 그 자체로 beneficial 유익한, 이익이 되는 act upon ~에 따라 실행에 옮기다, ~에 따라 행동하다 a sense of accomplishment 성취감 phenomenon 현상 affective forecasting 정서적 예측 predict 예측하다 in the present 현재 assume (그럴 것이라고) 생각하다, 추측하다 put into action 실행에 옮기다 fulfill 이행하다, 수행하다 envision 마음 속에 그리다 either A or B: A 또는 B 둘 중 하나 procrastinate 미루다 get discouraged 좌절하다, 의욕을 잃다 quit 그만두다 form 형성하다 focus on ~에 집중하다 goal 목표 at a time 한번에 break down into ~로 쪼개다, ~로 부수다 achieve 달성하다 task 일

60 주제/목적

What is the article all about?

(a) how to make a fresh start each year
(b) why people fail to make resolutions
(c) when it is time to quit unhealthy habits
(d) what makes resolutions difficult to keep

이 기사문은 무엇에 관한 글인가?

(a) 매년 새로운 시작을 하는 방법
(b) 사람들이 결심을 못하는 이유
(c) 불건전한 습관을 끊어야 하는 시기
(d) 결심한 것을 지키기 어렵게 만드는 것

정답 (d)

해설 첫 번째 문장에서 매년 새해에 많은 미국인들이 완수하지 못하는 결심을 한다고(At the beginning of every year, many Americans make resolutions that they fail to follow through on) 언급하고, 첫 문단의 마지막 문장에 사람들이 습관을 바꾸려고 애쓰는 이유가 있고, 그 이유가 인간의 두뇌의 작동 방식과 연관되어 있다고(There are several reasons why people struggle to change their habits, and those reasons are connected to how the human brain works) 언급하여 기사문 전체가 결심한 것을 지키기 어렵게 만드는 것이 무엇인지 알아보는 것에 관한 것임을 알 수 있습니다. 따라서 (d)가 정답입니다.

어휘 fresh start 새 출발 unhealthy 불건전한

❌ 오답 피하기

많은 사람들이 매년 새해에 결심을 한다는 것을 보아 결심을 하는 행위 자체를 하지 못하는 것이 아님을 알 수 있습니다. 따라서 (b)는 오답입니다.

---

61 추론

Based on the text why, most likely, is it hard to work new habits into a daily schedule?

(a) The brain needs time to adjust to changes.
(b) People do not have time for additions to their routine.
(c) The existing connections between neurons cannot be broken.
(d) People are naturally inclined to give up when challenged.

지문에 따르면, 일상의 일정에 새로운 습관을 넣는 것이 어려운 이유는 무엇일 것 같은가?

(a) 뇌가 변화에 적응할 시간이 필요하다.
(b) 사람들이 일상 활동에 추가되는 일을 위한 시간이 없다.
(c) 신경 세포들 사이의 기존 연결이 깨질 수 있다.
(d) 사람들은 도전을 받으면 포기하는 자연스러운 경향이 있다.

정답 (a)

해설 질문의 키워드인 hard to work new habits into a daily schedule은 두 번째 문단에 Until we incorporate resolutions into our daily routines, they many be difficult to stick to 문장을 패러프레이징 한 것입니다. 이 문장 앞에 우리의 뇌에 있는 신경 세포들 사이의 연결은 우리의 습관을 담당하고 있으며, 이러한 연결이 필수적으로 영구적이지 않은 반면에 우리가 한 습관을 더욱 더 자주 반복할 수록 그 연결은 점점 더 강해진다고(The connections between neurons in our brain are responsible for our habits and, while these connections are not necessarily permanent, they do become stronger the more often we repeat a habit) 언급한 문장을 통해서 새로운 습관을 형성하기 위해서는 자주 반복해서 신경 세포의 연결을 강하게 만들어야 한다는 것을 알 수 있습니다. 즉 반복을 한다는 것은 두뇌에 새로운 습관에 적응할 시간을 주는 것과 같은 의미이므로 정답은 (a)입니다.

어휘 work A into B: A를 B에 포함시키다, A를 B에 넣다 adjust to ~에 적응하다 addition 추가되는 것 existing 기존의 naturally 자연스럽게 be inclined to 동사원형: ~하는 경향이 있다 challenged 도전을 받은

패러프레이징

work new habits into a daily schedule → incorporate resolutions into our daily routines

According to the article, how do people boost their mood when making resolutions?

(a) by reminding themselves to think positively
(b) by thinking about their past accomplishments
(c) by imagining the benefits of transformation
(d) by planning many enjoyable activities

기사에 따르면, 사람들은 결심할 때 어떻게 기분을 나아지게 만드는가?

(a) 자신에 대해 긍정적으로 생각하도록 상기시킴으로써
(b) 과거에 성취했던 것을 생각함으로써
(c) 변화가 가져다 주는 이익을 상상함으로써
(d) 많은 즐거운 활동을 계획함으로써

정답 (c)

해설 질문의 키워드인 boost their mood는 세 번째 문단에서 언급된 for people feel better about themselves와 연결됩니다. 해당 문단에서 사람들이 기분을 좋아지게 만드는 방법으로 언급된 것은 인생에서 긍정적인 변화를 만들 수 있는 것, 예를 들어 체중을 줄이는 것이나 운동을 더 많이 하는 것과 같은 것에 대해 단순히 생각하는 것이 성취감을 준다는 것(Simply thinking about making a positive change in one's life, such as losing weight or exercising more, gives one a sense of accomplishment) 입니다. 이를 통해 인생에서 긍정적인 변화에 대해 생각해보는 것만으로 기분이 좋아진다는 것을 알 수 있으므로 정답은 (c)입니다.

어휘 boost one's mood ~의 기분을 나아지게 하다 remind 상기시키다 past 과거의 benefit 혜택, 이득 transformation 변화 enjoyable 즐거운 activity 활동

패러프레이징

simply thinking about making a positive change → imagining the benefits of transformation

According to the fourth paragraph, why do most people abandon their New Year's resolutions?

(a) because they are unsure of how to take action
(b) because they do not feel as good as expected
(c) because they never felt positive about the plan
(d) because they did not expect to encounter obstacles

네 번째 문단에 따르면, 대부분의 사람들이 새해 결심을 포기하는 이유는 무엇인가?

(a) 실천하는 방법을 모르기 때문에
(b) 기대했던 것만큼 기분이 좋지 않기 때문에
(c) 그 계획에 대해 긍정적으로 느껴본 적이 없기 때문에
(d) 장애물을 마주칠 것이라고 예상하지 않았기 때문에

정답 (b)

해설 질문의 키워드 abandon their New Year's resolution은 네 번째 문단 마지막 문장에 언급된 quit이라는 단어와 연결됩니다. 해당 문장에서는 사람들은 결심을 이행하는 시간이 되었을 때-그리고 그 행위가 그들이 마음 속에 그렸던 긍정적인 기분을 주지 않을 때, 많은 사람들은 미루거나 좌절을 하고 그만둘 것이라고(when the time comes to fulfill the resolution—and the act does not give the positive feeling they envisioned—many people will either procrastinate or get discouraged and quit) 언급되어 있습니다. 이를 통해 사람들이 결심한 대로 실행에 옮길 때 생각했던 기분이 들지 않으면 포기한다는 것을 알 수 있으므로 정답은 (b)입니다.

어휘 abandon 그만두다, 버리다 be unsure of ~을 모르다, ~에 대해 확신하지 못하다 take action 실천하다 encounter 마주치다, 만나다 obstacle 장애물

패러프레이징

the act does not give the positive feeling the envisioned → they do not feel as good as expected

---

64 세부 정보

What can people do to ensure that their resolutions are successful?

(a) try not to make too many changes at once
(b) complete the most complicated tasks first
(c) avoid rushing through the smaller steps
(d) share plans with as many people as possible

사람들은 그들이 결심한 것이 반드시 성공적이게 하기 위해서 무엇을 할 수 있는가?

(a) 한번에 너무 많은 것을 바꾸지 않도록 노력한다
(b) 가장 복잡한 일을 먼저 완료한다
(c) 더 작은 움직임을 통해 급히 움직이는 것을 피한다
(d) 가능한 많은 사람들과 계획을 공유한다

정답 (a)

해설 문맥상 결심은 새로운 습관을 만드는 것이기에 질문의 키워드인 resolutions are successful은 마지막 문단에서 언급된 form new habits and feel good about doing them을 패러프레이징한 것입니다. 해당 문장에서 새로운 습관을 형성하고 그 습관을 하는 것에 대해 기분이 좋아지기 위한 가장 좋은 방법 중 하나는 한번에 하나의 목표에만 집중하는 것이라고(One of the best ways to form new habits and to feel good about doing them is to focus on only one goal at a time) 언급되어 있으므로 이를 통해 한번에 하나의 목표에만 집중하는 것으로 새해 결심을 성공적으로 유지할 수 있음을 알 수 있습니다. 따라서 정답은 (a)입니다.

어휘 ensure 반드시 ~이게 하다, 보장하다 make a change 변화시키다 at once 한번에 complete 완료하다 complicated 복잡한 rush 급히 움직이다 step (목표 달성을 위한) 움직임, 조치 share 공유하다 as ~ as possible 가능한 한

패러프레이징

• form new habits and feel good about doing them → resolutions are successful
• focus on only one goal at a time → not to make too many changes at once

마지막 문단에서 if the goal is a large one, to break it down into smaller, easier-to-achieve tasks라는 문장으로 목표의 크기가 크다면 달성하기 쉬운 것으로 작게 나눠서 하라고 언급되어 있습니다. 이것은 한번에 하나의 목표를 차례대로 달성하기 위한 조치일 뿐 급히 움직이는 것을 피하기 위한 것은 아니므로 (c)는 오답입니다.

---

65 동의어

In the context of the passage, continual means _____ .

(a) quiet
(b) frequent
(c) tempting
(d) lengthy

해당 단락의 문맥에서 continual이 의미하는 것은?

(a) 조용한
(b) 빈번한
(c) 솔깃한, 유혹적인
(d) 길이가 긴

정답 (b)

해설 해당 문장에서 continual은 '실패'라는 의미의 명사 failures를 수식하고 있고, 이 실패는 앞 문장에서 언급한 새해의 결심을 완수하지 못하는 것을 의미합니다. 즉, 사람들이 새해가 될 때마다 결심을 하고 그것을 완수하지 못하는 것을 반복적으로 한다는 것을 의미하기 위해 continual을 쓴 것이므로 continual은 '반복적인', '계속되는'이라는 의미임을 알 수 있습니다. 반복은 곧 실행 횟수가 빈번한 것이므로 정답은 (b)입니다.

---

66 동의어

In the context of the passage, fulfill means _____ .

(a) release
(b) line up
(c) prevent
(d) carry out

해당 단락의 문맥에서 fulfill이 의미하는 것은?

(a) 내보내다
(b) 줄을 서다
(c) 예방하다
(d) 수행하다

정답 (d)

해설 해당 문장에서 fulfill은 '결심'이라는 the resolution을 목적어로 가지고 있는 동사이므로 문맥상 '실행에 옮기다', '이행하다'라는 의미를 나타냅니다. 따라서 선택지 중에서 '수행하다'라는 의미를 나타내는 (d)가 정답입니다.

PART 3

ONLINE DISINHIBITION

67 Online disinhibition is a psychological phenomenon in which people who communicate online feel less restrained and express themselves more freely than they would in real-life interactions. Thus, people may act completely different when interacting with others online. The term was first used in 2004 by psychology professor John Suler when he published the article, "The Online Disinhibition Effect."

This phenomenon can manifest in one of two ways: benign disinhibition or toxic disinhibition. In benign disinhibition, online interactions can have positive effects on the people involved. For example, **68** some people are able to freely express themselves on the Internet without feeling embarrassed or anxious. People who are shy or who belong to marginalized groups can easily find others with similar interests, develop friendships, and feel safe.

On the other hand, when the disinhibition is of the toxic kind, online interactions tend to have negative effects on the people involved. Toxic disinhibition occurs when people act cruelly online, using **72** foul language or harsh insults that can be hurtful to those who are on the receiving end.

There are several factors that influence online disinhibition. **69** One of these is the feeling of anonymity. When people believe that they can separate their actions on the Internet from their real-life identity, they are more confident about opening up. People feel like they can say anything online because they think that those actions will have no effect on their real lives.

온라인 탈억제

온라인 탈억제는 온라인으로 의사소통하는 사람들이 억제된 감정을 덜 느끼고 실제 생활의 상호교류에서 표현하는 것보다 더 자유롭게 그들 자신을 표현하는 심리적 현상이다. 그러므로, 사람들은 온라인에서 다른 사람들과 교류할 때 완전히 다르게 행동할 지도 모른다. 이 용어는 심리학 교수 존 슐러가 2004년 "온라인 탈억제 효과"라는 기사를 기고했을 때 처음 사용되었다.

이 현상은 양호한 탈억제 또는 중독성의 탈억제라는 두 가지 방식 중 하나로 나타난다. 양호한 탈억제에서 온라인 상호교류는 관여되어 있는 사람들에게 긍정적인 효과를 미칠 수 있다. 예를 들어, 몇몇 사람들은 쑥스러움이나 불안감을 느끼지 않고 인터넷에 자신을 자유롭게 표현할 수 있다. 부끄러워 하거나 소외된 단체에 속한 사람들은 비슷한 관심사를 가진 사람들을 쉽게 찾을 수 있고, 우정을 키우고, 안도감을 느낄 수 있다.

다른 한편으로는, 탈억제가 중독성의 유형일 때, 온라인 교류는 관여되어 있는 사람들에게 부정적인 효과를 미치는 경향이 있다. 중독성의 탈억제는 사람들이 듣는 입장에 있는 사람들의 마음을 상하게 할 수 있는 천박한 말이나 듣기 싫은 욕설을 사용하면서, 온라인에서 잔인하게 행동할 때 발생한다.

온라인 탈억제에 영향을 주는 요인에는 몇 가지가 있다. 그것들 중 하나는 익명성이라고 느끼는 것이다. 사람들은 실생활 속의 자신의 신원으로부터 인터넷에서의 행동을 분리시킬 수 있다고 생각할 때 마음을 터놓는 것에 대해 더 자신감을 가진다. 사람들은 온라인에서 뭐든지 말할 수 있다고 생각하는데, 그것은 그들이 그러한 행동이 자신의 실생활에 아무런 영향을 끼치지 않을 것이라고 생각하기 때문이다.

Online interactions that do not happen in real time also affect online disinhibition. **70** Unlike in real-time communication, if someone knows that what they are posting will not be seen by the recipient right away, they might worry less about being unkind and decide to send **73** inconsiderate messages. However, in some cases, delayed communication might also give the sender an opportunity to compose messages with more care.

Finally, it is impossible to see other people's facial expressions or hear their tone of voice online. **71** This lack of nonverbal cues that would otherwise be present in face-to-face interactions can cause a person to forget that they are still talking to a real human with real emotions.

실시간으로 발생하지 않는 온라인 상호교류는 또한 온라인 탈억제에 영향을 준다. 실시간 의사소통과는 달리, 만약 누군가 그들이 게시하는 것이 수신자에 의해 곧바로 보여지지 않을 것이라는 것을 안다면, 그들은 불친절하게 구는 것에 대해 신경을 덜 쓰고 사려 깊지 못한 메시지를 보내기로 결정할지도 모른다. 하지만, 몇몇 경우에, 지연된 의사소통은 또한 발신자에게 더 많은 배려를 가지고 작성할 기회를 줄 수도 있다.

마지막으로, 온라인에서는 다른 사람의 표정을 보거나 목소리의 어조를 들을 수 없다. 그렇지 않고 직접 마주하는 상호교류에서는 존재하는 이러한 비언어적 신호의 결핍은 한 사람으로 하여금 여전히 그들이 실제 감정을 지닌 사람에게 말을 하고 있다는 것을 잊어버리게 할 수도 있다.

어휘 disinhibition 탈억제 psychological 심리적인 phenomenon 현상 communicate 의사 소통하다 restrained 억제된, 억압된 express 표현하다 freely 자유롭게 real-life 실생활, 현실 interaction 상호교류 term 용어 psychology 심리학 publish 출간하다, 발간하다 manifest 나타내다, 분명하게 보이다 benign 양호한, 양성의 toxic 중독성의, 독성의, 유독한 have effects on ~에 영향을 미치다 involved 관여되어 있는 embarrassed 쑥스러운, 어색한 anxious 불안한 shy 부끄러운 belong to ~에 속하다 marginalized 소외된 interest 관심사 feel safe 안도감을 느끼다 occur 발생하다 cruelly 잔인하게, 잔혹하게 foul 천박한, 상스러운 harsh 듣기 싫은, 귀에 거슬리는 insult 모욕, 욕설 hurtful 마음을 상하게 하는 those who ~하는 사람들 on the receiving end 듣는 입장에 있는, 당하는 입장에 있는 factor 요인 influence 영향을 주다 anonymity 익명성 separate 분리하다 identity 신원, 신분 confident 자신감 있는 open up 마음을 터놓다 in real time 실시간으로 post 게시하다 recipient 수신인 right away 곧바로, 즉시 worry 신경쓰다, 염려하다 inconsiderate 사려 깊지 못한 delayed 지연된 sender 발신자 opportunity 기회 compose 작성하다 care 배려 facial expression 표정 tone 어조 lack 결핍, 부족 nonverbal 비언어의 cue 신호 otherwise 그렇지 않으면, 달리 present 존재하는 face-to-face 직접 만나서 하는, 대면하는 cause + 목적어 + to부정사: (목적어가) ~하도록 초래하다

67 주제/목적

What is the article mainly about?

(a) the change of personality a person undergoes when online
(b) the benefits of limiting internet screen time
(c) the important considerations of online dating
(d) the origin of a psychological internet phenomenon

이 기사문은 주로 무엇에 관한 글인가?

(a) 한 사람이 온라인에 있을 때 겪는 성격의 변화
(b) 인터넷 스크린 시간 제한의 이점
(c) 온라인 데이팅의 중요한 고려 사항
(d) 심리적 인터넷 현상의 기원

정답 (a)

해설 첫 문장에서 온라인 탈억제는 온라인으로 의사소통하는 사람들이 억제된 감정을 덜 느끼고 실제 생활의 상호교류에서 표현하는 것보다 더 자유롭게 그들 자신을 표현하는 심리적 현상이라고(Online disinhibition is a psychological phenomenon in which people who communicate online feel less restrained and express themselves more freely than they would in real-life interactions) 언급하였으므로 온라인에서 의사 소통할 때 심리적인 상태가 달라지는 것에 대해 이야기하고 있음을 알 수 있습니다. 따라서 정답은 (a)입니다.

어휘 personality 성격 undergo 겪다 benefit 이점, 혜택 limit 제한하다 screen time 전자기기의 화면 켜짐 시간, 사용 시간 consideration 고려 사항 origin 기원, 유래

패러프레이징

people who communicate online feel less restrained and express themselves more freely than they would in real-life interactions → the change of personality ~ when online

Based on the second paragraph, why do some people find it easier to communicate online?

(a) They can express themselves without feeling guilty.
(b) They can befriend others with shared concerns.
(c) They can be more supportive of strangers.
(d) They can avoid interacting with certain groups.

두 번째 문단에 따르면, 몇몇 사람들이 온라인으로 의사 소통하는 것을 더 쉽다고 느끼는 이유는 무엇인가?

(a) 죄책감 없이 그들 자신을 표현할 수 있다.
(b) 공통 관심사를 가지고 있는 다른 사람과 친구가 될 수 있다.
(c) 낯선 사람들에게 도움을 더 많이 줄 수 있다.
(d) 특정 단체와 교류를 하는 것을 피할 수 있다.

정답 (b)

해설 질문의 키워드 some people find it easier to communicate online은 두 번째 문단에 있는 문장 some people are able to freely express themselves on the Internet without feeling embarrassed or anxious을 패러프레이징한 것입니다. 정답의 단서를 찾기 위해 다음 문장을 보면, 부끄러워 하거나 소외된 단체에 속한 사람들은 비슷한 관심사를 가진 사람들을 쉽게 찾을 수 있고, 우정을 키우고, 안도감을 느낄 수 있다고(People who are shy or who belong to marginalized groups can easily find others with similar interests, develop friendships, and feel safe) 하는 문장에서 공통 관심사를 가진 사람들이 친구가 될 수 있다는 것을 알 수 있으므로 정답은 (b)입니다.

어휘 express 표현하다 guilty 죄책감 befriend 친구가 되어주다, ~와 친구가 되다 shared 공유된, 공통의 concern 관심사 supportive 지원하는, 도와주는 stranger 낯선 사람, 이방인 interact with ~와 상호 교류하다 certain 특정한

패러프레이징

- some people are able to freely express themselves on the Internet without feeling embarrassed or anxious
  → some people find it easier to communicate online
- others with similar interest, develop friendships → befriend others with shared concerns

---

69 세부 정보

According to the fourth paragraph, why are some people able to separate their online behavior from their real-life identity?

(a) because their complete freedom is guaranteed
(b) because their actions have no lasting effects on anyone
(c) because their personal data can be concealed
(d) because their posts will not be seen by their family

네 번째 문단에 따르면, 몇몇 사람들이 실생활의 신원으로부터 자신의 온라인 행동을 분리할 수 있는 이유는 무엇인가?

(a) 그들의 완전한 자유가 보장되기 때문에
(b) 그들의 행동이 누구에게도 지속적인 영향을 끼치지 않기 때문에
(c) 그들의 개인 정보가 감춰질 수 있기 때문에
(d) 그들의 게시물이 그들의 가족에게 보여지지 않을 것이기 때문에

정답 (c)

해설 질문의 키워드 separate their online behavior from their real-life identity는 네 번째 문단의 세 번째 문장 앞에 언급되어 있는데, 실생활의 신원으로부터 자신의 온라인 행동을 분리할 수 있는 원인은 그 앞 문장에서 익명성(anonymity)라고 언급되어 있습니다. 따라서 자신의 신원에 관한 정보는 인터넷에서 알 수 없기 때문이므로 정답은 (c)입니다.

어휘 behavior 행동 complete 완전한 guarantee 보장하다 lasting 지속되는 personal 개인의 conceal 감추다, 숨기다

❌ 오답 피하기

네 번째 문단 마지막 문장에는 온라인에서 무엇이든 말할 수 있다고 생각하는 사람들은 그러한 행동이 자신의 실생활에 아무런 영향을 미치지 않을 것이라고 생각하기 때문이라고 언급되어 있습니다. 그런 행동을 한 사람 자신에게 영향을 미치지 않을 것이라고 생각할 뿐 그 외에 다른 사람에게 미치는 영향에 대해서는 언급된 것이 없기 때문에 (b)는 오답입니다.

What is most likely true about people who use real-time online communication methods?

(a) They are more creative with their messages.
(b) They spend more time composing responses.
(c) They tend to be more mindful of what they say.
(d) They feel closer emotionally to the recipients.

실시간 온라인 의사 소통 방법을 사용하는 사람들에 관해 사실인 것은 무엇일 것 같은가?

(a) 메시지에 대해 좀 더 창의적이다.
(b) 답변을 작성하는 데 더 많은 시간을 보낸다.
(c) 그들이 말하는 것에 더 의식하는 경향이 있다.
(d) 수신인들에게 감정적으로 더 가깝게 느낀다.

정답 (c)

해설 질문의 키워드인 real-time online communication methods에 관해 언급된 다섯 번째 문단에서 Unlike in real-time communication라는 구문으로 실시간 의사소통의 상황과 반대되는 것을 언급하였습니다. 이 문장에서 만약 누군가 그들이 게시하는 것이 수신자에 의해 곧바로 보여지지 않을 것이라는 것을 안다면, 그들은 불친절하게 구는 것에 대해 신경을 덜 쓰고 사려 깊지 못한 메시지를 보내기로 결정할지도 모른다고(if someone knows that what they are posting will not be seen by the recipient right away, they might worry less about being unkind and decide to send inconsiderate messages) 언급하였으므로, 이와 반대되는 실시간 의사소통 방법을 사용하는 사람들은 메시지 수신자에게 신경을 더 많이 쓰고 사려 깊은 메시지를 보낼 것임을 유추할 수 있습니다. 따라서 이와 같은 의미를 나타내는 (c)가 정답입니다.

어휘 method 방법, 방식 creative 창의적인 spend + 시간 + -ing: ~하면서 시간을 보내다 response 답변, 응답 tend to 동사원형: ~하는 경향이 있다 mindful 의식하는, 유념하는 emotionally 감정적으로 recipient 수신인

How does the lack of nonverbal cues online affect people?

(a) by making them forget that they are living a real life
(b) by making it harder to interpret tone of voice
(c) by making them rely on their emotions when interacting
(d) by making it easier to disregard others' feelings

온라인에서의 비언어적 신호의 결핍은 사람들에게 어떻게 영향을 주는가?

(a) 현실의 삶을 살고 있다는 것을 잊게 만듦으로써
(b) 목소리의 어조를 이해하는 것을 더 어렵게 만듦으로써
(c) 상호 교류할 때 그들의 감정에 의존하도록 만듦으로써
(d) 다른 사람의 감정을 무시하는 것을 더 쉽게 만듦으로써

정답 (d)

해설 질문의 키워드인 the lack of nonverbal cues는 마지막 문단에서 직접 마주하는 상호교류에서는 손재하는 이러한 비언어적 신호의 결핍은 한 사람으로 하여금 여전히 그들이 실제 감정을 지닌 사람에게 말을 하고 있다는 것을 잊어버리게 초래할 수도 있다고(This lack of nonverbal cues that would otherwise be present in face-to-face interactions can cause a person to forget that they are still talking to a real human with real emotions) 설명되었습니다. 여기서 실제 감정을 가진 사람에게 말하고 있다는 것을 잊어버린다는 것은 사람의 감정을 신경 쓰지 않고 말하는 경우를 의미하므로 (d)가 정답입니다.

어휘 affect 영향을 주다 live a life 삶을 살다 interpret 이해하다 rely on ~에 의존하다 disregard 무시하다 feeling 감정, 기분

---

72 동의어

In the context of the passage, foul means _____.

(a) direct
(b) offensive
(c) strict
(d) complex

해당 단락의 문맥에서 foul이 의미하는 것은?

(a) 직접적인
(b) 모욕적인, 불쾌한
(c) 엄격한
(d) 복잡한

정답 (b)

해설 해당 문장에서 foul은 문맥상 온라인에서 잔혹하게 행동하는 사람들이 사용하는 언어(language)를 수식하는 형용사로 사용되었습니다. 그 뒤에 언급된 듣기 싫은 욕설(harsh insults)와도 유사한 의미를 나타낸다는 것을 알 수 있으므로 foul은 부정적인 의미로 사용되었습니다. 따라서 선택지 중에서 명사 language를 수식할 수 있으면서 '불쾌한'과 유사한 의미를 나타내는 형용사인 (b) offensive가 정답입니다.

---

73 동의어

In the context of the passage, inconsiderate means _____.

(a) rude
(b) forgetful
(c) instant
(d) disapproving

해당 단락의 문맥에서 inconsiderate가 의미하는 것은?

(a) 무례한
(b) 쉽게 잊혀질
(c) 즉각적인
(d) 못마땅해 하는

정답 (a)

해설 해당 문장에서 inconsiderate는 문맥상 불친절하게 구는 것에 걱정하지 않는 사람이 보내는 메시지(messages)를 수식하는 형용사로 쓰였습니다. 따라서 unkind와 유사한 의미로 사용될 수 있는 '무례한'이라는 의미를 나타내는 형용사 (a) rude가 정답입니다.

Celine Mitchell
9162 Belleview Street
Golden Valley Homes
Canyon Country, CA

Dear Ms. Mitchell:

As you are aware, we held our annual homeowners association meeting last Saturday. 74 We are writing this letter to tell you about our revised rules based on residents' suggestions and recommendations. The new guidelines are as follows:

1. The gate at the main entrance to our community will now remain closed at all times. Property owners must 79 notify security before a visitor is scheduled to arrive so that the visitor can be placed on a permanent or temporary guest list. Any visitor not listed will be denied access to the community. 75 This is to ensure the safety of all residents and to prevent any suspicious people from entering our community.

2. The association fee will be increased from $300 per month to $350 per month. This is to accommodate extra personnel for the 24/7 security measures implemented for our growing community and 76 to change our garbage collection service from once to twice a week.

3. Excessive noise coming from any residence that causes a disturbance to neighboring houses is strictly prohibited. First-time offenders will receive a written warning, while 77 a $100 fine will be given to repeat offenders.

4. 78 Residents are now required to park in their private garage or carport, unless their home is not equipped with one. In addition, on-street parking is allowed on only one side of the road. This is to prevent traffic congestion and to allow easy passage

셀린 미첼
벨뷰 스트리트 9162
골든 밸리 홈즈
캐년 컨트리, 캘리포니아주

미첼 씨께

아시다시피, 저희는 연례 주택소유주 협회 회의를 지난 토요일에 가졌습니다. 저희는 귀하에게 거주민들의 제안과 권고를 기반으로 한 수정된 규칙에 대해 말씀드리기 위해 이 편지를 쓰고 있습니다. 새로운 지침은 다음과 같습니다.

1. 저희 커뮤니티로 들어오는 주출입구에 있는 정문은 이제 항상 닫힌 상태로 유지될 것입니다. 소유주들은 방문자가 도착하기로 예정되기 전에 경비부서에 알려서 방문자가 영구적인 또는 일시적인 방문자 목록에 자리할 수 있도록 해야 합니다. 목록에 적히지 않은 방문자는 커뮤니티로의 접근이 거부될 것입니다. 이것은 모든 거주민들의 안전을 보장하고 저희 커뮤니티로 수상한 사람들이 들어오는 것을 막기 위한 것입니다.

2. 협회비가 월 300달러에서 350달러로 인상될 것입니다. 이것은 점점 커지는 커뮤니티를 위해 시행되는 하루 24시간, 주 7일의 보안 조치를 위한 추가 인력을 수용하기 위한 것이며, 쓰레기 수거 서비스를 주 1회에서 2회로 변경하기 위한 것입니다.

3. 주변의 주택에 방해를 일으키는 세대에서 나오는 과도한 소음은 엄격하게 금지됩니다. 최초 1회 위반자는 서면 경고를 받을 것이며, 반면에 반복적인 위반자들에게는 100달러의 벌금이 주어질 것입니다.

4. 거주민들은 자신의 집에 개인 차고 또는 간이 차고가 갖춰져 있지 않은 것이 아니라면 개인 차고 또는 간이 차고에 주차해야 합니다. 게다가, 노상 주차는 도로의 한 쪽에만 허용됩니다. 이것은 교통 체증을 예방하고 긴급 차량들의 용이한 통행을 가능

of emergency vehicles. Owners of improperly parked vehicles will be subjected to fines and towing fees at their own **80** expense.

We expect your full cooperation on these matters. Thank you.

Sincerely,
Mark Andrews
President
Golden Valley Homeowners Association

하도록 하기 위한 것입니다. 제대로 주차되지 않은 차량의 소유주들은 개인의 비용으로 벌금과 견인비의 대상이 될 것입니다.

저희는 이러한 문제들에 대해 귀하의 전적인 협조를 기대합니다. 감사합니다.

안녕히 계세요.
마크 앤드류스
회장
골든 밸리 주택소유주 협회

어휘 aware 알고 있는, 의식하고 있는 hold (행사 등을) 열다, 개최하다 annual 해마다의, 연례의 association 협회 revised 개정된, 수정된 based on ~을 기반으로 하여, ~에 따라 resident 거주민 suggestion 제안 recommendation 권고, 추천 guideline 가이드라인, 지침(서) as follow 다음과 같은 entrance 입구 community 커뮤니티, 공동 생활체 remain + 형용사: ~한 상태로 유지되다 at all times 항상, 언제나 property 재산, 건물, 부동산 owner 소유주 notify 알리다, 통보하다 security 보안, 경비(부서) be scheduled to 동사원형: ~하기로 예정되어 있다 so that (목적) ~하도록 하다 place 목적어 on the list: (목적어)를 목록에 넣다 permanent 영구적인 temporary 일시적인, 임시의 list 명단에 포함시키다 deny 거부하다 access 접근(권) ensure 보장하다 fee 요금 accommodate 받아들이다, 수용하다 24/7 주 7일 하루 24시간 measure 조치 implement 시행하다 garbage collection 쓰레기 수거 excessive 과도한, 지나친 disturbance 방해, 소란 strictly 엄격하게 prohibit 금지하다 offender 위반자 written warning 서면 경고 fine 벌금 be required to 동사원형: ~해야 하다, ~하는 것이 요구되다 private 개인적인, 사적인 carport 간이 차고 be equipped with ~을 갖추고 있다 in addition 게다가 on-street park 노상 주차 prevent 예방하다, 방지하다 traffic congestion 교통 체증, 교통 혼잡 easy passage 용이한 통행 emergency vehicle 긴급 차량 improperly 부적절한, 제대로 하지 않고 be subject to ~의 대상이다, ~을 받다 towing 견인, 끌기 at one's own expense 개인 비용으로, 자신의 비용으로 full cooperation 전적인 협조

Why did Mark Andrews write a letter to Celine Mitchell?

(a) to tell her about an upcoming community meeting
(b) to ask for her suggestions for new community guidelines
(c) to advise her of a problem within their community
(d) to inform her about the new rules in their community

마크 앤드류스 씨가 셀린 미첼 씨에게 편지를 쓴 이유는 무엇인가?

(a) 다가오는 커뮤니티 회의에 대해 말해주기 위해
(b) 새로운 지침에 대한 제안을 요청하기 위해
(c) 커뮤니티 내의 한 문제점에 대해 그녀에게 알리기 위해
(d) 커뮤니티의 새로운 규칙에 대해 알려주기 위해

정답 (d)

해설 첫 문단에서 We are writing this letter to ~ 라는 구문으로 편지를 쓰는 목적을 알려주고 있습니다. 이 문장에 따르면 거주민들의 제안과 권고를 기반으로 한 수정된 규칙에 대해(about our revised rules based on residents' suggestions and recommendations) 알려주기 위함이라고 언급되어 있으며, 그 뒤에 새로운 지침은 다음과 같다며(The new guidelines are as follows) 4개의 규칙에 대해 설명하고 있으므로 (d)가 정답입니다.

어휘 upcoming 다가오는 ask for ~을 요청하다 advise + 목적어 + of: ~에게 (목적어)를 알리다 inform ~에게 알리다

What was most likely true about visitors to the community before the first new regulation was created?

(a) Some of them received a background check.
(b) They had their own code to the front gate.
(c) Some of them intended to do harm.
(d) They could only be put on a temporary list

첫 번째 신규 규정이 만들어지기 전에 커뮤니티에 방문하는 방문객들에 대해 사실인 것은 무엇일 것 같은가?

(a) 방문객 중 몇몇은 신원 조사를 받았다.
(b) 방문객들은 정문에서 고유 코드를 받았다.
(c) 방문객 중 몇몇은 해가 되는 행동을 하려 하였다.
(d) 방문객들은 임시 목록에 포함되는 것만 가능했다.

정답 (c)

해설 질문에서 언급한 첫 번째 규정은 정문이 항상 닫혀 있게 될 것이라는 것인데, 이 규정이 생긴 목적에 대해 모든 거주민들의 안전을 보장하고 저희 커뮤니티로 수상한 사람들이 들어오는 것을 막기 위한 것(This is to ensure the safety of all residents and to prevent any suspicious people from entering our community)이라고 설명하고 있습니다. 이는 이

규정이 생기기 전에는 안정이 보장되지 않았고, 수상한 사람이 커뮤니티 내로 들어오려고 했다는 것을 유추할 수 있습니다. 따라서 정답은 (c)입니다.

어휘 regulation 규정 background check 신원 조사 code 코드, 암호 intend to 동사원형: ~하려 하다, ~할 작정이다
do harm 해를 입히다, 손해를 끼치다

---

76 세부 정보

How has the association decided to make the community's handling of its trash better?

(a) by hiring a different company
(b) by placing security cameras near waste bins
(c) by increasing service frequency
(d) by introducing a daily pickup system

협회는 커뮤니티의 쓰레기 처리를 더 잘 하기 위해 어떤 결정을 하였는가?

(a) 다른 업체를 고용함으로써
(b) 쓰레기통 근처에 보안 카메라를 배치함으로써
(c) 서비스 빈도를 높임으로써
(d) 일일 수거 제도를 도입함으로써

정답 (c)

해설 질문의 키워드인 handling of its trash는 쓰레기 수거에 관련하여 설명하고 있는 세 번째 문단에 언급되어 있습니다. 해당 문장에 따르면 쓰레기 수거 서비스를 주 1회에서 2회로 바꾸었다고(to change our garbage collection service from once to twice a week) 설명하고 있습니다. 이를 통해 서비스 횟수가 증가한 것을 알 수 있으므로 정답은 (c)입니다.

어휘 handling 처리 trash 쓰레기 hire 고용하다 place 놓다, 배치하다 security camera 보안 카메라 waste bin 쓰레기통
frequency 빈도 introduce 도입하다 daily 매일의, 일일의 pickup 수거 system 제도

패러프레이징

- garbage collection service → handling of its trash
- change ~ from once to twice a week → increasing service frequency

---

What will happen to residents who cause excessive noise more than once?

(a) Monthly fees will be increased.
(b) Legal steps will be taken immediately.
(c) A written warning will be issued.
(d) An appropriate fine will be imposed.

1회 이상 과도한 소음을 일으킨 거주민들에게는 어떤 일이 일어날 것인가?

(a) 월 회비가 인상될 것이다.
(b) 법적인 조치가 즉시 취해질 것이다.
(c) 서면 경고가 발급될 것이다.
(d) 적절한 벌금이 부과될 것이다.

정답 (d)

해설 질문의 키워드 excessive noise는 네 번째 문단에서 관련된 내용을 확인할 수 있습니다. 과도한 소음을 일으키는 것은 엄격히 금지된다고 하였는데, 첫 번째 위반자는 서면 경고를, 반복적인 위반자에게는 100달러의 벌금이 주어질 것이라고 (a $100 fine will be given to repeat offenders) 언급되어 있습니다. 따라서 벌금이 부과될 것이라고 언급한 (d)가 정답입니다.

어휘 more than once 1회 이상 monthly 월간의, 매월의 legal 법적인 step 조치 immediately 즉시 issue 발급하다, 발행하다 appropriate 적절한 impose 부과하다

패러프레이징

• repeat offenders → residents who cause excessive noise more than once
• will be given → will be imposed

When, most likely, would residents be allowed to park on the street?

(a) when their house does not include a carport
(b) whenever spaces are available
(c) when their family has multiple vehicles
(d) whenever traffic is minimal

거주민들에게 노상 주차가 허용되는 것은 언제일 것 같은가?

(a) 자신의 주택에 간이 차고가 포함되지 않을 때
(b) 공간이 이용 가능할 때마다
(c) 가족들이 2대 이상의 차량을 소유할 때
(d) 교통량이 매우 적을 때마다

정답 (a)

해설 질문의 키워드인 '노상 주차'(park on the street)는 다섯 번째 문단에 언급되어 설명되어 있습니다. 해당 문단에 따르면 거주민들은 자신의 집에 개인 차고 또는 간이 차고가 갖춰져 있지 않은 것이 아니라면 개인 차고 또는 간이 차고에 주차해야 한다고(Residents are now required to park in their private garage or carport, unless their home is not equipped with one) 언급되어 있습니다. 여기서는 개인 차고나 간이 차고가 없는 경우에 주차를 어떻게 해야 하는지에 대해서는 설명하지 않았지만 바로 뒤의 문장에서 노상 주차는 도로의 한 쪽에만 허용된다고(on-street parking is allowed on only one side of the road)라고 언급한 것으로 보아, 노상 주차는 개인 차고나 간이 차고가 없는 거주민들에게 허용한다는 것을 유추할 수 있습니다. 따라서 (a)가 정답입니다.

어휘 space 공간 available 이용 가능한 multiple 다수의, 2개 이상의 traffic 교통량 minimal 아주 적은, 최소의

79 동의어

In the context of the passage, notify means _____.

(a) limit
(b) contact
(c) fight
(d) expect

해당 단락의 문맥에서 notify가 의미하는 것은?

(a) 제한하다
(b) 연락하다
(c) 싸우다
(d) 기대하다

정답 (b)

해설 해당 문장에서 notify는 security를 목적어를 가지고 있는 동사로 쓰였으며, 문맥상 주택소유주가 예정된 방문자가 도착하기 전에 경비부서에 알려야 한다는 내용을 나타냅니다. 따라서 이와 유사한 의미를 나타낼 수 있는 '연락하다'라는 의미를 나타내는 (b) contact가 정답입니다.

80 동의어

In the context of the passage, expense means _____.

(a) budget
(b) value
(c) cost
(d) insurance

해당 단락의 문맥에서 expense가 의미하는 것은?

(a) 예산
(b) 가치
(c) 비용
(d) 보험

정답 (c)

해설 해당 문장에서 expense는 at their own expense라는 전치사구의 명사로 쓰였으며, 문맥상 제대로 주차하지 않는 차주에게 견인 비용을 자신의 비용으로 지불해야 한다는 것을 언급하고 있음을 알 수 있습니다. 따라서 expense는 '비용'의 의미를 나타내므로 유사한 의미를 나타내는 (c) cost가 정답입니다.

Grammar

1. (c)	**2.** (c)	**3.** (d)	**4.** (a)	**5.** (b)	**6.** (a)	**7.** (b)	**8.** (d)	**9.** (c)	**10.** (b)
11. (a)	**12.** (b)	**13.** (d)	**14.** (c)	**15.** (b)	**16.** (a)	**17.** (d)	**18.** (a)	**19.** (a)	**20.** (b)
21. (c)	**22.** (b)	**23.** (d)	**24.** (a)	**25.** (c)	**26.** (d)				

Listening

27. (b)	**28.** (a)	**29.** (d)	**30.** (c)	**31.** (a)	**32.** (c)	**33.** (b)	**34.** (c)	**35.** (d)	**36.** (b)
37. (b)	**38.** (a)	**39.** (a)	**40.** (d)	**41.** (a)	**42.** (c)	**43.** (a)	**44.** (b)	**45.** (c)	**46.** (b)
47. (d)	**48.** (c)	**49.** (d)	**50.** (c)	**51.** (a)	**52.** (d)				

Reading & Vocabulary

53. (c)	**54.** (b)	**55.** (a)	**56.** (b)	**57.** (d)	**58.** (a)	**59.** (d)	**60.** (b)	**61.** (c)	**62.** (a)
63. (d)	**64.** (a)	**65.** (b)	**66.** (c)	**67.** (d)	**68.** (c)	**69.** (b)	**70.** (b)	**71.** (c)	**72.** (a)
73. (d)	**74.** (c)	**75.** (b)	**76.** (a)	**77.** (d)	**78.** (c)	**79.** (a)	**80.** (d)		

채점 계산표 [정답 개수 기재]		채점 계산 방법
Grammar	_____ / 26문항	Grammar 정답 개수 ÷ 26 × 100
Listening	_____ / 26문항	Listening 정답 개수 ÷ 26 × 100
Reading & Vocabulary	_____ / 28문항	Reading & Vocabulary 정답 개수 ÷ 28 × 100
총점	_____ / 80문항 ▶ _____ / 100점	총점: 각 영역 합산 정답 개수 ÷ 80 × 100 ＊소수점 이하는 올림 처리

TEST 02

GRAMMAR
LISTENING
READING & VOCABULARY

01 조동사

Unlike most other birds, turkey vultures have a very good sense of smell. Using this ability, they _____ detect meat from over a mile away and often arrive at a food source before other vulture species.

(a) must
(b) would
(c) can
(d) should

대부분의 다른 새들과 달리, 터키 독수리는 아주 좋은 후각을 지니고 있다. 이 능력을 이용해, 이들은 1마일 넘게 떨어진 곳에서 고기를 감지할 수 있으며 흔히 다른 독수리 종보다 먼저 먹잇감이 있는 곳에 도착할 수 있다.

정답 (c)

해설 문장의 의미에 어울리는 조동사를 고르는 문제입니다. this ability는 앞 문장에 언급된 '아주 좋은 후각'을 가리키며, 그러한 능력을 이용해 아주 먼 곳에서도 고기를 감지할 수 있다는 의미를 나타내야 알맞으므로 '~할 수 있다'라는 뜻으로 능력이나 가능성을 나타낼 때 사용하는 (c) can이 정답입니다.

어휘 unlike ~와 달리 vulture 독수리 ability 능력 detect ~을 감지하다, ~을 탐지하다 arrive 도착하다 source 공급원, 근원, 원천 species (동식물의) 종

02 시제 – 과거완료진행

Keith went to the optometrist for a checkup last week, and he is now wearing his new prescription eyeglasses. His eyesight _____ for three months before Keith decided to have his eyes checked.

(a) has been worsening
(b) worsens
(c) had been worsening
(d) will worsen

키스는 지난 주에 검진을 위해 검안사에게 갔으며, 현재 처방 받은 새 안경을 착용하고 있다. 키스가 눈을 검사 받기로 결정하기 전까지 그의 시력은 3개월 동안 계속 악화되고 있었다.

정답 (c)

해설 동사 worsen의 알맞은 형태를 고르는 문제입니다. 빈칸이 속한 주절은 before절보다 더 이전 시점의 일을 나타내야 합니다. 따라서, before절에 쓰여 있는 과거시제 동사 decided가 가리키는 과거 시점보다 더 이전의 과거 시점에 일어난 일을 나타낼 수 있는 과거완료진행시제 (c) had been worsening이 정답입니다.

어휘 optometrist 검안사 checkup 검진, 점검 prescription 처방(된 것) eyesight 시력 decide + to 동사원형: ~하기로 결정하다 have + 목적어 + p.p.: (목적어)를 ~되게 하다 worsen 악화되다

03 접속사

Times Square in New York City used to be called Longacre Square. The famous commercial intersection used this original name _____ The *New York Times* newspaper moved its headquarters to the area in 1904.

(a) since
(b) because
(c) when
(d) until

뉴욕 시에 있는 타임스 스퀘어는 전에 롱에이커 스퀘어라고 불렸다. 뉴욕 타임스 신문사가 1904년에 그 지역으로 본사를 옮기기 전까지 그 유명한 상업적 교차로는 이 원래의 명칭을 사용했다.

정답 (d)

해설 문장의 의미에 어울리는 접속사를 고르는 문제입니다. 빈칸 앞뒤 부분을 읽어 보면, '뉴욕 타임스 신문사가 1904년에 그 지역으로 본사를 옮기기 전까지 ~가 이 원래의 명칭을 사용했다'와 같은 의미를 구성해야 가장 자연스러우므로 '~하기 전까지'를 뜻하는 (d) until이 정답입니다.

어휘 **used + to 동사원형**: 전에 ~했다, ~하곤 했다 **commercial** 상업적인 **intesection** 교차로 **original** 원래의, 원본의, 독창적인 **headquarters** 본사 **since** ~한 이후로, ~하기 때문에

04 준동사 – to부정사

Hailey was picked up from school by her dad. She asked if they could grab some tacos, and her dad agreed _____ some on the way home.

(a) to buy
(b) buying
(c) to have bought
(d) having bought

헤일리는 학교로 데리러 오신 아빠의 차에 탔다. 그녀는 함께 타코를 먹으러 갈 수 있는지 물었고, 아빠는 집으로 가는 길에 타코를 좀 구입하는 데 동의하셨다.

정답 (a)

해설 동사 buy의 알맞은 형태를 고르는 문제입니다. 빈칸 앞에 과거 시제로 쓰여 있는 동사 agree는 to부정사를 목적어로 취하므로 (a) to buy가 정답입니다.

어휘 **pick up** ~을 차로 데리러 가다 **ask if** ~인지 묻다 **grab** (간단히) ~을 먹다 **agree + to 동사원형**: ~하는 데 동의하다 **on the way** 가는 길에, 도중에

A hummingbird's heart beats at an average rate of 1,200 beats per minute. The human heart, _____ sixty to one hundred times per minute, is significantly slower by comparison.

(a) who only beats
(b) which only beats
(c) that only beats
(d) what only beats

벌새의 심장은 분당 1,200비트의 평균 속도로 뛴다. 분당 겨우 60~100회밖에 뛰지 않는, 인간의 심장은 그에 비해 상당히 더 느리다.

정답 (b)

해설 선행사인 사물 명사 human heart를 뒤에서 수식할 관계사절을 골라야 하므로 사물 명사를 수식할 수 있으면서 콤마와 함께 삽입되는 구조에 쓰일 수 있는 관계사 which가 이끄는 (b) which only beats가 정답입니다.

어휘 hummingbird 벌새 beat v. (심장이) 뛰다, 두드리다 n. 비트, 박자 rate 속도, 등급, 비율, 요금 significantly 상당히, 많이 by comparison 그에 비해, 비교상으로

❌ 오답 피하기

(c)의 that은 콤마와 함께 삽입되는 구조에 쓰일 수 없으며, (d) what은 선행사를 수식하지 않습니다.

Masood was thinking about going to the beach next weekend, but he is having second thoughts because rain is expected. If the forecast were to improve, Masood _____ to the coast as planned.

(a) would go
(b) would have gone
(c) will go
(d) will have gone

마수드는 다음 주말에 해변에 갈 생각을 하고 있었지만, 비가 예상되기 때문에 다시 생각해 보고 있다. 일기 예보가 개선되게 된다면, 마수는 계획대로 바닷가에 갈 것이다.

정답 (a)

해설 동사 go의 알맞은 형태를 고르는 문제입니다. If절의 동사가 가정법 과거를 나타내는 과거시제(were)일 때, 주절의 동사는 「would/could/might + 동사원형」과 같은 형태가 되어야 알맞으므로 (a) would go가 정답입니다.

어휘 have second thoughts 다시 생각해 보다, 재고하다 expect ~을 예상하다 be + to 동사원형: ~하게 되다, ~할 예정이다, ~해야 하다 improve 개선되다, 향상되다 as planned 계획대로

07 시제 - 현재완료진행

Frank's sister told him that there are no chemical elements starting with the letter J. Unconvinced, he _____ at the periodic table for the last five minutes, trying to prove her wrong.

(a) will stare
(b) has been staring
(c) stares
(d) had been staring

프랭크의 여동생은 그에게 글자 J로 시작하는 화학 원소가 없다고 말했다. 납득하지 못해서, 그는 지난 5분 동안 주기율표를 계속 응시하면서, 그녀가 틀렸음을 증명하려 하고 있다.

정답 (b)

해설 동사 stare의 알맞은 형태를 고르는 문제입니다. 빈칸 뒤에 위치한 「for the last + 시간/기간」 전치사구는 현재완료진행형 동사와 어울리므로 (b) has been staring이 정답입니다.

어휘 chemical element 화학 원소 letter 글자 unconvinced 납득하지 못한 periodic table (화학) 주기율표 prove A wrong: A가 틀렸음을 증명하다 stare ~을 응시하다

08 가정법 과거완료

Keeley recently repainted her living room with blue paint, but she does not like the new look. If she had known that the color would make the room look so dark, she _____ a different shade.

(a) will use
(b) would use
(c) will have used
(d) would have used

킬리가 최근 자신의 거실을 파란색 페인트로 다시 칠했지만, 그 새로운 모습을 마음에 들어 하지 않고 있다. 그녀가 그 색이 거실을 그렇게 어두워 보이게 만들 줄 알았다면, 그녀는 다른 색조를 이용했을 것이다.

정답 (d)

해설 동사 use의 알맞은 형태를 고르는 문제입니다. If절의 동사가 had known과 같이 가정법 과거완료를 나타내는 「had p.p.」일 때, 주절의 동사는 「would/could/might + have p.p.」와 같은 형태가 되어야 알맞으므로 (d) would have used가 정답입니다.

어휘 recently 최근 look n. 모습, 외관 v. ~하게 보이다, ~한 것 같다 make + 목적어 + 동사원형: (목적어)를 ~하게 만들다 shade 색조

The Leaning Tower of Pisa is tilted because of the soft soil that it was built on. _____, it was also this flexible soil that protected the tower from at least four strong earthquakes.

(a) In other words
(b) Therefore
(c) At the same time
(d) Otherwise

피사의 사탑은 그것이 서 있는 곳의 약한 토양 때문에 기울어져 있다. 그와 동시에, 그 탑을 최소 네 차례의 강한 지진으로부터 보호해 준 것도 바로 이 탄력있는 토양이었다.

정답 (c)

해설 빈칸에 알맞은 접속부사를 고르는 문제이므로 앞뒤 문장들의 의미 관계를 확인해야 합니다. 빈칸 앞에는 약한 토양이 피사의 사탑에 미치는 부정적인 영향이, 빈칸 뒤에는 그 토양이 미친 긍정적인 영향이 각각 쓰여 있습니다. 이는 동시에 미치는 양면적인 영향을 말하는 흐름이므로 '그와 동시에'라는 의미로, 고려해야 하는 대조적인 사실을 말할 때 사용하는 (c) At the same time이 정답입니다.

어휘 tilted 기울어진 soil 토양, 흙 it is A that: ~한 것이 바로 A이다 protect A from B: B로부터 A를 보호하다 at least 최소한, 적어도 earthquake 지진 in other words 다시 말해서 therefore 따라서, 그러므로 otherwise 그렇지 않으면, 그 외에는, 달리

Timothy has a photo album in which he gathers pictures of his friends. He bought it as a freshman and, by the time he eventually graduates, he _____ memories to the book for four years.

(a) is adding
(b) will have been adding
(c) will add
(d) has been adding

티모시는 친구들의 사진을 모아 넣는 사진 앨범을 하나 갖고 있다. 그는 그것을 신입생일 때 구입했는데, 그가 마침내 졸업할 때쯤이면, 그 책에 4년 동안 추억들을 추가하게 될 것이다.

정답 (b)

해설 동사 add의 알맞은 형태를 고르는 문제입니다. 빈칸 앞에 위치한 by the time he eventually graduates과 같이 by the time이 이끄는 절에 현재시제 동사(graduates)가 쓰이면 주절에 미래완료진행시제로 된 동사를 함께 사용하므로 (b) will have been adding이 정답입니다. 참고로, by the time이 이끄는 절에 과거시제 동사가 쓰이면 주절에 과거완료시제 또는 과거완료진행시제로 된 동사를 함께 사용합니다.

어휘 gather ~을 모으다 by the time ~할 때쯤이면 eventually 마침내 graduate 졸업하다 add A to B: A를 B에 추가하다

11 관계사절

Some people assume that Mars is a hot planet because of its red color, but the planet is actually colder than Earth. This is because the extremely thin atmosphere _____ does not retain any heat.

(a) that the planet possesses
(b) what the planet possesses
(c) when the planet possesses
(d) where the planet possesses

어떤 사람들은 화성이 그 붉은 색 때문에 뜨거운 행성이라고 추정하지만, 그 행성은 사실 지구보다 더 차갑다. 그 이유는 그 행성이 소유하고 있는 극도로 얇은 대기가 어떤 열도 유지하고 있지 않기 때문이다.

정답 (a)

해설 atmosphere 같은 사물 명사를 수식할 관계사절을 고를 때 관계대명사 that 또는 which가 이끄는 절은 「that[which] + 불완전한 절」의 구조로, 그리고 관계부사 where가 이끄는 절은 「where + 완전한 절」의 구조로 쓰여야 합니다. 따라서, that 뒤에 타동사 possesses의 목적어가 빠진 불완전한 절 the planet possesses이 쓰인 (a) that the planet possesses이 정답입니다.

어휘 assume that ~라고 추정하다, ~라고 생각하다 planet 행성 extremely 극도로, 대단히, 매우 thin 얇은, 가는 atmosphere 대기 retain ~을 유지하다, ~을 함유하다 possess ~을 소유하다

❌ 오답 피하기

관계대명사 what은 선행사(관계사절의 수식을 받는 명사)를 가지지 않는 관계대명사입니다.

12 가정법 과거

Donna has been earning a good salary translating documents from French to English. However, if she were to learn German, she _____ the opportunity to attract even more customers.

(a) will have
(b) would have
(c) will have had
(d) would have had

도나는 문서를 프랑스어에서 영어로 번역하면서 많은 급여를 받고 있다. 하지만, 그녀가 독일어를 배우게 된다면, 그녀는 훨씬 더 많은 고객들을 끌어들일 수 있는 기회를 갖게 될 것이다.

정답 (b)

해설 동사 have의 알맞은 형태를 고르는 문제입니다. if절의 동사가 가정법 과거를 나타내는 과거시제(were)일 때, 주절의 동사는 「would/could/might + 동사원형」과 같은 형태가 되어야 알맞으므로 (b) would have가 정답입니다.

어휘 earn (돈) ~을 벌다, ~을 얻다 translate ~을 번역하다 however 하지만, 그러나 be + to 동사원형: ~하게 되다, ~할 예정이다, ~해야 하다 have the opportunity + to 동사원형: ~할 기회를 갖다 attract ~을 끌어들이다 even (비교급 수식) 훨씬

Monowi is a town in Nebraska that has a population of one. As the town's only resident, Elsie Eiler's duties involve _____ as Monowi's mayor and librarian.

(a) to act
(b) having acted
(c) to have acted
(d) acting

모노위는 네브라스카에 위치한 마을로서, 인구가 1명이다. 이 마을의 유일한 주민으로서, 엘시 아일러의 직무는 모노위의 시장이면서 사서의 역할을 하는 것을 수반한다.

정답 (d)

해설 동사 act의 알맞은 형태를 고르는 문제입니다. 빈칸 앞에 쓰여 있는 동사 involve는 동명사를 목적어로 취하므로 (d) acting 이 정답입니다.

어휘 population 인구 resident 주민 duty 직무, 임무 involve ~을 수반하다, ~와 관련되다 act as ~의 역할을 하다 mayor 시장

Norah's computer monitor appeared to be broken but, when the technician checked it, he found a very simple issue. Had Norah known that the monitor was simply not plugged in, she _____ the problem herself.

(a) would fix
(b) will have fixed
(c) would have fixed
(d) will fix

노라의 컴퓨터 모니터는 고장 난 것처럼 보였지만, 기술자가 그것을 점검했을 때, 아주 간단한 문제를 발견했다. 노라가 그 모니터의 전원 플러그가 단지 꽂혀 있지 않았다는 사실을 알았다면, 그녀가 직접 그 문제를 바로잡았을 것이다.

정답 (c)

해설 동사 fix의 알맞은 형태를 고르는 문제입니다. Had Norah known은 가정법 과거완료를 구성하는 If Norah had known에서 If가 생략되고 주어와 had가 도치된 구조입니다. 따라서, If절의 동사가 「had p.p.」일 때 주절의 동사로 사용하는 「would/ could/ might + have p.p.」의 형태가 빈칸에 쓰여야 알맞으므로 (c) would have fixed가 정답입니다.

어휘 appear to be + 형용사: ~한 것처럼 보이다, ~한 것 같다 broken 고장 난, 망가진, 깨진 issue 문제, 사안 plug in ~의 전원 플러그를 꽂다 oneself (부사처럼 쓰여) 직접 fix ~을 바로잡다, ~을 고치다

15 준동사 – to부정사

Contrary to popular belief, sweat does not have any odor. However, when bacteria that live on the skin mix with the sweat, waste matter is produced, and this causes sweat _____ bad.

(a) smelling
(b) to smell
(c) having smelled
(d) to have smelled

일반적인 생각과 대조적으로, 땀은 어떤 냄새도 지니고 있지 않다. 하지만, 피부에 살고 있는 박테리아가 땀과 섞이면 노폐물이 생성되며, 이것이 땀에서 좋지 않은 냄새가 나도록 초래한다.

정답 (b)

해설 동사 smell의 알맞은 형태를 고르는 문제입니다. 빈칸 앞에 위치한 동사 cause는 '~에게 …하도록 초래하다'를 뜻하는 「cause + 목적어 + to 동사원형」의 구조로 쓰이므로 (b) to smell이 정답입니다.

어휘 contrary to ~와 대조적으로 popular 일반적인, 대중적인, 인기 있는 odor 냄새, 악취 however 하지만, 그러나 mix with ~와 섞이다 waste matter 노폐물 smell + 형용사: ~한 냄새가 나다

❌ 오답 피하기

to부정사 또는 동명사를 고르는 준동사 유형의 문제에서 빈칸 앞에 sweat과 같은 명사가 위치할 경우 대부분 to부정사가 정답입니다.

16 조동사

James cannot find his house keys. He _____ have checked that they were in his pocket before he left the office, but he forgot to do so.

(a) should
(b) can
(c) must
(d) will

제임스는 자신의 집 열쇠를 찾을 수 없다. 그는 사무실을 나서기 전에 그것들이 자신의 주머니에 있는지 확인했어야 했지만, 그렇게 하는 것을 잊었다.

정답 (a)

해설 문장의 의미에 어울리는 조동사를 고르는 문제입니다. 빈칸이 속한 문장 후반부에 위치한 but절에 '그렇게 하는 것을 잊었다'는 말이 쓰여 있어 빈칸이 속한 주절이 '~이 주머니에 있는지 확인했어야 했다'와 같은 의미를 나타내야 하므로 '~했어야 했다'라는 과거에 대한 후회를 뜻하는 「should have p.p.」의 구조가 쓰여야 합니다. 따라서 (a) should가 정답입니다.

어휘 leave ~에서 나가다, ~에서 떠나다 forget + to 동사원형: ~하는 것을 잊다 must have p.p. ~한 것이 틀림없다

Hawaiian pizza actually originated in Canada, not Hawaii. In the 1960s, Canadian Sam Panopoulos _____ with a pizza recipe when he decided to put canned pineapple on pizza and call it "Hawaiian pizza."

(a) experiments
(b) would experiment
(c) has been experimenting
(d) was experimenting

하와이안 피자는 사실 하와이가 아니라 캐나다에서 유래했다. 1960년대에, 샘 파노풀로스라는 캐나다인이 한 가지 피자 조리법을 실험하고 있었을 때 캔에 들어 있는 파인애플을 피자에 올려 놓으면서 그것을 "하와이안 피자"로 부르기로 결정했다.

정답 (d)

해설 동사 experiment의 알맞은 형태를 고르는 문제입니다. 빈칸 뒤에 과거시제 동사(decided)를 포함한 when절이 쓰여 있어 이 when절이 가리키는 과거 시점에 실험하는 일이 일시적으로 진행되던 상황을 나타내야 자연스러우므로 이러한 의미로 쓰이는 과거진행시제 (d) was experimenting이 정답입니다.

어휘 originate 유래하다, 비롯되다 recipe 조리법 decide + to 동사원형: ~하기로 결정하다 canned 캔에 들어 있는 experiment 실험하다

Trevor is bored with his economics class and is thinking of quitting. If the teacher were to deliver more interesting lectures, Trevor _____ to attend the class.

(a) would likely continue
(b) will likely continue
(c) would likely have continued
(d) will likely have continued

트레버는 경제학 수업이 지루해서 그만둘 생각을 하고 있다. 그 교사가 더 흥미로운 강의를 하게 된다면, 트레버는 아마 계속 수업에 출석할 것이다.

정답 (a)

해설 동사 continue의 알맞은 형태를 고르는 문제입니다. If절의 동사가 가정법 과거를 나타내는 과거시제(were)일 때, 주절의 동사는 「would/could/might + 동사원형」과 같은 형태가 되어야 알맞으므로 (a) would likely continue가 정답입니다.

어휘 bored 지루한 economics 경제학 quit 그만두다 be + to 동사원형: ~하게 되다, ~할 예정이다, ~해야 하다 deliver (강의, 연설 등) ~을 하다 continue + to 동사원형: 계속 ~하다 attend ~에 출석하다, ~에 참석하다 likely 아마

19 준동사 – 동명사

Lydia intends to lose weight but does not want to drop red meat from her diet. Her dietitian recommends _____ to white meat and fish instead because they contain less fat.

(a) switching
(b) to switch
(c) having switched
(d) to have switched

리디아는 체중을 감량할 작정이지만, 자신의 식단에서 붉은 고기를 빠트리고 싶어 하지는 않는다. 그녀의 영양사는 대신 흰살 고기와 생선으로 변경하도록 추천하고 있는데, 그것들이 지방을 덜 함유하고 있기 때문이다.

정답 (a)

해설 동사 switch의 알맞은 형태를 고르는 문제입니다. 빈칸 앞에 쓰여 있는 동사 recommend는 동명사를 목적어로 취하므로 (a) switching이 정답입니다.

어휘 intend + to 동사원형: ~할 작정이다, ~할 생각이다 drop ~을 빠트리다, ~을 빼다 dietitian 영양사 recommend -ing ~하도록 추천하다 switch to ~로 변경하다 instead 대신 contain ~을 함유하다, ~을 포함하다 fat 지방

❌ 오답 피하기

Recommend 뒤 목적어 자리에 빈칸이 위치할 경우 동명사가 정답이지만, 「recommend + 목적어 + 빈칸」의 구조처럼 recommend 뒤에 명사 목적어가 위치하고, 그 뒤에 빈칸이 위치할 경우 to부정사가 정답입니다.

20 가정법 과거완료

About 300 million years ago, Earth's seven continents were connected as one massive supercontinent called Pangaea. Had the continent not broken apart, ecosystems _____ very differently up to the present day.

(a) will likely have developed
(b) would likely have developed
(c) will likely develop
(d) would likely develop

약 3억년 전에, 지구의 대륙 일곱 개가 판게아라고 불리는 거대한 하나의 초대륙으로 연결되어 있었다. 그 대륙이 분리되지 않았다면, 생태계는 아마 오늘날에 이르기까지 아주 다르게 발달했을 것이다.

정답 (b)

해설 동사 develop의 알맞은 형태를 고르는 문제입니다. Had the continent not broken apart는 가정법 과거완료를 구성하는 If the continent had not broken apart에서 If가 생략되고 주어와 had가 도치된 구조입니다. 따라서, If절의 동사가 「had p.p.」일 때 주절의 동사로 사용하는 「would/could/might + have p.p.」의 형태가 빈칸에 쓰여야 알맞으므로 (b) would likely have developed가 정답입니다.

어휘 about 약, 대략 continent 대륙 connect ~을 연결하다 massive 거대한 break apart 분리되다, 분해되다 ecosystem 생태계 up to ~에 이르기까지 likely 아마 develop 발달하다, 발전하다

Willow trees contain salicin, a substance that transforms into salicylic acid, which is an ingredient of aspirin. This is why ancient beliefs prescribed that one _____ on willow bark to lessen fever and pain.

(a) is chewing
(b) chewed
(c) chew
(d) will chew

버드나무는 살리신산으로 탈바꿈하는 물질인, 살리신을 함유하고 있으며, 이는 아스피린의 재료이다. 이것이 바로 고대의 신앙에서 열과 통증을 완화하기 위해 버드나무 껍질을 씹도록 규정한 이유이다.

정답 (c)

해설 동사 chew의 알맞은 형태를 고르는 문제입니다. 빈칸은 동사 prescribed의 목적어 역할을 하는 that절의 동사 자리인데, prescribe와 같이 주장/요구/명령/제안 등을 나타내는 동사의 목적어 역할을 하는 that절에는 주어와 상관없이 동사원형만 사용하므로 (c) chew가 정답입니다.

어휘 willow tree 버드나무 contain ~을 함유하다, ~을 포함하다 substance 물질 transform into ~로 탈바꿈하다, ~로 변화하다 ingredient 재료, 성분 ancient 고대의 prescribe that ~하도록 규정하다 chew on ~을 씹다 bark (나무) 껍질 lessen ~을 완화하다

Rishi has been unable to attend school for three days because of the flu. When his classmate drops by in a few hours to lend him some of her notes, Rishi _____ in bed.

(a) was resting
(b) will be resting
(c) rests
(d) has been resting

리쉬는 독감 때문에 3일 동안 학교에 갈 수 없었다. 그의 친구가 자신의 노트중 일부를 그에게 빌려 주기 위해 몇 시간 후에 들를 때, 리쉬는 침대에 누워 쉬고 있을 것이다.

정답 (b)

해설 동사 rest의 알맞은 형태를 고르는 문제입니다. 「When + 주어 + 현재시제 동사(drops)」가 가리키는 미래 시점에 일시적으로 진행될 일을 나타낼 미래진행형 동사가 쓰여야 알맞으므로 (b) will be resting이 정답입니다.

어휘 be unable + to 동사원형: ~할 수 없다 attend ~에 출석하다, ~에 참석하다 flu 독감 drop by 들르다 in + 시간: ~ 후에 lend A B: A에게 B를 빌려 주다 rest 쉬다, 휴식하다

23 준동사 – to부정사

When flying on an airplane, our senses of smell and taste can decrease in sensitivity by more than 50 percent. This is why passengers tend _____ that in-flight meals taste bland.

(a) thinking
(b) to have thought
(c) having thought
(d) to think

비행기를 타고 날아갈 때, 우리의 후각과 미각은 민감성이 50퍼센트 이상 감소할 수 있다. 이것이 바로 승객들이 기내식에서 싱거운 맛이 난다고 생각하는 경향이 있는 이유이다.

정답 (d)

해설 동사 think의 알맞은 형태를 고르는 문제입니다. 빈칸 앞에 위치한 동사 tend는 to부정사와 어울려 '~하는 경향이 있다'라는 의미를 나타내므로 (d) to think가 정답입니다.

어휘 sense 감각, ~감 decrease in ~이 감소하다, ~이 하락하다 sensitivity 민감성 by (차이)~만큼, ~ 정도 tend + to 동사원형: ~하는 경향이 있다 taste + 형용사: ~한 맛이 나다 bland 싱거운, 밋밋한

24 시제 – 현재진행

There are plans to move our office to a bigger building because of our growing sales force. In fact, the president and department heads _____ the proposed locations at this very moment.

(a) are discussing
(b) discussed
(c) would discuss
(d) were discussing

늘어나는 영업 인력 때문에 더 큰 건물로 우리 사무실을 이전하려는 계획이 있다. 사실, 사장님과 부장님들께서 바로 지금 그 제안된 장소들을 논의하고 계신다.

정답 (a)

해설 동사 discuss의 알맞은 형태를 고르는 문제입니다. 빈칸 뒤에 위치한 at this very moment가 '바로 지금'이라는 의미로 현재 일시적으로 진행되는 일을 뜻하는 현재진행시제 동사와 어울려 쓰이므로 (a) are discussing이 정답입니다.

어휘 growing 늘어나는, 증가하는 force 인력 in fact 실제로, 사실 department head 부장 proposed 제안된 location 장소, 위치 at this very moment 바로 지금, 바로 이 순간

Our flight to the Maldives went through so much turbulence that a lot of passengers started to worry. However, the captain advised that everybody _____ calm, as the situation was under control.

(a) remains
(b) was remaining
(c) remain
(d) will remain

몰디브로 향하는 우리 항공기가 너무 많은 난기류를 겪어서 많은 승객들이 걱정하기 시작했다. 하지만, 기장은 모든 사람에게 차분함을 유지하도록 조언했는데, 그 상황이 통제되고 있었기 때문이었다.

정답 (c)

해설 동사 remain의 알맞은 형태를 고르는 문제입니다. 빈칸은 동사 advised의 목적어 역할을 하는 that절의 동사 자리인데, advise와 같이 주장/요구/명령/제안 등을 나타내는 동사의 목적어 역할을 하는 that절에는 주어와 상관없이 동사원형만 사용하므로 (c) remain이 정답입니다.

어휘 go through ~을 겪다, ~을 거쳐 가다 so A that B: 너무 A해서 B하다 turbulence 난기류 however 하지만, 그러나 advise that ~하도록 조언하다 calm 차분한, 침착한 under control 통제되는, 제어되는 remain + 형용사: ~한 상태를 유지하다

According to legend, goats were the first to experience the energizing effects of coffee. An ancient Ethiopian goat herder noticed that his goats became overly active every time they finished _____ on wild coffee beans.

(a) to feed
(b) having fed
(c) to have fed
(d) feeding

전설에 따르면, 염소가 커피의 에너지를 북돋우는 효과를 경험한 첫 번째 존재였다. 고대 에티오피아의 한 염소 목자는 자신의 염소들이 야생 커피 콩을 먹는 것을 끝마칠 때마다 지나치게 활동적인 상태가 되었다는 사실을 알아차렸다.

정답 (d)

해설 동사 feed의 알맞은 형태를 고르는 문제입니다. 빈칸 앞에 과거시제로 쓰여 있는 동사 finish는 동명사를 목적어로 취하므로 (d) feeding이 정답입니다.

어휘 according to ~에 따르면 legend 전설 energizing 에너지를 북돋우는 effect 효과, 영향 ancient 고대의 herder 목자, 목동 notice that ~임을 알아차리다, ~임에 주목하다 overly 지나치게 active 활동적인, 적극적인 every time ~할 때마다 feed on (동물이) ~을 먹다, ~을 먹고 살다

TEST 02 | Listening

PART 1

F: Wow, Marvin! **27** That tour of the Channel 8 News studio was impressive, wasn't it?

M: **27** I agree, Rose. I'm grateful our journalism professor gave us this rare opportunity to peek behind the scenes of a live news broadcast.

F: **28** What surprised me most was seeing how hectic the set seemed. Yet when you watch the news on TV, everything looks so smooth. The television crew worked frantically during the broadcast—the floor manager, camera operators, even the make-up artist.

M: Right, everyone works hard to make a finished product that looks easy. One thing that caught my attention was where the cameras were placed. They were set up far away from the news anchors because it's a better position for filming long shots. The camera operators just zoom in on the anchors whenever they need close-ups.

F: And all along, I thought the newscasters' close-ups and long shots were done by moving the cameras back and forth!

M: Me too. Keeping the cameras in one place seems much more efficient.

F: Yeah… Oh, and all the cameras are connected to the monitoring room, right?

M: That's right, Rose. **29** That huge wall of video screens shows images from all of the cameras so the director can see the set from every angle. I almost got dizzy watching so many screens at the same time!

여: 와우, 마빈! 채널 8 뉴스 스튜디오 견학이 인상적이지 않았어?

남: 동감이야, 로즈. 난 우리 저널리즘 교수님께서 뉴스 생방송 장면들의 이면을 엿볼 수 있는 이 흔치 않은 기회를 우리에게 주셔서 감사하게 생각해.

여: 내가 가장 놀라워했던 건 그 세트가 얼마나 정신없이 바빠 보였는지 확인한 거였어. 그렇지만 TV에서 뉴스를 보면, 모든 게 아주 순조롭게 보여. 텔레비전 방송국 직원들이 방송 중에 미친 듯이 일했잖아, 무대 감독과 카메라 기사, 심지어 메이크업 아티스트까지 말야.

남: 맞아, 모든 사람이 쉬워 보이는 최종 결과물을 만들기 위해 열심히 일하고 있어. 내 관심을 사로잡았던 한 가지는 카메라들이 배치된 곳이었어. 뉴스 앵커와 멀리 떨어진 곳에 설치되었는데, 롱샷을 촬영하기 더 좋은 위치이기 때문이야. 카메라 기사가 클로즈업이 필요할 때마다 앵커들을 확대하기만 하면 되거든.

여: 그리고 이제껏, 난 뉴스캐스터의 클로즈업과 롱샷이 카메라를 앞뒤로 움직여서 만들어지는 줄 알았어!

남: 나도. 카메라를 한 곳에 유지하는 게 훨씬 더 효율적인 것 같아.

여: 응… 아, 그리고 모든 카메라가 모니터실과 연결되어 있는 게 맞지?

남: 맞아, 로즈. 영상 스크린들이 있는 그 거대한 벽이 모든 카메라를 통해 나오는 이미지를 보여주기 때문에 연출자가 모든 각도에서 세트를 볼 수 있어. 난 그렇게 많은 스크린을 동시에 보면서 거의 어지러움을 느낄 뻔했어!

F: Me too, Marvin! And from the monitoring room, the news director chooses which camera shots are shown in the broadcast.

M: Amazing, isn't it?

F: Yup. I was also fascinated when the director showed us how the meteorologists use a green screen for their weather reports.

M: Ah, yes. The weather reporter just stood in front of the green screen, and the computer changed the map that shows up in the background.

F: **30** I always assumed the weather reporters were standing in front of a giant television screen that displayed the maps. **31** My little sister wants to be a meteorologist, so she'll be interested to hear about the green screen.

M: Really? I'd love to see her present the weather forecast on TV someday! That would be amazing. So, are there other parts of the tour that you enjoyed?

F: Definitely. I really enjoyed meeting Veronica Miller! I never thought I'd meet an award-winning reporter in person.

M: I think everybody in our class had a great time talking to Veronica Miller because she was very pleasant and was so willing to answer all our questions.

F: I agree. **32** I wasn't expecting her speaking voice to be so different from the formal voice she uses when she's reporting.

M: That's true. She's very professional on-screen but very warm and friendly in person.

여: 나도 그랬어, 마빈! 그리고 모니터실에서, 그 뉴스 연출자가 어느 카메라 장면이 방송으로 보여지는지 선택하잖아.

남: 놀랍지 않아?

여: 응. 난 그 연출자가 우리에게 일기 예보관이 어떻게 날씨 보도를 위해 녹색 스크린을 이용하는지 보여 주었을 때도 신기했어.

남: 아, 맞아. 기상캐스터는 그냥 그 녹색 스크린 앞에 서 있기만 하고, 컴퓨터가 배경에 나타나는 지도를 바꿨어.

여: 난 항상 기상캐스터가 지도를 표시하는 대형 텔레비전 스크린 앞에 서 있는 거라고 생각했어. 내 여동생이 일기 예보관이 되고 싶어 하기 때문에, 녹색 스크린 얘기를 들으면 흥미로워할 거야.

남: 정말? 언젠가 걔가 TV에서 일기 예보를 전하는 모습을 꼭 봤으면 좋겠어! 그렇게 되면 놀라울 거야. 그럼, 견학 시간 중에 또 즐거웠던 다른 부분들도 있어?

여: 당연하지. 베로니카 밀러 씨를 만난 게 정말 즐거웠어! 수상 경력이 있는 기자를 직접 만날 거라곤 전혀 생각하지 못했어.

남: 베로니카 밀러 씨가 너무 상냥하고 우리의 모든 질문에 아주 기꺼이 답변해 주셔서 우리 수업을 듣는 모두가 그분과 얘기하면서 아주 즐거운 시간을 보냈을 것 같아.

여: 동감이야. 말씀하시는 목소리가 보도할 때 이용하는 격식 있는 목소리랑 그렇게 다를 거라고는 예상하지 못했어.

남: 맞아. 화면상에서는 아주 전문적이시지만, 직접 만났을 때는 아주 따뜻하고 친절하셨어.

F: She gave us some great advice on how to be a top reporter. If we want to be successful like Veronica Miller, we have a lot of work ahead of us.

M: That's right, Rose. **33** To be the best broadcast journalists, we'll need to know how to do everything in the newsroom — not just how to read the news.

F: That's right, Marvin! Maybe next semester we should sign up for a video editing class.

여: 그분이 우리에게 최고의 기자가 되는 방법에 관해 몇몇 훌륭한 조언을 해 주셨잖아. 만일 우리가 베로니카 밀러 씨처럼 성공하기를 원한다면, 우린 앞으로 할 일이 많아.

남: 맞아, 로즈. 최고의 방송 기자가 되려면, 뉴스룸 내의 모든 걸 처리하는 방법을 알아야 할 거야, 단순히 뉴스를 읽는 방법뿐만 아니라.

여: 맞아, 마빈! 아마 다음 학기에는 우리가 영상 편집 강의를 신청해보는 게 좋을 것 같아.

어휘 **impressive** 인상적인 **rare** 흔치 않은, 드문 **opportunity + to 동사원형**: ~할 수 있는 기회 **peek behind** ~의 이면을 엿보다 **hectic** 정신없이 바쁜 **seem + 형용사**: ~한 것 같다, ~하게 보이다(= look + 형용사) **smooth** 순조로운 **frantically** 미친 듯이 **attention** 관심, 주의, 주목 **set up** ~을 설치하다 **zoom in on** (카메라로) ~을 확대하다 **all along** 이제껏, 내내 **efficient** 효율적인 **connect A to B**: A를 B에 연결하다 **angle** 각도 **dizzy** 어지러운 **choose** ~을 선택하다 **fascinated** 신기해 하는, 매료된 **meteorologist** 일기 예보관, 기상학자 **assume (that)** ~라고 생각하다, ~라고 추정하다 **display** (정보 등) ~을 표시하다, ~을 보여 주다 **see + 목적어 + 동사원형**: (목적어)가 ~하는 모습을 보다 **present** ~을 제공하다, ~을 제시하다 **award-winning** 수상 경력이 있는 **in person** 직접 (가서) **be willing + to 동사원형**: 기꺼이 ~하다 **expect + 목적어 + to 동사원형**: (목적어)가 ~할 것으로 예상하다 **formal** 격식 있는, 공식적인 **how + to 동사원형**: ~하는 방법 **semester** 학기 **sign up for** ~을 신청하다, ~에 등록하다 **editing** 편집

---

27 주제/목적

What are Rose and Marvin mainly talking about?

(a) their first experiences in an internship
(b) their impressions of an educational tour
(c) their plans to visit a broadcasting studio
(d) their dreams of becoming television actors

로즈와 마빈이 주로 무엇에 관해 이야기하고 있는가?

(a) 인턴 프로그램에 대한 각자의 첫 경험
(b) 교육용 견학에 대한 각자의 인상
(c) 각자의 방송 스튜디오 방문 계획
(d) 텔레비전 배우가 되려는 각자의 꿈

정답 (b)

해설 여자가 대화를 시작하면서 채널 8 뉴스 스튜디오 견학이 인상적이지 않았는지(That tour of the Channel 8 News studio was impressive, wasn't it?) 물은 뒤로 그에 대한 각자의 의견을 이야기하는 것으로 대화가 진행되고 있으므로 (b)가 정답입니다.

어휘 **impression** 인상, 감명

What surprised Rose the most about a live set?

(a) how different it looks on TV
(b) how rude the crew are
(c) how cold it feels in person
(d) how calm the anchors are

생방송 세트와 관련해 무엇이 로즈를 가장 놀라게 했는가?

(a) TV에서 얼마나 다르게 보이는지
(b) 그 담당 직원들이 얼마나 무례한지
(c) 직접 볼 때 얼마나 춥게 느껴지는지
(d) 앵커들이 얼마나 차분한지

정답 (a)

해설 여자가 대화 초반부에 자신이 가장 놀라워했던 것이 세트가 얼마나 정신없이 바빠 보였는지 확인한 것이었다고 언급하면서 TV에서 보는 뉴스는 모든 게 아주 순조롭게 보인다고 말하고 있습니다(What surprised me most was seeing how hectic the set seemed. Yet when you watch the news on TV, everything looks so smooth). 이는 실제와 TV에서의 모습이 아주 다르다는 뜻이므로 (a)가 정답입니다.

어휘 rude 무례한 calm 차분한, 침착한

패러프레이징

how hectic the set seemed / on TV, everything looks so smooth → how different it looks on TV

What made Marvin feel dizzy in the monitoring room?

(a) watching from a certain angle
(b) viewing brightly colored images
(c) looking through the cameras
(d) seeing multiple video screens

모니터실에서 무엇 때문에 마빈이 어지러움을 느꼈는가?

(a) 특정 각도에서 본 것
(b) 밝게 색이 조정된 이미지를 본 것
(c) 카메라를 통해 본 것
(d) 다수의 영상 스크린을 본 것

정답 (d)

해설 대화 중반부에 남자가 영상 스크린들이 있는 거대한 벽을 언급하면서 그렇게 많은 스크린을 동시에 보면서 거의 어지러움을 느낄 뻔했다고(That huge wall of video screens ~ I almost got dizzy watching so many screens at the same time!) 밝히고 있으므로 (d)가 정답입니다.

어휘 certain 특정한, 일정한 view ~을 보다 multiple 다수의, 다양한

(30) 세부 정보

How did Rose assume that studios displayed weather maps?

(a) by using a green screen backdrop
(b) by showing a paper map on screen
(c) by using a large television screen
(d) by projecting a computer screen

로즈는 스튜디오에서 어떻게 날씨 지도를 표시한다고 생각했는가?

(a) 녹색 스크린 배경을 이용함으로 써
(b) 스크린에 종이 지도를 보여 줌으 로써
(c) 대형 텔레비전 스크린을 이용함 으로써
(d) 컴퓨터 스크린을 비춰 줌으로써

정답 (c)

해설 여자가 대화 중반부에 기상캐스터가 지도를 표시하는 대형 텔레비전 스크린 앞에 서 있는 것으로 생각했다고(I always assumed the weather reporters were standing in front of a giant television screen that displayed the maps) 밝히 고 있으므로 (c)가 정답입니다.

어휘 **backdrop** 배경 **project** ~을 비추다, ~을 투사하다

❌ 오답 피하기

질문은 로즈가 어떻게 생각했는지를 묻고 있으므로 실제로 기상캐스터가 날씨 보도를 할 때 컴퓨터가 스크린에 지도를 비춰주 는 것을 언급한 (d)는 오답입니다.

Why will Rose's sister be interested in hearing about the studio tour?

(a) She hopes to be a weather reporter.
(b) She wants to be a news anchor.
(c) She hopes to become a set designer.
(d) She wants to be a director.

로즈의 여동생이 왜 스튜디오 견학에 관한 얘기를 듣는 데 관심이 있을 것인가?

(a) 기상캐스터가 되기를 바라고 있다.
(b) 뉴스 앵커가 되고 싶어 한다.
(c) 세트 디자이너가 되기를 바라고 있다.
(d) 연출자가 되고 싶어 한다.

정답 (a)

해설 여자가 대화 중반부에 여동생을 언급하면서 일기 예보관이 되고 싶어 하기 때문에 녹색 스크린 얘기를 들으면 흥미로워할 거라고(My little sister wants to be a meteorologist, so she'll be interested to hear about the green screen) 말하고 있으므로 (a)가 정답입니다.

패러프레이징

meteorologist → weather reporter

According to Rose, what was unexpected about Veronica Miller?

(a) that she looked the same without makeup
(b) that she behaved professionally
(c) that she sounded different in person
(d) that she dressed informally

로즈의 말에 따르면, 베로니카 밀러 씨와 관련해 무엇이 예상치 못한 것이었는가?

(a) 분장 없이도 동일하게 보였다는 점
(b) 전문적으로 행동했다는 점
(c) 직접 봤을 때 말투가 다르게 들렸다는 점
(d) 평상복 차림을 하고 있었다는 점

정답 (c)

해설 여자가 대화 후반부에 베로니카 밀러 씨가 말하는 목소리가 보도할 때 이용하는 격식 있는 목소리와 다를 거라고 예상하지 못했음을(I wasn't expecting her speaking voice to be so different from the formal voice she uses when she's reporting) 언급하고 있으므로 (c)가 정답입니다.

어휘 **unexpected** 예상치 못한, 뜻밖의 **behave** 행동하다, 처신하다 **dress informally** 평상복 차림을 하다

33 추론

What advice did Veronica Miller probably give the students?

(a) to make professional contacts
(b) to develop a varied skillset
(c) to gain academic qualifications
(d) to specialize in one role

베로니카 밀러 씨가 학생들에게 어떤 조언을 해 주었을 것 같은가?

(a) 직업상의 인맥을 만들어 둘 것
(b) 다양한 역량을 개발할 것
(c) 학문적 자격을 취득할 것
(d) 한 가지 역할을 전문으로 할 것

정답 (b)

해설 대화 후반부에 베로니카 밀러 씨의 조언과 관련해 이야기하면서 남자가 뉴스룸 내의 모든 걸 처리하는 방법을 알아야 할 거라고(To be the best broadcast journalists, we'll need to know how to do everything in the newsroom — not just how to read the news) 언급하고 있습니다. 이는 다양한 능력을 갖춰야 한다는 뜻이므로 (b)가 정답입니다.

어휘 contacts 인맥, 지인 관계 varied 다양한 skillset 역량, 능력 gain ~을 얻다, ~을 획득하다 qualification 자격(증) specialize in ~을 전문으로 하다

패러프레이징

know how to do everything in the newsroom → a varied skillset

Hello, dear customers! Thank you for your continued patronage of SunGrown Farmers Market, the biggest one-stop produce market in town. **34** We have recently launched SunGrown Online, so you can now buy our products without leaving the comfort of your home! Simply download the SunGrown Online app, install it onto your phone, and see what we have in store for you.

Shopping at SunGrown Online is a breeze! If you know exactly what you want, simply use our search function. **35** We have also added a special feature that will make your shopping so quick and easy: the SunGrown Basket is a feature for our customers who tend to order the same staple food items on a regular basis. With SunGrown Basket, just one click will add all of your preferred staples to an order.

Now, for the gardening enthusiasts, check out SunGrown Online's plant section. There, you can shop for a variety of colorful greenery and flowering plants supplied by the best growers in town. **36** For beginners, we also offer seedling sets complete with basic planting tools and care instructions. If you are not sure what type of plants to look for, check out the plant section's catalogue on the app for an overview of all our garden products.

SunGrown Kitchenette is known to most customers for its selection of hearty, delicious dishes. So, we have decided to take the Kitchenette online! Finally, you can have our fresh home-cooked meals delivered straight to your doorstep using SunGrown Online. You can also take a look at the weekly menu, which is posted in advance. However, **37** we suggest that you order ahead of time. The later you order, the more likely an item on the menu is to be sold out.

안녕하세요, 소중한 고객 여러분! 시에서 가장 규모가 큰 원스톱 농산물 시장인, 저희 선그로운 농산물 직판장에 대한 여러분의 지속적인 성원에 감사 드립니다. 저희가 최근 선그로운 온라인을 시작했으므로, 이제 편안한 여러분의 자택을 벗어나실 필요 없이 저희 제품을 구입하실 수 있습니다! 저희 선그로운 온라인 앱을 다운로드하신 다음, 전화기에 설치하시기만 하면, 저희가 여러분을 위해 매장에 보유하고 있는 것이 보이게 됩니다.

선그로운 온라인에서의 쇼핑은 식은 죽 먹기입니다! 원하시는 것을 정확히 알고 계시는 경우, 저희 검색 기능을 이용하시기만 하면 됩니다. 여러분의 쇼핑을 아주 신속하고 간편하게 만들어 드릴 특수 기능도 추가해 드렸는데, 선그로운 장바구니는 주기적으로 동일한 주요 식품을 주문하시는 경향이 있는 고객들을 위한 기능입니다. 선그로운 장바구니를 이용하시면, 단 한 번의 클릭으로 선호하시는 모든 주요 제품이 주문 사항에 추가될 것입니다.

이제, 원예 애호가들께서는, 선그로운 온라인의 식물 코너를 확인해 보시기 바랍니다. 그곳에서는, 우리 시에서 최고의 재배업자들이 제공해 드리는 다양한 다채로운 녹지 식물 및 꽃 식물을 쇼핑하실 수 있습니다. 초보자들을 위해, 기본적인 식수용 도구 및 관리 설명서가 완비된 묘목 세트도 제공해 드립니다. 어떤 종류의 식물을 찾고 계신지 확실치 않으실 경우, 저희의 모든 원예 제품에 대한 개요를 보실 수 있도록 앱에서 식물 코너의 카탈로그를 확인해 보시기 바랍니다.

선그로운 키치넷은 대부분의 고객들께 건강에 좋고 맛있는 다양한 요리들로 알려져 있습니다. 따라서, 저희가 이 키치넷을 온라인에서 제공해 드리기로 결정했습니다! 마지막으로, 여러분은 선그로운 온라인을 이용해 신선한 저희 가정식 식사를 여러분의 집 앞까지 곧장 배달시키실 수 있습니다. 또한 주간 메뉴도 확인해 보실 수 있는데, 그 메뉴는 미리 게시됩니다. 하지만, 저희는 예정보다 일찍 주문하시기를 권해 드립니다. 더 늦게 주문하실수록, 메뉴에 있는 제품이 품절될 가능성이 더 높습니다.

At SunGrown Farmers Market, **38** we believe that knowing where the products come from may help you feel assured that you're getting your money's worth. So, SunGrown Online also allows you to choose which farm grows your produce. After tapping an item, you can activate a drop-down menu showing the names of the farms that sell the item, with a brief description of each farm, including its size, method of farming, and location. **38** You may then choose to buy produce that comes from a particular farm.

We want to make sure that you get the freshest food items, so our products are delivered to us at dawn every day. **39** We therefore recommend that you place your orders no later than noon the day before. This allows us to plan ahead and receive only as much food as we need for the day, eliminating food waste and ensuring that our items are as fresh as possible. You may choose to pick up the goods yourself so you won't have to wait for the delivery, or you may have them delivered to your home for a small fee.

So, be among our satisfied customers who are already ordering our farm-fresh products online. Register with SunGrown Online now.

저희 선그로운 농산물 직판장에서는, 제품이 생산되는 곳을 알고 계시는 것이 여러분의 비용에 대한 가치를 얻고 있다는 안도감을 느끼게 해 드리는 데 도움이 될 수 있다고 생각합니다. 따라서, 저희 선그로운 온라인에서는 어느 농장이 여러분의 농산물을 재배하는지도 선택하실 수 있게 해 드립니다. 제품을 누르신 후, 규모와 재배 방식, 그리고 위치를 포함해, 각 농장에 대한 간략할 설명과 함께 해당 제품을 판매하는 농장명을 보여 드리는 드롭다운 메뉴를 활성화하실 수 있습니다. 그런 다음 특정 농장에서 생산되는 농산물을 구입하도록 선택하실 수 있습니다.

저희는 여러분께서 가장 신선한 식품을 받으시기를 원하므로, 저희 제품은 매일 새벽에 저희에게 배달됩니다. 저희는 그에 따라 늦어도 전날 정오까지는 주문해 주시기를 권해 드립니다. 이를 통해 저희가 미리 계획해 당일에 필요한 만큼만 많은 식품을 받아, 음식물 쓰레기를 없애고 저희 제품이 가능한 한 신선한 상태로 있도록 보장해 드릴 수 있습니다. 직접 상품을 가져 가시도록 선택하실 수 있으므로, 배송을 기다리실 필요가 없을 것이며, 또는 소액의 요금으로 댁까지 배송시키실 수도 있습니다.

자, 이미 온라인으로 저희 농장 직송 제품을 주문해 만족하고 계신 고객들 중 한 분이 되어 보시기 바랍니다. 지금 저희 선그로운 온라인에 등록해 보십시오.

어휘 continued 지속적인 patronage 성원, 애용 produce n. 농산물 recently 최근 launch ~을 시작하다, ~을 출시하다 install ~을 설치하다 breeze 식은 죽 먹기 function 기능 feature 특징 tend + to 동사원형: ~하는 경향이 있다 staple a. 주요한 n. 주식, 주요 산물 on a regular basis 주기적으로 preferred 선호하는 enthusiast 애호가, 열성적인 팬 a variety of 다양한 greenery 녹지 supply ~을 공급하다 seedling 묘목 complete with ~이 완비된 care 관리, 보살핌 instructions 설명(서), 안내(서) look for ~을 찾다 overview 개요, 개괄 be known for ~로 알려지다 decide + to 동사원형: ~하기로 결정하다 have + 목적어 + p.p.: (목적어)를 ~되게 하다 take a look at ~을 한 번 보다 post ~을 게시하다 in advance 미리, 사전에 ahead of time 예정보다 일찍 The 비교급, the 비교급: 더 ~할수록, 더 ~하다 more likely ~할 가능성이 큰 be sold out 품절되다, 매진되다 help + 목적어 + 동사원형: ~하도록 (목적어)를 돕다 feel assured that ~라는 점에 대해 안도감을 느끼다 worth 가치 allow + 목적어 + to 동사원형: (목적어)에게 ~할 수 있게 해 주다 grow ~을 재배하다 tap (살짝) ~을 누르다, ~을 두드리다 activate ~을 활성화하다 brief 간략한 description 설명 including ~을 포함해 method 방식 particular 특정한 make sure that (= ensure that) 반드시 ~하도록 하다, ~임을 확실히 하다 place one's order 주문하다 no later than 늦어도 ~까지는 eliminate ~을 없애다, ~을 제거하다 as A as possible: 가능한 한 A한[A하게] pick up ~을 가져 가다[오다] oneself (부사처럼 쓰여) 직접 farm-fresh 농장 직송의 register 등록하다

What is the talk all about?

(a) an online cooking course
(b) a local community garden
(c) an online shopping opportunity
(d) a local farm tour

담화가 모두 무엇에 관한 것인가?

(a) 온라인 요리 강좌
(b) 지역 공동체 텃밭
(c) 온라인 쇼핑 기회
(d) 지역 농장 견학

정답 (c)

해설 화자가 담화를 시작하면서 선그로운 온라인이라는 서비스를 소개하면서 집에서 편하게 제품을 구입할 수 있다고(We have recently launched SunGrown Online, so you can now buy our products without leaving the comfort of your home!) 밝힌 뒤로 그 기능 등과 관련해 설명하고 있으므로 (c)가 정답입니다.

어휘 **local** 지역의, 현지의 **community** 지역 공동체, 지역 사회 **opportunity** 기회

> **패러프레이징**
>
> SunGrown Online / buy our products without leaving the comfort of your home → an online shopping opportunity

How does the SunGrown Online app make shopping so quick?

(a) by having a simple setup process
(b) by providing a speedy payment method
(c) by highlighting popular products
(d) by remembering frequently bought items

선그로운 온라인 앱이 어떻게 쇼핑을 그렇게 신속하게 만들어 주는가?

(a) 간단한 설치 과정을 거침으로써
(b) 빠른 결제 방법을 제공함으로써
(c) 인기 제품을 강조함으로써
(d) 자주 구입하는 제품을 기억함으로써

정답 (d)

해설 화자가 담화 중반부에 쇼핑을 빠르고 쉽게 만드는 특수 기능을 추가하였다고 언급하면서 주기적으로 동일한 주요 식품을 주문하는 경향이 있는 고객들을 위한 기능인 선그로운 장바구니(We have also added a special feature that will make your shopping so quick and easy: the SunGrown Basket is a feature for our customers who tend to order the same staple food items on a regular basis)에 대해 설명하고 있습니다. 이는 주기적으로 주문하는 제품에 대한 정보를 기억하는 기능을 의미하므로 (d)가 정답입니다.

어휘 **process** (처리) 과정 **highlight** ~을 강조하다, ~을 집중 조명하다 **frequently** 자주, 빈번히

to order the same staple food items on a regular basis / just one click will add all of your preferred staples → remembering frequently bought items

36 세부 정보

What does SunGrown Online offer gardening enthusiasts?

(a) a collection of plant care videos
(b) starter kits for new gardeners
(c) a list of local plant growers
(d) plans for unique garden designs

선그로운 온라인이 원예 애호가들에게 무엇을 제공하는가?

(a) 식물 관리 동영상 모음
(b) 처음 원예를 시작한 사람들을 위한 초보자용 세트
(c) 지역 식물 재배업자들의 명단
(d) 독특한 정원 디자인을 위한 계획

정답 (b)

해설 담화 중반부에 화자가 초보자들을 위한 기본적인 식수용 도구 및 관리 설명서가 완비된 묘목 세트를 제공한다고(For beginners, we also offer seedling sets complete with basic planting tools and care instructions) 밝히고 있으므로 (b)가 정답입니다.

어휘 collection 모음, 수집(한 것들) kit 한 세트, 한 묶음 unique 독특한, 특별한

패러프레이징

For beginners / seedling sets complete with basic planting tools and care instructions → starter kits for new gardeners

Why, most likely, should customers order their meals in advance?

(a) to choose a delivery time
(b) to benefit from a wide selection
(c) to qualify for a discount
(d) to make special dietary requests

고객들이 왜 미리 자신들의 식사를 주문해야 할 것 같은가?

(a) 배송 시간을 선택하기 위해
(b) 다양한 종류의 혜택을 보기 위해
(c) 할인에 대한 자격을 얻기 위해
(d) 음식물에 관한 특별 요청을 하기 위해

정답 (b)

해설 화자가 담화 중반부에 가정식 식사 주문과 관련해 예정보다 일찍 주문하기를 권하면서 더 늦게 주문할수록 메뉴에 있는 제품이 품절될 가능성이 더 높다는 점을(we suggest that you order ahead of time. The later you order, the more likely an item on the menu is to be sold out) 이유로 언급하고 있습니다. 이는 품절되기 전에 제품의 종류가 가능한 한 다양할 때 주문하도록 권하는 것이므로 (b)가 정답입니다.

어휘 benefit from ~로부터 혜택을 보다, ~로부터 이득을 얻다 selection 선택(할 수 있는 종류) qualify for ~에 대한 자격이 있다 make a request 요청하다 dietary 음식물의, 식사의

How can customers be confident that they are getting their money's worth?

(a) They can buy from a preferred source.
(b) They can read customers' reviews.
(c) They can compare competitors' prices.
(d) They can register for a trial period.

고객들이 어떻게 비용에 대한 가치를 얻고 있다고 확신할 수 있는가?

(a) 선호하는 공급원을 통해 구입할 수 있다.
(b) 고객 후기를 읽어 볼 수 있다.
(c) 경쟁사의 가격을 비교해 볼 수 있다.
(d) 체험 기간에 등록할 수 있다.

정답 (a)

해설 질문의 키워드인 getting money's worth가 언급된 담화 후반부에 제품이 생산되는 곳을 알고 있으면 비용에 대한 가치를 얻고 있다는 안도감을 느끼게 하는 데 도움이 될 수 있다고(we believe that knowing where the products come from may help you feel assured that you're getting your money's worth) 언급되어 있습니다. 그리고 어느 농장이 농산물을 재배하는지 선택할 수 있게 해 주며, 청자에게 특정 농장에서 생산되는 농산물을 구입할 수 있도록 선택할 수 있다고(You may then choose to buy produce that comes from a particular farm) 설명하였습니다. 이는 고객이 선호하는 공급업체를 선택하는 방식을 뜻하므로 (a)가 정답입니다.

어휘 source 공급원, 원천, 근원 review 후기, 평가 compare ~을 비교하다 competitor 경쟁사, 경쟁자 trial 체험, 시험

패러프레이징

choose which farm grows your produce → buy from a preferred source

---

39 추론

Based on the talk, why, most likely, should customers order produce by noon?

(a) to get items while they are fresh
(b) to qualify for a refund
(c) to request same-day delivery
(d) to access free shipping

담화 내용에 따르면, 고객들이 왜 정오까지 농산물을 주문해야 할 것 같은가?

(a) 제품이 신선할 때 구입하기 위해
(b) 환불에 대한 자격을 얻기 위해
(c) 당일 배송을 요청하기 위해
(d) 무료 배송 서비스를 이용하기 위해

정답 (a)

해설 담화 후반부에 화자가 늦어도 전날 정오까지 주문하도록 권하면서 그 이유의 하나로 제품이 가능한 한 신선한 상태로 있도록 보장해 줄 수 있다는 점을(We therefore recommend that you place your orders no later than noon the day before. ~ ensuring that our items are as fresh as possible) 언급하고 있으므로 (a)가 정답입니다.

어휘 refund 환불(액) request ~을 요청하다 same-day 당일의 access ~을 이용하다, ~에 접근하다 free 무료의

패러프레이징

ensuring that our items are as fresh as possible → get items while they are fresh

PART 3

M: Hey, Christine! How's your event planning business doing?

F: Oh hello, Lawrence! I've been busy with the business lately. In fact, I need to meet some out-of-state clients this week.

M: It must be doing well! I'm happy for you.

F: Thanks. I'm having a bit of a problem, though. **40** Since I give a lot of presentations, my laptop is quickly filling up with files. I've been thinking about getting more storage for the files that I use in my promotional talks.

M: I see… I'm sure you use lots of slide shows, pictures, and large video files in your presentations. Have you come up with any good options yet?

F: Yes. I'm choosing between using external hard drive storage and online or cloud storage.

M: Maybe it would help if we discuss the pros and cons of each option.

F: Sounds good. Let's start with the first choice. **41** I think that using an external hard drive to store data is ideal for me since I give presentations during my business trips. I can retrieve documents directly from a hard drive and deliver talks wherever I am.

M: Right. With a hard drive, you can have faster access to files because you won't need to put in passwords or connect to the Internet to download the files.

남: 안녕하세요, 크리스틴 씨! 행사 기획 사업은 어떻게 되어 가고 있나요?

여: 아, 안녕하세요, 로렌스 씨! 그 사업으로 요즘 계속 바빴어요. 사실, 다른 주에 계신 몇몇 고객들을 이번 주에 만나 뵈어야 합니다.

남: 잘 되어 가고 있군요! 좋은 소식에 기쁩니다.

여: 감사합니다. 하지만, 약간의 문제가 있어요. 제가 발표를 많이 하기 때문에, 제 노트북 컴퓨터가 빠르게 파일들로 가득해 지고 있거든요. 제가 홍보용 연설에서 사용하는 파일들을 위해 더 많은 저장 공간을 확보하는 것에 관해 계속 생각해 보고 있어요.

남: 그러시군요… 분명 발표에서 슬라이드 쇼와 사진, 그리고 용량이 큰 동영상 파일을 많이 이용하시겠어요. 혹시 어떤 좋은 선택 사항이든 생각나신 게 있으신가요?

여: 네. 외장 하드 드라이브 저장 공간과 온라인 또는 클라우드 저장 공간을 이용하는 것 중에서 선택하려고요.

남: 아마 우리가 각각의 선택 사항이 지닌 장단점을 이야기해 보면 도움이 될 겁니다.

여: 좋은 생각이에요. 첫 번째 선택권부터 시작해 보죠. 데이터 저장을 위해 외장 하드 드라이브를 이용하는 게 제겐 이상적이라고 생각하는데, 제가 출장 중에 발표를 하기 때문이에요. 제가 어디에 있든 하드 드라이브에서 곧바로 문서를 꺼내 연설할 수 있어요.

남: 그렇죠. 하드 드라이브가 있으면, 파일을 더 빠르게 이용할 수 있는데, 비밀번호를 입력하거나 파일을 다운로드하기 위해 인터넷에 접속할 필요가 없을 것이기 때문이죠.

F: That's true. But `42` what I'm concerned about is that a hard drive can get damaged. I tend to rush when I'm about to give a talk, and I'm afraid the hard drive might get banged up in my bag. I wouldn't want to start a presentation only to learn that the drive isn't working.

M: Certainly not! Another thing about a hard drive is that it can get corrupted. As the storage device ages, files can start to degrade, or go bad, until they're not even usable anymore.

F: That can be a problem. Now, one advantage of online storage is that I don't need to carry anything else around with me. With this option, I can open files without having to attach my laptop to another device.

M: Good point. All you'll have to do is log into your account and click some buttons.

F: That's right.

M: And `43` `45` another convenient thing about cloud storage is that it's shareable. You just have to send a link to your clients, and they can access the documents you want to share.

F: That will work for me. I have many clients, and I won't need to email them one by one to send them files. However, one worry I have about online storage concerns the safety of my files.

M: Why's that?

F: Well, it's true that cloud storage hosts guarantee privacy and security. However, `44` I'm not really confident that my account can't be hacked.

여: 맞아요. 하지만 제가 우려하는 건 하드 드라이브가 손상될 수 있다는 점이에요. 저는 막 연설하려고 할 때 서두르는 경향이 있는데, 하드 드라이브가 제 가방 안에서 망가지게 될까봐 두려워요. 발표를 시작하는데 드라이브가 작동하지 않는다는 사실을 알게 되고 싶진 않을 거예요.

남: 당연히 그러고 싶지 않죠! 하드 드라이브와 관련해 또 다른 점은 오류가 날 수도 있다는 거예요. 저장 장치가 오래될수록, 파일들이 심지어 더 이상 이용할 수 없을 때까지 질적으로 저하되거나 형편없어지기 시작할 수 있어요.

여: 그럼 문제가 될 수 있죠. 자, 온라인 저장 공간의 한 가지 장점은 제가 다른 무엇도 직접 휴대하고 다닐 필요가 없다는 거예요. 이 선택으로, 제 노트북 컴퓨터를 또 다른 장치에 부착할 필요 없이 파일을 열 수 있죠.

남: 좋은 지적입니다. 계정에 로그인해서 버튼만 몇 개 클릭하시기만 하면 되죠.

여: 맞아요.

남: 그리고 클라우드 저장 공간과 관련해 편리한 또 다른 점은 공유가 가능하다는 겁니다. 고객들에게 링크를 전송하기만 하면, 공유하고자 하는 문서를 이용할 수 있죠.

여: 그게 제게 좋을 거예요. 제게 많은 고객들이 있는데, 그분들에게 파일을 보내 드리기 위해 일일이 이메일을 보내 드릴 필요가 없을 테니까요. 하지만, 제가 온라인 저장에 관해 갖고 있는 한 가지 걱정은 제 파일의 안전과 관련되어 있어요.

남: 왜 그런 걸까요?

여: 음, 클라우드 저장 호스트가 개인 정보 보호와 보안을 보장해 준다는 건 사실이에요. 하지만, 제 계정이 해킹 당할 리 없다고 정말로

I'm also skeptical of the claim that my files don't get leaked when they're in "the cloud."

M: That's actually a common concern. And another disadvantage I see with cloud storage is it's pretty expensive. You'll have to pay a subscription fee to use the service, plus upgrades for more storage.

F: And it's not just a one-time payment. I'll have to renew every year if I want to keep my storage. Hmm, this conversation has really helped me make a decision.

M: So what have you come up with?

F: 45 I think I'll choose the option that allows me to share files with my clients all at once. Thanks for the help, Lawrence!

M: You're welcome, Christine.

확신하지 못해요. 제 파일들이 "클라우드"에 있을 때 유출되지 않는다는 주장에 대해서도 회의적이고요.

남: 사실 흔한 우려 사항이죠. 그리고 제가 보는 클라우드 저장이 지닌 또 다른 단점은 꽤 비싸다는 점입니다. 그 서비스를 이용하려면 구독료를 결제해야 할 테고, 그에 더해 추가 저장 공간을 위한 업그레이드도 있죠.

여: 그리고 그게 단지 1회성의 결제도 아니에요. 제 저장 공간을 유지하기를 원할 경우에 매년 갱신해야 할 겁니다. 흠, 우리 대화가 결정을 내리는 데 제게 정말로 도움이 되었어요.

남: 그럼 어떤 생각이 드셨나요?

여: 제가 고객들과 모두 한꺼번에 파일을 공유할 수 있게 해 주는 선택 사항을 고를 것 같아요. 도와주셔서 감사해요, 로렌스 씨!

남: 별 말씀을요, 크리스틴 씨.

어휘 How's ~ doing?: ~는 어떻게 되어 가고 있나요? out-of-state 다른 주에 있는 a bit of 약간의, 조금의 fill up with ~로 가득 차다 storage 저장 (공간), 보관(소) promotional 홍보의, 판촉의 come up with (아이디어 등) ~을 생각해 내다, ~을 제시하다 choose ~을 선택하다 pros and cons 장단점 ideal 이상적인 retrieve (자료 등) ~을 꺼내다, ~을 되찾아 오다 access n. 이용 (권한), 접근 (권한) v. ~을 이용하다, ~에 접근하다 connect to ~에 연결되다 be concerned about ~에 대해 우려하다 get p.p. ~된 상태가 되다 damaged 손상된, 피해를 입은 tend + to 동사원형: ~하는 경향이 있다 rush 서두르다 be about + to 동사원형: 막 ~하려 하다 bang up ~을 망가뜨리다, ~을 손상시키다 only + to 동사원형: (결과적으로) ~하게 되다, ~할 뿐이다 work 작동하다, 효과가 있다 corrupt ~에 오류를 일으키다 age v. 오래되다, 낡아지다 degrade 질이 저하되다 not ~ anymore 더 이상 ~ 않다 advantage 장점(↔ disadvantage) carry + 목적어 + around: (목적어)를 갖고 다니다 without having + to 동사원형: ~할 필요 없이 attach A to B: A를 B에 부착하다 device 기기, 장치 Good point 좋은 지적입니다 All you'll have to do is + 동사원형: ~하기만 하면 될 것입니다 log into ~에 로그인하다 account 계정, 계좌 convenient 편리한 shareable 공유할 수 있는 one by one 일일이, 하나씩 concern ~와 관련되다 guarantee ~을 보장하다 be confident that ~라고 확신하다 be skeptical of ~에 대해 회의적이다 the claim that ~하다는 주장 leak ~을 유출시키다 subscription (서비스 등의) 가입, 구독 renew ~을 갱신하다 help + 목적어 + 동사원형: (목적어)가 ~하는 데 도움이 되다 make a decision 결정을 내리다 allow + 목적어 + to 동사원형: (목적어)가 ~할 수 있게 해 주다 all at once 모두 한꺼번에

40 세부 정보

Why has Christine been thinking about a new file storage option?

(a) Her desktop is disorganized.
(b) She would like better security.
(c) Her laptop has been slow lately.
(d) She needs space for work files.

크리스틴은 왜 새로운 파일 저장 선택 사항과 관련해 계속 생각하고 있는가?

(a) 자신의 데스크톱 컴퓨터가 체계적이지 못하다.
(b) 더 좋은 보안 상태를 원한다.
(c) 자신의 노트북 컴퓨터가 최근에 느려졌다.
(d) 업무용 파일을 위한 공간이 필요하다.

정답 (d)

해설 대화 초반부에 여자가 노트북 컴퓨터에 파일들이 가득해 지고 있다고 밝히면서 홍보용 연설에서 사용하는 파일들을 위해 더 많은 저장 공간을 확보하는 것에 관해 생각해 보고 있다고(I've been thinking about getting more storage for the files that I use in my promotional talks) 알리고 있으므로 (d)가 정답입니다.

어휘 disorganized 체계적이지 못한 would like ~을 원하다, ~으로 하고 싶다

패러프레이징

getting more storage for the files that I use in my promotional talks → needs space for work files

41 세부 정보

Why is using external hard drive storage ideal for Christine's business trips?

(a) because it provides easy access
(b) because it fits in her luggage
(c) because it is password-protected
(d) because it charges quickly

외장 하드 드라이브 저장 공간을 이용하는 것이 왜 크리스틴의 출장에 이상적인가?

(a) 더 수월한 접근성을 제공해 주기 때문에
(b) 자신의 짐에 크기가 적합하기 때문에
(c) 비밀번호로 보호되기 때문에
(d) 빠르게 충전되기 때문에

정답 (a)

해설 여자가 대화 초반부에 외장 하드 드라이브 저장 공간 이용이 이상적이라고 생각하는 이유로 출장 중에서 어디에 있든 하드 드라이브에서 곧바로 문서를 꺼낼 수 있다는 점을(I think that using an external hard drive to store data is ideal ~ I can retrieve documents directly from a hard drive and deliver talks wherever I am) 언급하고 있습니다. 이는 편리한 접근성을 말하는 것이므로 (a)가 정답입니다.

어휘 fit (크기 등이) 적합하다, 어울리다 luggage 짐, 수하물 charge 충전되다

패러프레이징

retrieve documents directly / wherever I am → provides easy access

---

42 세부 정보

What could be a problem if Christine uses a hard drive when giving presentations?

(a) that it could get lost
(b) that files could be deleted
(c) that it could become damaged
(d) that files could be stolen

크리스틴이 발표할 때 하드 드라이브를 이용하면 무엇이 문제가 될 수 있는가?

(a) 분실될 수 있다는 점
(b) 파일이 삭제될 수 있다는 점
(c) 손상될 수 있다는 점
(d) 파일이 도난될 수 있다는 점

정답 (c)

해설 대화 중반부에 여자가 하드 드라이브가 손상될 수 있다는 점이 우려된다고 말하면서 막 연설하려고 할 때 서두르는 경향이 있다고(~ what I'm concerned about is that a hard drive can get damaged. I tend to rush when I'm about to give a talk ~) 밝히고 있으므로 (c)가 정답입니다.

어휘 get lost 분실되다 delete ~을 삭제하다

---

43 세부 정보

According to Lawrence, how can using cloud storage be convenient for Christine?

(a) by enabling her to share files
(b) by allowing for faster software updates
(c) by keeping all her files in order
(d) by extending the laptop's battery life

로렌스의 말에 따르면, 클라우드 저장 공간을 이용하는 것이 어떻게 크리스틴에게 편리할 수 있는가?

(a) 파일을 공유할 수 있게 함으로써
(b) 더 빠른 소프트웨어 업데이트를 가능하게 함으로써
(c) 모든 파일을 순서에 맞게 유지하게 함으로써
(d) 노트북 컴퓨터의 배터리 수명을 연장함으로써

정답 (a)

해설 남자가 대화 중반부에 클라우드 저장 공간이 지닌 한 가지 편리한 점으로 공유 가능하다는 특징을(~ another convenient thing about cloud storage is that it's shareable) 언급하고 있으므로 (a)가 정답입니다.

어휘 enable + 목적어 + to 동사원형: (목적어)가 ~할 수 있게 해 주다 allow for ~을 가능하게 하다 in order 순서에 맞게 extend ~을 연장하다

> 패러프레이징
>
> shareable → enabling her to share files

44 세부 정보

Why is Christine worried about using cloud storage?

(a) because of limited access
(b) because of security concerns
(c) because of constant updates
(d) because of price increases

크리스틴이 클라우드 저장 공간을 이용하는 것과 관련해 걱정하는 이유가 무엇인가?

(a) 제한적인 이용 권한 때문에
(b) 보안 우려 때문에
(c) 지속적인 업데이트 때문에
(d) 가격 인상 때문에

정답 (b)

해설 여자가 대화 후반부에 자신의 계정이 해킹 당할 리 없다고 정말로 확신하지 못한다는(I'm not really confident that my account can't be hacked) 문제를 언급하고 있습니다. 이는 계정 보안 문제를 걱정하고 있다는 뜻이므로 (b)가 정답입니다.

어휘 limited 제한적인 constant 지속적인, 끊임없는 increase 인상, 증가

> 패러프레이징
>
> not really confident that my account can't be hacked → security concerns

What has Christine most likely decided to do after the conversation?

(a) buy a different laptop computer
(b) get a portable storage device
(c) subscribe to an online service
(d) bring paper files during her trips

크리스틴은 대화 후에 무엇을 하기로 결정했을 것 같은가?

(a) 다른 노트북 컴퓨터를 구입하는 일
(b) 휴대용 저장 장치를 구입하는 일
(c) 온라인 서비스에 가입하는 일
(d) 출장 중에 종이 파일을 챙겨 가는 일

정답 (c)

해설 대화 마지막 부분에 여자가 고객들과 모두 한꺼번에 파일을 공유할 수 있게 해 주는 선택 사항을 고를 것 같다고(I think I'll choose the option that allows me to share files with my clients all at once) 언급하고 있습니다. 이는 대화 중반부에 남자가 언급하는 클라우드 저장 공간의 장점에 해당하므로 (c)가 정답입니다.

어휘 portable 휴대용의 subscribe to (서비스 등) ~에 가입하다, ~을 구독하다

PART 4

Good morning, everyone. In honor of Emergency Preparedness Month and the first responders who risk their lives every day, welcome to the annual Disaster Management Conference.

Earthquakes, fires, and deadly storms can often happen with very little warning, so it is best to always be prepared. **46** Today, I would like to offer some advice on how to prepare for a disaster and deal with emergencies effectively.

The first tip is to set up your phone so it can receive emergency alerts. No one has time to stay glued to the news all day, and disaster tends to strike when you least expect it. We do, however, usually have our phones with us. That's why it's important to have official notifications from government agencies sent directly to you. **47** These notifications allow people to receive real-time updates about impending weather disturbances like storms and hurricanes.

The second tip is to attend emergency response training. Disasters can cause an array of injuries, so it is best to be prepared for such emergencies and learn what you can do to help. Having knowledge of basic medical treatments will come in handy in any emergency situation. **48** By attending disaster preparedness workshops, you can learn first aid skills, such as treating wounds and burns and performing CPR.

The third tip is to make a home emergency plan with your family. Safety starts at home, so make sure that every household member knows what to do. Let everyone know where they can find emergency supplies, such as candles for use when the power goes out. Point out all of the emergency exits in case you have to evacuate the house quickly.

안녕하세요, 여러분. 응급 상황 대비의 달과 매일 자신의 목숨을 걸고 있는 응급 구조원들을 기리는, 연례 재난 관리 컨퍼런스에 오신 것을 환영합니다.

지진과 화재, 그리고 치명적인 폭풍우는 흔히 아주 미미한 경고조차 없이 발생할 수 있으므로, 항상 대비하는 것이 최선입니다. 오늘, 저는 효과적으로 재난에 대비하고 응급 상황에 대처하는 방법에 관해 몇 가지 조언을 제공해 드리고자 합니다.

첫 번째 팁은 긴급 재난 메시지를 받을 수 있도록 전화기를 설정하시는 것입니다. 하루 종일 뉴스에 주의를 집중한 상태로 있을 시간이 있는 사람은 아무도 없으며, 재난은 전혀 예상하지 못할 때 들이 닥치는 경향이 있습니다. 하지만, 분명 평소에 우리 곁에는 전화기가 있습니다. 그것이 바로 정부 기관들에 의해 직접적으로 전송되는 공식 알림 메시지를 받는 것이 중요한 이유입니다. 이러한 알림 메시지들은 사람들에게 폭풍우과 허리케인 같이 임박한 기상 지각 변동과 관련된 실시간 정보를 받을 수 있게 해 줍니다.

두 번째 팁은 비상 대응 훈련에 참석하는 것입니다. 재난은 다양한 부상을 초래할 수 있으므로, 그러한 응급 상황에 대비하고 도움을 주기 위해 할 수 있는 것을 터득하는 것이 최선입니다. 기본적인 의학 치료에 대한 지식을 갖춰 두면 어떠한 응급 상황에서도 쓸모가 있을 것입니다. 재난 대비 워크숍에 참석함으로써, 상처 및 화상 치료와 심폐소생술 실시 같은 응급 처치 기술을 배울 수 있습니다.

세 번째 팁은 가족과 함께 가정용 비상 계획을 세워 두는 것입니다. 안전은 집에서 시작되므로, 반드시 가정 내 모든 구성원이 무엇을 해야 하는지 알고 있도록 하십시오. 모든 사람에게 전기가 나갔을 때 사용할 수 있는 양초 같은 비상 용품을 어디서 찾을 수 있는지 알려 주시기 바랍니다. 집에서 신속히 대피해야 하는 경우에 대비해 모든 비상구를 표시해 두십시오.

49 Children in particular should be oriented on where the exits are so they can follow the proper emergency procedure even if their parents are away.

The fourth tip is to make a communications plan. It can be alarming when disaster occurs while family members are away from home and separated from each other. Family members should therefore know how to get in touch with each other to find out everybody's whereabouts. **50** In some cases, communication may not be possible, so assign a meeting point where everyone can gather. Doing this could spare everyone the stress of not knowing where to go when an emergency happens.

The fifth tip is to prepare a disaster kit. In the confusion of the moment, you might not know which necessities to grab, nor will you have time to gather everything. Your kit must contain the basic needs like water, food, and medicine, and the supplies must be enough for at least two days. You can also pack a battery-operated radio so you can listen to the news. **51** The radio will let you receive rescue updates even during blackouts. A flashlight and whistle can be used to send out a signal when you need to call for help from your location.

Lastly, prepare your vehicle. As long as the roads are safe enough to drive on, your vehicle can be very useful during disasters. It will help your family evacuate immediately from dangerous areas and head towards safer places. **52** Always make sure that your car is in good condition and has extra emergency items like jumper cables, towing ropes, and a spare tire. You can also have a disaster kit ready in the car.

Thank you for attending the conference, and remember: you won't always know when a disaster is coming, but with just a little bit of planning, you can be ready for anything.

특히 아이들은 설령 부모가 부재 중이라 하더라도 적절한 비상 절차를 따를 수 있도록 비상구가 있는 곳과 관련해 위치를 파악하고 있어야 합니다.

네 번째 팁은 연락 계획을 세우는 것입니다. 가족 구성원들이 집에 있지 않아서 서로 떨어져 있는 동안 재난이 발생하는 경우에는 불안할 수 있습니다. 따라서, 가족 구성원들은 모두의 행방을 파악할 수 있도록 서로 연락할 방법을 알고 있어야 합니다. 어떤 경우에는, 연락이 가능하지 않을 수 있으므로, 모두가 모일 수 있는 만남의 장소를 지정해 두십시오. 이렇게 하시면 비상 사태가 발생하는 경우에 모두가 어디로 가야 하는지 알지 못하는 스트레스를 겪지 않을 수 있습니다.

다섯 번째 팁은 재난 대비 물품 세트를 준비하는 것입니다. 순간적으로 혼란스러울 때는, 어느 필수품을 가져 가야 할지 알지 못할 수도 있고, 모든 것을 챙길 시간도 없을 것입니다. 이 물품 세트는 반드시 물과 식량, 그리고 의약품 같은 기본적인 필수품을 포함해야 하며, 이 물품은 반드시 최소 이틀을 버티기에 충분해야 합니다. 뉴스를 들으실 수 있도록 배터리로 작동하는 라디오를 챙기실 수도 있습니다. 이 라디오는 심지어 정전 중에도 구조 소식을 듣게 해 줄 것입니다. 손전등과 호루라기는 여러분이 계시는 곳에서 도움을 요청할 필요가 있을 때 신호를 보내시는 데 쓰일 수 있습니다.

마지막으로, 차량을 준비하십시오. 도로가 운전하기에 충분히 안전하기만 하다면, 여러분의 차량은 재난 중에 매우 유용할 수 있습니다. 위험한 구역에서 즉시 대피해 더 안전한 장소로 향하도록 여러분의 가족에게 도움을 줄 것입니다. 항상 반드시 자동차가 좋은 상태로 유지되도록, 그리고 점퍼 케이블과 견인용 로프, 그리고 예비 타이어 같은 추가 비상 물품이 있도록 해 두시기 바랍니다. 또한 자동차에 재난 대피 물품 세트를 준비해 놓으실 수도 있습니다.

컨퍼런스에 참석해 주셔서 감사 드리며, 기억하셔야 하는 점은, 재난이 언제 닥칠지 항상 알지는 못하겠지만, 약간의 계획만으로도, 어떤 일에도 대비하실 수 있다는 사실입니다.

어휘 in honor of ~을 기리는 **emergency** 응급 상황, 비상 사태 **preparedness** 대비, 준비 **first responder** 응급 구조원 **risk one's life** ~의 목숨을 걸다 **annual** 연례적인, 해마다의 **disaster** 재난, 재해 **how + to 동사원형:** ~하는 방법 **deal with** ~에 대처하다, ~을 처리하다 **effectively** 효과적으로 **set up** ~을 설정하다, ~을 설치하다 **alert** 경고, 경보 **stay 형용사:** ~한 상태를 유지하다 **glued** 주의를 집중한, 눈을 떼지 않는 **tend + to 동사원형:** ~하는 경향이 있다 **strike** (재난, 질병 등이) 들이닥치다, 갑자기 발생하다 **notification** 알림 (메시지), 통지(서) **allow + 목적어 + to 동사원형:** (목적어)가 ~할 수 있게 해 주다 **real-time** 실시간의 **impending** 임박한, 곧 닥칠 **disturbance** 지각 변동, 소란, 장애 **response** 대응, 반응 **cause** ~을 초래하다 **an array of** 다양한 **injury** 부상 **treatment** 치료, 처치 **come in handy** 쓸모가 있다, 도움이 되다 **first aid** 응급 처치 **wound** 상처 **burn** 화상 **CPR** 심폐소생술 **make sure that** 반드시 ~하도록 하다, ~임을 확실히 해 두다 **let + 목적어 + know:** (목적어)에게 알리다 **supplies** 용품, 물품 **point out** ~을 표시하다, ~을 가리키다 **in case (that)** ~하는 경우에 (대비해) **evacuate** ~에서 대피하다 **in particular** 특히 **orient** ~에게 방향을 알리다 **follow** ~을 따르다 **proper** 적절한, 제대로 된 **procedure** 절차 **alarming** 불안한, 걱정스러운 **be separated from** ~와 떨어져 있다, ~에서 분리되다 **get in touch with** ~와 연락하다 **find out** ~을 파악하다, ~을 알아내다 **whereabouts** 행방, 소재 **assign** ~을 지정하다, ~을 배정하다 **spare A B:** A에게 B를 겪지 않게 하다 **confusion** 혼란, 혼동 **not A nor B:** A도 아니고 B도 아니다 **necessity** 필수품 **contain** ~을 포함하다 **at least** 최소한, 적어도 **pack** (짐 등) ~을 챙기다, ~을 꾸리다 **A-operated:** A로 작동하는 **rescue** 구조, 구출 **blackout** 정전 **call for** ~을 요청하다 **as long as** ~하기만 하면, ~하는 한 **enough + to 동사원형:** ~할 정도로 충분히 **head towards** ~로 향하다, ~로 가다 **jumper cable** 점퍼 케이블(자동차 배터리 충전용 케이블) **towing** 견인

---

46 주제/목적

What is the speaker mainly discussing?	화자는 주로 무엇을 이야기하고 있는가?
(a) avoiding unexpected illness	(a) 예기치 못한 질병을 피하는 것
(b) planning for dangerous situations	(b) 위험한 상황에 대비해 계획하는 일
(c) training to be a first responder	(c) 응급 구조원이 되기 위해 훈련 받는 일
(d) teaching emergency medicine	(d) 응급 의학을 가르치는 일

정답 (b)

해설 화자가 담화 초반부에 효과적으로 재난에 대비하고 응급 상황에 대처하는 방법에 관해 몇 가지 조언을 제공하겠다고(I would like to offer some advice on how to prepare for a disaster and deal with emergencies effectively) 밝힌 뒤로 관련 팁을 하나씩 소개하고 있으므로 (b)가 정답입니다.

어휘 avoid ~을 피하다 unexpected 예기치 못한, 뜻밖의 illness 질병 train 훈련 받다

> **패러프레이징**
>
> prepare for a disaster and deal with emergencies effectively → planning for dangerous situations

How can emergency alerts help one prepare for a disaster?

(a) by live streaming news reports
(b) by allowing time to order supplies
(c) by connecting to rescue services
(d) by providing key status updates

긴급 재난 문자 메시지가 어떻게 재난에 대비하는 데 도움을 줄 수 있는가?

(a) 뉴스 보도를 인터넷으로 생방송함으로써
(b) 물품을 주문할 시간을 허용함으로써
(c) 구조대와 연락됨으로써
(d) 중요한 상황 정보를 제공함으로써

정답 (d)

해설 담화 초반부에 화자가 긴급 재난 문자 메시지를 언급하면서 그 알림 메시지가 사람들에게 임박한 기상 지각 변동과 관련된 실시간 정보를 받을 수 있게 해 준다고(These notifications allow people to receive real-time updates about impending weather disturbances like storms and hurricanes) 알리고 있으므로 (d)가 정답입니다.

어휘 help + 목적어 + 동사원형: ~하는 데 (목적어)에게 도움을 주다 **stream** ~을 인터넷에서 방송하다 **connect to** ~와 연락되다, ~와 연결되다 **key** 중요한, 필수적인 **status** 상황

패러프레이징

allow people to receive real-time updates about impending weather disturbances → providing key status updates

---

Why should one attend disaster preparedness workshops?

(a) to find out how to avoid disasters
(b) to become a trained professional
(c) to learn how to care for injuries
(d) to borrow emergency equipment

재난 대비 워크숍에 왜 참석해야 하는가?

(a) 재난을 피하는 방법을 파악하기 위해
(b) 훈련된 전문가가 되기 위해
(c) 부상을 돌보는 방법을 배우기 위해
(d) 비상용 장비를 빌리기 위해

정답 (c)

해설 화자가 담화 중반부에 재난 대비 워크숍에 참석하면 상처 및 화상 치료와 심폐소생술 실시 같은 응급 처치 기술을 배울 수

있다는(By attending disaster preparedness workshops, you can learn first aid skills, such as treating wounds and burns and performing CPR) 점을 언급하고 있으므로 (c)가 정답입니다.

어휘 professional n. 전문가 care for ~을 돌보다, ~을 보살피다 borrow ~을 빌리다 equipment 장비

TEST 02

> **패러프레이징**
>
> learn first aid skills, such as treating wounds and burns → learn how to care for injuries

---

49 세부 정보

Based on the talk, what could a home emergency plan allow children to do on their own?

(a) contact neighbors for assistance
(b) put out a small fire
(c) find emergency supplies quickly
(d) exit the house safely

담화 내용에 따르면, 가정용 비상 계획이 아이들에게 스스로 무엇을 할 수 있게 해 줄 수 있는가?

(a) 도움을 받기 위해 이웃에게 연락하는 일
(b) 작은 불을 끄는 일
(c) 신속히 비상 용품을 찾는 일
(d) 안전하게 집에서 나가는 일

정답 (d)

해설 담화 중반부에 화자가 가정 비상 계획과 관련해 이야기하면서 아이들이 부모가 없을 때도 적절한 비상 절차를 따를 수 있도록 비상구의 위치를 파악하고 있어야 한다고(Children in particular should be oriented on where the exits are so they can follow the proper emergency procedure even if their parents are away) 말하고 있습니다. 이는 아이들 스스로 비상구를 찾아 대피하는 일을 의미하므로 (d)가 정답입니다.

어휘 contact ~에게 연락하다 assistance 도움, 지원 put out ~을 끄다 exit ~에서 나가다

> **패러프레이징**
>
> be oriented on where the exits are so they can follow the proper emergency procedure → exit the house safely

Why, most likely, is it important that families set an emergency meeting place?

(a) They might be unable to find help.
(b) They may lack transportation.
(c) They might lose contact.
(d) They may be in unfamiliar areas.

가족이 비상용 만남의 장소를 정하는 것이 왜 중요할 것 같은가?

(a) 도움을 구할 수 없을지도 모른다.
(b) 교통편이 부족해질 수 있다.
(c) 연락이 끊길지도 모른다.
(d) 익숙하지 않은 곳에 있을 수 있다.

정답 (c)

해설 화자가 담화 중반부에 가족 구성원 사이의 연락 계획과 관련해 이야기하면서 연락이 가능하지 않을 경우에 대비해 모두가 모일 수 있는 만남의 장소를 지정해 놓도록(In some cases, communication may not be possible, so assign a meeting point where everyone can gather) 당부하고 있으므로 (c)가 정답입니다.

어휘 **be unable + to 동사원형**: ~할 수 없다 **lack** ~이 부족하다 **transportation** 교통(편) **lose contact** 연락이 끊기다 **unfamiliar** 익숙하지 않은, 잘 알지 못하는

패러프레이징

communication may not be possible → might lose contact

How can a battery-operated radio be useful during a disaster?

(a) by keeping people informed
(b) by providing entertainment
(c) by allowing people to signal
(d) by charging other devices

배터리로 작동하는 라디오가 재난 중에 어떻게 유용할 수 있는가?

(a) 사람들에게 계속 정보를 알림으로써
(b) 오락거리를 제공해 줌으로써
(c) 사람들에게 신호를 보낼 수 있게 함으로써
(d) 다른 기기를 충전해 줌으로써

정답 (a)

해설 담화 후반부에 화자가 배터리로 작동하는 라디오를 언급하면서 정전 중에도 구조 소식을 듣게 해 준다(The radio will let you receive rescue updates even during blackouts) 장점을 알리고 있으므로 (a)가 정답입니다.

어휘 **keep + 목적어 + informed**: (목적어)에게 계속 알리다 **entertainment** 오락(거리) **signal** 신호를 보내다 **charge** ~을 충전하다 **device** 기기, 장치

52 세부 정보

What should one always make sure about his or her vehicle for emergencies?

(a) that it has an extra set of keys
(b) that it is full of gas
(c) that it has emergency snacks
(d) that it is in good shape

사람들이 비상 사태에 대비해 차량과 관련해 무엇을 확실히 해 두어야 하는가?

(a) 여분의 열쇠 꾸러미가 있도록 하는 것
(b) 연료가 가득한 상태로 있도록 하는 것
(c) 비상용 간식이 있도록 하는 것
(d) 좋은 상태로 있도록 하는 것

정답 (d)

해설 화자가 담화 후반부에 차량과 관련된 팁을 전하면서 항상 좋은 상태로 유지되도록 하라고(Always make sure that your car is in good condition) 조언하고 있으므로 (d)가 정답입니다.

어휘 be full of ~로 가득하다 in good shape 상태가 좋은

패러프레이징

in good condition → in good shape

❌ 오답 피하기

화자가 마지막 팁을 설명하면서 끝에 차 안에 재난 대피 물품 세트를 준비해 둘 수도 있다(You can also have a disaster kit ready in the car)라고 언급하는 것을 듣고 이를 비상용 간식(emergency snacks)과 연결하여 (c)를 정답으로 고를 수 있습니다. 하지만 이 문장은 부사 also를 사용하여 재난 대피 물품 세트를 두는 것은 추가적으로 준비할 수 있는 것을 덧붙여 설명한 것입니다. 질문의 키워드인 always make sure about his or her vehicle이 언급된 문장은 Always make sure that your car is in good condition이므로 (c)는 오답입니다.

PART 1

WANGARI MAATHAI

Wangari Maathai was a Kenyan educator, activist, and environmentalist **53** best known for being the first African woman to receive a Nobel Peace Prize. She founded the Green Belt Movement, an environmental organization that promotes the conservation of African forests.

Wangari Muta Maathai was born on April 1, 1940, in the town of Nyeri, Kenya. Maathai's awareness of the natural environment started when she was a child. Growing up, she spent time playing in streams and fetching water and firewood for her family. **54** Because her family obtained most of their necessities from the natural world, they associated nature with God and believed that the trees prevented disasters from happening to their land.

55 Although going to school was rare for girls at that time, Maathai was able to complete early education in various Catholic schools, finishing first in her classes. She qualified for a scholarship at Benedictine College in the United States, earning a degree in biology in 1964. She also **58** undertook doctoral courses in Germany and completed them in 1971 at the University of Nairobi, becoming the first woman in either East or Central Africa to earn a doctorate.

Maathai became an active member of the National Council of Women of Kenya, advocating for the rights of poor women whose lives were affected by the destruction of the country's natural resources. **56** Maathai sought to end the massive problem of deforestation by encouraging the village women to

왕가리 마타이

왕가리 마타이는 케냐의 교육가이자 활동가, 그리고 환경 운동가이며, 노벨 평화상을 수상한 최초의 아프리카 여성으로 가장 잘 알려져 있다. 그녀는 아프리카의 삼림 보존을 증진하는 환경 단체인, '그린 벨트 운동'을 설립했다.

왕가리 무타 마타이는 1940년 4월 1일에 케냐의 니에리라는 마을에서 태어났다. 자연 환경에 대한 마타이의 인식은 어렸을 때 시작되었다. 성장하면서, 그녀는 시냇물에서 놀기도 하고 가족을 위해 물과 땔감을 가져 가면서 시간을 보냈다. 그녀의 가족이 자연 세계에서 대부분의 필수품을 얻었기 때문에, 자연을 신과 연관 지었으며, 나무가 자신들의 땅에 재해가 발생하지 않게 막아 준다고 생각했다.

학교에 다니는 것이 당시의 여자 아이들에게는 흔치 않음에도 불구하고, 마타이는 다양한 가톨릭 학교에서 초기 교육을 이수할 수 있었으며, 자신의 반에서 1등으로 끝마쳤다. 그녀는 미국 베네딕틴 칼리지의 장학금에 대한 자격을 얻었으며, 1964년에 생물학 학위를 취득했다. 그녀는 또한 독일에서 박사 과정을 시작했고 1971년에 나이로비 대학교에서 이수하면서, 동아프리카 또는 중앙 아프리카에서 박사 학위를 취득한 최초의 여성이 되었다.

마타이는 케냐의 국가 여성 위원회의 적극적인 위원이 되어, 자국의 천연 자원 파괴로 인해 삶에 영향을 받은 가난한 여성들의 권리를 옹호했다. 마타이는 마을 여성들에게 나무를 심도록 권장함으로써 심각한 삼림 벌채 문제를 끝내려 했다. 이것이 그린 벨트 운동이 되었으며, 이는 곧 인접한 아프리카 국

plant trees. This became the Green Belt Movement, which was soon adopted by neighboring African countries. The organization has since planted over fifty-one million trees and provided thousands of women with a way to earn a living.

Maathai also led anti-government protests that led to her being arrested numerous times. In 1989, for example, **57** she staged a successful protest against the felling of trees in a recreational park that were being cleared to make room for a skyscraper. She was elected to Kenya's parliament in 2002 and **59** appointed as Assistant Minister in the Ministry for Environment and Natural Resources the following year. In 2004, Maathai received the Nobel Peace Prize for "her contributions to sustainable development, democracy, and peace."

When Maathai died in 2011, an award called the Wangari Maathai Forest Champion Award was launched with the purpose of recognizing others who contribute to the preservation and management of forests.

가들에 의해 채택되었다. 이 단체는 그 이후로 5천 백만 그루가 넘는 나무를 심어 왔으며, 수천 명의 여성들에게 생계를 유지할 방법을 제공해 왔다.

마타이는 또한 반정부 시위도 이끌었는데, 이는 그녀가 수 차례 체포되는 일로 이어졌다. 예를 들어, 1989년에는, 고층 건물에 필요한 공간을 마련하기 위해 제거되고 있던 한 휴양 공원의 나무 벌목에 반대하는 시위를 성공적으로 벌였다. 그녀는 2002년에 케냐 국회의원으로 선출되었으며, 이듬해에 환경 자원부 차관으로 선임되었다. 2004년에, 마타이는 "지속 가능한 개발과 민주주의, 그리고 평화에 대한 기여"로 노벨 평화상을 수상했다.

마타이가 2011년에 사망했을 때, '왕가리 마타이 포레스트 챔피언 상'이라고 불리는 상이 삼림 보존 및 관리에 기여하는 다른 이들을 인정하기 위한 목적으로 시작되었다.

어휘 activist 활동가 environmentalist 환경 운동가 best known for ~로 가장 잘 알려진 found ~을 설립하다 organization 단체, 기관 promote ~을 증진하다 conservation 보존, 보호 awareness 인식, 의식 grow up 성장하다, 자라다 stream 시내, 개울 fetch ~을 가져 오다 obtain ~을 획득하다, ~을 얻다(= earn) necessity 필수품 associate A with B: A를 B와 연관 짓다 prevent + 목적어 + from -ing: (목적어)가 ~하게 못하게 막다 disaster 재난, 재해 rare 흔치 않은, 드문 be able + to 동사원형: ~할 수 있다 complete ~을 이수하다, ~을 완료하다 qualify for ~에 대한 자격을 얻다 scholarship 장학금 degree 학위 biology 생물학 undertake ~을 시작하다, ~에 착수하다 either A or B: A 또는 B 둘 중의 하나 doctorate 박사 학위 active 적극적인, 활동적인 advocate for ~을 옹호하다 right 권리 affect ~에 영향을 미치다 destruction 파괴 resource 자원, 자산 seek + to 동사원형: ~하려 하다, ~하는 것을 추구하다 massive 심각한, 거대한 deforestation 삼림 벌채 encourage + 목적어 + to 동사원형: (목적어)에게 ~하도록 권장하다 plant ~을 심다 adopt ~을 채택하다 neighboring 인접한, 이웃의 provide A with B: A에게 B를 제공하다 way + to 동사원형: ~하는 방법 earn a living 생계를 유지하다 anti-government 반정부의 protest 시위 lead to ~로 이어지다 arrest ~을 체포하다 numerous 다수의, 수많은 stage a protest 시위를 벌이다 felling (나무의) 벌채, 벌목 make room 공간을 마련하다 skyscraper 고층 건물 elect ~을 선출하다 parliament 의회 appoint A as B: A를 B로 선임하다 contribution 기여, 공헌 sustainable 지속 가능한 democracy 민주주의 launch ~을 시작하다, ~에 착수하다 recognize ~을 인정하다 contribute to ~에 기여하다, ~에 공헌하다

What is Wangari Maathai best known for?

(a) becoming a famous politician
(b) founding religious organizations
(c) winning a prestigious award
(d) pioneering education reforms

왕가리 마타이는 무엇으로 가장 잘 알려져 있는가?

(a) 유명 정치인이 된 것
(b) 종교 단체를 설립한 것
(c) 권위 있는 상을 수상한 것
(d) 교육 개혁의 선구자가 된 것

정답 (c)

해설 첫 단락에 왕가리 마타이가 노벨 평화상을 수상한 최초의 아프리카 여성으로 가장 잘 알려져 있다는(best known for being the first African woman to receive a Nobel Peace Prize) 정보가 제시되어 있으므로 (c)가 정답입니다.

어휘 politician 정치인 religious 종교의 prestigious 권위 있는, 명망 있는 pioneer v. ~의 선구자가 되다, ~을 개척하다 reform 개혁

패러프레이징

receive a Nobel Peace Prize → winning a prestigious award

Why did Maathai's family have spiritual beliefs about nature?

(a) because they attended church regularly
(b) because they depended on it for their everyday needs
(c) because they experienced disasters frequently
(d) because they lacked access to it in their daily lives

마타이의 가족이 자연과 관련해 종교적 믿음을 갖고 있었던 이유는 무엇인가?

(a) 주기적으로 교회에 다녔기 때문에
(b) 일상에서 필요한 것들에 대해 그것에 의존했기 때문에
(c) 자주 재난을 경험했기 때문에
(d) 일상 생활 속에서 그에 대한 접근 기회가 부족했기 때문에

정답 (b)

해설 두 번째 단락에 자연 세계에서 대부분의 필수품을 얻었기 때문에 자연을 신과 연관지었다는(Because her family obtained most of their necessities from the natural world, they associated nature with God ~) 내용이 쓰여 있으므로 (b)가 정답입니다.

어휘 depend on ~에 의존하다 experience v. ~을 경험하다 frequently 자주, 빈번히 lack v. ~이 부족하다 access to ~에 대한 접근 (기회)

---

55 추론

Why, most likely, were Maathai's academic achievements unexpected?

(a) Females were rarely given access to education.
(b) She frequently argued with her teachers.
(c) Schools seldom accepted poor students.
(d) She initially performed poorly in her classes.

마타이의 학업적 성취가 왜 예기치 못한 일이었을 것 같은가?

(a) 여성들이 좀처럼 교육에 대한 접근 기회를 얻지 못했다.
(b) 자신의 교사들과 자주 언쟁했다.
(c) 학교들이 가난한 학생들을 거의 받지 않았다.
(d) 처음에는 반에서 성적이 좋지 못했다.

정답 (a)

해설 세 번째 단락에 학교에 다니는 것이 당시의 여자 아이들에게 흔치 않았음에도 불구하고 마타이가 다양한 가톨릭 학교에서 초기 교육을 완료한(Although going to school was rare for girls at that time, Maathai was able to complete early education ~) 사실이 쓰여 있습니다. 이는 당시의 여자 아이들에게 교육 기회가 많지 않았음을 의미하는 것이므로 (a)가 정답입니다.

어휘 achievement 성취, 업적 unexpected 예기치 못한 rarely 좀처럼 ~ 않다 argue 언쟁하다 seldom 거의 ~ 않다 accept ~을 받아들이다 initially 처음에

According to the fourth paragraph, how did the Green Belt Movement come to be?

(a) through a women's rights organization
(b) through the physical labor of women
(c) through a women's advocate in parliament
(d) through peaceful protests by women

네 번째 문단에 따르면, '그린 벨트 운동'은 어떻게 만들어지게 되었는가?

(a) 한 여성 권리 단체를 통해
(b) 여성들의 육체 노동을 통해
(c) 의회의 한 여성 옹호자를 통해
(d) 여성들의 평화적 시위를 통해

정답 (b)

해설 네 번째 단락에 마을 여성들에게 나무를 심도록 권장한 것이 '그린 벨트 운동'으로 이어진 사실이(Maathai sought to end the massive problem of deforestation by encouraging the village women to plant trees. This became the Green Belt Movement ~) 언급되어 있으므로 (b)가 정답입니다.

어휘 come + to 동사원형: ~하게 되다 physical 육체적인, 물리적인 labor 노동, 근로 advocate n. 옹호자, 지지자

> **패러프레이징**
>
> plant trees → physical labor

Why, most likely, did Maathai lead protests against the government?

(a) She was an advocate for social reform.
(b) She hoped to achieve public recognition.
(c) She was angry about its control over her career.
(d) She disapproved of environmental destruction.

마타이가 왜 정부에 반대하는 시위를 이끌었는가?

(a) 사회 개혁의 옹호자였다.
(b) 대중의 인정을 받기를 바랐다.
(c) 자신의 경력에 대한 통제와 관련해 화가 났다.
(d) 환경 파괴에 반대했다.

정답 (d)

해설 다섯 번째 문단에 반정부 시위의 한 가지 예시로 나무 벌채에 반대하는 시위를 성공적으로 벌였다는(she staged a successful protest against the felling of trees ~) 내용이 제시되어 있습니다. 이는 환경 파괴에 반대한 시위에 해당하므로 (d)가 정답입니다.

어휘 achieve recognition 인정 받다 control 통제, 제어 disapprove of ~에 반대하다

58 동의어

In the context of the passage, underd <u>undertook</u> means _____.

(a) pursued
(b) abandoned
(c) opposed
(d) recovered

해당 단락의 문맥에서 <u>undertook</u>이 의미하는 것은?

(a) 추구했다
(b) 버렸다, 포기했다
(c) 반대했다
(d) 회복했다, 되찾았다

정답 (a)

해설 undertook은 undertake의 과거형이며, 해당 문장에서 동사 undertook 뒤에 목적어로 박사 과정을 뜻하는 doctoral courses가 쓰여 있고 그 뒤에는 이것을 완료했다는 말이 쓰여 있습니다. 따라서, undertook이 그 과정을 시작했다는 의미를 나타내는 동사임을 알 수 있으며, 이는 그것을 추구했다는 뜻으로 볼 수 있으므로 (a)가 정답입니다.

59 동의어

In the context of the passage, <u>appointed</u> means _____.

(a) planned
(b) contacted
(c) promised
(d) chosen

해당 단락의 문맥에서 <u>appointed</u>가 의미하는 것은?

(a) 계획된
(b) 연락된, 접촉된
(c) 약속된
(d) 선택된

정답 (d)

해설 해당 문장에서 과거분사 appointed 뒤에 직책을 뜻하는 전치사구 as Assistant Minister(차관으로)가 쓰여 있어 appointed가 그러한 역할을 위해 선임된 것을 가리키는 단어임을 알 수 있으며, 이는 선택된 것과 같으므로 (d)가 정답입니다.

PART 2

STUDYING STUDENT ROUTINES

Getting up early for school is something most people are familiar with, but **60** research shows that delaying school start times by as little as an hour can lead to improvements in students' academic performance.

Surveys show that more than half of high school students in the US do not get enough sleep. This can be **65** detrimental to their overall development, especially in the case of adolescents, who need more sleep due to growth spurts. Health organizations therefore suggest that classes start no earlier than 8:30 a.m., to give students adequate sleep for their physical and mental health.

61 A study by the University of Washington set out to confirm the effects of adjusting school starting hours. For a period of two weeks, researchers worked with two sets of approximately ninety students each from two different high schools. One group followed the usual class schedule of starting at 7:50 a.m., and the other started almost an hour later, at 8:45 a.m.

62 Instead of asking students about their sleep routines, the researchers had them wear wrist monitors to collect data on movement and light exposure. The students also filled out a survey to report data such as daytime sleepiness and mood. The behavior of the students in class was observed with the help of two participating teachers.

The researchers found that **63(b)** the students who started school later got an average of thirty-four extra minutes of sleep. Although some people might have expected the late-start group to change their bedtimes accordingly—as teens are normally inclined to be night owls—**63(d)** both groups actually went to sleep around the same time.

학생들의 일상 연구

학교에 가기 위해 일찍 일어나는 것은 대부분의 사람들이 익숙한 일이지만, 연구에 따르면 학교 시작 시간을 적어도 1시간 정도 지연시키면 학생들의 학업 성적 향상으로 이어질 수 있는 것으로 나타난다.

설문 조사에 따르면 미국 내에서 절반이 넘는 고등학생들이 잠을 충분히 자지 못하는 것으로 나타난다. 이는 그들의 전반적인 성장에 해로울 수 있으며, 특히 급성장으로 인해 잠이 더 필요한 청소년의 경우에 그러하다. 보건 기구들은 그래서 학생들에게 신체적, 정신적 건강을 위해 충분한 수면 시간을 제공할 수 있도록 수업이 아무리 빨라도 오전 8시 30분에는 시작되어야 한다고 제안한다.

워싱턴 대학에서 학교 시작 시간을 조정하는 것의 영향을 확인하기 위한 연구에 착수했다. 2주의 기간에, 연구진은 각각 두 곳의 서로 다른 고등학교에 속한 약 90명의 학생들로 구성된 두 개의 조와 협업했다. 한 그룹은 오전 7시 50분에 시작하는 일반적인 수업 일정을 따랐고, 나머지 그룹은 거의 한 시간이나 더 늦은 오전 8시 45분에 시작했다.

학생들에게 각자의 일상적인 수면과 관련해 묻는 대신, 연구진은 움직임 및 빛에 대한 노출에 관한 데이터를 수집하기 위해 손목 측정 장치를 착용하게 했다. 이 학생들은 낮 시간의 졸음 및 기분 같은 데이터를 알릴 수 있도록 설문 조사지도 작성했다. 이 학생들이 보인 수업 시간 중의 행동은 두 명의 참여 교사가 제공한 도움으로 관찰되었다.

연구진은 더 늦은 시간에 학교를 시작한 학생들이 평균 34분을 추가로 잤다는 사실을 알게 되었다. 어떤 사람들은 늦게 시작한 그룹이 그에 따라 취침 시간을 변경할 것으로 예상했을지도 모르겠지만-십대들은 보통 저녁형 인간이 되는 경향이 있기 때문에-두 그룹 모두 실제로는 거의 같은 시간에 잠자리에 들었다.

63(c) The students with the later school start were less sleepy and more focused in class. **63(a)** Their final grades in biology class were 4.5 percent higher than those of students with an earlier school start.

The study has **66** established the potential benefits of scheduling classes to start at a later time. However, schools and parents are concerned about the challenges such a change could involve, such as insufficient time for afterschool activities and household chores. Nevertheless, **64** experts say that gaining improvements in the students' mental and physical development would be worth the effort.

학교 시작 시간이 더 늦은 학생들은 수업 중에 덜 졸려 했으며, 수업에 더 많이 집중했다. 그들의 생물학 수업 최종 점수는 학교 시작 시간이 더 빨랐던 학생들의 점수보다 4.5퍼센트 더 높았다.

이 연구는 수업을 더 늦은 시간에 시작하도록 일정을 정하는 것의 잠재적 이점을 규명했다. 하지만, 학교와 부모들은 방과후 활동 및 집안일을 위한 시간 부족과 같은, 그러한 변화가 수반할 수 있는 문제에 대해 우려하고 있다. 그럼에도 불구하고, 전문가들은 학생들의 정신적, 육체적 발달에 있어 개선을 이루는 것이 그만한 노력의 가치가 있을 것이라고 말한다.

어휘 routine 일상(적인 일) be familiar with ~에 익숙하다, ~을 잘 알다 delay ~을 지연시키다 by (차이) ~ 정도, ~만큼 as little as A: 적어도 A, 최소한 A lead to ~로 이어지다 improvement 개선, 향상 survey 설문 조사(지) detrimental 해로운 overall 전반적인 development 성장, 발전 in the case of ~의 경우에 adolescent 청소년 due to ~로 인해, ~ 때문에 growth spurts 급성장 organization 기구, 단체 suggest that ~라고 제안하다, ~임을 시사하다 no earlier than 아무리 빨라도 ~에는 adequate 충분한, 적절한 physical 육체적인 mental 정신적인 set out 착수하다, 시작하다 confirm ~을 확인해 주다 effect 영향, 효과 adjust ~을 조정하다, ~을 조절하다 approximately 약, 대략 follow ~을 따르다 instead of ~ 대신 have + 목적어 + 동사원형: (목적어)에게 ~하게 하다 collect ~을 수집하다, ~을 모으다 exposure 노출 fill out ~을 작성하다 behavior 행동, 행실 observe ~을 관찰하다 participating 참여하는 average 평균 might have p.p. ~했을지도 모르다 expect + 목적어 + to 동사원형: (목적어)가 ~할 것으로 예상하다 accordingly 그에 따라 be inclined + to 동사원형: ~하는 경향이 있다 night owl 저녁형 인간 focused 집중한, 초점이 맞춰진 grade 점수, 등급 biology 생물학 establish ~을 규명하다, ~을 확립하다 potential 잠재적인 benefit 이점, 혜택 however 하지만, 그러나 be concerned about ~와 관련해 우려하다 challenge (어려운) 문제, 도전 과제 involve ~을 수반하다, ~와 관련되다 insufficient 불충분한 household chore 집안일 nevertheless 그럼에도 불구하고 expert 전문가 gain ~을 이루다, ~을 얻다 worth the + 명사: ~할 가치가 있는

What is the article mainly about?

(a) how exercise can improve academic performance
(b) how daily schedules can affect student achievement
(c) how diet can influence examination results
(d) how school day length can impact student happiness

기사가 주로 무엇에 관한 것인가?

(a) 운동이 어떻게 학업 성적을 향상시킬 수 있는가
(b) 하루 일과가 어떻게 학생의 성취도에 영향을 미칠 수 있는가
(c) 식단이 어떻게 시험 결과에 영향을 미칠 수 있는가
(d) 학교 수업일의 길이가 어떻게 학생의 행복에 영향을 미칠 수 있는가

정답 (b)

해설 첫 문단에 학교 시작 시간을 1시간 지연시키면 학생들의 학업 성적 향상으로 이어질 수 있다는 연구 결과가(research shows that delaying school start times by as little as an hour can lead to improvements in students' academic performance) 지문의 주제로 제시되어 있으므로 이러한 의미에 해당하는 (b)가 정답입니다.

어휘 exercise 운동 affect ~에 영향을 미치다(= influence, impact) achievement 성취(도), 업적

패러프레이징

improvements in students' academic performance → student achievement

What was the purpose of the research conducted by the University of Washington?

(a) to assess the effects of reduced homework
(b) to confirm the connection between phone use and sleep
(c) to verify the benefits of delayed school starts
(d) to disprove a link between class size and performance

워싱턴 대학교에서 실시한 연구의 목적은 무엇이었는가?

(a) 줄어든 과제의 영향을 평가하는 것
(b) 전화기 사용과 수면 사이의 연관성을 확인하는 것
(c) 지연된 학교 시작 시간의 이점을 입증하는 것
(d) 학급의 크기와 성적 사이의 연관성이 틀렸음을 입증하는 것

정답 (c)

해설 세 번째 문단에 워싱턴 대학의 연구가 학교 시작 시간을 조정하는 것의 영향을 확인하기 위한 것임을(A study by the University of Washington set out to confirm the effects of adjusting school starting hours) 나타내는 말이 쓰여 있으므로 이러한 목적에 해당하는 (c)가 정답입니다.

어휘 conduct ~을 실시하다 assess ~을 평가하다 effect 영향, 효과 connection 연관성(= link) verify ~을 입증하다, ~을 확인하다 disprove ~이 틀렸음을 입증하다

TEST 02

> 패러프레이징
>
> confirm the effects of adjusting school starting hours → verify the benefits of delayed school starts

62 추론

Why, most likely, were the study's participants asked to wear wrist monitors?

(a) so their overnight activities could be recorded
(b) so their mood changes could be observed
(c) so their daytime naps could be tracked
(d) so their hormone levels could be detected

해당 연구의 참가자들이 왜 손목 측정 장치를 착용하도록 요청 받았을 것 같은가?

(a) 그들의 야간 활동이 기록될 수 있으므로
(b) 그들의 기분 변화가 관찰될 수 있으므로
(c) 그들의 낮잠이 파악될 수 있으므로
(d) 그들의 호르몬 수준이 감지될 수 있으므로

정답 (a)

해설 네 번째 문단에 학생들에게 각자의 일상적인 수면과 관련해 묻는 대신 움직임 및 빛에 대한 노출에 관한 데이터를 수집하려고 손목 측정 장치를 착용하게 했다는(Instead of asking students about their sleep routines, the researchers had them wear wrist monitors to collect data on movement and light exposure) 내용이 쓰여 있습니다. 이는 밤 시간대에 대한 관찰을 위한 것이므로 (a)가 정답입니다.

어휘 observe ~을 관찰하다 daytime 낮 시간의 nap 낮잠 track ~을 파악하다, ~을 추적하다 detect ~을 감지하다

Which of the following is NOT true about the late-start group?

(a) They did better in an assessment than their peers.
(b) They tended to get more sleep than they had before.
(c) They had better concentration in their lessons.
(d) They began going to bed later than they had before.

늦게 시작하는 그룹과 관련해 사실이 아닌 것은 무엇인가?

(a) 한 평가에서 또래들보다 더 잘했다.
(b) 이전에 그랬던 것보다 더 많이 자는 경향이 있었다.
(c) 수업 중에 더 좋은 집중력을 보였다.
(d) 이전에 그랬던 것보다 더 늦게 잠자리에 들기 시작했다.

정답 (d)

해설 다섯 번째 문단에 학교 시간이 늦어진 그룹이 취침 시간을 변경할 것으로 예상했을지도 모른다는 말과 함께 실제로는 두 그룹의 학생들이 모두 비슷한 시간대에 잤다는(both groups actually went to sleep around the same time) 말이 쓰여 있어 평소보다 더 늦게 잠들지는 않았음을 알 수 있으므로 (d)가 정답입니다.

어휘 assessment 평가 peer 또래, 동료 tend + to 동사원형: ~하는 경향이 있다 concentration 집중(력)

What do experts say about adopting later start times in school?

(a) that the benefits for students outweigh the inconveniences
(b) that it will result in very little change
(c) that the consequences for parents make it impractical
(d) that it will positively impact teachers

전문가들은 학교에서 더 늦은 시작 시간을 채택하는 것과 관련해 무슨 말을 하는가?

(a) 학생을 위한 이점이 불편함보다 더 크다는 점
(b) 변화를 거의 초래하지 않을 것이라는 점
(c) 부모에게 미치는 영향이 그것을 비현실적으로 만든다는 점
(d) 교사들에게 긍정적으로 영향을 미칠 것이라는 점

정답 (a)

해설 마지막 문단에 전문가들이 학생들의 정신적, 육체적 발달에 있어 개선을 이루는 것이 그만한 노력의 가치가 있을 것이라고 말한다는(experts say that gaining improvements in the students' mental and physical development would be worth the effort) 내용이 제시되어 있으므로 이에 해당하는 의미를 지닌 (a)가 정답입니다.

어휘 benefit 이점, 혜택 outweigh ~보다 더 크다, ~보다 더 중요하다 inconvenience 불편함 result in ~을 초래하다, ~라는 결과를 낳다 consequence 영향(력), 결과 impractical 비현실적인 positively 긍정적으로 impact ~에 영향을 미치다

패러프레이징

- gaining improvements in the students' mental and physical development → the benefits for students
- worth the effort → outweigh the inconveniences

65 동의어

In the context of the passage, detrimental means _____.

(a) unnatural
(b) harmful
(c) applicable
(d) general

해당 단락의 문맥에서 detrimental 이 의미하는 것은?

(a) 비정상적인, 부자연스러운
(b) 해로운, 유해한
(c) 해당되는, 적용되는
(d) 일반적인, 보편적인

정답 (b)

해설 해당 문장에서 detrimental 앞에 위치한 주어 This는 앞 문장에서 학생들이 잠을 충분히 자지 못한다고 말한 것을 가리키며, detrimental 뒤에는 전반적인 성장을 의미하는 전치사구가 쓰여 있습니다. 따라서, 잠을 충분히 자지 못하는 것이 성장에 좋지 못하다는 의미임을 알 수 있으며, 이는 해로운 것과 같으므로 (b)가 정답입니다.

66 동의어

In the context of the passage, established means _____.

(a) reconsidered
(b) installed
(c) demonstrated
(d) organized

해당 단락의 문맥에서 established 가 의미하는 것은?

(a) 재고했다
(b) 설치했다
(c) 증명했다, 시연했다
(d) 조직했다, 주최했다

정답 (c)

해설 해당 문장에서 동사 has established 뒤에 수업을 더 늦은 시간에 시작하도록 일정을 정하는 것의 잠재적 이점을 의미하는 말이 목적어로 쓰여 있습니다. 따라서, 연구를 뜻하는 주어 The study가 그러한 이점을 확인하게 해 주었다는 의미를 나타내는 것으로 볼 수 있으며, 이는 증명한 것과 같으므로 (c)가 정답입니다.

PART 3

PARROTFISH

Parrotfish are a group of fish species that thrive in shallow, tropical waters. They are characterized by their beak-like mouths, which resemble that of a parrot and give the group its name. Parrotfish are known for their ability to convert dead coral into fine white sand, which **72** constitutes the world's famous white beaches. Moreover, parrotfish are one of the key factors in maintaining the health of reefs. **67** The fish come in a wide range of vivid colors, including intricate combinations of green, blue, orange, and yellow that can change throughout their lives.

Parrotfish are also known to shift their sex as they mature, with most fish being born female and changing to male within a few years. Younger females breed more successfully, while **68** larger, fully developed males can effectively defend their offspring. Male fish can even change back to female when necessary.

Parrotfish are hunted by moray eels and reef sharks. In the daytime, they use their speed to evade predators but, **69** at night, some species cover their body in a clear "cocoon" of mucus before sleeping to conceal their smell and make them more difficult for predators to detect.

70 The fish spend most of the day feeding on algae that grows on the coral and can negatively affect its health. This practice helps provide space for new coral to grow, keeping the coral reefs thriving. Parrotfish also eat dead coral by grinding it with their tough, beak-like teeth. The undigested waste is **73** deposited onto the ocean floor and eventually finds its way onto beaches as fine white sand. Each parrotfish can produce up to 700 pounds of sand a year.

앵무고기

앵무고기는 얕은 열대 바다에서 번성하는 물고기 종의 한 무리이다. 이들은 새 부리 같은 입으로 특징지어지는데, 그것이 앵무새의 입과 닮아서 이 무리의 이름이 그러하다. 앵무고기는 죽은 산호를 고운 백색 모래로 탈바꿈시키는 능력으로 알려져 있는데, 이는 전 세계의 유명한 백사장들을 구성하고 있다. 더욱이, 앵무고기는 암초의 건강을 유지하는 데 있어 핵심적인 요소들 중 하나이다. 이 물고기는 아주 다양한 선명한 색상을 지니고 있는데, 초록색과 파란색, 오렌지색, 그리고 노란색의 복잡한 조합을 포함하며, 이는 이들의 삶 전반에 걸쳐 바뀔 수 있다.

앵무고기는 성숙해 가는 과정에서 자신의 성을 바꿀 수 있는 것으로도 알려져 있으며, 대부분의 물고기가 암컷으로 태어났다가 수년 내에 수컷으로 바꾼다. 더 어린 암컷들이 더 성공적으로 알을 낳는 반면, 더 크고 완전히 성장한 수컷들은 효과적으로 새끼들을 지킬 수 있다. 수컷 물고기는 심지어 필요 시에 다시 암컷으로 바뀔 수도 있다.

앵무고기는 곰치와 암초 상어에 의해 사냥 당한다. 낮 시간에는, 속도를 이용해 포식자들을 피하지만, 야간에, 일부 종은 냄새를 감추기 위해 잠들기 전에 깨끗한 점액 "보호막"으로 몸을 덮어 포식자들이 감지하기 더 어렵게 만든다.

이 물고기는 산호에서 자라면서 산호의 건강에 부정적으로 영향을 미칠 수 있는 해조류를 먹으면서 하루의 대부분을 보낸다. 이러한 행위는 새로운 산호가 자랄 공간을 제공해 주는 데 도움을 주어, 산호초가 계속 번성하게 해 준다. 앵무고기는 튼튼하고 새 부리 같은 이빨로 갈아서 죽은 산호를 먹기도 한다. 소화되지 않은 노폐물은 해저에 침전되며, 결국 고운 백색 모래로 해변에 흘러 들어간다. 각 앵무고기는 해마다 최대 700파운드의 모래를 만들어 낼 수 있다.

Although most parrotfish species are not classified as "endangered," their populations are nonetheless threatened. Some species, such as the bumphead parrotfish, are already rare in the Pacific Islands as they are continuously hunted and sold for aquarium displays and as delicacies. Destruction of their habitats is also one of the major threats to their populations. Various organizations are currently implementing measures to protect parrotfish, including regulating the extent of fishing and **71** informing the public of the fish's importance.

비록 대부분의 앵무고기 종이 "멸종 위기에 처한" 것으로 분류되지는 않지만, 이들의 개체군은 그럼에도 불구하고 위협 받고 있다. 범프헤드 앵무고기 같은 일부 종은 이미 태평양 제도에서 희귀한 상태인데, 지속적으로 사냥되어 수족관 전시용으로, 그리고 별미로 판매되고 있기 때문이다. 이들의 서식지 파괴도 개체군에 대한 주요 위협 요소들 중 하나이다. 다양한 기관이 현재 앵무고기를 보호하기 위한 조치를 시행하고 있으며, 어획 규모를 규제하고 일반인들에게 이 물고기의 중요성을 알리는 일을 포함한다.

어휘 species (동식물의) 종 thrive 번성하다 shallow 얕은 tropical 열대의 be characterized by ~로 특징지어지다 beak 새 부리 resemble ~을 닮다 be known for ~로 알려져 있다 ability + to 동사원형: ~할 수 있는 능력 convert A into B: A를 B로 탈바꿈시키다, A를 B로 전환하다 coral 산호 fine 고운, 미세한, 가는 constitute ~을 구성하다 factor 요소, 요인 maintain ~을 유지하다 reef 암초 a wide range of 아주 다양한 vivid 선명한, 생생한 including ~을 포함해 intricate 복잡한 combination 조합, 결합 be known + to 동사원형: ~하는 것으로 알려지다 shift ~을 바꾸다, 바뀌다 mature v. 성숙하다 effectively 효과적으로 defend ~을 지키다, ~을 방어하다 offspring (동물의) 새끼, 자식 when necessary 필요 시에 evade ~을 피하다 predator 포식자 cocoon 보호막 mucus 점액 conceal ~을 감추다, ~을 숨기다 detect ~을 감지하다 feed on ~을 먹다 algae 해조류 negatively 부정적으로 affect ~에 영향을 미치다 practice 행위, 습관, 관행, 실행 keep + 목적어 + -ing: (목적어)가 계속 ~하게 하다 grind ~을 갈다 undigested 소화되지 않은 deposit v. ~을 침전시키다 ocean floor 해저 eventually 결국, 마침내 find one's way onto ~로 흘러 들다 up to 최대 ~까지 be classified as ~로 분류되다 endangered 멸종 위기에 처한 populations 개체군 nonetheless 그럼에도 불구하고 threaten ~을 위협하다 continuously 지속적으로 delicacy 별미, 진미 destruction 파괴 habitat 서식지 threat 위협 (요소) organization 기관, 단체 currently 현재 implement ~을 시행하다 measures 조치 regulate ~을 규제하다, ~을 조절하다 extent 규모, 정도 inform A of B: A에게 B를 알리다 the public 일반인들, 대중

According to the first paragraph, what is true about parrotfish?

(a) They survive best at extreme depths.
(b) They eat the white sand around coral reefs.
(c) Their colors let them match their surroundings.
(d) Their appearance can transform over time.

첫 번째 문단에 따르면, 앵무고기와 관련해 사실인 것은 무엇인가?

(a) 극한의 깊이에서 가장 잘 생존한다.
(b) 산호초 주변의 백색 모래를 먹는다.
(c) 색이 주변 환경과 어울리게 해준다.
(d) 겉모습이 시간이 흐를수록 변할 수 있다.

정답 (d)

해설 첫 문단에 앵무고기가 아주 다양한 색을 지니고 있다는 사실과 함께 그 색이 일생에 걸쳐 바뀔 수 있다는 점이(The fish come in a wide range of vivid colors, including intricate combinations of green, blue, orange, and yellow that can change throughout their lives) 언급되어 있으므로 (d)가 정답입니다.

어휘 **survive** 생존하다 **extreme** 극한의, 극도의 **match** ~와 어울리다, ~와 일치하다 **surroundings** 주변 (환경) **appearance** 겉모습, 외관 **transform** 변하다, 탈바꿈하다

패러프레이징

a wide range of vivid colors / can change throughout their lives → appearance can transform over time

Why, most likely, is it helpful that parrotfish can change sex?

(a) Larger females are needed for reproduction.
(b) They can reach sexual maturity faster.
(c) Older males are needed to protect their young.
(d) They can achieve a more balanced population.

앵무고기가 성을 바꿀 수 있다는 점이 왜 도움이 되는가?

(a) 더 큰 암컷들이 번식하는 데 필요하다.
(b) 더 빠르게 성적 성숙에 이를 수 있다.
(c) 더 나이 많은 수컷들이 새끼를 보호하는 데 필요하다.
(d) 더욱 균형 잡힌 개체군을 이룰 수 있다.

정답 (c)

해설 두 번째 문단에 앵무고기가 성을 바꿀 수 있다는 특징과 관련해 더 크고 완전히 성장한 수컷들이 효과적으로 새끼들을 지킬 수 있다는(larger, fully developed males can effectively defend their offspring) 내용이 쓰여 있으므로 (c)가 정답입니다.

어휘 reproduction 번식, 생식 reach ~에 이르다 maturity 성숙 young n. 새끼 achieve ~을 이루다, ~을 달성하다

> **패러프레이징**
>
> defend their offspring → protect their young

69 세부 정보

According to the third paragraph, how do some parrotfish protect themselves from predators while sleeping?

(a) by hiding beneath the reef
(b) by masking their own scent
(c) by gathering in large numbers
(d) by giving off a foul odor

세 번째 문단에 따르면, 일부 앵무고기가 잠을 자는 동안 어떻게 포식자로부터 자신을 보호하는가?

(a) 암초 밑에 숨어서
(b) 자신의 냄새를 감춰서
(c) 대규모로 모여서
(d) 고약한 냄새를 풍겨서

정답 (b)

해설 세 번째 문단에 야간에 점액 보호막을 이용해 자신의 냄새를 감추는 방법이(at night, some species cover their body in a clear "cocoon" of mucus before sleeping to conceal their smell ~) 제시되어 있으므로 (b)가 정답입니다.

어휘 beneath ~ 밑에, ~ 아래에 mask v. ~을 감추다 scent 냄새, 향기 gather 모이다 give off (냄새, 빛 등) ~을 풍기다, ~을 발산하다 foul 고약한, 역겨운, 더러운 odor 냄새, 악취

> **패러프레이징**
>
> conceal their smell → masking their own scent

How do parrotfish help keep coral thriving?

(a) by attacking potential predators
(b) by removing damaging organisms
(c) by protecting beneficial algae
(d) by adding vital nutrients

앵무고기는 어떻게 산호가 계속 번
성하는 데 도움을 주는가?

(a) 잠재 포식자들을 공격함으로써
(b) 피해를 끼치는 생물체를 없앰으
  로써
(c) 유익한 해조류를 보호함으로써
(d) 필수 영양소를 추가함으로써

정답 (b)

해설 네 번째 문단에 앵무고기가 산호의 건강에 부정적으로 영향을 미칠 수 있는 해조류를 먹으면서 하루의 대부분을 보낸다고
(The fish spend most of the day feeding on algae that grows on the coral and can negatively affect its health) 쓰
여 있어 산호에 해로운 생물체를 없애 도움을 준다는 것을 알 수 있으므로 (b)가 정답입니다.

어휘 help + 동사원형: ~하는 데 도움을 주다 **potential** 잠재적인 **remove** ~을 없애다, ~을 제거하다 **damaging** 피해를 끼치는
organism 생물체 **beneficial** 유익한 **vital** 필수적인 **nutrient** 영양소

패러프레이징

feeding on algae that grows on the coral and can negatively affect its health → removing damaging organisms

What are some organizations doing to preserve parrotfish?

(a) breeding the creatures in captivity
(b) trying to relocate large populations
(c) working to raise public awareness
(d) advocating to ban fishing practices

일부 기관들이 앵무고기를 보호하기
위해 무엇을 하고 있는가?

(a) 그 생물을 사로잡아 사육하는 일
(b) 대규모 개체군을 이전하려 하는
  일
(c) 대중의 인식을 드높이려 노력하
  는 일
(d) 어획 관행 금지를 지지하는 일

정답 (c)

해설 마지막 문단에 앵무고기 보호를 위한 조치의 하나로 일반인들에게 그 물고기의 중요성을 알리는 일이(informing the
public of the fish's importance) 언급되어 있습니다. 이는 일반인들에게 그 물고기에 대한 인식을 드높이려는 것이므로
(c)가 정답입니다.

어휘 preserve ~을 보호하다, ~을 보존하다 **breed** ~을 사육하다, ~을 기르다 **creature** 생물 **relocate** ~을 이전하다 **raise**
awareness 인식을 드높이다 **advocate** 지지하다, 옹호하다 **ban** ~을 금지하다

informing the public of the fish's importance → raise public awareness

72 동의어

In the context of the passage, <u>constitutes</u> means _____.

(a) forms
(b) expresses
(c) serves
(d) inserts

해당 단락의 문맥에서 <u>constitutes</u>가 의미하는 것은?

(a) 구성하다, 형성하다
(b) 표현하다
(c) 제공하다, 봉사하다
(d) 삽입하다

정답 (a)

해설 해당 문장에서 constitutes 앞에 위치한 관계대명사 which는 바로 앞에 쓰여 있는 fine white sand(고운 백색 모래)를 가리키며, constitutes 뒤에는 목적어로 전 세계의 유명한 백사장들을 뜻하는 명사구가 쓰여 있습니다. 백색 모래는 백사장을 구성하는 요소이므로 '구성하다'를 뜻하는 또 다른 동사 (a) forms가 정답입니다.

73 동의어

In the context of the passage, <u>deposited</u> means _____.

(a) credited
(b) stored
(c) arranged
(d) released

해당 단락의 문맥에서 <u>deposited</u>가 의미하는 것은?

(a) 공을 인정 받은, 신뢰를 얻은
(b) 저장된, 보관된
(c) 조치된, 정렬된, 마련된
(d) 방출된, 배출된

정답 (d)

해설 해당 문장에서 deposited가 포함된 수동태 is deposited 앞뒤로 소화되지 않은 노폐물(The undigested waste)을 뜻하는 주어와 해저로의 이동과 관련된 onto 전치사구가 각각 쓰여 있습니다. 따라서, deposited가 소화되지 않은 노폐물이 빠져나와 해저 쪽으로 옮겨지는 움직임과 관련된 과거분사임을 알 수 있으므로 '방출된' 등을 뜻하는 (d)가 정답입니다.

PART 4

Audrey Hilton
Owner
Four Walls Printing Shop

Dear Ms. Hilton,

Good day! I am the manager of Mercer Office Supplies, and **74** I am writing to address the letter you sent us complaining about your recent order.

In the letter, you mentioned that **75** the parcel delivered to your shop on July 24 was missing two reams of XT 8.5-by-11-inch photo paper. Upon **79** consulting our records and making inquiries with our packaging staff, we have confirmed that the package sent to you was indeed incomplete.

On that particular date, **76** we experienced a glitch on our website due to the surge of orders we have been experiencing this graduation season. We have never had so many orders in the history of the company. This momentary malfunction affected the processing of orders and resulted in the incorrect quantity of paper being delivered to you.

I would like to apologize for our service issue. Moreover, I am requesting your patience in awaiting the delivery of the rest of your order. This is because **77** our supplier has temporarily **80** confined bulk orders of this particular product to one case per week, due to the current high demand. So, we will not be able to refill our stock until later this week. Rest assured that we will forward the remainder of your order to you as soon as possible.

78 To compensate for the inconvenience we have caused you, we will deliver four reams of the photo paper, two more than you initially ordered, to your address as soon as it is available.

오드리 힐튼
소유주
포 월즈 인쇄소

힐튼 씨께,

안녕하세요! 저는 머서 사무용품점의 매니저이며, 귀하의 최근 주문과 관련해 불만을 제기하시며 저희에게 보내신 편지를 처리하고자 편지를 씁니다.

이 편지에서, 귀하께서는 7월 24일에 귀하의 매장으로 전달된 배송품에 크기가 폭 8.5인치에 길이 11인치인 인화지 두 묶음이 빠져 있었다고 언급해 주셨습니다. 저희 기록도 참고하고 저희 포장 담당 직원에게도 문의하자마자, 귀하께 발송된 배송품이 실제로 미비한 상태였음을 확인했습니다.

그 특정일에, 저희가 이번 졸업 시즌에 계속 겪어오고 있는 주문 급증으로 인해 저희 웹 사이트에서 결함을 겪었습니다. 저희는 회사 역사상 그렇게 많은 주문을 받은 적이 전혀 없었습니다. 이 순간적인 오작동이 주문 처리 과정에 영향을 미치면서 부정확한 수량의 용지가 귀하께 전달되는 결과를 초래했습니다.

저희 서비스 문제에 대해 사과의 말씀 드리고자 합니다. 더욱이, 귀하의 나머지 주문품 배송을 기다리시는 데 있어 인내심을 요청 드립니다. 이는 저희 공급업체가 현재의 높은 수요로 인해, 이 특정 제품의 대량 주문을 주당 하나의 케이스로 일시적으로 제한해 두었기 때문입니다. 따라서, 저희는 이번 주 후반이나 되어야 저희 재고를 다시 채울 수 있을 것입니다. 저희가 가능한 한 빨리 귀하의 나머지 주문품을 전송해 드릴 것이므로 안심하시기 바랍니다.

저희가 귀하께 초래한 불편함에 대해 보상해 드리기 위해, 귀하께서 처음 주문하신 것보다 두 묶음 더 많은, 네 묶음의 인화지를 이용 가능해지는 대로 귀하의 주소로 배송 드리겠습니다.

We will email you when the products have arrived in our warehouse and are ready to ship. Please contact me by email if you have further questions.

Thank you very much for your understanding.

Regards,

Robert Kingsley
Robert Kingsley
Mercer Office Supplies

제품이 저희 창고에 도착해 발송해 드릴 준비가 되면 귀하께 이메일을 보내 드릴 것입니다. 추가 질문이 있으실 경우에 이메일로 제게 연락 주시기 바랍니다.

귀하의 양해에 대단히 감사 드립니다.

안녕히 계십시오.

로버트 킹슬리
머서 사무용품점

어휘 address (문제 등) ~을 해결하다, ~을 처리하다 complain 불만을 제기하다 recent 최근의 order 주문(품) mention that ~라고 언급하다 miss ~을 빠트리다 ream (종이의) 묶음 upon -ing ~하자마자 consult ~을 참고하다 inquiry 문의, 질문 confirm that ~임을 확인하다 indeed 실제로, 사실 incomplete 미비한, 불완전한 particular 특정한 glitch 결함, 작은 문제 due to ~로 인해, ~ 때문에 surge 급증, 급등 graduation 졸업(식) momentary 순간적인 malfunction 오작동, 기능 불량 affect ~에 영향을 미치다 processing 처리 (과정) result in + 목적어 + -ing: (목적어)가 ~하는 결과를 초래하다 incorrect 부정확한 quantity 수량 apologize for ~에 대해 사과하다 issue 문제, 사안 patience 인내(심) await ~을 기다리다 the rest of ~의 나머지(= the remainder of) supplier 공급업체, 공급업자 temporarily 일시적으로, 임시로 confine A to B: A를 B로 제한하다 bulk 대량의 current 현재의 demand 수요, 요구 not A until B: B나 되어야 A하다 be able + to 동사원형: ~할 수 있다 refill ~을 다시 채우다 stock 재고(품) Rest assured that ~이므로 안심하시기 바랍니다 forward ~을 전송하다 as soon as possible 가능한 한 빨리 compensate for ~에 대해 보상하다 inconvenience 불편함 cause A B: A에게 B를 초래하다 initially 처음에 as soon as ~하는 대로, ~하자마자 available 이용 가능한, 구입 가능한 contact ~에게 연락하다 further 추가적인, 한층 더 한

Why is Robert Kingsley writing to Audrey Hilton?

(a) to inform her about an issue with product quality
(b) to answer her inquiry about an estimate .
(c) to respond to her recent complaint about a delivery
(d) to verify the details of her last purchase

로버트 킹슬리 씨는 왜 오드리 힐튼 씨에게 편지를 쓰는가?

(a) 제품 품질 문제에 관해 알리기 위해
(b) 견적서와 관련된 문의에 답변하기 위해
(c) 배송과 관련된 최근의 불만 사항에 응답하기 위해
(d) 지난 구매품의 상세 정보를 확인하기 위해

정답 (c)

해설 첫 문단에 상대방이 최근 주문과 관련해 불만을 제기한 편지에 대해 처리하기 위해 편지를 쓴다고(I am writing to address the letter you sent us complaining about your recent order) 알리는 말이 목적에 해당합니다. 이는 고객의 불만에 응답하는 것이므로 (c)가 정답입니다.

어휘 inform ~에게 알리다 estimate 견적(서) respond to ~에 응답하다, ~에 반응하다 complaint 불만, 불평 verify ~을 확인하다, ~을 입증하다 details 상세 정보, 세부 사항

> **패러프레이징**
>
> address the letter you sent us complaining about your recent order → respond to her recent complaint about a delivery

What did Audrey mention in her letter?

(a) The product she ordered arrived damaged.
(b) The package in question was missing multiple items.
(c) The product she received was of poor quality.
(d) The package in question was delivered to the wrong address.

오드리 씨가 편지에서 무엇을 언급했는가?

(a) 자신이 주문한 제품이 손상된 상태로 도착했다는 점
(b) 문제의 배송품에 여러 제품이 빠져 있었다는 점
(c) 자신이 받은 제품이 품질이 좋지 못했다는 점
(d) 문제의 배송품이 엉뚱한 주소로 전달되었다는 점

해설 두 번째 문단에 상대방이 7월 24일에 매장으로 전달된 배송품에 크기가 폭 8.5인치에 길이 11인치인 인화지 두 묶음이 빠져 있었다고 언급한(the parcel delivered to your shop on July 24 was missing two reams of XT 8.5-by-11-inch photo paper) 사실이 쓰여 있으므로 (b)가 정답입니다.

어휘 **damaged** 손상된, 피해를 입은 **in question** 문제의 **multiple** 여럿의, 다수의 **of poor quality** 품질이 좋지 못한

패러프레이징

missing two reams of XT 8.5-by-11-inch photo paper → missing multiple items

---

76 세부 정보

Why did Mercer Office Supplies suffer a computer glitch?

(a) due to an increase in the number of sales
(b) due to an oversight of the maintenance staff
(c) due to an electrical outage from a storm
(d) due to an error made by the software programmers

머서 사무용품점은 왜 컴퓨터 결함을 겪었는가?

(a) 판매 수치의 증가로 인해
(b) 유지 관리 담당 직원의 간과로 인해
(c) 폭풍우에 따른 정전으로 인해
(d) 소프트웨어 프로그래머들이 저지른 실수로 인해

정답 (a)

해설 세 번째 문단에 주문 급증으로 인해 웹 사이트에서 결함을 겪은(we experienced a glitch on our website due to the surge of orders ~) 사실이 언급되어 있습니다. 이는 판매량의 증가에 따른 문제를 말하는 것이므로 (a)가 정답입니다.

어휘 **suffer** (부정적인 일 등) ~을 겪다, ~에 시달리다 **increase in** ~의 증가 **oversight** 간과, 실수 **maintenance** 유지 관리, 시설 관리 **electrical outage** 정전

패러프레이징

the surge of orders → an increase in the number of sales

Why, most likely, will the company's delivery of the remaining items be delayed?

(a) The employees are on strike.
(b) The supplier is being replaced.
(c) The office is temporarily closed.
(d) The current stock is limited.

나머지 제품에 대한 해당 회사의 배송이 왜 지연될 것 같은가?

(a) 직원들이 파업 중이다.
(b) 공급업체가 교체되고 있다.
(c) 사무실이 일시적으로 문을 닫았다.
(d) 현재의 재고가 제한적이다.

정답 (d)

해설 네 번째 문단에 배송 지연 문제를 언급하면서 공급업체에서 높은 수요에 따른 조치로 주당 하나의 케이스로 대량 주문을 일시적으로 제한했다고(our supplier has temporarily confined bulk orders of this particular product to one case per week ~) 알리는 내용이 제시되어 있습니다. 이는 현재 재고량이 제한되어 있음을 밝히는 것이므로 (d)가 정답입니다.

어휘 delay ~을 지연시키다 on strike 파업 중인 replace ~을 교체하다 limited 제한적인

패러프레이징

confined bulk orders of this particular product to one case per week → current stock is limited

---

How does Robert plan to make up for Audrey's inconvenience?

(a) by providing her with promotional gifts
(b) by offering her some money back
(c) by giving her more items than she paid for
(d) by sending her a better product

로버트는 어떻게 오드리의 불편함에 대해 보상해 줄 계획인가?

(a) 판촉용 선물을 제공함으로써
(b) 일부 환불을 제공함으로써
(c) 결제한 것보다 더 많은 제품을 제공함으로써
(d) 더 나은 제품을 보냄으로써

정답 (c)

해설 마지막 문단에 보상을 위해 처음 주문한 것보다 두 묶음 더 많은, 네 묶음의 인화지를 배송해 주겠다고(To compensate for the inconvenience we have caused you, we will deliver four reams of the photo paper, two more than you initially ordered ~) 제안하고 있으므로 (c)가 정답입니다.

어휘 make up for ~에 대해 보상하다 provide A with B: A에게 B를 제공하다

패러프레이징

deliver four reams of the photo paper, two more than you initially ordered → giving her more items than she paid for

79 동의어

In the context of the passage, consulting means _____.

(a) checking
(b) packing
(c) clearing
(d) forgetting

해당 단락의 문맥에서 consulting이 의미하는 것은?

(a) 확인하기
(b) 포장하기, 꾸리기
(c) 청소하기, 치우기
(d) 잊어 버리기

정답 (a)

해설 해당 문장에서 consulting our records는 바로 뒤에 and로 연결된 또 다른 동명사구와 마찬가지로 고객인 상대방이 제기한 문제의 원인을 파악하기 위한 방법에 해당합니다. 따라서, consulting our records가 회사의 기록을 확인해 보는 일을 의미하는 것으로 볼 수 있으므로 (a)가 정답입니다.

80 동의어

In the context of the passage, confined means _____.

(a) gathered
(b) weakened
(c) returned
(d) restricted

해당 단락의 문맥에서 confined가 의미하는 것은?

(a) 모았다
(b) 약화시켰다
(c) 반품했다, 반환했다
(d) 제한했다

정답 (d)

해설 해당 문장에서 confined 뒤에 대량 주문을 뜻하는 명사구와 특정 수량을 나타내는 to 전치사구, 그리고 높은 수요라는 원인을 나타내는 due to 전치사구가 쓰여 있습니다. 따라서, 높은 수요로 인해 공급업체에서 대량 주문이 가능한 수량을 제한해 놓았다는 의미인 것으로 생각할 수 있으므로 (d)가 정답입니다.

Grammar

1. (a)	2. (b)	3. (d)	4. (b)	5. (c)	6. (c)	7. (d)	8. (c)	9. (b)	10. (a)
11. (d)	12. (c)	13. (a)	14. (d)	15. (b)	16. (c)	17. (a)	18. (c)	19. (d)	20. (b)
21. (a)	22. (c)	23. (c)	24. (d)	25. (b)	26. (c)				

Listening

27. (b)	28. (c)	29. (a)	30. (b)	31. (d)	32. (a)	33. (c)	34. (a)	35. (d)	36. (c)
37. (b)	38. (c)	39. (a)	40. (d)	41. (a)	42. (b)	43. (d)	44. (c)	45. (a)	46. (b)
47. (c)	48. (d)	49. (a)	50. (b)	51. (b)	52. (d)				

Reading & Vocabulary

53. (b)	54. (a)	55. (c)	56. (d)	57. (b)	58. (c)	59. (a)	60. (b)	61. (d)	62. (a)
63. (c)	64. (d)	65. (b)	66. (a)	67. (d)	68. (a)	69. (c)	70. (b)	71. (d)	72. (a)
73. (c)	74. (c)	75. (b)	76. (b)	77. (a)	78. (d)	79. (c)	80. (d)		

채점 계산표 (정답 개수 기재)		채점 계산 방법
Grammar	_____ / 26문항	Grammar 정답 개수 ÷ 26 × 100
Listening	_____ / 26문항	Listening 정답 개수 ÷ 26 × 100
Reading & Vocabulary	_____ / 28문항	Reading & Vocabulary 정답 개수 ÷ 28 × 100
총점	_____ / 80문항 ▶ _____ / 100점	총점: 각 영역 합산 정답 개수 ÷ 80 × 100 *소수점 이하는 올림 처리

TEST 03

GRAMMAR
LISTENING
READING & VOCABULARY

01 접속부사

The identity of the poet who wrote *Sir Gawain and the Green Knight* is still unknown. _____, scholars have been able to determine that he lived in the West Midlands of England during the fourteenth century.

(a) However
(b) In conclusion
(c) Moreover
(d) For instance

「가윈 경과 녹색의 기사」를 쓴 시인의 신원은 여전히 미상이다. 하지만, 학자들은 그가 14세기에 잉글랜드의 웨스트 미들랜즈에 살았다는 사실을 밝혀낼 수 있었다.

정답 (a)

해설 빈칸에 알맞은 접속부사를 고르는 문제이므로 앞뒤 문장들의 의미 관계를 확인해야 합니다. 빈칸 앞에는 「가윈 경과 녹색의 기사」를 쓴 시인의 신원이 여전히 미상이라는 말이, 빈칸 뒤에는 학자들이 그가 살았던 지역을 밝혀냈다는 말이 각각 쓰여 있습니다. 이는 그 시인과 관련된 부정적인 정보와 긍정적인 정보가 이어지는 대조적인 흐름이므로 '하지만' 등의 의미로 대조나 반대를 나타낼 때 사용하는 (a) However가 정답입니다.

어휘 identity 신원, 정체 poet 시인 unknown 미상인, 알려져 있지 않은 scholar 학자 be able + to 동사원형: ~할 수 있다 determine that ~임을 밝혀내다 however 하지만, 그러나 in conclusion 마지막으로, 결론적으로 moreover 더욱이, 게다가 for instance 예를 들어

02 시제 – 과거진행

Mrs. Anderson nearly missed her package delivery last week. She _____ a sweater when the doorbell rang, and she was so absorbed in her task that she barely noticed the sound.

(a) will be knitting
(b) was knitting
(c) is knitting
(d) has been knitting

앤더슨 씨는 지난 주에 택배 배송품을 거의 놓칠 뻔했다. 그녀는 초인종이 울렸을 때 스웨터를 뜨개질하고 있었다. 그 일에 너무 몰두한 나머지 그 소리를 거의 알아차리지 못했다.

정답 (b)

해설 동사 knit의 알맞은 형태를 고르는 문제입니다. 빈칸 뒤에 과거시제 동사(rang)를 포함한 when절이 쓰여 있어 이 when 절이 가리키는 과거 시점에 뜨개질하는 행위가 일시적으로 진행되던 상황을 나타내야 자연스러우므로 이러한 의미로 쓰이는 과거진행시제 (b) was knitting이 정답입니다.

어휘 nearly 거의 miss ~을 놓치다, ~을 지나치다, ~에 빠지다 so A that B: 너무 A해서 B하다 absorbed 몰두한, 빠져 있는 task 일, 업무 barely 거의 ~ 않다 notice ~을 알아차리다 knit ~을 뜨개질하다

Scientists are using genome sequencing to explore de-extinction of species that have disappeared. Further advancements are still needed, but if researchers were to succeed, they _____ extinct animals, such as the woolly mammoth or the dodo.

(a) could have brought back
(b) will have brought back
(c) will bring back
(d) could bring back

과학자들은 사라진 종의 멸종 생물 복원을 탐구하기 위해 유전체 염기 서열 분석법을 이용하고 있다. 더 깊이 있는 발전이 여전히 필요하지만, 연구가들이 성공하게 된다면, 울리 매머드나 도도새 같이 멸종된 동물을 되살려낼 수 있을 것이다.

정답 (d)

해설 동사구 bring back의 알맞은 형태를 고르는 문제입니다. if절의 동사가 가정법 과거를 나타내는 과거시제(were)일 때, 주절의 동사는 「would/could/might + 동사원형」과 같은 형태가 되어야 알맞으므로 (d) could bring back이 정답입니다.

어휘 genome sequencing 유전체 염기 서열 분석법 explore ~을 탐구하다 de-extinction 멸종 생물 복원 species (동식물의) 종 disappear 사라지다 further 더 깊이 있는, 한층 더 한 advancement 발전, 진보 be + to 동사원형: ~하게 되다, ~할 예정이다, ~해야 하다 succeed 성공하다 extinct 멸종된 bring back ~을 되살리다, ~을 되돌리다

Jason's phone battery was very low on power when he left work yesterday. Because of this, he resisted _____ his phone until he could get home and charge it.

(a) to use
(b) using
(c) to have used
(d) having used

제이슨의 전화기 배터리 전력이 어제 그가 퇴근했을 때 매우 낮았다. 이것 때문에, 그는 집에 도착해 충전할 수 있을 때까지 전화기를 사용하는 것을 참았다.

정답 (b)

해설 동사 use의 알맞은 형태를 고르는 문제입니다. 빈칸 앞에 과거시제로 쓰여 있는 동사 resist는 동명사를 목적어로 취하므로 (b) using이 정답입니다.

어휘 low on power 전력이 낮은 resist -ing ~하는 것을 참다, ~하는 것을 견디다 charge ~을 충전하다

Maya often bakes as a way to relieve stress. She has a batch of chocolate cookies in the oven at the moment, and she _____ them out in about twenty minutes.

(a) will have been taking
(b) was taking
(c) will be taking
(d) has been taking

마야는 스트레스를 푸는 방법의 하나로 빵이나 과자를 굽는다. 그녀는 현재 오븐에 초콜릿 쿠키를 한 판 넣어 둔 상태이며, 약 20분 후에 꺼낼 것이다.

정답 (c)

해설 동사 take의 알맞은 형태를 고르는 문제입니다. 빈칸 뒤에 위치한 in about twenty minutes와 같은 「in + 시간/기간」 전치사구는 미래 시점을 나타내는 표현입니다. 따라서, 그 미래 시점에 일시적으로 진행될 일을 나타낼 미래진행형 동사가 쓰여야 알맞으므로 (c) will be taking이 정답입니다.

어휘 bake (빵이나 과자를) 굽다 way + to 동사원형: ~하는 방법 relieve (긴장 등) ~을 풀다, ~을 완화하다 batch 한 회분, 한 차례 at the moment 현재 in + 시간: ~ 후에 about 약, 대략

⊗ 오답 피하기

(a) will have been taking와 같은 미래완료진행형 동사는 과거나 현재에 시작된 일이 미래의 특정 시점까지 지속되는 것을 나타내므로 「in + 시간/기간」 전치사구와 함께 사용할 수 없습니다.

In parts of the Southern US, some homeowners paint their porch ceilings a distinct shade of light blue. The color, _____, is believed by some to confuse evil spirits and prevent them from entering a home.

(a) that is called "haint blue"
(b) what is called "haint blue"
(c) which is called "haint blue"
(d) who is called "haint blue"

미국 남부의 여러 지역에서는, 일부 주택 소유주들이 현관 천장을 독특한 색조인 연한 청색으로 칠한다. 이 색상은, "헤인트 블루"라고 불리는데, 어떤 사람들은 악령을 혼란스럽게 만들어 집에 들어가지 못하게 막아 준다고 여긴다.

정답 (c)

해설 사물 명사 color를 뒤에서 수식할 관계대명사절을 골라야 하므로, 사물 명사를 수식할 수 있으면서 콤마와 함께 삽입되는 구조에 쓰일 수 있는 관계대명사 which가 이끄는 (c) which is called "haint blue"가 정답입니다.

어휘 porch 현관 ceiling 천장 distinct 독특한, 뚜렷이 구별되는 shade 색조 be believed + to 동사원형: ~하는 것으로 여겨지다 confuse ~을 혼란스럽게 만들다, ~을 헷갈리게 하다 evil spirit 악령 prevent + 목적어 + from -ing: (목적어)가

~하지 못하게 막다

⊗ 오답 피하기

(a)의 that은 콤마 뒤에 쓰일 수 없고, (b)의 what은 명사를 수식하는 역할을 하지 않습니다.

---

07 시제 - 현재진행

The school's fire alarm started malfunctioning during the second period of the day and has continued to do so for the last hour. Steven cannot focus on his math problems while the alarm _____.

(a) rang
(b) has been ringing
(c) would ring
(d) is ringing

학교의 화재 경보기가 그날 2교시 중에 오작동하기 시작했으며, 마지막 한 시간 동안 계속 그렇게 오작동했다. 스티븐은 그 경보기가 울리는 동안 수학 문제에 집중하지 못하고 있다.

정답 (d)

해설 동사 ring의 알맞은 형태를 고르는 문제입니다. 빈칸이 속한 문장에서 주절에 현재시제 동사 cannot focus가 쓰여 있어 '~하는 동안'이라는 의미로 동시 진행 상황을 나타내는 while절에는 동일한 현재 시점에 진행 중인 일을 나타내는 현재진행형 동사가 쓰여야 알맞으므로 (d) is ringing이 정답입니다.

어휘 **fire alarm** 화재 경보기 **malfunction** 오작동하다 **continue + to 동사원형**: 계속 ~하다 **do so** (앞서 언급된 일에 대해) 그렇게 하다 **focus on** ~에 집중하다, ~에 초점을 맞추다 **while** ~하는 동안, ~인 반면 **ring** (종 등이) 울리다

Although never built, the Palace of the Soviets was intended to be a skyscraper topped with a statue of Vladimir Lenin. Had the building been completed, it _____ the world's tallest structure at that time.

(a) would be
(b) will have been
(c) would have been
(d) will be

전혀 지어지지는 않았지만, 소비에트 궁은 꼭대기에 블라드미르 레닌의 조각상이 있는 고층 건물이 될 계획이었다. 그 건물이 완성되었다면, 그 당시에 전 세계에서 가장 높은 구조물이 되었을 것이다.

정답 (c)

해설 be동사의 알맞은 형태를 고르는 문제입니다. 빈칸이 속한 주절 앞에 위치한 Had the building been completed는 가정법 과거완료 문장의 If절 If the building had been completed에서 If가 생략되고 had가 주어 앞으로 이동하면서 도치된 구조입니다. 따라서, 빈칸에 가정법 과거완료 문장의 주절에 쓰이는 「would/could/might + have p.p.」 형태의 동사가 쓰여야 알맞으므로 (c) would have been이 정답입니다.

어휘 **be intended + to 동사원형**: ~하도록 의도되다 **skyscraper** 고층 건물 **topped with** 꼭대기에 ~가 있는 **statue** 조각상 **complete** ~을 완성하다, ~을 완료하다 **structure** 구조(물) **at that time** 그 당시에

Driving while tired can be very dangerous. Road safety officers advise that drivers _____ to rest for a while if they find themselves feeling drowsy behind the wheel.

(a) are pulling over
(b) pull over
(c) will pull over
(d) pulled over

피곤한 상황에서 운전하는 것은 매우 위험할 수 있다. 도로 안전 담당관들은 운전자들이 운전석에서 자신도 모르게 졸음이 오는 느낌이 드는 경우에 잠시 동안 휴식할 수 있도록 길 한쪽에 차를 세우라고 조언한다.

정답 (b)

해설 동사구 pull over의 알맞은 형태를 고르는 문제입니다. 빈칸은 동사 advised의 목적어 역할을 하는 that절의 동사 자리인데, advise와 같이 주장/요구/명령/제안 등을 나타내는 동사의 목적어 역할을 하는 that절의 동사는 should 없이 동사원형만 사용하므로 (b) pull over가 정답입니다.

어휘 **while tired** 피곤한 상황에서 **advise that** ~하라고 조언하다 **rest** 휴식하다 **for a while** 잠시 동안 **find oneself -ing** 자신도 모르게 ~하다 **drowsy** 졸음이 오는, 나른한 **behind the wheel** 운전석에서

This year's creative writing competition is now underway. Participants _____ submit their entries by 12 p.m. next Friday, or their stories will not be reviewed by the judging panel.

(a) must
(b) can
(c) might
(d) would

올해의 창의적 글쓰기 경연 대회가 현재 진행 중입니다. 참가자들께서는 반드시 다음 주 금요일 오후 12시까지 참가작을 제출하셔야 하며, 그렇지 않으면 각자의 이야기가 심사 위원단에 의해 검토되지 않을 것입니다.

정답 (a)

해설 문장의 의미에 어울리는 조동사를 고르는 문제입니다. 빈칸이 속한 절이 '참가자들이 반드시 다음 주 금요일 오후 12시까지 참가작을 제출해야 한다'와 같은 의미를 구성해야 자연스러우므로 '반드시 ~해야 하다'라는 뜻으로 강제성이나 의무 등을 나타내는 조동사 (a) must가 정답입니다.

어휘 creative 창의적인 competition 경연 대회, 경기 대회 underway 진행 중인 participant 참가자 submit ~을 제출하다 entry 참가(작), 출품(작) by (기한) ~까지 review ~을 검토하다, ~을 살펴 보다 judging panel 심사 위원단

The interrobang is a punctuation mark that combines a question mark and an exclamation point. It was designed _____ a question asked in surprise or disbelief but has not been commonly adopted by writers.

(a) indicating
(b) to have indicated
(c) having indicated
(d) to indicate

감탄 의문 부호는 물음표와 느낌표를 결합한 구두점이다. 그것은 놀라움이나 의혹을 갖고 묻는 질문을 나타내기 위해 고안되었지만, 작가들에 의해 흔히 채택되지는 않았다.

정답 (d)

해설 동사 indicate의 알맞은 형태를 고르는 문제입니다. 빈칸 앞에 위치한 was designed는 to부정사와 어울려 '~하기 위해 고안되다, ~하도록 만들어지다'를 뜻하는 「be designed + to 동사원형」의 구조로 쓰이므로 (d) to indicate이 정답입니다.

어휘 interrobang 감탄 의문 부호 punctuation mark 구두점 combine ~을 결합하다, ~을 조합하다 exclamation point 느낌표, 감탄 부호 disbelief 의혹, 불신 commonly 흔히 adopt ~을 채택하다 indicate ~을 나타내다, ~을 가리키다

❌ 오답 피하기

Be caught를 제외한 수동태 형태 「be + p.p.(-ed)」 뒤에는 동명사가 아닌 to부정사가 위치합니다.

Suresh's friends invited him to a party but later revealed that everyone was wearing silly outfits. Suresh decided he would not go if it involved _____ a silly costume.

(a) having worn
(b) to wear
(c) wearing
(d) to have worn

수레시의 친구들이 그를 파티에 초대했지만, 모두가 우스꽝스러운 옷을 입는다는 사실을 나중에 밝혔다. 수레시는 그것이 우스꽝스러운 복장을 입는 것을 포함한다면 가지 않기로 결정했다.

정답 (c)

해설 동사 wear의 알맞은 형태를 고르는 문제입니다. 빈칸 앞에 과거시제로 쓰여 있는 동사 involve는 동명사를 목적어로 취하므로 (c) wearing이 정답입니다.

어휘 reveal that ~임을 밝히다, ~임을 드러내다 silly 우스꽝스러운, 바보 같은 outfit 옷, 의복 decide (that) ~하기로 결정하다 involve -ing ~하는 것을 포함하다 costume 복장, 의상

⊗ 오답 피하기

동명사 유형의 문제에서 (a) having worn과 같은 완료동명사는 정답으로 출제되지 않습니다.

Amber is hoping to receive an acceptance letter from the prestigious Wexman University. She also applied to a few smaller colleges in her home state _____ she gets rejected from her dream university.

(a) in case
(b) unless
(c) even though
(d) because

앰버는 명문대인 웩스먼 대학교로부터 입학 허가서를 받기를 바라고 있다. 그녀는 꿈에 그리던 대학교로부터 거절 당할 경우를 대비해 자신의 고향이 있는 주에 속한 몇몇 더 작은 대학교에도 지원했다.

정답 (a)

해설 문장의 의미에 어울리는 접속사를 고르는 문제입니다. 빈칸이 속한 문장이이 '꿈에 그리던 대학교로부터 거절 당할 경우에 대비해 ~ 몇몇 더 작은 대학교에도 지원했다'와 같은 의미를 구성해야 자연스러우므로 '~하는 경우에 (대비해)'를 뜻하는 접속사 (a) in case가 정답입니다.

어휘 acceptance letter 입학 허가서 prestigious 명문의, 권위 있는 apply to ~에 지원하다 get p.p. ~되다, ~된 상태가 되다 reject ~을 거절하다 in case (that) ~하는 경우에 (대비해) unless ~하지 않는다면, ~가 아니라면 even though 비록 ~하기는 하지만

14 시제 - 과거완료진행

The Winchester Mystery House is notable for its bizarre, sprawling architecture. It is said that construction crews _____ on the house nonstop for thirty-eight years until the owner died in 1922.

(a) have been working
(b) are working
(c) will have been working
(d) had been working

윈체스터 미스터리 하우스는 그 기이하고 사방으로 뻗어 있는 모양의 건축 양식으로 유명하다. 그 소유주가 1922년에 사망할 때까지 공사 인부들이 38년 동안 쉬지 않고 그 집에 대한 작업을 했던 것으로 전해진다.

정답 (d)

해설 동사 work의 알맞은 형태를 고르는 문제입니다. 빈칸 뒤에 '~할 때까지'를 뜻하는 접속사 until이 이끄는 절에 과거시제 동사(died)와 과거 시점 표현 in 1922가 쓰여 있어 더 이전의 과거에서부터 in 1922가 가리키는 과거 시점까지 작업이 지속되었던 것을 나타내야 하며, 이는 과거완료진행 동사로 표현하므로 (d) had been working이 정답입니다.

어휘 be notable for ~로 유명하다 bizarre 기이한 sprawling (모양 등이) 사방으로 뻗어 있는, 제멋대로 퍼져 있는 architecture 건축 (양식), 건축술 crew (함께 작업하는) 팀, 조 nonstop 쉬지 않고, 연속으로 owner 소유주

15 당위성을 나타내는 동사원형

Hurricanes and tropical storms can cause serious property damage. Experts advise that, when such weather systems are approaching, homeowners _____ preparations to minimize damage, such as taping or boarding up windows.

(a) will make
(b) make
(c) are making
(d) made

허리케인과 열대 폭풍우는 심각한 건물 피해를 초래할 수 있다. 전문가들은 그러한 기상계가 접근할 때, 주택 소유주들이 창문에 테이프를 붙이거나 판자로 막는 것과 같이, 피해를 최소화할 수 있도록 대비해야 한다고 조언한다.

정답 (b)

해설 동사 make의 알맞은 형태를 고르는 문제입니다. 빈칸은 동사 advise의 목적어 역할을 하는 that절의 동사 자리인데(when절은 that과 homeowners 사이에 삽입), advise와 같이 주장/요구/명령/제안 등을 나타내는 동사의 목적어 역할을 하는 that절의 동사는 should 없이 동사원형만 사용하므로 (b) make가 정답입니다.

어휘 tropical 열대의 cause ~을 초래하다 property 건물, 부동산, 자산 damage 피해, 손상 advise that ~하라고 조언하다 weather system 기상계, 일기계 approach 접근하다 make a preparation 대비하다, 준비하다 minimize ~을 최소화하다 board up ~을 판자로 막다

Jin is not happy with the quality of his assignment and has decided to rewrite it. If he were to submit the essay in its current condition, he _____ a very low score.

(a) would probably have received
(b) will probably have received
(c) would probably receive
(d) will probably receive

진은 자신의 과제물 수준에 만족하지 못해서 다시 쓰기로 결정했다. 그가 현재 상태로 에세이를 제출하게 된다면, 아마 아주 낮은 점수를 받을 것이다.

정답 (c)

해설 동사 receive의 알맞은 형태를 고르는 문제입니다. If절의 동사가 가정법 과거를 나타내는 과거시제(were)일 때, 주절의 동사는 「would/could/might + 동사원형」과 같은 형태가 되어야 알맞으므로 (c) would probably receive가 정답입니다.

어휘 quality 수준, 질, 품질 assignment 과제(물), 할당(된 것) decide + to 동사원형: ~하기로 결정하다 be + to 동사원형: ~하게 되다, ~할 예정이다, ~해야 하다 submit ~을 제출하다 current 현재의 receive ~을 받다

Ben and Nancy's first Christmas together is coming up, and Nancy is struggling to think of a good gift. Her friend suggested _____ Ben something handmade instead of a store-bought item.

(a) giving
(b) to give
(c) having given
(d) to have given

벤과 낸시가 처음으로 함께 하는 크리스마스가 다가오고 있는데, 낸시는 좋은 선물을 생각해 내는 데 힘겨워하고 있다. 그녀의 친구는 매장에서 구입한 제품 대신 손으로 만든 것을 벤에게 주는 것을 제안했다.

정답 (a)

해설 동사 give의 알맞은 형태를 고르는 문제입니다. 빈칸 앞에 과거 시제로 쓰여 있는 동사 suggest는 동명사를 목적어로 취하므로 (a) giving이 정답입니다.

어휘 struggle + to 동사원형: ~하는 데 힘겨워하다, ~하기 위해 발버둥치다 suggest -ing ~하라고 권하다, ~하도록 제안하다 instead of ~ 대신 store-bought 매장에서 구입한

❌ 오답 피하기

동명사 유형의 문제에서 (c) having given과 같은 완료동명사는 정답으로 출제되지 않습니다.

18 가정법 과거완료

When Kamila got home from work yesterday, she saw that the kitchen light bulb had burned out. Had her housemate let her know in advance, she _____ a replacement on the way home.

(a) will have bought
(b) would buy
(c) would have bought
(d) will buy

카밀라가 어제 퇴근하고 집에 갔을 때, 주방 전구가 꺼져 있는 것을 확인했다. 그녀의 동거인이 그녀에게 미리 알려 주었다면, 집에 가는 길에 교체품을 구입했을 것이다.

정답 (c)

해설 동사 buy의 알맞은 형태를 고르는 문제입니다. 빈칸이 속한 주절 앞에 위치한 Had her housemate let her know는 가정법 과거완료 문장의 If절 If her housemate had let her know에서 If가 생략되고 had가 주어 앞으로 이동하면서 도치된 구조입니다. 따라서, 빈칸에 가정법 과거완료 문장의 주절에 쓰이는 「would/could/might + have p.p.」 형태의 동사가 쓰여야 알맞으므로 (c) would have bought이 정답입니다.

어휘 light bulb 전구 burn out 다 꺼지다, 다 타버리다 let + 목적어 + know: (목적어)에게 알리다 in advance 미리, 사전에 replacement 교체(품), 대체(품) on the way 가는 길에, 오는 일에

19 시제 - 현재완료진행

The Japanese island of Aoshima, also known as "Cat Island," gets its name from its huge cat population. The island's human population, however, continues to fall and _____ since the decline of the local fishing industry.

(a) had been doing so
(b) is doing so
(c) will be doing so
(d) has been doing so

일본의 아오시마 섬은, "고양이 섬" 으로도 알려져 있으며, 엄청난 고양이 개체군으로 인해 그 이름을 얻었다. 하지만, 이 섬의 인구는 지속적으로 감소하고 있으며, 지역 어업의 쇠퇴 이후로 계속 그렇게 되어 오고 있다.

정답 (d)

해설 동사 do의 알맞은 형태를 고르는 문제입니다. 빈칸 뒤에 위치한 since the decline of the local fishing industry와 같이 '~한 이후로'를 뜻하는 「since + 명사(구)」 전치사구는 현재완료시제 동사 또는 현재완료진행시제 동사와 어울리므로 현재완료진행시제의 형태인 (d) has been doing so가 정답입니다.

어휘 known as ~라고 알려진 huge 엄청난, 막대한 population 개체군, 인구 however 하지만, 그러나 continue + to 동사원형: 지속적으로 ~하다 fall 감소하다, 하락하다 since ~ 이후로 decline 쇠퇴, 하락, 감소 local 지역의, 현지의 do so (앞서 언급된 일에 대해) 그렇게 하다

Beth spent three hours working on her motorcycle's engine. Unfortunately, when she attempted to fire it up, the engine completely failed _____, even after all her efforts.

(a) starting
(b) to start
(c) to have started
(d) having started

베스는 자신의 오토바이 엔진 작업에 세 시간을 보냈다. 안타깝게도, 시동을 걸어 보려 했을 때, 심지어 그녀의 모든 노력 후에도, 엔진이 완전히 시동이 걸리지 못했다.

정답 (b)

해설 동사 start의 알맞은 형태를 고르는 문제입니다. 빈칸 앞에 과거시제로 쓰여 있는 동사 fail은 to부정사와 어울려 '~하지 못하다, ~하는 데 실패하다'를 뜻하는 「fail + to 동사원형」의 구조로 쓰이므로 (b) to start가 정답입니다.

어휘 spend + 목적어 + -ing: ~하면서 (목적어)의 시간을 보내다 unfortunately 안타깝게도, 유감스럽게도 attempt + to 동사원형: ~하려 하다, ~하기를 시도하다 fire up ~의 시동을 걸다, ~을 작동시키다 completely 완전히 effort 노력

⊗ 오답 피하기

to부정사 유형의 문제에서 (c) to have started와 같은 완료부정사는 정답으로 출제되지 않습니다.

A popular style of cooking called sous vide entails immersing vacuum-sealed bags of food in temperature-controlled water. One advantage of the method is that the food _____ be left underwater for long periods without overcooking.

(a) can
(b) must
(c) should
(d) will

'수비드'라고 불리는 인기 있는 조리 방식은 진공 상태로 밀봉된 봉지에 담긴 음식을 온도 조절된 물 속에 담그는 일을 수반한다. 이 방식의 한 가지 장점은 그 음식을 과하게 익히지 않아도 오랫동안 물 속에 둘 수 있다는 점이다.

정답 (a)

해설 문장의 의미에 어울리는 조동사를 고르는 문제입니다. 빈빈칸이 속한 that절이 '음식을 과하게 익히지 않아도 오랫동안 물 속에 둘 수 있다'와 같은 의미로 어떤 장점이 있는지 설명하는 역할을 해야 알맞으므로 '~할 수 있다'라는 뜻으로 가능성을 나타내는 조동사 (c) can이 정답입니다.

어휘 entail -ing ~하는 것을 수반하다 immerse ~을 담그다 vacuum-sealed 진공 상태로 밀봉된 temperature-controlled 온도가 조절된 advantage 장점 method 방식 be left + 형용사: ~한 상태로 남겨지다 without -ing ~하지 않은 채로, ~하지 않고 overcook 너무 많이 익히다, 과조리하다

22 가정법 과거완료

Caroline prepared diligently for her conference presentation on childhood education but, while she was giving the speech yesterday, she left out important details. Had she not been so tired, she _____ a better presentation.

(a) will have delivered
(b) would deliver
(c) would have delivered
(d) will deliver

캐롤린은 아동 교육에 관한 자신의 컨퍼런스 발표를 위해 부지런히 준비했지만, 어제 연설을 하는 동안, 중요한 세부 사항을 빠뜨렸다. 그녀가 그렇게 피곤하지 않았다면, 더 나은 발표를 했을 것이다.

정답 (c)

해설 동사 deliver의 알맞은 형태를 고르는 문제입니다. 빈칸이 속한 주절 앞에 위치한 Had she not been은 가정법 과거완료 문장의 If절 If she had not been에서 If가 생략되고 had가 주어 앞으로 이동하면서 도치된 구조입니다. 따라서, 빈칸에 가정법 과거완료 문장의 주절에 쓰이는 「would/could/might + have p.p.」 형태의 동사가 쓰여야 알맞으므로 (c) would have delivered가 정답입니다.

어휘 diligently 부지런히, 열심히 presentation 발표(회) give a speech 연설하다 leave out ~을 빠뜨리다, ~을 배제하다 details 세부 사항, 상세 정보 deliver (발표 등) ~을 하다, ~을 전달하다

23 준동사 – to부정사

Frank's rubber plant has grown so quickly that it is now too big for its pot. He plans _____ it to a larger container with some fresh soil as soon as he can.

(a) transferring
(b) to have transferred
(c) to transfer
(d) having transferred

프랭크의 고무나무는 너무 빨리 자라서 지금은 그 화분에 비해 너무 크다. 그는 가능한 한 빨리 약간의 새로운 흙과 함께 더 큰 화분으로 그것을 옮겨 심을 계획이다.

정답 (c)

해설 동사 transfer의 알맞은 형태를 고르는 문제입니다. 빈칸 앞에 현재시제로 쓰여 있는 동사 plan은 to부정사를 목적어로 취하므로 (c) to transfer가 정답입니다.

어휘 grow 자라다, 성장하다 so A that B: 너무 A해서 B하다 plan + to 동사원형: ~할 계획이다 container 용기, 그릇 soil 흙, 토양 as soon as one can 가능한 한 빨리 transfer ~을 옮기다, ~을 이전하다

⊗ 오답 피하기

to부정사 유형의 문제에서 (b) to have transferred와 같은 완료부정사는 정답으로 출제되지 않습니다.

Lando has a lot in common with his friend Greta. However, unlike Greta, _____, Lando enjoys all kinds of meat and can regularly be found dining in the steak restaurant downtown.

(a) what is vegetarian
(b) which is vegetarian
(c) where is vegetarian
(d) who is vegetarian

랜도는 친구 그레타와 공통점이 많다. 하지만, 채식주의자인, 그레타와 달리, 랜도는 모든 종류의 고기를 즐기며, 시내에 있는 스테이크 레스토랑에서 식사하는 모습을 주기적으로 볼 수 있다.

정답 (d)

해설 사람 명사 Greta를 뒤에서 수식할 관계대명사절을 골라야 하므로 사람 명사를 수식할 수 있으면서 콤마와 함께 삽입되는 구조에 쓰일 수 있는 관계대명사 who가 이끄는 (d) who is vegetarian이 정답입니다.

어휘 have a lot in common with ~와 공통점이 많다 however 하지만, 그러나 unlike ~와 달리 regularly 주기적으로, 규칙적으로 be found -ing ~하는 모습이 보이다 vegetarian 채식주의자

❌ 오답 피하기

(a)의 what은 선행사를 수식하는 역할을 하지 않으며, (b)의 which와 (c)의 where는 사람 명사를 수식할 수 없습니다.

Amelia is struggling with a heavy course load this semester. If she were to drop one of her classes, she _____ more free time, but she likes her professors too much to do that.

(a) would have had
(b) would have
(c) will have
(d) will have had

아멜리아는 이번 학기에 많은 수업량으로 힘겨워하고 있다. 그녀가 수업들 중 하나를 수강 철회하게 된다면, 더 많은 여유 시간을 갖게 되겠지만, 그렇게 하기에는 그녀가 자신의 교수님들을 너무 많이 좋아한다.

정답 (b)

해설 동사 have의 알맞은 형태를 고르는 문제입니다. If절의 동사가 가정법 과거를 나타내는 과거시제(were)일 때, 주절의 동사는 「would/could/might + 동사원형」과 같은 형태가 되어야 알맞으므로 (b) would have가 정답입니다.

어휘 struggle with ~로 힘겨워하다 heavy (수량, 정도 등이) 많은, 심한 course load 수업량 be + to 동사원형: ~하게 되다, ~할 예정이다, ~해야 하다 drop ~을 수강 철회하다, ~을 중도 포기하다

Josh is at the immigration office to extend his visa, but there is a long line. Josh estimates that, by the time he is able to see an official, he _____ for over two hours.

(a) is waiting
(b) was waiting
(c) will have been waiting
(d) will be waiting

조쉬는 비자를 연장하기 위해 출입국 관리 사무소에 가 있지만, 줄이 길게 늘어서 있다. 조쉬는 관계자를 만날 수 있을 때쯤이면, 두 시간 넘게 계속 기다리고 있을 것으로 추정하고 있다.

정답 (c)

해설 동사 wait의 알맞은 형태를 고르는 문제입니다. by the time이 이끄는 절에 현재시제 동사(is)가 쓰이고 by the time과 연결되는 절에 「for + 기간」과 같은 기간 표현이 있으면, 그 절에 미래완료진행시제로 된 동사를 사용하므로 미래완료진행시제인 (c) will have been waiting이 정답입니다.

어휘 immigration office 출입국 관리 사무소, 이민국 extend ~을 연장하다 estimate that ~라고 추정하다 by the time ~할 때쯤이면 be able + to 동사원형: ~할 수 있다 official n. 관계자, 당국자

PART 1

M: Hey, Teresa.	남: 안녕, 테레사.
F: Oh, hi Eddie! How was the concert last night? I was sad that I couldn't go.	여: 아, 안녕, 에디! 어젯밤 콘서트는 어땠어? 난 갈 수 없어서 슬펐어.
M: Honestly, 27 it was probably a good thing you missed it.	남: 솔직히, 아마 그걸 놓친 게 잘된 일이었을 거야.
F: Really? Why? Was it not good?	여: 정말로? 왜? 재미 없었어?
M: It was okay once the main band, Hot New Panic, got started, but overall, 27 the whole experience was pretty disappointing, starting with the fact that I had to park 30 minutes away and walk.	남: 일단 주 밴드인 핫 뉴 패닉이 시작했을 때는 괜찮았는데, 전반적으로, 전체적인 경험이 꽤 실망스러웠어. 30분이나 멀리 떨어진 곳에 주차하고 걸어가야 했다는 사실부터 시작해서 말이야.
F: Isn't that normal for an outdoor stadium concert?	여: 야외 경기장 콘서트에선 그게 일반적이지 않아?
M: It is, but 28 there were no signs showing how to get to the location from the lot, and there weren't any shuttle buses. When I finally got there, it was hard to find the front gate to get in.	남: 그렇긴 하지만, 주차장에서 행사장으로 어떻게 가는지 보여 주는 표지판도 없었고, 셔틀 버스도 전혀 없었어. 마침내 그곳에 도착했을 땐, 입장하는 정문도 찾기 힘들었어.
F: Oh, that sounds really frustrating.	여: 아, 그럼 정말 불만스러웠을 것 같아.
M: It was, plus 29 there was only one line for everyone, including people who needed to buy a ticket, so it got really backed up. It took nearly two hours just to get through the gate.	남: 그랬어, 게다가 입장권을 구입해야 하는 사람들까지 포함해서, 모든 사람을 대상으로 줄이 하나뿐이었기 때문에, 정말 많이 밀렸어. 정문을 통과해서 들어가는 데에만 거의 두 시간이나 걸렸다니까.
F: Wow, Eddie. I can imagine that would be aggravating to have to wait for a long time just to get in.	여: 와우, 에디. 단지 입장하기 위해 오랫동안 기다려야 해서 짜증이 났을 거라는 게 상상이 돼.

I think the longest I ever waited was an hour, but there were multiple lines for people who did and didn't need to buy tickets. That concert was at an indoor venue, though, with assigned seats.

M: I would have expected a bit of a wait with people looking for their seats, but this concert was open admission. There were no seats for people to find. You could bring in your own chairs or blanket if you wanted, but most people wanted to stand near the stage like me.

F: **30** Were you able to get to the stage then, so you could at least see the bands up close?

M: **30** That was the best part, Teresa. I found a spot in the front row. The biggest issue was that the opening act was an hour late.

F: Oh no! Was there anyone else that could fill in and play while the crowd waited?

M: No. There was only the opening act and then the main band. The organizers were just walking around and not really saying anything. Some people in the crowd started booing and **31** others even left thinking that the whole thing was canceled.

F: But you stayed and waited to see what would happen, right?

M: Yeah, I was determined to stay until I saw Hot New Panic play. I paid a lot of money for the ticket, and it was one of the last shows before they retire. If I had missed this one, I would have to drive across the country to see their final show or just miss out completely. **32** Anyway, I didn't get home until well after midnight — that's why I'm so tired today.

내 생각에 내가 기다려 본 것 중에 가장 길었던 게 한 시간이었는데, 입장권을 사야 하는 사람들과 그렇지 않은 사람들을 위해 여러 줄이 있었어. 하지만, 그 콘서트는 지정 좌석이 있는 실내 행사장이었어.

남: 사람들이 자리를 찾느라 조금 기다릴 것이라고 예상했겠지만, 이 콘서트는 자유 입장이었어. 사람들이 찾아야 할 좌석이 없었거든. 원하면 개인 의자나 담요를 챙겨서 갈 수 있었지만, 대부분의 사람들은 나처럼 무대와 가까운 곳에 서 있고 싶어 했어.

여: 그럼 석어도 바로 가까이에서 밴드들을 볼 수 있게 무대 쪽으로 갈 수 있었어?

남: 그게 가장 좋은 부분이었어, 테레사. 내가 앞줄에서 자리를 하나 찾았거든. 가장 큰 문제는 오프닝 공연이 한 시간이나 늦었다는 거였어.

여: 아, 저런! 사람들이 기다리는 동안 대신해서 연주할 수 있는 다른 누구도 없었어?

남: 없었어. 오프닝 공연과 그 다음으로 주 공연 밴드만 있었어. 주최측 사람들은 그저 곳곳에서 걸어다니기만 하고 실제로는 어떤 말도 하지 않았어. 관객 속의 어떤 사람들은 야유하기 시작했고, 다른 사람들은 심지어 전부 취소되었다고 생각해서 돌아가기도 했어.

여: 하지만 남아서 무슨 일이 있을지 보려고 기다린 게 맞지?

남: 응, 핫 뉴 패닉이 공연하는 모습을 볼 때까지 남아 있기로 결심했지. 입장권을 사려고 많은 돈을 지불한데다, 이들이 은퇴하기 전에 하는 마지막 공연들 중 하나였거든. 이번 것을 놓쳤다면, 이들의 마지막 공연을 보기 위해 전국에 걸쳐 운전하고 다녀야 하거나 그냥 완전히 놓치게 될 거야. 어쨌든, 자정이 한참 지나서야 집에 갔는데, 그게 내가 오늘 이렇게 피곤한 이유야.

F: Well, Eddie, I think you made the right choice by staying, even if that meant being tired today! **33** Talking about this makes me want to listen to some Hot New Panic after work. I'm downloading their new single now.

M: Have fun with that, Teresa. As for me, I'm so tired I might crash before dinner.

여: 음, 에디, 내 생각엔 네가 남아 있음으로써 좋은 선택을 한 것 같아, 설사 그게 오늘 피곤한 걸 의미한다고 해도 말이야! 이렇게 얘기하고 나니까 퇴근 후에 핫 뉴 패닉이나 좀 들어 보고 싶어 지네. 지금 그들의 새 싱글을 다운로드하고 있어.

남: 즐겁게 들어, 테레사. 내 상태로 봐선, 난 너무 피곤해서 저녁 식사 전에 잠들지도 몰라.

어휘 How was A?: A는 어땠어? **miss** ~을 놓치다, ~을 지나치다, ~을 빠뜨리다 **get started** 시작하다 **overall** 전반적으로 **whole** 전체의 **the fact that** ~라는 사실 **sign** 표지(판), 안내판 **how + to 동사원형:** ~하는 방법 **get to** ~로 가다, ~에 도착하다 **lot** 주차장 **frustrating** 불만스럽게 만드는, 좌절하게 만드는 **plus** 게다가, 그에 더해 **including** ~을 포함해 **backed up** 밀려 있는, 정체되어 있는 **take** ~의 시간이 걸리다 **nearly** 거의 **aggravating** 짜증나게 하는, 화나게 하는 **multiple** 여럿의, 다수의 **venue** 행사장 **though** (문장 중간이나 끝에서) 하지만 **assigned** 지정된, 배정된 **would have p.p.** ~했을 것이다 **expect** ~을 예상하다 **a bit of** 약간의, 조금의 **look for** ~을 찾다 **admission** 입장(료) **be able + to 동사원형:** ~할 수 있다 **at least** 적어도, 최소한 **up close** 바로 가까이에서 **spot** 자리, 지점 **row** 줄, 열 **opening act** 오프닝 공연 **fill in** 대신하다 **organizer** 주최자, 조직자 **crowd** 사람들, 군중 **boo** 야유하다 **cancel** ~을 취소하다 **be determined + to 동사원형:** ~하기로 결심하다 **see + 목적어 + 동사원형:** (목적어)가 ~하는 모습을 보다 **retire** 은퇴하다 **miss out** 놓치다, 빠뜨리다 **completely** 완전히 **anyway** 어쨌든 **make a choice** 선택하다 **crash** 잠들다

---

(27) 세부 정보

Why did Eddie say it was a good thing Teresa missed the concert?

(a) because the weather was poor
(b) because it was difficult to get into the venue
(c) because the band was terrible
(d) because it was dangerous to be in the audience

에디는 왜 테레사가 콘서트를 놓친 것이 잘된 일이라고 말했는가?

(a) 날씨가 좋지 않기 때문에
(b) 행사장에 들어가기 힘들었기 때문에
(c) 밴드가 끔찍했기 때문에
(d) 관객 속에 있는 것이 위험했기 때문에

정답 (b)

해설 대화 초반부에 남자가 전반적으로 실망스러운 경험이었음을 언급하면서 그 첫 번째 이유로 30분이나 멀리 떨어진 곳에 주차하고 걸어가야 했다는 사실을(the whole experience was pretty disappointing, with the fact that I had to park 30 minutes away and walk) 말하고 있으므로 (b)가 정답입니다.

어휘 **terrible** 끔찍한 **audience** 관객, 청중, 시청자들

> **패러프레이징**

> park 30 minutes away and walk → it was difficult to get into the venue

---

28 세부 정보

What made parking a problem for Eddie?

(a) Traffic was heavy.
(b) Fees were high.
(c) Signage was poor.
(d) Spaces were limited.

무엇 때문에 주차가 에디에게 문제가 되었는가?

(a) 교통량이 많았다.
(b) 요금이 높았다.
(c) 안내 체계가 좋지 못했다.
(d) 공간이 제한적이었다.

정답 (c)

해설 남자가 대화 초반부에 주차장에서 행사장으로 가는 방법을 보여 주는 표지판이 없었다는(there were no signs showing how to get to the location from the lot) 문제를 언급하고 있으므로 (c)가 정답입니다.

어휘 traffic 교통(량), 차량들 heavy (수량, 정도 등이) 많은, 심한 signage 안내 체계, 표지(판) limited 제한적인

패러프레이징

there were no signs → Signage was poor

29 세부 정보

Why did it take Eddie so long to get into the venue?

(a) because there was a big line
(b) because he misplaced his original ticket
(c) because there was high security
(d) because he wanted to change his seat

왜 에디가 행사장에 들어가는 데 그렇게 오래 걸렸는가?

(a) 긴 줄이 있었기 때문에
(b) 원본 입장권을 분실했기 때문에
(c) 보안 수준이 높았기 때문에
(d) 좌석을 변경하고 싶었기 때문에

정답 (a)

해설 대화 초반부에 남자가 모든 사람을 대상으로 줄이 하나뿐이었기 때문에 정말 많이 밀려 있었다는 점을(there was only one line for everyone, including people who needed to buy a ticket, so it got really backed up) 오랜 시간이 걸린 이유로 언급하고 있으므로 (a)가 정답입니다.

어휘 take A B to do: A가 ~하는 데 B의 시간이 걸리다 misplace ~을 분실하다, ~을 둔 곳을 잊다

패러프레이징

only one line / got really backed up → there was a big line

What was the best part of the concert for Eddie?

(a) getting to go backstage
(b) being close to the band
(c) hearing all new music
(d) socializing with other fans

콘서트에서 무엇이 에디에게 가장 좋은 부분이었는가?

(a) 무대 뒤쪽 공간에 출입한 것
(b) 밴드와 가까운 곳에 있었던 것
(c) 완전히 새로운 음악을 들은 것
(d) 다른 팬들과 교류한 것

정답 (b)

해설 대화 중반부에 여자가 바로 가까이에서 밴드들을 볼 수 있게 무대 쪽으로 갈 수 있었는지(Were you able to get to the stage then, so you could at least see the bands up close?) 묻자, 남자가 그게 가장 좋은 부분이었다고(That was the best part) 밝히고 있으므로 (b)가 정답입니다.

어휘 socialize with ~와 교류하다, ~와 어울리다

패러프레이징

get to the stage / see the bands up close → being close to the band

How did the crowd react when they thought the concert had been canceled?

(a) Many of them yelled at the organizers.
(b) Some of them refused to leave.
(c) Many of them demanded a full refund.
(d) Some of them walked out.

관객들이 콘서트가 취소된 것으로 생각했을 때 어떻게 반응했는가?

(a) 그들 중 많은 이들이 주최측에 소리 쳤다.
(b) 그들 중 일부가 돌아가기를 거부했다.
(c) 그들 중 많은 이들이 전액 환불을 요구했다.
(d) 그들 중 일부가 걸어 나갔다.

정답 (d)

해설 남자가 대화 중반부에 어떤 사람들은 심지어 전부 취소되었다고 생각해서 돌아가기도 했다고(others even left thinking that the whole thing was canceled) 밝히고 있으므로 (d)가 정답입니다.

어휘 react 반응하다 yell 소리 치다 refuse + to 동사원형: ~하기를 거부하다 demand ~을 요구하다 refund 환불(액)

패러프레이징

others even left → Some of them walked out

32 세부 정보

Why is Eddie so tired today?

(a) because he arrived home late
(b) because he drove a long way
(c) because he stayed up all night
(d) because he danced for a long time

에디가 오늘 왜 그렇게 피곤한가?

(a) 집에 늦게 도착했기 때문에
(b) 먼 길을 운전했기 때문에
(c) 밤을 꼬박 새웠기 때문에
(d) 오랜 시간 춤을 췄기 때문에

정답 (a)

해설 대화 후반부에 남자가 자정이 한참 지나서야 집에 가는 바람에 오늘 피곤한 상태라고(I didn't get home until well after
midnight — that's why I'm so tired today) 알리고 있으므로 (a)가 정답입니다.

어휘 arrive 도착하다 stay up (늦게까지) 자지 않고 있다

패러프레이징

didn't get home until well after midnight → arrived home late

33 추론

What will Teresa probably do tonight?

(a) go to the band's concert
(b) have dinner with a friend
(c) listen to the band's music
(d) watch a movie at home

테레사는 오늘밤에 무엇을 할 것 같
은가?

(a) 그 밴드의 콘서트에 가는 일
(b) 친구와 저녁 식사하는 일
(c) 그 밴드의 음악을 듣는 일
(d) 집에서 영화를 보는 일

정답 (c)

해설 대화 후반부에 여자가 퇴근 후에 핫 뉴 패닉을 들어 보고 싶다고 밝히면서 지금 그들의 새 싱글을 다운로드하고 있나고
(Talking about this makes me want to listen to some Hot New Panic after work. I'm downloading their new
single now) 말하고 있으므로 (c)가 정답입니다.

Good morning, everyone! With questions arising over the quality of traditional wet and dry pet food, **34** we at Bark and Meow Pet Company are proud to introduce our newest fresh meal delivery service designed to ensure high-quality healthy meals for your pets. No longer do you have to serve your pet overly processed chunks that look nothing like the ingredients they supposedly contain. Bark and Meow is happy to do all the planning, mixing, and packaging for you. Let me explain.

Like all pet food, the package delivered to your home will contain the list of ingredients in each meal. However, unlike traditional pet food, not only are the ingredients familiar to you, but **35** our pet meals also look and smell similar to the food you might see on your own plate! We aim to not only keep your pets healthy, but also excited for mealtime — even when it comes to the pickiest of eaters.

Our website has a new tab for the meal delivery service where you can go and set up an account. After that, you're ready to start building your first order. Customers can browse through our list of fresh whole vegetables, whole grains, and meat, and then select ingredients based on their pets' dietary needs. For example, pets with sensitive stomachs may need easy-to-digest foods, like chicken and brown rice. **36** For those who aren't sure where to begin, we also have a menu full of signature meals to choose from. These are meals that have been taste-approved by our own pet family.

안녕하세요, 여러분! 전통적인 습식 반려동물 사료와 건식 사료의 품질에 대한 의문이 제기되고 있는 상황에서, 저희 바크 앤 미아오 펫 컴퍼니는 여러분의 반려동물을 위한 고품질 건강식을 보장해 드리기 위해 고안된 최신 신선한 음식 배달 서비스를 소개해 드리게 되어 자랑스럽습니다. 이제 더 이상 반려동물에게 재료와는 전혀 다르게 생긴 과도하게 가공된 음식을 줄 필요가 없습니다. 저희 바크 앤 미아오 사는 여러분을 위해 기꺼이 모든 계획과 혼합, 그리고 포장까지 해 드립니다. 제가 설명해 드리겠습니다.

모든 반려동물 사료와 마찬가지로, 여러분 댁에 배송되는 패키지는 각 음식에 성분표를 포함할 것입니다. 하지만, 전통적인 사료와 달리, 그 성분이 여러분께 익숙한 것일 뿐만 아니라, 저희 반려동물 음식은 여러분의 접시에서 보실 수 있을 법한 음식과 유사하게 보이고 냄새도 유사합니다! 저희는 여러분의 반려동물을 건강하게 유지해 드릴 뿐만 아니라, 식사 시간까지 즐겁게 유지해 드리는 것도 목표로 하고 있으며, 심지어 먹이에 대해 가장 까다로운 동물의 경우에도 마찬가지입니다.

저희 웹 사이트에는 음식 배송 서비스를 위한 새로운 탭이 있으며, 여러분은 그 탭으로 가서서 계정을 설정하실 수 있습니다. 그렇게 하시고 나면, 첫 주문의 진행을 시작할 준비가 됩니다. 고객들께서는 저희의 신선한 통채소와 통곡물, 그리고 육류에 대한 목록을 둘러 보신 다음, 반려동물의 식사에 필요로 하는 것을 바탕으로 재료를 선택하실 수 있습니다. 예를 들어, 위장이 민감한 반려동물은 닭고기와 현미 같은, 소화하기 쉬운 음식이 필요할 수 있습니다. 어디서부터 시작해야 할지 잘 모르시는 분들을 위해, 선택하실 수 있는 대표 음식들로 가득한 메뉴도 있습니다. 이것들은 저희 반려동물 가족에 의해 맛을 인정 받은 음식들입니다.

Once we make the meals from your pre-selected ingredients, we package them individually in reusable storage containers and pouches and then deliver them straight to your front door. **37** Your meals will arrive in an insulated container to ensure your pet's meals stay good for up to 24 hours from delivery until you are able to store them in your refrigerator or freezer. For a small fee, you can choose to receive the meals already frozen.

To get started with this service, simply go to our website to sign up for an account and select the meal delivery service. There, you will provide your address and payment information before making your pet's meal selections. **38** The cost per meal is based on the number of ingredients chosen as well as individual meal sizes selected.

For a limited time, you can receive two additional meals free with each order of ten meals. Our customer service center will send out an email alert 48 hours before your scheduled order is prepared and delivered. If your pet isn't happy with Bark and Meow meals, just cancel anytime. **39** Orders can be canceled by contacting customer service. We look forward to providing your pet with a yummy new mealtime experience.

일단 여러분께서 먼저 선택해 주신 재료들로 음식을 만들고 나면, 재활용 보관 용기 및 파우치에 개별 포장한 다음, 여러분의 문 앞까지 곧장 배송해 드립니다. 음식은 냉장실 또는 냉동실에 보관하실 수 있을 때까지 배송 후 최대 24시간 동안 반려동물 음식이 좋은 상태로 유지되도록 보장해 드리기 위해 보온 용기에 담겨 도착할 것입니다. 소액의 요금으로, 이미 냉동 처리된 음식을 받으시도록 선택하실 수 있습니다.

이 서비스를 시작하기 위해서는, 저희 웹 사이트로 가셔서 계정을 등록하신 다음, 음식 배송 서비스를 선택하시기만 하면 됩니다. 그곳에서, 반려동물 음식을 선택하시기 전에 여러분의 주소 및 결제 정보를 제공하시게 될 것입니다. 각 음식 비용은 선택된 재료의 숫자뿐만 아니라 선택된 개별 음식의 크기도 바탕으로 합니다.

한시적으로, 10개의 음식을 담은 각 주문에 대해 추가로 2개의 음식을 무료로 받으실 수 있습니다. 저희 고객 서비스 센터에서 여러분의 예정된 주문이 준비되어 배송되기 48시간 전에 이메일 알림 메시지를 발송해 드립니다. 여러분의 반려동물이 저희 바크 앤 미아오 음식에 만족하지 못하는 경우, 언제든지 취소하십시오. 주문은 고객 서비스 센터에 연락하셔서 취소하시면 됩니다. 저희는 여러분의 반려동물에게 맛있고 새로운 식사 시간 경험을 제공하기를 고대합니다.

어휘　**with + 목적어 + -ing:** (목적어)가 ~하면서, (목적어)가 ~하는 채로 **arise** (문제 등이) 제기되다, 떠오르다 **over** ~에 대해, ~을 두고 **traditional** 전통적인 **be proud + to 동사원형:** ~해서 자랑스럽다 **introduce** ~을 소개하다, ~을 도입하다 **designed + to 동사원형:** ~하도록 고안된, ~하기 위해 만들어진 **ensure** ~을 보장하다, 반드시 ~하도록 하다 **No longer do + 주어 + 동사원형:** 더 이상 (주어)가 ~ 않다 **overly** 지나치게 **processed** 가공 처리된 **chunk** 덩어리 **look nothing like** 전혀 ~ 같이 보이지 않다 **ingredient** 재료, 성분 **supposedly** 추정되어 **contain** ~을 포함하다 **packaging** 포장(재) **however** 하지만, 그러나 **not only A, but also B:** A뿐만 아니라 B도(= B as well as A) **familiar** 익숙한, 잘 아는 **similar to** ~와 유사한 **aim + to 동사원형:** ~하는 것을 목표로 하다 **when it comes to** ~와 관련해서, ~의 측면에 있어 **picky** 까다로운 **set up** ~을 설정하다, ~을 설치하다 **account** 계정, 계좌 **browse through** ~을 둘러 보다, ~을 훑어 보다 **whole** 통째의, 미정제된 **based on** ~을 바탕으로 **dietary** 음식물의, 식사의 **sensitive** 민감한 **stomach** 위장 **easy-to-digest** 소화하기 쉬운 **full of** ~로 가득한 **those who** ~하는 사람들 **signature** 대표적인 **choose from** ~에서 선택하다 **taste-approved** 맛을 인정 받은 **individually** 개별적으로, 각각 **reusable** 재활용 가능한 **storage** 보관, 저장 **container** 용기, 그릇 **insulated** 보온[보냉]의, 단열 처리된 **up to** 최대 ~의 **be able + to 동사원형:** ~할 수 있다 **store** ~을 보관하나, ~을 저장하다 **get started with** ~을 시작하다 **sign up for** ~을 신청하다, ~에 등록하다 **make a selection** 선택하다 **limited** 한정된, 제한적인 **free** 무료로 **alert** 알림 (메시지) **cancel** ~을 취소하다 **contact** ~에 연락하다 **look forward to -ing** ~하기를 고대하다 **yummy** 맛있는

What is the purpose of the presentation?

(a) to introduce a pet food service
(b) to promote a new pet store
(c) to announce a new pet care app
(d) to educate about pet nutrition

발표의 목적은 무엇인가?

(a) 반려동물 음식 서비스를 소개하는 것
(b) 새 반려동물 매장을 홍보하는 것
(c) 새 반려동물 관리 앱을 발표하는 것
(d) 반려동물 영양에 관해 교육하는 것

정답 (a)

해설 화자가 담화를 시작하면서 반려동물을 위한 최신 음식 배송 서비스를 소개한다고(we at Bark and Meow Pet Company are proud to introduce our newest fresh meal delivery service ~ for your pets) 밝히고 있으므로 (a)가 정답입니다.

어휘 promote ~을 홍보하다, ~을 촉진하다 c are 관리, 돌봄, 보살핌 nutrition 영양

Based on the talk, why, most likely, are these pet meals appealing?

(a) because the prices are low
(b) because of the way they taste
(c) because the portions are large
(d) because of the way they look

담화 내용에 따르면, 이 반려동물 음식이 왜 매력적일 것 같은가?

(a) 가격이 낮기 때문에
(b) 맛을 내는 방식 때문에
(c) 양이 많기 때문에
(d) 겉으로 보이는 방식 때문에

정답 (d)

해설 담화 초반부에 화자가 제품을 설명하면서 사람이 먹는 음식과 유사하게 보이고 냄새도 유사하다는(our pet meals also look and smell similar to the food you might see on your own plate!) 특징을 알리고 있으므로 (d)가 정답입니다.

어휘 appealing 매력적인 way 방식 portion 분량, 1인분

패러프레이징

look ~ similar to the food you might see on your own plate → the way they look

36 세부 정보

What can customers do if they are not sure where to begin?

(a) sign up for a trial account
(b) call customer support
(c) select from set meals
(d) meet with an expert

고객들이 어디서 시작해야 할지 잘 모를 경우에 무엇을 할 수 있는가?

(a) 체험용 계정을 신청하는 일
(b) 고객 지원부에 전화하는 일
(c) 세트 음식에서 선택하는 일
(d) 전문가와 만나는 일

정답 (c)

해설 화자가 담화 중반부에 어디서부터 시작해야 할지 잘 모르는 사람들을 위해 그들이 선택할 수 있는 대표 음식들로 가득한 메뉴도 있다고(For those who aren't sure where to begin, we also have a menu full of signature meals to choose from) 밝히고 있으므로 (c)가 정답입니다.

어휘 trial 체험, 시험 expert 전문가

패러프레이징

a menu full of signature meals to choose from → select from set meals

37 세부 정보

How does the company make sure the food does not go bad after delivery?

(a) It ships all meals frozen.
(b) It uses special packaging.
(c) It adds natural preservatives.
(d) It notifies buyers immediately.

이 업체는 어떻게 음식이 배송 후에 반드시 상하지 않게 하는가?

(a) 모든 음식을 냉동 상태로 배송한다.
(b) 특수 포장재를 사용한다.
(c) 천연 방부제를 추가한다.
(d) 구매자들에게 즉시 알린다.

정답 (b)

해설 담화 중반부에 화자가 배송 후 최대 24시간 동안 반려동물 음식이 좋은 상태로 유지되도록 보장하기 드리기 위해 보온 용기에 담겨 도착할 것이라고(Your meals will arrive in an insulated container to ensure your pet's meals stay good for up to 24 hours from delivery ~) 알리고 있습니다. 이는 특수 포장 용기에 담아 배송한다는 뜻이므로 (b)가 정답입니다.

어휘 ship ~을 배송하다 add ~을 추가하다 preservative 방부제 notify ~에게 알리다 immediately 즉시

패러프레이징

an insulated container → special packaging

What is the cost per meal based on?

(a) the frequency of orders
(b) the method of payment
(c) the variety of ingredients
(d) the species of pet

음식당 가격은 무엇을 바탕으로 하는가?

(a) 주문 빈도
(b) 결제 방식
(c) 재료의 종류
(d) 반려동물의 종

정답 (c)

해설 화자가 담화 후반부에 음식 비용이 선택된 재료의 숫자뿐만 아니라 선택된 개별 음식 크기도 바탕으로 한다고(The cost per meal is based on the number of ingredients chosen as well as individual meal sizes selected) 알리고 있으므로 (c)가 정답입니다.

어휘 frequency 빈도, 잦음 variety 종류, 다양함 species (동식물의) 종

패러프레이징

the number of ingredients / individual meal sizes → the variety of ingredients

How can customers cancel their orders?

(a) by reaching out to customer service
(b) by visiting a store branch
(c) by closing their account on the website
(d) by submitting an online form

고객들은 어떻게 주문을 취소할 수 있는가?

(a) 고객 서비스부에 연락해서
(b) 매장 지점을 방문해서
(c) 웹 사이트의 계정을 닫아서
(d) 온라인 양식을 제출해서

정답 (a)

해설 화자가 담화 맨 마지막 부분에 고객 서비스부에 연락해서 주문을 취소할 수 있다고(Orders can be canceled by contacting customer service) 알리고 있으므로 (a)가 정답입니다.

어휘 reach out to ~에 연락하다 branch 지점, 지사 submit ~을 제출하다 form 양식, 서식

패러프레이징

contacting customer service → reaching out to customer service

PART 3

M: Happy Friday, Elizabeth. Are you glad it's finally the weekend?

F: Hey, Johnny. Definitely! And Monday is a national holiday, so we have an additional day off.

M: I know. I'm leaving work now to head straight to the lake with friends. What are you planning to do?

F: I'm not sure actually. I completely forgot about the holiday until today, **40** so now I'm trying to decide if I want to head to the beach for the weekend or relax at home.

M: Well, let's talk it out. An advantage of going to the beach is having fun things to do like swimming and snorkeling.

F: That's true. Another great thing about the beach is the food. **41** The best seafood is at the restaurants near the beach, and I love to eat seafood when it's fresh.

M: **41** Me too! I love to eat fresh fish and crab at the beach. Plus, another good thing about going to the beach is the scenery. There is nothing more relaxing than gazing into the blue horizon and listening to the ocean waves.

F: True, Johnny. But **42** I'm a little reluctant to go because I would have to drive over six hours to get there.

M: It is a bit far. Another bad thing is that you would need to find a place to stay right away. Sometimes hotel rooms can be hard to find if you wait until the last minute and everyone else has the same idea about going to the beach.

남: 즐거운 금요일입니다, 엘리자베스 씨. 드디어 주말이 되어서 기쁘신가요?

여: 안녕하세요, 조니 씨. 물론이죠! 그리고 월요일이 공휴일이라서, 추가 휴무일이 하루 더 있어요.

남: 그러니까요. 저는 지금 퇴근하고 친구들과 곧장 호수로 갑니다. 뭘 하실 계획이세요?

여: 사실 잘 모르겠어요. 오늘까지 휴일에 대해서 완전히 잊고 있었기 때문에, 주말 동안 해변으로 가고 싶은지, 아니면 집에서 쉴지 지금 결정해 보려고 하는 중입니다.

남: 그럼, 그 얘기를 해 보죠. 해변에 가는 것의 한 가지 장점은 수영과 스노클링처럼 즐거운 것을 할 수 있다는 점이죠.

여: 맞아요. 해변과 관련해서 또 다른 아주 좋은 점은 음식이에요. 최고의 해산물은 해변과 가까운 레스토랑에 있는데, 제가 신선할 때 해산물을 먹을 걸 아주 좋아하거든요.

남: 저도요! 저는 해변에서 신선한 생선과 게를 먹는 걸 아주 좋아해요. 게다가, 해변으로 가는 것과 관련된 또 다른 좋은 점은 경치입니다. 푸른 수평선을 바라 보면서 바다의 파도 소리를 듣는 것만큼 느긋한 게 없죠.

여: 맞아요, 조니 씨. 하지만 전 가는 게 조금 망설여지는데, 그곳에 가려면 6시간 넘게 운전해야 할 것이기 때문이에요.

남: 좀 멀긴 하죠. 또 다른 좋지 않은 점은 당장 머무르실 곳도 찾아야 할 것이라는 사실이에요. 때때로 호텔 객실들은 마지막 순간까지 기다려야 하는 경우에 찾기 어려울 수 있고, 다른 모든 사람도 해변에 가는 것과 관련해서 같은 생각을 하잖아요.

F: Yeah, and because I would want to leave tonight, I would have to rush home to pack quickly. Maybe staying home is a better plan.

M: Well, Elizabeth, if you stay home, you can save money. That's always a plus!

F: Oh, absolutely. 43 Another good thing would be sleeping in every morning. Three days of extra rest might help me catch up on the hours of sleep I've missed since taking on that big project. If I were at the beach, I would want to be up early to enjoy some activities instead of sleeping in.

M: Yeah, and don't you live in a quiet neighborhood? I can imagine staying home would be much more relaxing than being at the beach with people being loud and partying. You might be able to recharge more if you stay home instead.

F: True, 44 but a major disadvantage of staying home is being bored. I haven't gone anywhere in weeks, and I think if I stay home, I might just end up working.

M: I know that project has been on your mind a lot lately.

F: It has. 44 And part of the reason my neighborhood is so quiet is because there is nothing to do there. I usually just come home and watch television.

M: There aren't any cafés or shops anywhere around you?

F: Nope. So I might regret staying home instead of using this time off to do something fun. 45 The weather right now is perfect for the beach. It would be a waste not to take advantage of it.

여: 네, 그리고 저는 오늘밤에 떠나길 원할 것이기 때문에, 서둘러 집으로 가서 빨리 짐을 꾸려야 할 거예요. 아마 집에 머물러 있는 게 더 나은 계획일 거예요.

남: 음, 엘리자베스 씨, 집에 머물러 계시면, 돈을 아끼실 수 있어요. 그건 언제나 이점이죠!

여: 아, 물론이죠. 또 다른 좋은 점은 매일 아침에 늦잠을 자는 일일 거예요. 3일 동안의 추가 휴식은 제가 그 중요한 프로젝트를 맡은 이후로 놓쳤던 수면 시간을 보충하는 데 도움이 될지도 몰라요. 제가 해변에 가 있는다면, 늦잠을 자는 대신 일찍 일어나서 몇몇 활동들을 즐기고 싶어 할 거예요.

남: 네, 그리고 조용한 지역에 살고 계시지 않나요? 집에 머물러 계시는 게 사람들이 시끄럽게 떠들고 파티를 하는 해변에 있는 것보다 훨씬 더 느긋할 거라는 게 상상이 돼요. 대신 집에 머물러 계시면 더 많이 재충전하실 수 있을지도 몰라요.

여: 맞아요, 하지만 집에 있는 것의 큰 단점은 지루하다는 거예요. 제가 몇 주 동안 아무데도 가지 않았기 때문에, 제 생각에 집에 있으면, 결국 그냥 일하게 될지도 몰라요.

남: 그 프로젝트가 최근에 당신 마음 속에 크게 자리잡고 있었다는 걸 알아요.

여: 그랬죠. 그리고 저희 동네가 그렇게 조용한 이유 중의 일부분은 그곳에 할 게 없기 때문이에요. 저는 평소에 그냥 집에 가서 텔레비전을 시청해요.

남: 주변에 어디에도 카페나 매장들이 전혀 없나요?

여: 없어요. 그래서 이 휴무를 이용해서 뭔가 재미있는 걸 하는 대신 집에 있는 걸 후회할지도 몰라요. 지금 날씨가 해변에 가기에 완벽하잖아요. 그걸 이용하지 않는 건 낭비일 거예요.

M: The weather is pretty amazing these days.

F: Plus, with this project I won't be able to take a vacation for another few months, and by then the weather will be much colder.

M: So, what do you think you'll do, Elizabeth?

F: 45 Honestly, Johnny, I think a change of scenery might be just what I need.

남: 요즘 날씨가 아주 놀랍긴 해요.

여: 게다가, 이 프로젝트 때문에 몇 달 동안 더 휴가를 갈 수 없을 텐데, 그때쯤이면 날씨가 훨씬 더 추워질 거예요.

남: 그럼, 어떻게 하실 생각이세요, 엘리자베스 씨?

여: 솔직히, 조니 씨, 기분 전환이 바로 제가 필요한 일일지도 모른다고 생각해요.

어휘 **day off** 휴일, 휴무 **head to** ~로 가다, ~로 향하다 **plan + to 동사원형:** ~할 계획이다 **completely** 완전히 **relax** 쉬다, 느긋하게 있다 **talk + 목적어 + out:** (목적어)를 이야기하다, (목적어)를 논의하다 **advantage** 장점(↔ disadvantage) **plus** ad. 게다가, 더욱이 n. 이점, 좋은 점 **scenery** 경치, 풍경 **There is nothing more A than B:** B만큼 A한 게 없다 **gaze into** ~을 바라 보다, ~을 응시하다 **horizon** 수평선, 지평선 **be reluctant + to 동사원형:** ~하기를 망설이다, ~하기를 주저하다 **would have + to 동사원형:** ~해야 할 것이다 **a bit** 조금, 약간 **rush** 서두르다 **pack** 짐을 꾸리다 **sleep in** 늦잠 자다 **extra** 추가의, 별도의 **rest** 휴식 **help + 목적어 + 동사원형:** (목적어)가 ~하는 데 도움을 주다 **catch up on** ~을 보충하다, (진행 등) ~을 따라잡다 **miss** ~을 놓치다, ~을 빠뜨리다 **take on** ~을 맡다 **neighborhood** 지역, 동네, 이웃 **with + 목적어 + -ing:** (목적어)가 ~하면서, (목적어)가 ~하는 채로 **be able + to 동사원형:** ~할 수 있다 **recharge** 재충전하다 **end up -ing** 결국 ~하게 되다 **regret -ing** ~하는 것을 후회하다 **time off** 휴가, 휴무 **take advantage of** ~을 이용하다 **by then** 그때쯤 **a change of scenery** 기분 전환

---

40 주제/목적

What concern is Elizabeth discussing with Johnny?

(a) whether to invite friends over
(b) whether to take an overseas vacation
(c) whether to join him on a trip
(d) whether to go away for the weekend

엘리자베스는 어떤 우려 사항을 조니와 이야기하고 있는가?

(a) 친구를 집으로 초대할지의 여부
(b) 해외로 휴가를 갈지의 여부
(c) 조니의 여행에 함께 할지의 여부
(d) 주말에 어디론가 떠날지의 여부

정답 (d)

해설 여자가 대화 초반부에 주말 동안 해변으로 가고 싶은지, 아니면 집에서 쉴지 지금 결정하려 한다고(now I'm trying to decide if I want to head to the beach for the weekend or relax at home) 밝히자, 남자가 그에 관해 이야기해 보자고 제안하고 있으므로 (d)가 정답입니다.

어휘 **concern** 우려, 걱정 **whether + to 동사원형:** ~할지(의 여부) **invite + 목적어 + over:** (목적어)를 집으로 초대하다 **overseas** 해외의 **join** ~와 함께 하다 **go away** (휴가 등을) 떠나다

패러프레이징

head to the beach for the weekend or relax at home → whether to go away

Based on the conversation, what do Elizabeth and Johnny both like to do at the beach?

(a) enjoy local cuisine
(b) lie in the sun
(c) read a good book
(d) wade in the water

대화 내용에 따르면, 엘리자베스와 조니 둘 모두 해변에서 무엇을 하는 것을 좋아하는가?

(a) 지역 요리를 즐기는 일
(b) 햇빛 아래에 누워 있는 일
(c) 좋은 책을 읽는 일
(d) 물 속을 헤치며 걷는 일

정답 (a)

해설 대화 초반부에 여자가 신선할 때 해산물을 먹을 걸 아주 좋아한다고(I love to eat seafood when it's fresh) 말하자, 남자 도 신선한 생선과 게를 먹는 걸 아주 좋아한다고(Me too! I love to eat fresh fish and crab at the beach) 밝히고 있는데, 해산물은 특정 지역의 요리로 볼 수 있으므로 (a)가 정답입니다.

어휘 local 지역의, 현지의 cuisine 요리 wade (물 등) ~을 헤치며 걷다, ~을 걸어서 건너다

패러프레이징

eat seafood / eat fresh fish and crab at the beach → enjoy local cuisine

What could make Elizabeth reluctant to visit the beach?

(a) the amount of traffic
(b) the length of the trip
(c) the cost of hotels
(d) the time of the year

무엇 때문에 엘리자베스가 해변을 방문하는 것을 망설이는가?

(a) 교통량
(b) 이동 길이
(c) 호텔 비용
(d) 일년 중의 시기

정답 (b)

해설 여자가 대화 중반부에 조금 망설여지는 이유로 가는 데 6시간 넘게 운전해야 한다고(I'm a little reluctant to go because I would have to drive over six hours to get there) 언급하고 있으므로 (b)가 정답입니다.

어휘 traffic 교통(량), 차량들 length (물리적, 시간적) 길이, 기간

패러프레이징

drive over six hours to get there → the length of the trip

43 세부 정보

How can Elizabeth make the most out of her vacation by staying home?

(a) by cleaning up her bedroom
(b) by working on a novel
(c) by hanging out with neighbors
(d) by catching up on sleep

엘리자베스는 어떻게 집에 머무르는 것으로 휴가를 최대한 이용할 수 있는가?

(a) 침실을 청소함으로써
(b) 소설 작업을 함으로써
(c) 이웃들과 어울려 시간을 보냄으로써
(d) 잠을 보충함으로써

정답 (d)

해설 대화 중반부에 여자가 3일 동안의 추가 휴식이 중요한 프로젝트를 맡은 이후로 놓쳤던 수면 시간을 보충하는 데 도움이 될 것이라는(Three days of extra rest might help me catch up on the hours of sleep I've missed ~) 장점을 말하고 있으므로 (d)가 정답입니다.

어휘 make the most out of ~을 최대한 이용하다 hang out ~와 어울려 시간을 보내다

44 세부 정보

Why would Elizabeth be bored if she stays home over the weekend?

(a) Her television is broken.
(b) Her favorite café is closed.
(c) Her local area is dull.
(d) Her housemate is away.

엘리자베스가 주말 동안에 걸쳐 집에 머물러 있으면 왜 지루할 것인가?

(a) 텔레비전이 고장 나 있다.
(b) 가장 좋아하는 카페가 닫았다.
(c) 그 지역이 따분하다.
(d) 함께 사는 사람이 부재 중이다.

정답 (c)

해설 여자가 대화 중반부에 집에 있는 것의 큰 단점이 지루하다고(a major disadvantage of staying home is being bored) 말한 다음, 그 동네에서 할 게 없다는 점을(part of the reason my neighborhood is so quiet is because there is nothing to do there) 밝히고 있으므로 (c)가 정답입니다.

어휘 broken 고장 난, 망가진, 깨진 dull 따분한, 재미없는 be away 부재 중이다, 떨어져 있다

> 패러프레이징
>
> bored / neighborhood is so quiet / nothing to do there → local area is dull

What has Elizabeth most likely decided to do?

(a) spend some time at the beach
(b) go to the office and work
(c) get some rest at her house
(d) try out a new hiking trail

엘리자베스는 무엇을 하기로 결정했을 것 같은가?

(a) 해변에서 시간을 보내는 것
(b) 사무실로 가서 일하는 것
(c) 집에서 휴식을 좀 취하는 것
(d) 새로운 등산로를 시험해 보는 것

정답 (a)

해설 여자가 대화 마지막 부분에 지금 날씨가 해변가에 가기에 완벽한 날씨이며 그걸 이용하지 않는 건 낭비일 것이라고(The weather right now is perfect for the beach. It would be a waste not to take advantage of it) 언급하였습니다. 그 후 대화 맨 마지막에 기분 전환이 바로 자신이 필요한 일일 것으로 생각한다고(I think a change of scenery might be just what I need) 언급하고 있습니다. 이는 집에 머물러 있지 않고 해변으로 가는 것을 의미하므로 (a)가 정답입니다.

어휘 decide + to 동사원형: ~하기로 결정하다 try out ~을 시험해 보다 trail 산길, 오솔길

PART 4

Welcome to our podcast, *Mental Health and You*. **46** More people are working from home than ever before, but these workers face a unique set of challenges. They find it hard to separate work life from personal life, and the pressure to be productive despite being at home can be intense. **46** Today we will give you some tips for managing stress while transitioning to working remotely.

47 The first tip is to keep the same schedule at home as you would in the office. Most people need a routine to feel productive and reduce stress. Wake up at your normal time and get ready just as you would if you were going into the office. Changing out of your pajamas is a way to tell your brain that it is now time to work.

48 Tip two is to set up a specific work area in your home. Try to use this space and equipment only for work. This allows you to have everything readily available so you won't get sidetracked by searching for necessary items. **48** This will not only help you simulate your previous working environment but also help you draw a line between work and home items, allowing you to remain focused on your tasks.

49 The third tip is to try working when you feel most productive. For example, some workers are morning people who are most productive early in the day. Arranging their workday so they can complete the most crucial or difficult tasks during that time helps create a sense of accomplishment. **49** It also reduces the frustration of trying to work on big tasks later in the day when it's easier to get distracted. Use your least productive part of the day for tasks that don't require much concentration, such as planning for the next day.

저희 팟캐스트 <정신 건강과 당신>에 오신 것을 환영합니다. 과거 그 어느 때보다 더 많은 사람들이 재택 근무를 하고 있지만, 이 근로자들은 일련의 특별한 어려움에 직면합니다. 그들은 업무 생활과 개인 생활을 분리하는 것을 어렵게 생각하며, 집에 있음에도 불구하고 생산적이어야 한다는 압박감이 극심할 수 있습니다. 오늘, 저희가 원격 근무로 전환하시는 과정에서의 스트레스를 관리하기 위한 팁을 몇 가지 전해 드리겠습니다.

첫 번째 팁은 사무실에 하실 법한 것과 동일한 일정을 집에서도 유지하시는 것입니다. 대부분의 사람들이 생산적인 기분을 느끼고 스트레스를 줄이기 위해서는 반복적인 일상이 필요합니다. 마치 사무실로 가시는 경우에 하실 법한 것처럼 평소의 시간에 일어나셔서 준비하십시오. 잠옷을 갈아입으시는 것은 여러분의 두뇌에 이제 일할 시간이라고 말하는 한 가지 방법입니다.

두 번째 팁은 집 안에 특정 업무 공간을 마련하는 것입니다. 이 공간과 장비를 오직 업무를 위해서만 이용하도록 하십시오. 이렇게 하시면 모든 것을 손쉽게 이용할 수 있게 해 줄 것이므로, 필요한 물건을 찾느라 샛길로 빠지지 않게 될 것입니다. 이는 이전의 업무 환경을 모방하는 데 도움을 줄 뿐만 아니라, 업무용 물품과 가정용 물품 사이에 선을 긋는 데 도움을 주어, 일에 초점이 맞춰진 상태로 유지하게 해 줄 것입니다.

세 번째 팁은 가장 생산적이라고 느껴지실 때 일을 해 보시는 것입니다. 어떤 근로자들은 하루 중 이른 시간에 가장 생산적인 아침형 인간입니다. 그들은 그 시간대에 가장 중대하거나 어려운 일을 완료할 수 있도록 근무일을 조정하는 것이 성취감을 만들어 내는 데 도움이 됩니다. 이는 또한 하루 중 집중력이 떨어지기 더 쉬운 늦은 오후에 중요한 일에 대한 작업을 하려 하는 좌절감도 줄여 줍니다. 하루 중 가장 덜 생산적인 시간대를 다음 날을 위한 계획 세우기 같이, 많은 집중력을 필요로 하지 않는 일에 쓰십시오.

50 The fourth tip is to set aside time to de-stress. Some workers feel like they need to prove that they're just as effective at home as they were in the office, which can actually lead to overworking. It is important to remember that a person does not need to be productive 100 percent of the time. **50** Try setting an alarm on your phone as a break reminder. Breaks are essential for mental well-being and overall work performance because they allow a person to recharge mentally before diving back into tasks.

51 The fifth tip for separating your work life from your personal life is to maintain an after-work ritual. When the workday is over, it can be difficult to feel like you are leaving work behind. For example, maybe going to the gym after work was a normal part of your routine, or if you commuted, there was a podcast or music playlist you would always listen to. **51** Continue to do these things to step out of your workday and back into your personal life.

52 The final tip for managing stress is to be gentle with yourself. Working from home might be a brand-new experience and it will take time to get into a good groove. Patience for others is important, but it is also important to be patient with yourself.

Thank you for listening to today's episode of *Mental Health and You*. We hope that we have given you some helpful tips on managing stress in a changing work environment.

네 번째 팁은 스트레스를 해소하기 위한 시간을 확보해 두시는 것입니다. 어떤 근로자들은 사무실에 있었을 때만큼 집에서도 유능하다는 것을 증명해야 할 필요가 있는 것처럼 느끼는데, 이는 사실 과로로 이어질 수 있습니다. 사람은 100퍼센트의 시간에 생산적일 필요가 없다는 사실을 기억하는 것이 중요합니다. 휴식 알림으로 여러분의 전화기에 있는 알람을 설정해 보십시오. 휴식 시간은 정신 건강과 전반적인 업무 수행 능력에 있어 필수적인데, 업무에 다시 몰두하기 전에 사람이 정신적으로 재충전할 수 있게 해 주기 때문입니다.

업무 생활과 개인 생활을 분리하기 위한 다섯 번째 팁은 퇴근 후의 의례적인 일을 유지하시는 것입니다. 근무일이 종료될 때, 일을 뒤에 남겨 두고 떠난다는 느낌이 들기 어려울 수 있습니다. 예를 들어, 아마 퇴근 후에 체육관에 가시는 것이 평소 일상의 일부분이었거나, 통근하셨을 경우, 항상 들으시곤 했던 팟캐스트나 음악 재생 목록이 있었을 것입니다. 근무일에서 벗어나 개인 생활로 돌아가실 수 있도록 이런 것들을 계속 하십시오.

스트레스 관리를 위한 마지막 팁은 여러분 자신에게 관대해지는 것입니다. 재택 근무는 완전히 새로운 경험일 수 있으며, 좋은 리듬을 타는 데 시간이 걸릴 것입니다. 다른 사람들에 대한 인내가 중요하긴 하지만, 여러분 자신에 대해 인내하는 것 또한 중요합니다.

저희 <정신 건강과 당신>의 오늘 방송분을 청취해 주셔서 감사 드립니다. 저희가 변화하는 업무 환경 속에서 스트레스를 관리하는 일에 관해 몇몇 도움이 되는 팁을 드렸기를 바랍니다.

어휘 　mental 정신적인　than ever before 과거 그 어느 때보다　face ~에 직면하다　a set of 일련의　unique 특별한, 독특한 find it + 형용사 + to 동사원형: ~하는 것을 (형용사)하게 생각하다　separate A from B: A와 B를 분리하다　pressure 압박(감)　intense 극심한, 강렬한　transition to ~로 전환하다　work remotely 원격으로 근무하다　routine 반복적인 일상(적인 것)　productive 생산적인　reduce ~을 줄이다, ~을 감소시키다　change out of ~을 갈아입다　way + to 동사원형: ~하는 방법　set up ~을 마련하다, ~을 설치하다, ~을 설정하다　specific 특정한, 구체적인　equipment 장비 allow + 목적어 + to 동사원형: (목적어)가 ~할 수 있게 해 주다　readily 손쉽게　available 이용 가능한　get sidetracked 샛길로 빠지다, 딴 데로 새다　necessary 필요한, 필수의　not only A but also B: A뿐만 아니라 B도　simulate ~을 모방 하다, ~처럼 보이게 하다　previous 이전의, 과거의　remain + 형용사: ~한 상태로 유지되다　focused on ~에 초점이 맞춰진, ~에 집중한　task 일, 업무　arrange ~을 조정하다, ~을 조치하다　crucial 중대한　help + 동사원형: ~하는 데 도움이 되다 accomplishment 성취, 달성　frestration 좌절(감), 불만　distracted 집중력이 떨어진, 정신이 산만해진　require ~을 필요로 하다　concentration 집중(력)　set aside (따로) ~을 확보하다, ~을 떼어 두다　de-stress 스트레스를 해소하다 prove that ~임을 증명하다　effective 유능한, 효과적인　lead to ~로 이어지다　break 휴식 (시간)　reminder (상기시키는) 알림, 메모　essential 필수적인　overall 전반적인　performance 수행 (능력), 실력, 성과, 실적　recharge 재충전하다　dive into ~에 몰두하다　maintain ~을 유지하다　ritual 의례(적인 것), 의식　leave + 목적어 + behind: (목적어)를 뒤에 남겨 두고 가다　commute 통근하다, 통학하다　continue + to 동사원형: 계속 ~하다　step out of ~에서 벗어나다　gentle 관대한 brand-new 완전히 새로운　get into a good groove 좋은 리듬을 타다　patience 인내(심)　epidose 한 회의 방송분

46　주제/목적

What is this podcast episode about?

(a) switching to new career
(b) adjusting to a new work arrangement
(c) making friends with colleagues
(d) learning to manage a heavy workload

이 팟캐스트는 무엇에 관한 것인가?

(a) 새로운 직업으로 바꾸는 것
(b) 새로운 업무 관련 조치에 적응하는 것
(c) 동료 직원과 친구가 되는 것
(d) 많은 업무량 관리법을 배우는 것

정답　(b)

해설　화자가 담화 초반부에 원격 근무로 전환하는 과정에서의 스트레스 관리를 위한 팁을 몇 가지 전하겠다고(we will give you some tips for managing stress while transitioning to working remotely) 밝히는 것으로 주제를 언급하고 있습니다. 이는 새로운 업무 환경으로의 변화에 대한 일종의 적응 방법에 해당하므로 (b)가 정답입니다.

어휘　switch to ~로 바꾸다　adjust to ~에 적응하다　arrangement 조치, 조정, 처리, 준비　colleague 동료 (직원)　heavy (수량, 정도 등) 많은, 심한　workload 업무량

패러프레이징

managing stress while transitioning to working remotely → adjusting to a new work arrangement

How can workers keep the same schedule at home as they would in the office?

(a) by ensuring a sufficient amount of sleep
(b) by making a detailed agenda
(c) by keeping a steady morning routine
(d) by setting up a recurring meeting

근로자들이 어떻게 사무실에서 하곤 했던 것과 동일한 일정을 집에서 유지할 수 있는가?

(a) 충분한 수면 시간을 보장함으로써
(b) 상세한 일정표를 만듦으로써
(c) 한결같은 오전 일상을 유지함으로써
(d) 반복적인 회의 시간을 마련함으로써

정답 (c)

해설 질문의 키워드인 사무실에서 하던 것처럼 집에서도 똑같은 일정을 유지하는 것이 첫 번째 팁을 설명하는 부분((The first tip is to keep the same schedule at home as you would in the office)에서 언급되었습니다. 그리고 생산적인 기분이 들도록 하고 스트레스를 줄이기 위해 반복적인 일상이 필요하다고(Most people need a routine to feel productive and reduce stress) 언급하였고 그 뒤에 부연설명으로 마치 사무실로 가는 경우에 하는 것처럼 평소의 시간에 일어나서 준비하라고(Wake up at your normal time and get ready just as you would if you were going into the office) 알리고 있습니다. 이는 오전 시간에 동일한 활동을 하는 것을 의미하므로 (c)가 정답입니다.

어휘 ensure ~을 보장하다, 반드시 ~하도록 하다 sufficient 충분한 detailed 상세한 agenda 일정표, 목록, 안건 steady 한결같은, 꾸준한 recurring 반복되는, 재발하는

> **패러프레이징**
>
> Wake up at your normal time and get ready just as you would if you were going into the office → keeping a steady morning routine

According to the talk, why should remote workers set up a specific place to work?

(a) to have privacy from family
(b) to ensure sufficient space
(c) to look professional in meetings
(d) to maintain concentration

담화 내용에 따르면, 원격 근무자들이 왜 특정 업무 공간을 마련해야 하는가?

(a) 가족과 분리된 사생활을 갖기 위해
(b) 충분한 공간을 보장하기 위해
(c) 회의에서 전문적으로 보이기 위해
(d) 집중력을 유지하기 위해

정답 (d)

해설 질문의 키워드인 특정 업무공간에 대한 언급은 두 번째 팁을 설명하는 부분(Tip two is to set up a specific work area in you home)에서 언급되었습니다. 그 후 그것은 이전의 업무 환경을 모방하는 데 도움을 줄 뿐만 아니라, 업무용 물품과 가정용 물품 사이에 선을 긋는 데 도움을 주어, 일에 초점이 맞춰진 상태로 유지하게 해 줄 것(This will not only help you simulate your previous working environment but also help you draw a line between work and home items, allowing you to remain focused on your tasks)이라고 밝히고 있습니다. 이는 집중력 유지에 좋다는 뜻이므로 (d)가 정답입니다.

어휘 privacy 사생활 maintain ~을 유지하다

> **패러프레이징**
>
> remain focused on your tasks → maintain concentration

49 추론

How, most likely, can one reduce the frustration of working on a big task?

(a) by choosing a productive time of day
(b) by working on it with colleagues
(c) by requesting feedback from a supervisor
(d) by dividing it into small pieces

어떻게 중요한 업무를 맡아 일하는 것에 대한 좌절감을 줄일 수 있는가?

(a) 하루 중 생산적인 시간대를 선택함으로써
(b) 동료 직원들과 함께 그것을 맡아 일함으로써
(c) 상사에게 의견을 요청함으로써
(d) 그것을 작은 부분들로 나눔으로써

정답 (a)

해설 담화 중반부에 화자가 가장 생산적이라고 느껴질 때 일을 하라는(to try working when you feel most productive) 조언을 전하면서, 그것이 오후 늦은 시간에 중요한 일에 대한 작업을 하는 좌절감도 줄여 준다고(It also reduces the frustration of trying to work on big tasks later in the day) 알리고 있으므로 (a)가 정답입니다.

어휘 choose ~을 선택하다 request ~을 요청하다 feedback 의견 supervisor 상사, 책임자, 감독 divide A into B: A를 B로 나누다

> **패러프레이징**
>
> try working when you feel most productive → choosing a productive time of day

TEST 03 Listening 191

According to the talk, what should workers set a phone alarm for?

(a) the end of the working day
(b) the time to take a break
(c) the moment to switch tasks
(d) the point when family return

담화 내용에 따르면, 근로자들은 무엇을 위해 전화기의 알람을 설정해야 하는가?

(a) 근무일의 종료
(b) 휴식을 취할 시간
(c) 업무를 바꾸는 순간
(d) 가족이 돌아오는 시점

정답 (b)

해설 화자가 담화 후반부에 휴식 알림으로서 전화기에 알람을 설정해 보도록(Try setting an alarm on your phone as a break reminder) 권하고 있으므로 (b)가 정답입니다.

어휘 take a break 휴식을 취하다 moment 때, 순간, 잠시 point 시점, 지점, 요소, 요점, 사항

패러프레이징

a break reminder → the time to take a break

Why is it helpful to maintain an after-work ritual?

(a) to ensure family interaction
(b) to transition back to personal time
(c) to maintain an active social life
(d) to focus on physical fitness

퇴근 후의 의례적인 일을 유지하는 것이 왜 도움이 되는가?

(a) 가족과의 교류를 보장하기 위해
(b) 개인 생활로 다시 전환하기 위해
(c) 적극적인 사회 생활을 유지하기 위해
(d) 신체적인 건강에 초점을 맞추기 위해

정답 (b)

해설 담화 후반부에 화자가 퇴근 후의 의례적인 일을 유지하도록(to maintain an after-work ritual) 조언하면서, 근무일에서 벗어나 개인 생활로 돌아갈 수 있도록 그런 일들을 계속 유지하라고(Continue to do these things to step out of your workday and back into your personal life) 알리고 있으므로 (b)가 정답입니다.

어휘 interaction 교류, 상호 작용 active 적극적인, 활동적인 physical 신체적인, 물리적인

패러프레이징

step out of your workday and back into your personal life → transition back to personal time

Why should employees be gentle with themselves when working from home?

(a) Their productivity will drop.
(b) They will miss their colleagues.
(c) Their stress will increase.
(d) They will need time to adjust.

직원들은 재택 근무를 할 때 왜 스스로에게 관대해야 하는가?

(a) 생산성이 떨어질 것이다.
(b) 동료들을 그리워할 것이다.
(c) 스트레스가 늘어날 것이다.
(d) 적응할 시간이 필요할 것이다.

정답 (d)

해설 화자가 마지막 팁으로 스스로에게 관대해지는 것을 언급하면서 재택 근무가 완전히 새로운 경험일 수 있고 좋은 리듬을 타는 데 시간이 걸릴 것이라고(The final tip for managing stress is to be gentle with yourself. Working from home might be a brand-new experience and it will take time to get into a good groove) 밝히고 있습니다. 이는 적응 시간이 필요하다는 의미이므로 (d)가 정답입니다.

어휘 drop 떨어지다, 하락하다 miss ~을 그리워하다 increase 늘어나다, 증가하다

패러프레이징

take time to get into a good groove → need time to adjust

PART 1

BILLIE HOLIDAY

Billie Holiday was an American jazz and swing singer. **53** Best known for her compelling and emotional vocal delivery as well as improvisational singing skills that brought her songs to life, she is widely seen as one of the most influential jazz singers of all time.

Eleanora Fagan, who later took the stage name Billie Holiday, was born on April 7, 1915, in Philadelphia, Pennsylvania. While her paternal parentage is disputed, American jazz musician Clarence Holiday is reported to be her father. He left not long after she was born, and she grew up with her mother in Baltimore, Maryland. Holiday's early life was marred by instability, leading her to drop out of school at the age of eleven and often get in trouble with the law. **54** She found peace in music and, as a young teenager, started singing in nightclubs in the Harlem neighborhood of New York.

Holiday's reputation grew with each performance. She made her recording debut at the age of eighteen, and it was then that she also reconnected with her father. In 1935, she was signed and began recording in earnest, showcasing her **58** flair for adapting her voice to fit a song's mood. **55** In 1938, Holiday made the potentially risky decision to work with Artie Shaw and his orchestra. In doing so, she became one of the first Black vocalists to work with a white orchestra. The increased exposure led her popularity to grow significantly.

In 1939, Holiday recorded her most controversial song, titled "Strange Fruit," about violence against African Americans in the American South.

빌리 홀리데이

빌리 홀리데이는 미국의 재즈 및 스윙 가수였다. 노래를 활기 넘치게 한 그녀의 강렬하고 감성적인 보컬 전달력뿐만 아니라 즉흥적인 노래 실력으로 가장 잘 알려져 있는, 그녀는 역사상 가장 영향력 있는 재즈 가수들 중 한 명으로 널려 여겨지고 있다.

나중에 빌리 홀리데이를 예명으로 가졌던, 엘레노라 페이건은 1915년, 4월 7일에 펜실베이니아 주, 필라델피아에서 태어났다. 아버지 쪽 혈통에 대한 논란이 있기는 하지만, 미국 재즈 음악가인 클래런스 홀리데이가 그녀의 아버지인 것으로 알려져 있다. 그는 그녀가 태어나고 얼마 되지 않아 떠났으며, 어머니와 함께 매릴랜드 주, 볼티모어에서 자랐다. 홀리데이의 어린 시절은 불안정으로 인해 망가지면서, 11살의 나이에 학교를 중퇴하고 자주 법과 관련해 곤경에 처하기에 이르렀다. 그녀는 음악 속에서 평화를 찾았으며, 어린 십대로서, 뉴욕의 할렘 지역에 있는 나이트클럽에서 노래하기 시작했다.

홀리데이의 명성은 공연을 할 때마다 높아졌다. 그녀는 18세의 나이에 음반 녹음으로 데뷔했으며, 아버지와 다시 연락이 닿은 것도 그때였다. 1935년에, 본격적으로 계약을 맺고 녹음하기 시작하면서, 자신의 목소리를 노래의 분위기에 적합하도록 맞추는 데 재능을 보였다. 1938년에, 홀리데이는 아티 쇼 및 그의 오케스트라와 협업하기로 하여 잠재적으로 위험한 결정을 내렸다. 그렇게 함으로써, 그녀는 백인 오케스트라와 협업하는 최초의 흑인 보컬리스트들 중 한 명이 되었다. 그러한 노출 증가로 인해 그녀의 인기는 상당히 올랐다.

1939년에, 홀리데이는 미국 남부의 아프리카계 미국인들을 대상으로 한 폭력에 관한, 가장 논란이 컸던 "이상한 과일"이라는 제목의 노래를 녹음했다.

The lyrics, combined with a slow tempo and emphasis on certain words, **56** created a hauntingly painful impression of the effects of racism, but the song met resistance in a still racially divided America. Nonetheless, the powerful feelings it evoked as well as its notoriety helped propel the song to fame.

그 가사는, 느린 템포 및 특정 단어에 대한 강조와 결합되어, 인종 차별 주의의 영향에 대한 잊을 수 없을 정도의 고통스러운 인상을 만들어 냈지만, 그 노래는 여전히 인종적으로 분리된 미국 내에서 반발에 부딪혔다. 그럼에도 불구하고, 그것이 자아내는 강렬한 느낌뿐만 아니라 그 악평까지도 그 노래가 명성이 나아가도록 도움을 주었다.

Throughout the 1940s and 1950s, Holiday continued to perform concerts, including multiple sold-out shows at New York's famous Carnegie Hall. On July 17, 1959, she died in New York City from health complications caused by **59** chronic alcohol and drug addiction. More than 3,000 people attended her funeral, including many famous jazz performers. **57** In 2000, she was inducted into the Rock and Roll Hall of Fame, which cemented her influential status.

1940년대와 1950년대에 걸쳐, 홀리데이는 뉴욕의 유명한 카네기 홀에서 열린 다수의 매진된 공연을 포함해, 지속적으로 콘서트를 열었다. 1959년 7월 17일에, 그녀는 만성적인 알코올 및 약물 중독에 의해 초래된 합병증으로 뉴욕 시에서 사망했다. 많은 유명 재즈 음악가들을 포함해, 3,000명이 넘는 사람들이 그녀의 장례식에 참석했다. 2000년에, 그녀는 로크롤 명예의 전당에 헌액되었으며, 그것은 그녀의 영향력 있는 지위를 공고히 해 주었다.

TEST 03

어휘 **known for** ~로 알려진 **compelling** 강렬한, 설득력 있는 **delivery** 전달(력) **as well as** ~뿐만 아니라 …도 **improvisational** 즉흥적인 **bring + 목적어 + to life:** (목적어)에 활기를 불어 넣다 **be seen as** ~로 여겨지다 **influential** 영향력 있는 **paternal** 아버지의 **parentage** 혈통 **disputed** 논란이 된 **be reported + to 동사원형:** ~하는 것으로 알려지다 **grow up** 자라다, 성장하다 **be marred by** ~에 의해 망가지다 **instability** 불안정 **lead to** ~로 이어지다 **drop out of** ~을 중퇴하다 **neighborhood** 지역, 이웃, 인근 **reputation** 명성(= fame) **reconnect with** ~와 다시 연락이 되다 **in earnest** 본격적으로 **showcase** ~을 선보이다 **flair** 재능, 재주 **adapt A to B:** A를 B에 맞추다, A를 B에 맞게 조정하다 **make a decision** 결정을 내리다 **potentially** 잠재적으로 **risky** 위험한 **in doing so** 그렇게 해서 **exposure** 노출 (효과) **lead to** ~로 이어지다 **popularity** 인기 **significantly** 상당히, 많이 **controversial** 논란이 많은 **violence** 폭력 **lyrics** 가사 **combined with** ~와 결합된 **emphasis on** ~에 대한 강조 **certain** 특정한, 일정한 **hauntingly** 잊을 수 없을 정도로 **painful** 고통스러운, 아픈 **impression** 인상, 감명 **effect** 영향, 효과 **racism** 인종 차별 주의 **meet resistance** 반발에 부딪히다 **divided** 분리된, 나뉜 **nonetheless** 그럼에도 불구하고 **evoke** ~을 자아내다 **notoriety** 악평, 악명 **help + 동사원형:** ~하는 데 도움을 주다 **propel** ~을 나아가게 하다, ~을 추진하다 **continue + to 동사원형:** 지속적으로 ~하다 **multiple** 다수의, 다양한 **sold-out** 매진된 **complication** 합병증 **cause** ~을 초래하다 **chronic** 만성적인 **addiction** 중독 **attend** ~에 참석하다 **funeral** 장례식 **be inducted into** ~에 헌액되다 **cement** v. ~을 공고히 하다 **status** 지위, 상태, 상황

What is Billie Holiday most remembered for?

(a) writing a famous American jazz song
(b) developing a distinctive vocal technique
(c) being the first female jazz singer in America
(d) having a controversial musical career

빌리 홀리데이는 무엇으로 가장 많이 기억되고 있는가?

(a) 유명한 미국 재즈 곡을 쓴 것
(b) 특유의 보컬 기술을 발전시킨 것
(c) 미국 최초의 여성 재즈 가수가 된 것
(d) 논란이 많은 음악 경력을 지닌 것

정답 (b)

해설 첫 문단에 빌리 홀리데이가 강렬하고 감성적인 보컬 전달력뿐만 아니라 즉흥적인 노래 실력으로 가장 잘 알려져 있다는 (Best known for her compelling and emotional vocal delivery as well as improvisational singing skills ~) 내용이 제시되어 있으므로 이러한 보컬 기술을 언급한 (b)가 정답입니다.

어휘 develop ~을 발전시키다, ~을 개발하다 distinctive 특유의, 특색 있는, 독특한

패러프레이징

compelling and emotional vocal delivery / improvisational singing skills → a distinctive vocal technique

Why did Holiday probably start singing in nightclubs?

(a) It brought her comfort when her life was difficult.
(b) It helped her cover her school tuition.
(c) It brought her public recognition when she was unknown.
(d) It helped her form valuable friendships.

홀리데이가 왜 나이트클럽에서 노래하기 시작했을 것 같은가?

(a) 삶이 어려워졌을 때 위안을 주었다.
(b) 학비를 충당하는 데 도움을 주었다.
(c) 무명이었을 때 대중적 인지도를 가져다 주었다.
(d) 소중한 우정을 형성하는 데 도움을 주었다.

정답 (a)

해설 두 번째 문단에 어렸을 때 힘겨웠던 시절을 이야기하면서 음악 속에서 평화를 찾았다는 사실과 함께 뉴욕의 할렘 지역에 있는 나이트클럽에서 노래하기 시작했다는(She found peace in music and, as a young teenager, started singing in nightclubs in the Harlem neighborhood of New York) 내용이 쓰여 있으므로 (a)가 정답입니다.

┌─────────────────────────┐
│ 패러프레이징 │
└─────────────────────────┘

found peace → brought her comfort

---

55 세부 정보

According to the text, how did Holiday make a breakthrough in her career?

(a) by introducing a new genre of music to audiences
(b) by recording a pioneering collaboration with her father
(c) by taking chances in her professional relationships
(d) by influencing the work of established artists

지문 내용에 따르면, 홀리데이는 어떻게 자신의 경력에서 돌파구를 마련했는가?

(a) 새로운 장르의 음악을 사람들에게 소개함으로써
(b) 아버지와 함께 선구적인 합작품을 녹음함으로써
(c) 직업적인 관계 속에서 기회를 잡음으로써
(d) 인정 받는 아티스트들의 작품에 영향을 미침으로써

정답 | (c)

해설 | 세 번째 문단에 본격적으로 계약을 맺고 활동하기 시작하면서 1938년에 아티 쇼 및 그의 오케스트라와 협업하기로 하여 잠재적으로 위험한 결정을 내린(In 1938, Holiday made the potentially risky decision to work with Artie Shaw and his orchestra) 사실이 언급되어 있습니다. 이를 통해 자신의 일과 관련된 기회를 놓치지 않으려 했다는 것을 알 수 있으므로 (c)가 정답입니다.

어휘 | make a breakthrough 돌파구를 마련하다 introduce ~을 소개하다 audiences 사람들, 관객, 청중, 시청자들
pioneering 선구적인 collaboration 합작(품), 협업 relationship 관계 influence ~에 영향을 미치다 established 인정 받는, 자리 잡은

┌─────────────────────────┐
│ 패러프레이징 │
└─────────────────────────┘

made the potentially risky decision to work with Artie Shaw and his orchestra → taking chances in her professional relationships

Based on the text, why, most likely, did some people dislike "Strange Fruit"?

(a) because it criticized a popular politician
(b) because they disapproved of its original composer
(c) because it promoted an illegal activity
(d) because they disagreed with its social message

지문 내용에 따르면, 일부 사람들이 왜 "이상한 과일"을 싫어했을 것 같은가?

(a) 인기 있는 정치인을 비판했기 때문에
(b) 원작자를 못마땅해 했기 때문에
(c) 불법 활동을 촉진했기 때문에
(d) 그 사회적 메시지에 동의하지 않았기 때문에

정답 (d)

해설 "이상한 과일"에 관해 설명하는 네 번째 문단에 그 노래가 인종 차별 주의의 영향에 대한 것이지만 여전히 인종적으로 분리된 미국 내에서 반발에 부딪혔다는(created a hauntingly painful impression of the effects of racism, but the song met resistance in a still racially divided America) 사실이 언급되어 있습니다. 이는 그 노래가 담고 있는 메시지에 동의하지 않는 사람들도 있다는 뜻이므로 (d)가 정답입니다.

어휘 criticize ~을 비판하다 politician 정치인 disapprove of ~을 못마땅해 하다 composer 작곡가 promote ~을 촉진하다 illegal 불법적인 disagree with ~에 동의하지 않다

What achievement proved Holiday's lasting legacy?

(a) having a famous concert hall named after her
(b) being honored by an artistic organization
(c) having her music featured in a popular film
(d) being commemorated by a renowned sculptor

어떤 업적이 홀리데이의 지속적인 유산을 증명하는가?

(a) 유명 콘서트 홀이 그녀의 이름을 따서 명명된 것
(b) 예술 단체에 의해 영예를 얻은 것
(c) 그녀의 음악이 유명 영화에 특별히 포함된 것
(d) 유명 조각가에 의해 기념된 것

정답 (b)

해설 마지막 문단 마지막 문장에 2000년에 로큰롤 명예의 전당에 헌액된 것이 홀리데이의 영향력 있는 지위를 공고히 해 주는 일이었음을(In 2000, she was inducted into the Rock and Roll Hall of Fame, which cemented her influential status) 의미한다는 내용이 쓰여 있으므로 (b)가 정답입니다.

어휘 achievement 업적, 성취 lasting 지속적인 legacy 유산 have + 목적어 + 과거분사: (목적어)를 ~되게 하다 name A after B: B의 이름을 따서 A를 명명하다 honor ~에게 영예를 주다 organization 단체, 기관 feature ~을 특별히 포함하다, ~을 특징으로 하다 commemorate ~을 기념하다 renowned 유명한 sculptor 조각가

패러프레이징

was inducted into the Rock and Roll Hall of Fame → being honored by an artistic organization

58 동의어

In the context of this passage, flair means _____.

(a) approval
(b) patience
(c) talent
(d) humor

해당 문단의 문맥에서 flair가 의미하는 것은?

(a) 승인, 인정
(b) 인내(심)
(c) 재능
(d) 유머

정답 (c)

해설 해당 문장에서 flair 앞에는 '~을 선보이다'를 뜻하는 동사 showcase의 분사가, 뒤에는 목소리를 노래의 분위기에 적합하도록 맞추는 것이 목적임을 의미하는 for 전치사구가 각각 쓰여 있습니다. 따라서, flair가 그러한 목적에 부합하는 능력 등을 나타내는 것으로 볼 수 있으므로 '재능'을 뜻하는 (c)가 정답입니다.

59 동의어

In the context of this passage, chronic means _____.

(a) regular
(b) unlikely
(c) flexible
(d) uncertain

해당 문단의 문맥에서 chronic이 의미하는 것은?

(a) 주기적인, 일반적인, 평소의
(b) 있을 것 같지 않은
(c) 유연한, 탄력적인
(d) 불확실한, 확신이 없는

정답 (a)

해설 해당 문장에서 chronic 뒤에 알코올 및 약물 중독을 의미하는 명사구 alcohol and drug addiction이 쓰여 있습니다. 이 명사구가 전치사 by의 목적어로서 사망 원인으로 제시되어 있어 chronic이 그러한 문제가 주기적으로 나타났거나 평소에 존재했음을 의미하는 형용사임을 알 수 있으므로 (a)가 정답입니다.

REMOTE WORKING BENEFITS

The COVID-19 pandemic compelled many businesses around the world to shift to a remote working model in order to avoid spreading infection. However, despite the unfortunate way in which remote working came to the forefront, **60** studies are showing that working from home has major benefits not just for workers, but for employers as well.

One major benefit of remote working is the decrease in commuting time. While obviously a benefit for employees, less time spent commuting also benefits businesses. The mental well-being of employees has been shown to be connected to a **65** surge in work productivity and a decrease in absenteeism. **61** Some employees commute an hour or more one way, arriving to work already stressed out. Commute length can also be a major factor in how often employees take sick days from work. When working from home, employees "arrive" to work fresh and ready to go in a relaxed environment.

Remote working options have also enabled companies to have more flexibility with regard to location. This is especially helpful when businesses are looking to recruit the best people to join their team. Previously, businesses would have to choose from a pool of either local candidates or those willing to uproot and move their lives to a new city, restricting the potential employee pool considerably. **62** With the ability to bring in exceptional individuals from across the nation, businesses benefit from a wealth of experienced candidates.

원격 근무의 이점

코로나 바이러스 감염증 대유행으로 인해 전 세계의 많은 업체들이 감염 확산을 피하기 위해 어쩔 수 없이 원격 근무 모델로 전환했다. 하지만, 원격 근무가 세상의 주목을 받게 된 유감스러운 방식에도 불구하고, 연구에 따르면 재택 근무가 근로자들뿐만 아니라 고용주들에게도 큰 이점이 있는 것으로 나타나고 있다.

원격 근무의 한 가지 주요 이점은 통근 시간의 감소이다. 분명 직원들에게 하나의 이점이기는 하지만, 통근하는 데 더 적은 시간이 소비되는 것은 업체에게도 유익하다. 직원들의 정신 건강은 업무 생산성의 급등 및 결근의 감소와 연관되어 있는 것으로 나타났다. 일부 직원들은 편도로 한 시간 이상 통근하면서, 이미 스트레스를 받은 상태로 직장에 도착한다. 통근 시간은 또한 직원들이 얼마나 자주 직장에서 병가를 내는지에 있어서도 주된 요인이 될 수 있다. 재택 근무를 할 때, 직원들은 느긋한 환경 속에서 생기 있고 일할 준비가 된 상태로 직장에 "도착한다".

원격 근무 옵션은 또한 회사들에게 장소와 관련된 더 많은 유연성을 가질 수 있게 해 주었다. 이는 특히 업체들이 팀에 합류할 최고의 인력을 모집하기를 바라고 있을 때 도움이 된다. 이전에는, 업체들이 지역에 사는 지원자들 또는 새로운 도시로 떠나 삶의 터전을 옮길 의향이 있는 사람들로 구성된 범주 내에서 선택해야 했기 때문에, 잠재적인 직원 범주가 상당히 제한되었다. 전국 각지의 뛰어난 인재들을 불러 모을 수 있는 능력을 지니고 있으면, 업체들은 경험 많은 풍부한 지원자들로부터 혜택을 얻는다.

Another major benefit to businesses is the potential to reduce operating costs. **63** With employees working from home, there is no need to budget for renting office space. This is especially handy for smaller businesses that may be operating in high-rent areas. One study estimated that businesses could save an average of $10,000 per employee per year with full-time remote working options.

While the **66** transition requires serious planning to enforce set work hours, ensure effective communication with employees, and provide office equipment for home use, **64** in the long run, remote working can improve efficiency and employee satisfaction, while allowing companies to build diverse and adaptable teams. With flexibility a key driver of success in the global market, this helps to make businesses more competitive.

업체들에 대한 또 다른 주된 이점은 운영비를 줄일 수 있는 잠재성이다. 직원들이 재택 근무를 하면, 사무실 공간 임대를 위한 예산을 잡을 필요가 없다. 이는 특히 임대료가 높은 지역에서 운영될 수 있는 더 작은 업체들에게 유익하다. 한 연구에서는 업체들이 정규직 원격 근무 옵션으로 직원 1인당 연간 평균 10,000달러를 아낄 수 있는 것으로 추정했다.

이러한 전환이 지정된 근무 시간을 시행하고, 직원들과의 효과적인 의사 소통을 보장하며, 재택용 사무 장비를 제공하기 위한 진지한 계획을 필요로 하기는 하지만, 장기적으로, 원격 근무는 효율성 및 직원 만족도를 향상시킬 수 있으면서, 회사들에게 다양하고 적응력이 높은 팀을 구축할 수 있게 해 준다. 세계 시장에서의 성공을 위한 핵심 원동력인 유연성이 있으면, 이는 업체들을 더욱 경쟁력 있게 만드는 데 도움이 된다.

TEST 03

어휘 remote working 원격 근무 benefit n. 이점, 혜택 v. ~에게 유익하다, 혜택을 보다 pandemic 대유행, 유행병 compel + 목적어 + to 동사원형: (목적어)가 어쩔 수 없이 ~하다 shift to ~로 전환하다, ~로 바꾸다 in order + to 동사원형: ~하기 위해 avoid -ing ~하는 것을 피하다 spread ~을 확산시키다 infection 감염 way 방식 come to the forefront 세상의 주목을 받다 as well ~도, 또한 decrease in ~의 감소 commute v. 통근하다 n. 통근 obviously 분명히 mental 정신적인 be connected to ~와 연관되다 surge 급증, 급등 absenteeism 결근 stressed out 스트레스를 받은 length 시간, 길이 factor 요인, 요소 take a sick day 병가를 내다 relaxed 느긋한, 여유로운 enable + 목적어 + to 동사원형: (목적어)에게 ~할 수 있게 해 주다(= allow + 목적어 + to 동사원형) flexibility 유연성, 탄력성 with regard to ~와 관련해 look + to 동사원형: ~하기를 바라다 recruit ~을 모집하다 previously 이전에, 과거에 pool (인력 등의) 범주, 집합 either A or B: A 또는 B 둘 중의 하나 local 지역의, 현지의 candidate 지원자, 후보자 willing + to 동사원형: ~할 의향이 있는, 기꺼이 ~하는 uproot (살던 곳에서) 떠나다 restrict ~을 제한하다 potential a. 잠재적인 n. 잠재성 considerably 상당히 ability + to 동사원형: ~할 수 있는 능력 exceptional 뛰어난, 이례적인 individual 사람, 개인 a wealth of 풍부한 budget v. 예산을 정하다 rent ~을 임대하다 handy 유익한, 유용한 operate 운영되다 estimate that ~라고 추정하다 transition 전환, 변환 enforce ~을 시행하다, ~을 집행하다 ensure ~을 보장하다 equipment 장비 in the long run 장기적으로 improve ~을 향상시키다, ~을 개선하다 efficiency 효율성 adaptable 적응할 수 있는, 적응력이 높은 driver 원동력, 동인 competitive 경쟁력 있는

What is the article mainly about?

(a) how employees have adapted to remote working
(b) how remote working can positively impact businesses
(c) how remote working helps the national economy
(d) how different industries can shift to remote working

기사가 주로 무엇에 관한 것인가?

(a) 직원들이 어떻게 원격 근무에 적응했는가
(b) 원격 근무가 어떻게 업체들에게 긍정적으로 영향을 미칠 수 있는가
(c) 원격 근무가 어떻게 국가 경제에 도움이 되는가
(d) 여러 다른 업계들이 어떻게 원격 근무로 전환할 수 있는가

정답 (b)

해설 첫 문단에 연구를 통해 재택 근무가 근로자들뿐만 아니라 고용주들에게도 큰 이점이 있는 것으로 나타났다고(studies are showing that working from home has major benefits not just for workers, but for employers as well) 언급한 뒤로 업체들에 대한 긍정적인 영향들을 설명하고 있으므로 (b)가 정답입니다.

어휘 **adapt to** ~에 적응하다 **positively** 긍정적으로 **impact** ~에 영향을 미치다

패러프레이징

working from home / benefits → remote working can positively impact

Based on the second paragraph, how, most likely, would working from home help reduce employee absence?

(a) by allowing workers to take more breaks
(b) by creating a peaceful work environment
(c) by providing more flexible working hours
(d) by eliminating stress from traveling to work

두 번째 문단에 따르면, 재택 근무는 어떻게 직원 결근을 줄이는 데 도움이 될 것 같은가?

(a) 직원들에게 더 많은 휴식을 취할 수 있게 함으로써
(b) 평화로운 업무 환경을 조성함으로써
(c) 더 탄력적인 근무 시간을 제공함으로써
(d) 직장으로 이동하는 스트레스를 없앰으로써

정답 (d)

해설 두 번째 문단에 어떤 직원들은 편도로 한 시간 이상 통근하면서 이미 스트레스를 받은 상태로 직장에 도착한다는(Some employees commute an hour or more one way, arriving to work already stressed out) 문제가 언급되어 있습니다. 따라서, 재택 근무는 통근에 따른 스트레스가 없어지는 이점이 있을 것으로 볼 수 있으므로 (d)가 정답입니다.

어휘 take a break 휴식을 취하다 flexible 탄력적인, 유연한 eliminate ~을 없애다, ~을 제거하다

---

62 세부 정보

According to the article, how does remote work benefit recruitment?

(a) It widens the range of potential candidates.
(b) It increases the chance of a candidate accepting the job.
(c) It simplifies the task of scheduling candidates for interview.
(d) It improves the prospect of a candidate staying in the position.

기사 내용에 따르면, 원격 근무가 어떻게 인력 모집에 유익한가?

(a) 잠재적인 지원자들의 범위를 확대해 준다.
(b) 지원자가 일자리를 받아들일 가능성을 높여 준다.
(c) 면접을 위해 지원자와 일정을 잡는 일을 간소화해 준다.
(d) 지원자가 해당 직책에 머물러 있을 가능성을 향상시켜 준다.

정답 (a)

해설 세 번째 문단에 장소와 관련된 더 많은 유연성을 언급하면서 전국 각지의 뛰어난 인재들을 불러 모을 수 있는 능력을(With the ability to bring in exceptional individuals from across the nation) 지닐 수 있는 이점을 언급하고 있습니다. 이는 모집 가능한 인력의 범위가 확대되는 것을 뜻하므로 (a)가 정답입니다.

어휘 widen ~을 확대하다, ~을 넓히다 range 범위, 종류 accept ~을 받아들이다 simplify ~을 간소화하다 task 일, 업무 prospect 가능성, 가망성

패러프레이징

the ability to bring in exceptional individuals from across the nation → widens the range of potential candidates

Based on the fourth paragraph, why might a small business choose a remote working model?

(a) to spend less time searching for a suitable office space
(b) to encourage employees to use their own computers
(c) to avoid facing unnecessarily high operating costs
(d) to allow managers to focus on expanding their departments

네 번째 문단에 따르면, 소기업이 원격 근무 방식을 선택할 수도 있는 이유는 무엇인가?

(a) 적합한 사무 공간을 찾는 데 시간을 덜 소비하기 위해
(b) 직원들에게 개인 컴퓨터를 이용하도록 권장하기 위해
(c) 불필요하게 높은 운영비에 직면하는 것을 피하기 위해
(d) 관리자들에게 각자의 부서를 확대하는 데 집중하도록 하기 위해

정답 (c)

해설 네 번째 문단에 원격 근무 방식으로 직원들이 재택 근무를 하면서 사무실 공간 임대 비용이 필요 없게 되어 더 작은 업체들에게 유익하다는 점이(With employees working from home, there is no need to budget for renting office space. This is especially handy for smaller businesses ~) 언급되어 있으므로 (c)가 정답입니다.

어휘 suitable 적합한, 알맞은 encourage + 목적어 + to 동사원형: (목적어)에게 ~하도록 권장하다 avoid -ing ~하는 것을 피하다 face ~에 직면하다 unnecessarily 불필요하게 focus on ~에 집중하다 expand ~을 확대하다, ~을 확장하다

패러프레이징

there is no need to budget for renting office space → avoid facing unnecessarily high operating costs

What is the purpose of the final paragraph?

(a) to give a specific example of a company with remote workers
(b) to remind readers of the disadvantages of remote working
(c) to show that employing remote workers is easy
(d) to argue that remote working is advantageous overall

마지막 문단의 목적은 무엇인가?

(a) 원격 근무자들이 있는 회사의 구체적인 예시를 제공하는 것
(b) 독자에게 원격 근무의 단점들을 상기시키는 것
(c) 원격 근무자들을 고용하는 것이 쉽다는 사실을 보여 주는 것
(d) 원격 근무가 전반적으로 이롭다는 점을 주장하는 것

정답 (d)

해설 마지막 문단에 장기적으로 원격 근무가 효율성 및 직원 만족도도 향상시키고 회사들에게도 다양하고 적응력이 높은 팀을 구축할 수 있게 해 준다는(~ in the long run, remote working can improve efficiency and employee satisfaction, while allowing companies to build diverse and adaptable teams) 점이 언급되어 있어 전반적으로 유익한 근무 방식임을 알 수 있으므로 (d)가 정답입니다.

어휘 specific 구체적인, 특정한 remind A of B: A에게 B를 상기시키다 disadvantage 단점 argue that ~임을 주장하다 advantageous 이로운, 유익한 overall 전반적으로

65 동의어

In the context of this passage, surge means _____.

(a) division
(b) rise
(c) breakdown
(d) gap

해당 문단의 문맥에서 surge가 의미하는 것은?

(a) 분할, 부서
(b) 증가, 상승
(c) 고장, 분해, 명세(서)
(d) 간격, 틈

정답 (b)

해설 해당 문장에서 surge in work productivity가 그 뒤에 and로 연결된 a decrease in absenteeism와 마찬가지로 직원들의 정신 건강이 미치는 긍정적인 영향을 나타내야 알맞습니다. 따라서, '직원 생산성의 증가'를 의미해야 자연스러우므로 (b)가 정답입니다.

66 동의어

In the context of this passage, transition means _____.

(a) change
(b) reduction
(c) profile
(d) conclusion

해당 문단의 문맥에서 transition이 의미하는 것은?

(a) 변화, 변경
(b) 감소, 할인
(c) 개요(서), 윤곽
(d) 결론, 결말

정답 (a)

해설 해당 문장에서 transition 뒤에 몇 가지 시행해야 하는 일들과 함께 진지한 계획이 필요하다는 말이 쓰여 있습니다. 이는 앞서 설명된 원격 근무를 실시하기 위한 계획이므로 transition이 원격 근무로 전환하는 것과 관련된 단어임을 알 수 있습니다. 따라서, '변화' 등을 뜻하는 (a) change가 정답입니다.

THE AMERICAN FLAG

The American flag is the national flag of the United States of America. Although the flag has always featured stars and stripes and the colors red, white, and blue, **67** the specific design has been altered more than twenty times since 1777.

68 Before 1776, America consisted of thirteen colonies under the rule of Great Britain. The emerging government in the colonies decided that a flag was needed to unite them as they fought for independence. The Flag Resolution of 1777 laid out the design for the new nation's first flag, with thirteen alternating red and white horizontal stripes and thirteen six-pointed white stars on a blue background to represent the original colonies.

69 As new states were added to the United States, more stars were added to the flag. The fiftieth and final star was added in 1960 when the state of Hawaii joined the union. The current design **72** retains thirteen red stripes, representing valor and bravery, and thirteen white stripes, representing purity and innocence. The blue background represents vigilance, perseverance, and justice. If a new state were admitted, the flag would need to be redesigned once more to accommodate the addition.

The United States has a Flag Code, or set of rules, that **70** outlines how the flag should be handled. For example, when a flag is worn out, it should be destroyed in a dignified manner, such as by burning. Additionally, the flag should never be used as clothing or bedding, nor should it be used for advertising purposes. It should never be displayed upside down unless to signal great danger, and it should never touch anything below it, such as the ground.

미국 국기

미국 국기는 미합중국의 국기이다. 비록 그 국기가 항상 별과 줄무늬, 그리고 붉은색과 흰색, 푸른색을 특징으로 해 오기는 했지만, 그 구체적인 디자인은 1777년 이후로 20번 넘게 변경되어 왔다.

1776년 전까지, 미국은 대영제국의 통치 하에 있는 13개의 식민지로 구성되어 있었다. 이 식민지들 사이에서 새롭게 떠오르던 정부는 독립을 위해 싸우는 과정에서 연합하기 위해 깃발이 필요하다는 결정을 내렸다. 1777년의 국기 결의안은 새로운 국가의 첫 국기에 대한 디자인을 제시했으며, 번갈아 위치하는 13개의 붉은색과 흰색 가로 줄무늬 및 6개의 뾰족한 끝을 가진 흰색 별 13개는 푸른색 배경 속에서 최초의 식민지들을 상징했다.

새로운 주들이 미국에 추가되면서, 더 많은 별이 국기에 추가되었다. 하와이 주가 이 연합에 합류한 1960년에 50번째이자 마지막 별이 추가되었다. 현재의 디자인은 용맹과 용감성을 상징하는 13개의 붉은색 줄무늬 및 순수성과 순결함을 상징하는 13개의 흰색 줄무늬를 유지하고 있다. 푸른색 배경은 경계와 인내, 그리고 정의를 상징한다. 새로운 주가 인정되는 경우, 이 국기는 이러한 추가를 수용하기 위해 한 번 더 재디자인되어야 할 것이다.

미국에는 국기를 어떻게 다뤄야 하는지 간략히 나타내는 국기 조례, 즉 일련의 규칙이 있다. 예를 들어, 국기가 닳아서 못 쓰게 된 경우, 소각 같은, 위엄 있는 방식으로 파기되어야 한다. 추가로, 국기는 의류나 침구류로 절대 사용하지 말아야 하며, 광고 목적으로도 쓰이지 말아야 한다. 아주 큰 위험에 대한 신호를 보내는 것이 아니라면 거꾸로 게양되지 말아야 하며, 지면 같이, 그 아래에 어떤 것도 닿지 말아야 한다.

There are various **73** <u>rituals</u> associated with the US flag. **71(a)** It is usually taken down during bad weather unless it is weather-resistant. **71(c)** If flown at night, it should be illuminated. **71(b)** The flag can be displayed every day but, during national holidays and days of remembrance in particular, it is flown to showcase patriotism. **71(d)** During times of national mourning, the flag is lowered to half-mast. This may be done following the death of a government official or a military member.

미국 국기와 연관된 다양한 의식이 존재한다. 일반적으로 날씨에 잘 견디는 것이 아니라면 악천후 중에는 내려진다. 밤에 휘날리는 경우에는, 조명을 비춰야 한다. 국기는 매일 게양될 수 있지만, 특히 국경일과 추모일 중에는, 애국심을 나타내기 위해 휘날린다. 국가 애도 기간 중에는, 국기를 조기로 낮춘다. 이는 정부 관계자 또는 군인의 사망 후에 이뤄질 수 있다.

어휘 feature ~의 특징을 이루다 stripe 줄무늬 specific 구체적인, 특정한 alter ~을 변경하다 consist of ~로 구성되다 colony 식민지 rule 통치 emerging 새롭게 떠오르는 decide that ~하기로 결정하다 unite ~을 연합하다, ~을 통일하다 independence 독립 lay out ~을 제시하다, ~을 설계하다, ~을 배치하다 alternating 번갈아 가면서 하는 horizontal 가로의, 수평의 pointed 뾰족한 represent ~을 상징하다, ~에 해당하다 add ~을 추가하다 join ~에 합류하다, ~에 가입하다 union 연합 current 현재의 retain ~을 유지하다 valor 용맹 bravery 용감, 용기 purity 순수(성) innocence 순결, 결백 vigilance 경계(심), 조심 perseverance 인내(심) justice 정의 admit ~을 인정하다, ~을 수용하다 accommodate ~을 수용하다 code 조례, 관례, 규범 outline ~을 간략히 설명하다, ~의 개요를 말하다 handle ~을 다루다, ~을 처리하다 worn out 닳아서 못 쓰게 된 destroy ~을 파기하다, ~을 파괴하다 dignified 위엄 있는 manner 방식 advertising 광고 (활동) display ~을 게양하다, ~을 게시하다 upside down 거꾸로 unless ~가 아니라면, ~하지 않는다면 signal ~에 대한 신호를 보내다, ~을 암시하다 ritual 의식, 의례적인 일 associated with ~와 연관된 take down ~을 끌어내리다, ~을 해체하다 weather-resistant 날씨에 잘 견디는 fly (깃발 등) ~을 휘날리다, ~을 달다(flown은 과거분사) illuminate ~에 조명을 비추다 remembrance 추모, 추도 in particular 특히 showcase ~을 나타내다, ~을 선보이다 patriotism 애국심 mourning 애도 lower ~을 낮추다, ~을 내리다 half-mast 조기, 반기(조의를 나타내기 위해 깃봉에서 기폭만큼 내려 게양) official n. 관계자, 당국자

Which statement best describes the US flag?

(a) Its colors have been adjusted frequently.
(b) It has remained unaltered since it was first conceived.
(c) Its basic elements have never been rearranged.
(d) It has taken on different looks over time.

어느 문장이 미국 국기를 가장 잘 설명하는가?

(a) 그 색들이 자주 조정되어 왔다.
(b) 처음 구상된 이후로 변경되지 않은 상태로 유지되어 왔다.
(c) 그 기본적인 요소들이 한 번도 재조정된 적이 없다.
(d) 시간이 흐르면서 여러 다른 모습을 띠게 되었다.

정답 (d)

해설 첫 문단에 구체적인 디자인이 1777년 이후로 20번 넘게 변경되어 왔다는(the specific design has been altered more than twenty times since 1777) 내용이 쓰여 있어 여러 다른 모습으로 변경되어 왔음을 알 수 있으므로 (d)가 정답입니다.

어휘 adjust ~을 조정하다, ~을 조절하다 remain + 형용사: ~한 상태로 유지되다 unaltered 변경되지 않은 conceive ~을 구상하다 element 요소 rearrange ~을 재조정하다, ~을 재배치하다 take on (특징, 모습 등) ~을 띠다

패러프레이징

has been altered more than twenty times → has taken on different looks over time

Why did the emerging government probably decide to create an official flag?

(a) to distance themselves from a ruling power
(b) to attract new immigrants to America
(c) to unite the colonies following a conflict
(d) to show their loyalty to Great Britain

새롭게 떠오르던 정부가 왜 공식 깃발을 만들기로 결정했을 것 같은가?

(a) 지배 세력과 거리를 두기 위해
(b) 새로운 이민자들을 미국으로 끌어들이기 위해
(c) 충돌 후에 식민지들을 연합하기 위해
(d) 대영제국에 충성심을 보여 주기 위해

정답 (a)

해설 두 번째 문단에 대영제국의 통치 하에 있던 13개의 식민지가 독립을 위해 싸우는 과정에서 연합하기 위해 깃발이 필요하다는 결정을 내린(Before 1776, America consisted of thirteen colonies under the rule of Great Britain. ~ a flag was needed to unite them as they fought for independence) 사실이 언급되어 있습니다. 따라서, 대영제국으로부터의 독립

에 해당하는 의미를 지니는 (a)가 정답입니다.

어휘 **official** 공식적인, 정식의 **distance oneself from** ~와 거리를 두다 **ruling power** 지배 세력 **attract** ~을 끌어들이다
immigrant 이민자 **following** ~후에 **conflict** 충돌, 갈등 **loyalty** 충성(심)

69 추론

What, most likely, would happen if a new state were added?

(a) The flag would feature more stripes.
(b) The stars would be made bigger.
(c) The flag would feature an additional star.
(d) The stripes would be made thicker.

새로운 주가 추가되는 경우에 무슨 일이 있을 것 같은가?

(a) 국기가 더 많은 줄무늬를 특징으로 할 것이다.
(b) 별이 더 크게 만들어질 것이다.
(c) 국기가 추가적인 별을 특징으로 할 것이다.
(d) 줄무늬가 더 두껍게 만들어질 것이다.

정답 (c)

해설 세 번째 문단에 새로운 주들이 미국에 추가될 때 더 많은 별이 그 깃발에 추가되는 방식으로(As new states were added to the United States, more stars were added to the flag) 디자인이 변경되었다고 쓰여 있으므로 (c)가 정답입니다.

어휘 **be made + 형용사**: ~하게 만들어지다 **additional** 추가적인 **thick** 두꺼운

According to the fourth paragraph, what does the Flag Code describe?

(a) how the flag can be properly used for advertising
(b) how individuals should show respect for the flag
(c) how the flag can be repaired if it becomes damaged
(d) how individuals should be punished for mistreating the flag

네 번째 문단에 따르면, 국기 조례가 설명하는 것은 무엇인가?

(a) 국기가 어떻게 광고용으로 적절히 쓰일 수 있는지
(b) 사람들이 어떻게 국기에 대해 경의를 표해야 하는지
(c) 국기가 손상되는 경우에 어떻게 수리할 수 있는지
(d) 사람들이 어떻게 국기를 잘못 다룬 것에 대해 처벌 받아야 하는지

정답 (b)

해설 네 번째 문단에 국기 조례가 있다는 말과 함께 그것이 국기를 어떻게 다뤄야 하는지 나타낸다고 언급하면서 위엄 있는 방식으로 파기하는 방법을(~ outlines how the flag should be handled. For example, when a flag is worn out, it should be destroyed in a dignified manner ~) 설명하고 있습니다. 이는 국기에 대한 경의를 표하는 방법을 알리는 것이므로 (b)가 정답입니다.

어휘 properly 적절히, 제대로 individual 사람, 개인 respect 경의, 존경(심) repair ~을 수리하다 damaged 손상된, 피해를 입은 punish ~을 처벌하다 mistreat ~을 잘못 다루다

패러프레이징

how the flag should be handled / in a dignified manner → how individuals should show respect for the flag

Which of the following is NOT an example of accepted flag use?

(a) taking the flag inside when a storm is coming
(b) having the flag on display for a holiday
(c) putting a spotlight on the flag when it is dark
(d) flying the flag upside down for national mourning

다음 중 용인되는 국기 이용법의 예시가 아닌 것은 무엇인가?

(a) 폭풍우가 다가올 때 국기를 실내로 가져 가는 것
(b) 공휴일에 국기를 게양하는 것
(c) 어두울 때 국기에 스포트라이트를 비추는 것
(d) 국가 애도를 위해 국기를 거꾸로 다는 것

정답 (d)

해설 마지막 문단에 국가 애도 기간 중에는 국기를 조기로 낮춘다고(During times of national mourning, the flag is lowered to half-mast) 쓰여 있으므로 (d)가 정답입니다. 거꾸로 다는 것은 네 번째 문단에 하지 말아야 하는 행위로 언급되어 있습니다.

어휘 accepted 용인되는, 받아들여지는 have + 목적어 + on display: (목적어)를 게양하다, (목적어)를 게시하다 spotlight 스포트라이트, 집중 조명

72 동의어

In the context of this passage, retains means _____.

(a) keeps
(b) identifies
(c) hangs
(d) manages

해당 문단의 문맥에서 retains가 의미하는 것은?

(a) 유지하다
(b) 확인하다, 알아보다
(c) 매달다, 걸다
(d) 관리하다

정답 (a)

해설 해당 문장에서 동사 retains 앞뒤로 현재의 디자인을 뜻하는 주어와 13개의 붉은색 줄무늬 및 13개의 흰색 줄무늬가 무엇을 상징하는지 설명하는 내용이 각각 언급되어 있습니다. 따라서, 동사 retains가 현재의 디자인이 그러한 특징들을 유지하고 있다는 의미를 나타내는 것으로 볼 수 있으므로 (a)가 정답입니다.

73 동의어

In the context of this passage, rituals means _____.

(a) stories
(b) areas
(c) customs
(d) sayings

해당 문단의 문맥에서 rituals가 의미하는 것은?

(a) 이야기
(b) 지역, 구역
(c) 관습, 세관
(d) 격언, 속담

정답 (c)

해설 해당 문장에서 rituals는 미국 국기와 연관되어 무엇이 다양하게 존재하는지를 나타냅니다. 그 뒤에 이어지는 문장들이 미국 국기가 일반적으로 이용되는 여러 가지 예시들을 설명하고 있어 rituals가 일종의 관습과 관련된 명사임을 알 수 있으므로 (c)가 정답입니다.

PART 4

Derek Martin
121 W. Clark St.
Newburg, TN

Dear Mr. Martin:

74 Thank you for contacting us via our website. Boom Pow Fitness is a gym with a friendly and welcoming atmosphere. We are **79** committed to the goal of making everyone feel comfortable about working to reach their fitness objectives and, as such, we regard all of our members as part of our fitness family. With that in mind, **74** let me address your queries.

Your inquiry mentioned that **75** you work long hours, and we understand how the week can fly by and your health can be neglected. That is why we offer convenient 24/7 membership access so you can fit exercise into your schedule. There are lockers available as well as showers if you desire a quick workout before heading to the office.

Our **80** spacious facility has ample room for our members to work out without feeling cramped. Everything is clean and well maintained, and we have an assortment of equipment for cardio and weight training. You expressed some nervousness about beginning your fitness journey, but **76** please do not worry. All weight machines come with guides showing how to perform each exercise.

데릭 마틴
W. 클락 스트리트 121번지
뉴버그, 테네시

마틴 씨께,

저희 웹 사이트를 통해 저희에게 연락 주셔서 감사합니다. 저희 붐 파우 피트니스는 친절하고 따뜻하게 맞이하는 분위기의 체육관입니다. 저희는 각자의 운동 목표를 달성하시도록 노력하시는 것과 관련해 모든 분께서 편안하게 느끼시도록 만들어 드리겠다는 목표에 전념하고 있으며, 그에 따라, 저희는 모든 회원들을 저희 피트니스 가족의 일원으로 여기고 있습니다. 이를 염두에 두고, 귀하의 문의 사항을 처리해 드리겠습니다.

귀하의 문의 사항에 귀하께서 장시간 근무하고 계신다고 언급되어 있으며, 저희는 어떻게 일주일이 순식간에 지나가면서 귀하의 건강이 등한시될 수 있는지 이해합니다. 그것이 바로 저희가 귀하께서 운동을 일정에 맞추실 수 있도록 하루 24시간 일주일 내내 편리한 회원 이용 권한을 제공해 드리는 이유입니다. 사무실로 향하시기에 앞서 간단한 운동을 원하시는 경우에 이용 가능한 사물함뿐만 아니라 샤워 시설도 있습니다.

널찍한 저희 시설은 저희 회원들께서 비좁은 느낌 없이 운동하실 수 있는 충분한 공간을 보유하고 있습니다. 모든 것이 깨끗하고 잘 유지 관리된 상태이며, 유산소 운동 및 웨이트 트레이닝에 필요한 각종 장비도 갖추고 있습니다. 귀하께서는 운동 여정을 시작하시는 것과 관련해 약간의 긴장감을 표하셨지만, 걱정하지 마십시오. 모든 웨이트 기계에는 각각의 운동을 실시하는 방법을 보여 주는 안내문이 딸려 있습니다.

Your request also mentioned an interest in more tailored help. **77** We have personal trainers who are happy to work with you to build a personalized fitness and nutrition plan. Additionally, we have a wide variety of fitness classes, such as yoga, Pilates, and cycling, that run from 5 a.m. to 7 p.m. every day of the week and are included in the price of your membership.

If this sounds like the fitness experience you were looking for, **78** please give me a call at 555-0167. I will tell you all about our membership plans and class options, and **78** we can set a time for you to tour our facilities or even try out one of our fitness classes.

Sincerely,

Cynthia Thompson

Cynthia Thompson
Assistant Manager, Boom Pow Fitness

귀하의 요청 사항에는 더 많은 맞춤 제공형 도움에 대한 관심도 언급되어 있었습니다. 저희는 개인 맞춤형 운동 및 영양 계획을 만들어 드리기 위해 기꺼이 함께 노력하는 개인 트레이너들을 보유하고 있습니다. 게다가, 요가와 필라테스, 그리고 자전거 타기 같은 아주 다양한 피트니스 강좌가 있으며, 이는 일주일에 매일 오전 5시부터 오후 7시까지 운영되며, 귀하의 회비에 포함되어 있습니다.

이 설명이 귀하께서 찾고 계시던 피트니스 경험인 것처럼 들리신다면, 555-0167번으로 제게 전화 주시기 바랍니다. 제가 저희 회원 약정 및 강좌 옵션에 관해 모두 말씀 드릴 것이며, 저희 시설을 견학하시거나 심지어 저희 피트니스 강좌들 중 하나를 체험해 보실 수 있도록 시간을 정하실 수도 있습니다.

안녕히 계십시오.

신시아 톰슨
부점장, 붐 파우 피트니스

어휘 contact ~에게 연락하다 via ~을 통해 atmosphere 분위기 be committed to ~에 전념하다 make + 목적어 + 동사원형: (목적어)가 ~하게 만들다 comfortable 편안한 reach ~에 이르다, ~에 도달하다 objective n. 목표, 목적 regard A as B: A를 B로 여기다 with A in mind: A를 염두에 두고 address v. (문제 등) ~을 처리하다, ~을 해결하다 query 문의, 질문(= inquiry) mention that ~라고 언급하다 fly by 순식간에 지나가다 neglect ~을 등한시하다, ~을 게을리하다 access 이용 (권한), 접근 (권한) fit A into B: A를 B에 맞추다 available 이용 가능한 as well as ~뿐만 아니라 …도 desire ~을 원하다 workout 운동 head to ~로 향하다, ~로 가다 spacious 널찍한 facility 시설(물) ample 충분한 cramped 비좁은 maintain ~을 유지 관리하다 an assortment of 각종 ~의 equipment 장비 cardio 유산소 운동, 심장 강화 운동 express ~을 표현하다 nervousness 긴장(감), 초조(함) come with ~이 딸려 있다, ~을 포함하다 how + to 동사원형: ~하는 방법 exercise 운동 interest in ~에 대한 관심 tailored 맞춰진 personalized 개인 맞춤형의 nutrition 영양 a wide variety of 아주 다양한 run 운영되다 incluce ~을 포함하다 sound like ~인 것처럼 들리다, ~인 것 같다 look for ~을 찾다 set ~을 정하다, ~을 설정하다 tour v. ~을 견학하다 try out ~을 체험하다, ~을 시험해 보다

Why is Cynthia Thompson writing to Derek Martin?

(a) to ask about his current workout goals
(b) to thank him for joining the fitness center
(c) to answer his questions about the gym
(d) to offer him a discount on a new membership

신시아 톰슨 씨가 왜 데릭 마틴 씨에 게 편지를 쓰는가?

(a) 그의 현재 운동 목표에 관해 물 어 보기 위해
(b) 피트니스 센터에 가입한 것에 대 해 감사의 인사를 하기 위해
(c) 체육관에 관한 질문에 답변하기 위해
(d) 신규 회원권에 대한 할인을 제공 해 주기 위해

정답 (c)

해설 첫 문단에 상대방인 데릭 씨가 웹 사이트를 통해 연락한 것에 대한 감사의 인사와 함께(Thank you for contacting us via our website) 데릭 씨의 문의 사항을 처리해 주겠다고(let me address your queries) 밝히는 말이 쓰여 있으므로 (c)가 정 답입니다.

어휘 current 현재의 join ~에 가입하다, ~에 합류하다

패러프레이징

address your queries → answer his questions

Based on the second paragraph, why might people fail to get enough exercise?

(a) because they think gym fees are too expensive
(b) because they lack time to focus on working out
(c) because they find it hard to get motivated
(d) because they lack interest in maintaining good health

두 번째 문단에 따르면, 사람들이 왜 충분히 운동하지 못할 수도 있는가?

(a) 체육관 요금이 너무 비싸다고 생 각하기 때문에
(b) 운동하는 데 집중할 시간이 부족 하기 때문에
(c) 동기가 부여되는 것이 어렵다고 생각하기 때문에
(d) 좋은 건강을 유지하는 것에 대한 관심이 부족하기 때문에

정답 (b)

해설 두 번째 문단에 장시간 근무를 하며 어떻게 일주일이 순식간에 지나가면서 건강이 등한시될 수 있는지 이해한다는(you work long hours, and we understand how the week can fly by and your health can be neglected) 내용이 쓰여 있습니다. 이는 운동하는 데 시간이 부족하다는 문제를 언급하는 것이므로 (b)가 정답입니다.

어휘 **fail + to 동사원형**: ~하지 못하다, ~하는 데 실패하다 **lack** ~이 부족하다 **focus on** ~에 집중하다, ~에 초점을 맞추다 **find it + 형용사 + to 동사원형**: ~하는 것이 …하다고 생각하다 **get motivated** 동기가 부여되다 **maintain** ~을 유지하다

패러프레이징

the week can fly by and your health can be neglected → lack time to focus on working out

76 추론

What, most likely, is Derek's concern about working out at the fitness center?

(a) the accessibility of convenient parking
(b) his lack of experience with gym equipment
(c) the quality of the exercise machines
(d) his prior challenges with past injuries

피트니스 센터에서 운동하는 것과 관련된 데릭 씨의 우려가 무엇일 것 같은가?

(a) 편리한 주차 공간 이용 가능성
(b) 체육관 장비에 대한 경험 부족
(c) 운동 기계의 품질
(d) 과거의 부상에 따른 이전의 힘겨움

정답 (b)

해설 세 번째 문단에 데릭 씨의 우려와 관련해 걱정하지 말라는 말과 함께 모든 웨이트 기계에 각각의 운동을 실시하는 방법을 보여 주는 안내문이 딸려 있다고(please do not worry. All weight machines come with guides showing how to perform each exercise) 알리는 말이 쓰여 있습니다. 이는 운동 기계 이용 방법을 걱정하는 것에 대해 안심시키는 말에 해당하므로 (b)가 정답입니다.

어휘 **accessibility** 이용 가능성, 접근 가능성 **convenient** 편리한 **parking** 주차 (공간) **quality** 품질, 질 **prior** 이전의, 사전의 **challenge** 힘겨움, 어려움, 도전 (과제) **past** 과거의, 지난 **injury** 부상

How can Derek enjoy a more customized gym experience?

(a) by consulting with experts about his workouts
(b) by having a daily session with a nutritionist
(c) by joining a program to monitor his weight loss
(d) by specifying his objectives in an online survey

데릭 씨는 어떻게 어떻게 맞춤 제공되는 체육관 경험을 더 많이 즐길 수 있는가?

(a) 그의 운동과 관련해 전문가와 상의함으로써
(b) 매일 영양사와 함께 하는 시간을 가짐으로써
(c) 자신의 체중 감소를 관찰할 수 있는 프로그램에 합류함으로써
(d) 온라인 설문 조사에서 자신의 목표를 명시함으로써

정답 (a)

해설 네 번째 문단에 개인 맞춤형 운동 및 영양 계획을 만들어 주기 위해 함께 노력하는 개인 트레이너들을 보유하고 있다고(We have personal trainers who are happy to work with you to build a personalized fitness and nutrition plan) 쓰여 있어 그 사람들의 도움을 받을 것으로 볼 수 있으므로 (a)가 정답입니다.

어휘 customized 맞춤 제공되는 consult with ~와 상의하다, ~에게 상담하다 expert 전문가 session (특정 활동을 위한) 시간 nutritionist 영양사 monitor v. ~을 관찰하다 specify ~을 명시하다 survey 설문 조사(지)

패러프레이징

personal trainers / a personalized fitness and nutrition plan → experts / a more customized gym experience

---

What will Cynthia do if Derek calls her?

(a) She will put him in touch with a personal trainer.
(b) She will email him membership documents to sign.
(c) She will send him a sample exercise plan.
(d) She will arrange a time to show him around the facility.

데릭 씨가 전화하는 경우에 신시아 씨가 무엇을 할 것인가?

(a) 개인 트레이너와 연락하게 해 줄 것이다.
(b) 서명해야 할 회원 가입 서류를 이메일로 보내 줄 것이다.
(c) 운동 계획표 샘플을 보내 줄 것이다.
(d) 시설물을 둘러 볼 수 있게 해 주는 시간을 마련할 것이다.

정답 (d)

해설 마지막 문단에 자신에게 전화하라는(please give me a call at 555-0167) 말과 함께 시설을 견학하거나 심지어 피트니스 강좌들 중 하나를 체험해 보는 시간을 정할 수도 있다고(we can set a time for you to tour our facilities ~) 알리고 있습니다. 따라서, 시설 견학 일정을 잡는 일을 뜻하는 (d)가 정답입니다.

어휘 put A in touch with B: A를 B와 연락하게 해 주다 arrange ~을 마련하다, ~을 조치하다

> **패러프레이징**
>
> set a time for you to tour our facilities → arrange a time to show him around the facility

---

79 동의어

In the context of the passage, committed means _____ .

(a) related
(b) attracted
(c) dedicated
(d) identical

해당 문단의 문맥에서 committed 가 의미하는 것은?

(a) 관련된
(b) 이끌린
(c) 전념하는
(d) 동일한

정답 (c)

해설 해당 문장에서 committed 뒤에 전치사 to와 함께 모든 사람을 편안하게 만들어 주는 것이 목표임을 나타내는 말이 쓰여 있습니다. 따라서, committed가 그러한 목표를 위해 최선을 다하는 것과 관련된 단어임을 알 수 있으며, 이는 전념하는 것과 같으므로 (c)가 정답입니다.

---

80 동의어

In the context of the passage, spacious means _____ .

(a) distinct
(b) bright
(c) elegant
(d) large

해당 문단의 문맥에서 spacious가 의미하는 것은?

(a) 독특한, 뚜렷이 다른
(b) 밝은
(c) 우아한
(d) 넓은

정답 (d)

해설 해당 문장에서 형용사 spacious는 바로 뒤에 위치한 명사 facility를 수식해 시설의 특징을 나타내야 하며, 그 뒤에 충분한 공간이 있다는 말이 쓰여 있어 이러한 특징과 관련되어야 알맞으므로 '넓은'을 뜻하는 (d) large가 정답입니다.

Grammar

1. (b)	**2.** (d)	**3.** (b)	**4.** (c)	**5.** (d)	**6.** (a)	**7.** (b)	**8.** (a)	**9.** (c)	**10.** (b)
11. (c)	**12.** (d)	**13.** (b)	**14.** (a)	**15.** (c)	**16.** (d)	**17.** (a)	**18.** (d)	**19.** (c)	**20.** (a)
21. (d)	**22.** (a)	**23.** (b)	**24.** (c)	**25.** (a)	**26.** (d)				

Listening

27. (b)	**28.** (d)	**29.** (a)	**30.** (c)	**31.** (d)	**32.** (b)	**33.** (a)	**34.** (a)	**35.** (b)	**36.** (c)
37. (d)	**38.** (a)	**39.** (b)	**40.** (d)	**41.** (c)	**42.** (a)	**43.** (d)	**44.** (b)	**45.** (c)	**46.** (c)
47. (b)	**48.** (d)	**49.** (a)	**50.** (c)	**51.** (b)	**52.** (a)				

Reading & Vocabulary

53. (a)	**54.** (c)	**55.** (b)	**56.** (b)	**57.** (d)	**58.** (c)	**59.** (a)	**60.** (d)	**61.** (b)	**62.** (b)
63. (c)	**64.** (a)	**65.** (d)	**66.** (c)	**67.** (b)	**68.** (a)	**69.** (c)	**70.** (d)	**71.** (d)	**72.** (c)
73. (a)	**74.** (b)	**75.** (d)	**76.** (b)	**77.** (a)	**78.** (c)	**79.** (a)	**80.** (d)		

채점 계산표 [정답 개수 기재]		채점 계산 방법
Grammar	_____ / 26문항	Grammar 정답 개수 ÷ 26 × 100
Listening	_____ / 26문항	Listening 정답 개수 ÷ 26 × 100
Reading & Vocabulary	_____ / 28문항	Reading & Vocabulary 정답 개수 ÷ 28 × 100
총점	_____ / 80문항 ▸ _____ / 100점	총점: 각 영역 합산 정답 개수 ÷ 80 × 100 *소수점 이하는 올림 처리

TEST 04

GRAMMAR
LISTENING
READING & VOCABULARY

01 시제 – 과거진행

Rosie broke her new phone on the way home last night. She _____ it when she fell asleep on the subway, and it slipped out of her hand.

(a) would hold
(b) was holding
(c) has been holding
(d) will hold

로지는 어젯밤에 집으로 가는 길에 새 전화기를 망가뜨렸다. 그녀가 지하철에서 잠들었을 때 그것을 붙잡고 있었는데, 그녀의 손에서 빠져 나갔다.

정답 (b)

해설 동사 hold의 알맞은 형태를 고르는 문제입니다. 빈칸 뒤에 과거시제 동사(fell)를 포함한 when절이 쓰여 있어 이 when절이 가리키는 과거 시점에 붙잡고 있던 상태가 일시적으로 지속되던 상황을 나타내야 자연스러우므로 이러한 의미로 쓰이는 과거진행시제 (b) was holding이 정답입니다.

어휘 break ~을 망가뜨리다, ~을 깨트리다 on the way 가는 길에, 오는 길에 fall asleep 잠들다 slip out of ~에서 빠져 나가다

02 관계사절

Chicken à la King is a dish of diced chicken cooked in a cream sauce with mushrooms and vegetables. The dish, _____, is often served over rice or noodles.

(a) what is easy to prepare
(b) who is easy to prepare
(c) that is easy to prepare
(d) which is easy to prepare

치킨 알라킹은 깍둑썰기 된 닭고기를 버섯과 채소를 곁들여 크림 소스에 조리한 요리이다. 이 요리는, 준비하기 쉬우며, 흔히 쌀 또는 면 위에 얹어 제공된다.

정답 (d)

해설 사물 명사 The dish를 뒤에서 수식할 관계사절을 고르는 문제입니다. 선택지 (a)~(d)를 보고 빈칸에 들어갈 관계사절이 관계대명사 뒤에 be동사 is와 형용사 easy, 그리고 to부정사 to prepare가 이어지는 구조임을 알 수 있습니다. 사물 명사를 수식하는 관계대명사는 which 또는 that인데, 빈칸 앞에 콤마가 있으므로 관계대명사 which로 시작하는 (d)가 정답입니다.

어휘 dice v. ~을 깍둑썰다, 주사위꼴로 자르다 serve (음식) ~을 제공하다, ~을 내오다 prepare ~을 준비하다

⊗ 오답 피하기

관계대명사 that은 콤마(,) 뒤에 사용할 수 없는 관계대명사입니다. 빈칸 앞에 콤마(,)가 있는 경우 that으로 시작하는 관계사절은 오답으로 소거합니다.

03 가정법 과거완료

Jupiter's gravity is so strong that it effectively protects Earth by deflecting comets that might otherwise hit our planet. If Jupiter had never existed, Earth _____ by many more comets by now.

(a) will likely have been struck
(b) would likely have been struck
(c) would likely be struck
(d) will likely be struck

목성의 중력은 너무 강해서 그렇지 않으면 우리 행성과 충돌할지도 모르는 혜성들의 방향을 바꿔 놓음으로써 효과적으로 지구를 보호해 준다. 만일 목성이 존재하지 않았다면, 지구는 지금쯤 더 많은 혜성들과 부딪쳤을 가능성이 있다.

정답 (b)

해설 동사 strike의 알맞은 형태를 고르는 문제입니다. If절의 동사가 had existed와 같이 가정법 과거완료를 나타내는 「had p.p.」일 때, 주절의 동사는 「would/could/might + have p.p.」와 같은 형태가 되어야 알맞으므로 (b) would likely have been struck이 정답입니다. likely와 같은 부사가 would/could/might과 have p.p. 사이에 위치할 수 있으므로 선택지에서 부사를 제외한 형태를 찾아 정답을 고르도록 합니다.

어휘 gravity 중력 so A that B: 너무 A해서 B하다 effectively 효과적으로 by (방법) ~함으로써, ~해서 deflect ~의 방향을 바꾸다 comet 혜성 otherwise 그렇지 않으면, 달리 exist 존재하다 likely 가능성 있는, ~할 것 같은 strike ~와 부딪치다 by now (과거) 지금쯤, 이제

❌ 오답 피하기

여기서 by now는 문맥상 '지금쯤 부딪쳤을 것이다'라는 내용을 나타내기 위해 쓰인 현재시점 직전의 과거시점을 언급하는 부사이므로 주절의 시제는 현재가 아닌 과거 시제입니다. 따라서 이 문제는 혼합가정법 문제로 오인하기 쉬운 가정법 과거완료 문제입니다.

04 준동사 - 동명사

Joe visited his friend in Calgary and intended to go home by 10 p.m. However, they were having so much fun that when they finally finished _____, it was already late, so Joe stayed the night.

(a) to have caught up
(b) having caught up
(c) catching up
(d) to catch up

조는 캘거리에 있는 친구를 방문했으며, 오후 10시까지 집으로 갈 생각이었다. 하지만, 그들이 너무 즐거운 시간을 보내는 바람에 못다한 얘기를 마침내 끝마쳤을 때, 이미 늦어서, 조는 하룻밤 묵었다.

정답 (c)

해설 동사구 catch up의 알맞은 형태를 고르는 문제입니다. 빈칸은 타동사 finished의 목적어 자리이며, finish는 동명사를 목적어로 취하여 '~하는 것을 끝마치다'라는 의미를 나타냅니다. 따라서 동명사인 (c) catching up이 정답입니다.

어휘 intend to 동사원형: ~할 생각이다, ~할 작정이다 by (기한) ~까지 however 하지만, 그러나 so A that B: 너무 A해서 B하다 catch up 못다한 얘기를 하다, (진행, 수준 등) ~을 따라잡다, ~을 만회하다

05 조동사

Magpies are some of the most intelligent birds and are known to be able to recognize themselves in a mirror. This is remarkable, as only a few animal species _____ identify themselves in such a way.

(a) would
(b) must
(c) should
(d) can

까치는 가장 지능적인 새들 중 일부이며, 거울에 비친 자신을 알아볼 수 있는 것으로 알려져 있다. 이는 놀라운 일인데, 오직 몇몇 동물 종만 그러한 방식으로 자신을 확인할 수 있기 때문이다.

정답 (d)

해설 빈칸에 들어갈 알맞은 조동사를 고르는 문제입니다. 빈칸 앞 문장에 거울에 비친 자신을 알아볼 수 있다고 언급되어 있어, 빈칸이 포함된 문장은 앞 문장과 마찬가지로 오직 몇몇 동물 종만 그런 방식으로 자신을 확인할 수 있다는 능력을 의미해야 알맞습니다. 따라서 '~할 수 있다'라는 의미로 능력을 나타내는 조동사 (d) can이 정답입니다.

어휘 intelligent 지능적인, 똑똑한 be known to 동사원형: ~하는 것으로 알려지다 be able to 동사원형: ~할 수 있다 recognize ~을 알아보다, ~을 인식하다 remarkable 놀라운, 주목할 만한 species (동식물의) 종 identify (신분 등) ~을 확인하다, ~을 알아보다 in such a way 그러한 방식으로

06 준동사 - to부정사

A partial solar eclipse will be happening today and will be visible from the town square. However, Derek and his astronomy club are planning _____ the event from the observatory because it offers a better view.

(a) to watch
(b) having watched
(c) watching
(d) to have watched

부분 일식이 오늘 일어날 것이며, 시내 광장에서 눈에 보일 것이다. 하지만, 데릭과 그의 천문학 동호회는 전망대에서 그 일을 지켜볼 계획을 세우고 있는데, 그것이 더 나은 시야를 제공해 주기 때문이다.

정답 (a)

해설 동사 watch의 알맞은 형태를 고르는 문제입니다. 빈칸은 타동사 are planning의 목적어 자리이며, plan은 to부정사를 목적

어로 취하여 '~할 계획이다'라는 의미를 나타냅니다. 따라서 to부정사인 (a) to watch가 정답입니다.

어휘 partial solar eclipse 부분 일식 visible 눈에 보이는 square 광장 however 하지만, 그러나 astronomy 천문학 observatory 전망대, 관측소

---

07 접속부사

The okapi lives in the jungles of the Congo and looks like a cross between a deer and a zebra. _____, it is actually the only living relative of the giraffe.

(a) Therefore
(b) However
(c) Otherwise
(d) Similarly

오카피는 콩고의 정글에 살고 있으며, 사슴과 얼룩말 사이의 잡종인 것처럼 보인다. 하지만, 그것은 사실 기린의 살아 있는 유일한 동족이다.

정답 (b)

해설 빈칸에 알맞은 접속부사를 고르는 문제이므로 앞뒤 문장들의 의미 관계를 확인해야 합니다. 빈칸 앞에는 오카피가 사슴과 얼룩말 사이의 잡종인 것처럼 보인다는 말이, 빈칸 뒤에는 사실 기린의 살아 있는 유일한 동족이라는 말이 각각 쓰여 있습니다. 이는 실제로 잡종이 아님을 밝히는 대조적인 흐름에 해당하므로 '하지만, 그러나'라는 의미로 대조나 반대를 나타내는 접속부사 (b) However가 정답입니다.

어휘 look like ~인 것처럼 보이다, ~인 것 같다 cross 잡종, 혼합 relative n. 동족, 친척 therefore 따라서, 그러므로 otherwise 그렇지 않으면, 그 외에는, 달리 similarly 유사하게, 마찬가지로

---

08 시제 – 미래완료진행

Margaret hates leaving her new cat on his own, but she had to run some errands today. By the time she gets home later, poor Tippy _____ alone for about five hours.

(a) will have been waiting
(b) has been waiting
(c) will wait
(d) is waiting

마가렛은 자신의 새 고양이를 혼자 남겨 두는 것이 싫지만, 오늘 심부름을 좀 하러 가야 했다. 그녀가 나중에 집에 돌아올 때쯤이면, 불쌍한 티피는 혼자 약 5시간 동안 기다리고 있게 될 것이다.

정답 (a)

해설 동사 wait의 알맞은 형태를 고르는 문제입니다. By the time이 이끄는 절에 gets와 같이 현재시제 동사가 쓰여 있고, 주절에 for about five hours와 같이 「for + 시간」 표현으로 지속 시간을 나타내는 구문이 있으면 그 시간 동안 계속 진행 중일 미래의 상태를 나타낼 미래완료진행형 동사가 필요하므로 (a) will have been waiting이 정답입니다.

어휘 on one's own 혼자, 자력으로 run errands 심부름하러 가다 by the time ~할 때쯤이면 about 약, 대략

Brianna has been baking for years, so she is always happy to give advice to those with less experience. She usually recommends _____ the baking journey with something simple, such as cupcakes.

(a) having started
(b) to start
(c) starting
(d) to have started

브리아나는 수년 동안 계속 빵과 쿠키를 구워 오고 있기 때문에, 경험이 더 적은 사람들에게 언제나 기꺼이 조언을 해 준다. 그녀는 대개 컵케이크 같이, 간단한 것으로 빵과 쿠키를 굽는 여정을 시작하는 것을 추천해 준다.

정답 (c)

해설 동사 start의 알맞은 형태를 고르는 문제입니다. 빈칸은 타동사 recommends의 목적어 자리이며, recommend는 동명사를 목적어로 취하여 '~하는 것을 추천하다'라는 의미를 나타냅니다. 따라서 동명사인 (c) starting이 정답입니다.

어휘 **those** (수식어구와 함께) ~하는 사람들 **usually** 대개, 평소에 **journey** 여정, 긴 여행

❌ 오답 피하기

recommend 뒤 목적어 자리에 빈칸이 위치할 경우 동명사가 정답이지만, 「recommend + 목적어 + 빈칸」의 구조처럼 recommend 뒤에 명사 목적어가 위치하고, 그 뒤에 빈칸이 위치할 경우 to부정사가 정답입니다.

Craig had a terrible time on his recent vacation to Scotland. His friend Arthur, _____, booked awful hotels, arranged unreliable transportation, and chose overpriced restaurants that were not very good.

(a) what organized everything
(b) who organized everything
(c) which organized everything
(d) that organized everything

크레이그는 스코틀랜드로 떠난 최근의 휴가 중에 끔찍한 시간을 보냈다. 모든 것을 준비해 준, 그의 친구 아서는 끔찍한 호텔을 예약했고, 신뢰할 수 없는 교통편을 마련했으며, 그렇게 좋지 않은데 너무 비싼 레스토랑들을 선택했다.

정답 (b)

해설 사람 명사 Arthur를 뒤에서 수식할 관계사절을 고르는 문제입니다. 선택지 (a)~(d)를 보고 빈칸에 들어갈 관계사절이 관계대명사 뒤에 타동사 organized와 목적어 everything이 이어지는 구조임을 알 수 있습니다. 사람 명사를 수식하는 관계대명사는 who 또는 that인데, 빈칸 앞에 콤마가 있으므로 관계대명사 who로 시작하는 (b)가 정답입니다.

어휘 **terrible** 끔찍한, 지독한(= awful) **recent** 최근의 **book** v. ~을 예약하다 **arrange** ~을 마련하다, ~을 조치하다 **unreliable** 신뢰할 수 없는 **transportation** 교통(편) **choose** ~을 선택하다 **overpriced** 너무 비싼 **organize** ~을 준비하다, ~을

조직하다, ~을 정리하다

11 준동사 – to부정사

Andy's musical instrument store almost closed last year, but he managed to keep it afloat by giving lessons to customers. Offering _____ people how to play music proved to be a profitable new line of business.

(a) to have taught
(b) having taught
(c) to teach
(d) teaching

앤디의 악기점은 작년에 거의 문을 닫을 뻔했지만, 고객들에게 레슨을 해 주는 것으로 간신히 연명했다. 사람들에게 음악을 연주하는 방법을 가르쳐 주겠다고 한 것이 수익성 있는 새로운 사업 노선인 것으로 드러났다.

정답 (c)

해설 동사 teach의 알맞은 형태를 고르는 문제입니다. 빈칸은 타동사 offer의 동명사인 Offering의 목적어 자리이며, offer는 to부정사를 목적어로 취하여 '~하겠다고 (제안)하다'라는 의미를 나타냅니다. 따라서 to부정사인 (c) to teach가 정답입니다.

어휘 musical instrument 악기 manage to 동사원형: 간신히 ~하다, 어떻게든 ~해내다 keep + 목적어 + afloat: (목적어)를 연명하다, (목적어)의 도산은 면하다 how to 동사원형: ~하는 방법 prove to 동사원형: ~하는 것으로 드러나다 profitable 수익성 있는

12 가정법 과거

Jim won last year's local marathon and became an instant celebrity. If he had more time to devote to training, he _____ the event every year, just to keep his fans happy.

(a) would probably have entered
(b) will probably enter
(c) will probably have entered
(d) would probably enter

짐이 작년에 열린 지역 마라톤 대회에서 우승하면서 순식간에 유명 인사가 되었다. 만일 그가 훈련에 전념할 시간이 더 많다면, 단지 자신의 팬들을 계속 기쁘게 해 주기 위해, 아마 매년 그 행사에 참가할 것이다.

정답 (d)

해설 동사 enter의 알맞은 형태를 고르는 문제입니다. If절의 동사가 가정법 과거를 나타내는 과거시제(had)일 때, 주절의 동사는 「would/could/might + 동사원형」과 같은 형태가 되어야 알맞으므로 (d) would probably enter가 정답입니다. probably 와 같은 부사가 would/could/might과 동사원형 사이에 위치할 수 있으므로 선택지에서 부사를 제외한 형태를 찾아 정답을 고르도록 합니다.

어휘 local 지역의, 현지의 instant 순식간의, 즉각적인 celebrity 유명 인사 devote to ~에 전념하다 keep + 목적어 + 형용사: (목적어)를 계속 ~하게 만들다, (목적어)를 ~한 상태로 유지하다 enter ~에 참가하다

---

13 시제 – 미래진행

When Reina arrives at Harvey's house for their date tonight, Harvey will not be there. Instead, he _____ late at the office, as he needs to finish a case report. Unfortunately, he forgot to tell Reina.

(a) has worked
(b) will be working
(c) works
(d) was working

레이너가 오늘밤 데이트를 위해 하비의 집에 도착할 때, 하비는 그곳에 있지 않을 것이다. 대신, 그는 사무실에서 늦게까지 일하고 있을 텐데, 그가 사례 보고서를 끝마쳐야 하기 때문이다. 안타깝게도, 그는 레이나에게 말하는 것을 잊었다.

정답 (b)

해설 동사 work의 알맞은 형태를 고르는 문제입니다. 빈칸 앞 문장에 시점 표현 tonight 및 미래를 나타내는 조동사 will과 함께 하비의 집에 있지 않을 것이라는 말이 쓰여 있습니다. 따라서 그 미래 시점에 일하고 있을 상황을 나타낼 수 있는 미래진행 시제 (b) will be working이 정답입니다.

어휘 instead 대신 case 사례, 경우 unfortunately 안타깝게도, 유감스럽게도 forget to 동사원형: ~하는 것을 잊다

---

14 준동사 – to부정사

Most cranberries are gathered in a process known as wet harvesting. In this process, the field is flooded and, after the vines are shaken, air pockets within the berries cause them _____ to the surface.

(a) to float
(b) floating
(c) having floated
(d) to have floated

대부분의 크랜베리는 습식 수확이라고 알려진 과정을 통해 거둬들여진다. 이 과정에서는, 밭을 침수시킨 다음, 그 덩굴식물을 흔들고 나면, 크랜베리 내부에 있는 공기 주머니가 그것을 수면으로 떠오르게 만든다.

정답 (a)

해설 동사 float의 알맞은 형태를 고르는 문제입니다. 빈칸 앞에 위치한 동사 cause는 「cause + 목적어 + to 동사원형」의 구조로 쓰여 '(목적어)가 ~하게 만들다, (목적어)가 ~하도록 초래하다'라는 의미를 나타내므로 (a) to float이 정답입니다.

어휘 gather ~을 거둬들이다, ~을 모으다 process (처리) 과정 harversting 수확 flood ~을 침수시키다 vine 덩굴나무 surface 수면, 표현 float 떠오르다, 뜨다

---

15 가정법 과거

Tardigrades may be tiny, but they are probably the toughest animals on Earth. For example, if one were to put a tardigrade in outer space, it _____ for decades.

(a) will likely survive
(b) will likely have survived
(c) would likely survive
(d) would likely have survived

완보류는 아주 작을 수 있지만, 아마 지구상에서 가장 끈질긴 동물일 것이다. 예를 들어, 누군가 완보류를 우주 공간에 갖다 놓게 된다면, 아마 수십 년 동안 생존할 것이다.

정답 (c)

해설 동사 survive의 알맞은 형태를 고르는 문제입니다. if절의 동사가 가정법 과거를 나타내는 과거시제(were)일 때, 주절의 동사는 「would/could/might + 동사원형」과 같은 형태가 되어야 알맞으므로 (c) would likely survive가 정답입니다. likely와 같은 부사가 would/could/might과 동사원형 사이에 위치할 수 있으므로 선택지에서 부사를 제외한 형태를 찾아 정답을 고르도록 합니다.

어휘 tardigrades 완보류(민물이나 습지 등에 사는 작은 벌레류) be to 동사원형: ~하게 되다, ~할 예정이다, ~해야 하다 outer space 우주 공간 decade 10년 likely 아마 survive 생존하다, 살아 남다

---

16 접속사

Fahrenheit 451 is a 1953 dystopian novel by Ray Bradbury in which books are censored and burned. Ironically, the book itself was also subjected to censorship in some places _____ it was judged to be offensive.

(a) even if
(b) although
(c) so that
(d) because

<화씨 451>은 레이 브래드버리의 1953년작 반이상향 소설이며, 그 소설에서 책들은 검열되고 불태워진다. 역설적이게도, 이 책 자체도 모욕적이라고 판단되었기 때문에 몇몇 곳에서 검열 대상이 되었다.

정답 (d)

해설 빈칸에 들어갈 알맞은 접속사를 고르는 문제입니다. 빈칸 앞뒤에 각각 위치한 절들이 '이 책 자체도 몇몇 곳에서 검열 대상이 되었다'와 '그것이 모욕적이라고 판단되었다'라는 의미를 나타냅니다. 따라서 빈칸 뒤에 위치한 절이 검열 대상이 된 이유에

해당하는 것으로 볼 수 있으므로 '~하기 때문에'라는 의미로 이유를 나타낼 때 사용하는 접속사 (d) because가 정답입니다.

어휘 dystopian 반이상향의 censor ~을 검열하다 ironically 역설적이게도 be subjected to ~의 대상이 되다 censorship 검열 be judged to 동사원형: ~하다고 판단되다, ~하다고 여겨지다 offensive 모욕적인, 불쾌한, 공격적인 even if 설사 ~한다 하더라도 although 비록 ~이기는 하지만 so that (목적) ~하도록, (결과) 그래서, 그래야

---

17 **가정법 과거완료**

Nigel forgot most of his lines in the final performance of the play last night and was embarrassed. If he had bothered to practice yesterday afternoon instead of playing video games, his performance _____ more smoothly.

(a) would have gone
(b) will go
(c) would go
(d) will have gone

나이젤은 어젯밤에 있었던 마지막 연극 공연에서 대부분의 대사를 잊어버려서 당황했다. 만일 그가 비디오 게임을 하는 대신 어제 오후에 애써 연습했다면, 그의 공연은 더 순조롭게 진행되었을 것이다.

정답 (a)

해설 동사 go의 알맞은 형태를 고르는 문제입니다. If절의 동사가 had bothered와 같이 가정법 과거완료를 나타내는 「had p.p.」일 때, 주절의 동사는 「would/could/might + have p.p.」와 같은 형태가 되어야 알맞으므로 (a) would have gone이 정답입니다.

어휘 line 대사 performance 공연, 연주(회) play 연극 embarrassed 당황한, 창피한 bother to 동사원형: 애써 ~하다, 일부러 ~하다 practice 연습하다 instead of ~ 대신 smoothly 순조롭게

---

18 **당위성을 나타내는 동사원형**

Helena saw a group of kids playing very close to a dangerous river. Fearing for their safety, she warned them of the risk and suggested they _____ somewhere else.

(a) are playing
(b) played
(c) will play
(d) play

헬레나는 한 무리의 아이들이 위험한 강과 아주 가까이에서 노는 모습을 봤다. 그들의 안전을 우려하여, 그녀는 그 위험 요소에 대해 경고하면서 어딘가 다른 곳에서 놀도록 권했다.

정답 (d)

해설 동사 play의 알맞은 형태를 고르는 문제입니다. 빈칸은 동사 suggested의 목적어 역할을 하는 that절의 동사 자리인데, suggest와 같이 주장/요구/명령/제안 등을 나타내는 동사의 목적어 역할을 하는 that절의 동사는 should 없이 동사원형만 사용하므로 동사원형인 (d) play가 정답입니다.

어휘   see + 목적어 + -ing: (목적어)가 ~하는 모습을 보다 close to ~와 가까이 fear for ~을 우려하다, ~을 염려하다 warn A of
B: A에게 B에 대해 경고하다 risk 위험 (요소) suggest (that) ~하도록 권하다, ~하도록 제안하다

19   준동사 – 동명사

Iguazu Falls, located on the border of Argentina and Brazil, is the largest waterfall system in the world. For those who enjoy _____ incredible natural wonders, it is a great bucket list addition.

(a) having visited
(b) to visit
(c) visiting
(d) to have visited

아르헨티나와 브라질의 국경에 위치한, 이과수 폭포는 전 세계에서 가장 큰 폭포이다. 믿을 수 없는 자연의 불가사의를 방문하기를 즐기는 사람들에게 있어, 이곳은 훌륭한 버킷 리스트 추가 대상이다.

정답   (c)

해설   동사 visit의 알맞은 형태를 고르는 문제입니다. 빈칸은 타동사 enjoy의 목적어 자리이며, enjoy는 동명사를 목적어로 취하여 '~하는 것을 즐기다'라는 의미를 나타냅니다. 따라서 동명사인 (c) visiting이 정답입니다.

어휘   located on ~에 위치한 border 국경, 경계(선) those who ~하는 사람들 incredible 믿을 수 없는 wonder 불가사의,
경이(로운 것) bucket list 버킷 리스트(죽기 전에 해 보고 싶은 것들을 적은 목록) addition 추가(되는 것)

20   가정법 과거완료

Mr. Davis's Friday afternoon statistics class is unpopular with students. Many of his past students maintain that if they had known beforehand how boring Mr. Davis was, they _____ a different class.

(a) would have chosen
(b) would choose
(c) will choose
(d) will have chosen

데이비스 씨의 금요일 오후 통계학 수업은 학생들에게 인기가 없다. 그의 과거 학생들 중 많은 이들은 데이비스 씨가 얼마나 지루한지 미리 알았다면, 다른 수업을 선택했을 것이라고 주장한다.

정답   (a)

해설   동사 choose의 알맞은 형태를 고르는 문제입니다. If절의 동사가 had known과 같이 가정법 과거완료를 나타내는 「had p.p.」일 때, if절과 연결되는 절의 동사는 「would/could/might + have p.p.」와 같은 형태가 되어야 알맞으므로 (a) would have chosen이 정답입니다.

어휘   statistics 통계학 unpopular with ~에게 인기가 없는 maintain that ~라고 주장하다 beforehand 미리, 사전에
choose ~을 선택하다

Yesterday, there was an escape from Grantville Prison. Four convicts are currently on the run, and police _____ them down with tracker dogs in the local woodland, where they are believed to be hiding out.

(a) will have been hunting
(b) hunted
(c) have hunted
(d) are hunting

어제, 그랜트빌 감옥에서 탈옥 사건이 있었다. 네 명의 재소자가 현재 도주 중이며, 경찰은 그들이 숨어 있는 것으로 여겨지는 지역 삼림 지대에서 추적견을 이용해 그들을 추적하고 있다.

정답 (d)

해설 동사 hunt의 알맞은 형태를 고르는 문제입니다. 빈칸 앞에 위치한 절에 '현재'를 뜻하는 부사 currently와 함께 현재 도주 중인 상태를 나타내는 말이 쓰여 있어 경찰이 현재 일시적으로 추적하는 일을 진행하고 있음을 뜻하는 동사가 필요하므로 이러한 의미를 나타낼 수 있는 현재진행시제 (d) are hunting이 정답입니다.

어휘 escape 탈출, 도피 convict 재소자 currently 현재 on the run 도주 중인 tracker 추적자, 사냥꾼 local 지역의, 현지의 be believed to 동사원형: ~하는 것으로 여겨지다 hide out 숨다, 은신하다

Due to the risk posed by box jellyfish and other marine stinging organisms, it is recommended that people _____ swimming off some Australian beaches at certain times of year.

(a) avoid
(b) are avoiding
(c) avoided
(d) will avoid

상자 해파리 및 다른 찌르는 해양 생물체들에 의해 가해지는 위험으로 인해, 사람들은 일년 중 특정 시기에 일부 호주 해변 앞바다에서 수영하는 것을 피하도록 권고되고 있다.

정답 (a)

해설 동사 avoid의 알맞은 형태를 고르는 문제입니다. 빈칸은 「it is ~ that절」 구조로 된 가주어/진주어 구문에서 진주어 역할을 하는 that절의 동사 자리인데, that 앞에 recommended와 같이 중요성/권고/필수/의무 등을 나타내는 형용사나 과거분사가 쓰이면 that절에 동사원형만 사용하므로 (a) avoid가 정답입니다.

어휘 due to ~로 인해, ~ 때문에 risk 위험 (요소) pose (위험, 문제 등) ~을 가하다, ~을 제기하다 marine 해양의 stinging 찌르는, 쏘는 organism 생물체 it is recommended that ~하도록 권장되다 certain 특정한, 일정한 avoid -ing ~하는 것을 피하다

23 시제 – 현재완료진행

Theresa may have to give up on her dream of becoming a juggler. She _____ for six months, but she still cannot keep three balls in the air for more than about five seconds.

(a) would practice
(b) has been practicing
(c) practices
(d) had been practicing

테레사는 저글러가 되겠다는 꿈을 포기해야 할지도 모른다. 그녀는 6개 월째 계속 연습해 오고 있지만, 여전 히 세 개의 공을 약 5초 이상 공중에 유지하지 못한다.

정답 (b)

해설 동사 practice의 알맞은 형태를 고르는 문제입니다. but절에 현재시제 동사 cannot keep과 현재 여전히 하지 못하고 있음 을 나타내는 말이 쓰여 있어 빈칸 뒤에 위치한 for six months가 과거에서부터 현재까지 계속 연습해 오고 있는 기간임을 알 수 있습니다. 과거에서부터 이어져 현재까지도 계속 진행되고 있는 중인 일은 현재완료진행 시제로 나타내므로 (b) has been practicing이 정답입니다.

어휘 may have to 동사원형: ~해야 할지도 모르다 give up on ~을 포기하다 juggler 저글러, 저글링하는 사람 about 약, 대략 practice 연습하다

24 조동사

In 2005, the municipal government of Rome passed new rules on animal welfare. One provision states that dog owners _____ walk their pets daily or face a fine equivalent to $625.

(a) would
(b) can
(c) must
(d) may

2005년에, 로마의 시정 당국은 동 물 복지에 관한 새로운 법을 통과시 켰다. 한 가지 조항은 견주는 반드시 자신의 반려동물을 매일 산책시켜야 하며, 그렇지 않으면 625달러 상당 의 벌금에 직면하게 된다고 명시하 고 있다.

정답 (c)

해설 문장의 의미에 어울리는 조동사를 고르는 문제입니다. 빈칸 뒤에 위치한 or 이하 부분은 '그렇지 않으면 625달러 상당의 벌 금에 직면하게 된다'라는 의미를 나타냅니다. 이는 반드시 지켜야 하는 일을 하지 않을 경우에 발생할 수 있는 부정적인 결 과이므로 '반드시 ~하다'라는 의미로 의무나 필요성을 나타내는 조동사 (c) must가 정답입니다.

어휘 municipal government 시정 당국 pass ~을 통과시키다 welfare 복지, 행복 provision 조항, 규정 state that ~라고 명시하다 walk ~을 산책시키다 face v. ~에 직면하다 fine n. 벌금 equivalent to ~ 상당의, ~에 상응하는

Lina finally got back to working on her thesis last week. For days, her air-conditioning unit _____ loud noises that prevented her from concentrating. Thankfully, someone eventually came to fix it.

(a) had been making
(b) is making
(c) will have made
(d) has been making

리나는 마침내 지난 주에 자신의 논문 작업을 다시 시작했다. 며칠 동안, 그녀의 에어컨 기기가 시끄러운 소음을 계속 만들어 내고 있어서 그녀가 집중하지 못하게 방해했다. 다행히, 누군가 결국 와서 그것을 고쳤다.

정답 (a)

해설 동사 make의 알맞은 형태를 고르는 문제입니다. 빈칸 뒤에 이어지는 that절에 과거시제 동사 prevented로 과거 시점에 방해한 사실을 나타내는 말이 쓰여 있어 빈칸 앞에 위치한 For days가 더 이전의 과거에서부터 그 과거 시점까지 이어진 기간임을 알 수 있습니다. 더 이전의 과거에서부터 특정 과거 시점까지 계속 이어진 일은 과거완료진행 시제로 나타내므로 (a) had been making이 정답입니다.

어휘 get back to ~로 돌아가다 work on ~에 대한 작업을 하다 thesis 논문 unit 기기 한 대 prevent + 목적어 + from -ing: (목적어)가 ~하지 못하게 방해하다 concentrate 집중하다 thankfully 다행히, 고맙게도 eventually 결국, 드디어 fix ~을 고치다

Assuming an average speed of about 25 mph, NASA estimates that if a person were to cycle to the moon, it _____ about 416 days to complete the journey.

(a) will take
(b) would have taken
(c) will have taken
(d) would take

시속 약 25마일의 평균 속도라는 가정 하에, NASA는 사람이 자전거를 타고 달에 가게 된다면, 그 여정을 완료하는 데 약 416일이 걸릴 것으로 추정하고 있다.

정답 (d)

해설 동사 take의 알맞은 형태를 고르는 문제입니다. if절의 동사가 가정법 과거를 나타내는 과거시제(were)일 때, if절과 연결되는 절의 동사는 「would/could/might + 동사원형」과 같은 형태가 되어야 알맞으므로 (d) would take가 정답입니다.

어휘 assuming ~라는 가정 하에, 가령 ~라면 about 약, 대략 estimate that ~라고 추정하다 be to 동사원형: ~하게 되다, ~할 예정이다, ~해야 하다 cycle 자전거를 타고 가다 complete ~을 완료하다 journey 여정, 긴 여행 take ~의 시간이 걸리다

PART 1

F: Hey Louis! Would you like some coffee?	여: 안녕하세요, 루이스 씨! 커피 좀 드시겠어요?
M: Hi Emily. Yes, that sounds great, thank you.	남: 안녕하세요, 에밀리 씨. 아주 좋습니다, 감사합니다.
F: I didn't know **27** you were back from your business trip already.	여: 벌써 출장에서 돌아 오신 줄 몰랐어요.
M: **27** I just got back a couple of days ago.	남: 며칠 전에 막 복귀했어요.
F: Where did you go again?	여: 어디로 가셨다고 하셨죠?
M: Barcelona.	남: 바르셀로나요.
F: Nice! **27** It's great how our company business takes us to so many cool places.	여: 잘됐네요! 회사 비즈니스 때문에 우리가 그렇게 많은 멋진 곳으로 다니는 방식이 너무 좋아요.
M: It really is. I loved getting sent to Hawaii last year. We had such a productive meeting with the client on the first day that we didn't need to do any follow-ups. **28** I was able to spend the rest of the trip on the beach. It was the best business trip I've ever had.	남: 정말 그래요. 저는 작년에 하와이로 보내져서 너무 마음에 들었어요. 저희가 첫째 날에 고객과 아주 생산적인 회의를 해서 어떤 후속 조치를 할 필요가 없었어요. 저는 그 출장의 나머지 시간을 해변에서 보낼 수 있었죠. 제가 그 동안 가 본 것 중에서 가장 좋은 출장이었어요.
F: **29** I think my favorite business trip was when I visited the company's branch in Singapore. It was the first time I'd been back there since childhood, so it gave me the opportunity to visit family and friends I hadn't seen in a long time.	여: 제 생각에 제가 가장 좋아했던 출장은 싱가포르에 있는 회사 지사를 방문했을 때였던 것 같아요. 어렸을 때 이후로 그곳에 다시 가 본 게 처음이었기 때문에, 오랫동안 보지 못했던 가족과 친구들을 방문할 기회를 제게 주었거든요.
M: I'm glad you had a chance to visit your childhood home. When I was sent to the Singapore branch, it was probably the worst business trip of my life.	남: 어린 시절의 고향을 방문하실 기회가 있으셨다니 기쁘네요. 제가 싱가포르 지사에 보내졌을 땐, 아마 제 인생에서 최악의 출장이었을 거예요.
F: Oh no! Why didn't you like Singapore?	여: 아, 저런! 왜 싱가포르가 마음에 들지 않으셨죠?

M: Don't get me wrong. The country was great. I just had a bit of bad luck. The air conditioner at my hotel was broken. It was so hot that I couldn't sleep at night.

F: Wow, that must have been rough. Singapore has a tropical climate, so the humidity makes it uncomfortable even if you wear light clothes and stay in the shade.

M: Yes. **30** I tried letting in some air from outside, but then a bunch of mosquitos flew in, and I got covered in bites. It was a nightmare, Emily.

F: I'm sorry you had such a bad experience, Louis. That reminds me of when I got sent to Alaska while I was working for my last employer. The building we worked in was freezing.

M: Was the heating system broken?

F: No, I don't think so. I was told that was the building's normal temperature. The other colleagues that I went with seemed to do just fine in the cold, but **31** I've lived in warm places my entire life, so the winter weather was really a problem for me.

M: Then you wouldn't want to visit some of the places I have on my wish list. **32** I've always wanted to visit Northern Canada.

F: Do you prefer cold places?

M: Not really. But **32** I've always wanted to try dog sledding.

F: Really? Why?

남: 오해는 하지 마세요. 그 국가는 아주 좋았어요. 전 그냥 조금 운이 없었어요. 제 호텔의 에어컨이 고장 났거든요. 너무 더워서 밤에 잠을 잘 수가 없었어요.

여: 와우, 그럼 틀림없이 힘드셨겠어요. 싱가포르가 열대 기후라서, 설사 가벼운 옷을 입고 그늘에 머물러 있는다 하더라도 습도 때문에 불편해지니까요.

남: 네. 바깥 공기를 좀 들어 오게 해 보려 했지만, 그때 모기 떼가 날아 들어와서, 모기 물린 자국으로 뒤덮였어요. 아주 끔찍한 일이었어요, 에밀리 씨.

여: 그렇게 좋지 못한 경험을 하셨다니 유감이네요, 루이스 씨. 그 얘기를 하시니까 제가 지난 회사에서 근무하던 중에 알래스카로 보내졌을 때가 다시 생각나네요. 저희가 일했던 건물이 몹시 추웠거든요.

남: 난방 시스템이 고장 났었나요?

여: 아뇨, 그런 것 같진 않아요. 그게 그 건물의 평소 온도라는 얘기를 들었어요. 함께 갔던 나머지 동료 직원들은 그 추위 속에서 그저 괜찮았던 것처럼 보였지만, 저는 평생을 따뜻한 곳에서 살아 왔기 때문에, 겨울 날씨가 제겐 정말 문제였어요.

남: 그러시면 제 희망 사항에 포함되어 있는 곳들 중 몇몇 곳은 방문하시고 싶지 않을 거예요. 저는 항상 캐나다 북부를 방문하고 싶었거든요.

여: 추운 곳을 선호하시나요?

남: 꼭 그렇진 않아요. 하지만 항상 개 썰매 타기를 해 보고 싶었거든요.

여: 정말인가요? 왜요?

M: I love huskies. I used to have one as a kid. He was super playful but, living in the city, it was hard to get all his energy out. The idea of having a pack of them pull me through the snow in their natural habitat sounds like so much fun.

F: Maybe you could convince the boss to send you to Northern Canada.

M: I'll bring it up at the next meeting!

F: Anyway, Louis, **33** a bunch of us are going out for dinner tonight to celebrate the end of the quarter. Want to join us?

M: **33** I'd love to, Emily. Thanks for the invitation!

F: Great. See you there!

남: 제가 허스키를 아주 좋아합니다. 어렸을 때 한 마리 키웠었어요. 굉장히 놀기 좋아했는데, 도시에서 살면, 그 모든 에너지를 분출하게 해 주기가 힘들었어요. 한 무리의 허스키들에게 자연 서식지에서 눈을 헤치며 저를 끌고 가게 하는 생각을 하면 아주 재미있을 것 같아요.

여: 아마 캐나다 북부로 보내 달라고 부장님을 설득해 보실 수도 있을 거예요.

남: 다음 회의 시간에 그 얘기를 꺼내 보려고요!

여: 어쨌든, 루이스 씨, 저희가 단체로 오늘밤에 이번 분기 마지막을 기념하기 위해 저녁 회식을 하러 가요. 함께 가시겠어요?

남: 꼭 가고 싶어요, 에밀리 씨. 초대 감사합니다!

여: 아주 좋습니다. 거기서 봐요!

어휘 **get p.p.** ~되다, ~된 상태가 되다 **such a 명사 that:** 너무 ~해서 …하다 **productive** 생산적인 **follow-up** 후속 조치 **be able to 동사원형:** ~할 수 있다 **the rest of** ~의 나머지 **branch** 지사, 지점 **opportunity to 동사원형:** ~할 수 있는 기회 **get + 목적어 + wrong:** (목적어)의 말을 오해하다 **a bit** 조금, 약간 **broken** 고장 난, 망가진, 깨진 **so A that B:** 너무 A해서 B하다 **rough** 힘든, 어려운 **tropical climate** 열대 기후 **humidity** 습도 **uncomfortable** 불편한 **shade** 그늘 **let in** ~을 들여 보내다 **a bunch of** 한 무리의, 한 묶음의, 다수의 **get covered in** ~로 뒤덮이다 **bite** 물린 자국 **nightmare** 아주 끔찍한 일, 악몽 **remind A of B:** A에게 B를 다시 생각나게 하다, A에게 B를 상기시키다 **employer** 회사, 고용주 **freezing** 몹시 추운 **colleague** 동료 (직원) **seem to 동사원형:** ~하는 것처럼 보이다, ~하는 것 같다 **do fine** 괜찮다, 잘 지내다 **entire** 전체의 **prefer** ~을 선호하다 **dog sledding** 개 썰매 타기 **used to 동사원형:** 전에 ~했다, ~하곤 했다 **super** 굉장히, 대단히 **playful** 놀기 좋아하는 **have + 목적어 + 동사원형:** (목적어)에게 ~하게 하다 **habitat** 서식지 **convince** ~을 설득하다 **bring + 목적어 + up:** (화제 등) (목적어)를 꺼내다 **celebrate** ~을 기념하다, ~을 축하하다 **quarter** 분기 **invitation** 초대(장)

What are Louis and Emily mostly discussing?

(a) study abroad programs
(b) work-related travel
(c) company branch locations
(d) mini-vacation spots

루이스와 에밀리는 주로 무엇을 이야기하고 있는가?

(a) 해외 유학 프로그램
(b) 업무 관련 출장
(c) 회사 지사들
(d) 단기 휴가 장소

정답 (b)

해설 에밀리가 대화 초반부에 루이스에게 출장에서 돌아왔는지 몰랐다며 인사하고 자신들이 회사 비즈니스 때문에 멋진 곳으로 많이 다니고 있어서 아주 좋다고(It's great how our company business takes us to so many cool places) 언급한 뒤로 서로 과거의 출장 경험과 관련해 이야기하고 있으므로 (b)가 정답입니다.

어휘 **A-related** A와 관련된 **branch location** 지사, 지점 **spot** 장소, 지점, 자리

> **패러프레이징**
>
> our company business takes us to so many cool places → work-related travel

What did Louis like most about his Hawaii trip?

(a) He stayed at a luxury hotel.
(b) He ate a lot of delicious food.
(c) He met the love of his life.
(d) He had plenty of time to relax.

루이스는 자신의 하와이 출장과 관련해 무엇을 가장 마음에 들어 했는가?

(a) 고급 호텔에 숙박했다.
(b) 맛있는 음식을 많이 먹었다.
(c) 일생의 사랑을 만났다.
(d) 휴식할 시간이 많이 있었다.

정답 (d)

해설 질문의 키워드인 Hawaii가 언급되는 부분에서 루이스가 작년에 하와이로 보내진 것이 너무 마음에 들었다고 밝히면서 첫째 날에 고객과 아주 생산적인 회의를 한 사실과 그로 인해 출장의 나머지 시간은 해변에서 보낼 수 있었다는 사실을(I loved getting sent to Hawaii last year. We had such a productive meeting with the client on the first day ~ I was able to spend the rest of the trip on the beach) 언급하고 있습니다. 따라서 쉴 수 있는 시간이 많았음을 나타내는 말이므로 (d)가 정답입니다.

어휘 **plenty of** 많은, 충분한 **relax** 휴식하다, 쉬다

29 세부 정보

Why was the Singapore trip Emily's favorite?

(a) because of the people she saw
(b) because of the work she accomplished
(c) because of the places she went
(d) because of the things she learned

에밀리가 싱가포르 출장을 가장 좋아했던 이유는 무엇인가?

(a) 자신이 본 사람들 때문에
(b) 자신이 완수한 일 때문에
(c) 자신이 갔던 장소들 때문에
(d) 자신이 배운 것들 때문에

정답 (a)

해설 질문의 키워드인 Singapore가 언급되는 부분에서 에밀리가 싱가포르 지사로의 출장이 가장 좋았다고 말하면서 그 이유로 오랫동안 보지 못했던 가족과 친구들을 만날 기회가 있었음을(I think my favorite business trip was when I visited the company's branch in Singapore ~ it gave me the opportunity to visit family and friends I hadn't seen in a long time) 밝히고 있습니다. 따라서 사람들을 만났던 기회와 관련해 언급한 (a)가 정답입니다.

어휘 accomplish ~을 완수하다, ~을 이루다

패러프레이징

visit family and friends → the people she saw

30 세부 정보

How did Louis try to deal with the Singapore heat?

(a) by wearing lighter clothes
(b) by purchasing an air conditioner
(c) by opening a window
(d) by finding a spot in the shade

루이스는 어떻게 싱가포르의 열기에 대처하려 했는가?

(a) 더 가벼운 옷을 착용함으로써
(b) 에어컨을 구입함으로써
(c) 창문을 열어 놓음으로써
(d) 그늘 속에 있는 자리를 찾음으로써

정답 (c)

해설 질문의 키워드인 Singapore가 언급되는 부분에서 루이스가 자신의 싱가포르 출장 경험을 이야기하면서 에어컨 고장 문제로 더웠던 밤에 바깥 공기를 들어 오게 하려 했다는(I tried letting in some air from outside) 말로 대처 방안을 언급하고 있으므로 (c)가 정답입니다.

어휘 deal with ~에 대서하다, ~을 처리하나 purchase ~블 구입하다

---

31 세부 정보

Why did Emily have problems with the cold in Alaska?

(a) because there were record low temperatures
(b) because she lost her winter clothes
(c) because the heater needed repair
(d) because she is used to warm places

에밀리는 왜 알래스카의 추위에 대해 문제가 있었는가?

(a) 기온이 기록적으로 낮았기 때문에
(b) 자신의 겨울 옷을 분실했기 때문에
(c) 난방기가 수리를 필요로 했기 때문에
(d) 따뜻한 곳에 익숙하기 때문에

정답 (d)

해설 질문의 키워드인 Alaska가 언급되는 부분에서 에밀리가 그곳의 추운 날씨와 관련해 자신은 평생을 따뜻한 곳에서 살아 왔기 때문에 겨울 날씨가 정말 문제라고(I've lived in warm places my entire life, so the winter weather was really a problem for me) 언급하고 있습니다. 이는 따뜻한 곳이 익숙하다는 뜻이므로 (d)가 정답입니다.

어휘 record low 기록적으로 낮은 temperature 기온, 온도 repair 수리 be used to 명사/동명사: ~에 익숙하다

패러프레이징

have lived in warm places my entire life → is used to warm places

오답 피하기

루이스가 난방 시스템이 고장 났는지 물을 때 heating과 broken을 언급한 것을 듣고 heater와 repair를 포함한 (c)를 정답으로 고르지 않도록 주의해야 합니다.

32 세부 정보

Why does Louis want to travel to Northern Canada?

(a) to explore natural attractions
(b) to try a new activity
(c) to research native animals
(d) to interview for a job

루이스는 왜 캐나다 북부로 출장 가고 싶어 하는가?

(a) 자연 명소를 탐험하기 위해
(b) 새로운 활동을 해 보기 위해
(c) 토종 동물을 연구하기 위해
(d) 취업 면접을 보기 위해

정답 (b)

해설 질문의 키워드인 Northern Canada가 언급되는 부분에서 루이스 씨가 항상 캐나다 북부를 방문하고 싶었다는(I've always wanted to visit Northern Canada) 말과 함께, 그 이유로 개 썰매 타기를 항상 해 보고 싶었다고(I've always wanted to try dog sledding) 언급하고 있습니다. 이는 그곳에서만 할 수 있는 특별한 활동이므로 (b)가 정답입니다.

어휘 explore ~을 탐험하다 attraction 명소, 인기 장서 native 토종의, 토착의

> 패러프레이징
>
> try dog sledding → try a new activity

33 추론

What will Louis probably do after work?

(a) have a meal with his colleagues
(b) head back home to rest
(c) celebrate his recent promotion
(d) prepare for a meeting

루이스는 퇴근 후에 무엇을 할 것 같은가?

(a) 동료 직원들과 식사한다
(b) 쉬기 위해 집으로 돌아간다
(c) 자신의 최근 승진을 기념한다
(d) 회의를 준비한다

정답 (a)

해설 대화 마지막 부분에 에밀리가 단체로 저녁 회식을 하러 간다고 밝히면서 함께 가고 싶은지 묻자(a bunch of us are going out for dinner tonight to celebrate the end of the quarter. Want to join us?), 루이스가 꼭 가고 싶다고 말하면서(I'd love to, Emily. Thanks for the invitation!) 동의하고 있으므로 (a)가 정답입니다.

어휘 recent 최근의 promotion 승진, 홍보, 판촉, 촉진

Hello, and 34 welcome to our tour of the brand-new Thompson School of Business at the University of Fontaine. As prospective students, you might be among the first to attend what we are sure will be one of the best business schools in the country. I'm delighted to be your guide today as we explore some of our state-of-the-art facilities.

We'll begin with our main lecture hall. In addition to regular class lectures, 35 this will also be the location for weekly presentations from successful area business owners. They will share with you their professional journeys and advise you on how to achieve your own success. We already have John Backer, CEO of Solar Blue Recycling, scheduled to be our very first guest speaker. You won't want to miss his recommendations on how to run sustainable businesses.

Across from the lecture hall is the Buckner Memorial Library, which offers an extensive catalogue of the most popular business publications. It features a state-of-the-art computer lab, and 36 it is the only library on campus that's open twenty-four hours a day, every day of the year, so students will always have a quiet place to study and do research.

Just outside the library doors is Fontaine Garden. This large outdoor space is a great place to relax between classes. At the heart of the garden, you'll see a large, bronze statue of General West Fontaine, the founder of the university, made possible through generous alumni donations. 37 He deserves to be recognized for his achievements in making education accessible to everyone. It may also be surprising to know that General Fontaine was a successful businessman in his day. He even had his own chain of hardware stores.

안녕하세요, 그리고 폰테인 대학교의 완전히 새로운 톰슨 경영 대학 견학 시간에 오신 것을 환영합니다. 장래의 학생으로서, 여러분은 저희가 전국 최고의 경영 대학들 중 하나가 될 것으로 확신하는 곳에 다니시는 첫 학생에 속하게 되실지도 모릅니다. 오늘 함께 몇몇 저희 최신 시설을 살펴 보는 과정에서 제가 여러분의 가이드가 되어 기쁩니다.

저희 본관 강당부터 시작해 보겠습니다. 정규 강의뿐만 아니라, 이곳은 또한 성공적인 지역 기업 소유주들의 주간 발표회를 위한 장소가 되기도 합니다. 그분들께서 각자의 직업 여정 이야기를 공유해 드리고 여러분만의 성공을 이루는 방법에 관해 조언해 드릴 것입니다. 이미 솔라 블루 리사이클링 사의 존 베이커 대표 이사님께서 저희의 가장 첫 번째 초청 연사가 되어 주실 예정입니다. 여러분은 지속 가능한 사업체 운영 방법에 관한 이분의 추천 사항들을 놓치고 싶지 않으실 것입니다.

이 강당 건너편에 있는 것은 버크너 기념 도서관으로서, 가장 인기 있는 비즈니스 관련 출판물에 대한 광범위한 도서 목록을 제공합니다. 이곳은 최신 컴퓨터실을 특징으로 하며, 캠퍼스 내에서 연중 매일, 하루 24시간 문을 여는 유일한 도서관이기 때문에, 학생들은 공부하고 연구할 수 있는 조용한 장소를 항상 가질 것입니다.

도서관 출입문 바로 바깥에는 폰테인 정원이 있습니다. 이 넓은 야외 공간은 수업들 사이에 쉴 수 있는 아주 좋은 장소입니다. 이 정원 한복판에서, 넉넉한 동문 기부금을 통해 가능해진, 대학 설립자 웨스트 폰테인 장군의 대형 동상이 보일 것입니다. 폰테인 장군은 모든 사람이 교육을 받을 수 있게 하셨다는 점에서 그 업적에 대해 인정받으셔야 마땅합니다. 폰테인 장군이 당시에 성공적인 사업가이셨다는 사실까지 아시게 되면 놀라워하실 수도 있습니다. 장군님은 심지어 개인 철물점 체인도 보유하셨습니다.

Just south of the garden is the student center. This is where you'll find a branch of the world-famous coffee chain, Redeye Coffee. **38** The coffee shop will be open every weekday from 6 to 11 a.m. so that students can grab a cup of their favorite hot beverage before classes start or choose from Redeye's selection of baked goods, including their famous chocolate espresso muffins.

Finally, we have the Thompson Dormitory. While the rest of the students at the university share a housing complex on the east side of the campus, the Thompson School of Business has its own dorm. This building features single rooms so students have extra privacy to focus on their studies.

Thank you for taking the campus tour. We hope you enjoyed it. Before you go, **39** we are pleased to share that incoming business students are invited to submit an essay about what inspires them to study business for a chance to win a month's worth of vouchers for free meals in the cafeteria. The top five entries will be awarded this valuable prize. We hope to see you soon!

정원 바로 남쪽에 있는 것은 학생 회관입니다. 이곳에서 세계적으로 유명한 커피 체인인 레드아이 커피의 지점을 발견하시게 될 것입니다. 이 커피 매장은 평일에 매일 오전 6시부터 11시까지 문을 열 것이므로 학생들이 수업 시작 전에 잠깐 각자 가장 좋아하는 따뜻한 음료를 한 잔 사갈 수 있으며, 또는 유명한 초콜릿 에스프레소 머핀을 포함해, 레드아이의 다양한 제과제품 중에서 고르실 수 있습니다.

마지막으로, 톰슨 기숙사가 있습니다. 대학의 나머지 학생들이 캠퍼스 동쪽 측면에 위치한 거주용 복합 건물에서 공동 생활하는 반면, 톰슨 경영 대학은 자체 기숙사가 있습니다. 이 건물은 1인실을 특징으로 하고 있어서 학생들이 각자의 공부에 집중할 수 있는 별도의 사생활을 누리게 됩니다.

캠퍼스 견학 시간에 와 주셔서 감사합니다. 즐거우셨기를 바랍니다. 가시기 전에, 경영대 신입생들은 구내식당에서 한 달 치의 무료 식사 쿠폰을 얻을 수 있는 기회를 위해, 경영학을 공부하도록 영감을 주는 것에 관한 에세이를 제출하도록 요청됩니다. 상위 5위까지의 제출작에 대해 이 소중한 상품이 수여됩니다. 곧 뵐 수 있기를 바랍니다!

어휘 brand-new 완전히 새로운 prospective 장래의, 장차 ~가 될 attend ~에 다니다, ~에 참석하다 explore ~을 살펴보다, ~을 탐사하다 state-of-the-art 최신의, 첨단의 facility 시설(물) in addition to ~뿐만 아니라, ~ 외에도 how to 동사원형: ~하는 방법 achieve ~을 이루다, ~을 달성하다 miss ~을 놓치다, ~을 지나치다 run ~을 운영하다 sustainable 지속 가능한 extensive 광범위한, 폭넓은 catalogue 도서 목록 publication 출판(물) feature ~을 특징으로 하다 relax 쉬다, 느긋하게 있다 statue 조각상 generous 넉넉한, 후한, 너그러운 alumni 동문, 동창 donation 기부(금) deserve to 동사원형: ~해야 마땅하다, ~을 받을 자격이 있다 recognize ~을 인정하다 achievement 업적, 성취, 달성 accessible 이용 가능한, 접근 가능한 branch 지점, 지사 grab 잠깐 ~하다 choose from ~에서 선택하다 one's selection of 다양한 the rest of ~의 나머지 dorm 기숙사 extra 별도의, 추가의 privacy 사생활 focus on ~에 집중하다 be invited to 동사원형: ~하도록 요청되다 submit ~을 제출하다 inspire + 목적어 + to 동사원형: (목적어)에게 ~하도록 영감을 주다 worth 가치, 값어치 voucher 쿠폰, 상품권 for free 무료로 entry 제출작, 출품작 award ~을 수여하다, ~을 주다 valuable 소중한, 가치 있는

What is the focus of the talk?	담화의 중점은 무엇인가?
(a) a tour for future students	(a) 미래의 학생들을 위한 견학
(b) a guide for new employees	(b) 신입 직원들을 위한 안내
(c) a tour for visiting parents	(c) 방문한 부모들을 위한 견학
(d) a guide for university faculty	(d) 대학 교수진을 위한 안내

정답 (a)

해설 화자가 담화를 시작하면서 톰슨 경영 대학 견학 시간에 온 것을 환영한다는 인사와 함께 청자들을 장래의 학생이라고(welcome to our tour of the brand-new Thompson School of Business at the University of Fontaine. As prospective students, you might be ~) 지칭하고 있으므로 (a)가 정답입니다.

어휘 faculty 교수진

패러프레이징

prospective students → future students

Why should students attend the weekly presentations?	학생들은 왜 주간 발표회에 참석해야 하는가?
(a) to earn extra credit	(a) 추가 학점을 받기 위해
(b) to learn from professionals	(b) 전문가들로부터 배우기 위해
(c) to meet other students	(c) 다른 학생들을 만나기 위해
(d) to practice public speaking	(d) 대중 연설을 연습하기 위해

정답 (b)

해설 질문의 키워드인 weekly presentations가 언급되는 부분에서 성공적인 기업 소유주들의 주간 발표회를 위한 장소임을 알리면서 그들 각자의 직업 여정 이야기도 공유해 주고 성공을 이루는 방법에 관해 조언해 준다고(~ for weekly presentations from successful area business owners. They will share with you their professional journeys and advise you on how to achieve your own success) 알리고 있습니다. 이는 이미 성공한 전문가들을 통해 배우는 것을 의미하므로 (b)가 정답입니다.

어휘 earn ~을 받다, ~을 얻다 credit 학점 professional n. 전문가 practice ~을 연습하다

패러프레이징

share with you their professional journeys and successful area business owners / advise you on how to achieve your own success → learn from professionals

What is unusual about the business school's library?

(a) It is open to local residents.
(b) It features rare publications.
(c) It is accessible at all times.
(d) It features a research lab.

경영 대학 도서관과 관련해 특이한 점은 무엇인가?

(a) 지역 주민들에게 개방된다.
(b) 희귀 출판물을 특징으로 한다.
(c) 항상 이용 가능하다.
(d) 연구실을 특징으로 한다.

정답 (c)

해설 질문의 키워드인 library가 언급되는 부분에서 연중 매일, 하루 24시간 문을 여는 도서관이라는(it is the only library on campus that's open twenty-four hours a day, every day of the year) 특징을 언급하고 있으므로 (c)가 정답입니다.

어휘 unusual 특이한, 유별난, 흔치 않은 local 지역의, 현지의 resident 주민 rare 희귀한, 드문 at all times 항상 research lab 연구실

패러프레이징

open twenty-four hours a day, every day of the year → accessible at all times

Why, most likely, does the school have a statue of General Fontaine?

(a) because of his business success
(b) because of his military service record
(c) because of his generous donations
(d) because of his educational contributions

학교에 왜 폰테인 장군의 조각상이 있을 것 같은가?

(a) 그의 사업적 성공 때문에
(b) 그의 군 복무 기록 때문에
(c) 그의 넉넉한 기부 때문에
(d) 그의 교육적 공헌 때문에

정답 (d)

해설 질문의 키워드인 a statue of General Fontaine가 언급되는 부분에서 모든 이가 교육을 받을 수 있게 만들었다는 점에서 그 업적에 대해 인정받아야 마땅하다는(He deserves to be recognized for his achievements in making education accessible to everyone) 말로 동상이 세워진 이유를 밝히고 있습니다. 이는 교육 분야에 대한 훌륭한 공헌을 언급하는 것이므로 (d)가 정답입니다.

어휘 service 복무, 재직, 봉사 contribution 공헌, 기여

패러프레이징

his achievements in making education accessible to everyone → his educational contributions

Why, most likely, would students go to the student center?

(a) to grab a quick breakfast
(b) to attend study groups
(c) to meet friends for lunch
(d) to sign up for tutoring

학생들이 왜 학생 회관에 갈 것 같은가?

(a) 간단한 아침 식사를 구입하기 위해
(b) 스터디 그룹에 참석하기 위해
(c) 친구들과 만나 점심 식사하기 위해
(d) 개인 지도를 신청하기 위해

정답 (a)

해설 질문의 키워드인 student center가 언급되는 부분에서 그곳에 있는 한 커피 매장을 소개하면서 평일에 매일 오전 6시부터 11시까지 문을 연다는 사실과 함께 학생들이 수업 시작 전에 따뜻한 음료를 사거나 머핀을 포함한 다양한 제과제품 중에서 선택할 수 있다고(The coffee shop will be open every weekday from 6 to 11 a.m. so that students can grab a cup of their favorite hot beverage before classes start or choose from Redeye's selection of baked goods ~) 알리고 있습니다. 이는 오전 시간에 간단한 아침 식사를 구입할 수 있다는 장점을 말하는 것이므로 (a)가 정답입니다.

어휘 sign up for ~을 신청하다, ~에 등록하다 tutoring 개인 지도, 과외

How can incoming students get vouchers for free meals?

(a) by visiting the housing office
(b) by entering a writing contest
(c) by taking the campus tour
(d) by completing a survey

신입생들은 어떻게 무료 식사 쿠폰을 받을 수 있는가?

(a) 기숙사 관리실을 방문함으로써
(b) 글쓰기 대회에 참가함으로써
(c) 캠퍼스 견학 시간을 이용함으로써
(d) 설문 조사지 작성 완료함으로써

정답 (b)

해설 화자가 담화 맨 마지막 부분에 경영대 신입생들에게 특정 주제로 된 에세이를 제출하도록 요청된다는 사실과 함께 그것이 구내식당에서 한 달 치의 무료 식사 쿠폰을 얻을 수 있는 기회임을(incoming business students are invited to submit an essay ~ for a chance to win a month's worth of vouchers for free meals in the cafeteria) 밝히고 있습니다. 따라서 (b)가 정답입니다.

어휘 free 무료의 enter ~에 참가하다 complete ~을 완료하다 survey 설문 조사(지)

패러프레이징

are invited to submit an essay → entering a writing contest

F: Marvin! 40 I never thought I'd see you here. How do you know the bride and groom?

M: Hey, Tina! I was roommates with the groom in college. What about you?

F: The bride is my cousin.

M: Wow, I never would've guessed. So, how have you been? Are you still working for the same company?

F: Yeah, full-time. But lately 45 I've been seriously considering quitting to go out on my own as a freelancer and be my own boss for a change.

M: I used to freelance before I got my current job. Maybe I could help you decide.

F: Great! I'd love to go over some of the pros and cons.

M: Sure. For starters, what's keeping you at your current job?

F: The biggest reason is that I have stability. I've worked hard to get where I am in the company. I'm responsible for a whole department, and I get lots of vacation time and health insurance benefits.

M: That's great. Having access to a retirement fund is what made me stay in my first corporate job so long.

F: Also, 41 I really love my coworkers and my bosses. We have a great office atmosphere, and we often socialize after work. So, I feel really lucky to have found a work environment with people I'm really comfortable around.

여: 마빈 씨! 이곳에서 볼 줄은 전혀 생각도 하지 못 했어요. 신랑과 신부를 어떻게 아세요?

남: 안녕하세요, 티나 씨! 대학 때 신랑과 룸메이트 였어요. 당신은요?

여: 신부가 제 사촌이에요.

남: 와우, 전혀 짐작도 못했을 거예요. 그래서, 어떻 게 지내셨나요? 여전히 같은 회사에서 근무하 고 계세요?

여: 네, 정규직으로요. 하지만 최근에 변화를 위해 프리랜서로서 따로 독립해 나가서 개인 사업을 하기 위해 그만두는 것을 심각하게 고려해 보고 있어요.

남: 제가 현재의 일자리를 얻기 전에 한때 프리랜서 로 일한 적이 있어요. 아마 제가 결정하시는 데 도움을 드릴 수 있을 거예요.

여: 잘됐네요! 몇몇 장단점을 꼭 짚어 보고 싶어요.

남: 네. 가장 먼저, 현재의 일자리에 계속 있게 해 주 는 것이 뭔가요?

여: 가장 큰 이유는 안정감이 있다는 점이죠. 전 회 사 내에서 현재의 위치를 얻기 위해 열심히 일 해 왔어요. 한 부서 전체를 책임지고 있고, 많은 휴가 시간과 건강 보험 혜택도 얻고 있고요.

남: 잘됐네요. 퇴직 연금을 이용할 수 있다는 게 제 가 첫 직장에서 그렇게 오래 머물러 있게 만들 어 준 것이에요.

여: 그리고, 동료 직원과 상사들이 정말 마음에 들 어요. 훌륭한 사무실 환경이 있고, 흔히 퇴근 후 에 서로 어울려요. 그래서, 함께 하기 정말 편한 사람들이 있는 업무 환경을 찾은 걸 정말 행운 이라고 느껴요.

M: Yeah, that's not something you get everywhere, Tina. So, why are you thinking about leaving?

F: Well, **42** **45** the main disadvantage of my current job is that I feel stuck in this career path. I want to try something completely different, like offering IT services. I've always loved solving people's computer problems.

M: That's a great idea!

F: So, **43** what was the best part about being a freelancer, Marvin?

M: **43** For me, it was the flexible hours. I had the freedom to choose when I worked. That meant I could go for a run in the afternoon before the kids got home from school, and then work again in the evenings if I wanted to. I was free to structure my day the way I wanted to, which improved my productivity.

F: That sounds so nice. I'm not a morning person, and it takes me four cups of coffee to wake up properly. If I could start work whatever time I wanted, I'd probably be a lot more productive.

M: You probably would. I find I do my best work at night, so I can definitely relate to that.

F: **44** Why did you end up going back to a traditional job?

M: Well, despite the benefits, **44** the drawback of being a freelancer is that you routinely have to network and put yourself out there to find jobs. I had to keep about five professional profiles updated online. Eventually, it became a bit too much of an effort.

F: Well, I'm glad things worked out for you in the end.

남: 네, 그건 모든 곳에서 얻게 되는 게 아니죠, 티나 씨. 그럼, 왜 떠날 생각을 하고 계신 거죠?

여: 그게, 현 직장의 주된 단점은 이 진로에만 갇혀 있는 느낌이 든다는 점이에요. 저는 완전히 다른 뭔가를 시도해 보고 싶어요, IT 서비스를 제공하는 일처럼요. 저는 항상 사람들의 컴퓨터 문제를 해결해 주는 걸 아주 좋아했거든요.

남: 아주 좋은 생각입니다!

여: 그럼, 프리랜서가 되는 것과 관련해서 뭐가 가장 좋은 부분인가요, 마빈 씨?

남: 제 경우엔, 탄력적 근무 시간이었어요. 언제 일할지 선택할 수 있는 자유가 있었거든요. 그건 아이들이 학교를 마치고 집에 오기 전에 오후에 달리기를 하러 간 다음, 제가 원하면 저녁 시간대에 다시 일할 수 있었다는 걸 의미하죠. 제가 원하는 방식으로 하루를 자유롭게 구성했는데, 그게 제 생산성을 향상시켜 주었죠.

여: 아주 좋은 것 같아요. 제가 아침형 인간은 아니라서, 제대로 정신이 들기 위해서 커피를 네 잔이나 마셔요. 언제든 제가 원하는 시간에 일을 시작할 수 있다면, 아마 훨씬 더 생산적일 거예요.

남: 아마 그러실 겁니다. 저는 밤에 일이 가장 잘 된다는 걸 알기 때문에, 그 부분에 분명 공감할 수 있어요.

여: 어째서 결국 예전 형태의 일자리로 돌아가시게 된 거죠?

남: 음, 그런 이점들에도 불구하고, 프리랜서가 되는 것의 단점은 일을 찾기 위해 일상적으로 교류 관계를 형성하고 특별히 애를 써야 한다는 점이에요. 저는 온라인에서 약 다섯 가지의 전문 프로필을 계속 업데이트해둬야 했어요. 결국, 좀 너무 과한 노력이 되었죠.

여: 음, 일이 결국 잘 풀리셔서 기쁘네요.

M: Thanks. It was a good move for me. So, do you think you're any closer to making your decision?

F: I think so. I know stability is important but, **45** at the end of the day, I feel like I need a change in my career. Thanks so much for your advice, Marvin!

M: Anytime, Tina!

남: 감사합니다. 제겐 신의 한 수였죠. 그럼, 결정을 내리시는 데 조금이라도 더 가까워지신 것 같으세요?

여: 그런 것 같아요. 안정감이 중요하긴 하지만, 결국에는, 제 경력에 있어 변화가 필요한 것 같아요. 조언 정말 감사합니다, 마빈 씨!

남: 별 말씀을요, 티나 씨!

어휘 **bride** 신부 **groom** 신랑 **What about you?** 당신은 어때요? **would have p.p.** ~했을 것이다 **consider -ing** ~하는 것을 고려하다 **quit** 그만두다 **on one's own** 독립해서, 혼자, 단독으로 **used to 동사원형:** (과거에) 한때 ~했다, ~하곤 했다 **freelance** v. 프리랜서로 일하다 **current** 현재의 **help + 목적어 + 동사원형:** (목적어)가 ~하는 것을 돕다 **go over** ~을 짚어 보다, ~을 검토하다 **pros and cons** 장단점 **stability** 안정(감) **be responsible for** ~을 책임지고 있다 **whole** 전체의 **insurance** 보험 **benefit** 혜택, 이점 **have access to** ~을 이용할 수 있다, ~에 접근할 수 있다 **retirement fund** 퇴직 연금 **atmosphere** 분위기 **socialize** 서로 어울리다 **comfortable** 편한, 편안한 **disadvantage** 단점(= drawback) **stuck in** ~에 갇혀 있는 **completely** 완전히, 전적으로 **solve** ~을 해결하다 **flexible** 탄력적인, 유연한 **choose** 선택하다 **go for** ~하러 가다 **structure** v. ~을 구성하다 **improve** ~을 향상시키다 **productivity** 생산성 **properly** 제대로, 적절히 **a lot** (비교급 강조) 훨씬 **find (that)** ~임을 알게 되다 **definitely** 분명히, 확실히 **relate to** ~에 공감하다 **end up -ing** 결국 ~하게 되다 **traditional** 전통적인, 예전에 하던대로의 **routinely** 일상적으로 **network** 교류 관계를 형성하다, 인적 관계를 형성하다 **put oneself out** 특별히 애쓰다 **keep + 목적어 + p.p.:** (목적어)를 ~된 상태로 유지하다 **about** 약, 대략 **eventually** 결국, 마침내 **a bit too much of** 좀 너무 과한 **things work out for** 일이 ~에게 잘 해결되다 **in the end** 결국, 결과적으로 **a good move** 신의 한 수, 뛰어난 조치 **close to** ~와 가까운

---

40 세부 정보

What event are Marvin and Tina attending?

(a) a college graduation
(b) a business convention
(c) a company retreat
(d) a wedding reception

마빈과 티나는 어떤 행사에 참석하고 있는가?

(a) 대학 졸업식
(b) 비즈니스 컨벤션
(c) 회사 야유회
(d) 결혼 피로연

정답 (d)

해설 티나가 대화를 시작하면서 예상치 못한 곳에서 만났음을 언급하는 말과 함께 신랑 신부를 어떻게 아는지(I never thought I'd see you here. How do you know the bride and groom?) 묻고 있으므로 (d)가 정답입니다.

어휘 **graduation** 졸업(식) **retreat** 야유회, 짧은 여행

❌ 오답 피하기

대화 초반부에 티나의 질문을 들은 마빈이 roommates와 college 같은 단어들을 말하는 것을 듣고 (a)를 정답으로 잘못 고르지 않도록 주의해야 합니다.

Why does Tina feel lucky to work for her current company?

(a) She has a beautiful office.
(b) She is paid generously.
(c) She likes her coworkers.
(d) She can retire early.

티나는 왜 현재의 회사에서 일하는 것을 행운이라고 느끼는가?

(a) 아름다운 사무실에 있다.
(b) 넉넉하게 급여를 받는다.
(c) 동료 직원들을 좋아한다.
(d) 조기 은퇴할 수 있다.

정답 (c)

해설 대화 중반부에 티나가 동료 직원과 상사들이 정말 마음에 든다고 밝히면서 그런 사람들과 함께 하는 업무 환경을 찾은 것이 정말 행운이라고(I really love my coworkers and my bosses. We have a great office atmosphere, and we often socialize after work. So, I feel really lucky ~) 밝히고 있으므로 (c)가 정답입니다.

어휘 generously 넉넉하게, 너그럽게 retire 은퇴하다

Why would Tina consider leaving?

(a) so she can explore a different field
(b) so she can improve her finances
(c) so she can return to a previous employer
(d) so she can complete her training

티나가 그만두기를 고려할 것 같은 이유는 무엇인가?

(a) 그래야 다른 분야를 살펴 볼 수 있으므로
(b) 그래야 자신의 재정 상태를 향상시킬 수 있으므로
(c) 그래야 이전의 회사로 돌아갈 수 있으므로
(d) 그래야 교육을 완료할 수 있으므로

정답 (a)

해설 티나가 대화 중반부에 현 직장의 주된 단점이 그 진로에만 갇혀 있는 느낌이 드는 점이라고 알리면서 IT 서비스를 제공하는 일 같이 완전히 다른 뭔가를 시도해 보고 싶다고(the main disadvantage of my current job is that I feel stuck in this career path. I want to try something completely different, like offering IT services) 언급하고 있습니다. 이는 다른 분야에서 일하고 싶다는 뜻이므로 (a)가 정답입니다.

어휘 explore ~을 살펴 보다, ~을 탐사하다 field 분야 finance 재정, 재무 previous 이전의, 과거의 employer 회사, 고용주 complete ~을 완료하다 training 교육, 훈련

패러프레이징

try something completely different → explore a different field

43

세부 정보

How did being a freelancer benefit Marvin?

(a) by allowing him to work anywhere
(b) by giving him time with his kids
(c) by allowing him to enroll in classes
(d) by giving him more freedom

프리랜서가 되는 것이 마빈에게 어떻게 유익했는가?

(a) 어디서든 일할 수 있게 함으로써
(b) 아이들과 보낼 시간을 제공함으로써
(c) 수업에 등록할 수 있게 함으로써
(d) 더 많은 자유를 제공함으로써

정답 (d)

해설 대화 중반부에 티나가 프리랜서로서 어떤 부분이 가장 좋았는지 묻자(what was the best part about being a freelancer, Marvin?), 마빈이 탄력적 근무 시간을 언급하면서 언제 일할지 선택할 수 있는 자유가 있었다고(For me, it was the flexible hours. I had the freedom to choose when I worked) 대답하고 있으므로 (d)가 정답입니다.

어휘 **benefit** v. ~에게 유익하다 **allow + 목적어 + to 동사원형:** (목적어)에게 ~할 수 있게 해 주다 **enroll in** ~에 등록하다

패러프레이징

flexible hours / had the freedom to choose when I worked → giving him more freedom

❌ 오답 피하기

마빈 씨가 대화 중에 자신의 아이들을 언급하기는 하지만, 아이들과 시간을 보내는 것을 프리랜서로서의 장점으로 말하지는 않고 있으므로 (b)는 오답입니다.

44

세부 정보

Why did Marvin eventually go back to a traditional job?

(a) to return to a regular routine
(b) to stop having to look for work
(c) to network with more people
(d) to gain access to benefits

마빈 씨가 왜 결국 예전 형태의 일자리로 돌아갔는가?

(a) 규칙적인 일상으로 돌아가기 위해
(b) 일을 찾아야 하는 것을 중단하기 위해
(c) 더 많은 사람들과 교류 관계를 형성하기 위해
(d) 혜택에 대한 이용 자격을 얻기 위해

정답 (b)

해설 질문의 키워드인 traditional job이 언급되는 부분에서 마빈은 프리랜서가 되는 것의 단점이 일을 찾기 위해 일상적으로 교류 관계를 형성하고 특별히 애를 써야 한다는(the drawback of being a freelancer is that you routinely have to network and put yourself out there to find jobs) 문제점을 언급하고 있습니다. 따라서 지속적으로 힘들게 일을 찾아야 하는 것을 중단하기 위해 예전 형태의 일자리로 돌아갔음을 알 수 있으므로 (b)가 정답입니다.

어휘 regular 규칙적인, 보통의 routine 일상 look for ~을 찾다 gain ~을 얻다 access to ~에 대한 이용 (자격), ~에 대한 접근 (권한)

> ❌ **오답 피하기**
>
> 일상적으로 교류 관계를 형성하는 것은 결국 프리랜서로서 지속적으로 일을 찾기 위한 과정의 하나로 언급되고 있어 예전 형태의 일자리로 돌아간 이유로 볼 수 없으므로 (b)는 오답입니다.

45 추론

What will Tina probably decide to do?

(a) take some vacation time
(b) interview at another company
(c) become a freelance worker
(d) keep her current position

티나는 무엇을 하기로 결정할 것 같은가?

(a) 쉬는 시간을 좀 갖는다
(b) 다른 회사에서 면접을 본다
(c) 프리랜서가 된다
(d) 현재의 직책을 유지한다

정답 (c)

해설 대화 맨 마지막 부분에 티나가 경력에 있어 변화가 필요한 것 같다는(I feel like I need a change in my career) 결론을 말하고 있습니다. 이는 대화 중반부에 티나가 완전히 다른 뭔가를 시도해 보고 싶다고 밝힌 것을 가리키는데, 대화 초반부에 티나가 최근에 프리랜서로서 일하는 것을 고려하고 있다고(I've been seriously considering quitting to go out on my own as a freelancer) 언급했으므로 (c)가 정답입니다.

어휘 decide to 동사원형: ~하기로 결정하다 position 직책, 일자리

Greetings, and welcome to the *Extra Education* podcast! This month, we've been focusing on extracurricular activities, and last week, I received a letter from a teacher asking me how to put on a school play. Luckily, I've had quite a bit of drama club experience over the years. **46** Allow me to walk you through everything you need to know to put together a fantastic school drama production.

47 The first step is to select a play. While it's tempting to pick one of your personal favorites, make sure it's something that your students can handle. I know a teacher who tried to put on a Shakespeare play with middle schoolers, and the kids barely understood any of the lines they were saying. It made the performances awkward, and I doubt the kids enjoyed themselves very much.

The next step is to assign responsibilities for the cast and crew. Remember, these are students and not professionals, so be careful not to hurt anyone's feelings. If a student isn't well-suited for their first choice, give them a rewarding responsibility doing something else. **48** It's important that they feel included. In one play that I organized at a local school, we had a student who wanted to act but had trouble projecting his voice enough for the audience to hear. He ended up doing a fantastic job overseeing tasks behind the scenes instead.

Step three, of course, is to hold plenty of rehearsals. Some students will have a difficult time remembering lines, so give them enough opportunity to practice and learn their staging. With regular rehearsals, everything will click into place.

안녕하세요, 그리고 <엑스트라 에듀케이션> 팟캐스트에 오신 것을 환영합니다! 이번 달에, 저희는 계속해서 방과 후 활동에 초점을 맞춰 오고 있으며, 지난 주에, 저는 한 교사분으로부터 학교 연극을 올리는 방법을 문의하는 내용의 편지를 받았습니다. 다행히, 제가 수년 동안 연극반을 해 본 경험이 꽤 있습니다. 환상적인 학교 연극 작품을 준비하시기 위해 알아 두셔야 하는 모든 것을 차근차근 설명해 드리겠습니다.

첫 단계는 연극을 선택하는 것입니다. 개인적으로 가장 좋아하시는 것들 중 하나를 고르시는 게 매력적이기는 하지만, 반드시 여러분의 학생들이 다룰 수 있는 것이어야 합니다. 제가 아는 한 교사분은 중학생들과 함께 셰익스피어 연극을 무대에 올리려 하셨는데, 그 아이들은 자신들이 말하는 대사의 어느 것도 거의 이해하지 못했습니다. 이로 인해 그 공연은 어색해졌는데, 저는 그 아이들이 그렇게 많이 즐거웠으리라고 생각하지 않습니다.

다음 단계는 출연진과 스태프들에게 책임을 배정하는 것입니다. 기억하셔야 하는 점은, 이들은 학생들이지 전문가가 아니기 때문에, 그 누구의 감정도 해치지 않게 주의하셔야 한다는 것입니다. 한 학생이 첫 번째 선택에 대해 아주 적합하지 않을 경우에, 그 학생에게 다른 뭔가를 하면서 보람을 느끼는 책임을 맡기십시오. 그 학생이 소속감을 갖는 것이 중요합니다. 제가 한 지역 학교에서 준비했던 연극에서는, 연기를 하고 싶어 했지만 관객들이 알아 들을 만큼 충분히 목소리를 전달하는 데 문제가 있었던 학생이 한 명 있었습니다. 그 학생은 결국 대신 무대 뒤의 일들을 총괄하는 환상적인 역할을 했습니다.

세 번째 단계는, 당연히, 충분한 예행 연습을 진행하시는 것입니다. 어떤 학생들은 대사를 기억하는 데 힘겨운 시간을 보낼 것이므로, 그 학생들에게 충분히 연습하면서 상연 과정을 익힐 기회를 주십시오. 주기적인 예행 연습을 통해, 모든 것이 딱 맞아 떨어지게 될 것입니다.

49 When I was in school, I used to practice my lines with my classmates during lunch. That really helped me to learn the more difficult parts of the script.

50 The fourth step is to build the set. A good set adds visual interest to performances, so it's important to spend time planning and building it. **50** To make things easier, ask if some of the parents have construction experience. Then, spend a weekend with the cast and crew — and some parent volunteers — building and painting the set.

51 The fifth step is to promote the event. Ask your students to post flyers around the community to spread the word. **51** For my first production, we were so focused on the play itself that we forgot to tell anyone other than our families that it was happening. After all that work preparing, we ended up performing in front of a small audience with a lot of empty seats!

52 The last step is to trust your students. By the time the show opens, you've already done your job as director. **52** Let your students do their thing, and don't panic if things don't go perfectly. One of the best performances I've ever seen was when an actor had to deal with the stage lights going out unexpectedly. I thought there would be a pause to fix them, but the actor just added a few lines about a storm in the area and made it feel like part of the show until the lights came back on. That was impressive, and it never would have happened if the director had jumped in to solve things.

So, there you have it: six steps to putting together the perfect school play. Time to get those audition sign-up sheets ready!

제가 학생이었을 때, 저는 반 친구들과 점심 시간에 대사를 연습하곤 했습니다. 그것이 대본에서 더 어려운 부분들을 익히는 데 정말 도움이 되었습니다.

네 번째 단계는 세트를 설치하는 일입니다. 좋은 세트는 공연에 대한 시각적 관심을 더해 주므로, 그것을 계획하고 설치하는 데 시간을 보내는 것이 중요합니다. 더 수월하게 하실 수 있도록, 몇몇 학부모님들께 건설 공사 경험이 있으신지 여쭤 보십시오. 그런 다음, 출연진 및 스태프, 그리고 몇몇 자원 봉사하시는 학부모님들과 세트를 만들고 페인트칠하시면서 주말을 보내 보십시오.

다섯 번째 단계는 그 행사를 홍보하는 일입니다. 입소문을 낼 수 있도록 학생들에게 지역 사회 곳곳에 전단을 붙이도록 요청하십시오. 제 첫 작품의 경우에, 저희가 연극 자체에 너무 집중하는 바람에 공연이 열린다는 사실을 저희 가족 외의 다른 사람에게 알리는 것을 잊었습니다. 그 모든 작업 준비 끝에, 저희는 결국 많은 좌석이 텅 비어 있는 상태로 소규모의 관객 앞에서 공연하게 되었습니다!

마지막 단계는 여러분의 학생들을 믿는 것입니다. 공연이 개막할 때쯤, 여러분께서는 연출자로서의 일을 이미 완료하신 것입니다. 학생들에게 그들의 일을 맡겨 두시고, 완벽히 진행되지 않더라도 당황하지 마십시오. 제가 본 가장 좋은 공연들 중 하나는 한 배우가 예기치 못하게 꺼진 무대 조명에 대처해야 했던 경우였습니다. 저는 그것을 고치기 위해 일시 중단이 될 줄 알았지만, 그 배우는 그저 그 지역 내의 폭풍우에 관해 몇 마디 대사를 추가했고, 조명이 다시 들어올 때까지 그것이 공연의 일부처럼 느끼게 만들었습니다. 그 모습은 인상적이었고, 연출자가 문제를 해결하기 위해 뛰어 들었다면 절대 일어나지 못했을 것입니다.

자, 여기까지가 완벽한 학교 연극을 준비하시는 여섯 가지 단계였습니다. 이제 오디션 참가 신청서를 준비해 두실 시간이군요!

어휘 **focus on** ~에 초점을 맞추다, ~에 집중하다 **extracurricular** 방과 후의, 정규 교과 외의 **how to 동사원형**: ~하는 방법 **put on a play** 연극을 무대에 올리다 **quite a bit of** 꽤 많이 **allow + 목적어 + to 동사원형**: (목적어)가 ~할 수 있게 해 주다 **walk A through B**: A에게 B를 차근차근 설명하다 **put together** ~을 준비하다, ~을 조립하다 **production** 제작(된 작품) **tempting** 매력적인, 솔깃한 **pick** ~을 고르다 **make sure (that)** 반드시 ~하도록 하다 **handle** ~을 다루다, ~을 처리하다 **barely** 거의 ~ 않다 **line** 대사 **awkward** 어색한, 곤란한, 골치 아픈 **doubt (that)** ~하다고 생각하지 않다, ~하는 데 의구심을 갖다 **assign** ~을 부여하다, ~을 배정하다 **responsibility** 책임(감) **cast** 출연진 **crew** 스태프 **professional** n. 전문가 **be careful (not) to 동사원형**: ~하도록(하지 않도록) 주의하다 **be well-suited for** ~에 아주 적합하다 **rewarding** 보람 있는 **feel included** 소속감을 갖다 **organize** ~을 준비하다, ~을 조직하다 **local** 지역의, 현지의 **have trouble -ing** ~하는 데 문제가 있다 **project** v. (소리 등) ~을 전하다 **end up -ing** 결국 ~하게 되다 **oversee** ~을 총괄하다 **task** 일, 업무 **hold** ~을 진행하다, ~을 개최하다 **rehearsal** 예행 연습 **opportunity to 동사원형**: ~할 수 있는 기회 **practice** 연습하다 **staging** 상연 **click into place** 딱 맞아떨어지다 **used to 동사원형**: (과거에) ~하곤 했다, 전에 ~했다 **script** 대본 **interest** 관심 **performance** 공연 **spend time -ing** ~하면서 시간을 보내다 **volunteer** 자원 봉사자 **promote** ~을 홍보하다 **post** ~을 붙이다, ~을 게시하다 **flyer** 전단 **spread the word** 입소문을 내다 **so A that B**: 너무 A해서 B하다 **forget to 동사원형**: ~하는 것을 잊다 **by the time** ~할 때쯤(이면) **panic** 당황하다 **go perfectly** 완벽히 진행되다 **deal with** ~에 대처하다, ~을 처리하다 **go out** (전기 등이) 나가다, 꺼지다 **unexpectedly** 예기치 못하게 **fix** ~을 고치다 **impressive** 인상적인 **would have p.p.** ~했을 것이다 **solve** ~을 해결하다 **there you have it** (설명 등의 마지막 순서에) 여기까지입니다 **get + 목적어 + ready**: (목적어)를 준비해 두다 **sign-up** 신청, 등록

46 주제/목적

What is the speaker mostly talking about?

(a) funding a student drama club
(b) acting in an afterschool play
(c) putting on a stage production
(d) persuading kids to do theater

화자는 주로 무엇에 관해 이야기하고 있는가?

(a) 학생 연극반에 자금을 제공하는 일
(b) 방과 후 연극에서 연기하는 일
(c) 무대 공연 작품을 올리는 일
(d) 연극 공연을 하도록 아이들을 설득하는 일

정답 (c)

해설 화자가 담화 초반부에 한 교사가 학교 연극을 올리는 방법을 문의한 것을 언급하면서 학교 연극 작품을 준비하기 위해 알아 둬야 하는 모든 것을 차근차근 설명해 주겠다고(Allow me to walk you through everything you need to know to put together a fantastic school drama production) 알린 뒤로 그 제작 과정을 단계별로 설명하고 있으므로 (c)가 정답입니다.

어휘 **fund** v. ~에 자금을 제공하다 **persuade** ~을 설득하다 **do theater** 연극 공연을 하다

패러프레이징

put together a fantastic school drama production → putting on a stage production

Based on the talk, what kind of play should a teacher probably select for middle schoolers?

(a) one with a lot of roles
(b) one that is manageable
(c) one with a lot of humor
(d) one that is challenging

담화 내용에 따르면, 교사는 중학생들을 위해 어떤 종류의 연극을 선택해야 할 것 같은가?

(a) 배역이 많이 있는 것
(b) 감당할 수 있는 것
(c) 유머가 많이 있는 것
(d) 도전 의식을 불러일으키는 것

정답 (b)

해설 담화 초반부에 화자가 첫 번째 단계로 연극을 선택하는 것을 언급하면서 반드시 학생들이 다룰 수 있는 것이어야 한다고 (The first step is to select a play. ~ make sure it's something that your students can handle) 알리고 있습니다. 이는 학생들이 감당할 수 있는 연극을 선택하도록 권하는 것이므로 (b)가 정답입니다.

어휘 manageable 감당할 수 있는 challenging 도전 의식을 불러일으키는, 까다로운

패러프레이징

can handle → manageable

How did the speaker make a particular student feel included?

(a) He assigned him a small role.
(b) He invited him to audition.
(c) He gave him time to practice.
(d) He let him work backstage.

화자는 어떻게 한 특정 학생이 소속감을 갖도록 만들었는가?

(a) 그에게 작은 배역을 배정했다.
(b) 오디션에 초대했다.
(c) 연습할 시간을 주었다.
(d) 무대 뒤에서 일하게 해 주었다.

정답 (d)

해설 질문의 키워드인 feel included가 언급되는 부분에서 화자는 소속감을 갖는 것의 중요성과 함께 한 학생과 관련된 일화를 소개하면서 목소리 전달 문제가 있었던 그 학생이 무대 뒤의 일들을 총괄하는 환상적인 역할을 했다고(~ had trouble projecting his voice enough for the audience to hear. He ended up doing a fantastic job overseeing tasks behind the scenes instead) 이야기하고 있으므로 (d)가 정답입니다.

어휘 particular 특정한, 특별한 let + 목적어 + 동사원형: (목적어)가 ~하게 해 주다

패러프레이징

overseeing tasks behind the scenes → work backstage

49 세부 정보

What helped the speaker to learn his lines?

(a) going over them with friends
(b) attending all the rehearsals
(c) practicing them backstage
(d) tying them to staging

무엇이 대사를 익히도록 화자에게
도움을 주었는가?

(a) 친구들과 함께 살펴 본 것
(b) 모든 예행 연습에 참석한 것
(c) 무대 뒤에서 연습한 것
(d) 대사를 발판에 묶어 매달아 놓은
것

정답 (a)

해설 담화 중반부에 화자가 자신이 학생이었을 때 반 친구들과 점심 시간에 대사를 연습했던 것이 정말 도움이 되었다는(When I was in school, I used to practice my lines with my classmates during lunch. That really helped me ~) 사실을 밝히고 있으므로 (a)가 정답입니다.

어휘 go over ~을 살펴 보다, ~을 검토하다 attend ~에 참석하다 tie A to B: A를 B에 묶어 매달다 staging 발판, 비계

패러프레이징

practice my lines with my classmates → going over them with friends

50 세부 정보

How does the speaker suggest making set construction easier?

(a) by hiring a professional team
(b) by keeping the design simple
(c) by asking parents to help
(d) by using items from past shows

화자는 어떻게 세트 설치 작업을 더
쉽게 만들도록 제안하는가?

(a) 전문 팀을 고용해서
(b) 디자인을 단순하게 유지해서
(c) 학부모들에게 돕도록 요청해서
(d) 과거의 공연 물품을 이용해서

정답 (c)

해설 질문의 키워드인 make set construction easier가 언급되는 부분에서 화자는 세트 설치와 관련해 더 수월하게 하려면 학부모님들에게 건설 공사 경험이 있는지 물어 보는 방법을(To make things easier, ask if some of the parents have construction experience) 언급하였습니다. 이는 학부모들에게 도움을 요청하는 것이므로 (c)가 정답입니다.

어휘 suggest -ing ~하도록 제안하다 hire ~을 고용하다 keep + 목적어 + 형용사: (목적어)를 ~하게 유지하다 ask + 목적어 + to 동사원형: (목적어)에게 ~하도록 요청하다 past 과거의, 지난

패러프레이징

ask if some of the parents have construction experience → asking parents to help

Why did the speaker's first production have such a small audience?

(a) because of a competing event
(b) because he failed to advertise
(c) because of a sudden storm
(d) because he had limited seating

화자의 첫 공연 작품은 왜 그렇게 관객이 적었는가?

(a) 경쟁하는 행사 때문에
(b) 광고하지 못했기 때문에
(c) 갑작스러운 폭풍우 때문에
(d) 좌석이 제한되어 있었기 때문에

정답 (b)

해설 질문의 키워드인 first production이 언급되는 부분에서 화자는 연극 자체에 너무 집중하는 바람에 공연이 열린다는 사실을 가족 외의 다른 사람에게 알리는 것을 잊었다고(For my first production, we were so focused on the play itself that we forgot to tell anyone other than our families that it was happening) 언급하고 있습니다. 따라서 연극 공연을 광고하지 못한 것이 관객이 적었던 이유임을 알 수 있으므로 (b)가 정답입니다.

어휘 competing 경쟁하는, 겨루는 fail + to 동사원형: ~하지 못하다, ~하는 데 실패하다 advertise 광고하다 sudden 갑작스러운 limited 제한적인 seating 좌석 (공간)

패러프레이징

forgot to tell anyone other than our families that it was happening → failed to advertise

---

According to the talk, what can a director do to show trust in students?

(a) let them solve problems on their own
(b) invite them to suggest favorite plays
(c) encourage them to stop the show if needed
(d) allow them to introduce the performance

담화 내용에 따르면, 연출자가 학생들에게 신뢰를 보여 주기 위해 무엇을 할 수 있는가?

(a) 스스로 문제를 해결하게 한다
(b) 가장 좋아하는 연극을 제안하도록 요청한다
(c) 필요할 경우에 공연을 중단하도록 권한다
(d) 공연을 소개할 수 있게 해 준다

정답 (a)

해설 질문의 키워드인 trust와 students가 언급되는 부분에서 화자는 마지막 단계로 학생들을 믿는 것을 언급하면서(The last step is to trust your students) 학생들에게 그들의 일을 맡겨 두라고(Let your students do their thing) 알리고 있습니다. 이는 공연과 관련해 학생들이 스스로 문제를 헤쳐 나가도록 맡겨 두라는 뜻이므로 (a)가 정답입니다.

어휘   show trust in ~에 대한 신뢰를 보이다   let + 목적어 + 동사원형: (목적어)가 ~하게 하다   solve ~을 해결하다   on one's own 스스로   invite + 목적어 + to 동사원형: (목적어)가 ~하도록 요청하다   encourage + 목적어 + to 동사원형: (목적어)가 ~하도록 권하다   if needed 필요할 경우에   allow + 목적어 + to 동사원형: (목적어)가 ~할 수 있게 해 주다   introduce ~을 소개하다

패러프레이징

Let your students do their thing → let them solve problems on their own

Reading & Vocabulary

PART 1

ROALD DAHL

53 Roald Dahl was a British writer best known for authoring children's fantasy books that mix clever storytelling with dark humor. His stories have been adapted into multiple films, plays, and television shows.

Dahl was born in 1916 in Cardiff, Wales, after his parents had emigrated from Norway. Unfortunately, when Dahl was three years old, both his sister and **54(a)** his father died unexpectedly. School was also a tough environment for Dahl, and **54(d)** he received poor grades. **54(b)** He was once punished by his headmaster for putting a mouse inside a jar of candy as a prank. Incidents like this were later used in his writing.

After graduating high school, Dahl avoided staying home and attending college, saying he preferred to take a job that would send him to "wonderful **58** faraway places." **55** He went to work for an oil company that sent him to Tanzania, Africa. Later, when World War II broke out, Dahl joined the Royal Air Force. While flying his first mission, he was forced to make a crash landing in Libya but was eventually rescued. The experience gave him material for his first short story collection, *Over to You: Ten Stories of Flyers and Flying*.

Initially, Dahl wrote for adults, but he later turned to children's literature. *James and the Giant Peach*, his first young adult novel, exemplifies Dahl's surreal, creative style. In the book, an impoverished young boy discovers an enormous magical peach. He befriends seven magically transformed insects and, together, they escape James's cruel aunts. James

로알드 달

로알드 달은 기발한 이야기 전개를 블랙 유머와 혼합한 아동용 판타지 도서를 집필한 것으로 가장 잘 알려져 있는 영국 작가였다. 그의 이야기는 다수의 영화와 연극, 그리고 텔레비전 프로그램으로 각색되어 왔다.

달은 부모님이 노르웨이에서 이주한 후, 웨일즈의 카디프에서 1916년에 태어났다. 안타깝게도, 달이 세 살이었을 때, 누나와 아버지가 모두 예기치 못하게 사망했다. 학교도 달에게는 힘든 환경이었으며, 그는 좋지 못한 성적을 받았다. 한 번은 장난 삼아 쥐 한 마리를 사탕 병에 넣었다가 교장 선생님에게 벌을 받기도 했다. 이런 일들은 나중에 그의 집필 활동에 이용되었다.

고등학교 졸업 후, 달은 집에 있으면서 대학교에 다니는 것을 피했고, "아주 멋진 멀리 떨어진 곳"으로 자신을 보내 줄 일자리를 얻는 것을 선호한다고 말했다. 그는 자신을 아프리카의 탄자니아로 보낸 한 정유회사에 일하러 갔다. 나중에, 2차 세계 대전이 발발했을 때, 달은 영국 공군에 입대했다. 자신의 첫 임무를 위해 비행하는 동안, 어쩔 수 없이 추락해 리비아에 착륙해야 했지만, 결국 구조되었다. 그 경험이 그에게 첫 단편 소설 모음집인 『오버 투 유: 비행사와 비행에 관한 10가지 이야기』에 대한 소재를 제공해 주었다.

처음에, 달은 성인을 위해 글을 썼지만, 나중에 아동 문학으로 눈을 돌렸다. 첫 청소년 소설인 『제임스와 거대한 복숭아』는 달의 초현실적이고 창의적인 문체를 잘 보여 주는 좋은 예이다. 이 책에서, 빈곤한 한 어린 소년이 거대한 마법 복숭아를 발견한다. 그는 마법으로 변신한 일곱 마리 곤충들과 친구가 되며, 함께, 제임스의 잔혹한 이모들에게서 달아

is an orphan, and **56** many of Dahl's stories involve missing parents, possibly inspired by the loss of his own father.

57 Dahl told his daughters stories every night, and he tried to incorporate details he knew children enjoyed: magic and adventure, along with grotesque elements. His nightly storytelling incorporated memories of his childhood trips to Norway, where he had discovered fantastic tales of trolls and sorcerers. Although his stories often lack a clear moral, many of the characters must use their imaginations to survive in a cruel world.

Dahl died in 1990 in Oxford, England. In 2023, many of his books were censored after being **59** deemed inappropriate for young readers. However, after public outcry, the books were reissued in their full versions. Despite ongoing debates over his work, Dahl remains one of the greatest children's storytellers of the twentieth century.

난다. 제임스는 고아이며, 달의 소설 대부분이 부모를 잃은 것과 관련되어 있는데, 아버지를 여읜 것에서 영감을 얻었을 가능성이 있다.

달은 매일밤 자신의 딸들에게 이야기를 해 주었으며, 아이들이 즐거워하는 것으로 알고 있던 세부 요소들, 즉 기괴한 요소들과 함께, 마법과 모험을 포함하려 했다. 그가 밤마다 해 준 이야기는 자신의 어렸을 적 노르웨이 여행에 대한 기억을 포함하고 있었는데, 그곳에서 그는 트롤과 마법사에 관한 환상적인 이야기들을 발견했다. 비록 그의 이야기가 종종 명확한 교훈이 부족하기는 하지만, 많은 등장인물들이 반드시 각자의 상상력을 이용해 잔인한 세계에서 생존한다.

달은 1990년에 잉글랜드의 옥스퍼드에서 사망했다. 2023년에, 많은 그의 도서들이 어린 독자들에게 부적합한 것으로 여겨진 후 검열되었다. 하지만, 대중의 항의 후에, 이 도서들은 온전한 버전으로 재발간되었다. 그의 작품을 두고 계속되는 논란에도 불구하고, 달은 20세기의 가장 위대한 아동 작가들 중 한 명으로 여전히 남아 있다.

TEST 04

어휘 best known for ~로 가장 잘 알려진 author v. ~을 집필하다 mix A with B: A와 B를 혼합하다 adapt ~을 각색하다 multiple 다수의, 다양한 play n. 연극 emigrate 이주하다 unfortunately 안타깝게도, 유감스럽게도 unexpectedly 예기치 못하게, 뜻밖에 receive ~을 받다 grade 성적, 점수, 등급 punish ~에게 벌을 주다 prank 장난 incident 일, 사건 avoid -ing ~하는 것을 피하다 prefer to 동사원형: ~하는 것을 선호하다 faraway 멀리 떨어진 break out (전쟁 등) 발발하다, 발생하다 mission 임무 be forced to 동사원형: 어쩔 수 없이 ~하다 make crash 추락하다 land v. 착륙하다 rescue ~을 구조하다 material 소재, 재료 initially 처음에 turn to (관심, 주의 등) ~로 돌리다 exemplify ~의 좋은 예가 되다 surreal 초현실적인 creative 창의적인 impoverished 빈곤한 discover ~을 발견하다 enormous 거대한 befriend ~와 친구가 되다 transform ~을 변모시키다 insect 곤충 escape ~에서 달아나다 cruel 잔혹한 orphan 고아 involve ~와 관련되다 inspire ~에게 영감을 주다 incorporate ~을 포함하다 details 세부 요소 grotesque 기괴한, 기이한 element 요소 tale 이야기 sorcerer 마법사 lack ~이 부족하다 moral 교훈, 도덕(성) imagination 상상(력) survive 생존하다 censor ~을 검열하다 be deemed 형용사: ~한 것으로 여겨지다 inappropriate 부적합한 outcry (대중의) 항의 reissue ~을 재발간하다 ongoing 계속되는 debate 논란, 논쟁, 토론 remain ~로 계속 남아 있다

What is Roald Dahl best known for?

(a) his tales for young audiences
(b) his timeless mystery movies
(c) his books for adult readers
(d) his acclaimed children's poetry

로알드 달은 무엇으로 가장 잘 알려져 있는가?

(a) 어린 독자들을 위한 이야기
(b) 시대를 초월한 미스터리 영화
(c) 성인 독자들을 위한 도서
(d) 호평을 받는 동시

정답 (a)

해설 질문의 키워드인 best known for는 지문의 첫 문단 best known for로 표현되어 있습니다. 해당 문장에 따르면 로알드 달은 아동용 판타지 도서를 집필한 것으로 가장 잘 알려져 있는 영국 작가라고(Roald Dahl was a British writer best known for authoring children's fantasy books ~) 소개되어 있으므로 어린 독자들을 위한 이야기를 의미하는 (a)가 정답입니다.

어휘 audience 독자들, 청중, 시청자들 timeless 시대를 초월한 acclaimed 호평을 받는, 찬사를 받는

> **패러프레이징**
>
> children's fantasy books → tales for young audiences

Which of the following is NOT mentioned in the article about Dahl's youth?

(a) He lost one of his parents at an early age.
(b) He got in trouble with a school administrator.
(c) He was taken away from his family as an infant.
(d) He performed poorly as a young student.

다음 중 달의 어린 시절과 관련해 기사에 언급되지 않은 것은 무엇인가?

(a) 어린 나이에 부모님 중 한 분을 잃었다.
(b) 학교 행정 책임자와 문제가 있었다.
(c) 갓난 아기일 때 가족과 멀리 떨어지게 되었다.
(d) 어린 학생일 때 성적이 좋지 못했다.

정답 (c)

해설 달의 어린 시절과 관련된 정보가 제시된 두 번째 문단에, 아버지의 예기치 못한 사망(his father died unexpectedly), 성적이 좋지 못했던 점(he received poor grades), 그리고 교장 선생님에게 벌을 받은 일(He was once punished by his headmaster)이 언급되어 있어 (a)와 (b), 그리고 (d)의 내용을 각각 확인할 수 있습니다. 하지만, 갓난 아기일 때 가족과 멀리 떨어져 지낸 것은 지문에 제시되어 있지 않으므로 (c)가 정답입니다.

어휘 get in trouble with ~와 문제가 있다 administrator 행정 책임자 infant 유아 perform poorly 성적이 좋지 못하다

Why, most likely, did Dahl move to another country?

(a) to attend a prestigious university
(b) to take a new position with his employer
(c) to serve as a member of the military
(d) to research material for his stories

달이 왜 다른 국가로 이주했을 것 같은가?

(a) 명문 대학교에 다니기 위해
(b) 회사에서 새로운 직책을 맡기 위해
(c) 군인의 한 명으로서 복무하기 위해
(d) 자신의 이야기에 필요한 소재를 조사하기 위해

정답 (b)

해설 질문의 키워드인 move to another country는 세 번째 문단에 sent him to Tanzania, Africa로 표현되었습니다. 해당 문장에서 자신을 아프리카의 탄자니아로 보낸 한 정유회사에 근무한(He went to work for an oil company that sent him to Tanzania, Africa) 사실이 언급되어 있어 한 회사에서 직책을 맡아 근무한 것을 의미하는 (b)가 정답입니다.

어휘 attend ~에 다니다, ~에 출석하다 prestigious 명문의, 권위 있는 position 직책, 일자리 employer 회사, 고용주 serve 복무하다, 재직하다 research ~을 조사하다, ~을 연구하다

> **패러프레이징**
>
> work for an oil company that sent him to Tanzania, Africa → take a new position with his employer

> ❌ **오답 피하기**
>
> 2차 세계 대전이 발발했을 때 군인으로서 복무한 사실이 언급되어 있기는 하지만 다른 국가로 이주해서 복무한 것은 아니므로 (c)는 오답입니다.

What is mentioned in the article as being a common theme in most of Dahl's stories?

(a) the search for a missing treasure
(b) the tragedy of growing up without a parent
(c) the quest for additional knowledge
(d) the struggle to overcome childhood poverty

기사에서 달의 이야기 대부분에서 일반적인 주제로서 언급된 것은 무엇인가?

(a) 사라진 보물 찾기
(b) 부모 없는 성장의 비극
(c) 추가적인 정보의 탐색
(d) 어린 시절의 가난을 극복하기 위한 힘겨움

정답 (b)

해설 질문의 키워드 common theme in most of Dahl's stories는 네 번째 문단에 many of Dahl's stories involve로 표현되어 있습니다. 해당 문장에 따르면 달의 소설 대부분이 부모를 잃은 것과 관련되어 있다는(many of Dahl's stories involve missing parents) 말로 그의 소설에 흔히 이용되는 주제가 언급되어 있으므로 (b)가 정답입니다.

어휘 treasure 보물 tragedy 비극 grow up 성장하다 quest 탐색, 탐구 struggle to 동사원형: ~하기 위한 힘겨움 overcome ~을 극복하다 poverty 가난

패러프레이징

missing parents → growing up without a parent

---

57 세부 정보

Based on the fifth paragraph, how, most likely, did Dahl develop his stories?

(a) by adapting lessons from well-known fairytales
(b) by recounting memories shared by his mother
(c) by observing everyday events in the world
(d) by entertaining his children at bedtime

다섯 번째 문단에 따르면, 달은 어떻게 자신의 이야기를 개발했는가?

(a) 잘 알려진 동화 속의 교훈을 각색함으로써
(b) 어머니와 함께 나눈 기억을 이야기함으로써
(c) 세상의 일상적인 사건들을 관찰함으로써
(d) 잠자리에 드는 시간에 자신의 아이들을 즐겁게 해 줌으로써

정답 (d)

해설 다섯 번째 문단에 아이들이 즐거워하는 것으로 알고 있는 세부 요소들을 포함해 매일 밤 자신의 딸들에게 이야기를 해 준(Dahl told his daughters stories every night, and he tried to incorporate details he knew children enjoyed ~) 방식이 언급되어 있으므로 잠자리에 드는 시간에 자신의 아이들을 즐겁게 해 준 일을 의미하는 (d)가 정답입니다.

어휘 develop ~을 개발하다, ~을 발전시키다 adapt ~을 각색하다 well-known 잘 알려진 fairytale 동화 recount ~을 이야기하다 observe ~을 관찰하다 entertain ~을 즐겁게 해 주다

패러프레이징

told his daughters stories every night / incorporate details he knew children enjoyed → entertaining his children at bedtime

In the context of the passage, <u>faraway</u> means _____.

(a) relaxing
(b) lost
(c) distant
(d) hidden

해당 단락의 문맥에서 <u>faraway</u>가 의미하는 것은?

(a) 느긋하게 해 주는, 마음 편한
(b) 잃어버린, 분실한
(c) 멀리 있는
(d) 숨겨진

정답 (c)

해설 해당 문장에서 명사구 wonderful faraway places는 전치사 to의 목적어로서 달이 보내질 장소들을 가리키며, faraway는 또 다른 형용사 wonderful과 함께 places를 수식해 그 장소의 특징을 나타냅니다. 바로 다음 문장에 아프리카의 탄자니아로 보내졌다는 사실이 쓰여 있어 '아주 먼' 등을 의미하는 형용사임을 알 수 있으므로 '멀리 있는'을 뜻하는 (c) distant가 정답입니다.

In the context of the passage, <u>deemed</u> means _____.

(a) judged
(b) made
(c) proven
(d) turned

해당 단락의 문맥에서 <u>deemed</u>가 의미하는 것은?

(a) 판단된
(b) 만들어진
(c) 판명된
(d) 돌려진, 거꾸로 된

정답 (a)

해설 해당 문장에서 deemed 뒤에 '부적합한'을 뜻하는 형용사 inappropriate이 쓰여 있어 being deemed inappropriate가 검열을 당한 이유임을 알 수 있습니다. 따라서 being deemed inappropriate가 '부적합한 것으로 생각되었음' 등을 뜻하는 것으로 볼 수 있는데, 이는 그러한 수준으로 판단되었다는 의미와 같으므로 '판단된'을 뜻하는 (a) judged가 정답입니다.

❌ 오답 피하기

검열을 거친 후에 부적합한 것으로 결정되어야 '판명되었다'라는 말로 표현할 수 있는데, after being deemed inappropriate은 검열 전의 과정에 해당하므로 (c)는 오답입니다.

PART 2

WHY BIRTHDAY CAKES ARE SERVED

At modern birthday parties, we eat cake and blow out birthday candles. Cake styles worldwide range from simple to **65** elaborate. This delicious treat is also available in countless flavors, from traditional vanilla to more exotic sweet and savory concoctions. **60** But how did the tradition of having cake on birthdays originate?

For much of human history, birthdays were not celebrated at all. **61** The first reference to such a celebration is the Bible's description of an Egyptian pharaoh's birthday that took place around 3000 BCE. However, it is likely that this celebration did not mark the pharaoh's birth date, but rather the date when he became ruler of Egypt and was thus born again as a god.

The ancient Greeks were the first to observe a public event with cake and candles. To celebrate Artemis, goddess of the moon, they made round cakes that represented the lunar sphere and topped these cakes with candles to imitate rays of moonlight. The ancient Romans used a similar unsweetened cake (made of flour, olive oil, nuts, and cheese) for birthdays, but only to **66** commemorate the fiftieth year—and **62** only if the citizen was a famous man. Women's birthdays were not celebrated until much later.

Kinderfest, a German holiday that began in the eighteenth century, is credited for popularizing birthday cakes as we know them today. Each birthday, children would receive a cake with lit candles signifying their age, with an extra candle to bestow good luck in the following year. That evening, after dinner, when the candles had nearly burned down, **63** the birthday child could blow them out, make a wish, and enjoy their treat.

생일 케이크가 제공되는 이유

현대의 생일 파티에서, 우리는 케이크를 먹고 생일 초를 불어서 끈다. 케이크 스타일은 단순한 것에서 부터 복잡한 것에 이르기까지 세계적으로 그 범위 가 다양하다. 이 맛있는 특별 음식은 또한 전통적인 바닐라에서부터 더 많은 이국적인 달콤함과 풍미 있는 혼합물에 이르기까지, 수없이 많은 맛으로도 이용 가능하다. 그런데 생일에 케이크를 먹는 전통 은 어떻게 유래했을까?

인류 역사의 많은 부분 동안, 생일은 전혀 기념되지 않았다. 이러한 기념 행사에 대한 최초의 참고 자료 는 기원전 3000년경에 열렸던 한 이집트 파라오의 생일에 대한 성경의 묘사이다. 하지만, 이 기념 행 사는 그 파라오의 생일을 기념한 것이 아니라, 그가 이집트의 통치자가 되어 그 결과로 한 명의 신으로 서 다시 태어난 날을 기념한 것일 가능성이 있다.

케이크와 양초로 공공 행사를 처음 기념한 사람들 은 고대 그리스인들이었다. 달의 여신인, 아르테미 스를 축하하기 위해, 그들은 달의 구체를 표현하는 둥근 케이크를 만들었으며, 달빛의 광선을 모방하 기 위해 이 케이크의 상단에 양초를 얹었다. 고대 로마인들은 생일을 위해 달지 않게 만든 유사한 케 이크를(밀가루와 올리브 오일, 견과류, 그리고 치즈 로 만든) 이용했지만, 오직 50세를 기념하기 위한 것이었으며, 해당 시민이 유명한 남성인 경우에만 해당되었다. 여성의 생일은 훨씬 더 나중에서야 기 념되었다.

18세기에 시작된 독일의 휴일인, 킨더페스트는 우 리가 오늘날 아는 바와 같이 생일 케이크를 대중화 시킨 것으로 인정받고 있다. 각 생일에, 아이들은 불을 붙여 자신의 나이를 나타내는 초가 있는 케이 크를 받곤 했으며, 이듬해에 대해 행운을 부여하는 별도의 초가 하나 더 있었다. 당일 저녁, 저녁 식사 를 마친 후, 초가 거의 타내려갔을 때, 생일인 아이 가 불어서 끄고 소원을 빈 다음, 그 특별 선물을 즐 길 수 있었다.

For decades, birthdays cake ingredients were costly and the baking process labor-intensive, limiting their popularity. However, with the Industrial Revolution came not only 64 mass production of ingredients that made them more affordable, but also a new ingredient, baking powder, which simplified the baking process. Ready-made cakes also became widely available for purchase. This made throwing a birthday party much easier, and has led to the birthday cake's worldwide popularity today.

수십 년 동안, 생일 케이크의 재료는 비싼 것이었고, 굽는 과정이 노동 집약적이었기 때문에, 그 인기가 제한되었다. 하지만, 산업 혁명으로 인해 더욱 저렴하게 만들어 준 재료들의 대량 생산이 이뤄졌을 뿐만 아니라, 굽는 과정을 간소화시킨 새로운 재료인, 베이킹 파우더까지 생겨났다. 다 만들어져 나오는 케이크 또한 널리 구매 가능하게 되었다. 이로 인해 생일 파티를 여는 것이 훨씬 더 쉬워졌으며, 오늘날 생일 케이크의 전 세계적인 인기로 이어져 왔다.

어휘 serve (음식 등) ~을 제공하다, ~을 내오다 range from A to B: A에서 B의 범위에 이르다 elaborate 복잡한, 정교한 treat 특별 음식, 특별 선물 available 이용 가능한 countless 수없이 많은 flavor 맛, 풍미 traditional 전통적인 exotic 이국적인 savory 풍미 있는, 맛있는 concoction 혼합물 tradition 전통 originate 유래하다 not ~ at all 전혀 ~ 않다 celebrate ~을 기념하다, ~을 축하하다(= commemorate) reference 참고 (자료) description 설명, 묘사 take place (행사 등) 열리다, 개최되다, 진행되다 it is likely that ~할 가능성이 있다 celebration 기념 행사, 축하 행사 ruler 통치자 thus 그 결과, 그러므로 ancient 고대의 observe ~을 기념하다, ~을 준수하다 represent ~을 표현하다 lunar 달의 sphere 구체, 구 top A with B: A의 상단에 B를 얹다 imitate ~을 모방하다 ray 광선, 빛 similar 유사한 unsweetened 달지 않게 만든 made of ~로 만들어진 not A until B: B나 되어야 A하다 be credited for (공로 등) ~에 대해 인정받다 popularize ~을 대중화시키다 signify ~을 나타내다, ~을 의미하다 bestow ~을 부여하다 make a wish 소원을 빌다 decade 10년 ingredient (음식) 재료, 성분 costly 비싼 labor-intensive 노동 집약적인 limit ~을 제한하다 popularity 인기 however 하지만, 그러나 Industrial Revolution 산업 혁명 not only A, but also B: A뿐만 아니라 B도 mass production 대량 생산 affordable 저렴한, 가격이 알맞은 simplify ~을 간소화하다 ready-made 다 만들어져 나오는 throw a party 파티를 열다 lead to ~로 이어지다

---

60 주제/목적

What is the article mainly about?

(a) the origin of a religious celebration
(b) the creator of a popular dessert item
(c) the symbolism behind a holiday event
(d) the evolution of a common tradition

기사가 주로 무엇에 관한 것인가?

(a) 종교적 기념 행사의 유래
(b) 인기 있는 디저트 제품의 창시자
(c) 한 휴일 행사의 이면에 존재하는 상징
(d) 흔한 전통의 발전

정답 (d)

해설 첫 번째 문단에 생일에 케이크를 먹는 전통이 어떻게 유래했을지(But how did the tradition of having cake on birthdays originate?) 질문을 던진 다음, 아주 오래 전의 과거에서부터 현재까지의 생일 축하 케이크와 관련해 문단별로 이야기하고 있으므로 (d)가 정답입니다.

어휘 origin 유래, 기원 religious 종교적인 creator 창시자, 만든 사람 symbolism 상징(주의) evolution 발전, 진화

What was the first historical mention of a birthday celebration?

(a) a tale inscribed on an ancient tablet
(b) a story told in a religious text
(c) a letter written by a famous ruler
(d) a poem dedicated to the gods

생일 기념 행사에 대한 최초의 역사적 언급은 무엇이었는가?

(a) 한 고대 명판에 새겨진 이야기
(b) 한 종교 서적에서 전해지는 이야기
(c) 한 유명 통치자가 쓴 편지
(d) 신들에게 바치는 시

정답 (b)

해설 질문의 키워드 first historical mention of a birthday celebration은 두 번째 문단에 The first reference to such a celebration으로 표현되어 있습니다. 해당 문장에 따르면 그러한 기념 행사에 대한 최초의 참고 자료는 기원전 3000년경에 열렸던 한 이집트 파라오의 생일에 대한 성경의 묘사라고(The first reference to such a celebration is the Bible's description of an Egyptian pharaoh's birthday ~) 언급되어 있으므로 (b)가 정답입니다.

어휘 inscribe ~을 새기다 tablet 명판 text 서적, 문서, 글, 문자 poem 시 dedicated to ~에게 바치는

> 패러프레이징
>
> the Bible's description → a story told in a religious text

How, most likely, did the ancient Romans decide whether someone would be celebrated with a cake?

(a) They based it on the time of day in which the party was held.
(b) They considered their reputation among other citizens.
(c) They based it on the time of year when the person was born.
(d) They considered their favorability among the gods.

고대 로마인들은 어떻게 누군가가 케이크로 축하를 받을 것인지 결정했는가?

(a) 하루 중에서 파티가 개최되는 시간을 바탕으로 했다.
(b) 다른 시민들 사이에서의 명성을 고려했다.
(c) 일년 중에서 그 사람이 태어난 때를 바탕으로 했다.
(d) 신들 사이에서의 호감도를 고려했다.

정답 (b)

해설 질문의 키워드 ancient Romans는 세 번째 문단에 그대로 제시되어 있습니다. 해당 문단에서 고대 로마인들이 이용한 케이크와 관련해 오직 50세를 기념하기 위한 것이었다는 점과 그 시민이 유명한 남성인 경우에만 해당되었다는 점이(only if the citizen was a famous man) 언급되어 있습니다. 유명한 남성이라는 말은 사람들 사이에서 명성이 높은 사람임을 의미

하므로 이러한 조건을 가리키는 (b)가 정답입니다.

어휘 whether ~인지 (아닌지) base A on B: A에 대해 B를 바탕으로 하다, A에 대한 바탕을 B에 두다 hold ~을 개최하다
consider ~을 고려하다 reputation 명성, 평판 favorability 호감도

> 패러프레이징
>
> famous → reputation among other citizens

63 세부 정보

When were eighteenth-century German children allowed to eat a special cake?

(a) once they had said all of their prayers
(b) on the morning of their birthday celebration
(c) after blowing out all of their candles
(d) before their midday meal was finished

18세기 독일의 아이들은 언제 특별 케이크를 먹도록 허용되었는가?

(a) 자신의 모든 기도를 말하자마자
(b) 생일 축하 파티가 있는 아침에
(c) 모든 초를 불어서 끈 후에
(d) 정오의 식사를 끝마치기 전에

정답 (c)

해설 질문의 키워드 eighteenth-century German children은 네 번째 문단에 그대로 제시되어 있습니다. 해당 문단에서 당시 독일에서 생일인 아이가 초를 불어서 끄고 소원을 빈 다음, 특별 선물, 즉 케이크를 즐길 수 있었다고(the birthday child could blow them out, make a wish, and enjoy their treat) 쓰여 있으므로 (c)가 정답입니다.

어휘 be allowed to 동사원형: ~하도록 허용되다 once ~하자마자, 일단 ~하는 대로 prayer 기도(문) midday 정오, 한낮

64 세부 정보

According to the article, what has made birthday cakes more popular over time?

(a) Prices of ingredients have fallen.
(b) Advertising efforts have increased.
(c) Home baking is making a comeback.
(d) People have acquired more spending money.

기사 내용에 따르면, 무엇 때문에 생일 케이크가 시간이 흐를수록 더 인기 있게 되었는가?

(a) 재료값이 하락했다.
(b) 광고 활동이 늘어났다.
(c) 집에서 굽는 것이 다시 인기를 얻고 있다.
(d) 사람들이 더 많은 용돈을 받았다.

해설 질문의 키워드 more popular는 다섯 번째 문단에 worldwide popularity로 표현되어 있습니다. 해당 문단에 산업 혁명으로 인해 케이크를 더욱 저렴하게 만들어 준 재료들의 대량 생산이 이뤄진 사실(mass production of ingredients that made them more affordable) 언급되어 있습니다. 따라서 재료값이 하락했음을 의미하는 (a)가 정답입니다.

어휘 advertising 광고 effort 활동, 노력 increase 늘어나다, 증가하다 make a comeback 다시 인기를 얻다 acquire ~을 받다, ~을 얻다

패러프레이징

more affordable → Prices ~ have fallen

---

65 동의어

In the context of the passage, elaborate means _____.

(a) tidy
(b) famous
(c) strong
(d) complex

해당 단락의 문맥에서 elaborate이 의미하는 것은?

(a) 말끔한, 잘 정돈된
(b) 유명한
(c) 강한, 튼튼한
(d) 복잡한

정답 (d)

해설 해당 문장에서 「range from A to B」는 'A에서 B의 범위에 이르다'라는 의미를 나타내므로 elaborate은 from 뒤에 쓰인 simple(간단한)과 대조적인 의미를 지니고 있음을 알 수 있습니다. 따라서 '간단한'과 대조되는 '복잡한'을 뜻하는 (d) complex가 정답입니다.

---

66 동의어

In the context of the passage, commemorate means _____.

(a) decorate
(b) find
(c) honor
(d) make

해당 단락의 문맥에서 commemorate이 의미하는 것은?

(a) 장식하다
(b) 찾다, 발견하다
(c) 기념하다, 기리다, 영예를 주다
(d) 만들다

정답 (c)

해설 해당 문장에서 to부정사구 to commemorate the fiftieth year는 고대 로마인들이 케이크를 이용한 목적을 나타내며, the fiftieth year가 '50세'를 의미하므로 commemorate이 '기념하다' 등을 의미하는 동사임을 알 수 있습니다. 따라서 '기념하다, 기리다' 등을 뜻하는 (c) honor가 정답입니다.

PART 3

THE TICHBORNE CLAIMANT

67 "The Tichborne Claimant" was a man who insisted he was the long-lost heir of a wealthy English family. The legal trials involving the man's claim were two of the longest and most controversial cases in Victorian-era England.

68 Roger Tichborne, son of Lady Tichborne, stood to inherit a vast fortune. In 1854, while sailing near South America, he was lost at sea. However, in 1863, encouraged by countless rumors and a fortune teller claiming Roger was still alive, Lady Tichborne placed advertisements in newspapers worldwide offering a reward for information about her son.

A man then known as Thomas Castro responded and wrote to Lady Tichborne, claiming to be Roger. He said that he had survived a shipwreck and was living in Australia. Despite many gaps in his tale, Lady Tichborne was eager to believe his story and invited him to visit. However, **69** many **72** speculated that grief for her lost son had made her irrational, and they questioned her mental state.

When Castro arrived in England, he was much shorter than Roger had been and had a much heavier frame. He was unable to communicate in French, a language that Roger had been raised speaking. Nonetheless, he resembled Roger in certain ways and **70** knew specific details of Roger's private life. So, Lady Tichborne accepted him and granted him a yearly allowance. When she died, the man sued for the entire family fortune.

The Tichborne family opposed Castro in court, calling him an imposter and using his appearance, lack of bilingualism, and absence of a tattoo on his left arm as evidence. But the British public generally disliked the aristocracy and instead took the side of the man seeking the Tichborne fortune.

티크본 청구인

"티크본 청구인"은 자신이 오랫동안 연락이 끊긴 한 부유한 영국 가문의 상속인이라고 주장한 한 남성이었다. 이 남성의 주장과 관련된 법정 재판이 빅토리아 시대 잉글랜드에서 가장 길고 가장 논란이 많았던 사건들 중 두 가지였다.

티크본 부인의 아들, 로저 티크본은 어마어마한 재산을 상속받을 것으로 보였다. 1854년에, 남아메리카 근처에서 항해하던 중에, 그는 바다에서 실종되었다. 하지만, 1863년에, 수없이 많은 소문 및 로저가 여전히 살아 있다고 주장하는 한 점쟁이에 의해 고무되어, 티크본 부인은 아들에 관한 정보에 대해 보상을 제공하겠다는 광고를 전 세계의 신문에 냈다.

그때 토머스 카스트로라고 알려진 한 남성이 반응을 보여 티크본 부인에게 편지를 보내, 로저라고 주장했다. 그는 난파선에서 살아 남아 호주에서 생활하고 있다고 말했다. 그의 이야기에 존재하는 많은 공백에도 불구하고, 티크본 부인은 그의 이야기를 간절히 믿고 싶어 했고 그에게 방문하도록 요청했다. 하지만, 많은 이들은 아들을 잃은 슬픔이 티크본 부인을 비이성적으로 만들었다고 추측했고, 티크본 부인의 정신 상태에 의구심을 품었다.

카스트로가 잉글랜드에 도착했을 때, 로저보다 훨씬 더 작았으며, 훨씬 더 육중한 체격을 지니고 있었다. 그는 로저가 자라면서 말했던 언어인 프랑스어로 소통하지 못했다. 그럼에도 불구하고, 그는 특정 측면에 있어 로저를 닮았고, 로저의 사생활에 대한 특정 세부 사항을 알고 있었다. 그래서, 티크본 부인은 그를 받아들였고, 그에게 해마다 용돈을 주었다. 티크본 부인이 사망했을 때, 이 남성은 가문의 재산 전체에 대해 소송을 제기했다.

티크본 가문은 그를 사기꾼이라고 부르면서 그의 외모와 2개 국어 능력의 부족, 그리고 왼쪽 팔의 문신 부재를 증거로 이용해, 법정에서 카스트로에게 이의를 제기했다. 하지만 영국의 대중은 일반적으로 귀족을 싫어했으며, 대신 티크본 가문의 재산을 차지하려는 이 남성의 편을 들었다.

Castro lost his second trial lawsuit. His true identity was revealed to be neither Roger Tichborne nor Thomas Castro. Instead, he was identified as Arthur Orton, a man wanted for horse theft and murder. He was sentenced to prison time for lying under oath. After his release, he died in poverty. Still, **71** he remained a popular folk hero for everyday people and was viewed by many as an innocent victim of **73** elite society.

카스트로는 2차 법정 소송에서 패했다. 그의 진짜 신분은 로저 티크본도, 토머스 카스트로도 아닌 것으로 밝혀졌다. 대신, 그의 신분은 말 절도 및 살인으로 수배 중이던 남성인 아서 오턴으로 확인되었다. 그는 법정에서의 선서를 한 상태에서 거짓 증언한 것에 대해 징역형을 선고받았다. 석방 후에, 그는 가난 속에 사망했다. 그럼에도 불구하고, 그는 여전히 일반인들에게 인기 있는 민중의 영웅으로 남아 있었으며, 많은 이들에 의해 엘리트 사회의 무고한 피해자로 여겨졌다.

어휘 claimant 청구인 insist (that) ~라고 주장하다 long-lost 오랫동안 연락이 끊긴, 오래 전에 잃어버린 heir 상속인 controversial 논란이 많은 case 사건, 경우, 사례 Victorian-era 빅토리아 시대의 stand to 동사원형: ~할 것으로 보이다, ~할 것 같다 inherit ~을 상속받다, ~을 물려받다 vast 어마어마한, 엄청난 fortune 재산 encouraged by ~에 의해 고무된 countless 수없이 많은 claim (that) ~라고 주장하다 place an advertisement 광고를 내다 reward 보상(금) known as ~라고 알려진 survive ~에서 살아 남다 shipwreck 난파(선) gap 공백, 간격, 차이 tale 이야기 be eager to 동사원형: ~하기를 간절히 바라다 invite + 목적어 + to 동사원형: (목적어)가 ~하도록 요청하다 speculate that ~라고 추측하다 grief 슬픔 irrational 비이성적인 question v. ~에 대해 의구심을 갖다 mental 정신의, 마음의 state 상태 much (비교급 수식) 훨씬 frame 체격, 뼈대 be unable to 동사원형: ~할 수 없다 communicate 의사 소통하다 raise ~을 키우다, ~을 기르다 nonetheless 그럼에도 불구하고 resemble ~을 닮다 in certain ways 특정 측면에 있어 specific 특정한, 구체적인 details 세부 요소, 상세 사항 accept ~을 받아들이다 grant ~을 주다, ~을 수여하다 allowance 용돈, 수당 sue 소송을 제기하다 entire 전체의 oppose ~에 이의를 제기하다, ~에 반대하다 imposter 사기꾼 lack 부족 bilingualism 2개 언어 사용 능력 absence 부재, 없음 tattoo 문신 evidence 증거 the public 일반인들 generally 일반적으로 aristocracy 귀족 take the side of ~의 편을 들다 trial lawsuit 법정 소송 identity 신분, 신원 be revealed to be A: A인 것으로 밝혀지다 neither A nor B: A도 B도 아닌 be identified as (신분 등) ~로 확인되다 wanted 수배 중인 be sentenced to prison time 징역형이 선고되다 lie under oath 법정 선서를 한 상태에서 위증하다 release 석방, 방출, 출시 poverty 가난 remain 여전히 ~로 남아 있다 folk hero 민중의 영웅 be viewed as ~로 여겨지다 innocent 무고한 victim 피해자

---

67 주제/목적

What is the main topic of the article?

(a) a woman who searched for a long-lost husband
(b) a man who tried to deceive a family
(c) a ship that was lost in a terrible storm
(d) a family fortune that was successfully stolen

기사의 주제는 무엇인가?

(a) 오랫동안 연락이 끊긴 남편을 찾던 여성
(b) 한 가문을 속이려 했던 남성
(c) 끔찍한 폭풍우 속에 사라진 선박
(d) 성공적으로 도난 당한 한 가족의 재산

정답 (b)

해설 첫 번째 문단에서 "티크본 청구인"이 자신이 오랫동안 연락이 끊긴 한 부유한 영국 가문의 상속인이라고 주장한 한 남성이

라고("The Tichborne Claimant" was a man who insisted he was the long-lost heir of a wealthy English family) 언급한 뒤로 이 남성의 사기 행위에 관해 이야기하고 있으므로 (b)가 정답입니다.

어휘 deceive ~을 속이다, ~을 기만하다 terrible 끔찍한

패러프레이징

a man who insisted he was the long-lost heir of a wealthy English family → a man who tried to deceive a family

❌ 오답 피하기

첫 번째 문단에 오랫동안 연락이 끊긴 사람은 티크본 가문의 상속인으로 언급되어 있고, 두 번째 단락에 그 사람이 티크본 부인의 아들이라고 쓰여 있으므로 (a)는 오답입니다.

68 세부 정보

What had Lady Tichborne's relative done that motivated her search?

(a) disappear while on a lengthy sailing voyage
(b) run away after an argument with friends
(c) insist on contacting a trusted fortune teller
(d) publish a mysterious letter in the newspaper

티크본 부인의 수색에 동기를 부여했던 티크본 부인의 인척이 했던 일은 무엇인가?

(a) 오랜 항해 여행 중에 사라졌다
(b) 친구와 언쟁 후에 도망쳤다
(c) 신뢰할 수 있는 점쟁이에게 연락하도록 주장했다
(d) 신문에 불가사의한 편지를 실었다

정답 (a)

해설 질문의 키워드 Lady Tichborne's relative는 두 번째 문단에 son of Lady Tichborne으로 표현되어 있습니다. 해당 문장에 따르면 티크본 부인의 아들, 로저 티크본이 1854년에 남아메리카 근처에서 항해하던 중에 바다에서 실종되었습니다(Roger Tichborne, son of Lady Tichborne, stood to inherit a vast fortune. In 1854, while sailing near South America, he was lost at sea). 따라서 이렇게 바다에서 사라진 것을 의미하는 (a)가 정답입니다.

어휘 relative n. 인척, 친척 motivate ~에게 동기를 부여하다 disappear 사라지다 lengthy 오랜, 너무 긴 voyage 여행 argument 언쟁, 주장 insist on ~을 주장하다 contact ~에게 연락하다 trusted 신뢰받는

패러프레이징

while sailing near South America, he was lost at sea → disappear while on a lengthy sailing voyage

Why, most likely, did Lady Tichborne believe Castro?

(a) because she recognized him instantly
(b) because he knew friends of the family
(c) because she was becoming mentally ill
(d) because he visited her in the hospital

티크본 부인이 왜 카스트로를 믿었을 것 같은가?

(a) 그녀가 그를 즉시 알아봤기 때문에
(b) 그가 가족의 친구들을 알았기 때문에
(c) 그녀가 정신 이상자가 되어 가고 있었기 때문에
(d) 그가 병원에 있던 티크본 부인을 방문했기 때문에

정답 (c)

해설 질문의 키워드 believe Castro는 세 번째 문단에 believe his story로 표현되어 있습니다. 해당 문단에 아들을 잃은 슬픔이 티크본 부인을 비이성적으로 만들었다는 추측과 함께 사람들이 티크본 부인의 정신 상태에 의구심을 품었다는(many speculated that grief for her lost son had made her irrational, and they questioned her mental state) 사실이 언급되어 있습니다. 따라서 이러한 정신적 문제를 이유로 제시한 (c)가 정답입니다.

어휘 recognize ~을 알아보다 instantly 즉시 ill 아픈, 병 든

패러프레이징

irrational / questioned her mental state → mentally ill

Which of the following is mentioned in the text about Castro?

(a) He weighed much less than Roger had.
(b) He spoke the same languages that Roger had spoken.
(c) He stood significantly taller than Roger had.
(d) He shared information only known to Roger and his family.

다음 중 지문에서 카스트로와 관련해 언급된 것은 어느 것인가?

(a) 로저보다 몸무게가 훨씬 더 가벼웠다.
(b) 로저가 사용했던 동일한 언어로 말했다.
(c) 로저보다 상당히 더 당당해 보였다.
(d) 오직 로저와 그의 가족에게만 알려져 있는 정보를 공유했다.

정답 (d)

해설 네 번째 문단에 카스트로가 로저의 사생활에 대한 특정 세부 사항을 알고 있었다는(knew specific details of Roger's private life) 내용이 쓰여 있습니다. 이는 로저 자신 및 그의 가족만 알고 있는 사적인 부분을 그 가족에게 언급했음을 의미하는 것이므로 (d)가 정답입니다.

어휘 **weigh** 무게가 ~이다 **stand tall** 당당해 보이다, 자신만만해 보이다 **significantly** 상당히, 많이

> **패러프레이징**
>
> knew specific details of Roger's private life → shared information only known to Roger and his family

71 세부 정보

Why did the British public side with Castro?	영국의 대중들은 왜 카스트로의 편을 들었는가?
(a) They were won over by his cleverness. (b) They distrusted the evidence against him. (c) They felt his imprisonment was cruel. (d) They preferred him over the family.	(a) 그의 영리함에 넘어갔다. (b) 그에 대한 증거를 불신했다. (c) 그의 징역형이 잔인하다고 느꼈다. (d) 그 가족보다 그를 더 좋아했다.

정답 (d)

해설 질문의 키워드 the British public은 여섯 번째 문단에 everyday people로 표현되어 있습니다. 해당 문장에 카스트로가 일반인들에게 인기 있는 민중의 영웅으로 남아 있었고 많은 이들에 의해 엘리트 사회의 무고한 피해자로 여겨졌다는 (he remained a popular folk hero for everyday people and was viewed by many as an innocent victim of elite society) 점이 언급되어 있습니다. 이는 카스트로에 대한 민중의 동정심을 나타내는 말에 해당하며, 그를 좋아하는 마음에서 비롯된 것으로 볼 수 있으므로 이러한 의미를 나타낸 선택지인 (d)가 정답입니다.

어휘 **side with** ~의 편을 들다 **win over** ~을 설득시키다, ~을 자기 편으로 끌어들이다 **cleverness** 영리함 **distrust** ~을 불신하다 **imprisonment** 징역형, 감금 **prefer A over B**: B보다 A를 더 좋아하다

In the context of the passage, speculated means

_____.

(a) forgot
(b) disagreed
(c) thought
(d) requested

해당 단락의 문맥에서 speculated
가 의미하는 것은?

(a) 잊었다
(b) 동의하지 않았다
(c) 생각했다
(d) 요청했다

정답 (c)

해설 해당 문장에서 동사 speculated 뒤에 이어지는 that절에 아들을 잃은 슬픔이 티크본 부인을 비이성적으로 만들었다는 내용이 쓰여 있습니다. 따라서 speculated는 주어 many가 가리키는 많은 사람들이 그러한 생각을 갖고 있었음을 나타내는 동사인 것으로 볼 수 있으므로 '생각했다'를 뜻하는 (c) thought이 정답입니다.

In the context of the passage, elite means _____.

(a) upper-class
(b) open
(c) modern-day
(d) old

해당 단락의 문맥에서 elite가 의미
하는 것은?

(a) 상류층의
(b) 개방된, 열린
(c) 현대의
(d) 늙은, 오래된, 구식의

정답 (a)

해설 해당 문장에서 elite 앞에 카스트로가 많은 이들에 의해 무고한 피해자로 여겨졌다는 내용이 쓰여 있어 elite society가 한 가문의 재산을 탐냈던 카스트로를 피해자로 만들 수 있는 사회 계층과 관련되어 것으로 볼 수 있습니다. 따라서 높은 사회 계층을 의미한다는 것을 알 수 있으므로 '상류층의'를 뜻하는 (a) upper-class가 정답입니다.

PART 4

Mr. Jack Reynolds
Department of Transportation
200 State Street
Watford, NY

Dear Mr. Reynolds,

I am contacting you in your capacity as Director of the Department of Transportation. **74** For the past month, increased traffic going past my apartment in the middle of the day has made it impossible for me to get work done from home. I hope you can find a solution for this issue.

A week ago, **75** I called your department seeking assistance. I was told that I would receive a call back from your office within two business days, but that call never came. Yesterday, I called again and was informed that the only way to **79** resolve this matter was to send a letter to the department. In the future, the department should tell citizens immediately when they must send a letter, rather than wasting their time with phone calls.

Although the area is quiet at night, with construction beginning on the new Watford Sports Stadium, the noise from construction trucks during the day is unacceptably loud. **76** This noise does not bother some residents because they are away at work during this time. However, I work from home as an illustrator, and the constant racket has made it impossible for me to concentrate in my apartment, even when I wear headphones.

I am especially annoyed because the stadium was a project that I and other residents personally opposed. **77** We spoke at the local townhall meeting about how building a new stadium was expensive and unnecessary. Our concerns were ignored at the time, and now they have been realized.

잭 레이놀즈 씨
교통부
스테이트 스트리트 200번지
왓포드, NY

레이놀즈 씨께,

교통부 책임자로서 귀하의 역할 측면에서 연락 드립니다. 지난 한 달 동안, 하루 중 한낮에 저희 아파트를 지나가는 교통량 증가로 인해 제가 집에서 일을 완료하는 것이 불가능해졌습니다. 귀하께서 이 문제에 대한 해결책을 찾아 주실 수 있기를 바랍니다.

일주일 전에, 저는 귀하의 부처에 도움을 요청하는 전화를 걸었습니다. 저는 영업일로 이틀 내에 귀하의 사무실로부터 다시 전화를 받을 것이라는 얘기를 들었지만, 그 전화는 전혀 오지 않았습니다. 어제, 저는 다시 전화했고, 이 문제를 해결할 수 있는 유일한 방법이 이 부처로 편지를 보내는 것이라는 통보를 받았습니다. 향후에는, 귀하의 부처는 전화 통화로 시간을 낭비하게 하는 대신, 즉시 시민들에게 언제 반드시 편지를 보내야 하는지 알려 주셔야 할 것입니다.

이 지역이 야간에는 조용하긴 하지만, 새로운 왓포드 스포츠 경기장에 대한 공사가 시작되면, 하루 중에 공사 트럭에서 발생되는 소음이 용납할 수 없을 정도로 큽니다. 이 소음이 어떤 주민들에게는 방해가 되지 않는데, 그들은 이 시간대에 직장에 가 있기 때문입니다. 하지만, 저는 삽화가로서 집에서 일하고 있어서, 지속적인 소음으로 인해 저희 아파트에서 집중하는 것이 불가능해졌으며, 심지어 제가 헤드폰을 착용하고 있는 경우에도 그렇습니다.

제가 특히 짜증스러운 이유는 이 경기장이 저와 다른 주민들이 개인적으로 반대했던 프로젝트였기 때문입니다. 저희는 지역 시청 회의에서 새로운 경기장을 짓는 일이 얼마나 많은 비용이 들고 불필요한지에 관해 이야기했습니다. 저희의 우려 사항들이 당시에는 무시되었으며, 지금 현실이 되었습니다.

I am aware that the next citywide election is in
November. **78** If I do not hear back from you within
the week about the current situation, I will feel
compelled to run for office myself in an aggressive
80 bid to replace you.

Sincerely,

Rebecca Donaldson

시 전체에 걸친 다음 선거가 11월에 있다는 사실을
알고 있습니다. 제가 현재의 상황과 관련해 귀하로
부터 일주일 내에 다시 소식을 듣지 못한다면, 귀하
를 대체하기 위한 적극적인 노력으로서 직접 출마
하고 싶은 충동을 느끼게 될 것입니다.

안녕히 계십시오.

레베카 도널드슨

어휘 contact ~에게 연락하다 capacity 역할, 지위, 역량, 수용력 traffic 교통(량), 차량들 make it + 형용사 + for 사람 + to
동사원형: (사람)이 ~하는 것이 (형용사)해지다 solution 해결책 issue 문제, 사안(= matter) seek ~을 구하다, ~을 찾다
assistance 도움, 지원 be told that ~라는 말을 듣다 be informed that ~라는 통보를 받다 resolve ~을 해결하다
immediately 즉시 rather than ~하는 대신, ~하는 것이 아니라 unacceptably 용납할 수 없을 정도로 bother ~을
방해하다 resident 주민 constant 지속적인 racket 큰 소음 concentrate 집중하다 annoyed 짜증이 난 oppose ~에
반대하다 local 지역의, 현지의 unnecessary 불필요한 concern 우려, 걱정 ignore ~을 무시하다 realize ~을 현실화하다
be aware that ~임을 알고 있다 citywide 시 전체의 current 현재의 situation 상황 feel compelled to 동사원형:
~하고픈 충동을 느끼다 run for office (공직에) 출마하다 oneself (부사처럼 쓰여) 직접 aggressive 적극적인, 공격적인
bid 노력, 입찰(액) replace ~을 대체하다, ~의 후임이 되다

74 주제/목적

Why is Rebecca Donaldson writing to Jack Reynolds?

(a) to inquire about an upcoming construction project
(b) to complain about a change in traffic noise
(c) to report safety issues in her apartment building
(d) to ask for clarification about a local parking law

레베카 도널드슨 씨가 왜 잭 레이놀즈 씨에게 편지를 쓰는가?

(a) 다가오는 공사 프로젝트에 관해 문의하기 위해
(b) 차량 소음의 변화와 관련해 불만을 제기하기 위해
(c) 자신의 아파트 건물 내에서 나타난 안전 문제를 알리기 위해
(d) 지역 주차법에 관한 해명을 요청하기 위해

정답 (b)

해설 첫 문단에 하루 중 한낮에 자신의 아파트를 지나가는 교통량 증가를(For the past month, increased traffic going past my apartment in the middle of the day ~) 언급하면서 그로 인해 발생한 문제를 설명하고 있습니다. 따라서 교통량의 변화에 따른 불만을 말하는 것이 목적임을 알 수 있으므로 (b)가 정답입니다.

어휘 inquire 문의하다 upcoming 다가오는, 곧 있을 complain 불만을 제기하다 ask for ~을 요청하다 clarification 해명 parking 주차

패러프레이징

increased traffic → a change in traffic noise

75 세부 정보

What was Rebecca told when she first contacted the Department of Transportation?

(a) that she might want to continue calling daily
(b) that she would likely receive a response letter
(c) that she might be better off writing a letter
(d) that she would be getting a call soon

레베카 씨가 처음 교통국에 연락했을 때 무슨 말을 들었는가?

(a) 매일 전화를 계속하면 좋을 것이라는 말
(b) 아마 답변서를 받을 것이라는 말
(c) 편지를 쓰는 편이 나을 수도 있다는 말
(d) 곧 전화를 한 통 받게 될 것이라는 말

정답 (d)

해설 질문의 키워드 contacted the Department of Transportation은 두 번째 문단에 called your department로 표현되어 있습니다. 해당 문장에서 도움을 요청하는 전화를 건 사실과 함께 영업일로 이틀 내에 다시 전화를 받을 것이라는 얘기를 들은 사실을(I called your department seeking assistance. I was told that I would receive a call back from your office within two business days) 밝히고 있습니다. 따라서 이러한 연락 방법을 언급한 (d)가 정답입니다.

어휘 continue -ing 계속 ~하다 likely 아마 be better off -ing ~하는 편이 낫다

패러프레이징

would receive a call back / within two business days → would be getting a call soon

❌ 오답 피하기

해당 문단에 레베카 씨가 두 번째 전화를 걸었을 때 편지를 써야 한다는 얘기를 들은 사실이 언급되어 있으므로 (c)는 오답입니다.

---

76 세부 정보

Why is the situation worse for Rebecca than for other residents?

(a) She has a longer commute to work.
(b) She spends a lot of time at home.
(c) She is often working late at night.
(d) She lives in a single-family home.

해당 상황이 왜 다른 주민들보다 레베카 씨에게 더 좋지 않은가?

(a) 직장으로 가는 통근 시간이 더 길다.
(b) 집에서 많은 시간을 보낸다.
(c) 자주 밤 늦게까지 일한다.
(d) 단독 주택에서 살고 있다.

정답 (b)

해설 질문의 키워드 other residents는 세 번째 문단에 some residents로 표현되어 있습니다. 해당 문장에 따르면 다른 주민들은 그 시간대에 직장에 가 있기 때문에 방해가 되지 않지만, 레베카 씨는 삽화가로서 집에서 일하고 있다는(This noise does not bother some residents because they are away at work during this time. However, I work from home as an illustrator) 사실을 알 수 있습니다. 따라서 집에서 보내는 시간이 많다는 것을 알 수 있으므로 (b)가 정답입니다.

어휘 commute 통근, 통학

패러프레이징

work from home as an illustrator → spends a lot of time at home

77 세부 정보

Why did Rebecca speak at the townhall meeting?

(a) to share that residents were against the project
(b) to request a change in the construction schedule
(c) to ask that the stadium be built in a different location
(d) to support a plan to repair residential buildings

레베카 씨가 시청 회의에서 발언을 했던 이유는 무엇인가?

(a) 주민들이 해당 프로젝트에 반대한다는 사실을 공유하기 위해
(b) 공사 일정의 변경을 요청하기 위해
(c) 해당 경기장을 다른 곳에 짓도록 요청하기 위해
(d) 주거용 건물들을 수리하려는 계획을 지지하기 위해

정답 (a)

해설 질문의 키워드 townhall meeting은 네 번째 문단에 그대로 제시되어 있습니다. 해당 문장에 레베카 씨와 주민들이 지역 시청 회의에서 새로운 경기장을 짓는 일이 얼마나 많은 비용이 들고 불필요한지에 관해 이야기했다는(We spoke at the local townhall meeting about how building a new stadium was expensive and unnecessary) 사실이 언급되어 있습니다. 이는 그 공사 프로젝트를 반대하는 이유를 밝힌 것이므로 이러한 의미로 쓰인 선택지 (a)가 정답입니다.

어휘 against ~에 반대하는 request ~을 요청하다 support ~을 지지하다 repair ~을 수리하다 residential 주거의

패러프레이징

how building a new stadium was expensive and unnecessary → against the project

78 추론

How, most likely, will Rebecca react if she does not hear back from Jack Reynolds?

(a) She will vote for a new Director of Transportation.
(b) She will decide to move away from Watford.
(c) She will try to become the next Director of Transportation.
(d) She will run for office as Mayor of Watford.

레베카 씨가 잭 레이놀즈 씨로부터 소식을 듣지 못하는 경우에 어떻게 반응할 것 같은가?

(a) 새 교통부 책임자에게 투표할 것이다.
(b) 왓포드에서 이사하기로 결정할 것이다.
(c) 차기 교통국 책임자가 되려 할 것이다.
(d) 왓포드 시장으로 출마할 것이다.

정답 (c)

해설 질문의 키워드 if she does not hear back from Jack Reynolds는 미지막 문단에 If I do not hear back from you로 표현되어 있습니다. 해당 문장에 따르면 레베카 씨는 레이놀즈 씨로부터 일주일 내에 다시 소식을 듣지 못하는 경우에 레이놀즈 씨를 대체하기 위해 직접 출마하려는 생각을 갖고 있음을(If I do not hear back from you within the week about the current situation, I will feel compelled to run for office myself in an aggressive bid to replace you) 알 수 있습니다. 첫 문단에 이 편지의 수신자인 레이놀즈 씨를 교통부 책임자로(Director of the Department of Transportation) 언급했으므로 다음 교통부 책임자가 되려 한다는 의미로 쓰인 (c)가 정답입니다.

어휘 react 반응하다 vote 투표하다 decide to 동사원형: ~하기로 결정하다 mayor 시장

패러프레이징

run for office myself in an aggressive bid to replace you → try to become the next Director of Transportation

⊗ 오답 피하기

해당 문장에 공직에 오르기 위한 선거에 출마한다는 말은 쓰여 있지만 그 직책이 왓포드 시장은 아니므로 (d)는 오답입니다.

---

79 동의어

In the context of the passage, resolve means _____.

(a) settle
(b) prefer
(c) choose
(d) propose

해당 단락의 문맥에서 resolve가 의미하는 것은?

(a) 해결하다, 처리하다
(b) 선호하다
(c) 선택하다
(d) 제안하다

정답 (a)

해설 해당 문장에서 resolve가 속한 that절은 레베카 씨가 도움을 요청하기 위해 교통부에 전화했을 때 통보 받은 내용을 나타냅니다. 또한, resolve 앞뒤에 '방법'을 뜻하는 명사 way와 레베카 씨의 문제를 가리키는 this matter가 쓰여 있어 교통부으로부터 전달 받은 문제 해결 방법을 언급하는 내용인 것으로 볼 수 있습니다. 따라서 '해결하다'를 의미하는 또 다른 동사 (a) settle이 정답입니다.

In the context of the passage, <u>bid</u> means _____ .

(a) cost
(b) image
(c) stop
(d) attempt

해당 단락의 문맥에서 <u>bid</u>가 의미하
는 것은?

(a) 비용
(b) 이미지
(c) 정지, 중단, 정거장
(d) 시도, 노력

정답 (d)

해설 해당 문장에서 bid가 속한 주절은 레이놀즈 씨로부터 일주일 내에 다시 소식을 듣지 못하는 경우에 레베카 씨가 취하려는
조치를 나타냅니다. bid 앞뒤에 '적극적인'을 뜻하는 형용사 aggresive와 레이놀즈 씨를 대체하겠다는 의미를 나타내는 to
부정사구가 쓰여 있는 것으로 볼 때, 그러한 an aggressive bid가 레이놀즈 씨를 대체하기 위한 적극적인 시도를 의미한다
는 것을 알 수 있으므로 (d)가 정답입니다.

TEST 04

Grammar

1. (a)	2. (c)	3. (d)	4. (b)	5. (a)	6. (c)	7. (b)	8. (b)	9. (a)	10. (d)
11. (d)	12. (c)	13. (b)	14. (d)	15. (b)	16. (c)	17. (d)	18. (c)	19. (a)	20. (b)
21. (a)	22. (d)	23. (a)	24. (c)	25. (a)	26. (b)				

Listening

27. (b)	28. (d)	29. (c)	30. (d)	31. (c)	32. (b)	33. (a)	34. (d)	35. (a)	36. (a)
37. (b)	38. (c)	39. (b)	40. (d)	41. (b)	42. (c)	43. (c)	44. (a)	45. (d)	46. (c)
47. (a)	48. (b)	49. (c)	50. (d)	51. (a)	52. (d)				

Reading & Vocabulary

53. (d)	54. (a)	55. (c)	56. (c)	57. (d)	58. (a)	59. (b)	60. (c)	61. (b)	62. (d)
63. (b)	64. (d)	65. (a)	66. (c)	67. (d)	68. (c)	69. (a)	70. (b)	71. (d)	72. (a)
73. (b)	74. (c)	75. (d)	76. (a)	77. (a)	78. (b)	79. (b)	80. (c)		

채점 계산표 [정답 개수 기재]		채점 계산 방법
Grammar	_____ / 26문항	Grammar 정답 개수 ÷ 26 × 100
Listening	_____ / 26문항	Listening 정답 개수 ÷ 26 × 100
Reading & Vocabulary	_____ / 28문항	Reading & Vocabulary 정답 개수 ÷ 28 × 100
총점	_____ / 80문항 ▸ _____ / 100점	총점: 각 영역 합산 정답 개수 ÷ 80 × 100 *소수점 이하는 올림 처리

TEST 05

GRAMMAR
LISTENING
READING & VOCABULARY

01 시제 - 미래진행

Carter has secured a volunteer position in Ecuador this summer, but it starts on the day of his upcoming graduation. Therefore, he _____ for the airport right after the morning ceremony.

(a) will be leaving
(b) will have left
(c) has been leaving
(d) would have left

카터는 올 여름에 에콰도르에 있는 자원 봉사 일자리를 확보했지만, 다가오는 졸업식 날짜에 시작한다. 따라서, 그는 오전의 졸업식 직후에 공항으로 떠나고 있을 것이다.

정답 (a)

해설 동사 leave의 알맞은 형태를 고르는 문제입니다. 빈칸 앞 문장의 but절에 현재시제 동사 starts로 다가오는 졸업식 날짜에 시작한다는 사실을 알리는 말이 쓰여 있는데, 이는 곧 있을 미래에 발생할 것으로 정해진 일을 나타내는 현재시제입니다. 따라서 빈칸 뒤에 위치한 right after the morning ceremony가 미래 시점임을 알 수 있으므로 미래에 일시적으로 진행될 일을 나타내는 미래진행시제 (a) will be leaving이 정답입니다.

어휘 secure ~을 확보하다 volunteer 자원 봉사자 position 일자리, 직책 upcoming 다가오는, 곧 있을 graduation 졸업(식) therefore 따라서, 그러므로 right after ~ 직후에 ceremony 기념 행사, 축하 행사 leave 떠나다, 출발하다

02 준동사 - to부정사

Tin was one of the first metals processed by humans. It was first used during the Bronze Age, when it was combined with copper _____ a mixture known as alloy bronze.

(a) to have created
(b) having created
(c) to create
(d) creating

주석은 인류에 의해 가공 처리된 최초의 금속들 중 하나였다. 그것은 청동기 시대에 처음 사용되었는데, 당시에 청동 합금이라고 알려진 혼합물을 만들어 내기 위해 구리와 결합되었다.

정답 (c)

해설 동사 create의 알맞은 형태를 고르는 문제입니다. 접속사 when 뒤로 주어 it과 수동태 동사 was combined, 그리고 with 전치사구가 쓰여져 있어 이미 when절의 구조가 완전한 상태입니다. 따라서 빈칸 이하 부분은 부가적인 요소인 수식어구의 역할을 해야 하며, '청동 합금이라고 알려진 혼합물을 만들어 내기 위해'라는 의미로 목적을 나타내는 to부정사구를 구성해야 알맞으므로 (c) to create이 정답입니다.

어휘 tin 주석 process ~을 가공 처리하다 combine A with B: A를 B와 결합하다 copper 구리 mixutre 혼합물 known as ~라고 알려진 allow bronze 청동 합금 create ~을 만들어 내다

03 접속사

In the 1960s, a rumor surfaced that the Japanese had renamed a town "Usa." The idea was that this had been done _____ they could export products labeled "Made in USA." The rumor was proven false.

(a) if
(b) even though
(c) unless
(d) so that

1960년대에, 일본이 한 마을을 "Usa"로 개명했다는 소문이 표면화되었다. 그 발상은 그들이 "Made in USA"라고 라벨 표기된 제품을 수출할 수 있도록 그렇게 했다는 것이었다. 이 소문은 거짓인 것으로 드러났다.

정답 (d)

해설 문장의 의미에 어울리는 접속사를 고르는 문제입니다. 빈칸이 속한 that절에서, 빈칸 앞에 위치한 절 this had been done(그렇게 했다)은 앞 문장에서 언급한 '한 마을을 "Usa"로 개명한 일'을 가리킵니다. 빈칸 뒤에 위치한 절이 '그들이 "Made in USA"라고 라벨 표기된 제품을 수출할 수 있었다'를 뜻하는 것으로 볼 때 '"Made in USA"라고 라벨 표기된 제품을 수출할 수 있도록 그렇게 했다'와 같은 의미를 구성해야 자연스러우므로 '~하도록'이라는 의미로 목적을 나타내는 접속사 (d) so that이 정답입니다.

어휘 rumor 소문 surface v. 표면화되다, 수면 위로 떠오르다 rename ~을 개명하다 export ~을 수출하다 label v. ~을 라벨로 표기하다 prove 형용사: ~인 것으로 드러나다 false 거짓의 even though 비록 ~이기는 하지만 unless ~하지 않는다면, ~가 아니라면

04 당위성을 나타내는 동사원형

My cousin Astrid wants to go somewhere warm for her winter vacation to escape Minnesota's freezing weather. Since my friends and I had already decided to go to Hawaii, I suggested that she _____ us.

(a) will join
(b) join
(c) is joining
(d) joined

내 사촌 애스트리드는 미네소타의 몹시 추운 날씨에서 벗어나기 위해 겨울 방학 동안 어딘가 따뜻한 곳으로 가고 싶어 한다. 내 친구들과 내가 이미 하와이로 가기로 결정했기 때문에, 난 그녀에게 우리와 함께 하자고 권했다.

정답 (b)

해설 동사 join의 알맞은 형태를 고르는 문제입니다. 빈칸은 동사 suggested의 목적어 역할을 하는 that절의 동사 자리인데, suggest와 같이 주장/요구/명령/제안 등을 나타내는 동사의 목적어 역할을 하는 that절의 동사는 should 없이 동사원형만 사용하므로 동사원형인 (b) join이 정답입니다.

어휘 somewhere 형용사: 어딘가 ~한 곳으로 escape ~에서 벗어나다, ~에서 탈출하다 freezing 몹시 추운, 얼어붙는 decide to 동사원형: ~하기로 결정하다 suggest that ~하자고 권하다, ~하자고 제안하다

Emery left last night's party early, just before the host entertained the guests with a few piano tunes. Had Emery stayed until the party ended, she _____ his performance.

(a) would have seen
(b) will see
(c) will have seen
(d) would see

에머리는 사회자가 몇몇 피아노 곡으로 손님들을 즐겁게 하기 직전에, 어젯밤 파티에서 일찍 떠났다. 에머리가 파티가 끝날 때까지 머물렀다면, 그녀는 그의 연주를 봤을 것이다.

정답 (a)

해설 동사 see의 알맞은 형태를 고르는 문제입니다. 빈칸이 속한 주절 앞에 위치한 Had Emery stayed는 가정법 과거완료 문장의 If절 If Emery had stayed에서 If가 생략되고 had가 주어 앞으로 이동하면서 도치된 구조입니다. 따라서, 빈칸에 가정법 과거완료 문장의 주절에 쓰이는 「would/could/might + have p.p.」 형태의 동사가 쓰여야 알맞으므로 (a) would have seen이 정답입니다.

어휘 host 사회자 entertain ~을 즐겁게 하다 tune 곡, 선율 performance 연주, 공연

Octopush is an aquatic sport that originated in England. Like hockey, it involves _____ a puck into a net. However, in this case, the sport takes place in a pool.

(a) to have pushed
(b) to push
(c) pushing
(d) having pushed

옥토푸시는 잉글랜드에서 유래한 수중 스포츠이다. 하키처럼, 이것은 네트 안으로 퍽을 밀어 넣는 것을 수반한다. 하지만, 이 경우에, 이 스포츠는 수영장에서 진행된다.

정답 (c)

해설 동사 push의 알맞은 형태를 고르는 문제입니다. 빈칸 앞에 쓰여 있는 동사 involves는 동명사를 목적어로 취하므로 (c) pushing이 정답입니다.

어휘 aquatic 수중의, 수상의 originate 유래하다 involve -ing ~하는 것과 관련되다, ~하는 것을 수반하다 however 하지만, 그러나 case 경우, 사례 take place 진행되다, 개최되다

07

가정법 과거

Ahmed will probably not be able to join the Greenburgh Fun Run on Saturday because he has a leg injury. However, if his leg were to heal faster than expected, he _____ in the event.

(a) would surely have participated
(b) would surely participate
(c) will surely participate
(d) will surely have participated

아메드는 다리 부상이 있기 때문에 아마 토요일에 있을 그린버그 자선 달리기 행사에 참가할 수 없을 것이다. 하지만, 그의 다리가 예상보다 더 빨리 낫게 된다면, 그는 분명 그 행사에 참가할 것이다.

정답 (b)

해설 동사 participate의 알맞은 형태를 고르는 문제입니다. if절의 동사가 가정법 과거를 나타내는 과거시제(were)일 때, 주절의 동사는 「would/could/might + 동사원형」과 같은 형태가 되어야 알맞으므로 (b) would surely participate이 정답입니다. surely와 같은 부사가 would/could/might와 동사원형 사이에 위치할 수 있으므로 선택지에서 부사를 제외한 형태를 찾아 정답을 고르도록 합니다.

어휘 **be able to 동사원형:** ~할 수 있다 **join** ~에 참가하다, ~에 합류하다 **injury** 부상 **however** 하지만, 그러나 **be to 동사원형:** ~하게 되다, ~할 예정이다, ~해야 하다 **heal** 낫다, 치유되다 **than expected** 예상보다 **surely** 분명히, 꼭 **participate in** ~에 참가하다

08

준동사 – to부정사

During its early months of operation, Silver Plate Restaurant struggled to attract customers. Luckily, the owners managed _____ this problem by advertising their business regularly on social media.

(a) having overcome
(b) to overcome
(c) overcoming
(d) to have overcome

운영 초기의 몇 달 동안, 실버 플레이트 레스토랑은 고객을 끌어들이는 데 힘겨워했다. 다행히, 소유주들이 소셜 미디어에 주기적으로 업체를 광고함으로써 이 문제를 극복해 낼 수 있었다.

정답 (b)

해설 동사 overcome의 알맞은 형태를 고르는 문제입니다. 빈칸은 타동사 managed의 목적어 자리이며, manage는 to부정사를 목적어로 취하여 '(간신히) ~해 내다, 어떻게든 ~하다'라는 의미를 나타냅니다. 따라서 to부정사인 (b) to overcome이 정답입니다.

어휘 **operation** 운영, 영업, 가동, 작동 **struggle to 동사원형:** ~하는 데 힘겨워하다, ~하려 애쓰다 **attract** ~을 끌어들이다 **by** (방법) ~함으로써, ~해서 **advertise** ~을 광고하다 **regularly** 주기적으로 **overcome** ~을 극복하다

Research has shown that attempts to hunt coyotes can cause them to breed in greater numbers. American ranchers, _____ to dislike coyotes, are typically cautioned to leave the creatures alone.

(a) who are known
(b) which are known
(c) that are known
(d) what are known

연구에 따르면 코요테를 사냥하려는 시도는 그들이 더 많은 숫자로 번식하는 것을 초래할 수 있는 것으로 나타났다. 코요테를 싫어하는 미국 목장 주인들은 일반적으로 그 생물체를 내버려 두라는 주의를 받는다.

정답 (a)

해설 사람 명사 American ranchers를 뒤에서 수식할 관계사절을 고르는 문제입니다. 선택지 (a)~(d)를 보고 빈칸에 들어갈 관계사절이 관계대명사 뒤에 수동태 동사 are known이 이어지는 구조임을 알 수 있습니다. 사람 명사를 수식하는 관계대명사는 who 또는 that인데, 빈칸 앞에 콤마가 있으므로 관계대명사 who로 시작하는 (a)가 정답입니다.

어휘 attempt to 동사원형: ~하려는 시도 cause + 목적어 + to 동사원형: (목적어)가 ~하는 것을 초래하다 breed 번식하다, 새끼를 낳다 rancher 목장 주인 typically 일반적으로 be cautioned to 동사원형: ~하라는 주의를 받다 leave + 목적어 + alone: (목적어)를 내버려 두다 creature 생물(체) be known to 동사원형: ~하는 것으로 알려지다

✖ 오답 피하기

관계대명사 that은 콤마(,) 뒤에 사용할 수 없는 관계대명사입니다. 빈칸 앞에 콤마(,)가 있는 경우 that으로 시작하는 관계사절은 오답으로 소거합니다.

Winona was invited to interview for the position of office assistant at a financial consulting firm. Right now, she _____ for the interview by reviewing the company's background and the specific job description.

(a) prepares
(b) has been preparing
(c) prepared
(d) is preparing

위노나는 한 재무 컨설팅 회사의 사무 보조 직책에 대한 면접 요청을 받았다. 바로 지금, 그녀는 그 회사의 배경 및 구체적인 직무 설명을 살펴보는 것으로 면접을 준비하고 있다.

정답 (d)

해설 동사 prepare의 알맞은 형태를 고르는 문제입니다. 빈칸 앞에 위치한 Right now가 '바로 지금'이라는 의미를 나타내어 현재 일시적으로 진행되는 일을 뜻하는 현재진행시제 동사와 어울려 쓰이므로 (d) is preparing이 정답입니다.

어휘 be invited to 동사원형: ~하라는 요청을 받다 position 직책, 일자리 assistant 보조, 조수 financial 재무의, 재정의 firm 회사, 업체 by -ing (방법) ~하는 것으로, ~함으로써 review ~을 살펴 보다, ~을 검토하다 specific 구체적인, 특정한 description 설명 prepare ~을 준비하다

11 가정법 과거완료

Last night, Xavier arrived at the railway station just minutes before the train was scheduled to depart for Portland. Had he missed it, he _____ to wait for hours at the station for the next ride.

(a) would have
(b) will have
(c) will have had
(d) would have had

어젯밤에, 자비에르는 기차가 포틀랜드로 출발하기로 예정된 것보다 불과 몇 분 전에 기차역에 도착했다. 그가 그 기차를 놓쳤다면, 다음 승차를 위해 역에서 몇 시간 동안 기다려야 했을 것이다.

정답 (d)

해설 동사 have의 알맞은 형태를 고르는 문제입니다. 빈칸이 속한 주절 앞에 위치한 Had he missed는 가정법 과거완료 문장의 If절 If he had missed에서 If가 생략되고 had가 주어 앞으로 이동하면서 도치된 구조입니다. 따라서 빈칸에 가정법 과거완료 문장의 주절에 쓰이는 「would/could/might + have p.p.」 형태의 동사가 쓰여야 알맞으므로 (d) would have had가 정답입니다.

어휘 arrive 도착하다 be scheduled to 동사원형: ~할 예정이다 depart 출발하다, 떠나다 miss ~을 놓치다, ~에 빠지다, ~을 지나치다 ride 승차, 타고 가기

12 조동사

Superstitions vary widely from culture to culture. According to some Italian and Portuguese beliefs, a person _____ invite bad luck by walking backwards, as this can alert the devil to their location.

(a) would
(b) should
(c) may
(d) must

미신은 문화마다 폭넓게 다양하다. 이탈리아와 포르투갈의 몇몇 믿음에 따르면, 뒤로 걷는 사람은 불운을 불러 올 지도 모르는데, 이것이 마귀에게 자신의 위치를 알릴 수 있기 때문이다.

정답 (c)

TEST 05

해설 빈칸에 들어갈 알맞은 조동사를 고르는 문제입니다. 빈칸이 속한 문장은 미신의 한 가지 예시를 말하는 내용으로서, 뒤로 걷는 것에 따라 발생힐 수 있는 좋지 못한 일을 의미해야 자연스럽습니다. 따라서 '~할 지도 모른다'라는 의미로 추측을 니디니는 조동사 (c) may가 정답입니다.

어휘 superstition 미신 vary 다양하다, 차이가 나다 from culture to culture 문화마다 according to ~에 따르면 belief 믿음, 생각, 신앙 by -ing (방법) ~함으로써, ~해서 alert A to B: A에게 B를 알리다 location 위치, 지점

13 당위성을 나타내는 동사원형

Although raccoons seem harmless, they sometimes carry viruses, despite the absence of obvious symptoms. Because of this, health experts advise that people _____ their hands if they come into contact with one.

(a) will wash
(b) wash
(c) washed
(d) are washing

비록 라쿤이 무해한 것처럼 보이기는 하지만, 명확한 증상의 부재에도 불구하고, 때때로 바이러스를 옮긴다. 이것 때문에, 의료 전문가들은 사람들에게 라쿤과 접촉하게 되는 경우에 손을 씻도록 조언하고 있다.

정답 (b)

해설 동사 wash의 알맞은 형태를 고르는 문제입니다. 빈칸은 동사 advise의 목적어 역할을 하는 that절의 동사 자리인데, advise와 같이 주장/요구/명령/제안 등을 나타내는 동사의 목적어 역할을 하는 that절의 동사는 should 없이 동사원형만 사용하므로 동사원형인 (b) wash가 정답입니다.

어휘 seem 형용사: ~한 것처럼 보이다, ~한 것 같다 harmless 무해한 carry (질병 등) ~을 옮기다 despite ~에도 불구하고 absence 부재, 없음, 결석 obvious 명확한 symptom 증상 expert 전문가 advise that ~하도록 조언하다 come into contact with ~와 접촉하게 되다

14 가정법 과거

Tamyra's homemade pizzas are delicious. Whenever she cooks for us, it feels like we are at a genuine Italian pizzeria. She often says that if she were able to, she _____ her own pizza restaurant.

(a) would have opened
(b) will open
(c) will have opened
(d) would open

타미라가 집에서 만든 피자는 맛이 좋다. 그녀가 우리에게 요리해 줄 때마다, 이탈리아의 정통 피자 전문점에 있는 것 같은 기분이 든다. 그녀는 자신이 할 수 있다면, 개인 피자 레스토랑을 열 것이라고 종종 말한다.

정답 (d)

해설 동사 open의 알맞은 형태를 고르는 문제입니다. if절의 동사가 가정법 과거를 나타내는 과거시제(were)일 때, 주절의 동사 는「would/could/might + 동사원형」과 같은 형태가 되어야 알맞으므로 (d) would open이 정답입니다.

어휘 whenever ~할 때마다 it feels like ~하는 것 같은 기분이다 genuine 정통의, 진짜의 pizzeria 피자 전문점 be able to 동사원형: ~할 수 있다

---

15 조동사

Leaving a dog's nails untended can lead to leg injuries, affecting the animal's long-term mobility. Therefore, pet owners _____ trim their dogs' nails regularly if they want to keep their pets healthy.

(a) could
(b) must
(c) might
(d) would

개의 발톱을 돌보지 않은 상태로 두 는 것은 다리 부상으로 이어질 수 있 으며, 그 동물의 장기적인 이동성에 영향을 미친다. 따라서, 반려동물 주 인은 자신의 반려동물을 건강하게 유지하기를 원한다면 개의 발톱을 주기적으로 손질해야 한다.

정답 (b)

해설 빈칸에 들어갈 알맞은 조동사를 고르는 문제입니다. 빈칸이 속한 문장이 결과를 나타내는 Therefore로 시작하고 있어 앞 문장에서 언급하는 다리 부상 및 이동성 관련 문제로 인해 개의 발톱을 반드시 주기적으로 손질해야 한다는 의무를 나타내 야 알맞습니다. 따라서 '반드시 ~해야 하다'라는 뜻으로 의무나 중요성 등을 나타낼 때 사용하는 (b) must가 정답입니다.

어휘 leave + 목적어 + 형용사: (목적어)를 ~한 상태로 두다 untended 돌보지 않은 lead to ~로 이어지다 injury 부상 affect ~에 영향을 미치다 long-term 장기적인 mobility 이동성, 가동성 therefore 따라서, 그러므로 trim ~을 손질하다, ~을 다듬다 regularly 주기적으로, 규칙적으로 keep + 목적어 + 형용사: (목적어)를 ~한 상태로 유지하다

---

16 시제 – 현재완료진행

The alternative rock band Dark Tide will hold its final performance this weekend. The band _____ at sold-out venues for two decades, and its final concert will be no exception.

(a) is performing
(b) had been performing
(c) has been performing
(d) performs

얼터너티브 록 밴드 다크 타이드가 이번 주말에 자신들의 마지막 공연 을 개최할 것이다. 이 밴드는 20년 동안 계속 매진된 행사장에서 공연 해 오고 있으며, 그들의 마지막 콘서 트도 예외가 아닐 것이다.

정답 (c)

해설 동사 perform의 알맞은 형태를 고르는 문제입니다. 첫 문장에 미래시제 동사 will hold를 통해 미래 시점에 마지막 공연을 개최할 것이라는 말이 쓰여 있어 빈칸 뒤에 위치한 for two decades가 과거에서부터 현재에 이르는 기간임을 알 수 있습

니다. 따라서 과거에서부터 현재까지 계속 이어져 오고 있는 일을 나타내는 현재완료진행 시제로 된 동사가 필요하므로 (c) has been performing이 정답입니다.

어휘 hold ~을 개최하다 performance 공연, 연주(회) sold-out 매진된 venue 행사장, 개최 장소 decade 10년 exception 예외 perform 공연하다, 연주하다

---

17 준동사 - 동명사

Due to the stressful workload, Homer wants to resign as his company's chief engineer. However, he intends to find a new job before quitting so that he does not risk _____ his sole source of income.

(a) to lose
(b) having lost
(c) to have lost
(d) losing

스트레스가 많은 업무량으로 인해, 호머는 소속 회사의 선임 엔지니어로서 사직하기를 원한다. 하지만, 자신의 유일한 수입원을 잃는 위험을 감수하지 않기 위해 그만두기 전에 새로운 직장을 찾을 생각이다.

정답 (d)

해설 동사 lose의 알맞은 형태를 고르는 문제입니다. 빈칸 앞에 쓰여 있는 동사 risk는 동명사를 목적어로 취하므로 (d) losing이 정답입니다.

어휘 due to ~로 인해 workload 업무량 resign 사직하다, 사임하다 however 하지만, 그러나 intend to 동사원형: ~할 생각이다, ~할 작정이다 quit 그만두다 so that (목적) ~하도록, (결과) 그래서, 그래야 risk -ing ~하는 위험을 감수하다 sole 유일한, 단 하나의 source 원천, 근원, 공급원 income 수입, 소득

---

18 시제 - 과거완료진행

The renovation of Watertown Public Library is underway. Some concerned patrons _____ about its deteriorating condition for years before a renovation project was finally approved last month.

(a) are worrying
(b) will be worrying
(c) had been worrying
(d) have been worrying

워터타운 공공 도서관의 개조 공사가 진행 중이다. 일부 우려하는 고객들은 개조 공사 프로젝트가 지난 달에 마침내 승인되기 전까지 수년 동안 그곳의 악화되는 상태에 대해 계속 걱정하고 있었다.

정답 (c)

해설 동사 worry의 알맞은 형태를 고르는 문제입니다. 빈칸 뒤에 '~하기 전에'를 뜻하는 접속사 before가 이끄는 절이 쓰여 있고, 이 before절의 동사 was가 과거시제입니다. 따라서 빈칸이 속한 주절은 그보다 더 이전에 발생한 일을 나타내야 하며, 특정

과거 시점보다 더 이전의 과거에 일어난 일은 과거완료진행 시제로 나타낼 수 있으므로 (c) had been worrying이 정답입니다.

어휘 renovation 개조, 보수 underway 진행 중인 concerned 우려하는, 걱정하는 patron 고객, 손님 deteriorating 악화되는 approve ~을 승인하다

---

19 준동사 – 동명사

While in college, Denzel will stay with his aunt in the city. He considered _____ his own apartment near campus, but he realized he could save money by staying with a relative.

(a) renting
(b) to have rented
(c) having rented
(d) to rent

대학교에 있는 동안, 덴젤은 그 도시에 계시는 고모와 함께 지낼 것이다. 그는 캠퍼스 근처에 있는 자신만의 아파트를 임대하는 것을 고려했지만, 친척과 함께 지냄으로써 돈을 절약할 수 있다는 사실을 알게 되었다.

정답 (a)

해설 동사 rent의 알맞은 형태를 고르는 문제입니다. 빈칸은 타동사 considered의 목적어 자리이며, consider는 동명사를 목적어로 취하여 '~하는 것을 고려하다'라는 의미를 나타냅니다. 따라서 동명사인 (a) renting이 정답입니다.

어휘 while ~하는 동안, ~인 반면 consider -ing ~하는 것을 고려하다 realize (that) ~임을 알게 되다, ~임을 깨닫다 by -ing (방법) ~함으로써, ~해서 relative 친척, 인척 rent ~을 임대하다

---

20 관계사절

The element Moscovium was discovered in 2003 by Russian and American scientists at the Joint Institute for Nuclear Research. This facility is in Moscow, _____ that the element is named after.

(a) what is the city
(b) which is the city
(c) that is the city
(d) where is the city

모스코븀이라는 원소는 2003년에 합동 원자핵 연구소의 러시아 과학자 및 미국 과학자들에 의해 발견되었다. 이 시설은 모스크바에 있으며, 이 원소는 이 도시의 이름을 따 명명된 것이다.

정답 (b)

해설 사물 명사 Moscow를 뒤에서 수식할 관계사절을 고르는 문제입니다. 선택지 (a)~(d)를 보고 빈칸에 들어갈 관계사절이 관계대명사 뒤에 be동사 is와 명사구 보어 the city가 이어지는 불완전한 구조임을 알 수 있습니다. 사물 명사를 수식하는 관계대명사는 which 또는 that인데, 빈칸 앞에 콤마가 있으므로 관계대명사 which로 시작하는 (b)가 정답입니다.

어휘 element 원소, 요소 discover ~을 발견하다 facility 시설(물) name A after B: B의 이름을 따서 A를 명명하다

21 가정법 과거완료

In 2011, the country of South Sudan was established upon separating from Sudan. If a referendum had not approved the split, Sudan _____ its title as the largest country in Africa.

(a) would have kept
(b) would keep
(c) will keep
(d) will have kept

2011년에, 남수단이라는 국가가 수단에서 분리되자마자 설립되었다. 국민 투표가 그 분리를 찬성하지 않았다면, 수단은 아프리카에서 가장 큰 국가로서의 칭호를 유지했을 것이다.

정답 (a)

해설 동사 keep의 알맞은 형태를 고르는 문제입니다. If절의 동사가 had not approved와 같이 가정법 과거완료를 나타내는 「had p.p.」일 때, 주절의 동사는 「would/could/might + have p.p.」와 같은 형태가 되어야 알맞으므로 (a) would have kept가 정답입니다.

어휘 establish ~을 설립하다, ~을 확립하다 upon -ing ~하자마자 separate from ~에서 분리되다 referendum 국민 투표, 총선거 approve ~을 찬성하다, ~을 승인하다 split 분리, 분할, 분열

22 접속부사

The Taino people of the Caribbean region were thought to have been wiped out by European colonizers in the 1500s. _____, a recent study revealed that fifteen percent of Puerto Ricans have Taino ancestry.

(a) Besides
(b) As a result
(c) In addition
(d) However

캐리비안 지역의 타이노족 사람들은 1500년대에 유럽 식민지 개척자들에 의해 말살된 것으로 여겨졌다. 하지만, 최근의 연구에 따르면 푸에르토리코 사람들의 15퍼센트가 타이노족 혈통을 지니고 있는 것으로 나타났다.

정답 (d)

해설 빈칸에 알맞은 접속부사를 고르는 문제이므로 앞뒤 문장들의 의미 관계를 확인해야 합니다. 빈칸 앞 문장에는 타이노족 사람들이 과거에 말살된 것으로 여겨졌다는 말이, 빈칸 뒤에는 푸에르토리코 사람들의 15퍼센트가 타이노족 혈통을 지니고

있다는 말이 각각 쓰여 있습니다. 이는 타이노족 혈통 유지와 관련해 서로 다른 정보를 언급하는 대조적인 흐름이므로 '하지만' 등의 의미로 대조나 반대를 나타낼 때 사용하는 (d) However가 정답입니다.

어휘 region 지역, 지방 be thought to 동사원형: ~하는 것으로 여겨지다 wipe out ~을 말살시키다, ~을 전멸시키다 colonizer 식민지 개척자 recent 최근의 reveal that ~임을 나타내다, ~임을 드러내다 ancestry 혈통, 가계

23 시제 – 과거진행

A production crew was stationed at the mall this morning to film a commercial starring a famous actress. When I walked by, the crew _____ equipment while the actress signed autographs for fans.

(a) was setting up
(b) will be setting up
(c) is setting up
(d) has been setting up

한 제작팀이 오늘 아침에 한 유명 여배우가 주연인 광고를 촬영하기 위해 쇼핑몰에 자리잡고 있었다. 내가 걸어서 지나갔을 때, 그 여배우가 팬들을 위해 사인을 해 주는 동안 그 팀이 장비를 설치하고 있었다.

정답 (a)

해설 동사구 set up의 알맞은 형태를 고르는 문제입니다. 빈칸 앞에 과거시제 동사(walked)를 포함한 When절이 쓰여 있어 이 When절이 가리키는 과거 시점에 장비를 설치하는 일이 일시적으로 진행되던 상황을 나타내야 자연스러우므로 이러한 의미로 쓰이는 과거진행시제 (a) was setting up이 정답입니다.

어휘 production 제작, 생산 crew (함께 작업하는) 팀, 조 station v. ~을 위치시키다, ~을 배치하다 film v. ~을 촬영하다 commercial n. 광고 (방송) star v. ~을 주연으로 하다 equipment 장비 while ~하는 동안, ~인 반면 sign an autograph 사인해 주다 set up ~을 설치하다, ~을 설정하다, ~을 준비하다

24 준동사 – to부정사

Now that his final exams are over, Ezra is excited to get back into the *Silver Striker* television series. He plans _____ all nine seasons over the summer break.

(a) to have watched
(b) watching
(c) to watch
(d) having watched

이제 기말 고사가 끝나서, 에즈라는 다시 <실버 스트라이커> 텔레비전 시리즈를 다시 볼 수 있게 되어 들떠 있다. 그는 여름 방학 동안에 걸쳐 아홉 개의 시즌을 모두 시청할 계획이다.

정답 (c)

해설 동사 watch의 알맞은 형태를 고르는 문제입니다. 빈칸은 타동사 plans의 목적어 자리이며, plan은 to부정사를 목적어로 취하여 '~할 계획이다'라는 의미를 나타냅니다. 따라서 to부정사인 (c) to watch가 정답입니다.

어휘 now that (이제) ~이므로 get back into ~을 다시 시작하다, ~로 돌아가다 plan to 동사원형: ~할 계획이다 over ~ 동안에 길처 summer break 여름 빙힉, 여름 휴가

25 가정법 과거

Saturn's rings occasionally disappear due to a tilt in the planet's axis. If someone were to view Saturn through a telescope during one of these periods, the planet _____ to have no rings at all.

(a) would seem
(b) will seem
(c) will have seemed
(d) would have seemed

토성의 고리는 그 행성 중심축의 기울기로 인해 이따금씩 사라진다. 만일 누군가가 이 기간들 중 한 번 동안 망원경을 통해 토성을 보게 된다면, 그 행성에 고리가 전혀 없는 것처럼 보일 것이다.

정답 (a)

해설 동사 seem의 알맞은 형태를 고르는 문제입니다. If절의 동사가 가정법 과거를 나타내는 과거시제(were)일 때, 주절의 동사는「would/could/might + 동사원형」과 같은 형태가 되어야 알맞으므로 (a) would seem이 정답입니다.

어휘 occasionally 이따금씩 disappear 사라지다 due to ~로 인해, ~ 때문에 tilt 기울기 planet 행성 axis (중심)축 be to 동사원형: ~하게 되다, ~할 예정이다, ~해야 하다 view ~을 보다 telescope 망원경 no ~ at all 전혀 ~ 않다 seem to 동사원형: ~하는 것처럼 보이다, ~하는 것 같다

26 시제 - 미래완료진행

Bailey is the most senior employee in her company, and she has no plans to resign anytime soon. By next year, she _____ there for ten years already.

(a) will be working
(b) will have been working
(c) is working
(d) has been working

베일리 씨는 소속 회사에서 가장 연장자인 직원이며, 당장은 사직할 계획이 없다. 내년쯤이면, 그녀는 그곳에서 벌써 10년째 계속 근무하고 있을 것이다.

정답 (b)

해설 동사 write의 알맞은 형태를 고르는 문제입니다. 빈칸 앞에 위치한 By next year가 미래시점을 나타내고 있고, 빈칸이 포함된 문장에 기간을 나타내는「for + 기간」표현인 for ten years가 쓰여 있어 10년 동안 계속 진행 중일 미래의 상태를 나타내는 미래완료진행형 동사가 필요하므로 (b) will have been working이 정답입니다.

어휘 senior 연장자의, 고위의, 선임의, 선배의 plan to 동사원형: ~하려는 계획 resign 사임하다, 사직하다 anytime soon 당장은 by ~쯤이면

Listening

PART 1

M: Hello, Rachel, I didn't know you shopped here.

F: Hi Craig! **27** I come to this grocery store when I'm visiting my sister. She lives nearby.

M: My place is around here too. Maybe we could all hang out sometime.

F: That sounds great! You know, last week I saw you shopping here. I tried to get your attention, but you had earphones in and didn't hear me.

M: Oh really? Sorry about that! When I shop, I like to listen to podcasts, so sometimes I don't know someone's talking to me unless I'm looking right at them.

F: I listen to podcasts when I'm doing chores, and it leads to the same problem. Earlier this week, I was gardening while listening to a show, and **28** I didn't hear my next-door neighbor walking up to me. She tapped me on the shoulder, and I was so surprised that I nearly fainted! I didn't want to surprise you like that.

M: Seeing you would have been a good surprise! By the way, I'm always looking for new podcasts — how do you find out about the ones you listen to?

F: There's a podcast especially for that! It's called *The New Podcast Podcast*, and every week the hosts discuss the best podcasts they've listened to recently.

남: 안녕하세요, 레이첼 씨, 이곳에서 쇼핑하시는 줄은 몰랐네요.

여: 안녕하세요, 크레이그 씨! 여동생 집을 방문할 때 이 식료품점에 와요. 여동생이 근처에 살거든요.

남: 저희 집도 이 주변에 있어요. 아마 언제 다같이 어울릴 수 있겠네요.

여: 아주 좋은 것 같아요! 있잖아요, 지난 주에 이곳에서 쇼핑하시는 걸 봤어요. 당신의 주의를 끌어 보려고 했는데, 이어폰을 끼고 계셔서 제 말을 듣지 못하셨어요.

남: 아, 정말인가요? 죄송합니다! 저는 쇼핑할 때, 팟캐스트를 듣는 걸 좋아해서, 때때로 제가 직접 쳐다보지 않으면 누군가가 제게 말을 걸고 있다는 걸 알지 못해요.

여: 저는 잡일을 할 때 팟캐스트를 듣는데, 같은 문제가 생겨요. 이번 주 초에는, 팟캐스트 쇼를 들으면서 정원에서 일하고 있었는데, 저희 옆집 사시는 이웃이 제게 걸어 오시는 소리를 듣지 못했어요. 그분이 제 어깨를 두드리셨는데, 너무 놀라는 바람에 거의 졸도할 뻔했어요! 저도 당신을 그렇게 놀라게 하고 싶지 않았어요.

남: 뵙게 되었다면 기분 좋은 놀라움이었을 거예요! 그건 그렇고, 저는 항상 새로운 팟캐스트를 찾고 있는데, 들으시는 것에 대해 어떻게 아시게 되나요?

여: 특별히 그런 부분을 위한 팟캐스트가 있어요! <더 뉴 팟캐스트 팟캐스트>라고 부르는데, 매주 진행자들이 각자 최근에 들어 본 최고의 팟캐스트를 이야기해요.

M: That sounds like a great way to find out about new shows! **29** What's your favorite podcast that you've discovered lately, Rachel?

F: 29 Well, Craig, I love podcasts where the guests tell spooky tales. There's one called *Bedtime Stories to Keep You Awake*, and it's great. Every episode features a different horror novel writer.

M: That sounds cool, but I'm not sure I could handle spooky stories! They could give me nightmares. Personally, I like comedy podcasts.

F: Oh really? I like comedy, too. Have you found a good one?

M: There are lots, but **30** my favorite is called *Only Half Joking*.

F: Is that the one where the hosts interview famous comedians?

M: No, actually. **30** Guests on the show are mostly young or up-and-coming comedians. It's a great way for newcomers to get exposure to a wider audience.

F: That sounds like fun. I'll look into it.

M: You should. **31** The best thing about *Only Half Joking* is that the host has been running the podcast for years, so there's tons of content to catch up on.

F: Oh, I love finding an interesting podcast with lots of episodes. But do you know what I *don't* love about podcasts?

M: Hmm… Is it when the host has an unpleasant speaking voice?

남: 그건 새로운 쇼에 대해 알아보기 아주 좋은 방법인 것 같네요! 최근에 발견하신 가장 마음에 드는 팟캐스트는 뭔가요, 레이첼 씨?

여: 음, 크레이그 씨, 저는 초대 손님들이 오싹한 얘기를 해 주는 팟캐스트를 아주 좋아해요. <잠을 깨워 드리는 잠자리 이야기>라고 부르는 게 있는데, 아주 재미있어요. 모든 에피소드가 다른 공포 소설 작가를 특징으로 해요.

남: 아주 좋은 것 같긴 하지만, 저는 오싹한 이야기를 감당할 수 있을지 잘 모르겠어요! 악몽을 꿀 수 있거든요. 개인적으로, 저는 코미디 팟캐스트를 좋아해요.

여: 아, 그래요? 저도 코미디를 좋아해요. 좋은 것을 찾으셨나요?

남: 많긴 한데, 제가 가장 좋아하는 건 <온리 하프 조킹>이라고 부르는 것이에요.

여: 진행자들이 유명 코미디언을 인터뷰하는 쇼인가요?

남: 실은, 아닙니다. 그 쇼의 초대 손님들은 대부분 젊거나 새롭게 떠오르는 코미디언들이에요. 신예들이 더 폭넓은 청자들에 대한 노출 효과를 얻을 수 있는 아주 좋은 방법이죠.

여: 재미있을 것 같아요. 저도 살펴 볼게요.

남: 그렇게 해 보세요. <온리 하프 조킹>의 가장 좋은 점은 진행자가 수년 동안 그 팟캐스트를 계속 운영해 오고 있어서, 따라잡아야 할 콘텐츠가 아주 많다는 거예요.

여: 아, 제가 에피소드가 많은 흥미로운 팟캐스트를 찾는 걸 아주 좋아해요. 하지만 제가 팟캐스트와 관련해서 정말 좋아하지 않는 게 뭔지 아세요?

남: 흠… 진행자가 듣기 싫은 목소리를 지니고 있는 경우인가요?

F: No. I'm not usually bothered by that. **32** My biggest problem with some podcasts is when guests go on tangents about random topics for long periods of time.

M: Oh, yeah, that happens pretty often, especially if the guests or hosts are close friends. They start talking about people they know or things they experienced that I'm unfamiliar with.

F: Exactly. I wish they'd stay focused on the episode's subject.

M: Agreed. Well, Rachel, I need to get home. My family's having a board game night, and I need to get everything set up.

F: Sounds good, Craig. Hey, **33** why don't you text me next week? You could come to my sister's house for dinner. She's a great cook.

M: **33** That sounds fun! I'll talk to you soon.

여: 아뇨. 그런 건 저는 보통 신경 쓰지 않아요. 몇몇 팟캐스트에 대한 제가 겪는 큰 문제는 초대 손님이 무작위의 주제와 관련해서 장시간 동안 옆길로 새는 경우입니다.

남: 아, 네, 그런 일이 꽤 자주 일어나죠, 특히 초대 손님이나 진행자들이 가까운 친구라면요. 서로 아는 사람이나 그들이 경험한 일인데 제가 잘 알지 못하는 것에 관해 이야기하기 시작하죠.

여: 바로 그거예요. 해당 에피소드의 주제에 계속 초점이 맞춰져 있으면 좋겠어요.

남: 동감입니다. 저, 레이첼 씨, 제가 집에 가야 합니다. 가족이 밤에 보드 게임을 하는데, 제가 모든 걸 준비해 둬야 해서요.

여: 재미있겠네요, 크레이그 씨. 있잖아요, 다음 주에 제게 문자 메시지 보내 보시면 어떨까요? 제 여동생 집에 저녁 식사하시러 오세요. 요리를 아주 잘 하거든요.

남: 재미있을 것 같네요! 곧 연락 드릴게요.

어휘 hang out 함께 어울리다, 함께 시간을 보내다 attention 주의, 주목, 관심 unless ~하지 않는다면, ~가 아니라면 chore 잡일, 허드렛일 lead to ~로 이어지다 garden v. 정원에서 일하다 hear + 목적어 + -ing: (목적어)가 ~하는 소리를 듣다 tap ~을 두드리다 faint 졸도하다, 기절하다 by the way (화제 전환 시) 그건 그렇고, 그런데 look for ~을 찾다 find out about ~에 관해 알아보다, ~에 관해 파악하다 recently 최근에 way to 동사원형: ~하는 방법 discover ~을 발견하다 spooky 오싹한, 으스스한 tale 이야기 episode (방송의) 에피소드, 1회분 feature ~을 특징으로 하다 handle ~을 감당하다, ~을 처리하다 up-and-coming 새롭게 떠오르는 newcomer 신예, 신입 exposure 노출 (효과) audience (시)청자들, 청중, 관객 look into ~을 살펴 보다, ~을 조사하다 run ~을 운영하다 catch up on (진행, 수준 등) ~을 따라잡다 usually 보통, 일반적으로 bother ~을 신경 쓰다 go on tangents 옆길로 새다 random 무작위의 be unfamiliar with ~을 잘 알다, ~에 익숙하다 stay + 형용사: ~한 상태를 유지하다 focused on ~에 초점이 맞춰진 subject 주제 get + 목적어 + p.p.: (목적어)를 ~되게 하다 set up ~을 준비하다, ~을 설치하다, ~을 설정하다 text v. ~에게 문자 메시지를 보내다

What are Rachel and Craig doing at the start of the conversation?

(a) hanging out at a party
(b) getting some groceries
(c) going to a concert
(d) shopping for clothes

레이첼과 크레이그는 대화 시작 부분에 무엇을 하고 있는가?

(a) 파티에서 서로 어울리는 일
(b) 식료품을 구입하는 일
(c) 콘서트에 가는 일
(d) 의류를 쇼핑하는 일

정답 (b)

해설 대화 초반부에 레이첼과 크레이그가 서로 쇼핑하는 상황임을 언급하고 있고, 특히 레이첼 씨가 식료품점에 와 있음을(I come to this grocery store when I'm visiting my sister. She lives nearby) 밝히고 있으므로 (b)가 정답입니다.

어휘 hang out 서로 어울리다, 함께 시간을 보내다

패러프레이징

come to this grocery store → getting some groceries

How did Rachel's neighbor surprise her?

(a) by accidentally bumping into her
(b) by sending her flowers
(c) by sharing some gardening tools
(d) by suddenly dropping by

레이첼의 이웃이 어떻게 그녀를 놀라게 했는가?

(a) 우연히 부딪쳐서
(b) 그녀에게 꽃을 보내서
(c) 몇몇 원예 도구를 공유해서
(d) 갑자기 들러서

정답 (d)

해설 질문의 키워드인 neighbor가 언급된 부분에서 레이첼이 옆집 사는 이웃이 자신에게 걸어 오는 소리를 듣지 못해서(I didn't hear my next-door neighbor walking up to me) 크게 놀랐던 일을 언급하고 있으므로 (d)가 정답입니다.

어휘 accidentally 실수로, 우연히 bump into ~와 부딪치다, ~와 우연히 만나다 suddenly 갑자기 drop by (잠깐) 들르다

패러프레이징

walking up to me → dropping by

29 세부 정보

What has been Rachel's favorite podcast lately?

(a) one that discusses horror films
(b) one that helps improve sleep
(c) one that features scary stories
(d) one that hosts famous actors

레이첼이 요즘 가장 좋아하는 팟캐스트는 무엇이었는가?

(a) 공포 영화를 이야기하는 것
(b) 수면 상태를 개선하는 데 도움을 주는 것
(c) 무서운 이야기를 특징으로 하는 것
(d) 유명 배우를 맞이하는 것

TEST 05

Who are the usual guests on Craig's favorite podcast?

(a) television comedy stars
(b) teachers of comedy writing
(c) retired stand-up comedians
(d) people who are new to comedy

크레이그가 가장 좋아하는 팟캐스트에서 통상적인 초대 손님은 누구인가?

(a) 텔레비전 코미디 스타들
(b) 희극 작문의 강사들
(c) 은퇴한 스탠드업 코미디언들
(d) 코미디를 처음 시작한 사람들

정답 (d)

해설 질문의 키워드인 Craig's favorite podcast가 언급된 부분에서 크레이그가 자신이 가장 좋아하는 것이 <온리 하프 조킹>이라고(my favorite is called *Only Half Joking*) 밝힌 다음, 그 쇼의 초대 손님들이 대부분 젊거나 새롭게 떠오르는 코미디언들이라고(Guests on the show are mostly young or up-and-coming comedians) 설명하고 있습니다. 이는 코미디를 시작한지 얼마 되지 않은 사람들로 볼 수 있으므로 (d)가 정답입니다.

어휘 usual 통상적인, 평소의, 보통의 retired 은퇴한

패러프레이징

young or up-and-coming comedians → people who are new to comedy

According to Craig, what is the best thing about the show, *Only Half Joking*?

(a) It changes hosts weekly.
(b) It features fun competitions.
(c) It has plenty of episodes.
(d) It invites audience feedback.

크레이그의 말에 따르면, <온리 하프 조킹>이라는 쇼와 관련해 가장 좋은 점은 무엇인가?

(a) 매주 진행자를 바꾼다.
(b) 재미있는 경쟁을 특징으로 한다.
(c) 에피소드가 많이 있다.
(d) 청자 의견을 요청한다.

정답 (c)

해설 질문의 키워드인 the best thing about the show, *Only Half Joking*이 언급된 부분에서 크레이그가 그 쇼의 진행자가 수년 동안 팟캐스트를 계속 운영해 오고 있어서, 따라잡아야 할 콘텐츠가 아주 많다는 사실을(The best thing about *Only Half Joking* is that the host has been running the podcast for years, so there's tons of content to catch up on) 알리고 있으므로 (c)가 정답입니다.

어휘 competition 경쟁, 시합, 대회 plenty of 많은 invite ~을 요청하다 feedback 의견

32 세부 정보

Why do some podcasts bother Rachel?

(a) because the episodes last too long
(b) because the conversations go off topic
(c) because the hosts interview too many guests
(d) because the speakers have annoying voices

왜 일부 팟캐스트가 레이첼을 신경 쓰이게 하는가?

(a) 에피소드들이 너무 오래 지속되기 때문에
(b) 대화가 주제에서 벗어나기 때문에
(c) 진행자들이 너무 많은 초대 손님을 인터뷰하기 때문에
(d) 화자들이 듣기 거북한 목소리를 지니고 있기 때문에

정답 (b)

해설 대화 중반부에 레이첼이 일부 팟캐스트와 관련된 문제를 언급하면서 초대 손님이 무작위의 주제와 관련해서 장시간 동안 옆길로 새는 경우를(My biggest problem with some podcasts is when guests go on tangents about random topics for long periods of time) 말하고 있습니다. 이는 주제에서 벗어난 이야기를 하는 경우를 의미하므로 (b)가 정답입니다.

어휘 last v. 지속되다 go off ~에서 벗어나다 annoying 거북하게 만드는, 짜증 나게 만드는

❌ 오답 피하기

레이첼이 자신이 싫어하는 것을 언급하는 부분에서 진행자가 초대 손님과 너무 오래 엉뚱한 얘기를 하는 것을 언급할 뿐, 인터뷰하는 초대 손님의 숫자와 관련해서는 이야기하지 않으므로 (c)는 오답입니다.

What will Rachel and Craig probably do next week?	레이첼과 크레이그는 다음주에 무엇을 할 것 같은가?
(a) have a meal together	(a) 함께 식사한다
(b) go to a family reunion	(b) 가족 모임에 간다
(c) hold a game night	(c) 게임의 밤 행사를 연다
(d) attend a cooking class	(d) 요리 강좌에 참석한다

정답 (a)

해설 질문의 키워드인 next week이 언급된 부분에서 레이첼이 다음 주에 문자 메시지로 연락하라고 제안하면서 자신의 여동생 집에 식사하러 오라고 말하자(why don't you text me next week? You could come to my sister's house for dinner. She's a great cook), 크레이그가 동의하고 있으므로(That sounds fun! I'll talk to you soon) (a)가 정답입니다.

어휘 reunion 모임, 재회, 재결합 hold ~을 열다, ~을 개최하다 attend ~에 참석하다

패러프레이징

come to my sister's house for dinner → have a meal together

Good day to all of you magicians out there! I'm pleased to announce that **34** we have officially opened ticket sales for the twenty-second annual Wizard Con, the biggest magicians' conference in the country. If you've never been to Wizard Con, allow me to tell you what it's all about and introduce some of the activities we have in store this year.

The original Wizard Con staple is, of course, the Trick Exchange, an open market for magicians to purchase props, equipment, and even trick guides. Popular makers of magic accessories will have booths set up in the main hall of the convention center. Company representatives will be available to demonstrate their products, answer questions, and take special orders for the unique items you may need for future performances. **35** If you order any custom-made items, the products will be created and shipped within no more than two business days, guaranteed.

Next up, we are encouraging all attendees to participate in our trick competition. This year, we're pleased to announce that we'll have a celebrity judge joining us. **36** Famous magician Max Hamilton, recently back from his sold-out European tour, will be joining our judging panel of specialists. Contestants will perform their own original tricks in front of the judges. If the panel is unable to determine how your trick was done, you will advance to the finals, which will be held later this year at the Starlight Palace Theater in Las Vegas. The winner of the final competition will receive a twenty-thousand-dollar prize.

Another popular part of Wizard Con is our annual fashion display. We know that in the magic business, style is an important part of your act. We'll be showcasing outfits that not only look great but also offer the special features magicians need — most

세상의 모든 마술사 여러분 안녕하세요! 전국에서 가장 규모가 큰 마술사 컨퍼런스인 제22회 연례 위저드 콘에 대한 입장권 판매를 공식적으로 개시했음을 알려 드리게 되어 기쁩니다. 저희 위저드 콘에 와 보신 적이 전혀 없으시다면, 제가 그 모든 것에 관해 알려 드리고 저희가 올해 마련한 몇몇 활동들도 소개해 드리겠습니다.

원래 위저드 콘의 주된 요소는, 당연히, '트릭 익스체인지'로서, 이는 마술사들이 소품과 장비, 심지어 마술 가이드까지 구입할 수 있는 공개 시장입니다. 마술 부대용품의 인기 있는 제조사들이 컨벤션 센터의 본관에 부스를 설치할 것입니다. 회사 대표자들이 각자의 제품을 시연하고, 질문에 답변해 드리며, 여러분께서 향후의 공연에 필요하실 수 있는 독특한 제품에 대한 특별 주문도 받을 수 있을 것입니다. 어떤 맞춤 제작 제품이든 주문하시는 경우, 해당 제품은 불과 이틀 만에 제작되어 배송된다는 점을 보장해 드립니다.

다음으로, 저희는 모든 참석자들께 저희 마술 경연 대회에 참가하시는 것을 권해 드립니다. 올해는, 유명 인사 한 분께서 심사 위원으로 함께 자리하실 것이라는 사실을 알려 드리게 되어 기쁩니다. 최근 전석 매진을 기록한 유럽 투어에서 돌아 오신, 유명 마술사 맥스 해밀턴 씨께서 저희 전문가 심사 위원단에 합류하실 예정입니다. 참가자들은 이 심사 위원들 앞에서 각자의 독창적인 마술을 공연하게 됩니다. 심사 위원단이 여러분의 마술이 어떻게 된 것인지 밝혀 내지 못하는 경우, 결선에 진출하시게 될 것이며, 이는 라스베가스의 스타라이트 팰리스 시어터에서 올 하반기에 개최됩니다. 결선 대회 우승자께서는 2만 달러의 상금을 받습니다.

위저드 콘의 인기 있는 또 다른 부분은 저희 연례 패션 전시회입니다. 저희는 마술 업계에서, 스타일이 여러분의 공연에서 중요한 일부분임을 알고 있습니다. 저희는 훌륭해 보일 뿐만 아니라, 마술사들이 필요로 하는 특별한 특징들, 그 중 가장 중요한,

importantly, secret pockets where you can hide anything from a handkerchief to a white rabbit. **37** All the outfits are available to buy, but supplies are limited. Don't wait too long to check out what we have in stock!

Finally, we at Wizard Con want to make our community as friendly and welcoming to children as possible. That's why **38** we have a special magic workshop for young ones interested in learning a few new skills. A crew of professional magicians will amaze your children with some basic magic before teaching them how to perform tricks themselves. Little ones can learn anything from card magic to pulling ping pong balls out of their ears!

We would love nothing more than to see the magic community grow, and that's why we're offering a special promotion on tickets. **39** For every two tickets you buy, you'll receive one extra for free. So, come on down to Wizard Con, and bring your friends along for a magical time!

손수건에서부터 흰토끼에 이르기까지 어떤 것이든 숨길 수 있는 비밀 주머니까지 제공해 드리는 복장을 선보일 것입니다. 모든 복장은 구입 가능하지만, 공급량은 제한되어 있습니다. 저희가 재고로 보유하고 있는 것을 확인하기 위해 너무 오래 기다리지 마십시오!

마지막으로, 저희 위저드 콘은 우리 지역 사회를 가능한 한 아이들에게 친절하고 따뜻한 곳으로 만들고 싶습니다. 그것이 바로 저희가 몇 가지 새로운 기술을 터득하는 데 관심이 있는 어린 마술사들을 위한 특별 마술 워크숍을 여는 이유입니다. 전문 마술사로 구성된 팀이 마술을 공연하는 방법을 직접 가르쳐 드리기 전에 몇몇 기본적인 마술로 여러분의 아이들을 놀라게 해 드릴 것입니다. 어린 마술사들은 카드 마술에서부터 귀에서 탁구공을 꺼내는 것에 이르기까지 어떤 것이든 배울 수 있습니다!

저희는 마술 업계가 성장하는 모습을 보는 것 외에는 더 이상 바라는 것이 없으며, 그것이 바로 저희가 입장권에 대해 특별 판촉 행사를 제공해 드리는 이유입니다. 구입하시는 모든 입장권 두 장에 대해, 무료로 추가 한 장을 더 받으시게 됩니다. 그렇게, 저희 위저드 콘에 찾아 오시기 바라며, 친구분들과 함께 오셔서 마법 같은 시간을 즐겨 보시기 바랍니다!

어휘 officially 공식적으로, 정식으로 annual 연례적인, 해마다의 allow + 목적어 + to 동사원형: (목적어)가 ~할 수 있게 해 주다 introduce ~을 소개하다 original 원래의, 독창적인 props 소품 equipment 장비 accessories 부대용품 have + 목적어 + p.p.: (목적어)를 ~되게 하다 set up ~을 설치하다, ~을 준비하다 representative n. 대표자, 직원 be available to 동사원형: ~할 수 있다 demonstrate ~을 시연하다, ~을 시범 보이다 unique 독특한, 특별한 performance 공연, 연기, 연주 custom-made 맞춤 제작의 no more than 불과 ~인, 겨우 ~인 guarantee ~을 보장하다 encourage + 목적어 + to 동사원형: (목적어)가 ~하도록 권하다 attendee 참석자 participate in ~에 참가하다 competition 경연 대회, 경기 대회 celebrity 유명인 judge 심사 위원 recently 최근 sold-out 매진된, 품절된 contestant (시합 등의) 참가자, 경쟁자 be unable to 동사원형: ~할 수 없다 determine ~을 밝혀 내다 advance to ~로 진출하다, ~로 나아가다 hold ~을 개최하다 receive ~을 받다 showcase ~을 선보이다 outfit 복장, 옷 not only A but also B: A뿐만 아니라 B도 feature 특징 supplies 공급량, 공급 물품 limited 제한된 have + 목적어 + in stock: (목적어)를 재고로 보유하다 as A as possible: 가능한 한 A한 welcoming (마음 등이) 따뜻한, 따뜻하게 맞이하는 crew (함께 작업하는) 팀, 조 amaze ~을 놀라게 하다 how to 동사원형: ~하는 방법 would love nothing more than to 동사원형: ~하는 것에는 외에 더 이상 바라는 것이 없다 see + 목적어 + 동사원형: (목적어)가 ~하는 모습을 보다 promotion 판촉 (행사), 홍보, 촉진 receive ~을 받다 extra 추가되는 것 for free 무료로 bring + 목적어 + along: (목적어)를 데려 오다

What is the talk mainly about?

(a) a magic shop opening
(b) a magician's charity event
(c) a brand-new magic show
(d) a convention for magicians

담화가 주로 무엇에 관한 것인가?

(a) 마술용품 매장 개장
(b) 한 마술사의 자선 행사
(c) 완전히 새로운 마술 쇼
(d) 마술사들을 위한 컨벤션

정답 (d)

해설 화자가 담화를 시작하면서 전국에서 가장 규모가 큰 마술사 컨퍼런스인 제22회 연례 위저드 콘에 대한 입장권 판매를 공식적으로 시작했음을(we have officially opened ticket sales for the twenty-second annual Wizard Con, the biggest magicians' conference in the country) 알린 후, 그 행사와 관련된 정보를 이야기하고 있으므로 (d)가 정답입니다.

어휘 charity 자선 (활동), 자선 단체 brand-new 완전히 새로운

패러프레이징

magicians' conference → convention for magicians

What do companies guarantee for special-order items?

(a) They promise rapid processing.
(b) They offer a two-year repair warranty.
(c) They promise free returns.
(d) They offer discounts on large orders.

업체들은 특별 주문 제품에 대해 무엇을 보장하는가?

(a) 빠른 처리를 약속한다.
(b) 2년 기간의 수리 보증을 제공한다.
(c) 무료 반품을 약속한다.
(d) 대량 주문에 대해 할인을 제공한다.

정답 (a)

해설 질문의 키워드인 special-order items가 custom-made items로 언급된 부분에서 어떤 맞춤 제작 제품이든 주문하는 경우에 제품이 불과 이틀 만에 제작되어 배송된다는 점을 보장한다고(If you order any custom-made items, the products will be created and shipped within no more than two business days, guaranteed) 알리고 있습니다. 이는 빠른 처리를 보장한다는 뜻이므로 (a)가 정답입니다.

어휘 promise ~을 약속하다 processing 처리 (과정) warranty 품질 보증(서) return 반품, 반환

패러프레이징

will be created and shipped within no more than two business days, guaranteed → promise rapid processing

Who will decide on the finalists for the trick competition?

(a) a panel of experts
(b) fellow contestants
(c) several celebrity judges
(d) all event attendees

누가 마술 대회 결선 진출자를 결정할 것인가?

(a) 전문가 위원단
(b) 동료 참가자들
(c) 여러 유명인 심사 위원들
(d) 모든 행사 참석자

정답 (a)

해설 질문의 키워드인 trick competition이 언급된 부분에서 유명 마술사 맥스 해밀턴 씨가 전문가 심사 위원단에 합류한다는 (Famous magician Max Hamilton, recently back from his sold-out European tour, will be joining our judging panel of specialists) 정보가 제시되므로 (a)가 정답입니다.

어휘 decide on ~을 결정하다 finalist 결선 진출자 expert 전문가 fellow 동료의, 또래의

패러프레이징

our judging panel of specialists → a panel of experts

❌ 오답 피하기

해당 부분에서 유명인으로 마술사 맥스 해밀턴 씨 한 명만 언급될 뿐, 나머지 심사 위원들도 유명인인지는 알 수 없으므로 (c)는 오답입니다.

37 세부 정보

Why might listeners hurry to see the fashion display?

(a) to meet a celebrity
(b) to purchase an outfit
(c) to enter a raffle
(d) to receive a free gift

청자들이 왜 패션 전시회를 보기 위해 서둘러야 할 수도 있는가?

(a) 유명인을 만나기 위해
(b) 옷 한 벌을 구입하기 위해
(c) 경품 추첨 행사에 참가하기 위해
(d) 무료 선물을 받기 위해

정답 (b)

해설 질문의 키워드인 fashion display가 언급된 부분에서 화자는 모든 복장이 구입 가능하지만 공급량이 제한되어 있기 때문에 너무 오래 기다리지 말라고(All the outfits are available to buy, but supplies are limited. Don't wait too long to check out what we have in stock!) 당부하고 있습니다. 이는 신속히 해당 의류 제품을 구입할 것을 알리는 것이므로 (b)가 정답입니다.

어휘 enter ~에 참가하다 raffle 경품 추첨 행사

outfits are available to buy → purchase an outfit

38 세부 정보

Why will the organizers hold a special magic workshop?

(a) to raise money for charity
(b) to promote a local academy
(c) to inspire kids to join in
(d) to advertise certain products

주최측이 특별 마술 워크숍을 개최할 이유는 무엇인가?

(a) 자선 기금을 마련하기 위해
(b) 지역 학교를 홍보하기 위해
(c) 아이들에게 함께 하도록 영감을 주기 위해
(d) 특정 제품을 광고하기 위해

정답 (c)

해설 질문의 키워드인 special magic workshop이 언급된 부분에서 새로운 기술을 터득하는 데 관심이 있는 어린 마술사들을 위한 특별 마술 워크숍을 연다는(we have a special magic workshop for young ones interested in learning a few new skills) 내용이 언급되었습니다. 이는 마술에 관심이 있는 아이들에게 함께 하도록 권장하기 위한 조치에 해당하므로 (c)가 정답입니다.

어휘 organizer 주최자, 조직자 raise money 기금을 마련하다, 모금하다 academy 학교, 학술원 promote ~을 홍보하다 local 지역의, 현지의 inspire + 목적어 + to 동사원형: (목적어)에게 ~하도록 영감을 주다 advertise ~을 광고하다 certain 특정한, 일정한

39 세부 정보

How can guests get a free ticket?

(a) by registering in advance
(b) by purchasing two at a time
(c) by posting on social media
(d) by joining the magicians' club

손님들은 어떻게 무료 입장권을 받을 수 있는가?

(a) 사전 등록함으로써
(b) 한 번에 두 장을 구입함으로써
(c) 소셜 미디어에 글을 게시함으로써
(d) 마술사 동호회에 가입함으로써

정답 (b)

해설 질문의 키워드인 free와 ticket이 언급된 부분에서 두 장을 구입하면 추가 한 장을 무료로 받는다고(For every two tickets you buy, you'll receive one extra for free) 알리고 있으므로 (b)가 정답입니다.

어휘 free 무료의 register 등록하다 in advance 미리, 사전에 post 글을 게시하다

every two tickets you buy → purchasing two at a time

PART 3

F: Hey Antonio! Are you here for the community college information event?

M: Hi Gina! Yeah, I'm signing up for some more classes. Is that what you're doing?

F: Yeah. Actually, your advice inspired me last Thanksgiving when you talked about continuing your education. **40** I thought, if my cousin loves taking these classes so much, I need to try it myself.

M: I'm certain you'll enjoy it!

F: I have a problem though. I only have time to take one class, and I'm torn between Contemporary American Literature and Marine Biology. You've taken several courses here. Could you help me decide?

M: I'd be happy to! Let's start with the literature course. Why do you want to take it?

F: Well, first of all, I love reading new books. With a contemporary literature course, I could catch up on all the great books that have been coming out recently.

M: I'm sure you'd be introduced to lots of new writing styles.

F: **41** I also think it would be good for me to be in a course where I'd be asked to write essays.

M: What? You want to write essays?

F: Yeah! I used to like writing, and I'm trying get back in the habit. I would enjoy writing essays, especially if they were about interesting books.

여: 안녕, 안토니오! 지역 대학 설명회 행사에 온 거야?

남: 안녕, 지나! 응, 몇몇 강좌에 더 등록하려고. 너도 등록할 거야?

여: 응. 실은, 지난 추수감사절에 교육을 지속하는 것에 관해 얘기했을 때 해준 조언이 나에게 영감을 주었어. 내 사촌이 이 강좌들을 수강하는 걸 아주 많이 좋아한다면, 나 자신도 시도해 볼 필요가 있겠다고 생각했어.

남: 분명 즐거울 거야!

여: 그런데 문제가 있어. 나는 강좌를 하나밖에 수강할 시간이 없는데, 현대 미국 문학과 해양 생물학 사이에서 고민 중이야. 너는 이곳에서 여러 강좌를 수강해 왔잖아. 내가 결정하는 데 도움을 줄 수 있겠어?

남: 기꺼이 그렇게 해 줄게! 문학 강좌부터 시작해 보자. 그걸 왜 수강하고 싶어?

여: 음, 가장 먼저, 나는 신간 도서를 읽는 걸 아주 좋아해. 현대 문학 강좌를 들으면, 최근에 계속 출간되고 있는 모든 훌륭한 도서들을 파악할 수 있을 거야.

남: 분명 많은 새로운 문체를 접하게 될 거야.

여: 그리고 내가 에세이를 쓰도록 요청 받게 될 강좌에 있으면 좋을 거라는 생각도 들어.

남: 뭐? 에세이를 쓰고 싶다고?

여: 응! 나는 전에 글쓰기를 좋아했는데, 다시 습관을 들여 보려고 해. 나는 에세이를 즐기면서 쓸 것 같아. 특히 그게 흥미로운 책에 관한 것이라면 말이야.

M: You'd certainly read interesting books, but the downside is that they could be challenging.

F: The books are difficult?

M: Well, 42 I took a course on twentieth-century novels here a few years ago. We read some books that were really hard to understand. The authors were experimenting with various writing styles, so I didn't know what they were trying to say.

F: If the books are too difficult, it might not be fun. 45 Maybe I should take Marine Biology.

M: 45 One advantage of that class is that it's run by Dr. Green. She's a great teacher, Gina. I know because I took one of her classes a while back.

F: What did you like about her, Antonio?

M: She made learning fun. 43 She believes that classes should be interactive, so we did lots of practical work. One time she took us to the state aquarium, and we got a special group tour. I even got to feed the dolphins!

F: A great teacher makes a huge difference, so that seems like a good option. 44 I'm just worried about the class schedule.

M: Do you have a scheduling conflict?

F: Well, kind of. You see, 44 I'm not a morning person, and the marine biology class is at 8 a.m.

M: An 8 a.m. class would be hard for anyone, whether you're a morning person or not. But who knows — maybe you'll find that a morning class is a nice way to start your day.

남: 분명 너는 흥미로운 책들을 읽겠지만, 단점은 그것들이 까다로울 수 있다는 점이야.

여: 그 책들이 어려워?

남: 난 이곳에서 몇 년 전에 20세기 소설에 관한 강좌를 하나 수강했어. 이해하기 정말 어려운 책들을 몇 권 읽었지. 저자들이 다양한 문체로 실험하고 있었기 때문에, 무슨 말을 하려고 하는 건지 알지 못했어.

여: 그 책들이 너무 어렵다면, 재미없을지도 모르겠다. 아마 해양 생물학을 수강해야 할 것 같아.

남: 그 강좌의 한 가지 장점은 그린 박사님께서 진행하신다는 점이야. 훌륭한 교육자이거든, 지나. 얼마 전에 그분 강좌들 중 하나를 들어서 알고 있어.

여: 그분의 무엇이 마음에 들었어, 안토니오?

남: 학습을 재미있게 만들어 주셨어. 수업이 상호작용하는 것이어야 한다고 생각하시기 때문에, 실습을 많이 했어. 한 번은 주립 수족관에 우리를 데리고 가셔서, 특별 단체 견학을 했어. 나는 심지어 돌고래들에게 먹이까지 주게 되었어!

여: 좋은 선생님이 엄청난 차이를 만들어 내지. 그래서, 그 수업이 좋은 선택일 것 같아. 난 단지 수업 일정이 걱정되네.

남: 일정 충돌 문제가 있어?

여: 음, 약간. 그러니까, 난 아침형 인간은 아닌데, 해양 생물학이 오전 8시에 있거든.

남: 오전 8시 수업은 누구에게나 힘들 거야, 아침형 인간이든 아니든 말이야. 하지만 누가 알겠어, 어쩌면 오전 수업이 하루를 시작하는 아주 좋은 방법이라는 사실을 알게 될지 말이야.

F: Yeah, possibly. And I've been wanting to start waking up earlier, anyway. Okay, I think I've made a decision.

M: Nice, Gina. What will you do?

F: I love to read, but 45 I want to learn from a professor who I know will be friendly and helpful. Thanks for your help, Antonio!

M: No problem. Let's get together after the semester starts and talk about how things are going.

F: Sounds great. See you later!

여: 응, 그럴 수 있지. 그리고 어쨌든 더 일찍 일어나는 걸 시작하고 싶었어. 좋아, 난 결정을 내린 것 같아.

남: 좋아, 지나. 뭘 할 거야?

여: 내가 책을 읽는 걸 아주 좋아하긴 하지만, 친절하고 도움이 될 거라는 사실을 알고 있는 교수님으로부터 배우고 싶어. 도와줘서 고마워, 안토니오!

남: 별 말씀을. 학기가 시작된 후에 만나서 어떻게 되어 가고 있는지 얘기해 보자.

여: 아주 좋은 생각이야. 나중에 봐!

어휘 sign up for ~에 등록하다, ~을 신청하다 inspire ~에게 영감을 주다 continue ~을 지속하다 oneself (부사처럼 쓰여) 직접 be certain (that) 분명 ~하다, ~하는 것을 확신하다 be torn between ~ 사이에서 고민하다 help + 목적어 + 동사원형: (목적어)가 ~하는 것을 돕다 contemporary 현대의, 동시대의 catch up on (진행, 수준 등) ~을 파악하다, ~을 따라잡다 recently 최근에 introduce ~을 소개하다 be asked to 동사원형: ~하도록 요청 받다 used to 동사원형: 전에 ~했다, ~하곤 했다 get back in the habit 다시 습관을 들이다 downside 단점 experiment 실험하다 advantage 장점, 이점 run ~을 진행하다, ~을 운영하다 interactive 상호 작용하는, 교류하는 practical work 실습 get to 동사원형: ~하게 되다 feed ~에게 먹이를 주다 make a difference 차이를 만들다 huge 엄청난, 거대한 seem like ~인 것 같다, ~인 것처럼 보이다 conflict 충돌, 상충 whether A or not: A이든 아니든 상관없이 way to 동사원형: ~하는 방법 anyway 어쨌든 make a decision 결정을 내리다 get together 만나다, 모이다 semester 학기 how things are going 어떻게 되어 가는지

---

40 세부 정보

Who inspired Gina to sign up for college classes?

(a) a student advisor
(b) a close coworker
(c) a former roommate
(d) a family member

누가 지나에게 대학 강좌에 등록하도록 영감을 주었는가?

(a) 학생 지도 교사
(b) 가까운 동료 직원
(c) 이전의 룸메이트
(d) 가족의 일원

정답 (d)

해설 대화 초반부에 지나가 자신의 사촌이 강좌들을 수강하는 걸 아주 많이 좋아한다면 자신도 시도해 볼 필요가 있겠다고 생각했다고(I thought, if my cousin loves taking these classes so much, I need to try it myself) 말하는 부분에서 자신에게 영감을 준 사람이 가족의 일원임을 알 수 있으므로 (d)가 정답입니다.

어휘 close 가까운 coworker 동료 (직원) former 이전의, 전직 ~의

> **패러프레이징**
>
> cousin → family member

---

41 세부 정보

Why does Gina think a literature course would be good for her?

(a) She could prepare for a degree program.
(b) She could practice her writing.
(c) She could study her favorite authors.
(d) She could meet fellow readers.

지나는 왜 문학 강좌가 자신에게 좋을 것이라고 생각하는가?

(a) 학위 프로그램에 대비할 수 있을 것이다.
(b) 글쓰기를 연습할 수 있을 것이다.
(c) 가장 좋아하는 작가들을 공부할 수 있을 것이다.
(d) 자신과 같은 독자들을 만날 수 있을 것이다.

정답 (b)

해설 대화 중반부에 문학 강좌와 관련해 이야기하는 부분에서 지나가 에세이를 쓰도록 요청 받게 될 강좌에 속해 있으면 좋을 거라고 생각한다는(I also think it would be good for me to be in a course where I'd be asked to write essays) 사실을 언급하고 있습니다. 이는 문학 강좌를 수강하는 동안 글쓰기를 연습할 기회가 있으면 좋겠다는 뜻을 나타내는 말이므로 (b)가 정답입니다.

어휘 degree 학위 practice ~을 연습하다 fellow 같은 처지에 있는, 동료의

> **패러프레이징**
>
> be asked to write essays → practice her writing

Why was Antonio's course on twentieth-century novels challenging?

(a) because of the strict professor
(b) because of the final exam
(c) because of the required texts
(d) because of the quick pace

20세기 소설에 관한 안토니오의 강좌는 왜 힘들었는가?

(a) 엄격한 교수 때문에
(b) 기말 시험 때문에
(c) 필수 교재 때문에
(d) 빠른 속도 때문에

정답 (c)

해설 질문의 키워드인 on twentieth-century novels가 언급된 부분에서 안토니오가 20세기 소설에 관한 강좌를 수강하면서 이해하기 정말 어려운 책들을 읽은 사실과 함께 무슨 말을 하려고 하는지 알지 못했다고(I took a course on twentieth-century novels here a few years ago. We read some books that were really hard to understand. ~ I didn't know what they were trying to say) 알리고 있습니다. 이는 수업 교재로 인해 겪은 어려움을 언급하는 것이므로 (c)가 정답입니다.

어휘 strict 엄격한 required 필수의, 필요한 text 교재, 문서, 글, 문자 (메시지) pace 속도

패러프레이징

some books → required texts

What did Antonio like about Dr. Green's course?

(a) the small-group projects
(b) the funny lectures
(c) the hands-on activities
(d) the light workload

안토니오가 그린 박사의 강좌와 관련해 무엇을 마음에 들어 했는가?

(a) 소규모 그룹 프로젝트
(b) 재미있는 강의
(c) 실습 활동
(d) 가벼운 학업량

정답 (c)

해설 대화 중반부에 그린 박사에 관해 이야기하는 부분에서 안토니오는 그린 박사가 수업이 상호 작용하는 것이어야 한다고 생각한다는 점과 함께 그로 인해 실습을 많이 한 사실을(She believes that classes should be interactive, so we did lots of practical work) 언급하고 있으므로 (c)가 정답입니다.

어휘 hands-on 실습의, 직접 해 보는 workload 학업량, 업무량

패러프레이징

practical work → hands-on activities

Why might taking the marine biology course be hard for Gina?

(a) because of the early start time
(b) because of the long commute
(c) because of the large class size
(d) because of the online format

해양 생물학을 수강하는 것이 지나에게 어려울지도 모르는 이유는 무엇인가?

(a) 이른 시작 시간 때문에
(b) 긴 통학 시간 때문에
(c) 큰 수업 규모 때문에
(d) 온라인 구성 방식 때문에

정답 (a)

해설 대화 중반부에 해양 생물학에 관해 이야기하는 부분에서 지나가 수업 일정과 관련해 걱정된다고(I'm just worried about the class schedule) 언급하였는데, 그 이유로 해양 생물학이 오전 8시에 시작한다는(I'm not a morning person, and the marine biology class is at 8 a.m.) 사실을 밝히고 있습니다. 이는 이른 시작 시간에 대한 걱정을 말하는 것이므로 (a)가 정답입니다.

어휘 commute 통학, 통근 format 구성 방식, 형식

패러프레이징

marine biology class is at 8 a.m. → early start time

What has Gina probably decided to do?

(a) enroll in both courses
(b) sign up for the literature course
(c) search for a new course
(d) take the marine biology course

지나는 무엇을 하기로 결정했을 것 같은가?

(a) 두 강좌에 모두 등록한다
(b) 문학 강좌에 등록한다
(c) 새로운 강좌를 찾아 본다
(d) 해양 생물학 강좌를 수강한다

정답 (d)

해설 대화 후반부에 지나가 친절하고 도움이 될 거라는 사실을 알고 있는 교수님으로부터 배우고 싶다고(I want to learn from a professor who I know will be friendly and helpful) 언급하고 있습니다. 이 교수님은 대화 중반부에 지나가 해양 생물학과 관련해 이야기하기 시작하자(Maybe I should take Marine Biology), 안토니오가 훌륭한 교육자라고 언급하는 그린 박사님을(One advantage of that class is that it's run by Dr. Green. She's a great teacher, Gina) 가리키므로 지나는 해양 생물학을 수강하기로 결정했음을 알 수 있습니다. 따라서 (d)가 정답입니다.

어휘 decide to 동사원형: ~하기로 결정하다 enroll in ~에 등록하다 search for ~을 찾다, ~을 검색하다

Welcome to another episode of *Enjoying Travel*, a podcast that helps you make traveling fun. Continuing with last week's topic of road trips, **46** today we'll cover a key element of any driving experience — the playlist. Here are six tips for making the perfect road trip playlist.

First, consider the length of your trip. Your playlist should be long enough that you don't need to keep repeating it. This is particularly important on long trips. Once, **47** I went on a five-hour road trip with friends along the California coast, but the playlist I made was only an hour long. Halfway through the trip, we'd already heard the same songs several times, and we were getting bored. To avoid this, make a playlist that matches the length of your drive.

Second, think about the atmosphere you want to create. If you're driving through the mountains, you might want to listen to something dramatic. On the other hand, if you're headed to the beach, cheerful summer music might be better. **48** A friend of mine was recently driving through the desert at sunset, which should have been relaxing, but the only music she had downloaded beforehand was heavy metal. It completely ruined the drive for her!

My third tip is to consider the preferences of your fellow passengers. Try to include something for everyone. That's not what my sister did on a trip we took to Los Angeles a few weeks ago. Her entire playlist was songs from Broadway musicals, which she likes to sing along with. I hate that stuff! **49** I asked her if we could listen to my classic rock mix, but she wouldn't put it on, and we started arguing about who had better taste in music. Don't assume that everyone in the car likes what you like.

여행을 즐겁게 만드는 데 도움을 드리는 팟캐스트, <여행 즐기기>의 또 다른 에피소드에 오신 것을 환영합니다. 지난 주의 주제였던 장거리 자동차 여행에 이어, 오늘은 모든 운전 경험의 핵심 요소인 플레이리스트를 다뤄 보겠습니다. 완벽한 자동차 여행용 플레이리스트를 만드는 여섯 가지 팁을 소개해 드리겠습니다.

첫째, 여행의 길이를 고려해 보십시오. 플레이리스트는 계속 반복할 필요가 없을 정도로 충분히 길어야 합니다. 이는 장거리 여행에서 특히 중요합니다. 한 번은, 제가 친구들과 함께 캘리포니아 해변을 따라 5시간 동안 자동차 여행을 떠났는데, 제가 만든 플레이리스트가 1시간밖에 되지 않았습니다. 그 여행의 중간쯤에, 저희는 이미 같은 노래들을 여러 차례 들은 상태였기 때문에, 지루해졌습니다. 이를 피하시려면, 운전 시간과 일치하는 플레이리스트를 만드십시오.

둘째, 만들고 싶은 분위기에 대해 생각해 보십시오. 산을 지나 운전하시는 경우, 뭔가 극적인 것을 듣고 싶어 하실 수도 있습니다. 반면에, 해변으로 향하시는 경우에는, 신나는 여름 음악이 더 나을지도 모릅니다. 제 친구 한 명은 최근 해질녘에 사막을 지나 운전하고 있었는데, 느긋함이 있어야 했지만, 그 친구가 미리 다운로드한 유일한 음악이 헤비메탈이었습니다. 그게 그 운전 시간을 완전히 망쳐 버렸죠!

세 번째 팁은 동승객들의 선호 사항을 고려해 보시는 것입니다. 모두를 위한 것을 포함해 보도록 하십시오. 제 여동생은 몇 주 전에 로스앤젤레스로 함께 떠났던 여행에서 그렇게 하지 못했습니다. 전체 플레이리스트가 자신이 따라 부르기 좋아하는, 브로드웨이 뮤지컬 곡들이었습니다. 저는 그런 걸 좋아하지 않거든요! 제가 제 고전 록 믹스를 들을 수 있는지 물어 봤지만, 여동생은 틀지 않았고, 저희는 누가 더 나은 음악 취향을 갖고 있는지에 관해 말다툼하기 시작했습니다. 자동차에 탄 모두가 여러분이 좋아하시는 것을 좋아한다고 생각하지 마십시오.

Fourth, make sure that whatever music you're taking is going to be accessible. Now that many of us use streaming services for music, you must consider internet coverage along your route. I have unlimited data, but that doesn't matter when there's no signal. **50** On last year's trip through the Rocky Mountains, I discovered that parts of my route had poor cell phone reception. I couldn't enjoy my streaming playlist, or even listen to the radio!

51 The fifth tip is that it's a good idea to incorporate familiar tunes in your playlist. If you only play new music, you might end up getting annoyed. I remember driving to Nevada and only downloading one set of tracks: a brand-new album by a band I liked. The album was terrible, and hearing it made me grumpy for the rest of the trip. That frustration could've been avoided if I had brought some old favorites.

My last recommendation concerns **52** changing up the track order to keep things interesting. If you plan the order carefully, knowing exactly which song follows which, you can create a playlist that flows like a work of art. However, **52** if you hit the "shuffle" button, the next song will always be a surprise. That way, you'll be more engaged, even on long car rides. This can breathe new life into a playlist, even if you've listened to it many times.

Every person is unique with different tastes. However, following these six tips will guarantee that every road trip is accompanied by an excellent playlist. Until next time, may all your travels be enjoyable.

넷째, 여러분께서 어떤 음악을 가져가시든 반드시 이용 가능하게 되도록 하십시오. 우리 대부분이 음악 스트리밍 서비스를 이용하고 있으므로, 경로상의 인터넷 접속 범위를 반드시 고려하시기 바랍니다. 제가 무제한 데이터를 이용하고 있지만, 신호가 없는 경우에는 중요하지 않습니다. 작년에 로키 산맥을 지났던 여행 중에, 저는 경로의 여러 구간에서 휴대 전화 수신 상태가 좋지 못했다는 사실을 알게 되었습니다. 저는 제 스트리밍 플레이리스트를 즐길 수도, 심지어 라디오를 청취할 수도 없었습니다!

다섯 번째 팁은 익숙한 곡을 플레이리스트에 포함하는 것이 좋은 아이디어라는 사실입니다. 오직 신곡만 틀어 놓는다면, 결국 짜증나시게 될지도 모릅니다. 제가 네바다로 운전해 가면서 오직 한 가지 일련의 트랙들만 다운로드한 게 기억이 나는데, 제가 좋아했던 한 밴드의 완전히 새로운 앨범이었습니다. 이 앨범이 끔찍했기 때문에 그걸 들으니까 나머지 여행 동안 투덜거리게 되었습니다. 제가 기존에 가장 좋아했던 몇몇 곡들을 가져갔다면 그런 불만은 피할 수 있었을 겁니다.

제 마지막 추천 사항은 흥미롭게 유지할 수 있도록 트랙 순서를 변경하는 것과 관련되어 있습니다. 어느 곳이 어느 곳 뒤에 이어지는지 정확히 알고, 순서를 신중히 계획하시면, 예술 작품처럼 흘러가는 플레이리스트를 만들어 내실 수 있습니다. 하지만, "무작위 재생" 버튼을 누르시는 경우, 다음 곡에 항상 놀라시게 될 것입니다. 그렇게 하시면, 심지어 장거리 자동차 여행 중에도, 더욱 몰입하시게 될 것입니다. 이는 플레이리스트에 새로운 생명을 불어넣을 수 있으며, 설사 여러 번 들으셨다 하더라도 그렇습니다.

각각의 사람은 서로 다른 취향을 지니고 있어 고유합니다. 하지만, 이 여섯 가지 팁을 따르시면 모든 자동차 여행에 훌륭한 플레이리스트가 동반된다는 점이 보장될 것입니다. 다음 시간까지, 여러분의 모든 여행이 즐겁기를 바랍니다.

어휘 episode (방송의) 에피소드, 1회분 help + 목적어 + 동사원형: (목적어)가 ~하도록 돕다 cover (주제 등) ~을 다루다 element 요소 consider ~을 고려하다 length (시간, 거리 등의) 길이 particularly 특히, 특별히 halfway through

TEST 05

~하는 중간에 avoid ~을 피하다 match ~와 일치하다, ~와 어울리다 atmosphere 분위기 on the other hand 반면에, 다른 한편으로는 be headed to ~로 향하다 cheerful 신나는, 쾌활한 recently 최근에 should have p.p. ~했어야 했다 relaxing 느긋하게 만드는, 여유로운 beforehand 미리, 사전에 completely 완전히, 전적으로 ruin ~을 망치다 preference 선호 (사항), 선호도 fellow 같은 입장에 있는, 동료의 include ~을 포함하다 entire 전체의 sing along with ~을 따라 부르다 stuff 것(들), 물건, 물체 mix 믹스, 섞은 것 argue 말다툼하다 taste 취향, 기호 assume that ~라고 생각하다, ~라고 추정하다 make sure that 반드시 ~하도록 하다 accessible 이용 가능한, 접근 가능한 now that (이제) ~이므로 coverage (서비스 등의) 적용 범위 unlimited 무제한의 matter v. 중요하다, 문제가 되다 discover that ~임을 알게 되다, ~임을 발견하다 reception 수신 (상태) incorporate ~을 포함하다 familiar 익숙한, 잘 아는 tune 곡, 곡조 end up -ing 결국 ~하게 되다 annoyed 짜증이 난 remember -ing ~한 것을 기억하다 brand-new 완전히 새로운 terrible 끔찍한 grumpy 투덜거리는 the rest of ~의 나머지 frustration 불만, 좌절 could have p.p. ~할 수도 있었다 favorite n. 가장 좋아하는 것 recommendation 추천 (사항) concern ~와 관련되다 order 순서 exactly 정확히 follow ~ 뒤에 이어지다, ~을 따르다 flow 흐르다 shuffle 무작위로 섞기 that way 그렇게 하면, 그런 방법으로 engaged 몰입한, 몰두한 breathe new life into ~에 새로운 생명을 불어 넣다 unique 고유한, 독특한 guarantee that ~임을 보장하다 be accompanied by ~이 동반되다

46 주제/목적

What is the talk mainly about?

(a) packing for a music festival
(b) creating a camping trip playlist
(c) choosing music for a road trip
(d) making playlists for friends

담화는 주로 무엇에 관한 것인가?

(a) 음악 축제를 위한 짐 꾸리기
(b) 캠핑 여행용 플레이리스트 만들기
(c) 자동차 여행용 음악 고르기
(d) 친구를 위한 플레이리스트 만들기

정답 (c)

해설 화자가 담화 시작 부분에 오늘은 모든 운전 경험의 핵심 요소인 플레이리스트를 다뤄 보겠다고 밝히면서 완벽한 자동차 여행용 플레이리스트를 만드는 여섯 가지 팁을 전하겠다고(today we'll cover a key element of any driving experience — the playlist. Here are six tips for making the perfect road trip playlist) 언급하고 있습니다. 이는 자동차 여행에 좋은 음악을 고르는 일을 의미하므로 (c)가 정답입니다.

어휘 pack 짐을 꾸리다, 짐을 싸다 choose ~을 선택하다

패러프레이징

making the perfect road trip playlist → choosing music for a road trip

Why did the speaker get bored during his drive along the California coast?

화자는 왜 캘리포니아 해변을 따라 운전하던 중에 지루해졌는가?

(a) because he failed to prepare enough music
(b) because he forgot to make a playlist
(c) because he remained on the same road
(d) because he decided to travel alone

(a) 충분한 음악을 준비하지 못했기 때문에
(b) 플레이리스트를 만드는 것을 잊었기 때문에
(c) 같은 도로에 계속 남아 있었기 때문에
(d) 혼자 여행하기로 결정했기 때문에

정답 (a)

해설 질문의 키워드인 drive along the California coast가 언급된 부분에서 화자는 친구들과 함께 캘리포니아 해변을 따라 5시간 동안 자동차 여행을 떠난 사실과 함께 자신이 만든 플레이리스트가 1시간밖에 되지 않았다는 점을(I went on a five-hour road trip with friends along the California coast, but the playlist I made was only an hour long) 밝히고 있습니다. 이는 여행 시간만큼 길이가 충분한 플레이리스트를 만들지 못한 것의 예시에 해당하므로 (a)가 정답입니다.

어휘 **fail to 동사원형**: ~하지 못하다, ~하는 데 실패하다 **forget to 동사원형**: ~하는 것을 잊다 **remain** 계속 남아 있다 **decide to 동사원형**: ~하기로 결정하다

패러프레이징

a five-hour road trip / the playlist I made was only an hour long → failed to prepare enough music

What problem did the speaker's friend have with her music during a drive through the desert?

화자의 친구가 사막을 지나 운전하던 중에 음악과 관련해 어떤 문제가 있었는가?

(a) It brought up bad memories.
(b) It set the wrong mood.
(c) It had poor sound quality.
(d) It made her sleepy.

(a) 나쁜 기억을 불러일으켰다.
(b) 엉뚱한 분위기를 만들었다.
(c) 음질이 좋지 못했다.
(d) 졸음이 오게 만들었다.

정답 (b)

해설 질문의 키워드인 friend와 drive through the desert가 언급된 부분에서 화자는 친구가 사막 여행 중에 느긋함이 있어야 했지만 음악이 헤비메탈이었기 때문에 그 시간을 완전히 망쳤다고(A friend of mine was recently driving through the desert at sunset, which should have been relaxing, but the only music she had downloaded beforehand was heavy metal. It completely ruined the drive for her!) 설명하고 있습니다. 이는 어울리지 않는 음악으로 인해 어색한 분위기 만들어진 것의 예시에 해당하므로 (b)가 정답입니다.

어휘 **bring up** ~을 불러일으키다 **set** ~을 만들어 내다, ~을 설정하다, ~을 결정하다

패러프레이징

should have been relaxing / completely ruined the drive → set the wrong mood

---

49 세부 정보

Why did the speaker argue with his sister about music?

(a) because she refused to stop singing along
(b) because she kept switching radio stations
(c) because she refused to play certain songs
(d) because she kept turning up the volume

화자가 음악과 관련해 여동생과 말다툼했던 이유는 무엇인가?

(a) 따라 부르는 것을 멈추기를 거부했기 때문에
(b) 계속 라디오 방송국을 바꿨기 때문에
(c) 특정 노래들을 틀기를 거부했기 때문에
(d) 계속 음량을 높였기 때문에

정답 (c)

해설 질문의 키워드인 argue와 sister가 언급된 부분에서 화자는 여동생이 틀어 놓은 브로드웨이 뮤지컬 곡들을 좋아하지 않아서 자신이 좋아하는 록 음악을 들을 수 있는지 물어 봤지만 여동생은 틀지 않았고 말다툼하게 되었다는(I asked her if we could listen to my classic rock mix, but she wouldn't put it on, and we started arguing ~) 일화를 소개하고 있습니다. 따라서 화자의 여동생이 특정 곡을 틀지 않아 말다툼했음을 알 수 있으므로 (c)가 정답입니다.

어휘 **refuse to 동사원형**: ~하기를 거부하다 **keep -ing** 계속 ~하다 **switch** ~을 바꾸다 **certain** 특정한, 일정한 **turn up the volume** 음량을 높이다

패러프레이징

asked her if we could listen to my classic rock mix, but she wouldn't put it on → refused to play certain songs

---

❌ 오답 피하기

해당 부분에서 sing along with라는 말이 등장하기는 하지만, 여동생이 따라 부르기 좋아하는 곡들을 틀었다는 말만 있을 뿐, 따라 부르기를 멈추는 것과 관련된 내용은 제시되지 않으므로 (a)는 오답입니다.

Why was the speaker unable to enjoy his playlist on last year's trip?

(a) because his car broke down
(b) because he ran out of data
(c) because his phone died
(d) because he had bad reception

화자는 왜 작년에 떠난 여행에서 플레이리스트를 즐길 수 없었는가?

(a) 자동차가 고장 났기 때문에
(b) 데이터가 부족해졌기 때문에
(c) 전화기가 작동하지 않았기 때문에
(d) 수신 상태가 좋지 못했기 때문에

정답 (d)

해설 질문의 키워드인 on last year's trip이 언급된 부분에서 화자는 경로의 여러 구간에서 휴대 전화 수신 상태가 좋지 못했기 때문에 자신의 스트리밍 플레이리스트를 즐길 수 없었다고(On last year's trip through the Rocky Mountains, I discovered that parts of my route had poor cell phone reception. I couldn't enjoy my streaming playlist ~) 언급하고 있으므로 (d)가 정답입니다.

어휘 **be unable to 동사원형**: ~할 수 없다 **break down** 고장 나다 **run out of** ~이 부족해지다, ~이 다 떨어지다 **die** (기계 등이) 작동을 멈추다

> **패러프레이징**
>
> had poor cell phone reception → had bad reception

> ❌ **오답 피하기**
>
> 해당 부분에서 데이터와 관련된 말이 있기는 하지만, 화자가 무제한 데이터를 이용한다는 사실만 언급될 뿐, 데이터 부족 문제로 인해 플레이리스트를 즐길 수 없었던 것은 아니므로 (b)는 오답입니다.

Based on the talk, what might listeners find annoying while in the car?

(a) too many unfamiliar songs
(b) songs with repetitive lyrics
(c) advertisements between songs
(d) songs with too much bass

담화 내용에 따르면, 청자들이 자동차에 타 있는 동안 무엇을 짜증난다고 생각할 수도 있는가?

(a) 너무 많은 익숙하지 않은 노래들
(b) 반복적인 가사가 있는 노래들
(c) 노래들 사이의 광고
(d) 베이스가 너무 많은 노래들

정답 (a)

해설 화자가 다섯 번째 팁을 소개하면서 익숙한 곡을 플레이리스트에 포함하는 것이 좋다고 말한 다음, 오직 신곡만 틀어 놓는다면 결국 짜증나게 될지도 모른다고(The fifth tip is that it's a good idea to incorporate familiar tunes in your playlist. If you only play new music, you might end up getting annoyed) 알리고 있습니다. 이는 익숙하지 않은 곡들이 너무 많으면 짜증날 수 있다는 뜻이므로 (a)가 정답입니다.

어휘 find + 목적어 + 형용사: (목적어)를 ~하다고 생각하다 unfamiliar 익숙하지 않은, 잘 알지 못하는 repetitive 반복적인 lyrics 가사 advertisement 광고

---

52 세부 정보

Based on the talk, how might someone create excitement on a long car ride?

(a) by changing styles often
(b) by trying out new bands
(c) by taking a friend's suggestions
(d) by mixing up the song order

담화 내용에 따르면, 장거리 자동차 여행에서 어떻게 흥겨움을 만들어 낼 수도 있는가?

(a) 자주 스타일을 바꿈으로써
(b) 새로운 밴드를 시도해 봄으로써
(c) 친구의 제안을 수용함으로써
(d) 곡 순서를 섞음으로써

정답 (d)

해설 화자가 마지막 추천 사항을 알리는 부분에서 흥미롭게 유지할 수 있도록 트랙 순서를 변경하는 것을(changing up the track order to keep things interesting) 언급한 다음, "무작위 재생" 버튼을 누르면 다음 곡에 항상 놀라게 될 것이라고(if you hit the "shuffle" button, the next song will always be a surprise) 밝히고 있습니다. 따라서 플레이리스트의 곡 순서를 섞는 것이 흥겨움을 만들어 내는 방법임을 알 수 있으므로 (d)가 정답입니다.

어휘 excitement 흥겨움, 신남 try out ~을 시도해 보다, ~을 시험해 보다 suggestion 제안, 의견

패러프레이징

changing up the track order → mixing up the song order

PART 1

HANK AARON

Hank Aaron was an American baseball player and civil rights champion. **53** He is best known for breaking baseball icon Babe Ruth's home run record and for holding his own record for thirty-three years.

Aaron was born in Mobile, Alabama, on February 5, 1934, during the Great Depression. Aaron and his siblings grew up in poverty. He enjoyed playing sports, but his parents could not afford to buy sports equipment, so **54** Aaron would practice baseball swings using everyday items, such as broomsticks and bottlecaps.

In 1954, after years of success in segregated high school and professional leagues, Aaron joined a Major League Baseball (MLB) team, the Milwaukee Braves. **55** In 1957, he was awarded the National League Most Valuable Player for leading his team to their only World Series Championship. Over a long career, he set a number of hitting records and, in the spring of 1974, he was on the verge of breaking one of MLB's most important milestones: the record for career home runs, which at the time was 714 and held by the legendary Babe Ruth.

On opening day, Aaron tied the record. Then, four days later, in front of a sold-out stadium, Aaron hit another home run and made history. Although it was a **58** momentous achievement, **56** many Americans were upset to see a Black man break Ruth's record. Aaron received letters from all over the country, many of which were racially threatening. That year, he set the Guinness World Record for the most mail sent to a private citizen. While he remained fearless under pressure, **57(c)** the highly publicized racist letters he received drew attention to a deep-rooted societal problem.

행크 아론

행크 아론은 미국의 야구 선수이자 인권 옹호자였다. 그는 야구 아이콘 베이브 루스의 홈런 기록을 경신한 것으로, 그리고 33년 동안 자신의 기록을 보유한 것으로 가장 잘 알려져 있다.

아론은 대공황 기간이었던 1934년, 2월 5일에, 앨라배마의 모빌에서 태어났다. 아론과 그의 형제들은 가난 속에서 자랐다. 그는 스포츠를 하는 것을 즐거워했지만, 그의 부모는 스포츠 장비를 구입할 여유가 없었기 때문에, 아론은 막대 빗자루와 병마개 같은 일상적인 물품을 이용해 야구 스윙을 연습하곤 했다.

1954년에, 인종 분리 고등학교 및 프로 리그에서 수년 동안의 성공을 거둔 끝에, 아론은 메이저리그 야구(MLB) 팀인 밀워키 브레이브스에 입단했다. 1957년에, 그는 소속 팀을 팀 유일의 월드 시리즈 챔피언 자리로 이끈 것에 대해 내셔널 리그 MVP를 수상했다. 오랜 선수 활동 기간에 걸쳐, 그는 수많은 타격 기록을 세웠으며, 1974년 봄에는, MLB에서 가장 중요한 이정표들 중 하나였던 개인 통산 홈런 기록을 경신하기 직전에 이르렀으며, 그 기록은 당시에 714개였으며, 전설적인 베이브 루스가 보유하고 있었다.

개막일에, 아론은 그 기록과 동률을 이뤘다. 그런 다음, 4일 후에, 전석 매진된 경기장에서, 아론은 홈런을 하나 더 치면서 역사를 만들었다. 이는 중대한 업적이었지만, 많은 미국인들은 흑인이 루스의 기록을 경신하는 모습을 보고 화가 났다. 아론은 전국 각지에서 온 편지를 받았으며, 그 대부분이 인종적으로 위협하는 내용이었다. 그해에, 그는 한 개인에게 가장 많은 우편물이 보내진 것에 대해 기네스 세계 기록을 세웠다. 그가 압력을 받는 상황에서도 여전히 두려움을 모르는 상태이기는 했지만, 그가 받은 널리 알려진 인종 차별주의적 편지들로 인해 깊게 뿌리 내리고 있던 사회 문제에 관심이 몰렸다.

In response, Aaron became determined to help
59 address race issues in America. After retiring
from baseball with 755 home runs, he donated
extensively to charities, dedicated his time to
creating scholarships for Black students, and
57(a) encouraged the MLB to develop more
diverse teams. These philanthropic efforts, partially
motivated by Aaron's personal struggles, also
honored the legacy of **57(b)** his friend, the late Martin
Luther King Jr., who had been killed for leading the
fight against racial inequality.

After spending many years as a business owner and
philanthropist, Hank Aaron died in January 2021.
Although his home run record was broken in 2007,
Aaron remains one of the greatest major league
players of all time and a role model for many.

그에 대한 대응으로, 아론은 미국 내의 인종 문제를 해결하는 데 도움을 주기로 결심하게 되었다. 755개의 홈런으로 야구계에서 은퇴한 후, 그는 자선 단체에 광범위하게 기부도 하고, 흑인 학생들을 위한 장학금을 만드는 데 시간을 쏟았으며, 더욱 다양한 팀을 만들도록 MLB에 권했다. 부분적으로 아론의 개인적 투쟁에 의해 동기가 부여되어, 이러한 박애주의적 노력은 친구이자 인종적 불평등에 맞선 싸움을 이끈 것으로 인해 죽임을 당한 고(故) 마틴 루터 킹 주니어의 유산을 기리는 것이었다.

사업가이자 박애주의자로서 오랜 시간을 보낸 후에, 행크 아론은 2021년 1월에 사망했다. 비록 그의 홈런 기록은 2007년에 깨졌지만, 아론은 여전히 역사상 가장 위대한 메이저리그 선수들 중 한 명이자 많은 이들의 롤 모델로 남아 있다.

어휘 civil right 인권, 시민권 champion 옹호자 be best known for ~로 가장 잘 알려져 있다 break ~을 경신하다, ~을 깨다 hold ~을 보유하다, ~을 소지하다 Great Depression 대공황 sibling 형제자매 grow up 자라다, 성장하다 poverty 가난 cannot afford to 동사원형: (시간, 금전적으로) ~할 여유가 없다 equipment 장비 practice ~을 연습하다 segregated 인종이 분리된 be awarded A: A를 수상하다, A가 수여되다 a number of 많은 (수의) on the verge of ~하기 직전인 milestone 이정표, 중대 사건 legendary 전설적인 tie ~와 동률을 이루다 sold-out 매진된, 품절된 momentous 중대한 achievement 업적, 성취, 달성 upset 화가 난 see + 목적어 + 동사원형: (목적어)가 ~하는 모습을 보다 racially 인종적으로 threatening 위협하는 remain 여전히 ~한 상태이다, 계속 ~한 상태로 남아 있다 fearless 두려움을 모르는 under pressure 압박을 받는 highly publicized 널리 알려진 racist a. 인종 차별주의적인 n. 인종 차별주의자 draw attention 관심을 끌다 in response 그에 대한 대응으로 determined 결심한 help + 동사원형: ~하는 데 도움을 주다 address v. (문제 등) ~을 해결하다, ~을 처리하다 issue 문제, 사안 retire 은퇴하다 donate ~을 기부하다 extensively 광범위하게 charity 자선 단체, 자선 행위 dedicate (시간, 노력 등) ~을 쏟다, ~을 바치다 scholarship 장학금 encourage + 목적어 + to 동사원형: (목적어)에게 ~하도록 권하다 diverse 다양한 philanthropic 박애주의적인, 자비로운 partially 부분적으로 motivate ~에게 동기를 부여하다 struggle 투쟁, 싸움, 힘겨움 honor ~을 기리다 late 고인이 된 legacy 유산 lead ~을 이끌다 inequality 불평등 philanthropist 박애주의자

What is Hank Aaron most famous for?

(a) breaking the record for the fastest pitch in baseball
(b) winning more awards than any baseball player before him
(c) having the longest career in baseball history
(d) hitting more home runs than any baseball player before him

행크 아론은 무엇으로 가장 유명한가?

(a) 야구에서 가장 빠른 투구에 대한 기록을 경신한 것
(b) 그보다 앞선 모든 야구 선수보다 더 많은 상을 받은 것
(c) 야구 역사에서 가장 긴 경력을 보유한 것
(d) 그보다 앞선 모든 야구 선수보다 더 많은 홈런을 친 것

정답 (d)

해설 질문의 키워드인 most famous for는 지문의 첫 문단에 best known for로 표현되어 있습니다. 해당 문장에 베이브 루스의 홈런 기록을 경신한 것으로, 그리고 33년 동안 자신의 기록을 보유한 것으로 가장 잘 알려져 있다고(He is best known for breaking baseball icon Babe Ruth's home run record and for holding his own record for thirty-three years) 쓰여 있으므로 가장 많은 홈런을 친 것을 언급한 (d)가 정답입니다.

어휘 be famous for ~로 유명하다 win an award 상을 받다

TEST 05

How did Aaron practice baseball during his childhood?

(a) by using common household objects
(b) by getting equipment from his older siblings
(c) by borrowing his neighbor's athletic gear
(d) by taking items from his school's sports department

아론은 어린 시절에 어떻게 야구를 연습했는가?

(a) 흔한 가정용 물품을 이용해서
(b) 형에게서 장비를 얻어서
(c) 이웃의 운동 장비를 빌려서
(d) 학교 운동부의 물품을 가져가서

정답 (a)

해설 질문의 키워드인 practice baseball가 그대로 제시된 두 번째 문단에 막대 빗자루와 병마개 같은 일상적인 물품을 이용해 야구 스윙을 연습하곤 했다고(Aaron would practice baseball swings using everyday items, such as broomsticks and bottlecaps) 언급되어 있습니다. 따라서 집에서 흔히 볼 수 있는 물품을 이용해 연습했다는 것을 알 수 있으므로 이러한 방식을 언급한 (a)가 정답입니다.

어휘 household 가정의 object 물품, 물체 borrow ~을 빌리다 athletic 운동의, 경기의 gear 장비, 복장

패러프레이징

using everyday items, such as broomsticks and bottlecaps → using common household objects

According to the text, which of the following is true of Aaron's major league career?

(a) He had previously played only on high school teams.
(b) He was named the best player for several seasons.
(c) He played an important role in his team's championship win.
(d) He struggled to stand out when he first began playing.

지문 내용에 따르면, 다음 중 아론의 메이저리그 경력에 대해 사실인 것은 어느 것인가?

(a) 이전에 오직 고등학교 팀에서만 활동했다.
(b) 여러 시즌 동안 최고의 선수로 지명되었다.
(c) 팀의 챔피언전 승리에서 중요한 역할을 했다.
(d) 처음 활동을 시작했을 때 두각을 나타내기 힘겨워했다.

정답 (c)

해설 질문의 키워드인 major league career가 그대로 제시된 세 번째 문단에 소속 팀을 월드 시리즈 챔피언 자리로 이끈 것에 대해 내셔널 리그 MVP를 수상했다는(In 1957, he was awarded the National League Most Valuable Player for leading his team to their only World Series Championship) 내용이 제시되어 있습니다. 이를 통해 팀이 챔피언이 되는 데 있어 중요한 역할을 했다는 것을 알 수 있으므로 (c)가 정답입니다.

어휘 previously 이전에, 과거에 be named A: A로 지명되다 play an important role in ~에 있어 중요한 역할을 하다 struggle to 동사원형: ~하는 데 힘겨워하다 stand out 두각을 나타내다, 두드러지다

❌ 오답 피하기

세 번째 문단에 고등학교 및 프로 리그에서 수년 동안 활동한 사실이 언급되어 있으므로 고등학교 팀에서만 활동했다는 의미로 쓰인 (a)는 오답입니다.

Why, most likely, did Aaron receive a lot of hate mail?

(a) because he performed poorly in an important game
(b) because he compared himself to another baseball player
(c) because he broke a record that was held by a white man
(d) because he was known for poor sportsmanship

아론이 왜 많은 혐오 우편물을 받았을 것 같은가?

(a) 중요한 경기에서 좋지 못한 성적을 냈기 때문에
(b) 자신을 다른 야구 선수와 비교했기 때문에
(c) 백인이 보유하고 있던 기록을 경신했기 때문에
(d) 좋지 못한 스포츠맨 정신으로 알려졌기 때문에

해설 질문의 키워드인 receive a lot of hate mail이 received letters와 racially threatening으로 제시된 네 번째 문단에 많은 미국인들이 루스의 기록을 흑인이 경신하는 모습을 보고 화가 났다는 사실과 함께, 아론이 전국 각지에서 받은 편지가 대부분 인종적으로 위협하는 내용이었다는(many Americans were upset to see a Black man break Ruth's record. Aaron received letters from all over the country, many of which were racially threatening) 내용이 제시되어 있습니다. 따라서 흑인인 아론이 백인인 루스의 기록을 경신한 것에 대해 위협적인 반응이 있었던 것으로 유추할 수 있으므로 (c)가 정답입니다.

어휘 perform poorly 좋지 못한 성적을 내다 compare A to B: A를 B와 비교하다

---

57 사실 확인

Which of the following is NOT mentioned as a factor in Aaron's decision to donate his time to charitable work?

(a) the lack of diversity on baseball teams
(b) the activist efforts of his friend
(c) the threats he received over his success
(d) the death of a former teammate

다음 중 자신의 시간을 자선 사업에 바치기로 한 아론의 결정에 있어 한 가지 요인으로 언급되지 않은 것은 어느 것인가?

(a) 야구 팀의 다양성 부족
(b) 친구의 활동가적인 노력
(c) 그가 자신의 성공에 대해 받은 위협
(d) 이전 팀 동료의 사망

정답 (d)

해설 다섯 번째 문단에서 더욱 다양한 팀을 만들도록 MLB에 권했다고(encouraged the MLB to develop more diverse teams) 언급한 부분과 친구이 마틴 루터 킹 주니어가 인종적 불평등에 맞선 싸움을 이끈 것으로 인해 죽임을 당했다고(his friend, the late Martin Luther King Jr., who had been killed for leading the fight against racial inequality) 밝힌 부분을 통해 (a)와 (b)를 각각 확인할 수 있습니다. 또한, 네 번째 문단에 아론이 받은 편지로 인해 인종 관련 문제에 관심이 몰렸다고(the highly publicized racist letters he received drew attention to a deep-rooted societal problem) 쓰여 있는 부분을 통해 (c)도 확인 가능합니다. 하지만, 팀 동료의 사망과 관련된 내용은 제시되어 있지 않으므로 (d)가 정답입니다.

어휘 factor 요인, 요소 decision to 동사원형: ~하려는 결정 charitable 자선의 lack 부족 activist 활동가 threat 위협, 협박 former 이전의, 전직 ~의

In the context of the passage, <u>momentous</u> means

_____.

(a) significant
(b) delayed
(c) necessary
(d) simple

해당 단락의 문맥에서 <u>momentous</u>
가 의미하는 것은?

(a) 중요한
(b) 지연된
(c) 필수적인
(d) 간단한

정답 (a)

해설 해당 문장에서 momentous가 속한 Although절의 주어 it은 앞선 문장에서 아론이 홈런 신기록을 세우면서 새 역사를 쓴 일을 가리키며, momentous가 수식하는 achievement는 '업적, 성취' 등을 의미합니다. 따라서 momentous는 아론의 홈런 신기록이 대단한 업적임을 나타내는 형용사임을 알 수 있으며, 이러한 의미에 해당하는 것으로서 '중요한'을 뜻하는 (a) significant가 정답입니다.

In the context of the passage, <u>address</u> means _____.

(a) wait for
(b) tackle
(c) complain about
(d) study

해당 단락의 문맥에서 <u>address</u>가 의
미하는 것은?

(a) ~을 기다리다
(b) 해결하다
(c) ~에 관해 불만을 제기하다
(d) 공부하다, 연구하다

정답 (b)

해설 해당 문장에서 address 뒤에 '인종 문제'를 뜻하는 명사구 race issues가 쓰여 있어 이 문장은 아론이 그 문제를 개선하거나 해결하는 데 도움을 주기로 결심했다는 의미를 구성해야 자연스럽습니다. 따라서 어떤 문제와 관련해 '해결하다, 처리하다' 등을 뜻하는 동사 (b) tackle이 정답입니다.

PART 2

THE INVENTION OF BARCODES

Today, the barcode is found everywhere: store products, library books, and even hospital wristbands. However, it has not always been this way. Before the barcode's invention, store items were priced manually, causing errors at checkout. Furthermore, without a dependable way to keep track of stock, retailers often failed to 65 detect theft. The retail industry needed a more efficient product-tracking system.

60 In the late 1940s, Joe Woodland and Bernard Silver devised the concept of the barcode, a mark that would allow machines to read product information. Sitting on a Miami beach, Woodland was inspired by a design he had sketched in the sand that was reminiscent of the dots found in Morse code. 61 By 1952, the two men had patented bullseye-shaped barcodes. However, the technology to read and process the information was not yet available.

The invention of the laser in the 1960s accelerated the development of barcode technology. In 1966, as more companies began to 66 pursue automation in checkout lines, the Kroger supermarket chain agreed to test a new system. 62 This spurred a competition to create the best barcode design. The Radio Corporation of America bought the patent for Woodland and Silver's bullseye design and began using it with laser scanners. 62 On July 3, 1972, the first bullseye barcode was tested at Kroger's Kenwood Plaza store in Cincinnati, to initial success.

However, problems soon followed. The bullseye barcode smudged easily, making it unreadable. In consideration of this issue, IBM employee George 63 Laurer created a new version: a striped barcode with a universal numbering system. On June 26, 1974, 63 the first item to be scanned using the new

바코드의 발명

오늘날, 바코드는 매장 제품, 도서관 서적, 그리고 심지어 병원용 손목밴드 등 모든 곳에 존재한다. 하지만, 항상 이런 방식이었던 것은 아니다. 바코드의 발명 이전에는, 매장 제품이 수작업으로 가격 표시가 되었기 때문에, 계산대에서 오류를 초래했다. 더욱이, 재고를 파악할 수 있는 신뢰할 만한 방법이 없어서, 소매업자들은 종종 절도를 감지하지 못했다. 소매 업계는 더욱 효율적인 제품 추적 시스템을 필요로 했다.

1940년대 말에, 조 우들랜드와 버나드 실버는 기계가 제품 정보를 판독할 수 있게 해 주는 표시인, 바코드라는 개념을 고안해 냈다. 마이애미의 한 해변에 앉아 있다가, 우들랜드는 자신이 모래사장에 스케치한 디자인에 의해 영감을 얻었으며, 그것은 모스 부호에 나타나는 점들을 연상시켰다. 1952년경, 두 남성은 과녁 모양의 바코드로 특허를 받았다. 하지만, 정보를 판독하고 처리하는 기술은 아직 이용할 수 없었다.

1960년대의 레이저 발명은 바코드 기술의 발전을 가속화시켰다. 1966년에, 더 많은 회사들이 계산대 줄의 자동화를 추구하기 시작하는 과정에서, 크로거 슈퍼마켓 체인이 새로운 시스템을 테스트하는 데 동의했다. 이는 최상의 바코드 디자인을 만들어 내기 위한 경쟁에 박차를 가했다. 라디오 코퍼레이션 오브 아메리카가 우들랜드와 실버의 과녁 디자인에 대한 특허를 사들였고, 레이저 스캐너로 이를 이용하기 시작했다. 1972년, 7월 3일, 최초의 과녁 모양 바코드가 크로거 사의 신시내티 켄우드 플라자 매장에서 테스트되어 최초의 성공에 이르렀다.

하지만, 문제들이 곧 뒤따랐다. 과녁 모양의 바코드는 쉽게 번져서, 판독할 수 없게 되었다. 이 문제를 고려해, IBM의 직원 조지 라우어가 새로운 버전을 만들어 냈는데, 바로 보편적인 번호 부여 시스템이 있는 줄무늬 모양의 바코드였다. 1974년, 6월 26일, 새 바코드를 이용해 스캔된 최초의 제품은 리글리

barcode was a packet of Wrigley's chewing gum, which had been chosen to show that the barcode could even be printed on very small packages.

Today, Laurer's barcode is still in use and has become essential in other areas, such as healthcare. Hospitals use barcodes on **64(a)** patient wristbands for accurate identification and on **64(b), (c)** prescription bottles for dosage and safety details. This application, which has elevated patient care and streamlined medical procedures, showcases the barcode's versatility and its global relevance in today's society.

사의 껌 한 통이었는데, 이것은 바코드가 심지어 아주 작은 포장지에도 인쇄될 수 있음을 보여 주기 위해 선택되었다.

오늘날, 라우어의 바코드는 여전히 이용되고 있으며, 의료 같은 다른 분야에서도 필수적인 것이 되었다. 병원에서는 정확한 신원 확인을 위한 환자 손목 밴드 및 복용량과 안전 상세 정보를 위한 처방약 병에 바코드를 이용하고 있다. 이러한 활용은, 환자 관리 수준을 높이고 의료 절차를 간소화해 온 것으로서, 오늘날의 사회에서 바코드가 지닌 다목적성 및 전 세계적인 적합성을 보여 준다.

어휘 invention 발명(품) wristband 손목밴드 way 방식, 방법 price v. 가격을 표시하다, 가격을 매기다 manually 수작업으로 casue ~을 초래하다 checkout 계산대 furthermore 더욱이, 게다가 dependable 신뢰할 수 있는 keep track of ~을 파악하다, ~을 추적하다 stock 재고(품) retailer 소매업자, 소매업체 fail to 동사원형: ~하지 못하다 detect ~을 감지하다, ~을 발견하다 theft 절도 efficient 효율적인 devise ~을 고안하다 allow + 목적어 + to 동사원형: (목적어)가 ~할 수 있게 해 주다 inspire ~에게 영감을 주다 reminiscent of ~을 연상시키는 dot 점 patent v. ~로 특허를 받다 n. 특허(권) bullseye-shaped 과녁 모양의 process ~을 처리하다 available 이용할 수 있는 accelerate ~을 가속화시키다 pursue ~을 추구하다 automation 자동화 agree to 동사원형: ~하는 데 동의하다 spur ~에 박차를 가하다 competition 경쟁 initial 최초의, 처음의 follow 뒤따르다 smudge 번지다, 얼룩지다 in consideration of ~을 고려해 issue 문제, 사안 striped 줄무늬 모양의 universal 보편적인, 일반적인 numbering 번호 부여 choose ~을 선택하다 in use 이용되는, 사용되는 essential 필수적인 patient 환자 accurate 정확한 identification 신원 확인 prescription 처방(약) dosage 복용량 details 상세 정보, 세부 사항 application 활용, 적용, 응용 elevate (수준 등) ~을 높이다, ~을 격상시키다 streamline ~을 간소화하다 procedure 절차 showcase ~을 보여 주다, ~을 선보이다 versatility 다목적성, 다재다능함 relevance 적합성, 관련성

60 주제/목적

What is the article mainly about?

(a) the impact of barcodes on retail sales
(b) the people who design barcodes today
(c) the history of the barcode system
(d) the person who created the barcode scanner

기사는 주로 무엇에 관한 것인가?

(a) 바코드가 소매 판매에 미치는 영향
(b) 오늘날 바코드를 디자인하는 사람들
(c) 바코드 시스템의 역사
(d) 바코드 스캐너를 만든 사람

정답 (c)

해설 두 번째 문단에서 1940년대 말에 조 우들랜드와 버나드 실버라는 사람들이 기계가 제품 정보를 판독할 수 있게 해 주는 표

시인 바코드라는 개념을 고안해 냈다고(In the late 1940s, Joe Woodland and Bernard Silver devised the concept of the barcode, a mark that would allow machines to read product informatio) 언급한 뒤로, 문단마다 바코드 개발과 관련해 시대별 변화를 이야기하고 있습니다. 따라서 바코드 시스템의 역사가 글의 주제임을 알 수 있으므로 (c)가 정답입니다.

어휘 **impact of A on B**: A가 B에 미치는 영향 **sales** 판매(량), 영업, 매출

❌ **오답 피하기**

지문에서 바코드 자체를 누가 만들었는지를 언급한 부분은 있지만, 누가 바코드 스캐너를 발명했는지는 언급한 부분은 없으므로 (d)는 오답입니다.

---

61 세부 정보

What prevented barcodes from being used in the 1950s?

(a) There was little demand for them.
(b) There was no way to scan them.
(c) There was a known flaw in their design.
(d) There was no consistent way to print them.

무엇이 1950년대에 바코드가 이용되지 못하게 막았는가?

(a) 그에 대한 수요가 거의 없었다.
(b) 그것을 스캔할 방법이 없었다.
(c) 그 디자인에 있어 알려진 결함이 있었다.
(d) 그것을 인쇄할 지속적인 방법이 없었다.

정답 (b)

해설 질문의 키워드인 in the 1950s는 두 번째 문단에 By 1952로 제시되어 있습니다. 해당 부분에 과녁 모양의 바코드로 특허를 받은 사실과 함께 정보를 판독하고 처리하는 기술은 아직 이용할 수 없었다는(By 1952, the two men had patented bullseye-shaped barcodes. However, the technology to read and process the information was not yet available) 문제점이 언급되어 있습니다. 이는 바코드만 만들어진 상태에서 그것을 스캔해 이용할 수 있는 방법이 없었다는 의미이므로 (b)가 정답입니다.

어휘 **prevent + 목적어 + from -ing**: (목적어)가 ~하지 못하게 막다 **demand** 수요, 요구 **flaw** 결함 **consistent** 지속적인, 일관된

패러프레이징

the technology to read and process the information was not yet available → There was no way to scan

When did Kroger's in Cincinnati first test barcode technology?

(a) before the bullseye shape was created
(b) after a universal numbering system was developed
(c) before lasers had become available
(d) after companies competed to make the best design

신시내티의 크로거 매장은 언제 처음 바코드 기술을 테스트했는가?

(a) 과녁 모양이 만들어지기 전에
(b) 보편적인 번호 부여 시스템이 개발된 후에
(c) 레이저가 이용 가능해지기 전에
(d) 회사들이 최상의 디자인을 만들기 위해 경쟁한 후에

정답 (d)

해설 질문의 키워드인 Kroger's in Cincinnati가 제시된 세 번째 문단에 1960년대에 최상의 바코드 디자인을 만들어 내기 위한 경쟁이 있었다고(This spurred a competition to create the best barcode design) 언급한 후, 1970년대에 크로거 사가 신시내치의 매장에서 과녁 모양의 첫 바코드를 테스트한 사실을(On July 3, 1972, the first bullseye barcode was tested at Kroger's Kenwood Plaza store in Cincinnati, to initial success) 밝히고 있습니다. 따라서 1960년대의 개발 경쟁 후에 1970년대에 테스트가 이뤄졌음을 알 수 있으므로 (d)가 정답입니다.

어휘 compete 경쟁하다

Why was chewing gum used to demonstrate Laurer's design?

(a) because it was produced by a partner company
(b) because it was particularly small
(c) because it was the store's bestselling item
(d) because it was visually appealing

라우어의 디자인을 보여 주는 데 껌이 이용된 이유는 무엇인가?

(a) 제휴 회사에 의해 만들어졌기 때문에
(b) 특히 작았기 때문에
(c) 그 매장의 베스트셀러 제품이었기 때문에
(d) 시각적으로 매력적이었기 때문에

정답 (b)

해설 질문의 키워드 chewing gum이 언급되는 네 번째 문단에 라우어가 새로운 버전의 바코드를 만들었다는(Laurer created a new version) 사실과 함께, 그것이 처음 이용된 제품으로 껌이 선택된 이유가 아주 작은 포장지에도 인쇄될 수 있음을 보여 주기 위해서라는 내용이(the first item to be scanned using the new barcode was a packet of Wrigley's chewing gum, which had been chosen to show that the barcode could even be printed on very small packages) 언급되었습니다. 따라서 껌의 작은 크기를 언급한 (b)가 정답입니다.

어휘 demonstrate ~을 보여 주다, ~을 입증하다, ~을 시연하다 particularly 특히, 특별히 visually 시각적으로 appealing 매력적인

on very small packages → particularly small

64 사실 확인

Which of the following is NOT implied about barcodes in the healthcare sector?

(a) They are used to track admitted patients.
(b) They help to reduce prescription errors.
(c) They are used to regulate medication dosages.
(d) They help to identify medical equipment.

다음 중 의료 분야의 바코드와 관련해 암시되지 않은 것은 어느 것인가?

(a) 입원한 환자들을 파악하는 데 이용된다.
(b) 처방 오류를 줄이는 데 도움이 된다.
(c) 약물 복용량을 규정하는 데 이용된다.
(d) 의료 장비를 확인하는 데 도움이 된다.

정답 (d)

해설 질문의 키워드 healthcare가 언급되는 다섯 번째 문단에 정확한 신원 확인을 위한 환자 손목밴드(patient wristbands for accurate identification) 및 복용량과 안전 상세 정보를 위한 처방약 병(prescription bottles for dosage and safety details)에 쓰인다는 정보가 제시되어 있어 (a)와 (b), 그리고 (c)의 내용을 확인할 수 있습니다. 하지만, 의료 장비 확인과 관련된 정보는 나타나 있지 않으므로 (d)가 정답입니다.

어휘 track ~을 파악하다, ~을 추적하다 admitted 입원한 reduce ~을 줄이다, ~을 감소시키다 regulate ~을 규정하다, ~을 조절하다 identify ~을 확인하다 equipment 장비

65 동의어

In the context of the passage, detect means _____.

(a) notice
(b) punish
(c) admit
(d) explain

해당 단락의 문맥에서 detect가 의미하는 것은?

(a) 알아차리다, 주목하다
(b) 처벌하다
(c) 인정하다, (입장 등을) 허락하다
(d) 설명하다

정답 (a)

해설 해당 문장은 바코드가 없었던 시대에 재고 파악과 관련해 발생한 문제점을 이야기하고 있으며, detect 뒤에 '절도'를 뜻하는 명사 theft가 쓰여 있어 failed to detect theft가 절도 문제를 파악하지 못했음을 의미한다는 것을 알 수 있습니다. 이는 그

러한 문제를 알아차리지 못한 것과 같으므로 '알아차리다'라는 의미를 나타내는 (a) notice가 정답입니다.

66 동의어

In the context of the passage, <u>pursue</u> means _____.

(a) ruin
(b) suspend
(c) seek
(d) repeat

해당 단락의 문맥에서 <u>pursue</u>가 의미하는 것은?

(a) 망치다
(b) 유예하다, 매달다
(c) 추구하다, 찾다
(d) 반복하다

정답 (c)

해설 해당 문장에서 pursue 뒤에 계산대와 관련된 자동화를 뜻하는 명사구 automation in checkout lines가 쓰여 있어 당시의 회사들이 자동화를 원했다는 의미로 볼 수 있습니다. 이는 그러한 이점을 추구한 것과 같으므로 '추구하다'라는 의미를 나타내는 (c) seek가 정답입니다.

PART 3

BANYAN TREE

The banyan tree is a species of fig tree and a member of the mulberry family. Found in India and Pakistan, it is notable for its aerial root system that grows above ground, for **67** the sweet fruit it produces, and for its unique relationship with fig wasps.

The name "banyan" may refer to many species of fig trees known as "strangler figs." **68** When a banyan seed lands on another tree, it grows into a vine that **72** extends toward the ground, wrapping around the tree and its roots. Eventually, the strangler fig will grow to encircle the original tree, killing it in the process.

As the banyan tree develops, it grows what are called aerial prop roots, which hang from its branches. **69** These roots grow into the ground, eventually hardening into thick wooden structures that look like tree trunks. However, all the trunks are connected to the original banyan. **69** A single banyan can expand outward into a broad area, creating what is often referred to as a banyan grove. The largest banyan tree currently alive is over 250 years old and can be found in Kolkata, India. With over 3,600 aerial roots, the tree covers roughly 3.5 acres, thus resembling an entire forest.

The banyan tree is pollinated by the fig wasp, a species that has evolved to have a close relationship with the tree. Figs initially develop as a structure called a syconium, or a pod with flowers on the inside. **70** Fig wasps lay their eggs inside these pods when the tree is producing pollen. The insects then transport pollen wherever they go. Later, pods are **73** dispersed by birds and other animals, which eat the mature figs.

반얀 트리

반얀 트리는 무화과 나무의 한 가지 종이자, 뽕나무 과의 일원이다. 인도와 파키스탄에서 발견되는, 이 나무는 지상에서 자라는 공중 뿌리 체계와 이 나무 가 만들어 내는 달콤한 과일, 그리고 무화과 말벌과 의 특별한 관계로 유명하다.

"반얀"이라는 명칭은 "교살 무화과 나무"라고 알려 진 무화과 나무의 많은 종을 가리킬 수 있다. 반얀 트리의 씨앗이 다른 나무 위에 내려 앉으면, 덩굴 식물로 자라면서 지면 쪽으로 확장하면서, 그 나무 와 뿌리를 휘감는다. 결국, 이 교살 무화과 나무는 자라서 원래의 나무를 둘러싸면서, 그 과정에서 그 나무를 죽이게 된다.

반얀 트리가 성장할 때, 공중 지주근이라고 부르는 것을 성장시키며, 이는 가지마다 매달린다. 이 뿌리 가 자라 땅속으로 들어가면서, 결국 두툼한 나무 구 조물로 경화되어 나무 몸통처럼 보이게 된다. 그런 데, 모든 몸통 부분은 원래의 반얀 트리와 연결되어 있다. 단 한 그루의 반얀 트리가 바깥쪽으로 확장해 넓은 구역에 이르면서, 흔히 반얀 수풀이라고 일컬 어지는 것을 형성한다. 현재 살아 있는 가장 큰 반 얀 트리는 250년이 넘었으며, 인도의 콜카타에서 찾아 볼 수 있다. 3,600개가 넘는 공중 뿌리를 지니 고 있는, 이 나무는 그 범위가 약 3.5에이커에 이르 고 있어서, 하나의 숲 전체와 닮아 있다.

반얀 트리는 무화과 말벌에 의해 수분되는데, 이 종 은 반얀 트리와 가까운 관계를 이루도록 진화해 왔 다. 무화과 나무는 처음에 은화과라고 부르는 구조 물, 즉 내부에 꽃들이 있는 꼬투리로 성장한다. 무 화과 말벌은 이 나무가 꽃가루를 만들어 내고 있을 때 이 꼬투리 내부에 알을 낳는다. 이 곤충은 그 후 자신이 가는 곳마다 꽃가루를 옮긴다. 그 이후에, 이 꼬투리들은 다 익은 무화과를 먹는 새와 다른 동 물들에 의해 흩어지게 된다.

The banyan is India's national tree and has great significance in the Hindu religion. According to Hindu mythology, **71(a)** the divine deity Krishna delivered a sermon while standing under a banyan tree. This speech — including its location — **71(c)** is described in the Bhagavad Gita scripture, one of the core Hindu texts. The banyan is often referred to as a "world tree" that grows upside down and **71(b)** provides blessings to those on Earth through its roots.

반얀 트리는 인도라는 국가를 상징하는 나무이며, 힌두교에서 대단한 중요성을 지니고 있다. 힌두교 신화에 따르면, 신성한 크리슈나신이 반얀 트리 아래에 서서 설교를 했다. 이 설교는, 그 장소를 포함해, 힌두교 핵심 성서들 중 하나인 바가바드 기타 경전에 묘사되어 있다. 반얀 트리는 흔히 거꾸로 자라는 "세계수"로 일컬어지고 있으며, 그 뿌리를 통해 지구상의 사람들에게 은총을 제공하고 있다.

어휘   species (동식물의) 종 fig tree 무화과 나무 mulberry 뽕나무 family (생물 분류상의) 과 be notable for ~로 유명하다 aerial 공중의 unique 특별한, 독특한 relationship 관계 wasp 말벌 refer to ~을 가리키다, ~을 일컫다 known as ~라고 알려진 seed 씨앗 land v. 내려앉다, 착륙하다 grow into ~로 자라다 vine 덩굴 식물 extend 확장하다, ~을 확장시키다 wrap ~을 휘감다, ~을 둘러싸다 eventually 결국, 마침내 encircle ~을 둘러싸다 process 과정 prop roots 지지근(지상부로 나와 있으면서 땅속으로 뻗어 들어가 줄기를 버티는 뿌리) hang from ~에 매달리다 branch 나뭇가지 harden 경화되다, 단단해지다 structure 구조(물) tree trunk 나무 몸통 be connected to ~와 연결되다 outward 바깥쪽으로 broad 넓은 be referred to as ~라고 일컬어지다 grove 수풀 currently 현재 cover ~의 범위에 이르다 roughly 약, 대략 thus 따라서, 그러므로 resemble ~을 닮다 entire 전체의 pollinate ~을 수분하다 evolve 진화하다, 발전하다 initially 처음에 syconium 은화과(무화과의 과실) pod (콩 등의) 꼬투리 lay one's eggs 알을 낳다 pollen 꽃가루, 화분 insect 곤충 transport ~을 옮기다 disperse ~을 흩어지게 하다 mature 성숙한, 다 익은 significance 중요성 religion 종교 according to ~에 따르면 mythology 신화 divine 신성한 deity 신 deliver a sermon 설교하다 including ~을 포함해 describe ~을 묘사하다 scripture 경전, 성전 core 핵심적인 text 성서, 문서, 글 upside down 거꾸로 blessing 은총, 은혜

---

67 주제/목적

What is the article mainly about?

(a) a tree that has edible leaves
(b) a poisonous tree species
(c) a tree that is becoming extinct
(d) a type of fruit-bearing tree

기사가 주로 무엇에 관한 것인가?

(a) 식용 잎이 있는 나무
(b) 독성이 있는 나무 종
(c) 멸종되고 있는 나무
(d) 과일을 맺는 나무의 일종

정답   (d)

해설   반얀 트리와 관련된 기본적인 정보를 제공하는 첫 문단에 달콤한 과일을 만들어 낸다는(the sweet fruit it produces) 내용이 제시되어 있으므로 이러한 특징을 언급한 (d)가 정답입니다.

어휘   edible 식용의, 먹을 수 있는 poisonous 독성이 있는 extinct 멸종된 fruit-bearing 과일을 맺는

패러프레이징

sweet fruit it produces → fruit-bearing

68 추론

How, most likely, do strangler figs get their name?

(a) from the method they use to get food
(b) from the twisted pattern of their roots
(c) from the way they eliminate other trees
(d) from the arm-like appearance of their vines

교살 무화과 나무는 어떻게 그 명칭을 얻었을 것 같은가?

(a) 먹을 것을 얻기 위해 이용하는 방법으로부터
(b) 꼬여 있는 뿌리 패턴으로부터
(c) 다른 나무를 제거하는 방식으로부터
(d) 팔처럼 생긴 덩굴 나무 모습으로부터

정답 (c)

해설 질문의 키워드인 strangler figs가 언급되는 두 번째 문단에 반얀 트리의 씨앗이 다른 나무에서 덩굴 식물로 자라면서 그 나무와 뿌리를 휘감아 죽이게 되는 과정이(When a banyan seed lands on another tree, ~ the strangler fig will grow to encircle the original tree, killing it in the process) 언급되어 있습니다. 따라서 이렇게 다른 나무를 죽여 없애는 방식으로부터 명칭을 얻은 것으로 볼 수 있으므로 (c)가 정답입니다.

어휘 method 방법, 방식 twisted 꼬여 있는, 뒤틀린 eliminate ~을 제거하다, ~을 없애다 arm-like 팔처럼 생긴 appearance 모습, 외관

69 세부 정보

According to the third paragraph, what makes up a banyan grove?

(a) the hardened roots of a single banyan tree
(b) the fallen leaves of many banyan trees
(c) the dried-out remains of several banyan trees
(d) the flowering branches of one banyan tree

세 번째 문단에 따르면, 무엇이 반얀 트리 수풀을 구성하는가?

(a) 단 한 그루의 반얀 트리 가진 경화된 뿌리
(b) 많은 반얀 트리에서 떨어진 잎
(c) 여러 반얀 트리의 말라 버린 유해
(d) 반얀 트리 한 그루에서 꽃을 피우는 가지

정답 (a)

해설 세 번째 문단 중반부에 뿌리가 경화되어 나무 몸통처럼 보이게 된다는 점과(These roots grow into the ground, eventually hardening into thick wooden structures that look like tree trunks) 단 한 그루의 반얀 트리가 바깥쪽으로 확장해 넓은 구역에 이르면서 반얀 수풀이라고 일컬어지는 것을 만든다는 점이(A single banyan can expand outward into a broad area, creating what is often referred to as a banyan grove) 언급되어 있습니다. 따라서 한 그루의 반얀 트리에서 나온 뿌리가 경화되고 확장하면서 반얀 수풀을 구성한다는 것을 알 수 있으므로 (a)가 정답입니다.

어휘 make up ~을 구성하다 fallen 떨어진 dried-out 말라 버린 remains 유해 flowering 꽃을 피우는

Based on the text, what can probably be said about fig wasps?

(a) They eat the pods produced by banyan trees.
(b) They carry pollen to and from their nests.
(c) They build their homes inside thick roots.
(d) They bring mature fruit to their hives.

지문 내용에 따르면, 무화과 말벌과 관련해 언급될 수 있는 것은 무엇인가?

(a) 반얀 트리가 만드는 꼬투리를 먹는다.
(b) 보금자리를 오가면서 꽃가루를 나른다.
(c) 두꺼운 뿌리 내부에 집을 짓는다.
(d) 다 익은 과일을 벌집으로 가져간다.

정답 (b)

해설 질문의 키워드인 fig wasps가 언급되는 네 번째 문단에 무화과 말벌이 반얀 트리의 꼬투리 내부에 알을 낳고, 가는 곳마다 그 꽃가루를 옮긴다는(Fig wasps lay their eggs inside these pods when the tree is producing pollen. The insects then transport pollen wherever they go) 내용이 쓰여 있습니다. 이를 통해 알을 낳은 보금자리와 꽃가루를 옮기는 외부 장소를 오가는 것으로 볼 수 있으므로 (b)가 정답입니다.

어휘 nest 보금자리, 둥지 hive 벌집

❌ 오답 피하기

해당 문단에 무화과 말벌이 꼬투리 안에 알을 낳는다는 말만 쓰여 있고 그것을 먹는지에 관한 정보는 제시되어 있지 않으며, 다 익은 무화과를 먹는 것은 새와 다른 동물들이라고 언급되어 있으므로 (a)와 (d)는 오답입니다.

Which is NOT stated in the final paragraph about a particular banyan tree's significance in Hindu mythology?

(a) It was the site of an important sermon.
(b) It is thought to be a source of divine blessings.
(c) It was referenced in a religious text.
(d) It is believed to house an important deity.

마지막 문단에서 특정 반얀 트리가 힌두교 신화에서 지니는 중요성과 관련해 언급되지 않은 것은 어느것인가?

(a) 중요한 설교 장소였다.
(b) 신성한 은총의 근원으로 여겨진다.
(c) 한 종교 문서에 언급되었다.
(d) 한 중요한 신에게 거처를 제공하는 것으로 여겨진다.

정답 (d)

해설 마지막 문단에서 신성한 크리슈나신이 설교를 한 장소로(the divine deity Krishna delivered a sermon while standing under a banyan tree) 언급한 부분에서 (a)를, 사람들에게 은총을 제공한다고(provides blessings) 말한 부분에서 (b)를, 그리고 힌두교에서 중요한 경전에 묘사되어 있다고(is described in the Bhagavad Gita scripture, one of the core Hindu texts) 밝히는 부분에서 (c)를 각각 확인할 수 있습니다. 하지만, 신에게 거처를 제공한다는 내용은 제시되어 있지 않으므로 (d)가 정답입니다.

어휘 **particular** 특정한 **site** 장소, 지점, 현장 **be thought to 동사원형:** ~하는 것으로 여겨지다(= be believed to 동사원형) **source** 근원, 원천 **reference** v. ~을 언급하다, ~을 인용하다 **house** v. ~에게 거처를 제공하다

---

72 동의어

In the context of the passage, extends means _____.

(a) stretches
(b) slows
(c) settles
(d) slides

해당 단락의 문맥에서 extends가 의미하는 것은?

(a) 늘어나다, 뻗다
(b) 둔화되다
(c) 자리잡다, 안정되다, 합의되다
(d) 미끄러지다

정답 (a)

해설 해당 문장에서 that 앞에 위치한 주절에는 다른 나무에 내려앉은 반얀 트리 씨앗이 덩굴 식물로 자란다는 말이, extends 뒤에는 '지면 쪽으로'를 뜻하는 전치사구와 다른 나무를 휘감는다는 내용을 담은 분사구가 각각 쓰여 있습니다. 따라서 extends는 덩굴 식물로 자라면서 지면 쪽으로 뻗어가는 모습을 나타내는 동사인 것으로 볼 수 있으므로 '늘어나다, 뻗다'를 뜻하는 (a) stretches가 정답입니다.

---

73 동의어

In the context of the passage, dispersed means _____.

(a) thrown
(b) spread
(c) known
(d) used

해당 단락의 문맥에서 dispersed가 의미하는 것은?

(a) 던져진
(b) 확산된
(c) 알려진
(d) 이용된

정답 (b)

해설 해당 문장에서 과거분사 dispersed 뒤에 '다 익은 무화과를 먹는 새와 다른 동물들에 의해'를 뜻하는 by 전치사구가 쓰여 있어 주어인 pods(꼬투리들)의 이동과 관련된 단어임을 알 수 있습니다. 따라서 무화과를 먹는 여러 동물들에 의해 이리저리 흩어지게 되는 것으로 볼 수 있습니다. 이는 확산되는 것과 같으므로 '확산된'을 뜻하는 (b) spread가 정답입니다.

PART 4

To: Diane Foster <diane.foster@marigoldhotel.com>
From: Horace Bramley <horace.bramley@
   wellnessretreats.com>
Subject: Wellness Spa Partnership

Dear Ms. Foster,

My name is Horace Bramley, and I am the owner of
Bramley's Wellness Retreats. **75** I produce retreat
experiences for overstressed workers in today's fast-
paced world. I am contacting you because I feel that
74 the Marigold would be the perfect location for
a wellness retreat, and I would love to partner with
you.

First, let me tell you about our retreats. We combine
physical activity and mindfulness practices to relieve
stress for corporate employees. For example, at a
recent retreat for business executives, we started the
day with aerobic exercise to work up a sweat and
then transitioned to gentle yoga poses. After lunch,
the clients meditated, focusing on releasing negative
emotions. We **79** cater to **75** clients who are in high-
intensity occupations and require an outlet for their
stress.

74 **76** When I was at your hotel, I felt an amazing
energy, in part due to the marvelous fragrances.
Each room had a gentle smell of exotic wood and
therapeutic oil, reminding me of an aromatherapy
session. I asked the desk clerk about the oils and
was told that you select them personally. Such
beautiful aromas would complement the relaxing spa
services I offer during my retreats.

수신: 다이앤 포스터 <diane.foster@
   marigoldhotel.com>
발신: 호레이스 브램리<horace.bramley@
   wellnessretreats.com>
제목: 웰니스 스파 사업 제휴

포스터 씨께,

제 이름은 호레이스 브램리이며, 저는 브램리스 웰
니스 리트리츠의 소유주입니다. 저는 빠른 속도로
흘러가는 현대 사회에서 지나치게 스트레스를 받는
직장인들을 위해 휴양 경험을 만들어 드리고 있습
니다. 제가 연락 드리는 이유는 매리골드 사가 건강
휴양을 위한 완벽한 장소가 될 것이라고 생각하기
때문이며, 귀사와 제휴 관계를 맺고 싶습니다.

우선, 저희 휴양 서비스에 관해 알려 드리겠습니다.
저희는 신체 활동과 마음 챙김 수련을 결합해 기업
직원들을 위해 스트레스를 해소해 드립니다. 예를
들어, 최근에 있었던 업체 임원 대상 휴양 서비스에
서, 저희는 땀을 흘릴 수 있도록 에어로빅 운동으로
하루를 시작한 다음, 가벼운 요가 동작으로 넘어갔
습니다. 점심 식사 후에는, 해당 고객들께서 명상을
하시면서, 부정적인 감정들을 쏟아 내시는 데 초점
을 맞추셨습니다. 저희는 고강도의 직업을 갖고 계
셔서 스트레스 분출 수단을 필요로 하시는 고객들
의 요구를 충족시켜 드립니다.

제가 귀하의 호텔에 있었을 때, 놀라운 에너지를 느
꼈는데, 부분적으로는 굉장한 향 때문이었습니다.
각 객실에서 이국적인 나무 및 치유 효과가 있는 오
일의 부드러운 향이 나서, 방향 요법 시간이 떠올랐
습니다. 제가 그 오일들에 대해서 데스크 직원에게
물어 봤는데, 귀하께서 직접 그 오일들을 고르신다
는 얘기를 들었습니다. 그렇게 아름다운 향기는 제
가 저희 휴양 서비스 중에 제공해 드리는 느긋한 스
파 서비스를 보완해 줄 것입니다.

A few months ago, **77** I held a spa retreat at a small hotel, and this led to a substantial increase in their profits for that period. **77** At a larger hotel like the Marigold, you would easily see greater financial rewards if you were to start hosting retreats.

I would love to **80** establish an arrangement with terms that you find agreeable. I will be unavailable this weekend due to an out-of-town business trip, but feel free to email me, and **78** we can schedule a video conference to discuss the details next week.

Best,

Horace Bramley

몇 달 전에, 제가 한 작은 호텔에서 스파 휴양 서비스 시간을 열었는데, 이 행사가 그 기간 중의 그곳 수익에 있어 상당한 증가로 이어졌습니다. 매리골드 같이 규모가 더 큰 호텔에서는, 휴양 서비스를 주최하기 시작하시면 손쉽게 더 큰 금전적 보상을 경험하시게 될 것입니다.

저는 귀하께서 합당하다고 생각하시는 조건에 대한 협의 시간을 꼭 정했으면 합니다. 제가 이번 주말에 다른 지역으로 가는 출장으로 인해 시간은 나지 않겠지만, 언제든지 제게 이메일 보내 주시면, 다음 주에 세부 사항을 논의할 수 있도록 화상 통화 일정을 잡으실 수 있습니다.

안녕히 계십시오.

호레이스 브램리

어휘 retreat 휴양 (서비스), 야유회, 짧은 여행 overstressed 지나치게 스트레스를 받는 fast-paced 속도가 빠른 contact ~에게 연락하다 wellness 건강 would love to 동사원형: 꼭 ~하고자 하다, ~하고 싶다 partner with ~와 제휴 관계를 맺다 combine ~을 결합하다 physical 신체적인, 물리적인 mindfulness practices 마음 챙김 수련 recent 최근의 executive 임원, 이사 work up a sweat 땀을 흘리다 transition to ~로 넘어가다, ~로 전환되다 gentle 가벼운, 부드러운 meditate 명상하다 focus on ~에 초점을 맞추다 release ~을 쏟아 내다, ~을 방출하다 negative 부정적인 cater to ~의 요구를 충족하다 high-intensity 고강도의 occupation 직업 outlet 분출 수단 in part 부분적으로 due to ~로 인해, ~ 때문에 marvelous 굉장한, 믿을 수 없는 exotic 이국적인 therapeutic 치유 효과가 있는, 치료상의 remind A of B: A에게 B를 떠올리게 하다, A에게 B를 상기시키다 aromatherapy 방향 요법 session (특정 활동을 위한) 시간 select ~을 고르다 complement ~을 보완해 주다 relaxing 느긋하게 하는, 여유로운 hold ~을 개최하다, (행사 등을) 열다 lead to ~로 이어지다 substantial 상당한 increase in ~의 증가 profit 수익 reward 보상 be to 동사원형: ~하게 되다, ~해야 하다, ~할 예정이다 host ~을 주최하다 establish ~을 설정하다, ~을 확립하다 arrangement 협의, 조치, 처리, 준비 term 조건, 조항 find + 목적어 + 형용사: (목적어)를 ~하다고 생각하다 agreeable 합당한, 받아들일 수 있는 unavailable (사람) 시간이 없는, (사물 등) 이용할 수 없는 feel free to 동사원형: 언제든지 ~하세요 video conference 화상 회의 details 세부 사항, 상세 정보

Why is Horace Bramley writing to Diane Foster?

(a) to request a discount on a group reservation
(b) to invite her to one of his wellness retreats
(c) to propose a collaboration with her hotel
(d) to ask her to invest in his business

호레이스 브램리 씨는 왜 다이앤 포스터 씨에게 이메일을 쓰는가?

(a) 단체 예약에 대한 할인을 요청하기 위해
(b) 자신의 건강 휴양 서비스 중 하나에 초대하기 위해
(c) 포스터 씨의 호텔과 협업을 제안하기 위해
(d) 자신의 사업에 투자하도록 요청하기 위해

정답 (c)

해설 첫 문단에 상대방인 포스터 씨의 업체를 매리골드라고 지칭하면서 그곳과 꼭 제휴 관계를 맺고 싶다는(the Marigold would be the perfect location for a wellness retreat, and I would love to partner with you) 뜻을 나타내는 말이 쓰여 있습니다. 또한, 세 번째 문단에는 포스터 씨의 업체를 호텔이라고(When I was at your hotel) 언급하고 있어 포스터 씨가 운영하는 호텔과의 제휴 관계를 제안하는 이메일임 알 수 있습니다. 이는 일종의 협업 관계를 제안하는 것이므로 (c)가 정답입니다.

어휘 reservation 예약 propose ~을 제안하다 collaboration 협업, 공동 작업 ask + 목적어 + 동사원형: (목적어)에게 ~하도록 요청하다 invest in ~에 투자하다

┌─ 패러프레이징 ─
│ would love to partner with you → propose a collaboration
└

Why, most likely, do Horace's clients attend his retreats?

(a) because of their poor physical health
(b) because of their stressful family responsibilities
(c) because of their need for emotional support
(d) because of their busy professional lives

호레이스 씨의 고객들은 왜 그의 휴양 서비스 시간에 참석할 것 같은가?

(a) 좋지 못한 신체 건강 때문에
(b) 스트레스 받는 가족에 대한 책임감 때문에
(c) 정서적 지지에 대한 필요성 때문에
(d) 바쁜 직장 생활 때문에

정답 (d)

해설 첫 문단에는 호레이스 씨의 휴양 서비스가 빠른 속도로 흘러가는 현대 사회에서 지나치게 스트레스를 받는 직장인들을 위한 것이라는(I produce retreat experiences for overstressed workers in today's fast-paced world) 말이 쓰여 있고, 두 번째 문단에는 그 고객들이 고강도 직업을 갖고 있음을(clients who are in high-intensity occupations) 밝히는 내용이 있습니다. 따라서 바쁘게 직장 생활을 하는 고객들이 그 휴양 시간에 참석할 것으로 생각할 수 있으므로 (d)가 정답입니다.

어휘 **attend** ~에 참석하다 **responsibility** 책임(감) **emotional** 정서적인 **support** 지원, 지지

> ### ❌ 오답 피하기
>
> 많은 스트레스를 받는 사람들이 서비스 대상임을 언급하고 있기는 하지만, 그것이 가족 문제와 관련되어 있는지는 알 수 없으며, 휴양 서비스의 일환으로 에어로빅 등의 신체 활동을 하는 시간이 있다는 정보가 제시되어 있으므로 (a)와 (b)는 오답입니다.

76 세부 정보

According to the third paragraph, why was Horace impressed with the Marigold Hotel?

(a) because of the soothing scents in the building
(b) because of the skilled musicians that performed there
(c) because of the beautiful paintings in the rooms
(d) because of the abundance of plants in the lobby

세 번째 문단에 따르면, 호레이스 씨는 왜 매리골드 호텔에 깊은 인상을 받았는가?

(a) 건물 내에서 나는 진정 효과가 있는 향 때문에
(b) 그곳에서 공연하는 숙련된 음악가들 때문에
(c) 객실마다 놓인 아름다운 그림들 때문에
(d) 로비에 놓은 많은 식물들 때문에

정답 (a)

해설 세 번째 문단에 상대방인 포스터 씨의 호텔인 매리골드 호텔에 갔을 때 놀란 이유로 굉장한 향을 언급하면서 각 객실에서 오일의 부드러운 향이 났던 사실을(When I was at your hotel, I felt an amazing energy, in part due to the marvelous fragrances. Each room had a gentle smell of exotic wood and therapeutic oil ~) 밝히고 있으므로 (a)가 정답입니다.

어휘 **be impressed with** ~에 깊은 인상을 받다 **soothing** 진정 효과가 있는 **scent** 향, 향기 **skilled** 숙련된, 능숙한 **perform** 연주하다, 공연하다 **the abundance of** 많은, 풍부한

패러프레이징

marvelous fragrances / a gentle smell of exotic wood and therapeutic oil → soothing scents

Based on the fourth paragraph, what advantage does the Marigold probably have over other hotels?

(a) It features more available rooms.
(b) It has a more impressive architectural design.
(c) It features more experienced staff.
(d) It has a more flexible reservation policy.

네 번째 문단에 따르면, 매리골드는 다른 호텔들에 비해 어떤 장점을 지니고 있을 것 같은가?

(a) 더 많은 이용 가능한 객실을 특징으로 한다.
(b) 더 인상적인 건축 디자인을 지니고 있다.
(c) 더 경험이 많은 직원들을 특징으로 한다.
(d) 더 탄력적인 예약 정책이 있다.

정답 (a)

해설 네 번째 문단에 호레이스 씨가 과거에 작은 호텔에서 열었던 행사를(I held a spa retreat at a small hotel) 언급한 다음, 매리골드 호텔이 규모가 더 크다는(At a larger hotel like the Marigold) 사실을 이야기하고 있습니다. 이를 통해 매리골드에 객실이 더 많다는 점을 알 수 있으므로 이러한 특징을 언급하는 (a)가 정답입니다.

어휘 advantage 장점, 이점 over (비교) ~에 비해, ~보다 feature ~을 특징으로 하다 available 이용 가능한 experienced 경험 많은 flexible 탄력적인, 유연한 policy 정책, 방침

패러프레이징

a larger hotel like the Marigold → features more available rooms

How does Horace suggest discussing the terms of their agreement?

(a) by meeting during his weekend trip to the hotel
(b) by arranging a call for the following week
(c) by connecting during a weekend conference
(d) by having lunch the following week

호레이스 씨는 어떻게 합의 조건을 논의하도록 제안하는가?

(a) 해당 호텔로 떠나는 자신의 주말 출장 중에 만나서
(b) 다음 주로 통화 일정을 정해서
(c) 주말 컨퍼런스 중에 연락해서
(d) 다음 주에 점심 식사를 하면서

정답 (b)

해설 질문의 키워드인 discuss와 terms가 제시되는 마지막 문단에 다음 주에 세부 사항을 논의할 수 있도록 화상 통화 일정을 잡을 수 있다는(we can schedule a video conference to discuss the details next week) 말로 논의 방식을 제안하는 내용이 쓰여 있으므로 이러한 방식에 해당하는 (b)가 정답입니다.

어휘 suggest -ing ~하도록 제안하다 arrange ~의 일정을 정하다, ~을 조치하다 call 통화, 전화 following 다음의 connect 연락하다, 연결되다

79 동의어

In the context of the passage, <u>cater to</u> means _____.

(a) promote
(b) serve
(c) separate
(d) provide

해당 단락의 문맥에서 <u>cater to</u>가 의미하는 것은?

(a) 홍보하다, 촉진하다, 승진시키다
(b) 서비스를 제공하다, 봉사하다
(c) 분리하다
(d) 제공하다

정답 (b)

해설 해당 문장에서 cater to 뒤에 목적어로 '고객들'을 뜻하는 명사 clients가 쓰여 있으며, 이 명사를 수식하는 who절에 고강도의 직업을 갖고 있어서 스트레스 분출 수단을 필요로 한다는 내용이 쓰여 있습니다. 주어가 호레이스 씨의 업체를 가리키는 We인 것으로 볼 때 그러한 고객들이 필요로 하는 바를 충족해 준다는 의미를 구성하는 것이 가장 자연스러우며, 이는 일종의 서비스를 제공하거나 봉사하는 것과 유사한 의미로 볼 수 있으므로 (b) serve가 정답입니다.

80 동의어

In the context of the passage, <u>establish</u> means _____.

(a) fight for
(b) allow
(c) set up
(d) review

해당 단락의 문맥에서 <u>establish</u>가 의미하는 것은?

(a) ~을 위해 싸우다
(b) 허용하다, 허락하다
(c) 정하다, 마련하다, 설치하다
(d) 살펴 보다, 검토하다

정답 (c)

해설 해당 문장에서 동사 establish 뒤에 '협의, 조치, 조정' 등을 뜻하는 명사 arrangement가 목적어로 쓰여 있고, 그 뒤에 with terms라는 전치사구가 위치해 있어 establish가 조건에 대한 협의와 관련되어 있다는 것을 알 수 있습니다. 또한, 다음 문장에 논의 일정을 잡는 방법을 제안하는 내용이 쓰여 있는 것으로 볼 때, establish an arrangement가 '협의 시간을 마련하다'를 의미하는 것으로 생각할 수 있으므로 (c) set up이 정답입니다.

Grammar

1. (c)	2. (c)	3. (d)	4. (b)	5. (a)	6. (b)	7. (c)	8. (d)	9. (a)	10. (b)
11. (b)	12. (a)	13. (d)	14. (c)	15. (b)	16. (b)	17. (a)	18. (c)	19. (d)	20. (c)
21. (c)	22. (b)	23. (d)	24. (a)	25. (a)	26. (d)				

Listening

27. (b)	28. (c)	29. (d)	30. (c)	31. (d)	32. (a)	33. (b)	34. (d)	35. (b)	36. (a)
37. (c)	38. (a)	39. (d)	40. (c)	41. (a)	42. (b)	43. (d)	44. (b)	45. (d)	46. (a)
47. (a)	48. (c)	49. (d)	50. (c)	51. (b)	52. (b)				

Reading & Vocabulary

53. (d)	54. (a)	55. (b)	56. (c)	57. (b)	58. (b)	59. (c)	60. (a)	61. (c)	62. (a)
63. (c)	64. (d)	65. (d)	66. (b)	67. (b)	68. (c)	69. (d)	70. (a)	71. (d)	72. (c)
73. (a)	74. (d)	75. (b)	76. (a)	77. (b)	78. (c)	79. (a)	80. (d)		

채점 계산표 (정답 개수 기재)		채점 계산 방법
Grammar	_____ / 26문항	Grammar 정답 개수 ÷ 26 × 100
Listening	_____ / 26문항	Listening 정답 개수 ÷ 26 × 100
Reading & Vocabulary	_____ / 28문항	Reading & Vocabulary 정답 개수 ÷ 28 × 100
총점	_____ / 80문항 ▶ _____ / 100점	총점: 각 영역 합산 정답 개수 ÷ 80 × 100 • 소수점 이하는 올림 처리

TEST 06

GRAMMAR
LISTENING
READING & VOCABULARY

Grammar

01 조동사

While hummingbirds are known as the smallest migrating bird, they have other special qualities. They are also the only birds that _____ fly backwards, using wings that beat up to 4,000 times per minute.

(a) would
(b) must
(c) can
(d) could

벌새는 가장 작은 철새로 알려져 있는 반면에 그 새들은 다른 특성을 가지고 있다. 그들은 뒤로 날 수 있는 유일한 새이기도 하는데, 1분당 최대 4000회까지 날개를 퍼덕인다.

정답 (c)

해설 빈칸에 들어갈 알맞은 조동사를 고르는 문제입니다. 빈칸 앞 문장은 벌새가 철새 중에서 가장 작은 새라고 알려져 있다는 내용을 언급하였으며, 그 뒤에 또다른 특성을 소개하는데, 벌새가 뒤로 난다는 것을 언급하였습니다. 이는 벌새의 능력을 나타내는 것이므로 '뒤로 날 수 있다'라는 의미를 나타내는 것이 적절합니다. 따라서 '~할 수 있다'라는 의미를 나타내는 조동사 (c) can이 정답입니다.

어휘 hummingbird 벌새 be known as ~로(서) 알려져 있다 migrating bird 철새 quality 특성, 자질 backwards 뒤로 beat (날개를) 퍼덕이다 up to 최대 ~까지 per ~당, ~마다

02 준동사 – 동명사

Jonathan and his friends want to see a movie on Friday night. Unfortunately, they all like completely different types of films, which makes _____ a movie difficult.

(a) to choose
(b) to have chosen
(c) choosing
(d) having chosen

조나단과 그의 친구들은 금요일 밤에 영화를 보고 싶어한다. 불행히도 그들은 모두 전혀 다른 종류의 영화를 좋아하는데, 그것이 영화를 고르는 것을 어렵게 만든다.

정답 (c)

해설 동사 choose의 알맞은 형태를 고르는 문제입니다. 빈칸은 which로 시작하는 관계대명사절에서 타동사 make 뒤에 위치하고 있으며, 빈칸 뒤에는 choose의 목적어로 쓰이는 a movie가 위치해 있습니다. 그 뒤에 타동사 choose에는 필요하지 않은 형용사 difficult가 위치해 있는 것을 보고 이 관계사절에서 make가 5형식 동사로 쓰여 「make + 목적어 + 목적격보어(형용사)」의 구조를 나타내고 있음을 알 수 있습니다. 따라서 빈칸은 5형식의 목적어 자리이므로 동명사인 (c) attending이 정답입니다.

어휘 unfortunately 불행히도, 안타깝게도 completely 완전히, 전혀 film 영화

⊗ 오답 피하기

5형식의 목적어 자리에는 to부정사가 위치하지 못하고, 「5형식 동사 + it + 목적격보어 + to부정사」의 구조로 목적어 자리에
가목적어 it을 쓰고 진목적어인 to부정사는 목적격보어 뒤에 위치합니다.
ex) make choosing a movie difficult = make it difficult to choose a movie

03 가정법 과거완료

The novel *Lightforce* was highly anticipated, but the author, Brad Bickley, could not finish it due to writer's block. Had the book been completed, it _____ launched at a celebrity event last month.

(a) would be
(b) will be
(c) will have been
(d) would have been

소설 『라이트포스』는 상당히 기대되는 작품이었는데, 작가인 브래드 비클리는 작가의 절필감으로 인해 그것을 완료할 수 없었다. 그 책이 완성되었다면, 그것은 지난 달에 유명 인사 행사에서 출시했을 것이다.

정답 (d)

해설 be동사의 알맞은 형태를 고르는 문제입니다. Had the book been은 가정법 과거완료를 구성하는 If the book had been 에서 If가 생략되고 주어와 had가 도치된 구조입니다. 따라서, If절의 동사가 「had p.p.」일 때 주절의 동사로 사용하는 「would/could/might + have p.p.」의 형태가 빈칸에 쓰여야 알맞으므로 (d) would have been이 정답입니다.

어휘 highly anticipated 상당히 기대되는 due to ~로 인해 writer's block 작가의 절필감, 글길이 막힘 complete 완료하다, 완성하다 launch 출시하다

04 시제 – 과거완료진행

The city of Istanbul is one of the largest and oldest in the world. Until 1453, it was known as "Constantinople" and _____ as the capital of the Byzantine Empire.

(a) has been serving
(b) had been serving
(c) would serve
(d) will have served

이스탄불은 가장 크고 오래된 도시 중 하나이다. 1453년까지, 그 도시는 "콘스탄티노플"로 알려져 있었으며, 비잔틴 제국의 수도로서의 역할을 하였다.

정답 (b)

해설 동사 serve의 알맞은 형태를 고르는 문제입니다. 등위접속사 and로 연결된 앞문장에 과거시제 동사 was known을 통해 "콘스탄티노플"로 일러진 것이 과거 시점이다는 깃을 알 수 있고 그 이전부터 비잔틴 제국의 수도였음을 알 수 있으므로 빈칸이 속한 문장은 was known보다 앞선 과거시점을 나타내야 합니다. 따라서 빈칸에 들어갈 시제는 특정 과거보다 더 먼저 일어난 일을 나타내는 과거완료진행시제가 되어야 하므로 (b) had been serving이 정답입니다.

어휘 be known as ~로(서) 알려져 있다 capital 수도 empire 제국 serve 역할을 하다

05 준동사 – to부정사

Rebecca is replying to a friend's email invitation to a party at his house next Friday night. Rebecca is eager _____, but only if she can take a guest along with her.

(a) to go
(b) to have gone
(c) going
(d) having gone

레베카는 다음 주 금요일 밤 친구의 집에서 있을 파티에 대한 초청 이메일에 답장을 쓰고 있다. 레베카는 파티에 가기를 열망하지만, 그녀가 초대손님을 한 명 데리고 갈 수 있을 경우에만 가능하다.

정답 (a)

해설 동사 go의 알맞은 형태를 고르는 문제입니다. 빈칸은 형용사 eager 뒤에 위치해 있으며, 형용사 eager는 be동사, to부정사와 함께 쓰여 「be eager to 동사원형」의 구조로 '~하기를 열망하다'라는 의미를 나타냅니다. 따라서 to부정사인 (a) to go가 정답입니다.

어휘 reply to ~에 답장을 쓰다, ~에 답변하다 invitation 초대 be eager to 동사원형: ~하기를 열망하다, 정말로 ~하고 싶어하다 only if ~해야만, ~할 경우에만 한해 along with ~와 함께

❌ 오답 피하기

선택지가 모두 to부정사, 동명사로 구성되어 있고 형용사 뒤에 빈칸이 있는 경우 to부정사가 정답입니다. 단, to have p.p와 같은 형태는 정답으로 출제되지 않습니다.

06 관계사절

Dogs understand us reasonably well when we communicate with them. This is because their advanced language processing, _____, allows them to comprehend words, tone, context, and gestures.

(a) who resembles ours
(b) which resembles ours
(c) that resembles ours
(d) what resembles ours

개는 우리가 그들과 의사소통을 할 때 상당히 잘 우리를 이해한다. 이것은 그들의 발전된 언어 처리과정 때문인데, 그것은 우리의 것과 유사하다. 그리고 이 언어 처리과정은 그들이 단어, 어조, 맥락, 그리고 몸짓을 이해하게 한다.

정답 (b)

해설 사물 명사 their advanced language processing을 뒤에서 수식할 관계사절을 고르는 문제입니다. 선택지 (a)~(d)를 보고 빈칸에 들어갈 관계사절이 관계대명사 뒤에 타동사 resembles와 목적어 ours가 이어지는 구조임을 알 수 있습니다. 사물 명사를 수식하는 관계대명사는 which 또는 that인데, 빈칸 앞에 콤마가 있으므로 관계대명사 which로 시작하는 (b)가 정답입니다.

어휘 reasonably 상당히, 꽤 communicate with ~와 의사소통하다 advanced 고급의, 발전된 processing 처리 과정 allow + 목적어 + to 동사원형: (목적어)가 ~하게 하다 comprehend 이해하다 tone 어조, 말투 context 맥락, 문맥 gesture 몸짓 resemble ~와 유사하다, ~을 닮다

---

07 가정법 과거

Iceland is very active geologically and has many hot springs that are popular with swimmers. If the country's volcanic activity were ever to cease, Icelanders _____ one of their favorite methods of relaxation.

(a) will lose
(b) will have lost
(c) would lose
(d) would have lost

아이슬란드는 지질학적으로 매우 활성화 된 지역이며, 수영 애호가들에게 인기 있는 많은 온천을 가지고 있다. 그 나라의 화산 활동이 멈춘다면, 아이슬란드 사람들은 그들이 가장 좋아하는 휴식 방법 중 하나를 잃을 것이다.

정답 (c)

해설 동사 lose의 알맞은 형태를 고르는 문제입니다. If절의 동사가 가정법 과거를 나타내는 과거시제(were)일 때, 주절의 동사는 「would/could/might + 동사원형」과 같은 형태가 되어야 알맞으므로 (c) would lose가 정답입니다.

어휘 active 활발한, 활성화 된 geologically 지질학적으로 hot spring 온천 popular with ~에게 인기 있는 swimmer 수영 애호가, 수영선수 volcanic 화산의 activity 활동 cease 멈추다, 중단되다 relaxation 휴식

---

08 접속사

Mark and Jen wanted to do some outdoor exercise this afternoon, but it is pouring rain outside. They are going to wait it out and play tennis in the park's indoor stadium _____ the rain stops.

(a) after
(b) whereas
(c) because
(d) until

마크와 젠은 오늘 오후에 야외 운동을 하고 싶어했다. 하지만 지금 밖에는 비가 퍼붓고 있는 중이다. 그들은 비가 끝나기를 기다릴 것이고, 비가 멈출 때까지 공원의 실내 체육관에서 테니스를 할 것이다.

정답 (d)

해설 빈칸에 들어갈 알맞은 접속사를 고르는 문제입니다. 빈칸 앞에 설명된 상황은 마크와 젠이 야외 운동을 하고 싶어했는지 지금 비가 내리고 있는 중이며, 그들은 비가 끝나기를 기다릴 것이라며 실내 체육관에서 테니스를 할 것이라고 언급되어 있습니다. 빈칸 뒤에는 비가 멈춘다는 내용이 현재시제로 쓰여져 있으므로 문맥상 '비가 멈출 때까지 테니스를 할 것이다'라는 의미를 나타내는 것이 가장 자연스럽습니다. 따라서 '~까지'를 나타내는 부사절 접속사 (d) until이 정답입니다.

어휘 outdoor 야외의, 실외의 pour 퍼붓다 outside 밖에서 be going to 동사원형: ~할 것이다 wait out 끝나기를 기다리다 indoor stadium 실내 체육관 whereas 반면에

---

09 시제 – 현재진행

The International Cheese-Making Competition begins tomorrow in Paris. Right now, competitors from more than twenty different countries _____ in the city, ready to demonstrate their dazzling expertise.

(a) are arriving
(b) arrive
(c) had been arriving
(d) would arrive

국제 치즈 만들기 대회가 내일 파리에서 시작된다. 바로 지금, 20개국 이상의 대회 참가자들이 파리에 도착하고 있으며, 그들은 그들의 현란한 전문 기술을 보여줄 준비가 되어 있다.

정답 (a)

해설 동사 arrive의 알맞은 형태를 고르는 문제입니다. 빈칸 앞에 위치한 Right now가 '바로 지금'이라는 의미를 나타내어 현재 일시적으로 진행되는 일을 뜻하는 현재진행시제 동사와 어울려 쓰이므로 (a) are arriving이 정답입니다

어휘 competition 대회, 경쟁 competitor (대회) 참가자, 경쟁자 demonstrate 보여주다, 발휘하다 expertise 전문 기술, 전문 지식

---

10 준동사 – to부정사

Alice has been calling her doctor for several days. She has decided that if she is not able _____ him by tomorrow, she will make an appointment with another doctor.

(a) reaching
(b) to reach
(c) having reached
(d) to have reached

앨리스는 며칠 동안 그녀의 의사에게 전화를 하고 있다. 만약 그녀가 내일까지 그와 연락이 되지 않는다면, 그녀는 다른 의사와 진료 예약을 할 것이라고 결심했다.

정답 (b)

해설 동사 reach의 알맞은 형태를 고르는 문제입니다. 빈칸은 형용사 able 뒤에 위치해 있으며, 형용사 able은 be동사, to부정사와 함께 쓰여 「be able to 동사원형」의 구조로 '~할 수 있다'라는 의미를 나타냅니다. 따라서 to부정사인 (b) to reach가 정답입니다.

어휘 **be able to 동사원형**: ~할 수 있다 **by** ~까지(완료, 기한) **make an appointment** 예약하다, 약속을 잡다 **reach** 연락이 되다, ~에 닿다

ⓧ 오답 피하기

선택지가 모두 to부정사, 동명사로 구성되어 있고 형용사 뒤에 빈칸이 있는 경우 to부정사가 정답입니다. 단, to have p.p.와 같은 형태는 정답으로 출제되지 않습니다.

---

11 시제 – 현재완료진행

Tamil, which is spoken in parts of India, Sri Lanka, and Singapore, is one of the oldest continuously spoken languages in the world. It is estimated that people _____ Tamil since 2500 BCE.

(a) are speaking
(b) have been speaking
(c) will be speaking
(d) had been speaking

인도 일부 지역, 스리랑카, 그리고 싱가포르에서 사용되는 타밀어는 지속적으로 사용되는 가장 오래된 언어 중 하나이다. 기원전 2500년부터 사람들이 타밀어를 사용해왔다고 추정된다.

정답 (b)

해설 동사 speaking의 알맞은 형태를 고르는 문제입니다. 빈칸이 포함된 문장 마지막에 위치한 「since + 과거시점」을 나타내는 since 2500 BCE가 '기원전 2500년부터'라는 의미를 나타내어 과거 시점에 시작하여 현재에도 진행 중인 동작이나 행동을 나타내는 현재완료진행형 동사와 어울리므로 (b) have been speaking이 정답입니다.

어휘 **continuously** 지속적으로, 계속 **it is estimated that** ~라고 추정된다 **BCE** 기원전

ⓧ 오답 피하기

「since + 과거시점」은 현재완료진행시제의 단서가 되기도 하지만 과거완료진행시제의 단서가 될 수 있습니다. 주변의 시제가 과거시제이고, since 뒤에 쓰인 과거시점이 특정과거시점보다 더 앞선 시점일 경우, 빈칸에 들어갈 시제는 과거완료진행시제입니다.

12 가정법 과거완료

Before going to bed last Thursday, Justin noticed that the batteries in his alarm clock were dead. If he had not replaced them, he _____ his appointment the following morning.

(a) might have missed
(b) will miss
(c) might miss
(d) will have missed

지난 목요일에 잠자리에 들기 전에, 저스틴은 그의 알람 시계의 배터리가 방전되었다는 것을 알았다. 만약 그가 그것들을 교체하지 않았다면 그는 그 다음날 아침에 그의 약속을 놓쳤을지도 모른다.

정답 (a)

해설 동사 miss의 알맞은 형태를 고르는 문제입니다. If절의 동사가 가정법 과거완료를 나타내는 과거완료시제(had p.p.)일 때, 주절의 동사는 「would/could/might + have + p.p.」와 같은 형태가 되어야 알맞으므로 (a) might have missed가 정답입니다.

어휘 go to bed 잠자리에 들다 notice 알아차리다 dead (배터리가) 방전된, 다 쓴 appointment 약속, 예약 following morning 다음날 아침

13 준동사 - 동명사

Natalie has arrived at the arena to see her favorite band, but their tour bus has broken down, causing a delay. She does not mind _____, though, as they are amazing in concert.

(a) to have waited
(b) having waited
(c) to wait
(d) waiting

나탈리는 그녀가 가장 좋아하는 밴드를 보기 위해 그 공연장에 도착하였다. 하지만 그들의 투어버스가 고장이 났고, 공연을 지연시켰다. 그래도 그녀는 그들이 콘서트에서는 대단하기 때문에 기다리는 것을 개의치 않았다

정답 (d)

해설 동사 wait의 알맞은 형태를 고르는 문제입니다. 빈칸 앞에 쓰여 있는 동사 mind는 동명사를 목적어로 취하므로 (d) waiting이 정답입니다.

어휘 arena 공연장, 경기장 cause 일으키다, 발생시키다 delay 지연, 지체 mind 상관하다, 개의하다 amazing 대단한, 놀라운

14 시제 – 미래진행

Colin canceled his old gym membership because the drive to that gym took too long. He is looking around at other gyms and _____ to a new one next week.

(a) switched
(b) has been switching
(c) will be switching
(d) would switch

콜린은 그가 오래 다닌 체육관으로 운전해서 가는 것이 너무 오래 걸려서 그 체육관의 회원권을 취소하였다. 그는 다른 체육관들을 둘러보고 있는 중이며, 다음 주에 새로운 곳으로 바꿀 것이다.

정답 (c)

해설 동사 switch의 알맞은 형태를 고르는 문제입니다. 빈칸이 속한 문장 앞에 미래시점을 나타내는 부사 next week이 쓰여 있으므로 빈칸이 속한 문장의 시제는 미래시제임을 알 수 있습니다. 따라서 보기 중에서 미래를 나타낼 수 있는 미래진행시제 (c) will be switching이 정답입니다.

어휘 cancel 취소하다 membership 회원권 drive to ~로 운전해서 가는 것 look around at ~을 둘러보다 switch to ~로 바꾸다, ~로 전환하다

15 준동사 – to부정사

Peacocks are among the world's largest flying birds, weighing up to thirteen pounds. At night, they perch in trees. However, they choose _____ their nests on the ground.

(a) building
(b) to build
(c) having built
(d) to have built

공작은 가장 큰 날 수 있는 새 중 하나이며, 체중이 최대 13 파운드까지 될 수 있다. 야간에 그들은 나무에 앉아 있다. 하지만, 그들의 둥지를 땅 위에 짓는 것을 선택한다.

정답 (b)

해설 동사 build의 알맞은 형태를 고르는 문제입니다. 빈칸 앞에 쓰여 있는 동사 choose는 to부정사를 목적어로 취하므로 (b) to build가 정답입니다.

어휘 peacock 공작 weigh 체중이 ~이다 up to 최대 ~까지 nest 둥지 on the ground 땅 위에, 지면에 build 짓다

Peter is about to complete his tenth marathon. He began long-distance running to improve his physical health, but he discovered he also loved racing. This coming September, he _____ in marathons for over two years.

(a) is competing
(b) will have been competing
(c) will be competing
(d) has been competing

피터는 그의 10번째 마라톤을 막 완주하려 하고 있다. 그는 그의 신체적 건강을 향상시키기 위해 장거리 달리기를 시작하였다. 하지만 그는 또한 자신이 경주하는 것을 좋아한다는 것을 알게 되었다. 다가오는 9월에, 그는 2년이 넘는 기간 동안 마라톤에 참가해오는 중일 것이다.

정답 (b)

해설 동사 compete의 알맞은 형태를 고르는 문제입니다. 빈칸 앞에 위치한 This coming September가 미래시점을 나타내고 있고, 빈칸이 포함된 문장에 for over two years와 같이 「for + 기간」 표현으로 기간을 나타내는 구문이 있으므로 2년 이상 동안 계속 진행 중일 미래의 상태를 나타낼 미래완료진행형 동사가 필요하므로 (b) will have been competing이 정답입니다.

어휘 be about to 동사원형: 막 ~하려고 하다, ~할 참이다 complete 완료하다 long-distance 장거리의 improve 향상시키다 physical 신체의 discover 알게 되다, 발견하다 race 경주하다 coming 다가오는 compete (대회에) 참가하다, 경쟁하다

Maria wants to get a puppy. Her best friend, Jemima, advised that she _____ one from a local shelter rather than buying one from a pet store.

(a) adopt
(b) adopted
(c) is adopting
(d) will adopt

마리아는 강아지 한 마리를 가지기를 원한다. 그녀의 절친, 제미마는 그녀가 애완동물 매장에서 한 마리를 사는 것보다 차라리 지역의 한 동물 보호소에서 한 마리를 입양해야 한다고 조언했다.

정답 (a)

해설 동사 adopt의 알맞은 형태를 고르는 문제입니다. 빈칸은 과거시제로 쓰인 동사 advised의 목적어 역할을 하는 that절의 동사 자리인데, advise와 같이 주장/요구/명령/제안/조언 등을 나타내는 동사의 목적어 역할을 하는 that절의 동사는 should 없이 동사원형만 사용하므로 동사원형인 (a) adopt가 정답입니다.

어휘 puppy 강아지 advise 충고하다, 조언하다 local 지역의 shelter 동물 보호소 rather than ~하는 것보다 (차라리) pet store 애완동물 매장 adopt 입양하다

18 관계사절

The Declaration of Independence was drafted by American statesman and attorney Thomas Jefferson, _____ the third US president and the founder of the University of Virginia.

(a) that was also
(b) which was also
(c) who was also
(d) what was also

미국의 독립 선언문은 미국 정치인이자 변호사인 토마스 제퍼슨에 의해 초안이 작성되었는데, 그는 또한 제 3대 미국 대통령이자 버지니아 대학교의 창립자였다.

정답 (c)

해설 사람 명사 attorney Thomas Jefferson을 뒤에서 수식할 관계사절을 고르는 문제입니다. 선택지 (a)~(d)를 보고 빈칸에 들어갈 관계사절이 관계대명사 뒤에 be동사 was와 부사 also가 이어지는 구조임을 알 수 있습니다. 사람 명사를 수식하는 관계대명사는 who 또는 that인데, 빈칸 앞에 콤마가 있으므로 관계대명사 who로 시작하는 (c)가 정답입니다.

어휘 Declaration of Independence 독립 선언문 draft 초안을 작성하다 statesman 정치인 attorney 변호사 founder 설립자, 창립자

> ❌ **오답 피하기**
>
> 관계대명사 what은 선행사(관계사절의 수식을 받는 명사)를 가지지 않는 관계대명사입니다.

19 시제 – 과거진행

Chelsea was leaving her apartment in a hurry to meet her friends when she realized that she _____ her keys. Shaking her head at her forgetfulness, she rushed back to retrieve them.

(a) is missing
(b) has been missing
(c) will have been missing
(d) was missing

첼시는 그녀가 열쇠를 놓고 왔다는 것을 깨달았을 때 그녀의 친구를 만나기 위해 서둘러 그녀의 아파트를 떠나고 있던 중이었다. 그녀의 건망증에 머리를 흔들면서, 그녀는 열쇠를 되찾아 오기 위해 서둘러 되돌아 갔다.

정답 (d)

해설 동사 missing의 알맞은 형태를 고르는 문제입니다. 빈칸 앞에 과거시제 동사(realized)를 포함한 when절이 쓰여 있어 이 when절이 가리키는 과거 시점에 준비하는 일이 일시적으로 진행되던 상황을 나타내야 자연스러우므로 이러한 의미로 쓰이는 과거진행시제 (d) was missing이 정답입니다.

어휘 in a hurry 서둘러, 급하게 realize 깨닫다, 알아차리다 shake 흔들다 forgetfulness 건망증 rush back 서둘러 되돌아 가다 retrieve 되찾다, 회수하다

William Shakespeare is considered one of the greatest writers in history. Some people have argued that his works _____ have been written by another author, but experts have thoroughly dismissed that claim.

(a) should
(b) will
(c) may
(d) can

윌리엄 셰익스피어는 역사상 가장 위대한 작가 중 한 명으로 여겨진다. 몇몇 사람들은 그의 작품들이 다른 작가의 의해 쓰여졌을지도 모른다고 주장했지만, 전문가들은 그 주장을 철저하게 묵살하였다.

정답 (c)

해설 빈칸에 들어갈 알맞은 조동사를 찾는 문제입니다. 빈칸 뒤에 have p.p. 형태의 have been written이 쓰인 것을 보고 과거 시점에 관한 조동사 표현인 「조동사 + have p.p.」 구문이 쓰였음을 알 수 있습니다. 그리고 빈칸이 포함된 문장에서 몇몇 사람들이 셰익스피어의 작품이 다른 작가의 의해 쓰여졌다고 주장했다는 내용이 언급되어 있는데, 여기서 쓰인 동사가 '주장 하다'라는 의미의 argue가 쓰였으므로 자신의 생각 또는 추측을 주장하는 내용을 나타내기 위해 '~했을지도 모른다'라는 의 미를 나타내는 것이 문맥상 적절합니다. 따라서 '~했을지도 모른다'라는 과거에 대한 추측을 나타내는 조동사 may have p.p.가 사용되었음을 알 수 있으므로 정답은 (c) may입니다.

어휘 be considered (as) ~로 여겨지다 in history 역사상 argue 주장하다 work 작품 author 작가 expert 전문가 thoroughly 철저하게 dismiss 묵살하다, 무시하다 claim 주장 may have p.p. ~했을지도 모른다 should have p.p. ~했어야 했다

Although Bill is looking for a new house, his financial advisor has reservations about such a purchase. He suggests that Bill _____ for a while until house prices decrease significantly.

(a) will wait
(b) waited
(c) wait
(d) is waiting

비록 빌이 새로운 집을 찾아보고 있지만, 그의 재정 자문가는 그러한 구매에 대해 의구심을 갖고 있다. 그는 빌에게 주택 가격이 상당히 떨어질 때까지 잠시 동안 기다려야 한다고 제안하였다.

정답 (c)

해설 동사 wait의 알맞은 형태를 고르는 문제입니다. 빈칸은 현재시제로 쓰인 동사 suggests의 목적어 역할을 하는 that절의 동사 자리인데, suggest와 같이 주장/요구/명령/제안/조언 등을 나타내는 동사의 목적어 역할을 하는 that절의 동사는 should없이 동사원형만 사용하므로 동사원형인 (c) wait가 정답입니다

어휘 look for ~을 찾다 financial advisor 재정 자문가 have reservations about ~에 대해 의구심을 갖다 suggest 제안하다 for a while 잠시 동안 price 가격 decrease 감소하다 significantly 상당히

22 가정법 과거

James loves cats, but he already has too many strays staying at his home. Still, if he were to move to a larger place, he _____ every abandoned cat in his neighborhood.

(a) will rescue
(b) would rescue
(c) will have rescued
(d) would have rescued

제임스는 고양이를 정말 좋아하지만, 그는 이미 너무 많은 유기동물들을 집에 데리고 있다. 아직도, 만약 그가 좀 더 큰 장소로 이사를 한다면, 그는 그의 동네에 모든 버려진 고양이들을 구조할 것이다.

정답 (b)

해설 동사 rescue의 알맞은 형태를 고르는 문제입니다. If절의 동사가 가정법 과거를 나타내는 과거시제(were)일 때, 주절의 동사는 「would/could/might + 동사원형」과 같은 형태가 되어야 알맞으므로 (b) would rescue가 정답입니다.

어휘 stray 유기 동물, 길 잃은 동물 still 그래도, 아직도 abandoned 버려진, 유기된 neighborhood 동네, 이웃, 인근 rescue 구조하다

23 접속부사

Leroy usually drives the same two-hour route every year to see his family for Christmas. _____, this year, heavy flooding in the area forced him to take a much longer, more roundabout drive.

(a) Likewise
(b) Therefore
(c) Otherwise
(d) However

리로이는 매년 크리스마스에 그의 가족을 보기 위해 똑같은 2시간 거리를 대개 운전해서 간다. 하지만, 올해, 그의 지역에 발생한 심한 홍수는 그로 하여금 어쩔 수 없이 훨씬 더 길고, 더 많이 우회하는 경로로 가도록 하였다.

정답 (d)

해설 빈칸에 들어갈 알맞은 접속부사를 고르는 문제입니다. 빈칸 앞 문장은 매년 크리스마스에 가족을 보기 위해 2시간이 걸리는 거리는 운전해서 간다는 내용이며, 빈칸 뒤의 내용은 심한 홍수로 인해 더 길고, 더 많이 우회하는 길로 갔다는 내용이므로 빈칸 앞뒤의 내용이 서로 상반되는 상황을 설명한다는 것을 알 수 있습니다. 따라서 '하지만'이라는 의미로 상반되는 상황을 나타낼 때 사용하는 접속부사 (d) However가 정답입니다.

어휘 route 경로, 노선 heavy (양, 정도가) 심한 flooding 홍수 force + 목적어 + to 동사원형: 어쩔 수 없이 (목적어)로 하여금 ~하게 하다, (목적어)가 억지로 하게 하다

German forces came close to winning World War I in its early stages. Had it not been for the efforts of the Belgian Army, the Germans _____ the Allies, a group of powerful countries.

(a) would probably have defeated
(b) will probably defeat
(c) will probably have defeated
(d) would probably defeat

독일군은 1차 세계 대전의 초기 단계에서 거의 승리할 뻔하였다. 벨기에군의 노력이 없었더라면, 어쩌면 독일군이 강대국 단체인 연합군을 패배 시켰을 것이다.

정답 (a)

해설 동사 defeat의 알맞은 형태를 고르는 문제입니다. Had it not been는 가정법 과거완료를 구성하는 If it had not been에서 If가 생략되고 주어와 had가 도치된 구조입니다. 따라서, If절의 동사가 「had p.p.」일 때 주절의 동사로 사용하는 「would/could/might + have p.p.」의 형태가 빈칸에 쓰여야 알맞으므로 (a) would probably have defeated가 정답입니다. 참고로 probably와 같은 부사가 있더라도 「would/could/ might + have p.p.」의 형태만 갖추어져 있으면 되므로 혼동하지 않도록 주의합니다.

어휘 force 군대 come close to 거의 ~하게 되다 stage 단계 if it had not been for ~가 없었더라면 effort 노력, 활동 defeat 패배 시키다 the Allies 연합군

Ever since Janice got her license, her mom has been really nervous about letting her drive. Nonetheless, last Friday night, her mom risked _____ Janice the keys to the family car.

(a) giving
(b) to give
(c) to have given
(d) having given

재니스가 면허를 얻은 후로 계속, 그녀의 엄마는 그녀가 운전하도록 하는 것에 대해 정말 불안해 해왔다. 그럼에도 불구하고, 지난 금요일 밤에, 그녀의 엄마는 위험을 각오하고 가족용 차량의 키를 재니스에게 주었다.

정답 (a)

해설 동사 give의 알맞은 형태를 고르는 문제입니다. 빈칸 앞에 쓰여 있는 동사 risk는 동명사를 목적어로 취하므로 (a) giving이 정답입니다.

어휘 license 면허, 허가(증) nervous 불안한, 신경 쓰이는, 초조한 let + 목적어 + 동사원형: (목적어가) ~하도록 하다 nonetheless 그럼에도 불구하고 risk -ing: 위험을 각오하고 ~하다, 감행하다

Marcus has been frightened of the woods ever since he saw a horror movie set in the forest. If he were to overcome his fear, he _____ his friends on a camping trip next weekend.

(a) to will join
(b) will have joined
(c) would have joined
(d) would join

마커스는 숲을 배경으로 하는 공포 영화를 본 이후로 계속 숲을 무서워 해왔다. 그가 공포를 극복할 수 있다면, 그는 다음 주 주말에 그의 친구들과 함께 캠핑 여행을 할 것이다.

정답 (d)

해설 동사 join의 알맞은 형태를 고르는 문제입니다. If절의 동사가 가정법 과거를 나타내는 과거시제(were)일 때, 주절의 동사는 「would/could/might + 동사원형」과 같은 형태가 되어야 알맞으므로 (d) would join이 정답입니다.

어휘 frightened of ~을 무서워하는 horror movie 공포 영화 set in ~를 배경으로 하는 forest 숲 overcome 극복하다 fear 공포 join 함께하다, 동참하다

PART 1

F: Hey, Sam! **27** I didn't expect to run into you at the department store. I hardly ever see you outside of work.

M: Hi, Tina. **27** I just moved to this neighborhood. Wow, your cart is full of stuff.

F: **28** I'm buying Christmas presents early this year to get my shopping done before the rush. I hate shopping in crowded stores during the holiday season. But I'll have to hide these gifts in the attic. My kids still believe in Santa, so I can't let them know that I'm buying their presents.

M: How old are your kids?

F: Four and six years old.

M: Did you believe in Santa Claus when you were growing up?

F: Yes! I wrote letters to him every year. My parents would pretend to mail them to the North Pole.

M: What did you write in your letters? Did you just ask for gifts?

F: I didn't ask, but I still wanted to get them. So, **29** I told Santa about the things I had done that year. I said I had been doing my chores and had straight As in school. I figured that would help me get all the presents I wanted.

M: When did you find out that Santa Claus wasn't real?

여: 안녕, 샘! 백화점에서 너를 마주칠 줄을 예상치 못했어. 회사 밖에서 너를 거의 본적이 없어.

남: 안녕, 티나. 난 이 동네로 막 이사를 왔어. 와, 네 카트는 물건으로 가득 차 있구나.

여: 난 혼잡해지기 전에 내 쇼핑을 끝내려고 올해에는 일찍 크리스마스 선물을 사고 있어. 나는 연휴 기간동안 붐비는 매장에서 쇼핑하는 것을 싫어해. 하지만 나는 다락방에 이 선물들을 숨겨야 할 것이야. 우리 아이들이 아직도 산타를 믿고 있거든. 그래서 나는 내가 그들의 선물을 사고 있다는 걸 그들이 알게 할 수 없어.

남: 네 아이들이 몇 살이니?

여: 4살과 6살이야.

남: 너는 자랄 때 산타를 믿었어?

여: 응! 난 매년 그에게 편지를 썼어. 나의 부모님은 북극으로 편지를 부치는 척 하곤 했어.

남: 편지에 뭐라고 썼어? 그냥 선물을 요청했어?

여: 요청하지 않았어. 하지만 나는 그래도 그것들을 가지고 싶었어. 그래서 나는 산타에게 내가 그 해에 내가 했던 일들에 대해 이야기 했지. 나는 내가 하기 싫은 일을 했고 학교에서 전과목 A를 받았다고 말했어. 나는 그게 내가 원했던 선물을 받도록 도움이 될 것이라고 생각했어.

남: 너는 산타 클로스가 진짜가 아니라는 걸 언제 알게 되었어?

F: When I was five. **30** I found a doll that I had asked for in my parents' closet, but the next morning, it was wrapped up and said, "from Santa."

M: Did you tell them you knew Santa Claus didn't exist?

F: No, I didn't want to stop getting gifts from him! I pretended I believed in Santa Claus until my parents told me the truth when I was eight. When did you realize that Santa was imaginary?

M: I never believed in Santa Claus. **31** My parents didn't think that it was right to lie to me.

F: Oh wow, Sam. Was it hard not getting gifts from Santa when your friends did?

M: No, my parents still gave me gifts. They just weren't "from Santa." I thought it was strange that my friends believed in something as impossible as a man delivering gifts to every child in the world. It just didn't seem realistic.

F: But Santa Claus is magical. And magic is fun to believe in as a child.

M: Maybe, Tina. But I have always been the sort of person who wants to know the truth about everything.

F: Were you ever tempted to tell your friends the truth about Santa Claus?

M: Well, my friend Sarah once asked me if Santa Claus was imaginary. She said she snuck down to the living room one Christmas Eve and saw her father assembling a train set "from Santa."

여: 내가 5살 때였어. 나는 부모님의 옷장에서 내가 요청했던 인형을 발견했어. 하지만, 다음날 아침 그게 포장되어 있었고 거기엔 "산타로부터"라고 적혀 있었어.

남: 부모님께 산타 클로스가 존재하지 않는다는 알고 있다고 말했어?

여: 아니, 난 산타로부터 선물을 받는 것을 그만두고 싶지 않았어. 부모님이 내가 8살 때 나에게 진실을 말해줄 때까지 산타 클로스를 믿는 척했어. 너는 산타 클로스가 상상의 인물이라는 것을 언제 깨달았어?

남: 나는 산타 클로스를 전혀 믿지 않았어. 나의 부모님은 나에게 거짓을 말하는 것이 옳다고 생각하지 않았어.

여: 와, 샘. 친구들이 산타로부터 선물 받을 때 너는 받지 못하는 게 힘들지 않았어?

남: 아니, 나의 부모님은 그래도 나에게 선물을 주셨어. 그 선물들은 그저 "산타로부터의" 선물이 아니었을 뿐이야. 나는 친구들이 전세계의 모든 아이들에게 선물을 배달하는 사람이라는 불가능한 것을 믿는다는 게 이상했어. 그건 그저 현실적으로 보이지 않았어.

여: 하지만 산타 클로스는 마법을 쓰잖아. 마법은 어린 아이로선 믿기에 재밌지.

남: 그럴지도 모르지, 티나. 하지만 나는 항상 모든 것에 대해 진실을 알고 싶어하는 그런 사람이야.

여: 친구들에게 산타 클로스에 관한 진실을 말하고 싶지는 않았어?

남: 음, 내 친구 사라가 한번은 나에게 산타 클로스가 상상의 인물인지 물었어. 그녀는 어느 크리스마스 이브에 거실로 살금살금 내려갔는데, 그녀의 아빠가 "산타로부터" 온 기차를 조립하고 있는 것을 봤대.

F: What did you tell Sarah?

여: 사라에게 뭐라고 말했어?

M: 32 I told her to ask her parents! Christmas was such a big event in her family. Their house was covered in Christmas decorations. 32 I didn't want to spoil their fun.

남: 나는 그녀의 부모님에게 물어보라고 말했어! 크리스마스는 그녀의 가족에게 정말 큰 행사였어. 그들의 집은 크리스마스 장식으로 덮여져 있었어. 난 그들의 즐거움을 망치고 싶지 않았어.

F: That was nice of you. Hey, I'm buying these presents now, but 33 after I'm done loading them into my car, would you like to grab coffee next door?

여: 그건 친절한 행동이었어. 난 이 선물들을 지금 살거야. 그런데 내가 그것들을 내 차에 싣고 난 후에 옆집에서 잠깐 커피 한잔 할까?

M: 33 Sure, Tina, that'd be great. But let me help you put your presents in the car. Then we can walk to the coffee shop together.

남: 물론이지, 티나. 그거 좋겠다. 하지만 너의 선물들을 자동차에 넣는 것을 도와줄게. 그러고 나서 우리는 같이 커피숍으로 걸어갈 수 있어.

F: Thanks, Sam!

여: 고마워, 샘!

어휘 run into 우연히 마주치다 department store 백화점 hardly ever 거의 ~하지 않는 neighborhood 동네, 인근 get + 목적어 + done: (목적어)를 끝내다, 완료하다 rush 혼잡 crowded 붐비는, 혼잡한 attic 다락 believe in ~을 믿다 pretend to 동사원형: ~하는 척하다 mail ~에게 편지를 부치다 Noth Pole 북극 ask for 요청하다 chore 하기 싫은 일, 허드렛일 straight As 전과목 A figure 생각하다 find out 알아내다 closet 옷장 wrap 포장하다 exist 존재하다 truth 진실, 사실 imaginary 상상의, 가상적인 deliver 배달하다 realistic 현실적인 magical 마법을 쓰는 sort of 그런 종류의 be tempted to 동사원형: ~하고 싶어지다, ~하라고 유혹받다 once 한번, 예전에 sneak down 살금살금 내려가다 assemble 조립하다 be covered 덮여있다 decoration 장식 spoil 망치다 be nice of you 넌 친절하구나 load ~을 싣다 grab 잠깐 ~하다

---

27 세부 정보

What are Sam and Tina doing at the start of the conversation?

(a) working at a department store
(b) shopping in their neighborhood
(c) going to a holiday party
(d) exchanging their presents

샘과 티나는 대화를 시작할 때 무엇을 하고 있었는가?

(a) 백화점에서 일하고 있었다.
(b) 그들의 동네에서 쇼핑하고 있었다.
(c) 연휴 파티에 가고 있었다.
(d) 선물을 교환하고 있었다.

정답 (b)

해설 대화가 시작될 때 티나가 샘에게 백화점에서 마주칠 줄을 예상하지 못했다고(I didn't expect to run into you at the department store) 언급하는 부분에서 대화 장소가 백화점인 것을 알 수 있으며, 그 뒤에 샘이 이 동네로 막 이사왔으며, 티나의 가득 찬 카트를 언급하는 부분(I just moved to this neighborhood. Wow, your cart is full of stuff)을 통해 그들이 같은 동네에서 쇼핑 중이었음을 알 수 있습니다. 따라서 정답은 (b)입니다.

어휘 **exchange** 교환하다

Why is Tina buying her presents early?

(a) to take advantage of big sales
(b) to buy items before they sell out
(c) to avoid large crowds of people
(d) to pay for things a little at a time

티나가 선물을 일찍 사고 있는 이유는 무엇인가?

(a) 대규모 할인을 이용하기 위해서
(b) 매진이 되기 전에 물건들을 사기 위해서
(c) 많은 사람들이 붐비는 것을 피하기 위해서
(d) 물건들을 한 번에 조금씩 사기 위해서

정답 (c)

해설 대화 초반부에 티나가 혼잡 전에 크리스마스 선물을 일찍 사는 것(I'm buying Christmas presents early this year to get my shopping done before the rush)에 대해 연휴 기간 동안 사람들이 매장에서 붐비는 것을 싫어한다고(I hate shopping in crowded stores during the holiday season) 언급한 것을 듣고 사람들이 많은 것을 피하고 싶은 것임을 알 수 있습니다. 따라서 정답은 (c)입니다.

어휘 **take advantage of** ~을 이용하다 **sell out** 매진되다 **large crowds of people** 많은 사람들이 붐비는 것 **pay for** ~에 대해 지불하다 **at a time** 한 번에

> **패러프레이징**
>
> hate ~ in crowded stores → avoid large crowds of people

What did Tina do in her letters to Santa?

(a) She requested presents for others.
(b) She listed all the toys that she wanted.
(c) She asked for a trip to see the elves.
(d) She pointed out her good behavior.

티나는 산타에게 보내는 편지에 무엇을 하였는가?

(a) 다른 사람들을 위한 선물을 요청했다.
(b) 그녀가 원했던 모든 장난감을 목록으로 작성했다.
(c) 요정들을 볼 수 있는 여행을 요청했다.
(d) 그녀의 착한 행동을 언급했다.

정답 (d)

해설 샘이 티나가 편지에 무엇을 썼는지 묻자 티나는 선물을 요청한 것이 아니라 자신이 그 해에 했던 것을 말했다고 하며, 하기 싫은 일을 한 것, 학교에서 전과목 A를 받을 것을 적었다고(I told Santa about the things I had done that year. I said I had been doing my chores and had straight As in school) 언급한 것으로 보아 자신이 했던 착한 행동을 썼음을 알 수 있으므로 (d)가 정답입니다.

어휘 request 요청하다 others 다른 사람들 list 목적으로 작성하다, 나열하다 elf 요정 point out 언급하다, 지적하다 behavior 행동

패러프레이징

doing my chores and had straight As in school → her good behavior

---

How did Tina first learn that Santa Claus was imaginary?

(a) by overhearing a friend talking
(b) by finding out from her parents
(c) by discovering a hidden present
(d) by seeing her dad wrap her gift

티나는 산타 클로스가 상상의 인물이라는 것을 어떻게 처음 알게 되었는가?

(a) 친구가 말하는 것을 우연히 들음으로써
(b) 그녀의 부모님으로부터 알아냄으로써
(c) 숨겨진 선물을 발견함으로써
(d) 그녀의 아빠가 그녀의 선물을 포장하는 것을 목격함으로써

정답 (c)

해설 샘이 티나에게 산타가 진짜가 아닌 것을 언제 알았냐는 질문에 티나가 다섯 살 때였다고 말하는 부분에서 산타가 상상의 인물임을 알게 된 경위를 설명하였습니다. 자신이 요청했던 인형을 부모님의 옷장에서 발견했는데, 다음날 "산타로부터"라는 메모로 포장되어 있었다고(I found a doll that I had asked for in my parents' closet, but the next morning, it was wrapped up and said, "from Santa.") 말하는 부분을 통해 숨겨진 선물을 발견한 것으로 산타에 대한 진실을 알게 되었음을 알 수 있습니다. 따라서 정답은 (c)입니다.

어휘 overhear 우연히 듣다 find out 알아내다 discover 발견하다 hidden 숨겨진

> **✕ 오답 피하기**
>
> 티나가 부모님의 옷장에서 인형을 발견하고 난 후 그 다음날 아침에 그 인형이 포장되어 있었다고(the next morning, it was wrapped up) 하였으므로 그녀의 아빠가 포장하는 것을 직접 본 것은 아님을 알 수 있습니다. 그래서 (d)는 오답입니다.

31 추론

What, most likely, did Sam's parents say about Santa Claus?

(a) that he was always watching
(b) that he was a magical figure
(c) that he was kind to all children
(d) that he was entirely fictional

샘의 부모님은 산타 클로스에 대해 뭐라고 말했을 것 같은가?

(a) 그가 항상 지켜보고 있었다는 것
(b) 그가 마법을 쓰는 인물이었다는 것
(c) 그가 모든 아이들에게 친절했다는 것
(d) 그는 완전히 허구의 인물이었다는 것

정답 (d)

해설 샘이 자신의 부모님이 산타에 대해 말하는 부분에서 부모님이 자신에게 거짓말하는 것이 옳다고 생각하지 않으셨다고(My parents didn't think that it was right to lie to me) 말하는 부분에서 그의 부모님이 티나의 부모님과 달리 산타가 존재하지 않는다는 사실을 직접 샘에게 말했음을 유추할 수 있습니다. 따라서 정답은 (d)입니다.

어휘 watch 지켜보다 magical 마법의, 마법을 쓰는 figure 인물 entirely 완전히 fictional 허구의, 상상의

Why did Sam refuse to tell his friend the truth about Santa?

(a) He worried about ruining a celebration.
(b) He was afraid her parents would be angry.
(c) He worried it would affect their relationship.
(d) He was afraid she would tell other children.

샘이 그의 친구에게 산타에 관한 진실을 말하기를 거부한 이유는 무엇이었는가?

(a) 기념 행사를 망치는 것을 걱정하였다.
(b) 그의 부모님이 화를 낼까봐 두려웠다.
(c) 친구와의 관계에 영향을 끼칠 것을 걱정하였다.
(d) 그녀가 다른 친구들에게 말할까봐 두려웠다.

정답 (a)

해설 샘이 그의 친구 사라가 크리스마스 이브에 거실에서 기차를 조립하고 있는 그녀의 아빠를 본 것을 말하면서 산타가 진짜가 아닌지 샘에게 물어보았다고 하였습니다. 그러나 샘은 사라에게 진실을 말하지 않고 그녀의 부모님에게 물어보라고(I told her to ask her parents!) 하면서 크리스마스가 그녀의 가족에게 정말 큰 행사였고(Christmas was such a big event in her family), 그들의 즐거움을 망치고 싶지 않았다고(I didn't want to spoil their fun) 말하는 것을 통해 그 가족의 기념 행사를 망치는 것을 걱정했음을 알 수 있습니다. 따라서 정답은 (a)입니다.

어휘 **refuse to 동사원형**: ~하기를 거부하다 **worry about** ~을 걱정하다 **ruin** 망치다 **celebration** 기념 행사 **be afraid** 두려워하다 **affect** 영향을 끼치다 **relationship** 관계

> **패러프레이징**
>
> • such a big event → a celebration
> • spoil → ruining

What will Tina and Sam probably do next?

(a) continue gift shopping
(b) have coffee nearby
(c) wrap some presents
(d) drive to a local café

티나와 샘은 그 후에 무엇을 할 것 같은가?

(a) 선물 쇼핑을 계속한다
(b) 근처에서 커피를 마신다
(c) 몇몇 선물을 포장한다
(d) 지역의 카페로 운전해서 간다

정답 (b)

해설 대화의 마지막 부분에서 티나가 짐을 다 싣고 난 후에 옆집에서 커피를 마시자는 제안(after I'm done loading them into my car, would you like to grab coffee next door)을 하였으며, 샘은 Sure이라고 동의의 대답을 하였으므로 대화 후에 티나와 샘은 근처에서 커피를 마실 것임을 알 수 있습니다. 따라서 정답은 (b)입니다.

어휘 continue 계속하다 nearby 근처에서 drive to ~로 운전해서 가다 local 지역의

패러프레이징

next door → nearby

❌ 오답 피하기

카페(café)로 간다는 내용이 언급된 (d)가 혼동될 수 있으나 (d)에 쓰인 동사 drive는 차를 운전해서 이동하는 것을 나타내는 것이며, 티나가 바로 옆집에서(next door) 커피를 마시자고 하였으므로 차로 이동할 필요가 없음을 알 수 있습니다. 따라서 (d)는 오답입니다.

34 Welcome to the grand reopening of the Sharpsboro Historical Battlefield site. As you may know, this site has been closed for the past year so that we could completely update all the attractions. I'm excited to tell you about all of its new features!

First, we've continued our practice of holding a daily re-enactment of the battle itself, fought between an inexperienced band of American rebels and highly trained British forces. Soldiers on both sides are played by local theater students. **35** They'll be happy to answer any questions you have about life as a soldier in colonial times, but please, hold your questions until after the re-enactment is finished. Also, the students begin rehearsing for their next show an hour after the battle's end, so please wrap up your questions by then.

Next, you can tour the field hospital where we recreate what conditions were like for wounded soldiers. Here, **36** we will ask a volunteer from the group to lie down on a bed and pretend to be operated on by our cast of doctors and nurses. We will have you change into a hospital gown before participating. We use fake blood and bandages to reenact the dressing of wounds, and we don't want you to get messy!

Later, you can take a ride on the Sharpsboro Railroad. Though railway trains didn't exist during the Revolutionary War, we've created this one specifically for our guests. It will take you across the entire fifty-acre battlefield. Watch out, though. There may be some surprises during the trip, such as a staged robbery by armed bandits. Though every seat offers an equal view of the landscape and action, please note that the train is an authentic coal-powered steam train. So, **37** sensitive passengers sitting in the front of the train may experience some respiratory irritation from the exhaust. Don't worry,

샤프스보로 전쟁 역사 현장의 재개장에 오신 것을 환영합니다. 아시다시피, 이 현장은 모든 명소들을 완전히 최신화 시킬 수 있도록 하기 위해 지난 해 동안 문을 닫았습니다. 저는 여러분에게 모든 새로운 특징들에 대해 말씀드리게 되어 흥분이 됩니다!

첫 번째로, 저희는 경험이 없는 미국 반란군과 고도의 훈련을 받은 영국군 간의 전투 자체를 매일 재연하는 연습을 계속해왔습니다. 양 측의 병사들은 현지 연극과 학생들에 의해 연기될 것입니다. 그들은 식민지 시절의 병사로서의 삶에 대해 여러분이 묻는 질문에 기꺼이 답변해드릴 것입니다. 하지만, 부디, 재연이 마친 후가 될 때까지 질문을 보류해주시기 바랍니다. 또한, 그 학생들은 전투가 끝나고 한 시간 후에 다음 쇼를 위해 리허설을 시작하므로, 그 때까지 질문을 완료해주시기 바랍니다.

다음으로, 여러분은 저희가 예전의 상태 그대로 재현한 부상병들을 위한 야전 병원을 둘러 보실 수 있습니다. 여기서, 저희는 둘러 보시는 분들 중에서 침대에 누워서 저희 의사 역할의 배우와 간호사 역할의 배우들에게 수술을 받는 척 하실 자원자 한 분을 요청드릴 것입니다. 참가하시기 전에 병원 가운으로 갈아 입으시도록 할 것입니다. 저희는 상처를 치료하는 것을 재현하기 위해 가짜 혈액과 붕대를 사용합니다. 그리고 저희는 여러분이 더러워지는 것을 원하지 않습니다!

이후에, 여러분은 샤프스보로 레일로드에 탑승하실 수 있습니다. 비록 독립 전쟁 중에는 기차가 존재하지 않았지만, 저희는 이것을 저희 고객을 위해 특별히 만들었습니다. 이 열차는 50 에이커 넓이의 전장 전체에 걸쳐 여러분을 데려다 줄 것입니다. 그래도, 조심하세요. 이 여행 중에는 무장한 노상 강도에 의한 연출된 강도 사건과 같은 몇몇 놀랄 만한 일들이 있을 수 있습니다. 비록 모든 좌석이 풍경과 액션에 대한 동일한 시야를 제공하지만, 기차가 실제로 석탄을 용하는 증기 기관열차이라는 점을 알아 두시기 바랍니다. 그래서, 기차의 앞에 앉으시는 민감한 승객들께서는 배기가스로 인해 호흡

though. There are plenty of seats in the back.

Finally, you can enter our large-format theater, where you can feel immersed in a feature-length documentary about the battle itself. **38** Following the documentary, all guests are invited to a full colonial-style dinner at General LeGarde's mansion. This dinner will feature food that was authentic to the period and will be hosted by an actor playing the role of the General himself. **Feel free to speak with the General during the meal.** Perhaps he can give you some insight into his surprising victory over the invading British army.

Those are the newest features of our battlefield tour. If you wish to purchase items at our gift shop following the tour's conclusion, just follow your guide to the shop near the exit. **39** You can get a special one-time-only discount on any item, just by saying the General's code phrase "send fresh horses" to the cashier at the shop. **Thanks, and have a great time!**

에 불편을 겪으실 수도 있습니다. 하지만, 걱정 마세요. 뒤쪽에는 충분한 좌석이 있습니다.

마지막으로, 여러분은 저희의 대형 영화관에 입장하실 수 있습니다. 그 곳에서 여러분은 그 전투 자체에 관한 장편 다큐멘터리 영화에 몰입하실 수 있습니다. 다큐멘터리 영화 후에, 모든 고객들은 르가르드 장군의 저택에서 완전히 식민지 시대 형식의 저녁 식사에 초대됩니다. 이 저녁 식사는 실제 그 시대의 음식을 특색으로 선보일 것이며, 장군 역할을 연기하는 배우에 의해 진행될 것입니다. 식사 시간 동안 장군님과 자유롭게 이야기를 나눠보세요. 어쩌면 그가 영국 침략군을 물리친 놀라운 승리에 대한 어떤 통찰력을 여러분에게 줄 수 있을지도 모릅니다.

이것들이 저희 전장 투어의 최신 특징들입니다. 여러분이 투어가 종료된 후에 기념품 매장에서 물건을 구매하시고 싶으시다면, 여러분의 안내원을 따라가서 출구 가까이에 있는 매장으로 가시기 바랍니다. 여러분은 매장의 계산원에게 장군의 암구호 "생기 넘치는 말을 보내라"를 말하는 것만으로 모든 물품에 대해 단 1회의 특별 할인을 받으실 수 있습니다. 감사합니다. 즐거운 시간 보내시기 바랍니다!

어휘 reopening 재개장 historical 역사적인, 역사와 관련된 battlefield 전장, 싸움터 site 현장, 장소 past 지난, 과거의 so that ~ can 그래서 ~할 수 있도록 completely 완전히 update 최신화 하다 attraction 명소, 인기거리 be excited to 동사원형: ~하게 되어 흥분되다, ~해서 신나다 feature 특징 hold 보류하다, 가지고 있다 daily 매일의, 일상의 reenactment 재현 battle 전투 inexperienced 경험이 없는, 미숙한 band (군) 부대, 군대 rebel 반란군 highly 매우, 대단히 trained force 군대, 병력 soldier 병사 theater 연극, 극장 colonial 식민지의 rehearse 리허설 하다, 예행 연습하다 wrap up 끝내다, 마치다 field hospital 야전 병원 condition 상태 wounded 부상 당한, 부상 입은 volunteer 자원자 lie down 눕다 pretend to 동사원형: ~하는 척 하다 operate 수술하다 cast 출연진, 배우진 change into ~로 갈아입다 fake 가짜의, 위조의 bandage 붕대 reenact 재현하다 dress (상처를) 치료하다 wound 상처 get messy 더러워지다 railway train 기차 exist 존재하다 Revolutionary War 미국 독립 전쟁 specifically 특별히 entire 전체의 watch out 조심하세요 staged 연출된 robbery 강도 사건 armed 무장한 bandit 노상 강도 equal 동일한 view 시야, 경관 note that ~임을 알아 두세요, ~에 주목하세요 authentic 진짜의, 진품의 coal-powered 석탄으로 움직이는 steam train 증기 기관차 sensitive 민감한, 예민한 passenger 승객 in the front of ~의 앞쪽에 respiratory 호흡의 irritation 불편, 짜증, 염증 exhaust 배기 가스 plenty of 충분한 large-format 대형의 feel immersed in ~에 몰입되다, ~에 집중하다 feature-length 장편 영화 길이의 mansion 저택 feature 특색으로 내보이다 period 기간 host 진행하다, 주최하다 general 장군 insight 통찰력, 견해 victory 승리 invading 침략하는 army 군대 purchase 구매하다 following ~후에 conclusion 종료 guide 안내원 exit 출구 code phrase 암구호 fresh 생기 넘치는 cashier 계산원

What is the main subject of the talk?

(a) a celebration of a war hero
(b) the making of a historical film
(c) a tour of a war museum
(d) the reopening of a historical site

담화의 주제는 무엇인가?

(a) 전쟁 영웅에 대한 기념 행사
(b) 역사 영화 제작
(c) 전쟁 박물관 투어
(d) 역사적 장소의 재개장

정답 (d)

해설 화자가 담화의 시작 부분에서 샤프스보로 전쟁 역사 현장의 재개장에 오신 것을 환영한다고(Welcome to the grand reopening of the Sharpsboro Historical Battlefield site) 언급하였으므로 역사적 장소가 다시 개장하는 것에 대한 담화임을 알 수 있습니다. 따라서 정답은 (d)입니다.

어휘 celebration 기념 행사 hero 영웅 museum 박물관

❌ 오답 피하기

담화 첫 부분에서 담화가 일어나는 장소를 museum(박물관)이 아니라 site라고 언급하였으므로 (c)는 오답입니다.

When can guests speak with the soldiers?

(a) when the park opens
(b) after their performance
(c) before the intermission
(d) as they are rehearsing

고객들이 병사들과 이야기를 나눌 수 있는 것은 언제인가?

(a) 공원이 개장할 때
(b) 병사들의 공연 후에
(c) 중간 휴식 시간 전에
(d) 그들이 예행 연습할 때

정답 (b)

해설 질문의 키워드인 the soldiers는 전투 재연을 공연하는 연극과 학생들을 가리킵니다. 이들과 이야기를 나누는 것은 담화 중에서 병사로서의 삶에 대한 질문에 답을 해줄 것이라는(They'll be happy to answer any questions you have) 부분을 듣고 알 수 있습니다. 이에 대해 화자는 재연을 마친 후가 될 때까지 질문을 보류해달라고(hold your questions until after the re-enactment is finished) 요청합니다. 이를 통해 전투 재연이 끝나고 이야기를 나눌 수 있음을 알 수 있으므로 정답은 (b)입니다.

어휘 performance 공연 intermission 중간 휴식 시간

패러프레이징

• reenactment → performance
• They'll be happy to answer any questions you have → speak with the soldiers

전투 재연이 끝나고 1시간 후 다음 공연을 위해 리허설을 하므로 그때까지 질문을 마쳐달라는(the students begin rehearsing for their next show an hour after the battle's end, so please wrap up your questions by then) 것을 통해 질문을 할 수 있는 시간이 전투 재연 공연과 리허설 사이의 중간 휴식 시간(intermission)임을 알 수 있습니다. 하지만 (c)는 '중간 휴식 시간 전'을 나타내므로 오답입니다.

36 세부 정보

What must hospital volunteers do before they participate?

(a) change into other clothes
(b) sign a legal form
(c) watch a training video
(d) get a doctor's note

병원에서의 자원자들은 참가하기 전에 무엇을 해야 하는가?

(a) 다른 의상으로 갈아 입는다
(b) 법적인 문서에 서명한다
(c) 교육 영상을 시청한다
(d) 의사의 진단서를 받는다

정답 (a)

해설 질문의 키워드인 hospital volunteers는 화자가 야전 병원에 대해 설명하는 중에 침대에 누워서 의사, 간호사 역할의 배우들에게 수술을 받는 척 할 자원자를 요청할 것(we will ask a volunteer from the group to lie down on a bed and pretend to be operated on by our cast of doctors and nurses)이라고 언급하는 부분에서 확인할 수 있습니다. 그 뒤에 화자가 자원자는 참가하기 전에 병원 가운으로 갈아 입도록 할 것(We will have you change into a hospital gown before participating)이라고 말하는 부분에서 옷을 갈아 입어야 하는 것이 언급되므로 (a)가 정답입니다.

어휘 sign 서명하다 legal form 법적인 문서(양식) training 훈련, 교육 a doctor's note 진단서

37 추론

Why, most likely, would some guests sit at the back of the train?

(a) to experience less engine noise
(b) to volunteer for the robbery
(c) to avoid breathing in the smoke
(d) to get the most scenic view

몇몇 승객이 기차의 뒤쪽에 앉을 이유는 무엇일 것 같은가?

(a) 엔진 소음을 덜 듣기 위해서
(b) 강도 사건에 자원하기 위해서
(c) 연기를 마시는 것을 피하기 위해서
(d) 가장 경치가 좋은 시야를 얻기 위해서

정답 (c)

해설 질문의 키워드인 the back of the train은 기차를 타고 전장 전체를 다니는 기차에 대해 설명하는 부분의 마지막에 언급되었습니다. 해당 부분의 앞에서 화자는 기차의 앞에 앉는 민감한 승객들은 배기가스로 인해 호흡에 불편을 겪으실 수도 있다고 언급하고, 뒤쪽에는 충분한 좌석이 있다고(sensitive passengers sitting in the front of the train may experience some respiratory irritation from the exhaust. ~ There are plenty of seats in the back) 설명하였습니다. 이를 통해 기차의 뒤쪽에 앉는 승객은 기차의 배기가스를 피할 수 있음을 알 수 있으므로 (c)가 정답입니다.

어휘 experience 겪다 noise 소음 smoke 연기 scenic 경치가 좋은

> **패러프레이징**
>
> exhaust → smoke

---

38 세부 정보

What takes place following the documentary?

(a) a meal hosted by an actor
(b) a tour of the general's mansion
(c) a colonial-style cooking class
(d) a speech from the film's director

다큐멘터리 영화 후에 무슨 일이 일어나는가?

(a) 배우에 의해 진행되는 식사
(b) 장군의 저택 투어
(c) 식민지 시대 형식의 요리 강의
(d) 영화 감독의 강연

정답 (a)

해설 질문의 키워드 following the documentary는 화자가 "Following the documentary"라고 말하는 부분에서 언급됩니다. 그 후에 화자는 모든 고객이 르가르드 장군 저택에서의 식민지 시대 형식의 저녁 식사에 초대된다고(all guests are invited to a full colonial-style dinner at General LeGarde's mansion) 설명합니다. 이 저녁 식사는 장군 역할을 연기하는 배우에 의해 진행될 것이라고(This dinner ~ will be hosted by an actor playing the role of the General himself) 설명하므로 (a)가 정답입니다.

어휘 take place 발생하다, 일어나다 meal 식사 cooking class 요리 강의 speech 강연, 연설 director 감독, 연출자

> **⊗ 오답 피하기**
>
> 장군의 저택에서의 저녁 식사(dinner)라고 언급하였으므로 tour나 cooking class가 언급된 (b), (c)를 오답으로 소거합니다.

How can visitors receive a discount at the gift shop?

(a) They can download an app.
(b) They can arrive at a certain time.
(c) They can join a mailing list.
(d) They can mention a specific phrase.

방문객들은 기념품 매장에서 어떻게 할인을 받을 수 있는가?

(a) 앱을 다운로드 받을 수 있다.
(b) 특정 시간에 도착할 수 있다.
(c) 정기 우편물 수신자 명단에 가입할 수 있다.
(d) 특정 문구를 말할 수 있다.

정답 (d)

해설 질문의 키워드인 receive a discount at the gift shop은 담화의 마지막 부분에서 화자가 1회의 특별 할인을 받을 수 있다 (You can get a special one-time-only discount on any item)고 말하는 부분에서 확인할 수 있습니다. 그 뒤에 할인 방법에 대해서는 매장의 계산원에게 "생기 넘치는 말을 보내라"라는 장군의 암구호를 말하는 것(just by saying the General's code phrase "send fresh horses" to the cashier at the shop)이라고 설명하므로 (d)가 정답입니다.

어휘 **certain** 특정한 **mailing list** 우편물 수신자 명단 **mention** 말하다, 언급하다 **specific** 특정한, 구체적인

패러프레이징

saying the General's code phrase → mention a specific phrase

M: Hi, Diana. How come you're in the dorms? I thought I was the only person here during break.

F: Hey, Jackson! 40 I left my parents' house as soon as Christmas was over. I wanted to a get a head start on work for next semester's classes.

M: Nice. I just like the peace and quiet.

F: It is pretty quiet here. Oh, guess what? When I was home, I found out I got a year-long internship at a museum in Madrid. It begins as soon as I graduate.

M: Wow! That's amazing!

F: To prepare myself, 41 I just signed up for a virtual Spanish class that meets weekly online. My language class is only four months long, though, so I'm wondering if it's a better idea to go to Madrid and learn the language once I'm there.

M: Well, let's discuss the pros and cons of taking a language class here versus learning Spanish once you're abroad.

F: Okay, so one advantage of taking the class here would be that I'd know some Spanish when I arrive. I'd be able to ask for directions and go shopping for groceries.

M: Right. In my experience, though, Diana, basic language classes aren't that helpful.

F: Oh, why's that, Jackson?

M: Well, 42 I took one semester of French before going to Paris. The instructor was great, but when I got there, the locals spoke so fast that I couldn't understand anything.

남: 안녕, 다이애나. 어째서 너는 기숙사에 있어? 내가 휴가 기간 동안 여기 있는 유일한 사람인 줄 알았어.

여: 안녕, 잭슨! 40 나는 크리스마스가 끝나자마자 부모님 댁을 떠났어. 다음 학기의 수업에 대해 유리한 출발을 하고 싶었거든.

남: 좋네. 난 그저 평온함과 조용한 것이 좋아.

여: 여기 정말 조용하다. 아, 그거 알아? 내가 집에 있을 때 마드리드에 있는 박물관에서 1년 기간의 인턴십을 받았다는 것을 알게 됐어. 그건 내가 졸업하자마자 시작해.

남: 와! 그거 놀라운데!

여: 나 자신을 준비시키기 위해서, 41 온라인으로 일주일마다 만나는 가상 스페인어 수업에 막 등록했어. 그래도 나의 언어 수업은 단 4개월 짜리인데, 그래서 나는 일단 스페인에 가서 그 언어를 배우는 게 더 좋은 생각인지 궁금해.

남: 음, 여기서 언어 수업을 듣는 것과 일단 스페인으로 가서 스페인어를 배우는 것의 장점과 단점에 대해서 이야기해보자.

여: 좋아, 그래서 여기서 수업을 듣는 것의 한 가지 장점은 내가 도착하면 내가 스페인어를 조금 알 것이라는 거야. 나는 방향을 묻고 식료품을 사러 쇼핑을 갈 수 있겠지.

남: 맞아. 그런데 내 경험상 말이야, 다이애나, 언어의 기초 수업은 그렇게 도움이 되지 않아.

여: 오, 이유가 뭐야, 잭슨?

남: 음, 42 난 파리로 가기 전에 프랑스어 수업을 1학기 동안 들었어. 강사는 훌륭했지만, 내가 그곳에 도착했을 때, 현지인들이 너무 빨리 말해서 나는 아무 것도 이해하지 못했어.

F: That's too bad. Native speakers do speak really fast.

M: All I could really understand was "Hello" and "Goodbye." I was too embarrassed to ask people to slow down.

F: So, maybe there isn't any point in taking Spanish here at the school if I'm going to be confused all the time anyway.

M: Maybe. But 43 I do remember that the French people I met appreciated that I was at least trying to learn the language.

F: Yeah, I've heard that it's a good idea to at least try.

M: So, what are some of the advantages of waiting to learn the language when you get there?

F: Luckily, everyone at the museum where I'll be interning already speaks English, so they wouldn't expect me to be fluent.

M: That is lucky.

F: And 44 there will be several other interns there who speak Spanish and can help me learn as I go.

M: That's great!

F: The other thing is that I have a full load of classes already, and I need to finish my senior thesis before I can graduate. I don't know if adding a language class to my packed schedule is a good idea.

M: True. Getting your project done is the most

여: 그거 안됐다. 원어민들은 정말 빨리 말해.

남: 내가 정말 이해할 수 있던 것은 "안녕" 그리고 "잘가"였어. 나는 너무 쑥스러워서 사람들에게 천천히 말해달라고 요청하지 못했어.

여: 그래서, 어쨌든 내가 항상 혼란을 겪을 거라면 이 곳의 학교에서 스페인어를 듣는 것은 의미가 없을지도 모르겠어.

남: 아마도. 하지만 내가 분명히 기억하는 건 내가 만났던 프랑스 사람들이 내가 최소한 그 언어를 배우려고 노력하고 있었다는 것을 인정해줬다는 거였어.

여: 그래, 최소한 시도를 하는 것이 좋은 생각이라는 것은 들은 적 있어.

남: 그래서, 기다렸다가 네가 그곳에 가서 그 언어를 배우는 것에 대한 장점은 뭐야?

여: 운이 좋게도, 내가 인턴직을 할 그 박물관에 있는 모든 사람들이 이미 영어를 말한다는 거야. 그래서 그들은 내가 유창할 것이라고 기대하지 않을 거야.

남: 그건 다행이네.

여: 그리고 스페인어를 말하는 다른 인턴들이 몇 명 있을 거라서, 그들이 내가 가서 배우는 것을 도와줄 수 있어.

남: 그거 굉장하네!

여: 또 다른 점은 난 이미 수업을 가득 듣고 있고, 내가 졸업하기 전에 나는 졸업 논문을 완료해야 한다는 거야. 가득 찬 내 일정에 언어 수업을 추가하는 게 좋은 생각인지 모르겠어.

남: 맞아. 너의 계획을 완료하는 것이 중요한 것이

important thing. And, of course, when you go to Madrid, you'll learn the language just by interacting with people every day.

F: Still, I'd feel embarrassed starting from scratch like that.

M: Well, people like helping newcomers. I'm sure the people you meet would be happy to see that you're eager to learn from them.

F: Maybe you're right.

M: So, have you decided what to do?

F: I think **45** I'd like to focus on my thesis without worrying about classes that aren't absolutely necessary.

M: That's a wise decision, Diana.

F: Thanks for your help, Jackson!

지. 그리고, 물론 네가 마드리드에 가면, 매일 사람들과 교류하면서 언어를 배우게 될 거야.

여: 그래도, 그렇게 아무런 사전 준비 없이 시작하는 게 쑥쓰럽다고 느낄거야.

남: 음, 사람들은 새로 온 사람들을 돕는 것을 좋아해. 네가 만나는 사람들이 네가 간절히 그들에게 배우려고 하는 것을 보고 기뻐할 거라고 확신해.

여: 네 말이 맞을지도 몰라.

남: 그래서, 무엇을 하기로 결정했어?

여: 내 생각에 난 절대적으로 필요한 것이 아닌 수업에 대해 걱정하지 않고 나의 논문에 집중하고 싶은 것 같아.

남: 그거 현명한 결정이야, 다이애나.

여: 도와줘서 고마워, 잭슨!

어휘　How come ~? 어째서 ~?, 왜 ~?　dorm 기숙사　break (짧은) 휴가　as soon as ~하자마자　get a head start 유리한 출발을 하다　semester 학기　peace 평온함　pretty 꽤　a year-long 1년 기간의　graduate 졸업하다　prepare oneself 자신을 준비시키다　sign up for ~에 등록하다　virtual 가상의　weekly 매주의, 일주일마다　worder if ~인지 궁금하다　pros and cons 장점과 단점　versus ~에 비해, ~대　abroad 해외에서　advantage 장점　directions 방향　grocery 식료품　helpful 도움이 되는, 유용한　instructor 강사　local 현지인　native 원어민의　too 형용사 to 동사원형: 너무 ~해서 ~할 수 없다　embarrassed 쑥쓰러운　slow down 속도를 늦추다, 천천히 하다　point 의미　confused 혼란을 느끼는　appreciate (진가를) 알아보다, 인정하다　at least 최소한　luckily 운이 좋게도, 다행히도　fluent (언어가) 유창한　a full load of ~가 가득한　senior thesis 졸업 논문　packed 가득 찬　project 계획　get + 목적어 + done: (목적어)를 완료하다　interact 교류하다　start from scratch 아무 준비 없이 시작하다　newcomer 새로 온 사람, 신입　be happy to 동사원형: 기꺼이 ~하다　be eager to 동사원형: ~하기를 열망하다, 간절히 ~하고 싶어하다　would like to 동사원형: ~하고 싶다　without -ing ~하지 않고　worry about ~에 대해 걱정하다　absolutely 절대적으로　necessary 필요한　wise 현명한

Why did Diana leave her parents' house?

(a) to start an internship
(b) to return to her job
(c) to study for classes
(d) to visit her friend

다이애나가 부모님 집을 떠난 이유
는 무엇인가?

(a) 인턴십을 시작하기 위해
(b) 그녀의 직장으로 돌아오기 위해
(c) 수업에 대한 공부를 하기 위해
(d) 그녀의 친구를 방문하기 위해

정답 (c)

해설 다이애나는 크리스마스가 끝나자마자 부모님 집을 떠났다고(I left my parents' house as soon as Christmas was over)
고 언급하고 나서, 다음 학기의 수업에 대해 공부하는 것에 유리한 출발을 하고 싶었다고(I wanted to a get a head start
on work for next semester's classes) 설명했습니다. 이를 통해 다이애나가 부모님 집을 떠난 것은 다음 학기에 대한 공부
를 하기 위한 것임을 알 수 있으므로 (c)가 정답입니다.

어휘 return 돌아오다

What type of class did Diana sign up for?

(a) an online class
(b) a required class
(c) an advanced class
(d) a popular class

다이애나가 등록한 것은 어떤 종류
의 강의인가?

(a) 온라인 강의
(b) 필수 강의
(c) 상급 강의
(d) 인기 강의

정답 (a)

해설 다이애나는 마드리드에서의 인턴십에 대비하기 위해 일주일마다 온라인으로 만나는 가상 스페인어 강의를 등록했다고(I
just signed up for a virtual Spanish class that meets weekly online)고 언급하였습니다. 따라서 (a)가 정답입니다.

어휘 required 필수의 advanced 상급의, 고급의 popular 인기 있는

Why did Jackson find language classes to be less useful than
he expected?

잭슨이 자신이 기대했던 것보다 언
어 강의가 덜 유용하다고 생각한 이
유는 무엇인가?

TEST 06

(a) He had trouble understanding the instructor.

(b) He was unable to develop good listening skills.

(c) He had trouble learning correct pronunciation.

(d) He was unable to remember the content.

(a) 강사를 이해하는 데 문제가 있었다.

(b) 우수한 듣기 실력을 발달시킬 수 없었다.

(c) 정확한 발음을 배우는 데 문제가 있었다.

(d) 강의 내용을 기억할 수 없었다.

정답 (b)

해설 질문의 키워드인 잭슨의 언어 강의는 잭슨이 파리에 가기 전에 프랑스 수업을 1학기 동안 들었다고(I took one semester of French before going to Paris) 언급한 부분에서 확인할 수 있습니다. 그 뒤에 잭슨은 강사는 좋았지만, 파리에 도착해서 현지인들이 말을 너무 빨리해서 이해할 수 있는 것이 없었다고(The instructor was great, but when I got there, the locals spoke so fast that I couldn't understand anything) 언급하는 것을 통해 잭슨이 현지인의 말을 잘 듣지 못한 것이 문제가 있었음을 알 수 있습니다. 따라서 정답은 (b)입니다.

어휘 find + 목적어 + 형용사: (목적어)가 ~하다고 생각하다 trouble -ing ~하는 데 문제가 있다 be unable to 동사원형: ~할 수 없다 correct 정확한, 맞는 pronunciation 발음 content 내용

패러프레이징

the locals spoke so fast that I couldn't understand anything → unable to develop good listening skills

---

43 세부 정보

According to Jackson, what did the local French people appreciate?

(a) his stories about travel

(b) his interest in local culture

(c) his knowledge of food

(d) his efforts to communicate

잭슨에 따르면 현지 프랑스 사람들이 인정했던 것은 무엇이었는가?

(a) 그의 여행에 관한 이야기

(b) 현지 문화에 대한 그의 관심

(c) 음식에 관한 그의 지식

(d) 의사 소통하려는 그의 노력

정답 (d)

해설 질문의 키워드인 the local French people appreciate는 자신이 만났던 프랑스 사람들이 그가 그 언어를 최소한 배우려고 했던 것을 인정해줬다는 것을 기억한다고(I do remember that the French people I met appreciated that I was at least trying to learn the language) 말하는 부분에서 확인할 수 있습니다. 이를 통해 프랑스 사람들은 잭슨의 노력을 인정했다는 것을 알 수 있으므로 (d)가 정답입니다.

어휘 interest 관심 knowledge 지식 effort 노력 communicate 의사 소통하다

패러프레이징

trying to learn the language → efforts to communicate

Who would help Diana communicate on her trip?

(a) her extended family
(b) her new coworkers
(c) her future roommate
(d) her local hosts

다이애나의 여행에서 다이애나를 도울 사람은 누구인가?

(a) 그녀의 대가족
(b) 그녀의 새로운 동료
(c) 그녀의 룸메이트가 될 사람
(d) 그녀의 현지 집주인

정답 (b)

해설 다이애나는 자신을 도와줄 사람으로 스페인을 말하는 다른 인턴 직원들을 언급(there will be several other interns there who speak Spanish and can help me learn as I go)하였습니다. 이를 통해 그녀가 스페인어를 말하는 것을 도울 사람은 그녀의 새로운 동료들임을 알 수 있으므로 (b)가 정답입니다.

어휘 communicate 의사 소통하다 extended family 대가족 coworker 동료 직원 future 미래의, 향후의 host 집주인

> **패러프레이징**
>
> several other interns → new coworkers

What has Diana probably decided to do?

(a) brainstorm ideas for a project
(b) start working on her new course
(c) download a language app
(d) concentrate on her senior thesis

다이애나는 무엇을 하기로 결정했을 것 같은가?

(a) 프로젝트에 대해 아이디어를 떠올리는 것
(b) 새로운 강좌에 대해 공부하기 시작하는 것
(c) 언어 앱을 다운로드 하는 것
(d) 졸업 논문에 집중하는 것

정답 (d)

해설 대화의 마지막 부분에서 무엇을 하기로 결정했는지 잭슨이 묻자, 다이애나는 절대적으로 필요한 것이 아닌 수업에 대해 걱정하지 않고 나의 논문에 집중하고 싶다고(I'd like to focus on my thesis without worrying about classes that aren't absolutely necessary) 언급하였습니다. 이를 통해 논문에 집중할 것이라는 것을 알 수 있으므로 (d)가 정답입니다.

어휘 brainstorm (아이디어 등을) 떠올리다, 마구잡이로 생각해내다 course 강의, 강좌 concentrate on ~에 집중하다

Hi, I'm Edward Ramirez, and **46** I've been invited to speak today about my experience writing and illustrating children's books. You might know me from my most popular book, *Edward's Escape*, which is about my experience growing up in Brooklyn, New York. Today, I have a few tips to offer about writing and illustrating books for children.

First, think about the child you used to be. Your childhood interests can be great topics for books. **47** *Edward's Escape* takes place on the fire escape where I used to sit and watch the activity in the city around me. My inspiration for the book came from thinking about how children observe the world around them. I remember wondering about my neighbors and watching different scenes from our apartment's small metal staircase high above the street.

Second, rather than try to write a perfect story, be playful. I was inspired to write by books I read as a kid, **48** including my favorite, which featured an imaginary story between a shark and seal who always hung out together. Children love to be surprised, and you will be more successful if you take risks with your story. This is something you can see in *Edward's Escape* when Edward uses his imagination to come up with stories about the strangers he sees walking by on the street below.

My third tip concerns illustrations. Rather than trying to capture the exact image that you describe in your story, allow the illustrations to capture what cannot be said in words. When Edward pictures the street, the drawings show much more than what is written in words. **49** For example, when a Chinese food delivery man walks by, the illustrations show Edward imagining that the cartoon dragon on the man's bag comes to life and flies through the streets.

안녕하세요, 저는 에드워드 라미레즈입니다. 저는 오늘 아동 도서를 쓰고, 그 삽화를 그리는 것에 대한 저의 경험에 대해 말씀드리기 위해 초대받았습니다. 여러분은 뉴욕의 브룩클린에서 자란 저의 경험에 대한 책인 『에드워드의 탈출』이라는 저의 가장 인기 있는 책으로 저를 아실지도 모르겠습니다. 오늘, 저는 아이들을 위한 책을 쓰고 삽화를 그리는 것, 대한 몇 가지 팁을 제공해드리겠습니다.

첫 번째로, 여러분이 과거에 어떤 아이었는지 생각해보세요. 여러분의 어렸을 적 관심은 책을 위한 아주 좋은 주제가 될 수 있습니다. 『에드워드의 탈출』은 제가 앉아서 제 주위의 도시에서의 활동을 지켜보곤 했던 비상 계단에서 생겨났습니다. 그 책에 대한 영감은 아이들이 그들 주변의 세상을 어떻게 관찰하는지 생각하는 것에서 유래하였습니다. 저는 제 이웃들에 대해 궁금해하고, 길에서 높이 떠 있는 저희 아파트의 작은 철제 계단에서 각기 다른 장면들을 지켜봤던 것을 기억합니다.

두 번째, 완벽한 이야기를 쓰려고 노력하기 보다는, 놀아 보려고 해보세요. 저는 항상 함께 많은 시간을 보내던 상어와 바다표범 사이의 상상의 이야기를 특징으로 했던, 제가 가장 좋아했던 책을 포함해서, 제가 어렸을 때 읽었던 책들에 의해 글을 쓰려는 영감을 받았습니다. 아이들은 놀라게 되는 것을 좋아해서, 여러분들은 여러분의 이야기에 과감해진다면 더 성공할 것입니다. 이것은 『에드워드의 탈출』에서 에드워드가 자신의 아래의 길을 걷는 낯선 사람들을 보면서 이야기를 떠올리기 위해 그의 상상력을 사용할 때 볼 수 있는 것입니다.

저의 세 번째 팁은 삽화에 관한 것입니다. 여러분의 이야기에 여러분이 묘사하는 정확인 이미지를 포착하려고 노력하기 보다는, 삽화가 단어로 표현될 수 없는 것을 포착하게 하세요. 에드워드가 길을 묘사할 때, 그림은 단어로 쓰여진 것보다 더 많은 것을 보여줍니다. 예를 들어, 중국 음식 배달원이 걸어갈 때, 삽화는 에드워드가 그 사람의 가방에 그려진 만화풍의 용이 살아 움직여서 길 사이를 날아다니는 것을 상상하는 것을 보여줍니다.

Though illustrations are important, they won't work if you aren't thinking about language and style choices, which brings me to my fourth piece of advice. Children like clever rhymes and easy words that they can read to themselves, but they also like learning new words. **50** Try to challenge children without overwhelming them. For example, I like to introduce at least one challenging word in each story that's new to my readers. In *Edward's Escape*, children learn the word "pedestrian" when I talk about the people walking by.

My fifth tip is to make sure your story is engaging. The plot of *Edward's Escape* isn't complicated, but there are some elements of mystery. **51** For instance, when a woman with a clipboard shows up at his apartment building, Edward wants to find out who she is. She's just there to read the electric meter, but Edward doesn't know that. That little mystery makes the story more interesting.

This brings me to my last tip. Make your characters as real as possible. Edward is a relatable character, which matters more than what happens to him in the story. Children care about Edward because he's curious like they are. **52** They really love finding characters like themselves on the pages of a book. That can go a long way in getting children excited about a story!

I hope these tips are helpful as you embark on the journey of writing for children. You'll find that it brings out the child in you, too!

삽화가 중요하긴 하지만, 여러분이 언어와 문체 선택에 대해 생각하지 않으면, 삽화는 효과가 없을 것입니다. 이것이 저의 네 번째 조언입니다. 아이들은 기발한 운율과 그들이 스스로에게 읽어줄 수 있는 쉬운 단어들을 좋아할 뿐만 아니라 새로운 단어를 배우는 것도 좋아합니다. 너무 압도적이지 않게 아이들에게 도전하려고 해보세요. 예를 들어, 저는 각각의 이야기에 독자들에게 새로운 단어를 최소한 하나를 소개하는 것을 좋아합니다. 『에드워드의 탈출』에서, 걸어다니는 사람들에 말할 때 아이들은 "보행자"라는 단어를 배웁니다.

저의 다섯 번째 팁은 여러분의 이야기가 반드시 관심을 사로잡도록 하라는 것입니다. 『에드워드의 탈출』의 줄거리는 복잡하지 않지만, 거기에는 미스터리의 몇몇 요소들이 있습니다. 예를 들어, 클립보드를 가지고 있는 한 여자가 그의 아파트에 나타났을 때, 에드워드는 그녀가 누구인지 알아내고 싶어합니다. 그녀는 단지 전기 계량기를 읽기 위해 거기에 있을 뿐이지만, 에드워드는 그것을 모릅니다. 그러한 작은 미스터리가 이야기를 좀 더 재미있게 만듭니다.

이제 저의 마지막 팁입니다. 여러분의 등장인물들을 가능한 한 진짜처럼 만드세요. 에드워드는 공감대를 형성하는 인물이며, 그것이 이야기 속에서 그에게 일어나는 일보다 더 중요합니다. 아이들은 에드워드가 자신들만큼 호기심이 많기 때문에 에드워드에게 관심을 가집니다. 아이들은 책의 페이지에서 그들과 같은 등장인물을 찾는 것을 정말 좋아합니다. 그것이 아이들을 이야기에 흥미를 가지도록 하는 것에 큰 도움이 될 수 있습니다.

이 팁들이 여러분이 아이들을 위한 글쓰기라는 여정을 시작하실 때 도움이 되길 바랍니다. 그 여정이 여러분 속에 있는 아이도 끌어낸다는 것을 알게 되실 겁니다!

어휘 illustrate 삽화를 그리다 grow up 자라다, 성장하다 offer 제공하다 used to (과거에) ~하곤 했다 take place 발생하다, 일어나다 fire escape 비상 계단 activity 활동 inspiration 영감 come from ~로부터 오다, 유래하다 observe 관찰하다 wonder 궁금해하다 scene 장면 metal 철제의, 금속의 staircase 계단 rather than ~하기 보다는 be inspired to 동사원형: ~하려는 영감을 받다 feature 특징으로 하다 imaginary 상상의, 허구의 shark 상어 seal 바다 표범 hang out 시간을 보내다 take risk with ~에 과감해지다, ~에 위험을 감수하다 imagination 상상력 come up with ~을 생각해내다

stranger 낯선 사람 walk by 걸어 지나가다 below 아래에 concern ~에 관한 것이다 illustration 삽화 capture 포착하다 exact 정확한 describe 묘사하다 allow + 목적어 + to 동사원형: (목적어)가 ~하도록 하다 cartoon 만화 come to life 살아 움직이다 work 효과가 있다 style 문체, 어투 clever 기발한 rhyme 운율, 음조가 비슷한 글자 challenge 도전하다 overwhelm 압도하다 at least 최소한 pedestrian 보행자 make sure 반드시 ~하게 하다 engaging (관심을) 사로잡는 plot 줄거리 complicated 복잡한 element 요소 mystery 미스터리, 추리 소설 show up 나타나다 find out 알아내다 electric meter 전기 계량기 character 등장 인물 as 형용사 as possible: 가능한 한 ~한 matter 중요하다 care about ~에 대해 관심을 갖다 curious 호기심 많은 go a long way in ~하는 것에 큰 도움이 되다 embark on ~을 시작하다, 착수하다 journey 여정, 여행 bring out 끌어내다

---

46 주제/목적

What is the talk mainly about?

(a) how to create books for kids
(b) how to publish kids' books
(c) how to get kids to read books
(d) how to review kids' books

담화는 주로 무엇에 관한 것인가?

(a) 아이들을 위한 책을 만드는 방법
(b) 아동 도서를 출간하는 방법
(c) 아이들이 책을 읽게 하는 방법
(d) 아동 도서의 후기를 작성하는 방법

정답 (a)

해설 화자가 담화 첫 부분에서 아동 도서를 쓰고 삽화를 그리는 경험에 대해 이야기하기 위해 초대 받았다(I've been invited to speak today about my experience writing and illustrating children's books)고 언급하였습니다. 이를 통해 이 담화가 아동 도서를 만드는 방법에 관한 것임을 알 수 있으므로 (a)가 정답입니다.

어휘 hot to 동사원형: ~하는 방법 create 만들다, 제조하다 publish 출간하다 review 후기를 작성하다, 검토하다

> **✖ 오답 피하기**
> 책을 출간하는 방법(how to publish)은 출판사가 작가로부터 원고를 받고, 인쇄를 하고 판매하는 과정에 관한 것이므로 (b)는 오답입니다.

---

47 세부 정보

Where does the speaker's book take place?

(a) on a building's fire escape
(b) in a haunted house
(c) on a skyscraper's roof
(d) in a famous museum

화자의 책은 어디서 발생하였는가?

(a) 건물의 비상 계단에서
(b) 유령이 나오는 집에서
(c) 고층 건물의 옥상에서
(d) 유명한 박물관에서

정답 (a)

해설 화자가 자신의 책 『에드워드의 탈출』에 대해 언급하면서 자신이 앉아서 도시의 활동을 지켜보던 비상 계단에서 발생하였다고(Edward's Escape takes place on the fire escape where I used to sit and watch the activity in the city around me) 설명하였습니다. 따라서 정답은 (a)입니다.

어휘 haunted 유령이 나오는 skyscraper 고층 건물

What is featured in the speaker's favorite childhood book?

(a) an imaginary person
(b) a true story
(c) an unlikely friendship
(d) a strange creature

화자가 가장 좋아하는 어린 시절의 책은 무엇을 특징으로 하는가?

(a) 상상의 인물
(b) 실화
(c) 예상 밖의 우정
(d) 이상한 생명체

정답 (c)

해설 화자가 어린 시절 가장 좋아했던 책에 대해 설명하는 부분에서 그 책이 상상의 이야기를 포함하고 있는데, 그 이야기가 항상 함께 시간을 보내는 상어와 바다 표범 사이의 이야기라고(which featured an imaginary story between a shark and seal who always hung out together) 언급하였습니다. 화자가 상상의 이야기(imaginary story)라고 언급한 것으로 보아 상어와 바다 표범이 항상 어울릴 만큼 친해질 수 없음을 알 수 있습니다. 이는 발생할 가능성이 적은, 예상 밖의 우정에 관한 것이므로 (c)가 정답입니다.

어휘 unlikely 예상 밖의, 발생할 가능성이 적은 friendship 우정 creature 생명체, 존재

패러프레이징

imaginary → unlikely

How do readers know that Edward is using his imagination?

(a) He pretends he is a delivery man.
(b) He sees an animal driving a car.
(c) He pretends he is in another country.
(d) He sees a cartoon coming to life.

에드워드가 상상력을 이용하고 있다는 것을 독자들은 어떻게 아는가?

(a) 그가 배달원인 척 한다.
(b) 그는 동물이 자동차를 운전하는 것을 본다.
(c) 그가 다른 나라에 있는 척 한다.
(d) 그는 만화가 살아 움직이는 것을 본다.

정답 (d)

해설 질문의 키워드인 imagination은 화자가 일러스트에 대해 설명하면서 자신의 상상력을 이용했던 경험에 대해 말할 때 언급됩니다. 화자는 자신의 책 『에드워드의 탈출』의 일러스트에 관한 예시를 들면서 중국 음식 배달원의 가방에 그려진 만화풍의 용 그림이 살아 움직여서 길 사이를 날아다니는 것(For example, when a Chinese food delivery man walks by, the illustrations show Edward imagining that the cartoon dragon on the man's bag comes to life and flies through the streets)을 언급하였습니다. 따라서 정답은 (d)입니다.

어휘 pretend ~인 척하다

50 세부 정보

Based on the talk, how might writers challenge young readers?

(a) by introducing a puzzle
(b) by using complex characters
(c) by introducing new vocabulary
(d) by using sudden plot twists

담화에 따르면, 작가들은 어떻게 어린 독자들에게 도전하는가?

(a) 퍼즐을 소개함으로써
(b) 복잡한 등장인물을 사용함으로써
(c) 새로운 어휘를 소개함으로써
(d) 줄거리의 갑작스러운 전환을 사용함으로써

정답 (c)

해설 화자는 아이들을 압도하지 말고 그들에게 도전을 하려고 노력하라(Try to challenge children without overwhelming them)고 언급한 뒤, 자신은 독자들에게 생소한 단어를 최소한 하나씩 각 이야기에 소개하는 것을 좋아한다(I like to introduce at least one challenging word in each story that's new to my readers)고 언급하였습니다. 이를 통해 화자는 새로운 단어를 어린 독자에게 소개시키는 것으로 독자에게 도전하는 것임을 알 수 있으므로 (c)가 정답입니다.

어휘 complex 복잡한 vocabulary 어휘 sudden 갑작스러운 twist 전환, 반전

패러프레이징

one challenging word ~ that's new to my readers → new vocabulary

51 세부 정보

What mystery does Edward want to solve?

(a) the history of his apartment building
(b) the identity of a strange woman
(c) the contents of a hidden container
(d) the secret lives of his parents

에드워드가 해결하고 싶어하는 미스터리는 무엇인가?

(a) 아파트 건물의 역사
(b) 낯선 여성의 정체
(c) 숨겨진 용기의 내용물
(d) 부모님의 비밀스러운 삶

정답 (b)

해설 화자가 미스터리에 대해 설명하면서, 그의 작품 『에드워드의 탈출』 속에 등장하는 한 여자를 예시로 언급하였습니다. 클립보드를 든 여자가 에드워드의 아파트에 나타났을 때, 그는 그녀가 누구인지 알고 싶어했다고(For instance, when a woman with a clipboard shows up at his apartment building, Edward wants to find out who she is) 언급한 부분에서 에드워드가 여성의 정체에 대한 미스터리를 풀고 싶어했다는 것을 알 수 있습니다. 따라서 정답은 (b)입니다.

어휘 solve 풀다, 해결하다 identity 정체, 신원 content 내용물 hidden 숨겨진 container 용기

패러프레이징

- wants to find out → want to solve
- who she is → identity of strange woman

---

52 추론

According to the speaker, what, most likely, gets children excited about reading?

(a) being able to answer questions
(b) finding something familiar in the characters
(c) knowing how the tale will end
(d) believing that the stories are real

화자에 따르면, 아이들이 독서에 흥미를 가지도록 하는 것을 무엇일 것 같은가?

(a) 질문에 대답할 수 있는 것
(b) 등장 인물들에게서 친숙한 것을 찾는 것
(c) 이야기가 어떻게 끝날지 아는 것
(d) 이야기가 진실이라고 믿는 것

정답 (b)

해설 담화 마지막 부분에서 아이들을 이야기에 흥미를 가지도록 하는 데 큰 도움이 될 수 있을 것(That can go a long way in getting children excited about a story!)이라고 언급한 곳에서 질문의 키워드 get children excited about reading을 확인할 수 있습니다. 이 문장에서 언급된 주어 That은 그 앞문장에서 아이들은 책에서 자신들과 닮은 등장인물을 찾는 것을 정말 좋아한다(They really love finding characters like themselves on the pages of a book)는 것을 가리키므로 정답은 (b)입니다.

어휘 familiar 친숙한, 익숙한 tale 이야기 real 진짜의

패러프레이징

finding characters like themselves → finding something familiar in the characters

Reading & Vocabulary

PART 1

CHARLIE CHAPLIN

Charlie Chaplin was an English actor and director who rose to fame during the silent film era. **53** He is known for his iconic comedy character "the Little Tramp," an innocent but mischievous individual dressed in a tattered suit and derby hat who appeared in numerous movies.

Charles Spencer Chaplin was born on April 16, 1889, in London, England. His childhood was difficult. His father left when he was very young, and **54** his mother, a music hall entertainer, was often unable to provide for Charlie and his brother. However, **54** her passion for performing inspired her son, and young Charlie soon harbored ambitions to be an actor.

Chaplin's talent secured him a spot in a British comedy troupe but, after traveling with the group to the US, his focus **58** shifted to comic movies. In 1914, he signed a contract with Keystone Studios in Los Angeles. For one production, he chose enormous pants, an undersized coat and hat, and a fake mustache from the studio's vast costume selection. Chaplin claimed that once he put on those accessories, he knew who his new character was, and "the Little Tramp" was born.

As this new character, Chaplin rose to stardom. The Little Tramp was low in social status but possessed perfect manners, and **55** audiences saw themselves in the character's daily struggles against authority figures. By 1918, Chaplin was earning a movie star's salary. He wrote, directed, and starred in *The Gold Rush*, a comedy that is now considered one of history's greatest silent films.

찰리 채플린

찰리 채플린은 무성 영화 시대에 명성을 날린 영국의 배우이자 감독이었다. 그는 "작은 트램프"라는 그의 상징적인 코미디 캐릭터로 유명한데, 그는 수많은 영화에 출연한 낡을 대로 낡은 정장을 입고 중산 모자를 쓴, 순수하지만 짓궂은 인물이다.

찰스 스펜서 채플린은 영국의 런던에서 1889년 4월 16일에 태어났다. 그의 어린 시절은 힘겨웠다. 그의 아버지는 그가 아주 어렸을 때 떠났고, 음악당 예능인이었던 그의 어머니는 종종 그와 그의 동생을 부양할 수 없었다. 하지만, 공연에 대한 그녀의 열정은 그녀의 아들에게 영감을 주었고, 어린 찰리는 곧 배우가 되겠다는 야망을 품었다.

채플린의 재능은 영국의 코미디 공연단의 한 자리를 확보하게 하였지만, 공연단과 함께 미국에 다녀온 뒤로, 그의 초점은 코믹 영화로 바뀌었다. 1914년, 그는 로스앤젤레스에 있는 키스톤 스튜디오와 계약을 맺었다. 한 영화 제작에서 그는 스튜디오의 방대한 의상 선정에서 막대하게 큰 바지, 작은 코트와 모자, 그리고 가짜 수염을 골랐다. 채플린은 그런 액서세리를 착용하자마자, 이 새로운 캐릭터가 누구인지 알았다고 주장했고, "작은 트램프"가 탄생하였다.

이 새로운 캐릭터로, 채플린은 스타덤에 올랐다. 작은 트램프는 사회적 지위는 낮지만 완벽한 예절을 갖추고 있었고, 관객들은 그 캐릭터가 권력자에 대항하는 일상 속에서 분투하는 것을 보고 그들 자신을 보았다. 1918년쯤, 채플린은 인기 영화 배우의 급여를 벌고 있었다. 그는 코미디 영화 <황금광 시대>의 극본, 연출, 주연을 맡았으며, 이 영화는 현재 역사상 최고의 무성 영화 중 하나로 여겨진다.

After 1927, movies began featuring sound, but Chaplin swore that audiences would never hear the Tramp talk. So, he retired the character. In 1940, he appeared in his first speaking role as the lead in the political parody *The Great Dictator*. Chaplin plays a dual role as both dictator Adolf Hitler and the barber who is mistaken for him. **56** The barber eventually embraces the confusion, using the attention and notoriety to argue for compassion and peace over discriminatory behavior.

In later life, **57** Chaplin was accused of having **59** ties to Communist figures during a time when the US government viewed that political ideology as dangerous. In response, Chaplin relocated to Switzerland in political protest, where he died in 1975. Today, he is remembered as one of the greatest stars of the silent film era and as an actor who revolutionized on-screen comedy.

1927년 이후, 영화는 소리를 특징으로 나타내기 시작했지만, 채플린은 관객들이 절대로 트램프가 말하는 것을 듣지 않을 것이라고 맹세했다. 그래서, 그는 그 캐릭터를 은퇴시켰다. 1940년에, 그는 <위대한 독재자>라는 정치 패러디 영화에서 최초로 말하는 역할로 주연을 맡아 출연하였다. 채플린은 독재자 아돌프 히틀러와 히틀러로 오해 받는 이발사로서 1인 2역을 맡았다. 이발사는 결국 그 혼란을 받아들이고, 차별적인 행동보다는 연민과 평화를 위해 변론하는 것에 그 관심과 악명을 사용한다.

말년에, 채플린은 미국 정부가 그 정치적 이데올로기를 위험한 것으로 바라보았던 시기 중에 공산주의 인사들과 유대 관계를 맺고 있는 것으로 고소되었다. 이에 대응하여, 그는 정치적 항의로 스위스로 이주하였으며, 그곳에서 1975년에 사망하였다. 오늘날, 그는 무성 영화 시대의 가장 위대한 스타 중 한 명이자 영화에서의 코미디에 혁신을 일으켰던 배우로 기억되고 있다.

어휘 actor 배우 director 영화 감독 rise to fame 명성을 날리다 silent film 무성 영화 era 시대 iconic 상징적인 character 캐릭터, 등장 인물 innocent 순수한, 순진한 mischievous 짓궂은 individual 사람, 개인 dressed in ~을 입은 tattered 낡은 대로 낡은, 누더기가 된 suit 정장 derby hat 중산 모자 appear 출연하다 numerous 수많은 entertainer 예능인, 연예인 be unable to 동사원형: ~할 수 없다 provide for ~을 부양하다 passion 열정 inspire 영감을 주다, 격려하다 harbor (생각 등을) 품다 ambition 야망, 야심 secure 확보하다, 얻어 내다 spot 자리 troupe 극단 shift 바꾸다, 옮기다 sign 서명하다 contract 계약서 enormous 막대한, 거대한 undersized 보통보다 작은 fake 가짜의 mustache 콧수염 vast 방대한 costume 의상 selection 선정, 모음 claim 주장하다 once ~하자마자 put on ~을 착용하다 rise to stardom 스타덤에 오르다, 스타가 되다 social status 사회적 지위 possess 소유하다, 가지고 있다 manners 예절, 예의 audience 관객 struggle 투쟁, 분투 against ~에 대항하여 authority figure 권력자, 막강한 실력자 earn 얻다, 벌다 salary 급여 star 주연을 맡다 feature 특징으로 내보이다 swear 맹세하다 retire 은퇴시키다 political 정치적인 parody 패러디 dictator 독재자 dual role 1인 2역 barber 이발사 be mistaken for ~으로 오해받다 eventually 결국 embrace 수용하다, 받아 들이다 confusion 혼란, 혼동 notoriety 악명 argue for ~을 찬성하다, ~을 위해 변론하다 compassion 동정, 연민 discriminatory 차별적인 behavior 행동 in later life 말년에 be accused of ~으로 비난받다, ~으로 고소[고발]되다 have a tie to ~와 관련을 가지다, ~와 유대 관계를 맺다 government 정부 ideology 이데올로기, 이념 in response 이에 대응하여 relocate 이주하다 protest 항의 revolutionize 혁신을 일으키다 on-screen 영화에서의

According to the article, what is Charlie Chaplin best known for?

(a) portraying a famous historical figure onscreen
(b) appearing in the first silent movie
(c) producing award-winning romantic comedies
(d) developing a humorous film character

기사에 따르면, 찰리 채플린은 무엇으로 가장 유명한가?

(a) 역사적으로 유명한 인물을 영화에서 연기한 것
(b) 최초의 무성 영화에 출연한 것
(c) 상을 받은 로맨틱 코미디를 제작한 것
(d) 재미있는 영화 캐릭터를 개발한 것

정답 (d)

해설 질문의 키워드인 best known for는 지문의 첫 문단 known for로 표현되어 있습니다. 해당 문장에 따르면 그의 상징적인 코미디 캐릭터 "작은 트램프"로 유명하다(He is known for his iconic comedy character "the Little Tramp)고 언급되어 있습니다. 이를 재미있는 영화 캐릭터(a humorous film character)라고 표현한 (d)가 정답입니다.

어휘 portray (영화 등에서) 연기하다 figure 인물 onscreen 영화에서 award-winning 상을 받은, 수상한 humorous 재미있는, 웃긴

패러프레이징

his iconic comedy character → a humorous film character

Based on the second paragraph, why, most likely, did Chaplin decide to become a performer?

(a) because he admired his mother's profession
(b) because he was persuaded to by an acting agent
(c) because he wanted to follow in his brother's footsteps
(d) because he had dreams of becoming wealthy

두 번째 문단에 따르면, 채플린이 연기자가 되겠다고 결심한 이유는 무엇일 것 같은가?

(a) 그의 어머니의 직업을 존경했기 때문에
(b) 연기 에이전트에 의해 설득되었기 때문에
(c) 그의 형의 발자취를 따라가고 싶었기 때문에
(d) 부유해지고 싶다는 꿈이 있었기 때문에

정답 (a)

해설 두 번째 문단에서 질문의 키워드 become a performer에 대해서 문단 마지막 부분에 음악당의 예능인이었던 채플린의 어머니가 가진 공연을 향한 열정이 그녀의 아들에게 영감을 주었고, 어린 찰리가 곧 배우가 되겠다는 열망을 품었다(her passion for performing inspired her son, and young Charlie soon harbored ambitions to be an actor)라고 설명한 부분에서 언급되었습니다. 이를 통해 찰리 채플린은 그의 어머니의 직업을 보고 배우가 되었음을 알 수 있으므로 정답은 (a) 입니다.

어휘 performer 연기자, 공연자 admire 존경하다 profession 직업 be persuaded 설득되다 follow one's footstep ~의 발자취를 따라가다 wealthy 부유한

---

55 세부 정보

Why did audiences relate to Chaplin's "Little Tramp" character?

(a) They understood his ongoing romantic struggles.
(b) They identified with his everyday challenges.
(c) They aspired to reach his high social status.
(d) They supported his respect for government authority.

관객이 채플린의 "작은 트램프"라는 캐릭터에 공감하였던 이유는 무엇인가?

(a) 관객들은 그의 계속되는 낭만적인 분투를 이해했다.
(b) 관객들은 그의 일상의 도전에 동질감을 가졌다.
(c) 관객들은 그의 높은 사회적 지위에 이르기를 열망하였다.
(d) 관객들은 정부 권력에 대한 그의 존경심을 지지하였다.

정답 (b)

해설 질문의 키워드인 "Little Tramp" character에 대해 설명한 네 번째 문단에서 채플린이 연기하는 "Little Tramp" 캐릭터가 권력자에 대항하여 매일 고군분투하는 것을 보고 관객들이 자기 자신을 보았다(audiences saw themselves in the character's daily struggles against authority figures)는 부분에서 관객들이 "Little Tramp"라는 캐릭터를 동질감을 느꼈다는 것을 알 수 있습니다. 따라서 정답은 (b)입니다.

어휘 relate to ~에 공감하다 ongoing 계속되는 romantic 낭만적인, 연애의 struggle 분투, 노력 identify with ~에 동질감을 가지다, ~와 동일시하다 everyday 일상의 challenge 도전 aspire to 동사원형: ~하기를 열망하다 reach 이르다, 도달하다 support 지지하다, 도와주다 respect 존경심 government authority 정부 권력

패러프레이징

audiences saw themselves in the character's daily struggles~ → identified with his everyday challenges

❌ 오답 피하기

네 번째 문단에서 언급된 the character's daily struggles against authority figures에서 "Little Tramp"라는 캐릭터가 정부 권력자에게 대항하였다는 것을 알 수 있으므로, 정부 권력자에게 존경심을 보였다는 내용을 나타내는 (d)는 오답입니다.

In *The Great Dictator*, what did the barber's acceptance of his new identity allow him to do?

(a) escape his many previous mistakes
(b) launch a campaign for public office
(c) encourage greater kindness in society
(d) draw more attention to his business

<위대한 독재자>에서 이발사가 새로운 신분을 받아들인 것은 그가 무엇을 하게 하였는가?

(a) 그의 많은 이전의 실수들로부터 벗어났다
(b) 관공서를 향한 사회적 운동을 시작하였다
(c) 사회에 더 많은 친절함을 장려하였다
(d) 그의 사업에 더 많은 관심을 끌어 모았다

정답 (c)

해설 <위대한 독재자>에 대해 언급된 다섯 번째 문단에서 그 영화에서 찰리 채플린이 연기한 1인 2역 중 하나인 이발사는 아돌프 히틀러에 똑같이 생겨서 많은 오해를 받았다는 내용을 확인할 수 있습니다. 그 뒤에 결국 그 이발사는 자신을 히틀러로 혼동하는 것을 받아들이고 그것을 이용하여 차별적인 행동보다는 연민과 평화를 위해 변론하였다고(The barber eventually embraces the confusion, using the attention and notoriety to argue for compassion and peace over discriminatory behavior) 언급되어 있습니다. 이를 통해 이발사는 사람들 사이에 차별보다는 더 많은 친절이 있도록 노력했음을 알 수 있습니다. 따라서 정답은 (c)입니다.

어휘 acceptance 수용, 받아 들임 identity 신분, 신원 allow + 목적어 + to 동사원형: (목적어)가 ~하도록 하다 escape 벗어나다, 탈출하다 previous 이전의 launce 시작하다 campaign 사회적 운동, 캠페인 public office 관공서 encourage 격려하다, 장려하다 draw 끌다 business 사업, 영업장

┌─ 패러프레이징 ─
│ • embrace → acceptance
│ • compassion and peace → kindness
└─

How did Chaplin respond to the US government's accusations?

(a) by quitting a political party
(b) by relocating to another country
(c) by making a protest movie
(d) by resorting to legal action

채플린은 미국 정부의 고소에 어떻게 반응하였는가?

(a) 정당을 탈퇴함으로써
(b) 다른 국가로 이주함으로써
(c) 항의하는 영화를 만듦으로써
(d) 법적인 조치에 의지함으로써

정답 (b)

해설 미국 정부가 공산주의자들과의 유대로 채플린을 고소하였다는 내용이 언급된 마지막 문단에서 그에 대한 대응으로 스위스로 이주하였다(in response, Chaplin relocated to Switzerland in political protest)고 설명되었습니다. 따라서 정답은 (b)입니다.

어휘 respond to ~에 반응하다 accusation 고소, 고발, 비난 quit 그만두다 political party 정당 resort to ~에 의지하다, ~에 호소하다 legal action 법적인 조치

❌ 오답 피하기

Chaplin relocated to Switzerland in political protest를 보고 정치적 항의의 뜻에서 스위스로 이주하였다는 것은 알 수 있으나, 이것이 항의하는 영화를 만든 것을 의미하는 하지 않으므로 (c)는 오답입니다.

In the context of the passage, shifted means _____.

(a) worked
(b) changed
(c) listened
(d) planned

해당 단락의 문맥에서 shifted가 의미하는 것은?

(a) 일했다
(b) 바꿨다
(c) 들었다
(d) 계획했다

정답 (b)

해설 해당 문장에서 shifted는 '그의 초점'이라는 his focus라는 주어의 동사로 사용되었으며, 그 뒤에 to comedy movies라는 전치사구가 '코미디 영화로'라는 의미를 나타내므로 문맥상 코미디 극단에서 활동하던 채플린이 코미디 영화로 그의 관심을 바꾸었다는 의미를 나타낸다는 것을 알 수 있습니다. 따라서 '바꾸다'라는 의미를 나타내는 동사 change의 과거형 (b) changed가 정답입니다.

In the context of the passage, <u>ties</u> means _____.

(a) disruptions
(b) additions
(c) connections
(d) intentions

해당 단락의 문맥에서 <u>ties</u>가 의미하는 것은?

(a) 방해
(b) 추가
(c) 연관성
(d) 의도

정답 (c)

해설 해당 문장에서 ties는 having이라는 동명사의 목적어로 쓰였으며, 그 뒤에 '공산주의 인물들에'라는 의미를 나타내는 전치사구 to Communist figures가 있으므로 문맥상 채플린이 공산주의 인물들과의 관계를 가지고 있는 것으로 고소되었다는 내용임을 알 수 있습니다. 따라서 ties가 관계를 나타내는 명사로 쓰였으므로 선택지 중 '연관성'이라는 의미를 나타내는 명사 (c) connections가 정답입니다.

PART 2

60 WHY HOT DOGS ARE RARELY SOLD IN FAST-FOOD RESTAURANTS

패스트푸드점에서 핫도그가
거의 판매되지 않는 이유

Hot dogs—sausages served on a split roll—are one of America's most popular foods. Hot dogs, like hamburgers, originated in Germany, but they are now commonly associated with American cuisine. Many fast-food restaurants, such as McDonald's and Burger King, built their businesses by selling hamburgers. However, 60 it is rare for an American fast-food chain to sell hot dogs.

갈라진 롤에 소시지가 들어있는 핫도그는 미국에서 가장 인기있는 음식 중 하나이다. 햄버거처럼 핫도그는 독일에서 유래했지만, 지금은 흔히 미국 음식과 연관되어 있다. 맥도날드와 버거킹과 같은 많은 패스트푸드 식당들은 햄버거를 판매함으로써 사업을 일으켰다. 하지만, 미국의 패스트푸드 체인점이 핫도그를 판매하는 것은 드문 일이다.

So, why are fast-food hot dogs so unpopular? 61 Although some restaurants have attempted to market hot dogs, most have been surprisingly unsuccessful. The "McHotDog" vanished from the McDonald's menu shortly after its release, and endeavors by other chains also flopped, with a newspaper review calling Burger King's hot dog "a disgusting disgrace." 61 But, like hamburgers, hot dogs are simple to prepare, so they seem like a perfect fit for fast-food restaurants.

그래서, 핫도그가 그렇게 인기가 없는 이유는 무엇일까? 비록 몇몇 식당이 핫도그를 판매하려고 시도했지만, 대부분이 놀랍게도 성공하지 못했다. "맥핫도그"는 출시 직후 맥도날드의 메뉴에서 사라졌고, 다른 체인점들의 시도 또한 완전히 실패하였는데, 한 신문의 리뷰에서는 버거킹의 핫도그를 "역겨운 망신"이라고 불렀다. 하지만, 햄버거처럼, 핫도그는 준비하기에는 간단해서, 패스트푸드 식당에는 완벽하게 맞는 것처럼 보인다.

Interestingly, the food's preparation might be what has led to its failure. 62 Fast-food hamburgers with buns can remain warm and edible under heat lamps for about fifteen minutes, allowing them to be ready before a customer even places an order. But hot dogs sweat moisture, turning their bread soggy very quickly. This means they must be either served to a restaurant-goer immediately or kept separate from their buns, which 65 hinders service, making for long lines and unhappy patrons.

흥미롭게도, 그 음식의 준비가 그 실패를 초래한 것일지도 모른다. 빵이 있는 패스트푸드 햄버거는 약 15분 동안 열등 아래에서 따뜻하고 먹을 수 있는 상태로 있을 수 있어서, 고객이 주문을 하기 전에 햄버거를 준비된 상태가 되도록 할 수 있었다. 하지만 핫도그는 물기가 스며 나와서, 빵을 아주 빠르게 축축하게 만든다. 이것은 핫도그가 식당 이용자들에게 즉시 제공되어야 하거나, 그 빵을 따로 분리하여 보관해야 한다는 것을 의미하는데, 이것이 음식 제공을 저해하여 긴 줄을 서게 하고, 단골 손님들을 언짢게 만드는 것이다.

63 Hot dogs are also prepared differently based on regional preferences. For instance, many restaurants in Chicago, where hot dogs are loaded with toppings, discourage putting ketchup on their "dogs." But elsewhere in America, ketchup is

핫도그는 또한 지역별 선호에 따라 다르게 준비된다. 예를 들어 시카고에 있는 많은 식당들의 핫도그는 토핑으로 채워지는데, 이것이 그들의 핫도그 위에 케첩을 올리지 못하게 한다. 하지만 미국의 다른 곳에서는, 케첩은 토핑으로 받아들여진다.

66 acceptable as a topping. In New York, hot dogs often come with sauerkraut and, in the Southwestern United States, they are typically served with mayonnaise and bacon. These differences in local tastes make it difficult for chain restaurants to offer a single product that can be prepared quickly.

Hot dogs first became popular in the US during the early 1900s. **64** They were often sold at seaside resorts or state fairs, so Americans came to associate them with leisure and summer weather. People enjoy grilling them at family picnics and ordering them at baseball games. A mental link between hot dogs, relaxation, and the outdoors may help explain why customers are less interested in buying them from fast-food restaurants.

뉴욕에서, 핫도그는 종종 사우어크라우트와 함께 나오며, 미국의 남서부에서는, 일반적으로 마요네즈와 베이컨이 함께 제공된다. 이러한 지역적 취향의 차이는 빠르게 준비되어야 하는 단 하나의 제품을 체인 레스토랑이 제공하는 것을 어렵게 만든다.

핫도그는 1900년대 초에 미국에서 최초로 인기를 얻었다. 핫도그는 종종 해변 리조트나 주 박람회에서 판매되었고, 그래서 미국인들은 핫도그를 여가와 여름 날씨에 연관 짓게 되었다. 사람들은 가족 나들이에서 그릴로 핫도그를 굽는 것과 야구 경기장에서 핫도그를 주문하는 것을 좋아한다. 핫도그, 휴식, 그리고 야외에 대한 머리 속에서의 연결은 고객들이 패스트푸드 식당에서 핫도그를 사는 것에 대한 관심이 적은 이유를 설명하는 데에 도움을 줄 수 있다.

어휘 split 나뉘어진, 갈라진 roll (빵) 롤 originate 비롯되다, 유래하다 commonly 흔히 be assoicated with ~와 관련되어 있다 cuisine 요리 business 사업 rare 드문, 희귀한 chain 체인점 unpopular 인기 없는 attempt to 동사원형: ~하려고 시도하다 market 판매하다, 시장에 내놓다 surprisingly 놀랍게도 vanish 사라지다 shortly after 곧, 머지 않아 release 출시 endeavor 시도, 노력 flop 완전히 실패하다, 주저 앉다 review 후기, 검토 disgusting 역겨운 disgrace 망신, 수치 prepare (음식을) 준비하다 seem like ~처럼 보이다 perfect fit 완벽하게 맞는 것, 딱 맞는 것 interestingly 흥미롭게도 preparation (음식의) 준비 lead to ~로 이어지다, ~을 초래하다 failure 실패 bun (작고 둥글납작한) 빵 remain + 형용사: ~한 태로 남아 있다 edible 먹을 수 있는 heat lamp 열등, 적외선등 place an order 주문하다 sweat 물기가 스며 나오다 moisture 물기, 수분 turn + 목적어 + 형용사: (목적어)를 ~하게 바꾸다 either A or B: A 또는 B restaurant-goer 식당 이용고객 immediately 즉시 separate 분리된 hinder 방해하다, ~을 못하게 하다 unhappy 언짢은 patron 단골 손님 based on ~에 기반하여 regional 지역의 preference 선호(도) for instance 예를 들면 be loaded with ~로 채워지다, ~을 가지고 있다 topping (음식 위에 얹는) 토핑, 고명 discourage 의욕을 꺾다, 못하게 막다 elsewhere 다른 곳에서 acceptable 받아 들여지는 sauerkraut 사우어크라우트(독일의 양배추 발효 음식) typically 일반적으로 taste 취향 single 하나의 seaside 해변 state fair 주 박람회 leisure 여가 활동 grill 그릴에 굽다, 불에 굽다 mental link 머리 속에서의 연결, 정신적인 연결 관계 relaxation 휴식 be less interested in ~에 관심이 적은

60 주제/목적

What is the article mainly about?

(a) the limited market for hot dogs
(b) the increasing popularity of hot dogs
(c) the overall history of hot dogs
(d) the ingredients included in hot dogs

이 기사문은 주로 무엇에 관한 글인가?

(a) 핫도그의 한정적인 시장
(b) 핫도그에 대한 증가하는 인기
(c) 핫도그의 전반적인 역사
(d) 핫도그에 포함된 재료

정답 (a)

해설 기사의 제목이 WHY HOT DOGS ARE RARELY SOLD IN FAST-FOOD RESTAURANTS로, '패스트푸드 식당에서 핫도그가 거의 팔리지 않는 이유'로 정해져 있으며, 핫도그에 대해 설명하고 있는 첫 문단의 마지막 부분에서 많은 미국의 패스트푸드 체인점에서 햄버거를 판매하고 있지만, 핫도그를 파는 것은 드물다(it is rare for an American fast-food chain to sell hot dogs)고 언급한 것으로 보아 햄버거에 비해 핫도그의 시장이 한정적이라는 것을 알 수 있습니다. 따라서 정답은 (a)입니다.

어휘 limited 제한된, 한정적인 increasing 증가하는 popularity 인기 overall 전반적인 ingredient (음식) 재료

61 세부 정보

Based on the second paragraph, why might the failure of fast-food hot dogs be surprising?

(a) because they are inexpensive to produce
(b) because they are well-received by customers
(c) because they are relatively easy to make
(d) because they are highly rated in restaurant reviews

두 번째 문단에 따르면, 패스트푸드 핫도그의 실패가 놀라운 이유는 무엇일 수 있는가?

(a) 생산 비용이 저렴하기 때문에
(b) 고객들에게 잘 받아들여지기 때문에
(c) 상대적으로 만들기 쉽기 때문에
(d) 식당 후기에서 높은 평가를 받기 때문에

정답 (c)

해설 두 번째 문단에서 몇몇 패스트푸드 식당들이 핫도그를 판매하려고 시도하였지만 놀랍게도 성공하지 못했다고 언급한 부분에서 질문의 키워드인 failure of fast-food hot dogs be surprising를 확인할 수 있습니다. 그리고 문단 마지막 부분에서 햄버거처럼 핫도그가 준비하기에는 간단해서 패스트푸드 식당에 완벽하게 잘 맞는 것으로 보인다고(But, like hamburgers, hot dogs are simple to prepare, so they seem like a perfect fit for fast-food restaurants) 언급한 내용을 통해 '놀랍게도 성공하지 못했다'고 말한 것은 만들기 쉽기 때문에 성공할 것으로 예상하였지만 그렇게 하지 못했다는 것을 알 수 있으므로 정답은 (c)입니다.

어휘 failure 실패 inexpensive (비용이) 저렴한 well-received 잘 받아들여지는 relatively 상대적으로 highly rated 높게 평가되는

62 세부 정보

According to the article, what makes selling fast-food hamburgers convenient?

(a) They remain edible after preparation.
(b) They can be cooked with a heat lamp.
(c) They require only a few ingredients.
(d) They are prepared using basic equipment.

기사에 따르면, 패스트푸드 햄버거를 파는 것을 편리하게 만드는 것은 무엇인가?

(a) 준비가 끝난 후에 먹을 수 있는 상태로 남아있다.
(b) 열등으로 조리될 수 있다.
(c) 몇 가지의 재료만 필요하다.
(d) 기본적인 장비를 사용하여 준비된다.

정답 (a)

해설 세 번째 문단에서 질문의 키워드인 Fast-food hamburgers에 대해 패스트푸드 햄버거는 열등 아래에서 약 15분 동안 따뜻하고 먹을 수 있는 상태로 유지될 수 있다고(Fast-food hamburgers with buns can remain warm and edible under heat lamps for about fifteen minutes) 설명하고 있으므로 정답은 (a)입니다.

어휘 convenient 편리한 remain (~한 상태로) 남아 있다 edible 먹을 수 있는 preparation (요리) 준비 heat lamp 열등, 적외선등 require 필요로 하다 ingredient (음식의) 재료 equipment 장비

❌ 오답 피하기

Heat lamp로 조리를 한다는 내용은 언급되어 있지 않으므로 (b)는 오답입니다.

What is suggested in the fourth paragraph about hot dog toppings in the United States?

(a) that they are only popular in certain regions
(b) that they should be added in a specific order
(c) that they vary widely in different parts of the country
(d) that they have become increasingly expensive

네 번째 문단에서 미국 핫도그의 토핑에 관해 알 수 있는 것은 무엇인가?

(a) 특정 지역에서만 인기가 있을 뿐이라는 것
(b) 특정 주문에 추가되어야 한다는 것
(c) 미국 내 다른 지역에서 상당히 다양하다는 점
(d) 점점 더 비싸졌다는 것

정답 (c)

해설 네 번째 문단에서 핫도그는 지역의 선호도에 기반하여 다르게 준비되어야 한다(Hot dogs are also prepared differently based on regional preferences)고 언급되어 있고, 그 뒤로 시카고와 뉴욕, 미국 남서부에서의 핫도그 위에 올리는 토핑에 대해 예시를 들어 설명하고 있습니다. 이를 통해 미국 지역마다 토핑이 다양하다는 것을 알 수 있으므로 (c)가 정답입니다.

어휘 **popular** 인기 있는 **certain** 특정한 **specific** 특정한, 구체적인 **order** 주문 **vary widely** 상당히 다양하다 **increasingly** 점점 더 **expensive** 값비싼

패러프레이징

prepared differently based on regional preferences → vary widely in different parts of the country

TEST 06

How did hot dogs come to be associated with leisure?

(a) They were initially served at baseball games.
(b) They were originally eaten on national holidays.
(c) They were initially eaten only in the summer.
(d) They were originally sold at outdoor locations.

핫도그가 어떻게 여가 활동과 연관되게 되었는가?

(a) 처음에 야구 경기에서 제공되었다.
(b) 원래 국경일에 먹던 것이었다.
(c) 처음에 여름에만 먹던 것이었다.
(d) 원래 야외 지점에서 판매되었다.

정답 (d)

해설 질문의 키워드 associated with leisure는 다섯 번째 문단의 미국인이 핫도그를 여가 활동과 연관시키게 되었다(Americans came to associate them with leisure)라고 언급한 문장에 나타나 있습니다. 그 앞에 핫도그와 여가 활동의 연관성에 대한 이유로 핫도그가 종종 해변 리조트나 주 박람회에서 판매되었다(They were often sold at seaside resorts or state fairs)고 언급되어 있으므로 이를 야외 지점에서 판매되었다고 표현한 (d)가 정답입니다.

어휘 **be associated with** ~와 관련되다 **initially** 처음에, 애초에 **originally** 원래 **national holiday** 국경일 **outdoor location** 야외 지점, 실외 장소

패러프레이징

sold at seaside resorts or resorts or state fairs → sold at outdoor locations

❌ 오답 피하기

People enjoy grilling them at family picnics and ordering them at baseball games라는 문장에서 야구 경기장에서 주문하는 것을 즐긴다는 의미를 나타내었는데 이는 야구 경기장에서 최초로 핫도그가 판매 또는 제공된 것을 의미하는 것이 아니므로 (a)는 오답입니다.

---

65 동의어

In the context of the passage, hinders means _____.

(a) expands
(b) invites
(c) creates
(d) delays

해당 단락의 문맥에서 hinders가 의미하는 것은?

(a) 확장하다
(b) 초대하다
(c) 만들다
(d) 지연시키다

정답 (d)

해설 해당 문장에서 hinders는 '핫도그가 식당 이용객들에게 즉시 제공되거나 빵을 분리하여 보관해야 한다는 것을 의미한다'는 관계대명사 which가 가리키는 앞문장의 전체 내용을 주어로 가지는 동사로 쓰였습니다. 그 뒤에 식당에서의 음식이 나오는 것을 가리키는 service가 목적어로 쓰였으며, 긴 줄을 만들고 단골 손님들을 언짢게 만든다는 내용이 있으므로 문맥상 hinders는 식당에서 핫도그를 주문 시 시간이 지체된다는 것을 의미합니다. 따라서 보기 중에서 '지연시키다'라는 의미를 나타내는 동사 delay의 현재시제 (d) delays가 정답입니다.

In the context of the passage, <u>acceptable</u> means
_____.

(a) valuable
(b) suitable
(c) visible
(d) believable

해당 단락의 문맥에서 <u>acceptable</u>
이 의미하는 것은?

(a) 소중한
(b) 알맞은, 적절한
(c) 보이는
(d) 그럴 듯한

정답 (b)

해설 해당 문장에서 acceptable은 문맥상 시카고를 제외한 미국에서는 핫도그의 토핑으로서 케첩에 대해 '받아 들여질 수 있다'
는 의미로 쓰였습니다. 이는 케첩이 토핑으로서 적절하다는 의미이므로 보기 중에서 '알맞은, 적절한'이라는 의미를 나타내
는 형용사 (b) suitable이 정답입니다.

PART 3

THE CATHEDRAL OF JUSTO GALLEGO

The Cathedral of Justo Gallego, also called "the Cathedral of Junk," is a religious building in Madrid, Spain. Covering 8,000 square feet, with a dome rising 130 feet in the air, **67** it was created nearly single-handedly as an act of spiritual devotion by a former monk.

Justo Gallego joined a monastery as a young man. In 1961, **68** after falling ill with tuberculosis, he requested permission to leave his religious order and seek treatment. Gallego vowed that if he survived his condition, he would realize his dream of building a religious shrine. He recovered and, without any formal training, began building the cathedral on land that he had inherited from his family.

Gallego designed the building in an unusual style. He avoided straight lines in his plans, instead favoring curves and circles. **69** As an explanation for this design, Gallego stated that God made all things round, including the planets and the earth. He also used unusual construction techniques. To make the cathedral's columns, he filled empty paint cans with concrete. To make stained glass windows, he smashed discarded colored glass into tiny pieces, then painstakingly glued the fragments into complex patterns.

Most of the materials used for the cathedral were recycled everyday objects or **72** surplus materials donated by local companies. Though Gallego mainly funded his work through donations, **70** he also received $45,000 from the Coca-Cola Company, which used his partially built cathedral in an advertisement. Following the commercial, approximately 1,000 tourists began visiting the cathedral each day.

후스토 갈레고 대성당

"쓰레기의 대성당"이라고도 불리는 후스토 갈레고 대성당은 스페인의 마드리드에 있는 종교적인 건물이다. 공중으로 130 피트의 높이로 서 있는 돔을 가지고 8000 평방 피트에 걸쳐 있는 이 대성당은 전직 수도사의 종교적인 헌신의 행위로서 거의 혼자의 힘으로 지어졌다.

후스토 갈레고는 젊은 시절에 수도원에 들어갔다. 1961년, 결핵에 걸린 후로 그의 수도회를 떠나 치료를 받으러 가기 위한 허락을 요청하였다. 갈레고는 만약 그의 질병 상태를 견뎌 낸다면, 그는 성당을 짓겠다는 그의 꿈을 실현시킬 것이라고 맹세하였다. 그는 회복하였고, 정식 교육도 받지 않은 채, 그가 가족으로부터 물려받은 땅에 대성당을 짓기 시작하였다.

갈레고는 독특한 방식으로 건물을 디자인하였다. 그는 그의 설계도에서 직선을 피하였고, 그 대신에 곡선과 원을 편애하였다. 이 디자인에 대한 설명으로 갈레고는 신은 행성과 지구를 포함해서 만물을 둥글게 만들었다고 말했다. 그는 또한 독특한 건축 공법을 사용하였다. 대성당의 기둥을 만들기 위해, 그는 비어 있는 페인트통에 콘크리트를 채웠다. 스테인드글라스 창문을 만들기 위해, 그는 버려진 색유리를 작은 조각으로 부수었고, 그 뒤에 그 조각들을 복잡한 패턴으로 공들여 붙였다.

대성당에 사용된 대부분의 재료들은 재활용된 일상 용품이거나 현지 기업들에 의해 기부된 잔여 자재였다. 비록 갈레고는 주로 기부를 통해 그의 작업의 자금을 충당하였지만, 그는 또한 코카콜라 컴퍼니로부터 4만 5천달러를 받았으며, 그 회사는 지어진 대성당의 일부를 광고에 사용하였다. 광고 후에, 대략 1,000명의 관광객들이 매일 대성당을 방문하기 시작하였다.

For decades, Gallego worked on the cathedral daily, with little outside assistance. **71** When local authorities **73** deemed the building to be structurally unsound, there were fears that, when Gallego died, the still-unfinished building would be demolished. To avoid this, Gallego arranged to donate the building to a nonprofit agency. After Gallego's death in 2021, **71** the organization began making repairs, saving the cathedral from destruction. Its members committed to completing the cathedral, and construction is ongoing to this day, according to Gallego's plans. However, the building is not registered as a church. Instead, it serves as a meditative space for followers of all religions.

수 십년동안, 갈레고는 거의 외부의 도움 없이 매일 대성당 작업을 하였다. 지방 정부 당국이 그 대성당이 구조적으로 불안정하다고 생각하였을 때, 갈레고가 사망하면 미완성의 대성당이 철거될 것이라는 두려움이 있었다. 이를 피하기 위해 갈레고는 비영리 단체에 대성당을 기부하는 것으로 처리하였다. 2021년 갈레고의 사망 이후, 그 단체는 수리를 하기 시작하였고, 대성당을 파괴되는 것에서 구해내었다. 그 단체의 회원들은 대성당을 완성하는 데 전념했으며, 그 공사는 갈레고의 설계에 따라 지금까지도 계속되고 있다. 하지만, 그 건물은 교회로 등록되지 않았다. 대신, 모든 종교의 신봉자들을 위한 명상의 공간으로서 역할하고 있다.

어휘 cathedral 대성당 junk 쓰레기, 쓸모없는 물건 religious 종교적인 cover 걸치다, 포함시키다 square 평방의, 제곱의 dome 돔, 반구형 지붕 single-handedly 혼자의 힘으로, 단독으로 spiritual 종교적인 devotion 헌신 former 이전의 monk 수도사 join 합류하다, 들어가다 monastery 수도원 fall ill with ~라는 병에 걸리다 tuberculosis 결핵 request 요청하다 permission 허락 religious order 수도회 treatment 치료 vow 맹세하다 survive ~을 견디다, ~에서 살아남다 condition 질병 상태 realize 실현시키다 shrine 성당, 성지 formal 정식의 training 교육, 훈련 inherit 상속받다, 물려받다 design 디자인하다, 고안하다 unusual 독특한, 특이한 straight 곧은, 일직선의 plan 설계도 favor 편애하다, 찬성하다 curve 곡선 circle 원 explanation 설명 state 말하다, 진술하다 round 둥글게 planet 행성 the earth 지구 construction 건축, 공사 technique 기술 column 기둥 fill 채우다 stained glass 스테인드글라스 smash 부수다, 박살내다 discarded 버려진 tiny 작은 painstakingly 공들여, 힘들여 glue (접착제로) 붙이다 fragment 조각 complex 복잡한 pattern 패턴, 무늬 materials 재료 recycled 재활용된 everyday object 일상 용품 surplus 과잉의, 여분의, 잔여의 donate 기부하다 mainly 주로 fund 자금을 충당하다 through ~을 통해 donation 기부 partially 일부, 부분적으로 advertisement 광고 following ~후에 commercial (상업) 광고 approximately 대략 tourist 관광객 decade 10년 work on ~에 대해 작업을 하다, ~에 공을 들이다 daily 매일 little 거의 ~ 않는 assistance 도움, 지원 authorities 정부 당국 deem 여기다, 생각하다 structurally 구조적으로 unsound 불안정한 fear 두려움 still-unfinished 미완성의 demolish 철거하다, 무너뜨리다 arrange (일을) 처리하다 nonprofit agency 비영리 단체 organization 조직, 단체 make a repair 수리하다 save A from B: A를 B로부터 구해내다 destruction 파괴 commit to -ing ~하는 데 전념하다 ongoing 계속되는, 진행 중인 to this day 지금까지도 according to ~에 따라 register 등록하다 instead 그 대신에 serve as ~로서 역할을 하다 meditative 명상적인 space 공간 follower 신봉자 religion 종교

Based on the first paragraph, why did Justo Gallego probably build the cathedral?

(a) to raise awareness of recycling
(b) to show his religious faith
(c) to stay active in retirement
(d) to attract tourists to his home

첫 번째 문단에 따르면 후스토 갈레고가 대성당을 지은 이유는 무엇일 것 같은가?

(a) 재활용에 대한 인식을 높이기 위해서
(b) 그의 종교적 신념을 보여주기 위해서
(c) 은퇴하여 활동적으로 지내기 위하여
(d) 그의 집으로 관광객을 끌기 위하여

정답 (b)

해설 첫 번째 문단에서 후스토 갈레고가 대성당을 지은 이유에 대해서 종교적인 헌신의 행위(it was created ~ as an act of spiritual devotion by a former monk)라고 언급하였습니다. 이를 통해 대성당을 지은 것은 종교적인 신념에 따른 행동이었음을 알 수 있으므로 (b)가 정답입니다.

어휘 raise awareness 인식을 높이다 recycling 재활용 faith 신념 stay active 활동적으로 지내다 in retirement 은퇴하여 attract 끌다

패러프레이징

spiritual devotion → religious faith

What caused Gallego to leave the monastery?

(a) He experienced a disturbing dream.
(b) He was ordered to by his supervisor.
(c) He needed to address a serious illness.
(d) He was advised to by a family member.

갈레고가 수도원을 떠나게 한 것은 무엇이었는가?

(a) 그는 충격적인 꿈을 꾸었다.
(b) 그는 그의 상사에게 떠나라는 명령을 받았다.
(c) 그는 심각한 질병에 대처해야 했다.
(d) 그는 가족 중 일원으로부터 떠나라는 조언을 들었다.

정답 (c)

해설 두 번째 문단에 갈레고가 수도원을 떠나기 위한 허락을 요청하였다는 내용의 문장이 있는데 그 이유는 결핵에 걸려 치료하기 위한 것(after falling ill with tuberculosis, he requested permission to leave his religious order and seek treatment)이었다고 언급되어 있습니다. 따라서 정답은 (c)입니다.

어휘 cause + 목적어 + to 동사원형: (목적어)가 ~하는 것을 초래하다 disturbing 충격적인, 불안감을 주는 be ordered to 동사원형: ~하라는 명령을 받다 supervisor 상사, 감독, 관리관 need to 동사원형: ~해야 하다, ~할 필요가 있다 address 다루다, 대처하다 illness 질병 be advised to 동사원형: ~하라는 조언을 듣다

패러프레이징

seek treatment → address a serious illness

---

69 추론

Based on the third paragraph, what probably influenced Gallego's choice for the style of the cathedral?

(a) his desire to simplify its construction
(b) his attempt to model it after a famous building
(c) his goal for it to be attractive to visitors
(d) his effort to imitate natural shapes in its design

세 번째 문단에 따르면, 무엇이 대성당의 양식에 대한 갈레고의 선택에 영향을 주었을 것 같은가?

(a) 공사를 간소화시키고 싶은 갈망
(b) 유명한 건물을 따라 만들고자 하는 시도
(c) 대성당이 방문객들에게 매력적으로 보이기 위한 목표
(d) 설계에 자연의 모양을 모방하고자 하는 노력

정답 (d)

해설 세 번째 문단에서 갈레고가 독특한 양식으로 대성당을 디자인하였다고 언급하면서, 직선을 피하고 곡선과 원을 사용하였다고 합니다. 이러한 디자인에 대한 설명으로 갈레고는 신이 행성과 지구를 포함해서 만물을 둥글게 만들었다고 말했다는 (As an explanation for this design, Gallego stated that God made all things round, including the planets and the earth) 부분에서 갈레고는 자연의 모습을 모방하여 그 대성당을 설계했음을 알 수 있습니다. 따라서 정답은 (d)입니다.

어휘 influence 영향을 주다 choice 선택 desire 갈망, 바람 simplify 단순화시키다, 간소화하다 attempt 시도 model after ~을 본떠서 만들다 goal 목표 attractive 매력적인 effort 노력 imitate 모방하다 natural 자연의 shape 모양

패러프레이징

made all things round including ~ the earth → natural shape

70 세부 정보

Why did the Coca-Cola Company contribute to Gallego's building costs?

(a) because it used the site in promotional materials
(b) because it had to pay for damage it caused
(c) because it wanted to make a charitable donation
(d) because it put advertisements up at the location

코카콜라 컴퍼니가 갈레고의 건축 비용에 기여한 이유는 무엇인가?

(a) 홍보 자료에 그 장소를 사용했기 때문에
(b) 그 회사가 입힌 피해에 대해 보상해야 했기 때문에
(c) 자선적인 기부를 하기를 원했기 때문에
(d) 그 위치에 광고를 게시했기 때문에

정답 (a)

해설 네 번째 문단에서 갈레고가 코카콜라 컴퍼니로부터 45,000달러를 받았는데, 그 회사가 그 대성당의 지어진 일부를 광고에 사용하였다고(he also received $45,000 from the Coca-Cola Company, which used his partially built cathedral in an advertisement) 언급되어 있습니다. 이를 통해 코카콜라 컴퍼니가 갈레고에게 건축 비용으로 45,000달러를 준 이유가 그 회사의 홍보 자료에 대성당을 사용하기 위해서였다는 것을 알 수 있습니다. 따라서 정답은 (a)입니다.

어휘 contribute 기여하다, 기부하다 cost 비용 site 장소 promotional 홍보의 materials 자료 pay for ~에 대해 지불하다 damage 피해, 손해 make a donation 기부하다 charitable 자선의, 자선적인 put up ~을 게시하다

패러프레이징

• his partially built cathedral → the site
• in an advertisement → in promotional materials

오답 피하기

used his partially built cathedral in an advertisement는 갈레고가 짓고 있던 대성당의 일부를 광고에 사용하였다는 의미이므로, 대성당에 광고를 게시한 것과는 다릅니다. 따라서 (d)는 오답입니다.

71 세부 정보

How did a nonprofit agency save the cathedral?

(a) by registering it as a church
(b) by purchasing it from the owner
(c) by opening it to the public
(d) by making it structurally safe

비영리 단체는 어떻게 그 대성당을 구해내었는가?

(a) 교회로 등록함으로써
(b) 소유주로부터 매입함으로써
(c) 대중에게 공개함으로써
(d) 구조적으로 안전하게 만듦으로써

정답 (d)

해설 마지막 문단에서 갈레고가 사망하면 정부 당국에서 구조적으로 불안정하다고 여기는 대성당을 철거할지도 모른다는 두려움이 있었다고 언급되어 있습니다. 그래서 갈레고는 대성당을 한 비영리 단체에게 기부하였고, 갈레고의 사망 후에 이 비영리 단체는 수리를 시작하여 대성당이 파괴되는 것으로부터 구해냈다고(the organization began making repairs, saving the cathedral from destruction) 설명하고 있습니다. 따라서 비영리 단체가 대성당을 수리한 것은 구조적으로 안정적으로 만들어 철거되지 않도록 한 것이므로 정답은 (d)입니다.

어휘 owner 소유주, 주인 open to the public 대중에게 공개하다 safe 안전한

TEST 06

72 동의어

In the context of the passage, surplus means _____.

(a) costly
(b) written
(c) extra
(d) learning

해당 단락의 문맥에서 surplus가 의미하는 것은?

(a) 값비싼
(b) 쓰여진
(c) 여분의
(d) 학습하는

정답 (c)

해설 해당 문장에서 surplus는 문맥상 후스토 갈레고 대성당에 사용된 재료로 언급된 현지 회사에 의해 기부된 재료를 설명하면서 쓰인 형용사입니다. 회사에서 필요한 재료를 기부하는 것은 더 이상 그 재료가 필요하지 않은 것이라는 의미이므로, surplus는 '잔여의', '여분의'라는 의미를 나타낸다는 것을 알 수 있습니다. 따라서 선택지 중에서 이와 같은 의미를 나타내는 형용사 (c) extra가 정답입니다.

73 동의어

In the context of the passage, deemed means _____.

(a) judged
(b) hoped
(c) promised
(d) forced

해당 단락의 문맥에서 deemed가 의미하는 것은?

(a) 판단했다
(b) 희망했다
(c) 약속했다
(d) 강요했다

정답 (a)

해설 해당 문장에서 deemed는 지방 정부 당국(local authorities)을 주어로, 후스토 갈레고 대성당을 목적어로 가지는 과거시제의 동사로 사용되었습니다. 문맥상 지방 정부 당국이 그 대성당을 구조적으로 불안정하다고 생각했다는 의미로 이해되므로, 이와 문맥상 유사한 의미로 '판단하다'라는 의미를 나타내는 동사 judge의 과거형 (a) judged가 정답입니다.

PART 4

TO: Baggage Services <baggageservices@defiantair. com>

FROM: Emma Lewis <emma.lewis@sparklemail. com>

SUBJECT: Baggage Issue

Dear Sir or Madam:

Last Sunday, I flew from Tokyo to Los Angeles aboard Defiant Airlines. **74** When I arrived in Los Angeles, my luggage was declared lost. It has been three days now, and I have still not received it. I am contacting the Baggage Services Department to resolve the issue.

When my suitcase failed to appear on the carousel, I went to the nearest Defiant desk to seek assistance. However, upon hearing my situation, **75** staff suggested only that I wait in case someone had taken it by accident. Apparently, such errors are often noticed within minutes, and bags are quickly returned. I waited as instructed, but without success.

After returning to the desk, I was given a claim number. The agent then told me that if my suitcase could not be located and returned within twenty-four hours, I would be given a voucher to purchase clothing. This was helpful but **79** insufficient, **76** as I needed replacement items immediately. I was traveling for business, and I hadn't worn my usual professional clothing because it was such a long flight.

Furthermore, I am an architect, and I had packed miniature architectural models for my **80** imminent project, a multi-million-dollar skyscraper in Los Angeles. When my luggage failed to reach its destination, **77** I was forced to put off meetings with my biggest client, placing my project in jeopardy. If the models are not returned, I will have to reproduce

수신인: 수화물 서비스 <baggageservices@ defiantair.com>

발신인: 엠마 루이스 <emma.lewis@sparklemail. com>

제목: 수화물 문제

담당자님께

지난 일요일, 저는 데피앙트 항공을 이용하여 도쿄에서 로스앤젤레스로 비행하였습니다. 제가 로스앤젤레스에 도착했을 때, 저의 수화물이 분실되었다고 신고되었습니다. 지금 3일째인데, 저는 아직도 그것을 받지 못했습니다. 저는 이 문제를 해결하기 위해 수화물 서비스 부서로 연락 드리고 있습니다.

저의 여행가방이 수화물 컨베이어 벨트에 나타나지 못했을 때, 저는 도움을 구하기 위해 가장 가까운 데피앙트 항공사 접수처로 갔습니다. 하지만, 저의 상황에 대해 듣자마자, 직원은 우연히 누군가가 그것을 잘못 가져갔을 경우에 대비해서 기다리라고만 제안하였습니다. 분명히, 그런 실수는 흔히 몇 분 내에 알게 되고, 가방은 빠르게 반환됩니다. 일러 주신대로 저는 기다렸지만, 성과는 없었습니다.

제가 접수처로 돌아온 후 저는 접수 번호를 받았습니다. 그리고 나서 그 직원은 제 여행가방의 위치를 파악할 수 없어서 24시간 이내에 돌아올 수 없게 된다면 저는 옷을 구매할 상품권을 받을 것이라고 말했습니다. 이건 도움이 되긴 하지만 충분하지 않았습니다. 왜냐하면 저는 그 즉시 대체품이 필요했기 때문입니다. 저는 출장 중이었고, 장거리 비행이었기에 제가 평소에 입는 직업 상의 의복을 입고 있지 않았습니다.

더욱이, 저는 건축가이며, 로스앤젤레스의 수백만 달러의 고층 건물에 대한 임박한 프로젝트를 위해서 축소 건축 모형을 챙겼었습니다. 제 수화물이 목적지에 도착하지 못했을 때, 저는 어쩔 수 없이 저의 최대 고객과의 회의를 미룰 수밖에 없었으며, 그것은 제 프로젝트를 위기에 처하게 하였습니다. 그 모형이 돌아오지 않으면, 저는 그것을 다시 만들어

them, and this will involve considerable expense, for which I will hold Defiant responsible.

I have called Defiant daily without receiving any updates. **78** Should my luggage be permanently misplaced, I will be forced to sue your airline for all damages inflicted on me by the loss. Therefore, if my suitcase is not returned to me, you will hear from my attorney.

Sincerely,

Emma Lewis

야 할 것이고, 그것은 상당한 비용을 수반할 것이며, 이것은 제가 데피앙트 항공사에 책임을 물을 것입니다.

저는 데피앙트 항공사에 매일 전화하였으나 새로운 소식은 받지 못했습니다. 제 수화물을 영영 찾을 수 없게 된다면, 저는 그 분실로 저에게 끼친 모든 손해를 귀 항공사에 청구할 수밖에 없습니다. 그러므로, 저희 여행가방이 저에게 돌아오지 않는다면, 귀사는 저의 변호사로부터 연락을 받을 것입니다.

안녕히 계세요.

엠마 루이스

어휘 **baggage** 수화물 **issue** 문제 **aboard** 탑승하여 **declare** 신고하다 **lost** 분실된 **contact** 연락하다 **resolve** 해결하다 **department** 부서 **suitcase** 여행 가방 **fail to 동사원형**: ~하지 못하다 **appear** 나타나다 **carousel** 수화물 컨베이어 벨트 **desk** 접수처, 안내처 **seek** 구하다 **assistance** 도움, 지원 **upon -ing** ~하자마자 **situation** 상황 **suggest** 제안하다 **in case** ~의 경우에 대비하여 **by accident** 우연히 **apparently** 명백히 **error** 실수 **within** ~내에 **as instructed** 안내받은 대로, 알려준 대로 **without success** 성과 없이 **be given** 받다 **agent** 직원, 대리인 **locate** 위치를 찾다 **voucher** 상품권, 교환권 **purchase** 구입하다 **insufficient** 불충분한 **replacement** 대체 **immediately** 즉시 **travel for business** 출장 가다 **usual** 평소의, 보통의 **professional** 직업의, 전문적인 **furthermore** 더욱이 **architect** 건축가 **pack** (짐을) 꾸리다, 싸다 **miniature** 축소 모형 **architectural** 건축의 **imminent** 임박한 **multi-million** 수백만의 **skyscraper** 고층 건물 **luggage** 수화물 **reach** 도달하다 **destination** 목적지 **be forced to 동사원형**: 어쩔 수 없이 ~하다, ~할 수밖에 없다 **put off** 연기하다, 미루다 **place + 목적어 + in jeopardy**: (목적어)를 위험에 처하게 하다 **reproduce** 재생산하다, 다시 만들다 **involve** 수반하다 **considerable** 상당한 **expense** 비용 **hold responsible for** ~에 대해 책임을 묻다 **daily** 매일 **permanently** 영구적으로, 영영 **misplace** 찾지 못하다, 분실하다 **sue** 청구하다, 고소하다 **damage** 피해, 손해 **inflict** 가하다, 끼치다 **loss** 분실, 손실 **therefore** 따라서, 그러므로 **attorney** 변호사

---

74 주제/목적

Why is Emma Lewis writing to Defiant Airlines?

(a) to inquire about luggage restrictions
(b) to complain about damaged property
(c) to get excess baggage fees refunded
(d) to locate belongings lost on a trip

엠마 루이스 씨가 데피앙트 항공사에게 편지를 쓰는 이유는 무엇인가?

(a) 수화물 제한에 대해 문의하기 위해
(b) 재산 피해에 대해 불만을 제기하기 위해
(c) 초과 수화물 요금을 환불 받기 위해
(d) 여행 중 분실물의 위치를 찾기 위해

정답 (d)

해설 편지의 목적은 첫 문단에 언급되어 있습니다. 엠마 루이스 씨는 비행기를 타고 로스앤젤레스에 도착하였으나 자신의 수화물이 분실된 것을 알게 되었고 3일이 지나도 수화물을 받지 못해서 이 문제를 해결하기 위해 연락하고 있다고(When I arrived in Los Angeles, my luggage was declared lost. It has been three days now, and I have still not received it. I am contacting the Baggage Services Department to resolve the issue) 언급하고 있습니다. 여기서 말하는 이 문제(the issue)에 대한 해결은 분실된 자신의 수화물을 찾는 것이므로 정답은 (d)입니다.

어휘 inquire 문의하다 restriction 제한 complain 불만을 제기하다, 불평하다 damaged property 재산 피해 get refunded 환불 받다 excess 초과한, 과도 fee 요금 locate ~의 위치를 찾다 belongings 소지품 on a trip 여행 중에

❌ 오답 피하기

편지의 마지막에 피해에 대한 보상에 대한 언급이 있지만, 자신의 여행 가방이 영구적으로 분실될 경우에 피해에 대한 청구를 할 것이라고(Should my luggage be permanently misplaced, I will be forced to sue your airline for all damages inflicted on me by the loss) 언급하였으므로 아직 피해에 대한 불만을 제기하는 것이 아님을 알 수 있습니다. 따라서 (b)는 오답입니다.

---

75 세부 정보

What did the staff suggest may have occurred?

(a) Emma put the wrong label on her case.
(b) Another passenger mistook Emma's luggage for their own.
(c) Emma waited in the wrong location.
(d) A staff member dropped Emma's bag in error.

직원은 무슨 일이 일어났을지도 모른다고 제안하였는가?

(a) 엠마가 그녀의 가방에 잘못된 라벨을 붙였다.
(b) 다른 승객이 엠마의 수화물을 자신의 것으로 오해했다.
(c) 엠마가 잘못된 위치에서 기다렸다.
(d) 한 직원이 실수로 엠마의 가방을 떨어뜨렸다.

정답 (b)

해설 두 번째 문단에서 엠마의 상황을 듣고서 항공사의 직원이 다른 사람이 우연히 가져갔을 경우에 대비해서 기다리라고 제안했다고(staff suggested only that I wait in case someone had taken it by accident) 언급한 부분을 보고 직원은 누군가가 엠마의 여행 가방을 착각하여 잘못 가져갔다고 생각했음을 알 수 있습니다. 따라서 정답은 (b)입니다.

어휘 may have p.p. ~했을 지도 모른다 label 라벨 mistake 오해하다 location 위치 drop 떨어뜨리다 in error 실수로

패러프레이징

someone had taken it by accident → another passenger mistook Emma's luggage for their own

Why, most likely, did Emma require additional clothing?

(a) because she had professional engagements to attend
(b) because she had been unprepared for the cold weather
(c) because she had left her jacket on the plane
(d) because she had traveled in her business suit

왜 엠마는 추가 의상이 필요할 것 같은가?

(a) 그녀가 참가해야 할 직업 상의 업무가 있었기 때문에
(b) 그녀가 추운 날씨에 준비가 되어 있지 않았기 때문에
(c) 그녀가 비행기에 그녀의 재킷을 놔뒀기 때문에
(d) 그녀가 사무복을 입고 이동했기 때문에

정답 (a)

해설 세 번째 문단에서 옷(clothing)에 언급된 부분은 엠마가 대체할 물품이 당장 필요하다고 하면서, 자신은 현재 출장 중이며, 장거리 비행이라 비행 중에는 평소에 입는 직업 상의 의복을 입고 있지 않았다고(as I needed replacement items immediately. I was traveling for business, and I hadn't worn my usual professional clothing because it was such a long flight) 언급하였습니다. 이를 통해 엠마는 업무 상 착용해야 하는 옷이 필요하다는 것을 알 수 있으므로 (a)가 정답입니다.

어휘 require 필요로 하다, 요구하다 additional 추가의 engagement 업무, 약속 attend 참가하다 unprepared 준비되지 않은 business suit 작업복

❌ 오답 피하기

엠마의 편지 중에 I hadn't worn my usual professional clothing. 라는 문장에서 직업 상의 의복을 착용하지 않았음을 알 수 있습니다. Professional clothing이 business suit로 패러프레이징 되었다고 볼 수 있지만, 그녀는 비행기에서 사무복을 입고 있지 않았으므로 (d)는 오답입니다.

What put Emma's architectural project at risk?

(a) the loss of several valuable documents
(b) the need to postpone meetings with a client
(c) the accidental breakage of her models by the airline
(d) the fact that she was unable to reach her coworkers

엠마의 건축 프로젝트를 위험에 빠트린 것은 무엇인가?

(a) 귀중한 몇몇 문서의 분실
(b) 고객과의 회의를 연기해야 할 필요성
(c) 항공사에 의한 그녀의 모형의 우발적 파손
(d) 그녀가 동료 직원에게 연락할 수 없었다는 사실

정답 (b)

해설 질문의 키워드인 put Emma's architectural project at risk는 네 번째 문단에서 엠마가 어쩔 수 없이 자신의 가장 큰 고객과의 회의를 연기해야 했고, 자신의 프로젝트를 위기에 처하게 하였다고(I was forced to put off meetings with my biggest client, placing my project in jeopardy) 언급한 부분에서 확인할 수 있습니다. 이를 통해 엠마는 고객과의 회의를 미뤄야 했기 때문에 자신의 프로젝트가 위험에 빠졌다고 볼 수 있으므로 (b)가 정답입니다.

어휘

> **패러프레이징**
>
> placing my project in jeopardy → put Emma's architectural project at risk

---

78 세부 정보

According to the letter, what will Emma do if the situation is not resolved?

(a) refuse to fly with the airline again
(b) call the airline every day for updates
(c) bring a legal case against the airline
(d) visit the airline's offices in person

편지에 따르면, 상황이 해결되지 않을 경우 엠마는 무엇을 할 것인가?

(a) 그 항공사의 비행편을 다시 이용하기를 거부한다
(b) 최신 소식을 위해 매일 항공사에 전화한다
(c) 항공사를 상대로 법적 소송을 제기한다
(d) 항공사 사무실을 직접 방문한다

정답 (c)

해설 편지의 마지막 부분에서 엠마는 자신의 수화물이 영구적으로 찾지 못하게 될 경우, 분실로 인해 자신에게 끼친 모든 피해에 대해 항공사에게 청구할 것이라고(Should my luggage be permanently misplaced, I will be forced to sue your airline for all damages inflicted on me by the loss) 언급하였습니다. 여기서 sue는 '고소하다', '청구하다'라는 의미로 법적 소송을 의미하는 동사입니다. 따라서 (c)가 정답입니다.

어휘 refuse to 동사원형: ~하기를 거부하다 bring a legal case 법적 소송을 제기하다 against ~을 상대로, ~에 대항하여
in person 직접

In the context of the passage, <u>insufficient</u> means

_____.

(a) unsatisfactory
(b) inaccurate
(c) unavoidable
(d) included

해당 단락의 문맥에서 <u>insufficient</u>가
의미하는 것은?

(a) 만족스럽지 못한
(b) 정확하지 않은
(c) 피할 수 없는
(d) 포함된

정답 (a)

해설 해당 문장에서 insufficient는 항공사 직원이 말하길, 엠마의 여행 가방이 24시간 내에 돌아오지 않는다면, 옷을 구입할 상품권을 받을 것이라고 했다는 문장 뒤에 엠마는 그 도움이 되었다(helpful)고 했으나 그 뒤에 역접의 접속사 but이 있으므로 insufficient가 helpful과 반대의 의미를 나타낸다는 것을 알 수 있습니다. 따라서 문맥상 항공사에서 제공될 상품권으로는 '충분하지 않다'라는 의미를 나타낸다고 볼 수 있으므로 선택지 중에서 '만족스럽지 못한'이라는 의미를 나타내는 형용사 (a) unsatisfactory가 정답입니다.

In the context of the passage, <u>imminent</u> means _____.

(a) finished
(b) affordable
(c) common
(d) upcoming

해당 단락의 문맥에서 <u>imminent</u>가
의미하는 것은?

(a) 완료된
(b) 감당할 수 있는
(c) 흔한
(d) 다가오는

정답 (d)

해설 해당 문장에서 imminent는 엠마의 프로젝트(project)를 수식하는 형용사로 사용되었으며, 그 프로젝트는 건축가인 엠마가 수백만 달러의 고층 건물에 대한 것임을 알 수 있습니다. 그리고 그 프로젝트를 위해 고객과의 회의가 있었으나 수화물에 들어 있는 축소 모형이 분실되어 고객과의 회의를 연기해야 하는 상황임을 설명하고 있습니다. 이를 통해 이 프로젝트는 가까운 시일 내에 고객과의 회의를 시작으로 진행되어야 하는 프로젝트이므로, '임박한'이라는 의미를 나타낸다는 것을 알 수 있습니다. 따라서 선택지 중에 이와 유사한 의미로 '다가오는'이라는 의미를 나타내는 형용사 (d) upcoming이 정답입니다.

TEST 06

Grammar

1. (b)	**2.** (a)	**3.** (d)	**4.** (c)	**5.** (b)	**6.** (d)	**7.** (b)	**8.** (b)	**9.** (a)	**10.** (a)
11. (d)	**12.** (c)	**13.** (c)	**14.** (b)	**15.** (d)	**16.** (c)	**17.** (a)	**18.** (a)	**19.** (d)	**20.** (b)
21. (c)	**22.** (d)	**23.** (c)	**24.** (a)	**25.** (b)	**26.** (a)				

Listening

27. (c)	**28.** (a)	**29.** (c)	**30.** (d)	**31.** (a)	**32.** (b)	**33.** (d)	**34.** (d)	**35.** (c)	**36.** (b)
37. (c)	**38.** (a)	**39.** (b)	**40.** (c)	**41.** (b)	**42.** (b)	**43.** (d)	**44.** (c)	**45.** (a)	**46.** (a)
47. (d)	**48.** (a)	**49.** (b)	**50.** (a)	**51.** (d)	**52.** (c)				

Reading & Vocabulary

53. (a)	**54.** (d)	**55.** (a)	**56.** (c)	**57.** (c)	**58.** (b)	**59.** (d)	**60.** (a)	**61.** (c)	**62.** (b)
63. (b)	**64.** (d)	**65.** (c)	**66.** (d)	**67.** (a)	**68.** (d)	**69.** (c)	**70.** (b)	**71.** (b)	**72.** (a)
73. (c)	**74.** (d)	**75.** (b)	**76.** (a)	**77.** (c)	**78.** (b)	**79.** (a)	**80.** (d)		

채점 계산표 (정답 개수 기재)		채점 계산 방법
Grammar	_____ / 26문항	Grammar 정답 개수 ÷ 26 × 100
Listening	_____ / 26문항	Listening 정답 개수 ÷ 26 × 100
Reading & Vocabulary	_____ / 28문항	Reading & Vocabulary 정답 개수 ÷ 28 × 100
총점	_____ / 80문항 ▸ _____ / 100점	총점: 각 영역 합산 정답 개수 ÷ 80 × 100 ＊소수점 이하는 올림 처리

TEST 07

Grammar

01 시제 - 과거진행

Megan had planned to have dinner at her favorite Italian restaurant but chose to cook instead. She _____ ingredients for her creamy pasta sauce when she realized she did not have any cream or milk.

(a) has been gathering
(b) was gathering
(c) would gather
(d) is gathering

메건은 그녀가 가장 좋아하는 이탈리아 식당에서 저녁을 먹을 계획이었으나 대신 요리하기로 선택했다. 그녀는 크림 파스타 소스를 위한 재료를 모으던 중 크림이나 우유가 없다는 것을 깨달았다.

정답 (b)

해설 동사 gather의 알맞은 형태를 고르는 문제입니다. 빈칸 뒤에 과거시제 동사(realized)를 포함한 when절이 쓰여 있어 이 when절이 가리키는 과거 시점에 준비하는 일이 일시적으로 진행되던 상황을 나타내야 자연스러우므로 이러한 의미로 쓰이는 과거진행시제 (b) was gathering이 정답입니다

어휘 plan 계획하다 choose 선택하다 cook 요리하다 gather 모으다 ingredient 재료 creamy 크림 같은 realize 깨닫다

02 관계사절

Finished in 1931, *The Persistence of Memory* is one of Salvador Dali's most famous oil paintings. Art critics interpret the three melting clocks in the painting, _____, as signifying the fluidity of time.

(a) which were inspired by melting cheese
(b) that were inspired by melting cheese
(c) who were inspired by melting cheese
(d) what were inspired by melting cheese

1931년에 완성된 <기억의 지속>은 살바도르 달리의 가장 유명한 유화 중 하나이다. 미술 비평가들은 녹는 치즈에서 영감을 받은 이 그림의 세 개의 녹아 내리는 시계를 시간이 유동적이라는 것을 의미한다고 해석한다.

정답 (a)

해설 사물 명사 the painting을 뒤에서 수식할 관계사절을 고르는 문제입니다. 사물 명사를 수식하는 관계대명사는 which 또는 that인데, 빈칸 앞에 콤마가 있으므로 관계대명사 which로 시작하는 (a)가 정답입니다.

어휘 finished 완성된 persistence 지속 memory 기억 interpret 해석하다 melting 녹는 famous 유명한 oil painting 유화 art critic 미술 비평가 melting 녹는 inspired 영감을 받은 signify 의미하다 fluidity 유동성

03 당위성을 나타내는 동사원형

Dave is having trouble at work after accidentally breaking the company laptop. His employer is demanding that he _____ for the repair, or else the laptop's cost will be deducted from his next paycheck.

(a) paid
(b) is paying
(c) will pay
(d) pay

데이브는 실수로 회사 노트북을 망가뜨린 후 직장에서 어려움을 겪고 있다. 그의 고용주는 노트북 수리비를 지불하라고 요구하며, 그렇지 않으면 다음 급여에서 노트북 비용을 공제하겠다고 했다.

정답 (d)

해설 동사 pay의 알맞은 형태를 고르는 문제입니다. 빈칸은 동사 is demanding의 목적어 역할을 하는 that절의 동사 자리인데, demand와 같이 주장/요구/명령/제안 등을 나타내는 동사의 목적어 역할을 하는 that절의 동사는 should없이 동사원형만 사용하므로 동사원형인 (d) pay가 정답입니다.

어휘 have trouble 어려움을 겪다 work 직장 accidentally 실수로 break 고장 내다 laptop 노트북 컴퓨터 employer 고용주 demand 요구하다 pay 지불하다 repair 수리 or else 그렇지 않으면 cost 비용 deduct 공제하다 next 다음 paycheck 급여

04 가정법 과거

The red supergiant star Betelgeuse will inevitably explode one day. Although the star is nearly 650 light-years away, if it were to explode, it _____ from Earth, even in the daytime.

(a) will be visible
(b) would have been visible
(c) would be visible
(d) will have been visible

적색 초거성 베텔게우스는 언젠가는 불가피하게 폭발할 것이다. 이 별은 거의 650광년이나 떨어져 있지만 폭발한다면 지구에서 낮에도 보일 것이다.

정답 (c)

해설 be동사와 형용사 visible의 알맞은 형태를 고르는 문제입니다. If절의 동사가 가정법 과거를 나타내는 과거시제(were)일 때, 주절의 동사는 「would/could/might + 동사원형」과 같은 형태가 되어야 알맞으므로 (c) would be visible이 정답입니다.

어휘 supergiant 초거성, 굉장히 큰 별 Betelgeuse 베텔게우스 inevitably 불가피하게, 필연적으로 explode 폭발하다 one day 언젠가 although 비록 ~이지만 nearly 거의 light-year 광년 away 떨어져 visible 눈에 보이는 even 심지어 daytime 낮

05 준동사 - 동명사

Gostra is a traditional Maltese game dating back to the Middle Ages. The game involves _____ along a greasy wooden pole to grab one of three flags attached to the end.

(a) to have run
(b) running
(c) having run
(d) to run

고스트라는 중세 시대로 거슬러 올라가는 몰타의 전통 게임이다. 이 게임은 기름기가 많은 나무 기둥을 따라 달려가 끝에 붙어 있는 세 개의 깃발 중 하나를 잡는 게임이다.

정답 (b)

해설 동사 run의 알맞은 형태를 고르는 문제입니다. 빈칸은 타동사 involves의 목적어 자리이며, involve는 동명사를 목적어로 취하여 '~하는 것을 수반하다'라는 의미를 나타냅니다. 따라서 동명사인 (b) running이 정답입니다.

어휘 traditional 전통적인 Maltese 몰타의 dating back 거슬러 올라가다 Middle Ages 중세 involve 포함하다, 수반하다 greasy 미끄러운 wooden 나무로 된 pole 기둥 grab 잡다 flag 깃발 attached 붙어 있는

06 시제 - 미래진행

Lara fell down in the street and sprained her wrist. Unfortunately, this means she cannot work her usual job as a massage therapist, so she _____ at home for a few weeks until her wrist heals.

(a) will have been staying
(b) stays
(c) has stayed
(d) will be staying

라라는 길에서 넘어져 손목을 삐었다. 안타깝게도 이로 인해 라라는 평소 마사지 치료사로 하던 일을 할 수 없게 되어 손목이 회복될 때까지 몇 주 동안 집에 머무를 것이다.

정답 (d)

해설 동사 stay의 알맞은 형태를 고르는 문제입니다. 빈칸이 속한 문장 뒤에 시간 부사절 접속사 until과 해당 접속사절에 현재시제동사(heals)가 쓰였으므로 빈칸이 속한 문장의 시제는 미래시제임을 알 수 있습니다. 따라서 보기 중에서 미래를 나타낼 수 있는 미래진행시제 (d) will be staying이 정답입니다.

어휘 fall down 넘어지다 sprain 삐다 wrist 손목 unfortunately 불행하게도 mean 의미하다 usual 평소의 job 일 massage therapist 마사지 치료사 stay 머물다 until ~까지 heal 회복되다

The peregrine falcon is considered the fastest animal in the world. While diving to hunt, it _____ reach speeds of up to 240 miles per hour, which is comparable to a Formula 1 racecar.

(a) shall
(b) can
(c) should
(d) must

송골매는 세계에서 가장 빠른 동물로 여겨진다. 사냥을 위해 급강하할 때는 시속 최대 240마일까지 도달할 수 있으며, 이는 포뮬러 1 경주용 자동차에 필적한다.

정답 (b)

해설 빈칸에 들어갈 알맞은 조동사를 고르는 문제입니다. 빈칸이 속한 문장은 송골매가 다이빙을 할 때 최대 시속 240마일까지의 속도에 도달한다는 내용인데, 이것은 송골매가 가진 비행 능력을 나타내는 것이므로 '~할 수 있다'라는 의미를 나타내는 것이 적절합니다. 따라서 정답은 (b) can입니다.

어휘 peregrine falcon 송골매 consider 여기다 fast 빠른 dive (급)강하하다 hunt 사냥하다 reach 도달하다 speed 속도 up to 최대 mile 마일 per ~당 be comparable to ~에 필적하다, ~와 비교할 수 있다 racecar 경주용 차

After trying many new software programs, the manager found SurveyScape to be the only program _____ all of the company's needs. Therefore, it was installed on every workplace computer last week.

(a) what fulfilled
(b) that fulfilled
(c) who fulfilled
(d) when fulfilled

많은 새로운 소프트웨어 프로그램을 사용해 본 후에, 매니저는 서베이스케이프가 회사의 모든 요구 사항을 충족하는 유일한 프로그램이라는 것을 알게 되었다. 따라서, 그 프로그램은 지난 주에 모든 업무용 컴퓨터에 설치되었다.

정답 (b)

해설 사물 명사 the only program을 수식할 관계사절을 고르는 문제입니다. 사물 명사를 수식하는 관계대명사는 which 또는 that인데, (a)~(d) 중에는 which로 시작하는 관계사절이 없으므로 정답은 (b) that fulfilled입니다.

어휘 manager 관리자 fulfill 충족하다 need 요구 therefore 따라서 install 설치하다 workplace 직장

❌ 오답 피하기

관계부사 when은 시간을 나타내는 명사를 선행사로 가지며, 관계부사 when 뒤에는 주어와 동사, 목적어/보어 등 필요한 문장 성분이 갖춰져야 합니다.

Wally's sales pitch was cut short after everyone was asked to leave the building for a scheduled pest control treatment. Had he been informed ahead of time, he _____ his meeting with the client.

(a) would have rescheduled
(b) will reschedule
(c) would reschedule
(d) will have rescheduled

월리의 구매 권유는 예정된 해충 방제 처리를 위해 모두가 건물에서 나가도록 요청 받은 후 중단되었다. 만약 그가 미리 알았다면, 고객과의 회의를 다시 잡았을 것이다.

정답 (a)

해설 동사 reschedule의 알맞은 형태를 고르는 문제입니다. Had he been은 가정법 과거완료를 구성하는 If he had been에서 If가 생략되고 주어와 had가 도치된 구조입니다. 따라서, If절의 동사가 「had p.p.」일 때 주절의 동사로 사용하는 「would/could/might + have p.p.」의 형태가 빈칸에 쓰여야 알맞으므로 (a) would have rescheduled가 정답입니다.

어휘 sales pitch 구입 권유 cut short 중단되다, 갑자기 끝내다 scheduled 예정된 pest 해충 control 방제 treatment 처리 inform 알리다 ahead 미리 reschedule 다시 잡다

Determined to quit her job, Charlotte began writing her resignation letter. She _____ it for almost an hour before she realized she wanted to stay at the company after all.

(a) had been working on
(b) works on
(c) has been working on
(d) would work on

직장을 그만두기로 결심한 샬롯은 사직서를 쓰기 시작했다. 결국 자신이 회사에 남고 싶다는 것을 깨닫기 전에 그녀는 거의 한 시간 동안 사직서에 공을 드리고 있던 중이었다.

정답 (a)

해설 동사구 work on의 알맞은 형태를 고르는 문제입니다. 빈칸이 속한 문장에 「for + 기간」으로 기간을 나타내는 표현 for almost an hour와 시간 부사절 접속사 before, 그리고 과거시제동사(realized)가 위치해 있는 것을 통해, 샬롯이 사직서를 거의 1시간 동안 작업하던 것은 그녀가 회사에 남고 싶다는 것을 깨닫기 이전에 있었던 일임을 알 수 있습니다. 따라서 빈칸에 들어갈 시제는 realized보다 더 먼저 일어난 일을 나타내는 과거완료진행시제가 되어야 하므로 (a) had been working on이 정답입니다.

어휘 determined 결심한 quit 그만두다 resignation 사직서 work on ~에 공을 들이다, ~에 대한 작업을 하다 realize 깨닫다 stay 남다 after all 결국

Moai are giant stone statues of human figures carved by the Rapa Nui people of Easter Island. In some cases, the head is the only visible part _____ the torsos are wholly or partially buried.

모아이는 이스터섬의 라파누이 사람들이 조각한 거대한 인간 형상의 석상이다. 어떤 경우에는 몸통이 완전히 또는 부분적으로 묻혀 있기 때문에 머리만 보이는 경우도 있다.

(a) so that
(b) until
(c) even if
(d) because

정답 (d)

해설 빈칸에 들어갈 알맞은 접속사를 고르는 문제입니다. 빈칸 앞의 주절의 내용은 모아이 석상 중 몇몇은 머리 부위만 보인다는 내용이며, 빈칸이 포함된 부사절의 내용은 몸통이 전체 또는 일부가 묻혀 있다는 내용이므로 '몸통 전체 또는 일부가 묻혀 있기 때문에 머리 부위만 보인다'라는 결과와 원인의 순서로 이어진 문장임을 알 수 있습니다. 따라서 정답은 원인 또는 이유를 나타내는 접속사 (d) because입니다.

어휘 giant 거대한 statue 석상 figure 형상 carve 조각하다 visible 보이는 torso 몸통 wholly 완전히 partially 부분적으로 bury 묻다

This year, Neil's company is celebrating its fiftieth anniversary, and a committee has been put in charge of the upcoming party. They _____ activities for the past two weeks but have plenty more to do.

올해 닐의 회사는 창립 50주년을 맞이하여, 다가오는 파티를 담당할 위원회를 구성하였다. 그들은 지난 2주 동안 활동을 계획해 왔지만, 해야 할 일이 아직 많이 남아 있다.

(a) had been planning
(b) are planning
(c) have been planning
(d) will have planned

정답 (c)

해설 동사 plan의 알맞은 형태를 고르는 문제입니다. 빈칸 뒤에 위치한 「for the past + 기간」은 '지난 ~동안'이라는 의미로 과거 시점에 시작하여 해당 기간을 거쳐 현재에도 진행 중인 동작이나 행동을 나타내는 현재완료진행형 동사와 어울리므로 (c) have been planning이 정답입니다.

어휘 celebrate 기념하다 anniversary 기념일 committee 위원회 charge 책임 upcoming 다가오는 plan 계획하다 activity 활동 past 지난 plenty 많이

Waumat is an initiation rite of the Sateré-Mawé indigenous group in Brazil. The ritual requires boys _____ the stings of bullet ants, which cause a burning, throbbing sensation that typically lasts for about twenty-four hours.

(a) enduring
(b) to have endured
(c) to endure
(d) having endured

와우맷은 브라질의 사테레-마웨 토착민들의 성년식이다. 그 의식은 남자 아이들에게 독개미에게쏘인 상처를 견디는 것을 요구하는데, 그것은 일반적으로 24시간 동안 지속되는 불에 타는 듯한 욱씬거리는 느낌을 일으킨다.

정답 (c)

해설 동사 endure의 알맞은 형태를 찾는 문제입니다. 빈칸 앞에 위치한 동사 requires은 「require + 목적어 + to 동사원형」의 구조로 쓰여 '(목적어)에게 ~하도록 요구하다'라는 의미를 나타내므로 to부정사 (c) to endure가 정답입니다.

어휘 initiation rite 성년식 indigenous group 토착민, 토착집단 ritual 의식, 의례 require + 목적어 + to 동사원형: (목적어)에게 ~하도록 요구하다 sting (곤충의 침, 가시에) 쏘인 상처 bullet ant 독개미 cause 일으키다, 발생시키다 burning 불에 타는 듯한 throbbing 욱씬거리는, 고동치는 sensation 느낌, 감각 typically 일반적으로 last 지속되다

At the age of eight, Steve became frightened when he jumped into the ocean and the waves were stronger than expected. Since then, he has disliked _____ in open water. He prefers pools instead.

(a) having swum
(b) swimming
(c) to swim
(d) to have swum

여덟 살 때 스티브는 바다에 뛰어들었을 때 예상보다 파도가 강해서 겁을 먹었다. 그 이후로, 그는 탁 트인 물에서 수영하는 것을 좋아하지 않게 되었다. 대신 그는 수영장을 선호한다.

정답 (b)

해설 동사 swim의 알맞은 형태를 고르는 문제입니다. 빈칸은 타동사 disliked의 목적어 자리이며, dislike는 동명사를 목적어로 취하여 '~하는 것을 싫어하다'라는 의미를 나타냅니다. 따라서 동명사인 (b) swimming이 정답입니다.

어휘 become 되다 frightened 겁먹다 jump 뛰어들다 ocean 바다 wave 파도 strong 강한 expect 예상하다 since 이후로 dislike 좋아하지 않다 open 탁 트인, 널따란 prefer 선호하다 pool 수영장 instead 대신

15

Using simulators, astronomers can predict the effect of an asteroid hitting Earth. For example, if an asteroid the size of Mount Everest were to collide with Earth, it _____ widespread devastation and even mass extinctions.

(a) will likely have caused
(b) would likely have caused
(c) will likely cause
(d) would likely cause

천문학자들은 시뮬레이터를 사용하여 소행성이 지구에 충돌할 때의 영향을 예측할 수 있다. 예를 들어, 에베레스트 산 크기의 소행성이 지구와 충돌한다면 광범위한 황폐화와 심지어 대규모 멸종을 초래할 가능성이 있다.

정답 (d)

해설 동사 cause의 알맞은 형태를 고르는 문제입니다. If절의 동사가 가정법 과거를 나타내는 과거시제(were)일 때, 주절의 동사는 「would/could/might + 동사원형」과 같은 형태가 되어야 알맞으므로 (d) would likely cause가 정답입니다. likely와 같은 부사가 would/could/might와 동사원형 사이에 위치할 수 있으니 선택지에서 부사를 제외한 형태를 찾아 정답을 고르도록 합니다.

어휘 simulator 시뮬레이터 astronomer 천문학자 predict 예측하다 effect 영향 asteroid 소행성 hit 충돌하다 example 예 collide 충돌하다 likely 가능성이 있다 cause 초래하다 widespread 광범위한 devastation 황폐(상태) even 심지어 mass 대규모 extinction 멸종

16

조동사

Bowling is a sport that is probably rooted in religious practice. Around the fourth century, Germans _____ roll a stone to knock down clubs that represented nonbelievers. This ritual signified the cleansing of sins.

(a) should
(b) might
(c) would
(d) must

볼링은 아마도 종교적인 관행에서 유래된 스포츠일지도 모른다. 4세기쯤, 독일인들은 돌을 굴려 비신자들을 나타내는 곤봉을 쓰러뜨리곤 했다. 이 의식은 죄를 씻어내는 것을 의미했다.

정답 (c)

해설 빈칸에 들어갈 알맞은 조동사를 고르는 문제입니다. 빈칸 앞에 쓰인 전치사구 Around the fourth century가 과거시점을 나타내고 있으며, 문맥상 독일인들이 돌을 굴려서 비신자들을 나타내는 곤봉들을 쓰러뜨렸다는 것을 의미하므로 빈칸에는 과거의 행동을 나타내는 조동사가 적절합니다. 따라서 선택지 중에서 '~하곤 했다'라는 의미로 과거의 불규칙적인 행동을 나타내는 (c) would가 정답입니다.

어휘 rooted in ~에서 유래된, ~에 뿌리 내린 religious 종교적인 practice 행위, 관행 around 약, ~쯤 roll 굴리다 knock down 쓰러뜨리다 club 곤봉 represent 나타내다, 해당하다 nonbeliever 비신자, 종교를 믿지 않는 사람 ritual 의식 signify 의미하다 cleansing 씻어냄, 정화, 세정 sin 죄

17 시제 - 미래완료진행

Chan is in the middle of a speech that has lasted far too long. By the time he finishes, his very restless audience _____ to him for an hour and a half.

(a) will have been listening
(b) will be listening
(c) has been listening
(d) is listening

챈은 너무 오래 지속되는 연설의 중간에 있다. 그가 연설을 마칠 무렵에는 매우 안절부절한 청중이 한 시간 반 동안 그의 말을 듣고 있었을 것이다.

정답 (a)

해설 동사 listen의 알맞은 형태를 고르는 문제입니다. 빈칸 앞에 위치한 「By the time + 주어 + 현재시제동사(finishes)」가 미래 시점을 나타내고 있고, 빈칸이 포함된 문장에 for an hour and a half와 같이 「for + 기간」 표현으로 기간을 나타내는 구문이 있으므로 1시간 30분 동안 계속 진행 중일 미래의 상태를 나타낼 미래완료진행형 동사가 필요하므로 (a) will have been listening이 정답입니다.

어휘 speech 연설 last 지속되다 far 너무 restless 가만히 있지 않는 audience 청중

18 당위성을 나타내는 동사원형

Linda will need more time to complete her thesis. She needs to do heavy revisions after one of the panelists advised that Linda _____ the focus of the discussion section.

(a) change
(b) changed
(c) is changing
(d) will change

린다는 논문을 완성하기 위해 더 많은 시간이 필요할 것이다. 논문 심사 위원 중 한 명이 토론 부분의 주안점을 변경해야 한다는 조언을 한 후 린다는 대대적인 수정을 해야 한다.

정답 (a)

해설 동사 change의 알맞은 형태를 고르는 문제입니다. 빈칸은 동사 advised의 목적어 역할을 하는 that절의 동사 자리인데, advise와 같이 주장/요구/명령/제안 등을 나타내는 동사의 목적어 역할을 하는 that절의 동사는 should없이 동사원형만 사용하므로 동사원형인 (a) change가 정답입니다

어휘 complete 완성하다 thesis 논문 heavy 대량(다량)의 revision 수정 panelist 패널리스트 advise 조언하다 focus 주안점, 초점 discussion 토론 section 부분

19 가정법 과거완료

Tech-Newton, a startup technology company, canceled its expansion after failing to reach sales targets. Had the company sold more products, it _____ enough money to fund the new factory.

(a) will make
(b) would make
(c) will have made
(d) would have made

스타트업 기술 회사인 테크뉴튼은 매출 목표를 달성하지 못한 후 회사의 확장을 취소했다. 이 회사가 더 많은 제품을 판매했다면 새 공장에 자금을 제공할 충분한 수익을 올렸을 것이다.

정답 (d)

해설 동사 make의 알맞은 형태를 고르는 문제입니다. Had the company sold는 가정법 과거완료를 구성하는 If the company had sold에서 If가 생략되고 주어와 had가 도치된 구조입니다. 따라서, If절의 동사가 「had p.p.」일 때 주절의 동사로 사용하는 「would/could/ might + have p.p.」의 형태가 빈칸에 쓰여야 알맞으므로 (d) would have made가 정답입니다.

어휘 startup 스타트업, 신생 기업 technology 기술 cancel 취소하다 expansion 확장 fail 실패하다 reach 달성하다 target 목표 product 제품 fund ~에 자금을 제공하다

20 준동사 – 동명사

A famous adage says that laughter is the best medicine. Psychologists have long agreed with this, as they regard _____ as an effective way to relieve anxiety and reduce feelings of depression.

(a) to laugh
(b) laughing
(c) to have laughed
(d) having laughed

유명한 격언에 따르면 웃음은 최고의 약이라고 한다. 심리학자들은 오랫동안 이에 동의해 왔는데, 그들은 웃음을 불안을 완화하고 우울감을 줄이는 효과적인 방법으로 여기기 때문이다.

정답 (b)

해설 동사 laugh의 알맞은 형태를 고르는 문제입니다. 빈칸은 타동사 regard의 목적어 자리이며, regard는 동명사를 목적어로 취하여 '~하는 것을 여기다'라는 의미를 나타냅니다. 따라서 동명사인 (b) laughing이 정답입니다.

어휘 famous 유명한 adage 격언 laughter 웃음 medicine 약 psychologist 심리학자 agree 동의하다 regard 여기다 laugh 웃다 effective 효과적인 way 방법 relieve 완화하다 anxiety 불안 reduce 줄이다 feeling 감정 depression 우울

21 준동사 – to부정사

Tom's cat, Chito, escaped last week and has still not returned. After putting up posters around the neighborhood and receiving no news, Tom has decided _____ a reward in the hope of bringing Chito home.

(a) having offered
(b) to have offered
(c) to offer
(d) offering

톰의 고양이 치토가 지난주에 탈출한 후 아직 돌아오지 않고 있다. 동네 곳곳에 포스터를 붙였지만 아무 소식도 받지 못하자 톰은 치토를 집으로 데려오길 바라는 마음으로 포상금을 제공하기로 결정했다.

정답 (c)

해설 동사 offer의 알맞은 형태를 고르는 문제입니다. 빈칸은 타동사 has decided의 목적어 자리이며, decide는 to부정사를 목적어로 취하여 '~하기로 결정하다'라는 의미를 나타냅니다. 따라서 to부정사인 (c) to offer가 정답입니다.

어휘 escape 탈출하다 still 아직 return 돌아오다 put up 붙이다, 게시하다 poster 전단지 neighborhood 동네 receive 받다 decide 결정하다 offer 제공하다 bring 데려오다

22 접속부사

Symbiosis refers to a biological interaction between two species that is usually of benefit to both. _____, clownfish deter predators from sea anemones and, in return, benefit from the shelter provided by the anemones.

(a) Otherwise
(b) By contrast
(c) Meanwhile
(d) For instance

공생은 보통 2개의 종이 양쪽 모두 혜택을 받는 생물학적 교류 관계를 지칭한다. 예를 들어, 흰동가리는 포식 동물들로 하여금 말미잘을 단념시키게 하며, 그 답례로 말미잘이 제공하는 주거지로부터 혜택을 받는다.

정답 (d)

해설 빈칸에 알맞은 접속부사를 고르는 문제이므로 앞뒤 문장들의 의미 관계를 확인해야 합니다. 빈칸 앞 문장은 공생이 무엇인지 정의를 나타내고 있으며, 빈칸 뒤의 문장은 흰동가리와 말미잘의 관계를 설명하고 있습니다. 문맥상 흰동가리와 말미잘은 공생 관계로 볼 수 있으므로, 공생 관계의 예시를 나타낸 것임을 알 수 있습니다. 따라서 선택지 중에서 '예를 들어'라는 의미로 예시를 나타낼 때 사용되는 접속부사 (d) For instance가 정답입니다.

어휘 symbiosis 공생 refer to ~을 지칭하다, ~을 나타내다 biological 생물학적인 interaction 교류 species 종 benefit 혜택, 이익 clownfish 흰동가리 deter 단념시키다, 그만두게 하다 predator 포식자, 포식 동물 sea anemone 말미잘 in return 대신에, 답례로 otherwise 그렇지 않으면 by contrast 대조적으로 meanwhile 그 동안에, 한편 for instance 예를 들어

Although Vanessa wants to practice law, she is worried that she might have flunked the bar exam. If she were to receive a failing grade, she _____ making alternative career plans.

(a) would have begun
(b) will have begun
(c) would begin
(d) will begin

바네사는 변호사 일을 하고 싶지만, 변호사 시험에서 낙제했을까 봐 걱정하고 있다. 만약 그녀가 낙제 점수를 받게 된다면, 그녀는 다른 진로 계획을 세우기 시작할 것이다.

정답 (c)

해설 동사 begin의 알맞은 형태를 고르는 문제입니다. if절의 동사가 가정법 과거를 나타내는 과거시제(were)일 때, 주절의 동사는 「would/could/might + 동사원형」과 같은 형태가 되어야 알맞으므로 (c) would begin이 정답입니다.

어휘 although 비록 ~이지만 practice law 변호사 일을 하다 flunk 낙제하다 bar exam 변호사 시험 receive 받다 failing 낙제 grade 점수 alternative 대안적인

Andrea is an avid horticulturalist. Today, she will host a party for her gardening club. She _____ her azaleas and boxwoods right now so she can show them off to her guests.

(a) is pruning
(b) has been pruning
(c) would prune
(d) will have pruned

안드레아는 열렬한 원예가이다. 오늘 그녀는 자신의 원예 동호회를 위해 파티를 열 것이다. 그녀는 손님들에게 자랑하기 위해 지금 자신의 진달래와 회양목을 가지치기를 하고 있다.

정답 (a)

해설 동사 prune의 알맞은 형태를 고르는 문제입니다. 빈칸 앞에 위치한 right now가 '바로 지금'이라는 의미를 나타내어 현재 일시적으로 진행되는 일을 뜻하는 현재진행시제 동사와 어울려 쓰이므로 (a) is pruning이 정답입니다.

어휘 avid 열렬한, 열심인 horticulturalist 원예가 host 열다 gardening 원예 prune 가지치기하다 azalea 진달래 boxwood 회양목 right now 지금

When Thea was young, her father often taught her simple household repairs. For example, she once learned _____ a clogged sink, which is very useful now that she lives alone.

(a) to have fixed
(b) to fix
(c) fixing
(d) having fixed

테아가 어렸을 때, 그녀의 아버지는 종종 그녀에게 간단한 집 수리를 가르쳐주곤 했다. 예를 들어, 그녀는 막힌 싱크대를 고치는 것을 배운 적이 있는데, 지금 혼자 살고 있는 그녀에게 매우 유용하다.

정답 (b)

해설 동사 fix의 알맞은 형태를 고르는 문제입니다. 빈칸은 타동사 learned의 목적어 자리이며, learn은 to부정사를 목적어로 취하여 '~하는 것을 배우다'라는 의미를 나타냅니다. 따라서 to부정사인 (b) to fix가 정답입니다.

어휘 household 집안 repair 수리 example 예시 once 한때 learn 배우다 fix 고치다 clogged 막힌 sink 싱크대

The film critic gave a big-budget movie a terrible review for its mediocre story. He wrote that if the acting had been as bad as the writing, he probably _____ the theater before the movie ended.

(a) would have left
(b) will have left
(c) would leave
(d) will leave

그 영화 평론가는 대규모 예산의 영화에 대해 그저 그런 스토리로 혹평을 남겼다. 그는 만약 연기가 각본만큼 나빴다면 아마 영화가 끝나기 전에 극장을 나갔을 것이라고 썼다.

정답 (a)

해설 동사 leave의 알맞은 형태를 고르는 문제입니다. If절의 동사가 had been과 같이 가정법 과거완료를 나타내는 「had p.p.」일 때, 주절의 동사는 「would/could/might + have p.p.」와 같은 형태가 되어야 알맞으므로 (a) would have left가 정답입니다.

어휘 critic 평론가 big-budget 대규모 예산 terrible 끔찍한 mediocre 그저 그런 acting 연기 as + 형용사 + as ~만큼 (형용사)한 theater 극장

PART 1

F: Paul, can we talk about our trip to Hapsville?

M: Sure, Maria. I'm excited about the trip. We've been talking about visiting Hapsville since we first got married!

F: 27 It'll be a long overdue city break, that's for sure.

M: What exactly do you want to discuss?

F: Well, I'm wondering if you'd want to do a city tour while we're there.

M: Actually, that hadn't crossed my mind. Exploring the city on a tour could be cool, given all the history there.

F: There are a few group tours available. One goes all day and covers the oldest buildings in the city. Maybe that one?

M: I like the idea of sightseeing. The only problem with a tour is that we won't have much say in where we go, and we might end up rushing from one place to another.

F: Good point. 28 Let's just wander the city on our own. That way, we can really get the most out of our trip!

M: Great idea. You know, 29 there's one place I'm eager to check out—the Hapsville Museum. A colleague of mine went there last summer and couldn't stop talking about how amazing it was!

여: 폴, 우리 합스빌 여행에 대해 얘기 좀 할 수 있을까?

남: 물론이지, 마리아. 난 여행이 정말 기대돼. 우리가 처음 결혼했을 때부터 합스빌에 가자고 얘기해왔잖아!

여: 한참 늦은 도심으로 떠나는 여행이 될 거라는 건 확실해.

남: 정확히 무엇을 논의하고 싶어?

여: 글쎄, 우리가 그곳에 있는 동안 당신이 시내 투어를 하고 싶지 않을까 해서 말이야.

남: 사실, 그런 생각은 해본 적이 없어. 투어를 하면서 도시를 둘러보는 것도 멋진 경험이 될 것 같아. 그곳의 모든 역사를 생각해보면 말야.

여: 이용 가능한 단체 투어가 몇몇 있어. 하루 종일 도시에서 가장 오래된 건물들을 둘러보는 투어도 있어. 그런 건 어때?

남: 나는 관광하는 게 좋아. 투어의 유일한 문제점은 우리가 어디로 갈지 결정할 수 없고 이곳에서 저곳으로 서둘러 이동만 하게 될 수도 있다는 거야.

여: 좋은 지적이야. 그냥 우리끼리 도시를 돌아다니자. 그렇게 하면 여행을 최대한 즐길 수 있을 거야!

남: 좋은 생각이야. 내가 정말 가보고 싶은 곳이 있는데 바로 합스빌 박물관이야. 지난 여름에 내 동료 중 한 명이 그곳에 갔는데 얼마나 대단한 곳인지 계속 이야기하더라고!

F: What's so special about it?

M: **29** They have a collection of complete dinosaur skeletons. I've always dreamed of seeing a real *T-rex* skeleton up close!

F: Dinosaurs, of course! I should've seen that coming.

M: I know. I'm a bit of a nerd. If the museum doesn't interest you, we don't have to go.

F: Actually, Paul, I'm totally up for it. There'll be plenty to see at the museum.

M: What I'm most looking forward to is the city's restaurants. Did you know that Hapsville was recently ranked among the top ten food destinations in the country?

F: Right. **30** We'd have lots of choices when it comes to dining out.

M: Yeah. But having too many options could be a problem.

F: **30** We should plan ahead. I suggest that we research restaurants with great reviews before we go. Then we can pick where we want to eat each day.

M: Smart thinking, Maria!

F: Hmm, it sounds like we'll be doing a lot of moving around. Do you think we'll be able to walk everywhere?

M: **31** Hapsville has good public transportation. There's a subway system for getting around quickly, and they also have buses for shorter distances.

여: 거기의 어떤 점이 특별한 거야?

남: 그곳은 공룡의 전체 골격 표본을 소장하고 있어. 난 진짜 티라노사우르스 골격을 가까이서 보는 게 꿈이었어!

여: 공룡이라, 당연하겠지! 그럴 줄 알았어야 했어.

남: 알아. 내가 좀 괴짜지. 박물관이 너의 흥미를 끌지 않는다면, 우리는 가지 않아도 돼.

여: 사실, 폴, 난 정말 가고 싶어. 박물관에는 볼거리가 많을 거야.

남: 내가 가장 기대하는 것은 그 도시의 식당들이야. 합스빌이 최근 미국 10대 음식 여행지로 선정되었다는 사실을 알고 있었어?

여: 맞아. 외식을 할 때 선택의 폭이 넓겠네.

남: 응. 하지만 선택지가 너무 많으면 문제가 될 수 있어.

여: 우린 미리 계획을 세워야 해. 가기 전에 리뷰가 좋은 레스토랑을 조사하는 게 좋을 것 같아. 그러면 매일 먹고 싶은 곳을 고를 수 있을 거야.

남: 좋은 생각이야, 마리아!

여: 흠, 이동을 많이 해야 할 것 같네. 우리가 모든 곳으로 걸어서 갈 수 있을 것 같아?

남: 합스빌은 대중교통이 잘 되어 있어. 빠르게 이동할 수 있는 지하철이 있고, 짧은 거리를 이동할 수 있는 버스도 있어.

F: ☒ Sounds convenient. I'll look online and see if we can get a transit card that covers all types of transportation.

M: That would definitely simplify things. Oh! I just realized I don't have my camera!

F: What happened to it?

M: ☒ I lent it to my brother, and he was supposed to return it before we left.

F: He'd better get it back to you soon. I want to take a bunch of photos there, and my phone's camera just isn't good enough.

M: ☒ Tell you what, I'll head over to his place right now.

F: All right, Paul. While you're gone, I'll do some research on those transit cards.

M: Sounds good, Maria. And ☒ let's not worry about cooking tonight. I'll grab some takeout on my way back.

F: That works for me!

여: 편리할 것 같네. 모든 종류의 교통수단을 이용할 수 있는 교통카드를 구할 수 있는지 온라인에서 알아볼게.

남: 그러면 확실히 일이 더 간단해지겠네. 아! 방금 나에게 카메라가 없다는 걸 깨달았어!

여: 어떻게 된 거야?

남: 내가 동생에게 빌려줬는데, 그는 우리가 떠나기 전에 그걸 돌려주기로 했어.

여: 곧 돌려주는 게 좋을거야. 거기서 사진을 많이 찍고 싶은데 내 휴대폰 카메라로는 충분하지 않아.

남: 그럼 내가 지금 바로 그의 집으로 가볼게.

여: 알았어, 폴. 네가 가는 동안 나는 교통카드에 대해 검색을 좀 해볼게.

남: 좋아, 마리아. 그리고 오늘 저녁 요리는 걱정하지 말자. 내가 돌아가는 길에 포장 음식을 좀 사올게.

여: 나도 좋아!

어휘 overdue 기한이 지난, 연체된 city break 도심을 떠나는 여행 cross (one's) mind 떠오르다, 스치다 sightseeing 관광, 구경 wander 돌아다니다, 방황하다 eager to 동사원형: 간절히 ~하고 싶어하는, 열망하는 up for it ~할 준비가 된, 하고 싶은 rank among ~에 속하다, ~의 순위에 오르다 dining out 외식 plan ahead 미리 계획하다, 사전에 준비하다 public transportation 대중교통, 공공교통수단 transit card 교통카드, 대중교통카드 takeout 포장 음식, 테이크아웃 convenient 편리한, 이용하기 쉬운 simplify 단순화하다, 간소화하다 colleague 동료, 직장 동료 collection 수집품, 모음 skeleton 해골, 골격 up close 가까이서, 직접 a bit of 약간 ~한, 조금 ~한 given ~을 고려하면, ~인 점에서 available 이용 가능한, 구할 수 있는 cover 다루다, 포함하다 rush 서두르다, 재촉하다 get the most out of 최대한 활용하다, 최대의 가치를 얻다 check out 확인하다, 방문하다 special 특별한, 독특한 recently 최근에, 얼마 전에 research 조사하다, 연구하다 suggest 제안하다, 권하다 grab (음식을) 사다, 재빨리 챙기다 head over 가다, 이동하다 better get 서둘러 ~하다, 빨리 ~하는 것이 좋다 looking forward to ~을 기대하다, 고대하다 smart thinking 똑똑한 생각, 현명한 아이디어 recently ranked 최근에 순위에 오른, 최근 평가된 plenty 많은, 충분한 option 선택, 옵션 cover all types of 모든 종류의 ~을 포함하다, 모든 유형의 ~을 아우르다

What are Paul and Maria mainly talking about?

(a) their dream honeymoon
(b) their most recent trip
(c) their upcoming vacation
(d) their favorite travel spot

폴과 마리아는 주로 무엇에 대해 이야기하고 있는가?

(a) 그들이 꿈꾸는 신혼여행
(b) 가장 최근에 다녀온 여행
(c) 다가오는 휴가
(d) 가장 좋아하는 여행지

정답 (c)

해설 대화 초반부에 마리아가 폴에게 합스빌로 가는 여행에 대해 이야기를 해보자고 제안하고, 폴이 결혼했을 때 이후로 합스빌에 방문하는 것에 대해 이야기를 해왔다고 언급하였습니다. 그 뒤에 마리아가 오랫동안 미뤄온 휴가가 될 것(It'll be a long overdue city break)이라고 언급한 것에서 이들이 이야기를 나누고 있는 합스빌 여행은 다가오는 휴가에 관한 것임을 알 수 있습니다. 따라서 정답은 (c)입니다.

어휘 mainly 주로, 대부분 upcoming 다가오는, 곧 있을 vacation 휴가, 여행 favorite 가장 좋아하는, 선호하는 spot 장소, 지점

According to the conversation, how can Paul and Maria get the most out of their trip?

(a) by making their own itinerary
(b) by participating in a group tour
(c) by traveling with their friends
(d) by hiring a private tour guide

대화에 따르면, 폴과 마리아는 어떻게 여행을 최대한 활용할 수 있는가?

(a) 자신들만의 여정을 만듦으로써
(b) 그룹 투어에 참여함으로써
(c) 친구들과 함께 여행함으로써
(d) 개인 여행 가이드를 고용함으로써

정답 (a)

해설 마리아가 폴에게 시티 투어를 원하는지 물어보았으나 폴은 관광하는 것이 좋다고 말한 뒤, 투어의 문제점을 언급하였습니다. 그러자 마리아가 그럼 스스로 도시를 돌아다니자고(Let's just wander the city on our own) 말하는 것을 통해 폴과 마리아는 자신들만의 여정대로 여행할 것임을 알 수 있습니다. 따라서 정답은 (a)입니다.

어휘 according to ~에 따르면, ~에 의하면 conversation 대화, 대담 get the most out of 최대한 활용하다, 최대의 가치를 얻다 itinerary 여행 일정, 계획 participate in ~에 참여하다, 참가하다 private 개인의, 사적인

> **패러프레이징**
>
> just wander the city on our own → making their own itinerary

Why does Paul want to check out the museum?

(a) It has life-like dinosaur models.
(b) It has the oldest dinosaur display.
(c) It has whole dinosaur skeletons.
(d) It has the biggest dinosaur display.

폴이 박물관을 살펴 보고 싶어하는
이유는 무엇인가?

(a) 실물과 같은 공룡 모형이 있다.
(b) 가장 오래된 공룡 전시물이 있
다.
(c) 공룡의 전체 골격이 전시되어 있
다.
(d) 가장 큰 공룡 전시물이 있다.

정답 (c)

해설 질문의 키워드인 the museum은 폴이 정말로 가고 싶은 곳이 한 군데 있는데 바로 합스빌 박물관이라고(there's one
place I'm eager to check out—the Hapsville Museum) 말하는 부분에서 언급됩니다. 마리아가 박물관에 관해 무엇이
특별한지 묻자 폴은 박물관이 공룡의 전체 골격 표본을 소장하고 있다고(They have a collection of complete dinosaur
skeletons) 언급하는 것을 통해 폴이 박물관으로 가고 싶어하는 이유를 알 수 있습니다. 따라서 정답은 (c)입니다.

어휘 **check out** 살펴보다, 확인하다 **life-like** 실물 같은, 생생한 **display** 전시, 진열 **skeleton** 골격, 해골 **whole** 전체의, 완전한
model 모형, 모델

패러프레이징

a collection of complete dinosaur skeletons → whole dinosaur skeletons

❌ 오답 피하기

폴의 말에 따르면 합스빌 박물관에는 공룡의 전체 골격 표본이 있다고 언급하였는데, 이는 공룡의 뼈를 전시한 것을 의미하므로
실물과 같은 모형 공룡과는 다릅니다. 따라서 (a)는 오답입니다.

What might be a challenge for Paul and Maria when it comes to
dining out in Hapsville?

(a) staying within their budget
(b) getting a reservation
(c) finding decent restaurants
(d) deciding where to eat

폴과 마리아가 합스빌에서 외식을
할 때 가장 어려운 점은 무엇인가?

(a) 예산 범위 내에서 식사하기
(b) 예약하기
(c) 괜찮은 레스토랑 찾기
(d) 식사 장소 결정하기

정답 (d)

해설 질문의 키워드인 dining out in Hapsville은 폴이 가장 기대하는 것이 그 도시의 식당들이라고 하자 마리아는 외식할 때 선택할 수 있는 식당이 너무 많다고(We'd have lots of choices when it comes to dining out) 말하는 부분에서 언급됩니다. 그 후에 마리아가 미리 계획을 세우고 후기(reviews)가 좋은 식당을 조사해서 매일 원하는 곳을 고르자고(We should plan ahead. I suggest that we research restaurants with great reviews before we go. Then we can pick where we want to eat each day)라고 말하는 것을 통해 폴과 마리아가 외식하기 전에 식사할 곳을 미리 정할 것임을 알 수 있습니다. 따라서 정답은 (d)입니다.

어휘 challenge 과제, 어려움 when it comes to ~에 관해서라면, ~에 대해 말하자면 dining out 외식, 밖에서 식사하기 budget 예산, 비용 reservation 예약 decent 괜찮은, 품질 좋은 decide 결정하다, 선택하다

> 패러프레이징
>
> pick where we want to eat → deciding where to eat

---

31 세부 정보

How will Paul and Maria get around the city?

(a) by taking public transportation
(b) by walking around
(c) by using ride-share services
(d) by renting a car

폴과 마리아는 어떻게 도시를 돌아 다닐 것인가?

(a) 대중 교통을 이용함으로써
(b) 걸어 다님으로써
(c) 차량 공유 서비스를 이용함으로써
(d) 자동차를 대여함으로써

정답 (a)

해설 질문의 키워드인 get around the city는 마리아가 이동을 많이 해야 할 것 같다고(it sounds like we'll be doing a lot of moving around) 말하는 부분에서 언급됩니다. 이에 폴은 합스빌에는 대중교통이 잘 되어 있다고 말하며 지하철과 버스를 언급합니다(Hapsville has good public transportation. There's a subway system for getting around quickly, and they also have buses for shorter distances). 이에 마리아가 편리할 것 같다고 대답하는 것을 통해 이 둘은 대중 교통을 이용할 것임을 알 수 있습니다. 따라서 정답은 (a)입니다.

어휘 get around 돌아다니다, 이동하다 public transportation 대중교통 walking around 돌아다니다, 걷다 ride-share services 차량 공유 서비스 rent 빌리다, 임대하다

Why is Paul going to his brother's place?

(a) to try to borrow a camera
(b) to get his camera back
(c) to ask for advice on cameras
(d) to have his camera fixed

폴은 왜 동생의 집으로 가는가?

(a) 카메라를 빌리러 가기 위해
(b) 카메라를 되찾기 위해
(c) 카메라에 대한 조언을 구하기 위해
(d) 카메라를 고치기 위해

정답 (b)

해설 폴은 자신의 카메라를 동생에게 빌려주었고, 자신이 떠나기 전에 돌려받기로 했다고(I lent it to my brother, and he was supposed to return it before we left) 언급하였습니다. 그 후에 폴은 지금 당장 동생의 집으로 가겠다고(Tell you what, I'll head over to his place right now) 말하는 것을 통해 빌려 주었던 카메라를 되찾으러 가는 것임을 알 수 있습니다. 따라서 정답은 (b)입니다.

어휘 borrow 빌리다 get back 돌려받다, 되돌려받다 advice 조언, 충고 fix 고치다, 수리하다

What will Paul and Maria probably do after Paul gets back?

(a) go out for dinner
(b) cook for the next day
(c) get some dessert
(d) have a meal at home

폴이 돌아온 후에 폴과 마리아는 무엇을 할 것 같은가?

(a) 저녁을 먹으러 나간다.
(b) 다음 날을 위해 요리를 한다.
(c) 디저트를 먹는다.
(d) 집에서 식사를 한다.

정답 (d)

해설 폴이 자신의 동생의 집으로 갈 것이라고 말하자 마리아는 교통카드에 대해 조사를 해보겠다고 말합니다. 그 후에 폴이 오늘 밤 요리하는 것은 걱정하지 말라며 돌아오는 길에 포장 음식을 사오겠다고(let's not worry about cooking tonight. I'll grab some takeout on my way back) 말하는 것을 통해 폴이 돌아오면 폴과 마리아는 집에서 식사를 할 것임을 알 수 있습니다. 따라서 정답은 (d)입니다.

어휘 probably 아마, 아마도 go out for 외출하여 ~을 하다 cook 요리하다 dessert 후식, 디저트 have a meal 식사를 하다

Hello, ladies and gentlemen. **34** I am here to announce the much-anticipated Festival of Stars—an extraordinary event dedicated to astronomy and the wonders of our night sky, to be held at the local convention center. Tickets go on sale today, so let me fill you in on the main features of the festival.

A festival dedicated to astronomy would be nothing without an opportunity to explore the starry world above. **35** The plaza outside the convention center will have five observatory booths, each containing a state-of-the-art telescope for viewing. These will be supervised by professional astronomers who will guide you through the night sky, revealing distant planets and star clusters that will leave you amazed. Of course, attendees are also welcome to bring their own telescopes and stargazing equipment, which can be set up in the plaza.

To add to the festival's opportunities for education, we have gathered respected astronomers and scientists to deliver lectures. Speakers are joining us from around the world to explain the mysteries of the cosmos and share their discoveries. Among the speakers will be retired astronaut Carl Jackson, who holds the record for the longest-ever spacewalk. **36** Carl will speak about his career and show his personal collection of photos from space. His talk promises to be spectacular!

There will also be interactive workshops around the convention hall providing guests with a variety of space-related, hands-on activities, such as building mini rockets and crafting models of the solar system. **37** Our younger attendees can also join the "Space Camp" workshop, where, among other things, they can design their own alien character and even get it printed on a T-shirt. Get ready to take home knowledge *and* special souvenirs.

안녕하세요, 신사 숙녀 여러분. 저는 지역 컨벤션 센터에서 개최될 천문학과 밤하늘의 경이로움을 주제로 한 특별 행사인 '별의 축제'를 소개해 드리고자 이 자리에 섰습니다. 오늘부터 티켓이 판매되기 시작하니 축제의 주요 특징에 대해 자세히 알려드리겠습니다.

천문학을 주제로 한 축제는 하늘의 별을 탐험할 수 있는 기회가 없다면 아무런 의미가 없을 것입니다. 컨벤션 센터 외부 광장에는 5개의 천문대 부스가 설치되며, 각 부스에는 최신식 망원경이 설치될 것입니다. 전문 천문학자가 밤하늘을 안내하며 멀리 떨어진 행성과 성단 등 놀라움을 자아낼 만한 별들을 보여줄 것입니다. 물론, 참가자들은 또한 개인 망원경과 별 관측 장비를 가져와 광장에 설치할 수 있습니다.

축제의 교육 기회에 덧붙여, 저명한 천문학자 및 과학자들을 초청하여 강연을 진행합니다. 전 세계에서 온 연사들이 우주의 신비를 설명하고 자신의 발견을 공유하기 위해 참여합니다. 연사 중에는 최장 우주유영 기록을 보유하고 있는 은퇴한 우주비행사 칼 잭슨 씨가 참여합니다. 칼 씨는 자신의 경력에 대해 이야기하고 우주에서 찍은 개인 사진 컬렉션을 보여줄 예정입니다. 그의 강연은 장관을 이룰 것으로 보입니다!

또한 컨벤션 홀 주변에서는 미니 로켓 만들기, 태양계 모형 만들기 등 우주와 관련된 다양한 체험 활동을 제공하는 인터랙티브 워크숍이 열릴 예정입니다. 어린이 참가자들은 또한 "스페이스 캠프" 워크숍에 참여할 수 있으며, 그 중에서도 자신만의 외계인 캐릭터를 디자인하고 티셔츠에 프린트할 수 있습니다. 지식과 특별한 기념품을 집으로 가져갈 준비를 하세요.

You won't want to miss the Stellar Dome planetarium shows, which are a highlight of the festival. In the Stellar Dome, you can recline in your seat and gaze up at the curved ceiling, which becomes a canvas for a projection of the night sky. But **38** these planetarium shows are more than just visuals. This year's shows are special because the world-famous Starplayer Orchestra has composed some innovative new accompaniment to the visual effects, and they'll be here performing live. These free shows will be held each night of the festival.

Finally, let me tell you about the prize drawing. The Festival of Stars presents an opportunity for one lucky guest to win the trip of a lifetime to Italy, the birthplace of Galileo, who was the father of astronomy and modern science. For a chance to win the trip, **39** attendees need to purchase a ticket for the raffle upon entry to the festival. The winner will be announced on the last day of the event.

Whether you're an experienced astronomer or a casual stargazer, the Festival of Stars promises to be unforgettable. Mark your calendars, and join us there!

축제의 하이라이트인 스텔라 돔 천체투영관 공연도 놓치고 싶지 않으실 거예요. 스텔라 돔에서는 좌석에 뒤로 기대어 곡선형 천장을 올려다볼 수 있는데, 이 천장은 밤하늘을 투영하는 캔버스가 됩니다. 하지만 이 천체투영관 공연은 단순한 시각적 볼거리 그 이상입니다. 올해의 공연은 세계적으로 유명한 스타플레이어 오케스트라가 시각 효과에 맞춰 혁신적인 새 반주를 작곡하고 라이브로 공연하기 때문에 더욱 특별합니다. 이 무료 공연은 축제 기간 동안 매일 밤 열립니다.

마지막으로 경품 추첨에 대해 말씀드리겠습니다. '별의 축제'는 천문학과 현대 과학의 아버지인 갈릴레오의 출생지인 이탈리아로 일생일대의 여행을 떠날 수 있는 행운의 기회를 한 분께 선사합니다. 여행에 당첨될 기회를 잡으려면 참가자들은 축제 입장 시 추첨 티켓을 구매해야 합니다. 당첨자는 행사 마지막 날에 발표됩니다.

숙련된 천문학자이든 별을 처음 보는 사람이든, '별의 축제'는 잊지 못할 추억을 약속드립니다. 달력에 표시해두고 축제에 참여해 보세요!

어휘 announce 발표하다, 알리다 much-anticipated 많이 기대된 extraordinary 비범한, 특별한 dedicated to ~에 헌신된, ~에 전념하는 wonder 경이, 놀라움 convention center 컨벤션 센터, 대회장 fill + 목적어 + in: (목적어)에게 정보를 제공하다, 알려주다 plaza 광장, 광장형 공간 observatory 천문대 state-of-the-art 최신식의, 최첨단의 telescope 망원경 supervise 감독하다, 지휘하다 guide + 목적어 + through: (목적어)를 안내하다, 인도하다 reveal 드러내다, 밝히다 attendee 참석자 stargazing 별을 관찰하는 것 equipment 장비, 기기 lecture 강의, 강연 mystery 신비, 불가사의 cosmos 우주 discovery 발견 astronaut 우주비행사 career 경력, 직업 spectacular 장관의, 멋진 interactive 상호작용하는 hands-on 실습의, 직접 체험하는 workshop 워크숍, 실습반 solar system 태양계 attendee 참석자 among other things 그 중에서도 planetarium 천체투영관 highlight 하이라이트, 가장 중요한 부분 recline 기대다, 눕다 canvas 캔버스, 화면 accompaniment 반주, 동반 perform 공연하다, 연주하다 raffle 추첨, 복권 birthplace 출생 unforgettable 잊을 수 없는, 기억에 남는 mark one's calendar 일정을 기록하다

34 주제/목적

What is the talk mainly about?	담화는 주로 무엇에 관한 것인가?
(a) an astronomy club gathering	(a) 천문학 클럽 모임
(b) an astronomy course	(b) 천문학 강좌
(c) a summer astronomy camp	(c) 여름 천문학 캠프
(d) an astronomy festival	(d) 천문학 축제

정답 (d)

해설 대화 초반부에 화자가 지역 컨벤션 센터에서 개최될 천문학과 밤하늘의 경이로움을 주제로 한 특별한 행사인 '별의 축제'를 소개해 드리고자 이 자리에 섰다고(I am here to announce the much-anticipated Festival of Stars—an extraordinary event dedicated to astronomy and the wonders of our night sky, to be held at the local convention center) 알리고 있으며, 또한 마지막에는 축제의 주요 특징에 대해 자세히 알려주겠다고(let me fill you in on the main features of the festival) 말하는 것을 통해 담화의 주제가 천문학 축제임을 알 수 있습니다. 따라서 정답은 (d)입니다.

어휘 gathering 모임, 집합 course 과정, 수업 camp 캠프, 야영 festival 축제, 행사

✖ 오답 피하기

담화 중반에 "Space Camp" workshop이 언급되지만, 이는 '별의 축제'(Festival of Stars)를 구성하는 하나의 요소에 해당하며, 담화에 축제가 열리는 계절이 여름인지 언급되지 않았으므로 (c)는 오답입니다.

35 세부 정보

How will visitors to the plaza learn about the night sky?	광장을 방문하는 사람들은 밤하늘에 대해 어떻게 배울 수 있는가?
(a) by viewing an interactive exhibit	(a) 인터랙티브 전시물을 관람함으로써
(b) by reading a booklet	(b) 책자를 읽음으로써
(c) by receiving expert instruction	(c) 전문가의 지도를 받음으로써
(d) by watching a video	(d) 영상을 시청함으로써

정답 (c)

해설 질문의 키워드 중 하나인 the plaza는 컨벤션 센터 외부 광장에는 최신식 망원경이 있는 5개의 천문대 부스가 있을 것이라고(The plaza outside the convention center will have five observatory booths, each containing a state-of-the-art telescope for viewing) 말하는 부분에서 언급됩니다. 그 뒤에 또다른 질문의 키워드인 the night sky에 대해 전문 천문학자가 밤하늘을 안내할 것이라고(These will be supervised by professional astronomers who will guide you through the night sky) 말하는 부분에서 언급됩니다. 이를 통해 밤하늘은 전문 천문학자의 도움으로 안내 받을 것임을 알 수 있으므로 정답은 (c)입니다.

36 세부 정보

What will astronaut Carl Jackson do during the talk?

(a) lecture on space technology
(b) share his past experiences
(c) debate with other scientists
(d) speak about his future plans

우주비행사 칼 잭슨 씨는 강연 중에 무엇을 할 것인가?

(a) 우주 기술에 대한 강연을 한다
(b) 자신의 과거 경험을 공유한다
(c) 다른 과학자들과 토론한다
(d) 자신의 미래 계획에 대해 말한다

정답 (b)

해설 화자가 은퇴한 우주 비행사 칼 잭슨 씨가 강연을 할 것임을 알리면서 칼 씨가 자신의 경력에 대해 이야기하고 우주에서 찍은 개인 사진 컬렉션을 보여줄 예정이라고(Carl will speak about his career and show his personal collection of photos from space) 설명합니다. 이는 칼 씨가 자신의 과거에 대한 이야기를 관객들에게 들려줄 것이라는 것을 의미하므로 정답은 (b)입니다.

어휘 **past experiences** 과거의 경험들 **debate** 토론하다, 논쟁하다 **future plan** 미래 계획

How can younger attendees get their own customized T-shirt?

(a) by ordering on the website
(b) by visiting the souvenir shop
(c) by participating in a workshop
(d) by signing up for a contest

어린 참가자는 어떻게 맞춤 티셔츠를 받을 수 있는가?

(a) 웹사이트에서 주문함으로써
(b) 기념품 가게를 방문함으로써
(c) 워크숍에 참여함으로써
(d) 콘테스트에 참가 신청함으로써

정답 (c)

해설 질문의 키워드인 younger attendees와 T-shirt는 화자가 어린이 참가자들이 참여할 수 있는 "스페이스 캠프" 워크숍에 대해 설명하는 중에 언급됩니다. 화자는 그 워크숍에서 자신만의 외계인 캐릭터를 디자인하고 티셔츠에 프린트할 수 있다고 (Our younger attendees can also join the "Space Camp" workshop, where, among other things, they can design their own alien character and even get it printed on a T-shirt) 설명하는데, 이를 통해 맞춤 티셔츠를 얻는 방법이 워크숍을 참석하는 것임을 알 수 있습니다. 따라서 정답은 (c)입니다.

어휘 customized 맞춤형의, 개인화된 souvenir 기념품 participate in 참여하다 contest 대회, 경연

패러프레이징

join the "Space Camp" workshop → participating in a workshop

Why are this year's planetarium shows special?

(a) They include original music.
(b) They feature innovative visual effects.
(c) They include live narration.
(d) They feature a new sound system.

올해의 천체투영관 공연이 특별한 이유는 무엇인가?

(a) 오리지널 음악이 포함되어 있다.
(b) 혁신적인 시각 효과를 제공한다.
(c) 라이브 내레이션이 포함되어 있다.
(d) 새로운 음향 시스템을 사용한다.

정답 (a)

해설 화자가 스텔라 돔 천체투영관 공연(Stellar Dome planetarium show)에 대해 설명하면서 올해의 공연이 특별한 이유로 세계적으로 유명한 스타플레이어 오케스트라가 시각 효과에 맞춰 혁신적인 새 반주를 작곡하고 라이브로 공연할 것이기 때문이라고(these planetarium shows are more than just visuals. This year's shows are special because the world-famous Starplayer Orchestra has composed some innovative new accompaniment to the visual effects, and they'll be here performing live) 설명하는 부분에서 올해 공연에는 공연에 맞춰진 오리지널 음악이 추가될 것임을 알 수 있습니다. 따라서 정답은 (a)입니다.

어휘 original 원본의, 독창적인 music 음악 innovative 혁신적인, 창의적인 visual effects 시각 효과

the world-famous Starplayer Orchestra has composed some innovative new accompaniment to the visual effects → include original music

오케스트라가 시각 효과에 맞춰 음악을 작곡했으며 그것을 라이브로 연주할 것이라는 것은 공연에 맞춰진 오리지널 음악이 추가된 것을 의미하는 것이기 때문에 공연 음향의 효과나 제어를 담당하는 음향 시스템과는 거리가 먼 개념입니다. 따라서 (d)는 오답입니다.

39 세부 정보

What must attendees do to enter the prize drawing?	경품 추첨에 응모하려면 참가자가 무엇을 해야 하는가?
(a) join a mailing list	(a) 메일링 리스트에 가입한다
(b) buy a raffle ticket at the event	(b) 이벤트에서 추첨권을 구매한다
(c) fill out an online form	(c) 온라인 양식을 작성한다
(d) donate money to a charity	(d) 자선 단체에 기부한다

정답 (b)

해설 질문의 키워드인 the prize drawing은 담화의 마지막 부분에서 언급됩니다. 화자는 경품 추첨(the prize drawing)에 대해 설명하면서, 참가자들은 축제 입장 시 추첨 티켓을 구매해야 한다고(attendees need to purchase a ticket for the raffle upon entry to the festival) 설명하는 부분을 통해 참가자들이 티켓 구매를 해야 한다는 것을 알 수 있습니다. 따라서 정답은 (b)입니다.

어휘 raffle ticket 추첨권, 복권 mailing list 이메일 목록 form 양식 donate 기부하다, 기증하다 charity 자선, 기부

F: Are you cold, James?	여: 추워, 제임스?
M: I'm good, Sarah. You can turn on the heater if you're chilly.	남: 난 괜찮아, 사라. 추우면 히터 켜도 돼.
F: Okay. Have you looked outside? It's already started snowing.	여: 알았어. 밖은 봤어? 벌써 눈이 내리기 시작했어.
M: Yep. **40** I'll need to clean the snow off the car tomorrow morning.	남: 응. 내일 아침에 차에 쌓인 눈을 치워야겠어.
F: Snow sure can be a hassle, but it helps me get into the holiday spirit.	여: 눈이 오면 귀찮긴 하지만 연휴 분위기를 만끽하는 데는 도움이 되지.
M: Now that you mention the holidays, Christmas is only a month away, and we still haven't decided whether to spend the holiday with your parents or take a short vacation to Silverview, just the two of us.	남: 연휴 얘기가 나왔으니 말인데, 크리스마스가 한 달밖에 안 남았는데 부모님과 함께 보낼지 아니면 우리 둘이서 실버뷰로 짧은 휴가를 갈지 아직 결정하지 못했어.
F: Let's talk it over.	여: 우리 논의 해보자.
M: Sure. First, let's go over the advantages of staying with your parents.	남: 응. 먼저, 부모님과 함께 지낼 때의 장점부터 살펴보자.
F: The main benefit is that my sister and her family will be there. It would be wonderful to celebrate Christmas with our little niece and nephew.	여: 가장 큰 장점은 언니와 언니의 가족이 함께 지낼 것이라는 점이야. 우리 꼬마 조카들과 함께 크리스마스를 기념하면 정말 좋을 것 같아.
M: I agree. **41** What I'd most look forward to is watching the kids take their new toys out of the boxes. Seeing the joy on their faces as they gather around the Christmas tree and unwrap their presents is priceless.	남: 나도 같은 생각이야. 내가 가장 기대하는 것은 아이들이 상자에서 새 장난감을 꺼내는 모습을 보는 거야. 크리스마스 트리 주위에 모여서 선물 포장을 풀 때 아이들의 얼굴에서 기쁨을 보는 것은 정말 값진 일이야.
F: I think they'll love the toys we got them.	여: 아이들이 우리가 준비한 장난감을 정말 좋아할 것 같아.
M: And don't forget, your mom's Christmas dinner is a huge plus! Her cooking's fantastic. I can't stop thinking about her crispy roasted potatoes.	남: 그리고 어머니의 크리스마스 저녁 식사가 큰 장점이 된다는 것도 잊지 마! 어머니의 요리는 정말 환상적이야. 어머니의 바삭한 구운 감자에 대한 생각을 멈출 수가 없어.

F: Mmm! She goes all out during the holidays.

M: But **42** the thing I'm really worried about is that space is pretty limited at your parents' house. I have a feeling we'd end up on that inflatable mattress again.

F: Oh, I remember how uncomfortable that was for you last time.

M: Yes, it gave me a terrible backache. And with your sister and her kids around, the place will probably be even more cramped.

F: Yeah, that's worth thinking about. Now, what are your thoughts on taking a Christmas trip to Silverview, James?

M: Well, Sarah, the town is in a beautiful location. We always enjoy going there for peace and quiet. It's the perfect spot for a relaxing Christmas Day walk in the countryside.

F: You're right. It's gorgeous there in the winter. Just like a Christmas card.

M: And **43** **45** we could go skating on the frozen lake. You've never tried that before.

F: **43** I've always been a bit hesitant about that. Isn't it dangerous? What if the ice started to crack?

M: Don't worry about falling through. I used to go skating there almost every winter, and the ice was always thick enough.

F: That's reassuring. **44** One drawback of going to Silverview, though, is that we only have a few days off work for Christmas, and it's a long drive back from there.

여: 음! 엄마는 연휴 동안 전력을 다하셔.

남: 하지만 내가 정말 걱정되는 건 네 부모님 댁의 공간이 꽤 협소하다는 거야. 나는 결국 또 공기 주입식 매트리스에서 자게 될 것 같은 느낌이 들어.

여: 지난번에 그게 너에게 얼마나 불편했는지 기억나.

남: 맞아, 그걸로 심한 요통을 얻었지. 그리고 언니와 아이들이 함께 있으면 아마 훨씬 더 비좁을 거야.

여: 응, 생각해 볼 만하네. 이제 실버뷰로 크리스마스 여행을 떠나는 것에 대해 어떻게 생각해, 제임스?

남: 글쎄, 사라, 이 마을은 아름다운 장소에 있지. 우리는 항상 평화롭고 조용한 곳에 가는 것을 좋아하잖아. 크리스마스에 시골에서 느긋하게 산책하기에 완벽한 장소야.

여: 맞아. 겨울에 그곳은 정말 멋져. 마치 크리스마스 카드 같아.

남: 그리고 우린 얼어붙은 호수에서 스케이트를 타러 갈 수도 있어. 넌 한 번도 시도해본 적 없잖아.

여: 난 항상 그건 좀 망설여졌어. 위험하지 않아? 얼음에 금이 가기 시작하면 어떡해?

남: 떨어지는 것에 대한 걱정은 하지 마. 거의 매년 겨울마다 스케이트를 타러 갔었는데, 얼음은 항상 충분히 두꺼웠거든.

여: 그거 안심이 되네. 하지만 실버뷰에 갈 때 한 가지 단점이 있다면 크리스마스에 며칠만 쉬고 거기서 돌아오는 길이 멀다는 거야.

M: **44** Yeah, that could cut our vacation short. We'd need to leave earlier than we'd like to beat the traffic. The roads are usually packed after the holidays.

F: And we'd still end up spending the whole day driving instead of enjoying our time off.

M: Discussing this has been helpful, but I'm still not sure what to do. What about you, Sarah?

F: **45** What I really want is a Christmas to remember. Do you think you can find some ice skates that will fit me?

M: Definitely! Are you sure?

F: Absolutely. I'll pass on the inflatable mattress this year!

남: 응, 그럼 휴가가 짧아질 수도 있겠네. 교통 체증을 피하려면 더 일찍 출발해야 할 것 같아. 연휴가 끝나면 보통 도로가 꽉 막히니까.

여: 그러면 휴가를 즐기는 대신에 하루 종일 운전하느라 시간을 보내게 되겠네.

남: 이것에 대해 논의하는 게 도움이 되긴 했지만 난 여전히 어떻게 해야 할지 잘 모르겠네. 넌 어때, 사라?

여: 내가 정말 원하는 건 기억에 남는 크리스마스야. 나에게 맞는 아이스 스케이트를 찾을 수 있을까?

남: 물론이지! 진심이야?

여: 물론이지. 올해는 공기 주입식 매트리스는 넘길게!

어휘 heater 히터, 난방기 chilly 추운, 쌀쌀한 hassle 번거로움, 어려움 holiday spirit 휴일 분위기 mention 언급하다, 말하다 vacation 휴가 talk it over 상의하다, 논의하다 go over 검토하다, 논의하다 benefit 이점, 혜택 niece 조카 (여자) nephew 조카 (남자) unwrap 포장을 풀다 priceless 매우 귀중한, 값진 huge 큰, 엄청난 plus 장점, 추가적인 것 go all out 전력을 다하다, 온갖 노력을 다하다 inflatable 공기 주입식의, 공기나 기체로 부풀리는 backache 허리 통증 cramped 비좁은, 좁은 hesitant 주저하는, 망설이는 reassuring 안심시키는, 확신을 주는 drawback 단점, 문제점 packed 가득 찬, 혼잡한 cut short 짧게 끝내다, 단축시키다 beat the traffic 교통 체증을 피하다 discuss 논의하다, 이야기하다 fit 딱 맞다 absolutely 완전히, 절대적으로 pass on 포기하다, 넘기다

40 세부 정보

What will James have to do in the morning?

(a) clear snow from the street
(b) buy cleaning supplies
(c) remove snow from the car
(d) get the car repaired

제임스는 아침에 무엇을 해야 하는가?

(a) 거리의 눈을 치운다
(b) 청소 용품을 구매한다
(c) 차에서 눈을 제거한다
(d) 자동차 수리을 받는다

정답 (c)

해설 대화 초반부에 사라가 눈이 오기 시작했다고 말하자 제임스는 내일 아침에 차에 있는 눈을 치워야겠다고(I'll need to clean the snow off the car tomorrow morning) 말하는 부분을 통해 제임스가 내일 아침 할 일이 무엇인지 알 수 있습니다. 따라서 정답은 (c)입니다.

어휘 clear 치우다, 제거하다 cleaning supplies 청소 용품 repair 수리하다, 고치다

> **패러프레이징**
>
> clean the snow off the car → remove snow from the car

---

41 **세부 정보**

What would James most look forward to about Christmas with their niece and nephew?

(a) decorating the tree together
(b) watching them open gifts
(c) making cookies together
(d) seeing them play with new toys

제임스가 조카들과 함께 하는 크리스마스에 가장 기대하는 것은 무엇인가?

(a) 함께 트리를 장식하는 것
(b) 조카들이 선물을 여는 것을 보는 것
(c) 함께 쿠키를 만드는 것
(d) 조카들이 새 장난감을 가지고 노는 것을 보는 것

정답 (b)

해설 사라가 조카들과 크리스마스를 기념하는 일이 아주 좋을 것이라고 말하자, 제임스는 자신이 가장 기대하는 것이 바로 그 아이들이 새 장난감을 박스에서 꺼내는 것을 보는 것(What I'd most look forward to is watching the kids take their new toys out of the boxes)이라고 말합니다. 이를 통해서 제임스가 크리스마스에 조카들이 크리스마스 선물 상자를 여는 것을 보고 싶어한다는 것을 알 수 있으므로 (b)가 정답입니다.

어휘 decorate 장식하다, 꾸미다 unwrap gifts 선물을 뜯다, 풀다 make cookies 쿠키를 만들다

> **패러프레이징**
>
> take their new toys out of the boxes → open gifts

> **⊗ 오답 피하기**
>
> 제임스가 말한 것은 아이들이 상자에서 새 장난감을 꺼내는 것(take their new toys out of the boxes)이라고 언급하였으므로 새 장난감을 가지고 노는 것은 나타내는 (d)는 오답입니다.

What worries James about staying at Sarah's parents' house?

(a) the uncomfortable sofa
(b) the crowded space
(c) the unfamiliar foods
(d) the noisy children

사라의 부모님 댁에 머무는 것에 대해 제임스가 걱정하는 것은 무엇인가?

(a) 불편한 소파
(b) 붐비는 공간
(c) 낯선 음식들
(d) 시끄러운 아이들

정답 (b)

해설 제임스가 가장 걱정하는 것은 사라의 부모님 댁의 공간이 꽤 협소하다는 것(the thing I'm really worried about is that space is pretty limited at your parents' house)이라고 말한 부분을 통해 제임스의 걱정거리는 사라의 부모님댁의 협소한 공간 문제임을 알 수 있습니다. 따라서 정답은 (b)입니다.

어휘 worry 걱정하다 crowded 붐비는, 혼잡한 space 공간

> **패러프레이징**
>
> space is pretty limited → the crowded space

Why might Sarah be hesitant to go skating on the lake?

(a) She dislikes putting on the gear.
(b) She is afraid of slipping on the ice.
(c) She dislikes the freezing weather.
(d) She is afraid of falling into the water.

사라가 호수에서 스케이트를 타는 것을 주저할 수도 있는 이유는 무엇인가?

(a) 그녀는 장비 착용을 싫어한다.
(b) 그녀는 얼음 위에서 미끄러지는 것을 두려워한다.
(c) 그녀는 추운 날씨를 싫어한다.
(d) 그녀는 물에 빠지는 것을 두려워한다.

정답 (d)

해설 제임스가 얼어붙은 호수에 스케이트를 타러 갈 수도 있다고 말하자, 사라는 스케이트를 타는 것에 대해서 좀 주저해왔다고(I've always been a bit hesitant about that) 말합니다. 그 후에 위험하지 않은지(Isn't it dangerous?), 얼음에 금이 가기 시작하면 어떻게 하는지(What if the ice started to crack?) 묻는 것으로 보아 사라가 걱정하는 것은 호수의 표면이 깨져서 물에 빠지는 것임을 알 수 있습니다. 따라서 정답은 (d)입니다.

어휘 hesitant 망설이는, 주저하는 slip 미끄러지다 fall into the water 물에 빠지다

Why would James and Sarah have a shorter vacation if they went to Silverview?

(a) because of the bad storm
(b) because of the packed hotels
(c) because of the travel time
(d) because of the holiday closures

제임스와 사라가 실버뷰에 간다면 그들이 더 짧은 휴가를 가지게 될 이유는 무엇인가?

(a) 심한 폭풍 때문에
(b) 꽉 찬 호텔 때문에
(c) 이동 시간 때문에
(d) 휴일 휴무 때문에

정답 (c)

해설 질문의 키워드인 Silverview는 사라가 실버뷰에 가는 것에 대한 단점을 언급하면서 크리스마스에 며칠밖에 쉬지 못하며, 돌아오는 길이 장거리 운전이라고(One drawback of going to Silverview, though, is that we only have a few days off work for Christmas, and it's a long drive back from there) 말하는 부분에서 언급됩니다. 그러자 제임스가 그게 자신들의 휴가를 짧게 만들어버릴 수 있다고(that could cut our vacation short) 말하는 부분을 통해 실버뷰로 갈 경우 휴가 기간이 짧아지는 이유가 바로 장거리 운전 여행임을 알 수 있습니다. 따라서 정답은 (c)입니다.

어휘 shorter 더 짧은 vacation 휴가 travel time 여행 시간 holiday closures 휴일 동안의 휴업, 문을 닫는 것

패러프레이징

a long drive back from there → the trave time

What have James and Sarah most likely decided to do?

(a) visit a town by themselves
(b) go to her parents' place
(c) stay at home by themselves
(d) drop by her friends' place

제임스와 사라는 무엇을 하기로 결정했을 것 같은가?

(a) 그들끼리만 한 마을을 방문한다
(b) 부모님 집에 간다
(c) 그들끼리만 집에 머무른다
(d) 친구들 집에 들른다

정답 (a)

해설 대화의 마지막 부분에서 사라는 자신이 원하는 것은 기억에 남는 크리스마스라고 하며, 자신에게 맞는 아이스 스케이트를 찾을 수 있다고 생각하냐고(Do you think you can find some ice skates that will fit me?) 제임스에게 묻습니다. 그러자 제임스는 물론이라고 답하는 것을 듣고 이 둘은 크리스마스에 아이스 스케이트를 타러 갈 것임을 알 수 있습니다. 그리고 그들의 앞선 대화에서 얼어 붙은 호수에서 스케이트를 탈 수 있는 곳으로 언급된 실버뷰(Silverview) 마을로 갈 것임을 알 수 있습니다. 따라서 정답은 (a)입니다.

어휘 decide 결정하다 drop by 잠깐 들르다

Hello, everyone. As a seasoned long-distance runner, **46** I'm thrilled to be here at the Mondale Sports Center to share my passion for marathon running. Covering twenty-six miles is no small task, and preparing for a marathon is all about dedication and hard work. **46** Here are some tips on how to prepare for this challenge.

47 The first tip is to create your own training program. Having coached many runners, I recommend a preparation period of sixteen to twenty weeks. But don't just get out there and try to run every day. First, decide which goals you'd like to meet each week, and build in some rest days. If you struggle with organizing your time, there are many great marathon training plans online that you can download.

The second tip is to include cross-training in your routine to boost overall fitness. While a marathon primarily involves running, that doesn't mean you should avoid other activities. **48** I spend most of my time at the gym lifting weights. I don't enjoy weight training, but it's a vital part of my preparation, as it strengthens my entire body. Trust me. You need more than a good pair of legs to complete a marathon.

The third tip is to choose the right footwear. With so many styles of running shoes available, **49** it's hard to choose the best ones. Personally, I've found it stressful to make that decision. But I feel less overwhelmed after paying a visit to a specialty running store. At the store, the skilled salespeople assess my running style on a treadmill and provide me with a range of shoe options to try. This personalized approach ensures that I find the perfect running shoes for my needs.

The fourth tip is to get into the right mindset on the morning of the marathon. Whatever you do, remember to keep things positive. Usually, I wake up

안녕하세요, 여러분. 노련한 장거리 달리기 선수로서 몬데일 스포츠 센터에서 마라톤에 대한 저의 열정을 공유하게 되어 매우 기쁩니다. 26마일을 달리는 것은 결코 쉬운 일이 아니며, 마라톤을 준비하는 것은 모두 헌신과 노력이 걸리는 일입니다. 이 도전을 어떻게 준비해야 하는지 몇 가지 팁을 알려드리겠습니다.

첫 번째 팁은 자신만의 훈련 프로그램을 만드는 것입니다. 많은 러너들을 지도해 온 저는 16주에서 20주의 준비 기간을 추천합니다. 하지만 무작정 밖에 나가서 매일 달리려고 하지 마세요. 먼저, 매주 달성하고 싶은 목표를 정하고 휴식일을 계획하세요. 시간을 계획하는 데 어려움을 겪는다면 온라인에서 다운로드할 수 있는 훌륭한 마라톤 훈련 계획이 많이 있습니다.

두 번째 팁은 전반적인 체력 향상을 위해 크로스 트레이닝을 루틴에 포함시키는 것입니다. 마라톤에는 주로 달리기가 수반되지만 그렇다고 해서 다른 활동을 피해야 한다는 의미는 아닙니다. 저는 대부분의 시간을 헬스장에서 중량 운동을 하며 보냅니다. 저는 웨이트 트레이닝을 즐기지는 않지만, 몸 전체를 강화하기 때문에 마라톤 준비에 필수적인 부분입니다. 제 말을 믿으세요. 마라톤을 완주하려면 좋은 다리보다 더 많은 것이 필요합니다.

세 번째 팁은 올바른 신발을 선택하는 것입니다. 다양한 스타일의 러닝화를 이용할 수 있어서, 최고의 러닝화를 선택하기가 어렵습니다. 개인적으로 저는 그런 결정을 내리는 것에 스트레스를 받았습니다. 하지만 러닝 전문 매장을 방문하고 나서는 덜 부담스러워졌습니다. 매장에서는 숙련된 판매원이 러닝 머신에서 제 달리기 방식을 평가하고 다양한 신발 선택권을 추천해 줍니다. 이 맞춤형 접근 방식을 통해 제 필요에 맞는 완벽한 러닝화를 확실히 찾을 수 있었습니다.

네 번째 팁은 마라톤 당일 아침에 올바른 마음가짐을 갖는 것입니다. 무슨 일을 하든 긍정적인 생각을 유지하는 것을 잊지 마세요. 보통 저는 일찍 일어

early and enjoy a cup of coffee and some breakfast while catching up on my social media. However, you might want to change your morning ritual for the day of the race. Once, **50** I made the mistake of opening my social media at the start of race day and saw an upsetting news story someone had uploaded. After that, I felt sick to my stomach and wasn't able to put all of my energy into running.

Tip number five is to listen to your body. Last year, I pushed through some mild knee pain during my runs because I was desperate to compete in the marathon I had signed up for. It was a huge mistake! **51** Midway through the actual race, I experienced unbearable pain and was forced to quit. I ended up with a severe knee injury that prevented me from running for four months. The lesson is clear: listen to your body's signals, and seek medical advice if needed.

The last tip is to recover properly after each practice run. Training for a marathon will be hard on your body, so proper rest and recovery are important. Some runners choose to meditate on their rest days, but that doesn't work for me. **52** Personally, I like visiting my local spa for a full-body massage. It soothes and relaxes my aching muscles after a run, offering the care my body needs after suffering such intense physical training.

Thanks for joining me. Good luck as you begin your marathon training journey.

나 커피 한 잔과 아침 식사를 즐기면서 소셜 미디어를 확인합니다. 하지만 마라톤 경주 당일에는 아침 습관을 바꾸는 것이 좋습니다. 한번은 경주가 시작될 때 소셜 미디어를 열어보는 실수를 저질렀는데, 누군가 올린 충격적인 뉴스를 본 적이 있습니다. 그 후 속이 울렁거려서 달리기에 온 힘을 쏟을 수 없었죠.

다섯 번째 팁은 내 몸에 귀를 기울이는 것입니다. 작년에 저는 등록한 마라톤 대회에 참가하고 싶다는 절박함 때문에 달리기 도중 가벼운 무릎 통증을 참았습니다. 그건 큰 실수였죠! 실제 경주 도중에 견딜 수 없는 통증이 찾아왔고 어쩔 수 없이 경기를 그만둬야 했습니다. 결국 무릎에 심각한 부상을 입어 4개월 동안 달리기를 할 수 없게 되었죠. 교훈은 분명합니다. 몸의 신호에 귀를 기울이고 필요한 경우 의사의 조언을 구해야 한다는 것입니다.

마지막 팁은 연습 달리기 후 적절한 회복을 하는 것입니다. 마라톤 훈련은 신체에 무리를 줄 수 있으므로 적절한 휴식과 회복이 중요합니다. 일부 달리기 선수들은 휴식일에 명상을 하기도 하지만 저에게는 효과가 없습니다. 개인적으로 저는 동네 스파에 가서 전신 마사지를 받는 것을 좋아합니다. 격렬한 육체적 훈련 후 지친 근육을 진정시키고 긴장을 풀어주며 몸에 필요한 관리를 제공합니다.

저와 함께해 주셔서 감사합니다. 마라톤 훈련 여정을 시작하는 여러분께 행운을 빕니다.

어휘 seasoned 경험이 풍부한, 노련한 long-distance 장거리의 be thrilled to 동사원형: ~해서 기쁘다, ~해서 짜릿한 기분을 느끼다 share 공유하다 passion 열정 marathon 마라톤 prepare for ~을 준비하다, ~에 대비하다 cover 가다, 이동하다 task 일, 과업 dedication 헌신, 전념 challenge 도전 coach 지도하다 recommend 권장하다, 추천하다 goal 목표 struggle 애쓰다, 힘들어하다 organizing 조직, 정리 routine 반복적인 일상, 반복하는 행동 boost 증진시키다, 향상시키다 primarily 주로 involve 수반하다, 포함하다 lift weights 역기를 들다 vital 중요한, 필수적인 strengthen 강화하다 entire 전체의 trust 믿다 a pair of 한 쌍의 footwear 신발 find it + 형용사 + to 동사원형: ~하는 것을 (형용사)하다고 느끼다 make a decision 결정을 내리다 feel less overwhelmed 부담을 덜 느끼다 pay a visit to ~을 방문하다 specialty 전문 assess 평가하다 treadmill 트레드밀, 러닝 머신 provide A with B: A에게 B를 제공하다 a range of 다양한 종류의 personalized 개인화된 approach 접근법 ensure 반드시 ~하게 하다, 보장하다 mindset 마음가짐 remember to 동사원형: ~할 것을 기억하다 positive 긍정적인 catch up with 따라 잡다, (밀린 것을) 확인하다 ritual 의식, 습관 upsetting 불안하게 만드는, 기분 나쁜 push through 강행하다, 끝까지 해내다 desperate 필사적인, 절망적인

TEST 07 Listening **449**

sign up for ~을 등록하다 midway through ~을 지나는 동안에 unbearable 참을 수 없는, 견딜 수 없는 be forced to 동사원형: 어쩔 수 없이 ~하게 되다, ~하기를 강요 받다 signal 신호 seek 구하다, 찾다 recover 회복하다 properly 제대로, 적절히 recovery 회복 meditate 명상하다 work for ~에 효과가 있다 personally 개인적으로 soothe 진정시키다, 달래다 aching 쑤시는, 통증이 있는 suffer 시달리다, 고통받다, 겪다 intense 강렬한, 극심한 physical 신체의 journey 여행, 여정

46 주제/목적

What is the talk mainly about?	담화는 주로 무엇에 관한 것인가?
(a) how to train for a marathon	(a) 마라톤을 위한 훈련 방법
(b) how to organize a marathon	(b) 마라톤을 조직하는 방법
(c) how to win a marathon	(c) 마라톤에서 우승하는 방법
(d) how to recover from a marathon	(d) 마라톤 후에 회복하는 방법

정답 (a)

해설 담화 초반부에 화자는 장거리 달리기 선수로서 마라톤을 향한 자신의 열정을 공유하게 되어 기쁘다고 언급하였으며(I'm thrilled to be here at the Mondale Sports Center to share my passion for marathon running), 청중들에게 이 도전, 즉 마라톤을 준비하는 방법에 대한 팁을 소개하겠다고(Here are some tips on how to prepare for this challenge) 말하는 부분에서 담화의 주제가 마라톤 경주에 대비하는 훈련 방법이라는 것을 알 수 있습니다. 따라서 정답은 (a)입니다.

어휘 train 훈련하다, 연습하다 marathon 마라톤 mainly 주로, 대개 talk 강연, 이야기 dedication 헌신, 전념 challenge 도전, 과제

패러프레이징

some tips on how to prepare for this challenge → how to train for a marathon

47 세부 정보

What is the first tip in the talk?	강연의 첫 번째 팁은 무엇인가?
(a) look online for races to enter	(a) 온라인에서 참가할 레이스를 찾아본다
(b) consult a running coach	(b) 러닝 코치와 상담한다
(c) find a partner to train with	(c) 함께 훈련할 파트너 찾는다
(d) make a practice schedule	(d) 연습 일정을 정한다

정답 (d)

해설 화자는 첫 번째 팁으로 자신만의 훈련 프로그램을 만드는 것(The first tip is to create your own training program)이라고 말합니다. 이는 자신만의 연습 일정을 정하는 것을 의미하므로 정답은 (d)입니다.

어휘 tip 팁, 조언 practice 연습, 훈련 schedule 일정 goal 목표 build in 포함시키다 rest day 휴식일

48 세부 정보

How does the speaker spend most of his time at the gym?

(a) He does weight training.
(b) He uses an exercise bike.
(c) He takes yoga classes.
(d) He walks on the treadmill.

화자는 체육관에서 대부분의 시간을 어떻게 보내는가?

(a) 웨이트 트레이닝을 한다.
(b) 운동용 자전거를 사용한다.
(c) 요가 수업을 듣는다.
(d) 러닝 머신 위에서 걷는다.

정답 (a)

해설 화자가 두 번째 팁을 설명하는 중에 질문의 키워드인 spend most of his time이 언급됩니다. 그는 체육관에서 대부분의 시간을 웨이트 트레이닝을 하면서 보낸다고(I spend most of my time at the gym lifting weights) 언급한 부분을 통해 정답이 (a)임을 알 수 있습니다.

어휘 **weight training** 웨이트 트레이닝, 중량 훈련

49 세부 정보

What does the speaker find to be stressful?

(a) trying different running styles
(b) getting a good pair of shoes
(c) shopping for exercise machines
(d) buying the right workout clothes

화자가 스트레스를 받는다고 생각하는 것은 무엇인가?

(a) 다양한 러닝 스타일을 시도하는 것
(b) 좋은 신발을 구입하는 것
(c) 운동기구 쇼핑
(d) 적합한 운동복을 구입하는 것

정답 (b)

해설 화자가 세 번째 팁인 올바른 신발을 고르는 것에 대해 설명하는 중에 질문의 키워드인 find to be stressful을 언급합니다. 화자는 최고의 신발을 고르는 것이 어렵다고(it's hard to choose the best ones) 말하며, 자신은 그러한 결정을 하는 것이 스트레스를 받는 일로 느꼈다고(I've found it stressful to make that decision) 말하는 것을 통해 화자가 자신에게 가장

좋은 신발을 고르는 일에 대해 스트레스를 받았다는 것을 알 수 있습니다. 따라서 정답은 (b)입니다.

어휘 try 시도하다 exercise machine 운동 기구 workout cloth 운동복

---

50 세부 정보

Based on the talk, what might runners want to avoid doing the morning of the race?

(a) reading online posts
(b) waking up too early
(c) eating a large breakfast
(d) drinking too much coffee

담화에 따르면, 달리기 선수들이 경주 당일 아침에 피해야 할 행동은 무엇인가?

(a) 온라인 게시물을 읽는 것
(b) 너무 일찍 일어나는 것
(c) 아침을 많이 먹는 것
(d) 커피를 너무 많이 마시는 것

정답 (a)

해설 질문의 키워드인 the morning of the race는 네 번째 팁을 설명하는 중에 언급됩니다. 화자가 경주 당일 실수로 소셜 미디어를 열었다가 누군가가 업로드한 충격적인 뉴스를 보았다고 말하며, 그 후에 속이 좋지 않아 달리기에 자신의 모든 에너지를 쓸 수 없었다고(I made the mistake of opening my social media at the start of race day and saw an upsetting news story someone had uploaded. After that, I felt sick to my stomach and wasn't able to put all of my energy into running) 말하는 부분에서 경주 당일에 피해야 하는 행동에 대해 언급하였습니다. 이를 통해 화자가 경주 당일 아침에는 온라인 게시물을 보는 것을 피하는 것을 권장하는 것을 알 수 있으므로 정답은 (a)입니다.

어휘 avoid 피하다 read 읽다 online 온라인 post 게시물, 글

---

51 세부 정보

Why was the speaker forced to quit midway through a race?

(a) He was exhausted.
(b) He felt mild knee pain.
(c) He broke a rule.
(d) He had a serious injury.

화자가 경주 도중에 중도 포기해야 했던 이유는 무엇인가?

(a) 그는 지쳐 있었다.
(b) 그는 가벼운 무릎 통증을 느꼈다.
(c) 그는 규칙을 어겼다.
(d) 심각한 부상을 입었다.

정답 (d)

해설 질문의 키워드인 forced to quit midway through a race는 화자가 다섯 번째 팁인 자신의 몸에 귀를 기울이라는 내용을 설명하는 중에 언급됩니다. 그는 가벼운 무릎 통증을 참고 마라톤 경주를 계속 하였고 결국 실제 경주 도중에 참을 수 없는 고통을 느껴 어쩔 수 없이 경주를 그만두었으며(Midway through the actual race, I experienced unbearable pain and was forced to quit), 이후 그는 심각한 무릎 부상을 입게 되었다고(I ended up with a severe knee injury) 말하는 부분을 통해 화자가 경주를 그만 둔 것은 심각한 무릎 부상 때문인 것을 알 수 있습니다. 따라서 정답은 (d)입니다.

어휘 **forced** 강제로, 억지로 **quit** 그만두다 **midway** 중간, 도중에 **serious** 심각한 **injury** 부상 **pain** 고통, 통증

패러프레이징

a severe knee injury → a serious injury

❌ 오답 피하기

화자가 마라톤 경주 중에 가벼운 무릎 통증을 무시하고 강행했다고(I pushed through some mild knee pain during my runs) 언급하였으나 이것은 심각한 부상으로 이어질 수 있다는 화자의 신체가 보내는 신호였으며 마라톤 도중에 그만 둔 직접적인 원인이 아닙니다. 따라서 (b)는 오답입니다.

---

52 세부 정보

How does the speaker like to relax between practice runs?

(a) by soaking in a hot bath
(b) by doing meditation
(c) by getting a massage
(d) by visiting his friends

화자는 연습 달리기 사이에 어떻게 휴식을 취하는 것을 좋아하는가?

(a) 뜨거운 욕조에 몸을 담그는 것으로써
(b) 명상을 하는 것으로써
(c) 마사지를 받음으로써
(d) 친구를 방문함으로써

정답 (c)

해설 질문의 키워드 practice run은 화자가 마지막 팁을 설명하는 중에 언급됩니다. 화자는 개인적으로 동네 스파에 가서 전신 마사지를 받는 것을 좋아한다고(Personally, I like visiting my local spa for a full-body massage)라고 말하는 부분을 통해서 화자가 연습 달리기 후에 마사지를 받는 것으로 휴식을 취한다는 것을 알 수 있습니다. 따라서 정답은 (c)입니다.

어휘 **relax** 휴식을 취하다 **soak** 담그다 **bath** 욕조

PART 1

GEORGIA O'KEEFFE

Georgia O'Keeffe was an American painter. She has been called the "mother of American modernism" and is **53** best known for her paintings of natural scenes, such as flowers and landscapes, often inspired by places she knew.

Born in Sun Prairie, Wisconsin, in 1887, O'Keeffe was the daughter of dairy farmers. As a young girl, she knew she wanted to be an artist and took lessons with a local watercolor painter. **54** She later studied in New York, where she won a scholarship to a summer school program for her painting, *Untitled (Dead Rabbit with Copper Pot)*. O'Keeffe's time in New York City enabled her to visit galleries that displayed work by experimental artists and photographers.

During these years in the city, O'Keeffe practiced a style known as imitative realism. Artists using this style tried to paint exactly what they saw, as if capturing a photograph. However, **55** O'Keeffe grew bored with this. Later, when she met artist Arthur Wesley Dow, who believed that art should be a form of self-expression, his influence led her to create abstract paintings that focused on moods and emotions rather than realism.

She pursued this new style, later known as modernism, while working as an art teacher in South Carolina. She was among the few painters in the world skilled at creating this type of art. In 1915, she mailed some of her drawings to a friend in New York, who shared them with **56** famous art critic, Alfred Stieglitz. Stieglitz realized that O'Keeffe's art was special and arranged high-profile showings of her

조지아 오키프

조지아 오키프는 미국의 화가였다. 그녀는 "미국 모더니즘의 어머니"라고 불려 왔으며, 그녀는 꽃과 풍경들과 같은 자연 경관을 그린 그림으로 가장 유명했는데, 그 풍경들은 종종 그녀가 알고 있던 장소에 영감을 받아 그린 것이었다.

1887년 위스콘신의 선 프레리에서 태어 났으며, 오키프는 낙농업자의 딸이었다. 어린 소녀였을 때, 그녀는 자신이 예술가가 되고 싶다는 것을 알았고, 지역의 수채화가에게 교습을 받았다. 그는 이후 뉴욕에서 공부하였으며, 그곳에서 그녀는 그녀의 그림 <무제(구리 냄비를 든 죽은 토끼)>로 여름 학교 프로프램에서 장학금을 받았다. 뉴욕 시에서 보낸 오키프의 시간은 그녀로 하여금 시험적인 예술가들과 사진작가들의 작품이 전시되어 있는 미술관을 방문할 수 있게 해주었다.

뉴욕에서의 이 몇 년 동안, 오키프는 모방적 사실주의로 알려진 방식을 연습하였다. 이 방식을 사용하는 예술가들은 마치 사진을 찍는 것처럼 그들이 본 것을 그대로 그리려고 노력하였다. 하지만, 오키프는 이것에 점점 권태를 느꼈다. 이후, 예술은 자기표현의 형식이 되어야 한다고 믿었던 화가 아서 위즐리 도우를 만났을 때, 그의 영향력은 그녀를 사실주의보다 기분과 감정에 초점을 둔 추상화를 그리도록 이끌었다.

그녀는 사우스캐롤라이나에서 미술 교사로 근무하는 동안 이 새로운 방식을 추구하였으며, 이후 이 방식은 모더니즘으로 알려졌다. 그녀는 이런 유형의 예술을 창조하는 것에 숙달된, 세계에서 몇 안 되는 화가 중 한 명이었다. 1915년에, 그녀는 뉴욕에 있는 친구에게 자신의 그림 몇 점을 우편으로 보냈는데, 그 친구는 그 그림들을 유명한 미술 평론가 알프레드 스티글리츠와 함께 보았다. 스티클리츠는

work. Soon, O'Keeffe became one of the most famous artists in the nation.

오키프의 예술이 특별하다는 것을 깨달았고, 세간의 이목을 끌만한 전시로 그녀의 작품을 선보일 자리를 마련하였다. 곧, 오키프는 미국에서 가장 유명한 예술가 중 한 명이 되었다.

O'Keeffe and Stieglitz married in 1924. Stieglitz loved his wife's art but **57** misunderstood its meaning. He interpreted the abstract forms in her paintings as an expression of her femininity, **which other critics agreed with.** **57** O'Keeffe, however, rejected this thinking as sexist and **58** distanced herself from these ideas by painting more recognizable images.

오키프와 스티클리츠는 1924년에 결혼하였으며, 스티클리츠는 아내의 예술을 사랑하였으나 그 의미를 제대로 이해하지 못했다. 그는 그녀의 그림 속 추상적인 형식을 그녀의 여성성에 대한 표현으로 해석하였고, 그것은 다른 평론가들도 동의하였다. 하지만 오키프는 이러한 성차별주의자로서의 생각을 거부하였으며, 좀 더 잘 알아볼 수 있는 그림을 그려 이러한 생각이 자신에게 개입되지 않도록 하였다.

Until her death in 1986, O'Keeffe continued to be a bold and experimental artist. She spent much of her life in New Mexico, where the harsh natural landscape inspired her. In 2014, a painting of a flower, *Jimson Weed/White Flower No. 1*, sold for $44.4 million. The continued value of her art is a reminder that she was not just an **59** eminent female modernist but also one of the greatest artists of the twentieth century.

1986년 사망할 때까지, 오키프는 대담하고 실험적인 예술가로 계속 활동하였다. 그녀는 뉴멕시코에서 생의 많은 날을 보냈으며, 그곳에서의 가혹한 자연 경관이 그녀에게 많은 영감을 주었다. 2014년에, 꽃 한 송이가 그려진 그림 <독말풀/흰꽃 No.1>이 4440만 달러에 판매되었다. 그녀의 예술에 대한 지속적인 가치는 그녀가 단지 탁월한 여성 모더니스트일 뿐만 아니라 20세기의 가장 위대한 예술가 중 한 명이라는 것을 상기시켜준다.

어휘 natural 자연의 scene 경관 landscape 풍경 inspire 영감을 주다 dairy farmer 낙농업자 take lessons 교습을 받다 watercolor painter 수채화가 win a scholarship 장학금을 받다 copper 구리, 청동 pot 냄비 enable + 목적어 + to 동사원형: (목적어)가 ~할 수 있게 하다 display 전시하다 work 작품 experimental 실험적인 imitative 모방적인 realism 사실주의 exactly 그대로, 정확하게 capture a photograph 사진을 찍다 grow bored 점점 지루함을 느끼다 form 형식, 양식 self-expression 자기표현 influence 영향력 abstract painting 추상화 focus on ~에 초점을 두다 mood 기분 emotion 감정 rather than ~보다는 pursue 추구하다 skilled at ~에 숙련된, ~에 능숙한 critic 평론가 arrange 마련하다, 준비하다 high-profile 세간의 이목을 끄는 showing 전시 misunderstand 오해하다, 잘 이해하지 못하다 interpret 해석하다, 이해하다 abstract 추상적인 femininity 여성성 agree with ~에 동의하다 reject 거절하다 sexist 성차별주의자 distance + 목적어 + from ~: ~가 (목적어)에게 개입하지 못하게 하다, (목적어)를 ~로부터 멀리 떨어뜨려 놓다 recognizable 잘 알아볼 수 있는 bold 대담한, 용감한 harsh 혹독한, 가혹한 continued 지속적인, 계속되는 value 가치 reminder 상기시켜 주는 것 not just A but also B: A일 뿐만 아니라 B도 eminent 저명한, 탁월한

What is Georgia O'Keeffe most famous for?	조지아 오키프는 무엇으로 가장 유명한가?
(a) creating paintings of the natural world (b) experimenting with different art mediums (c) inventing techniques for landscape painting (d) making sculptures using natural objects	(a) 자연에 대한 그림을 그리는 것 (b) 다른 예술 매개체로 실험하는 것 (c) 풍경화에 대한 기술을 발명하는 것 (d) 자연물을 이용하여 조각품을 만드는 것

정답 (a)

해설 질문의 키워드인 most famous for가 첫 문단에서 best known for로 언급되었습니다. 그 뒤에 언급되는 her paintings of natural scenes, such as flowers and landscapes가 정답의 단서이며, 이를 paintings of the natural world로 언급한 (a)가 정답입니다.

어휘 natural world 자연(계) experiment 실험하다 medium 매개, 매체 invent 발명하다 technique 기술, 기법 sculpture 조각 object 물체, 사물

패러프레이징

her paintings of natural scenes, such as flowers and landscapes → creating paintings of the natural world

When was O'Keeffe exposed to unconventional works of art?	오키프가 관습에 얽매이지 않은 예술품에 노출된 것은 언제인가?
(a) when she was working for a photographer (b) when she was a volunteer at an art gallery (c) when she was taking lessons from a local painter (d) when she was a student in a major city	(a) 사진작가와 작업하는 중일 때 (b) 화랑의 자원봉사자였을 때 (c) 지역의 한 화가에게 교습을 받는 중일 때 (d) 대도시에서 학생이었을 때

정답 (d)

해설 질문의 키워드 unconventional works of art는 두 번째 문단에서 work by experimental artists and photographers로 언급되었습니다. 실험적인 화가나 사진작가가 작업한 작품은 당시에 관습적이지 않은 방식을 보여줬음을 알 수 있습니다. 따라서 오키프가 이러한 작품들이 전시된 미술관을 방문할 수 있었던 시기가 뉴욕에서 장학금을 받으며 공부를 하고 있었던 때이므로 (d)가 정답입니다.

어휘 **be exposed to** ~에 노출되다, ~와 접촉하다 **unconventional** 관습에 얽매이지 않은, 색다른, 특이한 **volunteer** 자원봉사자 **art gallery** 미술관, 화랑 **major city** 대도시, 주요 도시

패러프레이징

experimental → unconventional

⊗ 오답 피하기

지역의 한 화가에서 교습을 받은 것은 오키프가 뉴욕으로 가기 전에 있었던 일이며, 그 시기에는 unconventional works of art에 대해 언급된 것이 없으므로 (c)는 오답입니다.

---

55 사실 확인

Which is NOT mentioned in the text about O'Keeffe's work after meeting Dow?

(a) It became boring to her after a while.
(b) It was influenced by the other artist's ideas.
(c) It departed from her realistic art style.
(d) It was an expression of her feelings

도우와 만난 후의 오키프의 작품에 대해 지문에서 언급되지 않은 것은 어느 것인가?

(a) 그 이후 한동안 그녀에게 지루하게 느껴졌다.
(b) 다른 예술가들의 생각에 영향을 받았다.
(c) 그녀의 사실주의적 예술 방식에서 벗어났다.
(d) 그녀의 감정 표현이었다.

정답 (a)

해설 질문의 키워드인 Dow는 세 번째 문단에서 오키프가 만난 화가 Arthur Wesley Dow를 가리키는 것을 알 수 있습니다. 예술을 자기표현의 방식으로 여기는 그와 만난 이후로 오키프는 그 전에 연습하고 있던 모방적 사실주의를 벗어나 추상화를 그리기 시작하였고, 기분과 감정에 초점을 두었다고 언급되어 있습니다. 그러나 오키프가 지루하게 생각했던 것은 모방적 사실주의(imitative realism)이므로 정답은 (a)입니다.

어휘 **boring** 지루하게 하는 **after a while** 그 후로 한 동안 **influence** 영향을 주다 **depart from** ~로부터 벗어나다 **realistic** 사실주의적인 **feeling** 감정, 기분

How did O'Keeffe initially rise to fame?

(a) by winning a notable art competition
(b) by sharing her work with a fellow teacher
(c) by getting the attention of an industry expert
(d) by sending her work to a high-profile gallery

오키프는 처음에 어떻게 유명해졌는가?

(a) 중요한 미술 대회에서 우승함으로써
(b) 그녀의 작품을 동료 교사들에게 보여줌으로써
(c) 업계의 전문가의 관심을 받음으로써
(d) 세간의 이목을 끄는 미술관에 그녀의 작품을 보냄으로써

정답 (c)

해설 질문의 키워드인 initially rise to fame은 네 번째 문단 마지막에 O'Keeffe became one of the most famous artists in the nation에서 언급되었습니다. 그녀가 이렇게 유명해진 것은 유명한 예술 평론가인 알프레드 스티글리츠가 그녀가 특별하다는 것을 알아보고 그녀의 작품에 대한 전시회를 마련했기 때문(Stieglitz realized that O'Keeffe's art was special and arranged high-profile showings of her work)이므로 (c)가 정답입니다.

어휘 initially 처음에, 애초에 rise to fame 명성을 날리다, 유명해지다 notable 중요한, 주목할 만한 art competition 미술 대회 fellow 동료 attention 주의, 관심 industry expert 업계의 전문가

패러프레이징

• rise to fame → became one of the most famous artists
• famous art critic → industry expert

Based on the fifth paragraph, why, most likely, did O'Keeffe change her painting style again?

(a) because she wanted her art to better reflect her femininity
(b) because she was inspired by advice from her husband
(c) because she was bothered by misconceptions about her art
(d) because she wanted to attract the attention of critics

다섯 번째 문단에 따르면, 오키프가 그녀의 화풍을 다시 바꾼 이유는 무엇일 것 같은가?

(a) 자신의 예술이 여성성을 더 잘 반영하기를 원했기 때문에
(b) 남편의 조언에 영감을 얻었기 때문에
(c) 그녀의 예술에 대한 오해에 신경이 쓰였기 때문에
(d) 평론가들의 관심을 끌고 싶었기 때문에

정답 (c)

해설 질문의 키워드 change her painting style again은 문맥상 추상적인 그림을 그리는 방식으로 화풍을 바꾸었던 오키프가 한 번 더 바꾼 것을 의미하는데, 다섯 번째 문단 마지막에 언급된 painting more recognizable images에서 recognizable 이라는 단어는 추상화를 뜻하는 abstract painting과 서로 상반된 의미이므로 오키프가 그림을 그리는 방식을 바꿨음을 알 수 있습니다. 이렇게 바꾼 이유는 남편과 다른 평론가들이 자신의 그림을 여성성의 표현으로 오해한 것(misunderstood its meaning. He interpreted the abstract forms in her paintings as an expression of her femininity, which other critics agreed with)을 거절하는 것에 비롯된 것이므로 (c)가 정답입니다.

어휘 **painting style** 화풍, 그림을 그리는 방식 **reflect** 반영하다 **be bother by** ~에 신경 쓰이다 **misconception** 오해 **attract** 끌다

> **패러프레이징**
>
> misunderstood → misconceptions

---

58 동의어

In the context of the passage, distanced means _____ .

(a) confused
(b) separated
(c) challenged
(d) identified

해당 단락의 문맥에서 distanced가 의미하는 것은?

(a) 혼동시켰다
(b) 분리하였다
(c) 이의를 제기하였다
(d) 신원을 확인하였다

정답 (b)

해설 해당 문장에서 distanced는 herself를 목적어로 두고, from these ideas라는 전치사구를 가지고 있는데, 문맥상 these ideas는 스티클리츠가 오키프의 예술의 의미를 여성성의 표현으로 보는 것을 의미합니다. 그래서 오키프는 더 잘 알아볼 수 있는 그림을 그렸다는 내용을 통해서 동사 distance는 그런 생각을 자신으로부터 떨어뜨렸다는 의미를 나타낸다고 볼 수 있습니다. 따라서 보기 중에서 '분리하다', '떼어놓다'라는 의미의 동사 separate의 과거형 (b) separated가 정답입니다.

---

59 동의어

In the context of the passage, eminent means _____ .

(a) casual
(b) threatening
(c) familiar
(d) leading

해당 단락의 문맥에서 eminent가 의미하는 것은?

(a) 무관심한
(b) 위협하는
(c) 익숙한
(d) 가장 중요한

해설 해당 문장에서 eminent는 조지아 오키프를 설명하는 내용에서 female modernist를 수식하는 형용사로 쓰였습니다. 그 앞에 언급된 주어 The continued value of her art로 보아 eminent는 오키프가 여성 모더니스트로서 높은 가치를 가진 인물임을 나타내는 단어로 쓰였음을 알 수 있으므로 보기 중에서 '가장 중요한', '선두하는'이라는 의미를 나타내는 (d) leading이 정답입니다.

PART 2

WHY DID EGYPTIANS MAKE 🔢60 MUMMIES?

One of the most common images associated with ancient Egypt is that of the mummy. 🔢60 Mummies, or preserved human remains, were created by Egyptians beginning about 5,000 years ago, and perhaps even earlier. Though we do not have direct records of the reasons for this practice, Egyptologists agree that these figures served a religious purpose related to beliefs about the afterlife.

🔢61 The earliest Egyptian mummies may have been created unintentionally. Egypt's climate is very hot and dry, without much rain. Because of this, 🔢61 some bodies that were buried in the desert did not decompose. Instead, they were preserved. This discovery may have provided inspiration to the ancient Egyptians, who then began studying how to replicate this effect.

Scholars say that by as early as 2600 BCE, Egyptians were intentionally preserving the bodies of the dead. They developed techniques for drying out corpses so they would not decompose. 🔢62(a) These methods involved removing the internal organs and 🔢65 coating the body in natron, a type of salt, for over a month. This dried the body and kept it free of bacteria. 🔢62(c) The body was then wrapped in sheets of linen and sometimes adorned with decorations. 🔢62(d) Rich, powerful individuals were commonly mummified, then buried in 🔢66 elaborate tombs with numerous passageways and chambers, such as the famous pyramids.

이집트인은 왜 미라를 만들었을까?

고대 이집트와 연관된 가장 흔한 그림 중에 하나는 미라의 그림이다. 미라, 혹은 보존된 인간의 유해는 이집트인들에 의해 약 5000년 전, 어쩌면 훨씬 더 이전에 만들어지기 시작하였다. 비록 이러한 관행의 이유에 대한 직접적인 기록을 가지고 있지 않지만 이집트학자들은 이 사람들이 사후 세계에 대한 믿음과 관련된 종교적 목적을 수행했다는 것에 동의한다.

초기 이집트 미라들은 의도치 않게 만들어졌을지도 모른다. 이집트의 기후는 아주 덥고 건조하며, 비가 많이 오지 않는다. 이것 때문에, 사막에 묻혔던 몇 몇 시체들이 부패하지 않았다. 대신에, 그 시체들은 보존되었다. 이 발견은 고대 이집트인들에게 영감을 주었을 지도 모르며, 그들은 그리고 나서 이러한 결과를 반복할 수 있는 방법을 연구하기 시작했다.

학자들은 기원전 2600년 정도 쯤, 이집트인들이 의도적으로 죽은 시체를 보존하고 있었다고 말한다. 그들은 시체가 부패되지 않도록 시체를 건조하는 기술을 발달시켰다. 이 방법은 인체 내부의 장기들을 제거하고, 소금의 한 종류인 탄산소다로 시체를 한 달 이상 뒤덮는 일을 수반하였다. 이는 시체를 건조시켰고 박테리아가 없는 상태로 유지시켰다. 그 후 시체는 여러 장의 인견으로 꽁꽁 싸였으며, 때때로 장식물들로 꾸며졌다. 부유하고, 권력이 있는 사람들은 흔히 미라로 만들어졌고, 그 후 유명한 피라미드와 같이 수많은 통로와 방이 있는 정교한 무덤에 묻혔다.

Historians generally agree that mummification served a religious purpose. It was thought that preservation of the body would help the individual enter the afterlife. **63** The dead person's soul, detached from the body, would be reunited with its physical form at a later time. Because the person would need their body even after death, it was important to keep it in good condition. These ideas about immortality may also be linked to the Egyptian god Osiris, who was said to have died and been reborn every year.

Ancient mummies continue to be a useful source of knowledge for modern-day researchers. Due to the success of the Egyptians at preserving human remains, **64** scientists have been able to use x-rays and biopsies to learn about the health of ancient people, including things like diet and disease. These findings give us a richer understanding of life in the ancient world.

역사학자들은 일반적으로 미라로 만드는 것이 종교적인 목적을 수행했다는 것에 동의한다. 시체의 보존은 그 사람이 사후 세계에 들어가는 것을 도울 것이라고 여겨졌다. 죽은 사람의 영혼은 육체로부터 떨어져서, 나중에 육신의 형태와 다시 재결합될 것이다. 그 사람은 사망 후에도 육체가 필요할 것이기 때문에, 양호한 상태로 육체를 유지시키는 것이 중요했다. 불멸에 대한 이런 사상 또한 이집트의 신 오시리스와 연관되어 있을 수 있으며, 그 신은 매년 죽었다가 부활한다고 전해졌다.

고대 미라들은 현대 연구자들에게는 계속해서 지식에 대한 유용한 원천이 되고 있다. 인간의 유해를 보존하는 것에 대한 이집트인들의 성공으로 인해, 과학자들은 식단과 질병 같은 것들을 포함하여 고대 사람들의 건강에 대해 알기 위해 엑스레이와 생체 검사를 사용할 수 있었다. 이러한 결과들은 고대 세계에서의 삶에 대한 더욱 풍부한 이해를 우리에게 전해준다.

어휘 common 흔한 associated with ~와 연관된 mummy 미라 preserved 보존된 remains (죽은 사람의) 유해 perhaps 어쩌면, 아마도 direct 직접적인 record 기록 practice 관행, 실천 Egyptologist 이집트학자 figure 인물, 사람 server a purpose 목적을 수행하다, 목적에 부합하다 religious 종교적인 related to ~에 관련된 belief 믿음, 신념 afterlife 사후 세계 may have p.p.: ~했을지도 모른다 unintentionally 의도치 않게, 무심결에 climate 기후 body 시체 bury 묻다 desert 사막 decompose 부패하다, 썩다 instead 대신에 preserve 보존하다 discovery 발견 inspiration 영감 replicate 모사하다, 복제하다 effect 결과, 효과 scholar 학자 intentionally 의도적으로, 고의로 corpse 시체 method 방법 remove 제거하다 internal 내부의 organ 장기, 조직 coat 덮다 natron 천연 탄산소다 dry 건조하다 free of ~가 없는 wrap 싸다, 포장하다 adorn 꾸미다, 장식하다 decoration 장식물 commonly 흔히 mummify 미라로 만들다 elaborate 정교한, 공을 들인 tomb 무덤 numerous 수많은 passageway 통로 chamber 방, 실 historian 역사학자 generally 일반적으로 mummification 미라화, 미라로 만드는 것 enter ~로 들어가다 detach from ~로부터 떨어지다 reunite 재결합하다 physical 신체적인 at a later time 나중에 immortality 불멸 be linked to ~에 연결되어 있다 reborn 다시 태어나는, 부활한 source 원천, 근원 modern-day 현대의 due to ~로 인해 biopsy 생체 검사 finding 결과, 결론 richer 더 풍부한, 더 풍요로운 understanding 이해

What is the article mainly about?

(a) a method of preserving the dead
(b) a significant archeological site
(c) a popular myth about the afterlife
(d) an annual religious ritual

기사문은 주로 무엇에 관한 것인가?

(a) 죽은 사람을 보존하는 방법
(b) 중요한 고고학적 유적지
(c) 사후 세계에 대한 유명한 신화
(d) 연례 종교 의식

정답 (a)

해설 지문의 제목에서 알 수 있듯이 지문의 주제는 미라(mummies)이며, 미라에 대해서 첫 문단에서 preserved human remains(보존된 인간의 유해)라고 설명한 뒤, 이어지는 문단에서 미라의 유래에서부터 미라가 만들어진 배경과 방법이 설명되고 있으므로 (a)가 정답입니다.

어휘 the dead 죽은 사람들, 망자 significant 중요한 archeological site 고고학적 유적지 popular 인기 있는, 유명한 myth (근거 없는) 신화 annual 연례의, 해마다의 ritual 의식, 의례

❌ 오답 피하기

지문에 사후 세계(afterlife)가 언급되었지만 미라가 만들어진 목적에 관해 언급되었을 뿐, 사후 세계에 대한 정의나 내용이 자세히 설명된 것이 아니므로 (c)는 오답입니다.

Based on the article, how were the first Egyptian mummies likely created?

(a) by being placed in freezing tombs
(b) by being exposed to thin mountain air
(c) by being buried deep in the sand
(d) by being sealed in airtight coffins

기사에 따르면, 최초의 이집트 미라는 어떻게 만들어졌을 것 같은가?

(a) 얼어붙은 무덤에 놓임으로써
(b) 희박한 산 공기에 노출됨으로써
(c) 모래 속에 묻힘으로써
(d) 진공의 관에 봉인됨으로써

정답 (c)

해설 질문의 키워드인 the first Egyptian mummies는 두 번째 문단 첫 부분에 The earliest Egyptian mummies로 언급되어 있습니다. 그 뒤에 some bodies that were buried in the desert did not decompose라는 문장에서 사막에 묻혔던 몇몇 시체들이 썩지 않았고, 그것이 고대 이집트인들에게 영감을 주었을 것이라고 언급하며 최초의 미라에 대해 추측하고 있습니다. 따라서 최초의 미라는 사막에 묻혀서 만들어졌으므로 (c)가 정답입니다.

패러프레이징

• the first Egyptian mummies → The earliest Egyptian mummies
• buried in the desert → buried deep in the sand

Which is NOT mentioned about the mummification process used by ancient Egyptians?

(a) It involved extracting parts from inside the body.
(b) It was done over a year-long period.
(c) It involved encasing the body in cloth.
(d) It was customary among the upper class.

고대 이집트인들이 사용한 미라화 과정에 관해 언급되지 않은 것은 어느 것인가?

(a) 시체 내부의 부위들을 추출하는 일을 수반했다.
(b) 1년이 넘는 기간이 걸려 완료된다.
(c) 천으로 시체를 감싸는 일을 수반했다.
(d) 상류층 사이에서 관례적인 일이었다.

정답 (b)

해설 미라화(mummification)에 대해 언급된 세 번째 문단에서 내부 장기를 제거하는 일을 수반했다(involved removing the internal organs)는 부분에서 (a)의 내용을 확인할 수 있습니다. 그리고 인견으로 싸였다는 점(wrapped in sheets of linen)에서 (c)를, 그리고 부유하고 권력이 있는 사람들이 흔히 미라가 되었다는 점(Rich, powerful individuals were commonly mummified)에서 (d)를 확인할 수 있습니다. 그런데 소금의 한 종류인 나트론으로 한 달 이상 덮는다(coating the body in natron, a type of salt, for over a month)고 언급된 부분에서 (b)의 내용이 지문과 다르다는 것을 알 수 있습니다. 따라서 정답은 (b)입니다.

어휘 process 과정, 절차 extract 추출하다 part 부위, 부분 year-long 1년 기간의, 1년이 걸리는 period 기간 encase 감싸다 cloth 옷감, 천 customary 관례적인, 습관적인 upper class 상류층, 고위 계급

패러프레이징

- removing the internal organs → extracting parts from inside the body
- wrapped in sheets of linen → encasing the body in cloth
- Rich, powerful individuals were commonly mummified → It was customary among the upper class

According to the fourth paragraph, why did ancient Egyptians believe that bodies should be preserved?

(a) because they would be inhabited by the soul of a god
(b) because they would be used by the deceased in the afterlife
(c) because they would otherwise spread deadly diseases
(d) because they would be used later in religious ceremonies

네 번째 문단에 따르면, 고대 이집트인들이 시체들이 보존되어야 한다고 믿었던 이유는 무엇인가?

(a) 신의 영혼이 임할 것이기 때문에
(b) 사후 세계에서 망자들에 의해 사용될 것이기 때문에
(c) 그렇지 않으면 치명적인 질병을 퍼트릴 것이기 때문에
(d) 이후에 종교적인 의식에서 사용될 것이기 때문에

정답 (b)

해설 네 번째 문단의 내용에 따르면, 죽은 자의 영혼이 나중에 육체적 형태와 재결합할 것이고, 그래서 그 사람은 죽은 후에도 자신의 육신이 필요할 것이기 때문에 육체를 양호한 상태로 유지하는 것이 중요하다고(The dead person's soul, detached from the body, would be reunited with its physical form at a later time. Because the person would need their body even after death, it was important to keep it in good condition) 언급되어 있습니다. 이를 통해 죽은 사람의 육신을 보존해야 하는 이유는 죽은 자들이 나중에 필요할 것이기 때문임을 알 수 있으므로 (b)가 정답입니다.

어휘 inhabit 살다, 존재하다 soul 영혼 the deceased 망자, 죽은 사람들 otherwise 그렇지 않으면 spread 퍼트리다 deadly 치명적인 disease 질병 ceremony 의식

패러프레이징

the person would need their body even after death → they would be used by the deceased in the afterlife

According to the final paragraph, what has helped scientists learn more about ancient people?

(a) using modern equipment to mummify animals
(b) trying to recreate the mummification process
(c) investigating the places where mummies have been stored
(d) carrying out medical procedures on mummies

마지막 문단에 따르면, 과학자들이 고대 사람들에 대해 더 많은 것을 알 수 있도록 도와준 것은 무엇인가?

(a) 동물을 미라로 만들기 위한 현대 장비를 사용한 것
(b) 미라화 과정을 재현하려고 노력한 것
(c) 미라가 저장된 장소를 조사한 것
(d) 미라에게 의료적 시술을 수행한 것

정답 (d)

해설 질문의 키워드인 scientist learn more about ancient people은 마지막 문단의 마지막 부분에서 과학자들이 고대 사람들의 건강에 대해 알기 위해 엑스레이와 생체 검사를 사용할 수 있었다(scientists have been able to use x-rays and biopsies to learn about the health of ancient people)는 문장에 언급되어 있습니다. 이를 통해 과학자들이 미라에 엑스레이를 사용하고 생체 검사를 해보았다는 것을 알 수 있으므로 (d)가 정답입니다.

어휘 equipment 장비 recreate 재현하다, 되살리다 investigate 조사하다 store 저장하다 carry out 수행하다 medical procedure 의료적 시술, 의료 방법

패러프레이징

use x-rays and biopsies → carrying out medical procedures

65 동의어

In the context of the passage, coating means _____.

(a) carrying
(b) calming
(c) covering
(d) cleaning

해당 단락의 문맥에서 coating이 의미하는 것은?

(a) 가지고 다니는 것
(b) 진정시키는 것
(c) 덮는 것
(d) 청소하는 것

정답 (c)

해설 해당 문장에서 coating은 타동사인 involved의 목적어 자리에 동명사 형태로 쓰였습니다. 문맥상 한 달 이상 나트론(natron)으로 시체를 처리하여 박테리아를 없애는 것으로 언급되어 있습니다. 이를 통해 나트론을 시체에 바르거나 덮는 것으로 이해할 수 있으므로 보기 중에서 '덮다'라는 의미를 나타내는 동사 cover의 동명사 형태인 (c) covering이 정답입니다.

66 동의어

In the context of the passage, elaborate means _____.

(a) busy
(b) temporary
(c) secret
(d) complex

해당 단락의 문맥에서 elaborate이 의미하는 것은?

(a) 바쁜
(b) 일시적인
(c) 비밀의
(d) 복잡한

정답 (d)

해설 해당 문장에서 elaborate는 무덤(tombs)이라는 명사를 수식하는 형용사로 사용되었으며, 그 뒤에 이 무덤은 수많은 통로와 방이 있다고 설명되어 있습니다. 이를 통해 이 무덤이 복잡한 구조를 가지고 있다고 볼 수 있으므로 보기 중에서 '복잡한'이라는 의미를 나타내는 형용사 (d) complex가 정답입니다.

PART 3

67 PEACHES

67 The peach tree, or *Prunus persica*, is a deciduous tree that grows a sweet, fleshy fruit. The tree has been domesticated for thousands of years and provides an important fruit crop for many across the world.

The peach belongs to the genus Prunus, which also includes fruit trees such as cherry and apricot. 68 It requires both moderately cold winters and warm summers in order to mature into a fruit-bearing tree, since blossoming is triggered by a period of cold. This means that peach trees cannot usually grow in tropical areas unless they are at high altitudes. Typically, peach trees begin fruiting after three years and can live for up to twenty.

Historians believe that the peach originated in China and was first 72 cultivated as a crop in Zhejiang Province as early as 6000 BCE. The fruit later spread throughout Asia and into the Middle East, Europe, and North America. 69 Because the peach grew so well in Persia, or modern-day Iran, the Romans thought that the fruit had originated there. They referred to the fruit as the "Persian apple," and this is the source of the persica part of its scientific name.

In addition to being a delicious food, peaches have 73 occupied an important place in the cultures of Asia and Europe. In Chinese mythology, for example, the fruit has been associated with immortality. 70 Legend tells of a celebration called the Feast of Peaches, which occurred every 6,000 years. The gods would gather to consume peaches that helped maintain their eternal life. Later, when peaches arrived in Europe, painters such as Vincent van Gogh and Claude Monet featured the fruit in many of their works. The beautiful peaches in these artworks came to be associated with ideas about health and well-being.

복숭아

복숭아 나무, 혹은 *프루너스 페르시카*는 달콤하고 다육질의 과일이 자라는 낙엽수이다. 이 나무는 수천 년 동안 재배되어 왔으며 전세계에서 많은 나라에서 주요 과일 작물을 제공한다.

복숭아는 살구속에 속하며, 그것은 또한 체리와 살구와 같은 과일 나무를 포함한다. 복숭아는 열매가 열리는 나무로 자라기 위해 적당히 추운 겨울과 따뜻한 여름이 모두 필요한데, 이는 개화가 추운 기간에 촉발되기 때문이다. 이는 복숭아 나무가 높은 고도에 있지 않는다면 열대 지역에서는 보통 자랄 수 없다는 것을 의미한다. 일반적으로, 복숭아 나무는 3년 후에 열매를 맺기 시작하며 최대 20년까지 살 수 있다.

역사학자들은 복숭아가 중국에서 유래했으며 기원전 6000년에 저장성에서 작물로서 처음 재배되었다고 믿고 있다. 그 이후 이 열매는 아시아 전역, 그리고 중동, 유럽, 북아메리카로 퍼졌다. 복숭아는 페르시아, 현대의 이란에서 매우 잘 자랐기 때문에, 로마인들은 그 과일이 그곳에서 유래했다고 생각했다. 그들은 이 과일을 "페르시아의 사과"라고 지칭했으며, 이것이 이 과일의 학술명에 있는 '페르시카' 부분의 근원이다.

맛있는 음식인 것과 더불어, 복숭아는 아시아와 유럽의 문화에 중요한 위치를 차지해왔다. 예를 들어, 중국 신화에서 이 과일은 불사와 연관되어 왔다. 전설에 따르면 6000년마다 발생하는 '복숭아 축제'라고 불리는 축하 행사가 있다고 한다. 신들은 그들의 영생을 유지하는 데 도움이 되는 복숭아를 먹기 위해 모였다고 한다. 이후에, 복숭아가 유럽에 도달하였을 때, 반 고흐와 클로드 모네와 같은 화가들이 그들의 많은 작품 속에 이 과일을 특징적으로 그렸다. 이 작품들 속의 아름다운 복숭아는 건강과 안녕에 관한 사상과 연관되게 되었다.

Today, peaches continue to be an important food item in many countries. However, peach crops are threatened by the changing global climate. Because peaches require such specific climatic conditions, **71** seasonal temperature fluctuations have harmed the crop in recent years, endangering this economically and culturally significant fruit.

오늘날, 복숭아는 계속해서 많은 국가에서 중요한 식품이 되고 있다. 하지만, 복숭아 작물은 세계 기후의 변화로 인해 위협을 받고 있다. 복숭아가 특정한 기후 조건을 필요로 하기 때문에, 계절 온도의 변동은 최근 몇 년간 이 작물에 해를 끼쳐 왔으며, 이 경제적으로 그리고 문화적으로 중요한 과일을 위태롭게 만들고 있다.

어휘 ┃ deciduous tree 낙엽수 grow 성장시키다, 자라게 하다 fleshy 다육질의, 두껍고 부드러운 domesticate 재배하다 crop 작물 belong to ~에 속하다 genus (생물 분류) 속 Prunus 살구속 apricot 살구 require 필요로 하다, 요구하다 moderately 적당하게 mature 성장하다, 자라나다 fruit-bearing 열매를 맺는, 열매가 열리는 blossoming 개화 trigger 촉발시키다 tropical 열대의 unless ~하지 않는다면 altitude 고도 typically 일반적으로 fruit 열매를 맺다 up to 최대 ~까지 historian 역사학자 originate 유래하다 cultivate 재배하다, 경작하다 spread 퍼지다 throughout 전역에, 도처에 modern-day 현대의 refer to ~을 지칭하다 source 근원, 원천 scientific name 학술명 in addition to ~에 더불어, ~뿐만 아니라 occupy 차지하다 mythology 신화 associated with ~와 연관된 immortality 불멸, 불사 celebration 행사, 기념 feast 축제, 연회 occur 발생하다, 일어나다 gather 모이다 consume 섭취하다, 먹다 maintain 유지하다 eternal life 영생 feature 특징으로 나타내다 work 작품 well-being 안녕, 행복 be threatened by ~에 위협받다 global 세계의 climate 기후 climatic condition 기후 조건 seasonal temperature 계절 온도 fluctuation 변동 harm 해를 끼치다, 손상시키다 endanger 위태롭게 하다, 위험에 빠뜨리다 economically 경제적으로 culturally 문화적으로

---

67 주제/목적

What is the article mainly about?

(a) the different characteristics of a type of fruit
(b) the economic impact of an important fruit crop
(c) the different varieties of a type of fruit
(d) the sudden decline of a common fruit crop

기사문은 주로 무엇에 관한 것인가?

(a) 한 종류의 과일의 다른 특징들
(b) 중요한 과일 작물의 경제적 영향
(c) 한 종류의 과일의 다른 품종들
(d) 흔한 과일 작물의 갑작스러운 감소

정답 ┃ (a)

해설 ┃ 제목을 통해 주제가 '복숭아'인 것을 알 수 있습니다. 첫 문단에서 복숭아에 대한 간략한 설명, 두 번째 문단에서 복숭아의 재배환경, 세 번째 문단에서 복숭아의 유래에 대해 설명하고 있으므로 전체적으로 복숭아의 특징에 대해 설명하는 글임을 알 수 있습니다. 따라서 정답은 (a)입니다.

어휘 ┃ characteristic 특징 economic 경제의, 경제성이 있는 impact 영향 variety (작물의) 품종 sudden 갑작스러운 decline 감소 common 흔한

According to the article, what enables peach trees to grow fruit?

(a) being situated in a specific type of soil
(b) receiving regular amounts of rainfall
(c) being planted during a particular season
(d) experiencing a well-timed change in temperature

기사에 따르면, 복숭아 나무가 열매를 자라는 것을 가능하게 하는 것은 무엇인가?

(a) 특정 유형의 토양에 위치하는 것
(b) 일정량의 강우를 받는 것
(c) 특정한 계절동안 심는 것
(d) 기온에 있어서 시의 적절한 변화를 겪는 것

정답 (d)

해설 질문의 키워드인 peach trees to grow fruit는 두 번째 문단에서 fruit-bearing tree로 언급되었습니다. 해당 문장에서 복숭아 나무가 열매를 자라게 하는 나무로 성장하기 위해서는 적당히 추운 겨울과 따뜻한 여름이 모두 필요하다는(It requires both moderately cold winters and warm summers in order to mature into a fruit-bearing tree) 내용이 언급됩니다. 이를 통해서 복숭아 나무가 계절에 맞는 기온 변화를 겪어야 한다는 것을 알 수 있으므로 (d)가 정답입니다.

어휘 enable + 목적어 + to 동사원형: (목적어)가 ~하는 것을 가능하게 하다 situated 자리 잡은, 위치한 specific 특정한 soil 토양, 땅 regular amount 일정량, 고정적인 양 rainfall 강우 planted 심어진 particular 특정한 experience 겪다 well-timed 시의 적절한, 때를 잘 맞춘 temperature 기온, 온도

패러프레이징

requires both moderately cold winters and warm summers → a well-timed change in temperature

Where did the peach get part of its scientific name?

(a) from an ancient myth about its creator
(b) from the region where it was first found
(c) from a mistaken belief about its origins
(d) from the person who first discovered it

복숭아가 학술명의 일부를 어디서 얻었는가?

(a) 복숭아의 창조자에 관한 고대 미신으로부터
(b) 최초로 발견된 지역으로부터
(c) 복숭아의 기원에 대한 잘못된 신념으로부터
(d) 복숭아를 최초로 발견했던 사람으로부터

정답 (c)

해설 질문의 키워드인 scientific name은 세 번째 문단 마지막 부분에 언급되었습니다. 해당 문장에서 복숭아의 학술명 중 일부인 persica가 페르시아에서 복숭아가 아주 잘 자라서, 로마인들이 복숭아를 "페르시아의 사과"라고 지칭하였다는(Because the peach grew so well in Persia, or modern-day Iran, the Romans thought that the fruit had originated there. They referred to the fruit as the "Persian apple,") 것에서 얻게 되었다고 설명하고 있습니다. 이를 통해 복숭아의 학술명이 복숭아의 기원을 오해한 로마인들에 의한 것임을 알 수 있으므로 (c)가 정답입니다.

어휘 creator 창조자, 창작자 region 지역 mistaken belief 잘못된 신념 origin 기원, 근원 discover 발견하다

---

70 세부 정보

Based on the article, how did peaches come to be associated with eternal life?

(a) through their documented use in ancient medicines
(b) through their portrayal in legends as a divine food
(c) through their recurring presence in ancient poetry
(d) through their depiction in many famous paintings

기사에 따르면, 복숭아는 어떻게 영생과 연관되게 되었는가?

(a) 고대 의학에서 문서화된 사용을 통해
(b) 전설 속에서 신성한 음식으로 묘사된 것을 통해
(c) 고대 시에서의 반복적인 등장을 통해
(d) 많은 유명한 그림에서 묘사된 것을 통해

정답 (b)

해설 질문의 키워드인 eternal life는 네 번째 문단에서 6000년 마다 열리는 '복숭아 축제' 신들이 모여 그들의 영생을 유지하는 데 도움이 되는 복숭아를 먹었다는(Legend tells of a celebration called the Feast of Peaches, which occurred every 6,000 years. The gods would gather to consume peaches that helped maintain their eternal life) 문장에서 언급되었습니다. 이 문장을 통해 복숭아가 전설 속에서 영생을 위한 신들이 먹는 과일로 묘사되었음을 알 수 있으므로 (b)가 정답입니다.

어휘 documented 문서화된 medicine 의학, 약 portrayal 묘사 divine 신성한, 신의 recurring 되풀이하여 발생하는 presence 존재, 있음 depiction 묘사

패러프레이징

The gods would gather to consume peaches ~ → a divine food

❌ 오답 피하기

복숭아가 유럽에 도달하여 반 고흐나 클로드 모네와 같은 유명 화가의 작품에 복숭아가 묘사되었다고 언급되었으나 이들의 그림에서 복숭아는 영생(eternal life)을 나타내는 것이 아니므로 (d)는 오답입니다.

Why, most likely, have supplies of peaches been reduced in recent years?

(a) The fruit is being damaged by invasive pests.
(b) The trees have been affected by environmental shifts.
(c) The fruit is spoiling faster due to new diseases.
(d) The trees have been threatened by the logging industry.

최근 몇 년간 복숭아의 공급이 줄어 든 이유는 무엇일 것 같은가?

(a) 그 과일이 침습적 해충에 의해 훼손되고 있다.
(b) 그 나무가 환경 변화에 의해 영 향을 받았다.
(c) 그 과일이 새로운 질병으로 인해 더 빠르게 상하고 있다.
(d) 그 나무가 벌목 산업에 의해 위 협받았다.

정답 (b)

해설 최근 몇 년간의 복숭아에 생긴 변화에 대한 언급은 마지막 문단에서 복숭아가 최근 몇 년간 계절적 기온 변동으로 해를 입 었다는(seasonal temperature fluctuations have harmed the crop in recent years) 내용의 문장에서 나타났습니다. 이 문장을 통해 계절적 기온 변동이 복숭아의 공급이 줄어들게 한 원인으로 유추할 수 있으므로 (b)가 정답입니다.

어휘 supply 공급 reduce 줄이다, 감소시키다 damage 손상시키다, 훼손하다 invasive 침습적인, 침략적인 pest 해충 affect 영향을 주다 environmental 환경의 shift 변화 spoil 상하다 due to ~로 인해 logging industry 벌목 산업

패러프레이징

seasonal temperature → environmental shifts

In the context of the passage, cultivated means _____.

(a) farmed
(b) impacted
(c) finished
(d) removed

해당 단락의 문맥에서 cultivated가 의미하는 것은?
(a) 경작되는
(b) 충격을 받은
(c) 완료된
(d) 제거된

정답 (a)

해설 해당 문장에서 cultivated는 복숭아가 기원전 6000년부터 작물로 재배되었음을 나타내는 문장에서 '재배된'이라는 의미를 나타내는 과거분사로 쓰였습니다. 따라서 보기 중에서 '경작되는', '재배되는'이라는 의미를 나타내는 (a) farmed가 정답입 니다.

In the context of the passage, occupied means _____.

(a) stolen
(b) regained
(c) held
(d) symbolized

해당 단락의 문맥에서 occupied가
의미하는 것은?

(a) 훔쳤다
(b) 되찾았다
(c) 잡고 있었다
(d) 상징했다

정답 (c)

해설 해당 문장에서 occupied는 그 앞에 위치한 have와 함께 주어를 peaches로 가지는 현재완료시제의 동사로 사용되었습니다. 목적어가 an important place이므로 문맥상 '복숭아가 중요한 자리에 있었다' 또는 '복숭아가 중요한 자리를 차지했다'는 의미를 나타내는 것을 알 수 있습니다. 따라서 보기 중에서 '잡고 있다', '보유하다'라는 의미를 나타내는 타동사 hold의 과거형 (c) held가 정답입니다.

PART 4

To: Burt Greenie <b.greenie@greenunicorn.net>
From: Dr. Tess Burrell <t.burrell@smilodonvet.com>
Subject: Taking Care of Spot

Dear Mr. Greenie,

This is Dr. Burrell, your veterinarian, following up about your visit today. As I mentioned earlier, your dog Spot has a bit of an upset stomach, but this is nothing serious. **74** Following the instructions below should get Spot feeling better in no time.

First, **75** remember to keep Spot relaxed and rested. This probably won't be difficult because he seems very tired from his illness. Limit his exercise to three short walks per day, plus additional outside time whenever he needs to go to the bathroom. We don't want him outside chasing after squirrels all day, as he needs to save his energy for recovery.

Remember to give him the pills that I prescribed today. These will help **79** settle his upset stomach. It can be difficult to get dogs to swallow pills, so be patient. **76** The best thing to do is put the pill in some soft dog food or a favorite treat and trick him into swallowing it. Try to use a healthy treat.

Finally, **77** feed Spot a **80** bland diet for a few weeks to boost his recovery. Rather than giving him his regular dog food, try plain white rice and boiled, skinless chicken, which will still provide a nutritious meal. You can also mix in pureed pumpkin from a can, like you would use for making pumpkin pie. Make sure it's plain pumpkin, though, without any added spices that could irritate his stomach. After recovery, you may resume feeding Spot his regular diet.

수신인: 버트 그리니 <b.greenie@greenunicorn.net>
발신인: 테스 버렐 박사 <t.burrell@smilodonvet.com>
제목: 스팟 간병

그리니 씨에게,

저는 귀하의 수의사 버렐 박사입니다. 금일 방문에 관해 덧붙여 설명 드립니다. 제가 이전에 말씀드린 대로, 귀하의 개 스팟은 약간의 배탈이 났습니다만, 심각한 것은 아닙니다. 아래의 지시 사항을 따라하시면 스팟은 곧 좋아질 것입니다.

우선, 스팟을 편안하게 하고 쉬게 하는 걸 기억하시기 바랍니다. 스팟이 배탈로 아주 피곤해 보이기 때문에 이것은 어쩌면 어렵지 않을 것입니다. 하루에 3회의 짧은 산책으로 운동을 제한하세요. 그리고 스팟이 화장실에 가야 할 때마다 추가로 야외 시간을 더하세요. 저희는 스팟이 회복을 위한 에너지를 아껴야 할 필요가 있기 때문에 그가 야외에서 하루 종일 다람쥐를 뒤쫓는 것을 원치 않습니다.

제가 오늘 처방해드린 약을 스팟에게 주는 것을 기억하시기 바랍니다. 이것은 그의 배탈을 진정시키는 데 도움이 될 것입니다. 개가 약을 삼키게 하는 것은 어려운 일이 될 수 있으므로, 인내심을 가지시기 바랍니다. 최고의 방법은 부드러운 사료 또는 가장 좋아하는 간식에 약을 넣어 그것을 삼키도록 속이는 것입니다. 건강에 좋은 간식을 이용하시길 바랍니다.

마지막으로, 회복력을 증대시키기 위해 몇 주간은 스팟에게 자극적이지 않은 식단으로 먹이시기 바랍니다. 그의 일반적인 사료를 주는 것 대신에, 일반 백미와 껍질이 없는 삶은 닭을 주시기 바라며, 이는 그래도 영양이 풍부한 식사가 될 것입니다. 또한 호박 파이를 만드실 때 사용하시는 것처럼 통조림으로 되어 있는 호박 퓨레를 섞어서 주셔도 됩니다. 그래도 그의 배를 자극시킬 수도 있는 양념이 첨가되지 않은, 아무 것도 섞이지 않은 호박인지 반드시 확인하시기 바랍니다. 회복 후에는 스팟에게 평소의 식단대로 먹이를 계속해서 주시면 됩니다.

Following these tips should put Spot on the path to a quick recovery. 78 If you have any other concerns or his condition doesn't improve over the next three days, please call me at the clinic. I will have my assistant check in after a few days. I hope Spot feels better soon.

이러한 팁들을 따르시면 스팟은 빠르게 회복할 것입니다. 다른 우려 사항이 있으시거나 그의 상태가 향후 3일 이상 개선되지 않는다면, 저희 병원으로 전화해주세요. 저는 제 조수가 며칠 후에 확인하도록 하겠습니다. 스팟이 얼른 낫길 바랍니다.

Best,

안녕히 계세요.

Dr. Tess Burrell

테스 버렐 박사

어휘 | taking care of ~을 돌보기, ~을 간호하기 veterinarian 수의사 follow up ~을 덧붙여 설명하다 mention 언급하다 a bit of 약간의 upset stomach 배탈 instruction 지시 (사항) in no time 당장, 금방, 곧 relaxed 편안한 probably 아마도, 어쩌면 illness 질병 limit 제한하다 short walk 짧은 산책 per day 하루에, 1일당 additional 추가의 chase after ~을 뒤쫓다, ~을 추격하다 squirrel 다람쥐 recovery 회복 pill 약, 알약 prescribe 처방하다 settle 진정시키다 swallow 삼키다 patient 인내심 있는 treat 간식, 먹이 trick 속이다 healthy 건강에 좋은 feed 먹이다, 먹이를 주다 bland 자극적이지 않은, 싱거운 boost 증대시키다, 돋우다 rather than ~보다는 regular 일반적인, 평소의 dog food 개 사료 plain 보통의, 아무것도 섞이지 않은 boiled 삶은 skinless 껍질이 없는 nutritious 영양분이 많은 pureed 퓨레로 만든 added 첨가된 spicy 양념 irritate 자극하다 stomach 배, 복부 put ~ on the path to ~로 가는 길로 들게 하다 concern 걱정, 우려 condition 상태 improve 개선되다, 향상되다 assistant 조수

---

74 주제/목적

Why is Dr. Burrell writing to Burt Greenie?

(a) to identify the symptoms of his dog's current illness
(b) to ask for details of his dog's current routine
(c) to suggest ways to prevent his dog's frequent stomach bugs
(d) to give him advice for his dog's recovery

버렐 박사가 버트 그리니 씨에게 편지를 쓰는 이유는 무엇인가?

(a) 그의 개의 현재 질병에 대한 증상을 확인하기 위해서
(b) 그의 개가 현재 하고 있는 반복적 일상에 대한 자세한 내용을 요청하기 위해서
(c) 그의 개의 잦은 장염을 예방하는 방법을 제안하기 위해서
(d) 그의 개의 회복을 위한 조언을 그에게 주기 위해서

정답 (d)

해설 편지의 첫 문단 마지막 부분에 지시 사항을 잘 따르면 버트 그리니 씨의 개 스팟이 금방 나아질 것이라고(Following the instructions below should get Spot feeling better in no time) 언급하였으므로 편지의 목적은 수의사가 아픈 개가 지켜야 하는 지시 사항을 전달하는 것임을 알 수 있습니다. 따라서 정답은 (d)입니다.

어휘 identify 확인하다, 밝히다 symptom 증상 current 현재의 ask for ~을 요청하다 details 자세한 내용 routine 매일 반복적으로 하는 일상 행동 suggest 제안하다 prevent 예방하다, 막다 frequent 잦은, 빈번한 stomach bug 장염 advice 조언, 충고

패러프레이징

get Spot feeling better → his dog's recovery

---

75 세부 정보

According to the letter, why would it be easy to keep Spot relaxed?

(a) He dislikes going outside most of the time.
(b) He lacks energy due to his health issues.
(c) He naturally has a quiet temperament.
(d) He is taking medicine that makes him sleepy.

편지에 따르면, 스팟이 편안한 상태를 유지하기 쉬운 이유는 무엇인가?

(a) 그는 대부분의 시간에 야외로 나가는 것을 싫어한다.
(b) 그는 건강 문제로 인해 에너지가 부족하다.
(c) 그는 선천적으로 조용한 기질을 가지고 있다.
(d) 그는 그를 졸리게 만드는 약을 먹고 있다.

정답 (b)

해설 질문의 키워드인 keep Spot relaxed는 지문의 두 번째 문단 첫 부분에서 remember to keep Spot relaxed and rested라는 문장에서 지시시항으로 언급되었습니다. 이것은 어렵지 않을 것이라고 말하면서 그가 아픈 것으로 인해 아주 피곤해 보이기 때문(This probably won't be difficult because he seems very tired from his illness)이라고 설명되어 있습니다. 이를 통해 스팟이 건강에 문제가 있어서 에너지가 없음을 알 수 있으므로 (b)가 정답입니다.

어휘 dislike ~을 싫어하다 go outside 야외로 나가다 lack 부족하다 energy 에너지, 힘 issue 문제 naturally 선천적으로, 천부적으로 temperament 기질 take medicine 약을 복용하다

패러프레이징

• won't be difficult → would it be easy
• he seems very tired from his illness → He lacks energy due to his health issues

How does Dr. Burrell suggest getting the dog to take medication?

(a) by hiding it in appetizing food
(b) by following it with a treat
(c) by cutting it into smaller pieces
(d) by mixing it into his water bowl

버렐 박사는 개가 약을 어떻게 먹는 것을 제안하는가?

(a) 먹음직스러운 음식에 숨김으로써
(b) 간식을 먹은 후에 이어서 먹임으로써
(c) 작은 조각으로 자름으로써
(d) 물 그릇에 넣고 섞음으로써

정답 (a)

해설 질문의 키워드인 take medication은 세 번째 문단에서 give him the pills로 언급되었습니다. 해당 문단에서 편지 발신인인 버렐 박사는 가장 좋은 방법은 부드러운 사료나 가장 좋아하는 간식에 약을 넣어서 그것을 삼키도록 스팟을 속이는 것 (The best thing to do is put the pill in some soft dog food or a favorite treat and trick him into swallowing it)이라고 설명하였습니다. 이를 통해 버렐 박사가 제안하는 약을 먹는 방법은 스팟이 좋아하는 음식에 약을 숨겨 한꺼번에 먹도록 하는 것이라는 것을 알 수 있으므로 (a)가 정답입니다.

어휘 suggest 제안하다 take medication 약을 복용하다 hide 숨기다 appetizing 먹음직스러운, 구미가 당기는 follow A with B: B 뒤에 A를 이어서 하다 cut ~ into smaller pieces ~을 작은 조작으로 자르다 mix 섞다 water bowl 물 그릇

> **패러프레이징**
>
> • take medication → give him the pills
> • some soft dog food or a favorite treat → appetizing food

Why, most likely, does Dr. Burrell recommend pausing Spot's regular diet?

(a) to adjust his meals for more nutritional value
(b) to remove the cause of his stomach irritation
(c) to increase his chances of healing quickly
(d) to avoid a reaction with his medications

버렐 박사가 스팟의 평소 식단을 잠시 멈출 것을 권고하는 이유는 무엇일 것 같은가?

(a) 영양가가 더 많은 식사로 조정하기 위해서
(b) 위장의 자극을 주는 원인을 제거하기 위해서
(c) 빠르게 회복할 가능성을 증가시키기 위해
(d) 그가 복용하는 약에 대한 반작용을 피하기 위해

정답 (c)

해설 질문의 키워드인 pausing Spot's regular diet는 네 번째 문단에서 Rather than giving him his regular dog food에서 언급되었습니다. 이 문단의 첫 문장에서 몇 주 동안 그의 회복력을 증대시키기 위해 자극적이지 않은 식단을 먹이라고(feed Spot a bland diet for a few weeks to boost his recovery) 언급하였습니다. 이를 통해 스팟이 평소의 식단을 잠시 멈춰야 하는 이유가 회복력을 증대시키기 위한 것임을 알 수 있으므로 정답은 (c)입니다.

어휘 recommend 권고하다, 추천하다 pause 잠시 멈추다 adjust 조정하다, 적응하다 nutritional value 영양가 remove 제거하다 cause 원인 stomach irritation 위장 자극 chance 가능성, 확률 healing 회복, 치유 reaction 반작용

패러프레이징

boost his recovery → increase his chances of healing quickly

❌ 오답 피하기

네 번째 문단의 Make sure it's plain pumpkin, though, without any added spices that could irritate his stomach이라는 문장에서 stomach irritation에 관한 내용이 언급되었으나 위장에 자극을 줄 수 있는 양념을 첨가하지 말라는 것이므로 위장 자극의 원인 제거가 아닌 그 원인이 될 수 있는 것을 피하는 것임을 알 수 있습니다. 따라서 (b)는 오답입니다.

---

78 세부 정보

According to the letter, what should Burt do if his pet does not get better after three days?

(a) take the dog to an emergency care clinic
(b) get in touch with the veterinarian directly
(c) bring the dog for a follow-up appointment
(d) call the doctor's assistant immediately

편지에 따르면 버트 씨는 그의 애완동물이 3일 후에 낫지 않으면 무엇을 해야 하는가?

(a) 개를 응급 치료 병원으로 데려간다
(b) 수의사에게 직접 연락한다
(c) 후속 진료 예약을 위해 개를 데리고 간다
(d) 즉시 의사의 조수에게 전화한다

정답 (b)

해설 마지막 문단에서 버렐 박사는 스팟의 상태가 3일 후에도 개선되지 않으면 자신에게 전화하라고(If you have any other concerns or his condition doesn't improve over the next three days, please call me at the clinic) 언급하였습니다. 따라서 정답은 (b)입니다.

어휘 pet 애완 동물 get better 낫다, 호전되다 emergency 응급, 긴급 get in touch with ~와 연락하다 directly 직접 follow-up 후속의 appointment 진료 예약 immediately 즉시

❌ 오답 피하기

마지막 문단에서 버렐 박사의 조수(assistant)에 대해 언급되어 있으나 이는 버렐 박사가 조수에게 며칠 후에 확인하라고 지시하는 내용이므로 버트 씨가 전화할 대상이 아님을 알 수 있습니다. 따라서 (d)는 오답입니다.

In the context of the passage, settle means _____ .

(a) calm
(b) push
(c) fill
(d) touch

해당 단락의 문맥에서 settle이 의미하는 것은?

(a) 진정시키다
(b) 밀다
(c) 채우다
(d) 만지다

정답 (a)

해설 해당 문장에서 settle은 문맥상 버렐 박사가 스팟에게 처방한 약이 그의 배탈에 도움이 될 것이라는 내용에서 쓰인 동사입니다. 이를 통해 settle은 질병이나 고통을 경감시키는 의미로 쓰인다는 것을 알 수 있으므로 보기 중에서 '진정시키다'라는 의미를 나타내는 동사 (a) calm이 정답입니다.

In the context of the passage, bland means _____ .

(a) constant
(b) liquid
(c) popular
(d) mild

해당 단락의 문맥에서 bland가 의미하는 것은?

(a) 끊임없는
(b) 액체 형태의
(c) 인기 있는
(d) (맛이) 순한, 약한

정답 (d)

해설 해당 문장에서 bland는 문맥상 버렐 박사가 스팟의 회복을 증대시키기 위해서 몇 주 동안 먹어야 하는 식단을 제안하는 내용에서 '식단'을 의미하는 명사 diet를 수식하는 형용사로 쓰였습니다. 이를 통해 bland는 '자극적이지 않은'이라는 의미를 나타내는 것이 적절하므로 보기 중에서 '(맛이) 순한, 약한'이라는 의미를 나타내는 (d) mild가 정답입니다.

시원스쿨 LAB